Peaceful Conquest

PEACEFUL CONQUEST

The Industrialization
of Europe 1760–1970

BY
SIDNEY POLLARD

OXFORD UNIVERSITY PRESS

Oxford University Press, Walton Street, Oxford OX2 6DP

LONDON   GLASGOW   NEW YORK   TORONTO
DELHI   BOMBAY   CALCUTTA   MADRAS   KARACHI
KUALA LUMPUR   SINGAPORE   HONG KONG   TOKYO
NAIROBI   DAR ES SALAAM   CAPE TOWN
MELBOURNE   AUCKLAND

and associate companies in
BEIRUT   BERLIN   IBADAN   MEXICO CITY   NICOSIA

Published in the United States
by Oxford University Press, New York

© *Oxford University Press 1981*

First published 1981
Reprinted with corrections 1982

British Library Cataloguing in Publication Data

Pollard, Sidney
  Peaceful conquest.
  1. Europe — Industries — History
  I. Title
  338'.094   HC240   80-41061
  ISBN 0-19-877093-6
  ISBN 0-19-877095-2 Pbk

Set in IBM Baskerville by Graphic Services, Oxford
Printed in Hong Kong

Preface

It is perhaps best to start with some words of warning on what this book is *not* about. It is, above all, not a comprehensive economic history of Europe, of the kind that would set out to present a balanced account of the past two hundred years in which each development which might conceivably be termed economic, and each country or region, received its due share of attention. It is, on the contrary, concerned solely with the process of industrialization, as it alights here or there in Europe, transforming and being transformed by the changing geographical setting and historical sequence in which it occurs. This means, on the one hand, that once a country or region is industrialized, it fades from these pages, except in so far as it affects the industrialization of others. It also means that the industrialization of Europe is seen as a single, and not a repetitive, process.

The process started in Britain and the industrialization of Europe took place on the British model; it was, as far as the Continent was concerned, a purely and deliberately imitative process. Even after the 1860s, when technological and organizational innovations came increasingly from other advanced countries also, and the continuing process could correctly be described as European or even as North Atlantic, to include the growing impact of North American originality, it was still a development from the base of the British model. Whether an alternative model might have been possible is no doubt an interesting question,[1] but it is a basic tenet of this book that Europe's industrialization occurred as an outgrowth of a single root with mutations caused by varying circumstances.

The essential core of the process described here was technological, consisting of a better way of producing things or the production of new things. Some of the technical innovations brought with them necessarily some other changes: factories, large concentrations of capital, new forms of labour discipline. These are considered here, but only in so far as they were an essential part of the basic technological transformation. This may seem to be a narrow way of describing the process of industrialization, too slight to carry the momentous transformation of Europe which is the theme of this book. But the European world was, over most of the period described here, a competitive world, and technological change, leading to lower real costs and prices, was enough to allow some industries and regions to expand at hitherto unknown rates, while others declined and died. These were momentous consequences; but the causes were, in essence, quite humble, and it is among these that this book finds its interest.

What of the first cause? How did it all start in Britain? It is a legitimate question, on which a large and inconclusive literature exists, but it is not our theme. We begin at the point at which the seeds have been sown and the apparently irresistible imitative process is set going.[2] In tracing this process, we are almost inevitably driven to consider supply rather than demand. At every stage, at any given point in time, there existed a certain market, largely, of course, created by previous development. The purpose of this study is to ask how it was met, and why it was met by one group of persons, or one region, or by one method of production, rather than another. Supply must rule supreme in such an investigation,[3] and it is for this reason that our interest centres on such factors as location, resources, methods of production, or trade policies. This is not an attempt to pre-empt the question whether supply or demand 'caused' the industrial revolution, such questions, as will be argued below, usually being put in the wrong way. It is merely to recognize that it was supply conditions which were determinant in the actual course taken by industrialization, which is our theme.

This book, further, is by deliberate choice not concerned with the social or cultural consequences of industrialization, though this does not mean that those themes are not of overwhelming historical significance. We need not even assume that industrialized countries are richer,[4] let alone happier, than agrarian. The apparent normative tone which inevitably creeps into histories of this kind, celebrating a rapid industrial transformation as 'success' and deploring its absence as 'failure' is merely instrumental within the story told, which is that of the industrialization process.

The next omission to be mentioned may perhaps be considered the least defensible of all: in being concerned with Europe only, we leave out the rest of the world. While in the early years of industrialization the absence of the USA may be a serious flaw, the omission of links with colonies and other overseas suppliers becomes ever more serious as the development of European industrialization proceeds. We are concerned here, after all, with a unique phase in the rise of world capitalism, and the limitation of our interest to one Continent implies nothing less than a serious distortion of the overall pattern. Beyond this warning, the need of every book to draw its limits somewhere, and the basic unity of the story told, must be our main excuses.

It should be noted, also, that we are here concerned with broad, secular developments, and not with cyclical or even shorter movements. This emphasis derives directly from the subject matter, but takes on particular significance in the discussion of the role of trade in industrialization for, with few exceptions, most trade and monetary theory is concerned with short-term change. Some heretical views in relation to standard theory arise directly from this contrast.

Several of the ideas of this book have been set out in an earlier essay[5] and have met with a mixed reception. The debt owed to the pioneer work of W. W. Rostow[6] will be obvious to many; the intellectual debt to E. A. Wrigley's earlier work[7] is greater still, and it is a matter for regret that so many of his fertile ideas were allowed to be neglected in favour of his later interest in population studies, distinguished though his contribution be in that field also.

All of us are in debt to Alexander Gerschenkron who more than any other scholar reintegrated a historical sense with the study of industrialization, after the two had threatened to part company when the latter lost itself in schematic and abstract concepts. While the present study builds on the Gerschenkron tradition, it is distinguished from it by two major features: one is the emphasis on the contemporaneous world, which Gerschenkron hints at rather than incorporates as a major element; and the other is the divergence from the almost axiomatic assumption of Gerschenkron, Kuznets, and others[8] that countries within their political boundaries are the only units within which it is worthwhile to consider the process of industrialization.

It is a major premiss of this study that this process, on the contrary, is essentially one of regions, operating in a European context, and that in the early phases, when the foundations were being laid for the industrial transformation of society, governments were at best irrelevant, and frequently took a negative part, in a development which drew its main driving force from outside the political and governmental sphere. Moreover, in its pioneering stage it helped, as it was helped by, the decline of state interference in economic life, which marked the transition from mercantilism to laissez-faire, or in Herbert Spencer's terms,[9] from 'militant' to 'industrial' society. The liberal interlude, however, did not last long and it gave way once more to a politically dominated phase of wars and economic warfare, made more destructive than the earlier mercantilism by the intervening changes, to be replaced, in turn, after 1945, by a new form of integration of powerful nation states, based on two Europes, not one. European industrialization is intimately and fundamentally bound up with this dialectical development, which in turn corresponds to distinct phases in the rise of world capitalism. The 'national' view of industrialization is thus an inadmissible backward projection from a differently organized world on to an earlier Europe.

Finally, some comments on the vexed question of historical causation must be made at this point, even if only far too briefly and inadequately, in order to obviate some possible later misunderstandings. Historical causal chains are long and convoluted, and it is possible to start work on them at different points, taking the preceding links for granted. It is an unfortunate fact that the larger part of historical controversy concerns, not the data or even their interpretation, but the different links with which historians begin their reasoning, not realizing that it is that which mainly divides them. This is therefore a plea for an understanding of the exact point of entry chosen in this book. Thus the neglect of the demand factor does not mean that demand is, in some eternal, abstract sense, of no significance: it merely means that this study takes it for granted, as an earlier link in the chain. Similarly, the belittling of the role of government in, say, providing a stable legal framework within which industrialization can take place, does not mean that it is in some immanent sense of no significance. But in our study, when we are faced with stable governments over large parts of Europe, but industrialization in only a few small regions of the Continent, that function could not help us in our quest for an explanation. It may explain, indeed, why Europe, and not Central Africa, saw the rise of modern industrialism, but that is not our topic.

Such an approach will assign little value to monocausal explanations, the concentration on a single link which can at best 'explain' an immediate narrow effect only. But if events or processes have many causes, it is also true that not all 'causes' have positive effects. The long list of 'causes' one used to find in textbooks all working in the same direction to explain why, for example, the mechanized cotton industry settled in Lancashire, greatly oversimplifies the picture. For one could also think of many factors present in eighteenth-century Lancashire inimical to the progress of mechanical spinning, which therefore must have developed in spite of them. This, indeed, is normal: whether the sum of potential 'causes' works in one direction or another is often a matter of knife-edge balance. Thus a region lying next to a successfully industrialized one is by that very fact subject to many influences encouraging its own industrialization, and many other inhibiting it. Which will prevail does not depend on one 'cause', but on the net effect of 'causes' pulling in different directions, and impinging on its own traditions and resources: 'relevance depends on context.'[10] Moreover, it often takes a small shift only in circumstances to turn a vicious circle into a virtuous one, and vice versa.

Finally, causes are themselves effects of earlier developments, while effects, no matter how derived and dependent, take on some life of their own and become causes. Both play these dual roles simultaneously, and which is which depends on the immediate context, the link at which one decides to enter the chain. This does not mean that all explanations are equally good, or equally worthless. On the contrary, some causes have much greater significance than others, and some affect the timing, others the value, others still the direction of events. Above all, the chain has a certain sequence: some links must, historically, occur before others.[11] This preface is not a plea for unhistorical thought or unscientific history; it is a plea to abstain from controversy which bypasses the issues instead of meeting them, because it has failed to note that there are different points of entry.

This study was made possible by a year freed from teaching and administrative duties and spent at the Zentrum für Interdisziplinäre Forschung, University of Bielefeld. I think with gratitude of that admirable and generous institution, which provided the comfortable working conditions, congenial colleagues, and pleasant surroundings in which work is but a pleasure. It would be invidious to single out too many of the very large number of people who have aided the project without sharing in any way its shortcomings. Among those who must be mentioned by name are the colleagues in the History Faculty of the University of Bielefeld, above all Jürgen Kocka, Reinhart Koselleck, and Hans-Ulrich Wehler, who helped far more than they realized; Waclaw Dlugoborski, colleague for one year at the Z.i.F.; Mrs R. A. Duncan, of the Department of Geography in the University of Sheffield, who drew the maps; G. Schlesiger, of the History Section of the Bielefeld University Library, who was helpful far beyond the call of duty, and E. Penke and A. C. Plänitz, the Bielefeld Z.i.F. librarians. By rights I should also include all the members of the vigorous History seminars at Bielefeld, the audiences in various Universities who listened and commented on lectures on some or other aspects of this book, my colleagues in the Z.i.F., and its directorate and staff; but I hope that they will, in consideration of the reader's patience, accept my collective and none the less sincere thanks for the stimulus and support derived from them.

Bielefeld/Sheffield 1979   Sidney Pollard

Contents

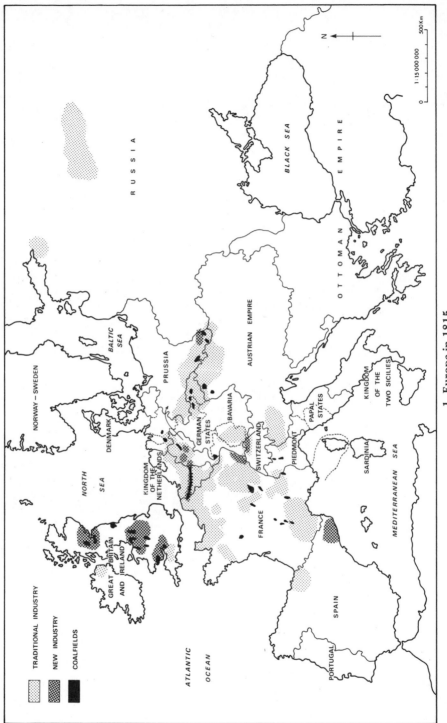

1. Europe in 1815

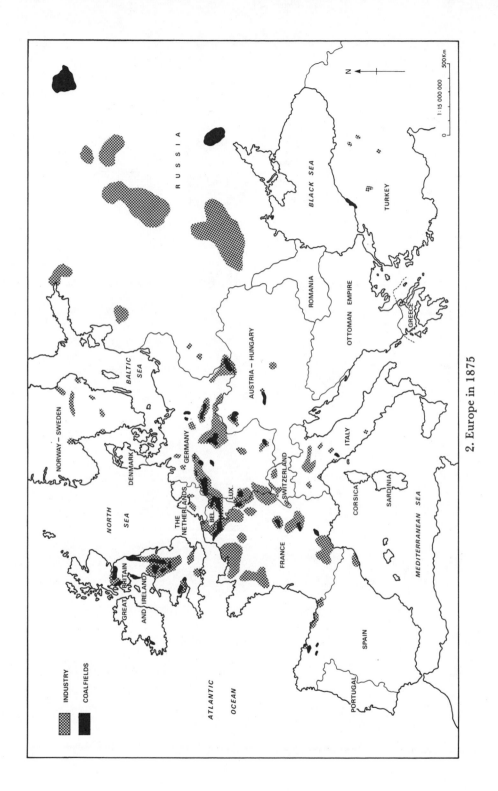

2. Europe in 1875

INDUSTRY

COALFIELDS

NORWAY – SWEDEN

RUSSIA

BALTIC
SEA

DENMARK

GERMANY

THE
NETHERLANDS

BEL.

LUX.

AUSTRIA – HUNGARY

SWITZERLAND

ROMANIA

BLACK SEA

OTTOMAN EMPIRE

TURKEY

GREECE

NORTH
SEA

GREAT
BRITAIN
AND IRELAND

FRANCE

ITALY

CORSICA

SARDINIA

MEDITERRANEAN SEA

SPAIN

PORTUGAL

ATLANTIC
OCEAN

N

500 Km.

1 : 15 000 000

0

Prologue

Chapter 1
The Industrial Revolution in Britain

By common consent, the first sustained process of industrialization is held to have occurred in Britain in the period c.1760 to c.1830 or 1850. Termed the industrial revolution, it is frequently taken to be the classical example of its kind, the standard of reference against which others may be judged. There is no shortage of books on the topic, nor is the subject exhausted: new data and new interpretations are constantly being added. However, from the early classical descriptions of Toynbee and Mantoux, to the recent standard works of Ashton, Deane, or Mathias,[1] these accounts tend to have one thing in common: they treat the British industrial revolution as a single national phenomenon.

Closer acquaintance reveals that industrialization in Britain was by no means a single, uninterrupted, and unitary, still less a nation-wide process. Different industries fared very differently at various periods; there were distinct phases of development; and far from being spread evenly across the country, the changes were highly concentrated geographically, creating significant spacial differentials at any one time. These have often been noted, the temporal sequences and varying industrial fortunes quite frequently, the regional element less so, but they have seldom been brought into an operative relationship with each other. It is the contention of this chapter that the interplay of time, industry, and region provides an important clue to the understanding of the actual historial events in Britain, and of the way in which industrialization spread to the rest of Europe. Since the regional element has been neglected in the past, it will have to be particularly emphasized, possibly beyond its due deserts, in this chapter.

Regional Specialization and Differentiation in the Traditional Economy

If we take our stand at any time before the particular changes associated with the industrial revolution have begun, say around 1750, we find no great and obvious differences between the more developed parts of the British Isles and the advanced regions on the Continent.[2] To many observers, indeed, then and now,[3] France seemed the richer and more promising economy. In both countries, most industries were geographically concentrated, that concentration having recently increased, and in both these concentrations were surrounded by overwhelmingly agricultural districts.

There are several types of reasons why such industrial concentrations were found in Britain in the mid-eighteenth century. Among the most important was the location of natural resources. There has been a tendency in recent years, nourished perhaps by the influence of theoretical economists on economic historians, to underrate the significance of such natural resources, possibly because they do not fit into neat theoretical schemes, or perhaps because we are misled by their lesser significance for industrial location in the later twentieth century into underrating their role in the eighteenth. But no one looking at Britain in 1750 can fail to see the critical part played by the availability of resources accessible to the then going technology. The interplay of history and geography here is complex. Scientific understanding and progress has a logic of its own, and coal, for example, in order to become part of an advancing economy, must be sufficiently accessible, both from the surface and from the pit mouth to the markets, for it to be raised before the technology which it would help to create and which could handle less accessible veins, had come into being.[4] The accessibility of resources itself has thus a technical–historical dimension. It may well be that the development of the Newcomen engine which allowed the exploitation of the deeper British coal pits in the mid-eighteenth century was a lucky accident that need not have happened,[5] but for the industrialization of Britain to have proceeded at the time, coal had to be there in the first place. Resources were a necessary, though not a sufficient, condition.

Among the resources determining industrial location, the most obvious are minerals. 'Cheap and plentiful' coal, remarked the observant Aikin in 1795, is 'an advantage inestimable to a manufacturing district'.[6] Coal attracted all industries requiring heat or power and the map of the British industrial revolution, it is well known, is simply the map of the coalfields, with the significant exception of the northeastern coalfield, which had less industry than its output warranted, and London, which had no local coal. But the two areas were linked by the constant sailings of the colliers that formed a large proportion of the British mercantile marine, thus forming the exception that confirmed the rule in a special and significant way. A similar relationship, on a smaller scale, existed between the Cumberland coalfield and Dublin. Other minerals responsible for industrial concentrations were copper, tin, and iron and, to a lesser extent, lead, salt, and fireclay. In an age when land transport was prohibitively expensive and even water transport difficult for anything as bulky as mineral ores or coal, only the need for fuel could move the metallurgical plants away from the pit mouths and it depended on current technology and costs whether, say, South Wales coal was brought to Cornwall, or Cornish copper ore to South Wales.

Next to minerals, it was water which located industry: water as a source of power, along the slopes of the Pennines, in North Wales, even in the West Midlands;[7] water used in textile processes, stressed by all who observed the woollen districts; and above all water for transport. The seaports that were channels of entry for colonial goods, like Bristol, Liverpool, or Glasgow thereby became the natural sites for industrial developments based on processing sugar, cotton, or tobacco.[8] Rivers, particularly those improved by navigation works, like the Aire and Calder which opened out the Yorkshire woollen district (1699 onwards) and the Don navigation which allowed the Sheffield region to flourish (1721-32), made possible other concentrations. Before long, canals were to become key features of yet other industrial areas like South Lancashire or parts of the West Midlands,[9] though it should be noted that, like navigation works, they were in part the results, as well as the causes, of local industrial development.

The produce of the soil was less commonly a location factor in Britain than in other countries, though sheep and flax had helped originally to determine the general areas of the woollen and linen industries.[10] Timber had long ceased to be a determining product: on the contrary, the search to overcome its shortage had an important effect in stimulating technical innovation.

The influence of agriculture, indeed, lay in a different, almost an opposite direction. There is a striking negative correlation between areas of agricultural comparative advantage and areas of industrialization: industrial employment settled very largely either in districts which never had much agricultural potential like the Pennine slopes, or those which had become disadvantaged by the agricultural changes of the previous century, like the Midland clay belt. That correlation, which has been commented on before,[11] has recently been put into its British context in a number of brilliant sketches by Eric Jones.[12]

Behind it lies the reasonable supposition that employers who have a choice will go to where the costs of factors of production, and labour in particular, are low, or that those who operate in districts where labour costs are low will enjoy a competitive advantage. Regions in which the supply price of labour, or the returns to the farmer's own time are low because of poor agricultural opportunities will therefore offer advantages to industrialists—advantages which, in their timing, depend on the development of a minimal transport system making this kind of regional agricultural specialization possible. Many, perhaps most, modern development theories assign an important role to a cheap labour supply as a favourable condition, while at later stages of industrialization, the quest for cheap labour is often the most powerful agent for shifting industrial locations, and therefore evening out industrial growth, between regions.

There is, however, a subtle but fundamental difference between the British experience and most models including cheap labour drawn from an agricultural sector of low productivity, or indeed between the British experience and that of many parts of the Continent of Europe in a phase of development which has become known as 'proto-industrialisation'.[13] There are, it is true, signs in earlier centuries that some of the areas less favoured for agricultural purposes took to industry as a refuge from a Malthusian threat,[14] but by the mid-eighteenth century the motive force was different. The preceding decades had seen a rise in agricultural efficiency and a fall in food prices, giving a strong upward push to the economy. Whether the additional real income arising out of the more productive farms was converted into higher demand for industrial or for agricultural goods may not be entirely clear,[15] but in either case there was no absolute deterioration of output for the dwellers in the less favoured regions and no Malthusian pressure, merely a failure to share in the bonanza of falling real costs. There was therefore a market for their labour, if not on the land, then partly and before long wholly in industry arising out of the additional incomes created on the land. Industrialists were looking for potential workers at least as hard as the latter were looking for work: there was a demand pull rather than a supply push in the good years around 1750. In the labour market it is important who takes the initiative.[16]

Thus we have accounts of immigration into the poorer and less favoured areas of Lancashire, by both skilled and unskilled men, to work on cotton and other textiles, rather than a desperate thronging by displaced peasants to find industrial work, and the 'enclosure movement in Lancashire tended not so much to drive workers into the towns as to help the spread of industry in the country'. Even then, local manufacturers had to place some of their spinning outside the county. The numbers of Sheffield's cutlers and nailmakers round about had also to be made up by immigration, and so had the metalworking trades of the West Midlands and even the iron industry of Furness. In the woollen trade, while the East Anglian weavers had to send out as far as Hertfordshire and Bedfordshire for spinning, the West Riding weavers went as far afield as the wild valleys of North Yorkshire, stockings were knitted in Westmorland and Durham, and the Midland Counties framework-knitting villages could make up their labour supply only by absorbing immigrants. North Wales attracted its first foreign entrepreneurs by its low wages, but even the Scottish and Irish linen industries were basically stimulated by market opportunities, as soon as local technical competence permitted, rather than by starvation. The objection to Pitt's Irish resolutions of 1785 from the English side was precisely that Ireland offered potentially strong competition since it enjoyed the advantages of lower labour costs and lower taxation.[17] Among mixed enterprises in agricultural/industrial areas, it seems, those located where agricultural advantages were declining, switched to a greater emphasis on industry, and vice versa.[18] As so often in economic development effects soon turned into causes, for the industries which had been attracted to the less favoured areas by lower factor costs, soon caused wages to rise above those in agricultural areas to continue the momentum of local growth under the more normal relationship between agricultural and industrial wages.[19]

Apart from natural advantages favouring one location rather than another, there might be those that might be called political. The activities of a capital city, above all London but also Dublin, and, to a lesser extent Edinburgh,[20] generated luxury demands from Court and government and a mass demand from soldiers, servants, and those who provided for them, which by themselves, as in other countries, amounted to a significant industrial concentration. Dockyards and arsenals were potentially centres of other such conglomerations, and if the industrial belts of Scotland and Ireland are to be denominated regions, the official encouragement of the linen industry there would be another politically determined location factor.

Once an industrial concentration had been created, 'external economies' emerged to enlarge the advantages and accelerate the spatial differentiation. Among the most powerful of them were the creation of an infrastructure, such as canals or roads that would benefit newcomers, supply industries including those that might provide capital goods,[21] markets and a knowledge of markets. Given the structure of mid-eighteenth century industry which distinguished itself from peasant crafts not so much by capital equipment as by the breeding-up of inimitable skills, the localization of skilled labour was of particular significance. By training, specialization, and division of labour, a flexible labour supply to individual employers and merchants was made possible, which provided an overwhelming advantage over any firm that might set up outside the constituted centre. Among textiles, much the most important of the manufacturing industries, the advantages of the localization of skills were particularly telling, as soon as a region became efficient enough to become an exporter to other areas in Britain or abroad. No one who reads Defoe's accounts of his travels in the 1720s can fail to be struck by the way in which towns, even villages, specialized in certain patterns or qualities, and in which skills in finishing and merchanting were tied to certain locations.[22] Even among the Midland nailmakers it was said that about twenty 'districts' existed, each making a different nail.[23]

These considerations are familiar. Discussions on external economies will be found in all standard texts on industrialization, and in descriptions of the British industrial revolution, among others, but in each case they will be applied to the country as a whole. In point of fact, however, they did not apply to the whole country, but to a few select areas. Much of the rest of the country followed different lines of development.

It must not be assumed that the system of localized industrialization had in any sense become fixed or regularized around 1750, before the industrial revolution. On the contrary, it was in a constant state of flux and development. While some industrial areas had a long tradition of manufacturing or mining, others were newly emerging.[24] Some regions and the key industries on which they were based, including the leading textiles, were themselves expanding rapidly if irregularly.

Scottish linen, produced along a crescent covering much of the lowlands and the coastal plain from the south-west to Aberdeen, registered a doubling of the yardage stamped for sale between 1730 and 1750, to be tripled again by 1800. Irish linen, made mainly in the north-east of the island, but spreading outward from there, increased its exports to Great Britain a hundredfold between 1700 and 1800, and more than eightfold even between 1728 and 1800. English linen production, scattered over four areas, is more difficult to estimate, but appears to have kept pace with the output of the other two countries combined. The industry remained rural, employing many part-time agriculturalists, it remained organized under the putting-out system, and until the end of the century there were no significant technical innovations. Yet British and Irish manufacturers succeeded in this period to drive the formerly dominant Dutch and Germans from a large part of this traditional British market.[25] While linen was the main import-replacing industry, wool was the chief home industry and the chief exporter; it provided 70% of English domestic exports in 1700 and still over 50% in 1770. The total output of that industry, starting from a much higher level in 1700, grew more slowly, by 150% over the century, but that modest increase hides the dramatic relocation of its main centre from the West Country and East Anglia to the West Riding of Yorkshire, which was well under way by 1750. The share of that region in the total output rose from 20% in 1700 to 60% in 1800. There was, incidentally, associated with it a similarly dramatic shift of its main foreign markets from Europe to the Mediterranean, and thence, from the 1750s, to America, over the same period.[26] Other growing textile industries included silk, stocking-knitting and, of course, the expanding mixed cotton and Manchester goods of Lancashire.

Framework-knitting, i.e. the knitting of stockings, gloves, and similar goods by machine, was one of those industries which had left London because of the obstructiveness of the guild, as well as the high wages ruling there, and had come to be concentrated in the three Midland counties of Nottinghamshire, Leicestershire, and Derbyshire, as the nucleus of another industrial region.[27] By the mid-eighteenth century the power of guilds had been on the wane for a long time, but they still had a nuisance value, though the system gave its dying kick about that time.[28] It was London wage levels which were more actively driving other industries, like shoemaking and silk-throwing, out of the capital, while others still, including shipbuilding, expanded with London's growth. Among the earliest to use capital-intensive mass production methods even before 1750 was London porter-brewing.[29]

While iron-mining and smelting remained dispersed, following ore, charcoal, and water-power to the more remote parts of the country, metal working was an industry which in its expansion became specialized and locationally concentrated. Sheffield began to monopolize much of cutlery and tools making in one single town; the metal-working district of the West Midlands, by contrast, was spread over several towns, each specializing in a small number of products. Nailing was a rural industry, surrounding both areas and helping to turn large stretches of country into semi-urban ribbon developments. Cementation steel had been a West Midland speciality; crucible steel, developed by Benjamin Huntsman in the 1740s, located steelmaking largely in Sheffield. The Potteries began about this time to absorb most of the productive capacity of the industry in the country, turning, rather like Sheffield had done a little earlier in the case of cutlery, a widely dispersed peasant industry into a set of skilled and polished crafts.[30]

There is further evidence for the instability of the regional industrial system in the fate of industries themselves, some of which grew, creating new concentrations, other continued in traditional industrial areas, while others still declined. Decline might be associated with the exhaustion of natural resources, or loss of competitiveness as new discoveries favoured other areas, as in the case of the Wealden iron industry or the industrial complex built up around the Whitehaven coalfield; it might be associated with transport changes, like the absorption of much formerly local port traffic by London; the inability or unwillingness to accept technical change as in the case of the knitting areas that refused to accept the frame; the loss of protection either by tariffs or distance, as in the case of the Scottish woollen industry; high wages and restrictions on entry, as in the case of the Exeter weavers; rising wages, as in London and some southern agricultural counties, or inability to follow the fashions, as in some towns in the West Country and East Anglia woollen districts.[31] In some areas, the spaces vacated by declining industries were filled by new ones: Coventry's skill of survival is well known.[32] Other areas became de-industrialized, like parts of East Anglia. However, it should be noted that the areas which lost their industrial concentrations had mostly part-time industrial workers and were generally too small to deserve the title of a region: indeed, no minimum standard of size or complexity such as determined industrial growth in later periods can as yet be clearly discerned in the shifting kaleidoscope of industrial specialization before 1750.

Yet there was at least one respect in which the traditional industrial regions exerted an economic influence comparable with that of later, firmer concentrations, and that was their relationship to the agriculturalists surrounding them. An industrial region makes two major kinds of demand on its rural vicinity: a demand for labour and a demand for food, and they tend to pull in opposite directions.

Most industry in the mid-eighteenth century was still of the domestic variety, and this was particularly so in the case of the largest, the textile industry. The finishing processes were increasingly coming to be performed in large workshops in towns, but weaving, a male occupation, was spread around the countryside, and spinning and other preparatory processes were also performed there by women and children, often on a part-time basis. As demand for industrial labour rose, the time which these people devoted to agriculture fell: Part-time textile workers became full time, formerly full-time agriculturalists took up the loom or the spinning wheel part time. The rhythm was different everywhere, sometimes the men leaving off farming first, sometimes the women and girls, but the direction of the change was everywhere the same: labour left the land.[33] Where paid labour had been employed on the farms, wages rose as men were tempted away to industry, and made local farming less competitive. In any case, rents rose. These deficiencies and disadvantages to farmers within industrial orbits were made good only to a very slight extent by manure from the towns, and extra labour at harvest time.

At the same time as the food supply from within and from the immediate surroundings of the industrial region fell, demand for it increased with the growth of a relatively well-paid population and the rise in the number of horses, to power the growing needs of transport. As rising demands were pressing on shrinking supplies, two types of reaction occurred: a transformation of land use within the region, and a rising demand for food and fodder imports from without.

Some of the northern textile regions had never been more than poor upland meadow and moss, but even where the land had once been arable, it tended to be converted back to pasture, for the weaver to keep his cow, his chickens, and above all his horse, which was every-where the heart of the transport system. This petty animal husbandry required little labour, though it helped to even out the work over the year, the weaver being enabled to see to his plot when work in industry was slack. It also reduced the need for specialized local dairy farming to supply the industrial population. However, the massive dovetailing of summer farm work and winter industry, which played such a large part on the Continent of Europe,[34] was of less importance in Britain: the arable fields were generally too far away from the towns.

The industrial region thus had to spread its tentacles outward. Where it found poor soil nearby, it attracted away its population, leaving it less populated than before.[35] But mostly it used the ring of regions around it to make up its food supply. Thus the Derbyshire upland region imported food from Nottinghamshire or even farther afield; West Riding grain came from Lincolnshire and the East and North Ridings and its horses also came from the East; Birmingham was supplied by the rural parts of Warwickshire; North Wales had to bring in food from nearby English counties; and Lancashire brought in food from Cheshire, Westmorland, Lincolnshire, Durham, Wales, and even Ireland.[36] In Ireland itself Ulster drew on Sligo and Mayor for its grain, though there was an even more important link in the fact that 'England's industrial expansion and Ireland's economic develop-ment in the eighteenth century are associated':[37] Irish agriculture was fostered by the existence of the English market as a whole.

Thus the industrial regions colonized[38] their agricultural neighbours in the same way that Britain was said to have colonized other countries, and the whole west to have colonized the Third World in our own day. They took from them some of their most active and adaptable labour, and they encouraged them to specialize in the supply of agricultural produce, sometimes at the expense of some pre-existing industry, running the risk thereby that this specialization would permanently divert the colonized areas from becoming industrial themselves.

Although some of the evidence for these developments is drawn from later in the eighteenth century, their beginnings were clearly present even around 1750. 'Traditional' Britain, far from being an undifferentiated agrarian society with a scattering of craft and dom-estic industry, exhibited a complex and shifting pattern of industrial concentration[39] with its own interrelationships, depending in turn on a growing role of transport, commerce, and credit. This pre-existing pattern helped to determine the distribution of the new industries. In as much as the juxtaposition of competing firms, the mutual stimulation of scientists and inventors in close personal contact, the direct influence of nearby markets played a part in lifting the pioneer country over the threshold of industrialization, regional concentration must share in the 'causes' of the industrial revolution in Britain. It was also to influence the actual sequence of events, once the industrial revolution had taken off.

The First Phase: the 1760s–1790s

In all standard accounts certain technical innovations in a number of key industries and economic sectors, together with a change in their organization and a rapid increase in their output, play a leading part in defining the onset of the industrial revolution. They help to distinguish it from the period which preceded and from contemporary economies such as the French, which failed to take these particular steps at the same time.

Every such list will contain the cotton industry in which new types of spinning-machine (Hargreaves' jenny, *c.* 1764, Arkwright's water-frame, patented in 1769, and Crompton's mule, patented in 1779), together with a bundle of other inventions relating to carding, roving, roller-printing, and chemical bleaching, among others, provided the classic case of revolutionary change. On the basis of a striking reduction in costs there followed a vast increase of the market at home and abroad, a change-over to the factory involving mass employment away from home and in a large building powered by a single motive power, innovations in marketing, in finance, in machine-building, and further concomitant changes, at least in part induced by cotton-spinning, such as labour migration and transport investment.

Another industry combining new technology with a remarkable increase in output was ironmaking. Here the key innovations were the coke-smelting process developed by Abraham Darby *c.* 1709 but introduced widely, after overcoming technical and other snags, only in the 1750s, and the puddling and rolling process, patented by Henry Cort in 1783 and 1784, which permitted large-scale production of the more useful refined (bar) iron. Again, new technology led not only to cost reductions and an unprecedented expansion of markets and sales, but also to other consequent changes. These included the relocation on the coalfields and the creation of large, capital-intensive integrated firms, with implications for migration, transport, and other economic sectors.

Other focuses of innovation will be found on most though not necessarily on all lists. The building of the first true steam-engine by James Watt in 1774 was perhaps the most spectacular technological achievement of the age and, by giving man for the first time in history large concentrations of power that were in some sense 'independent' of location, is held by some to have been the most significant innovation of all. However, even by 1800 the engine-building industry was still extremely small both in terms of output and employment. Coal-mining, it is true, registered an increase in output and played a central part in the whole process at least comparable with that of iron, but there was no significant technological breakthrough, though there were many piecemeal improvements. The same, on a much smaller scale, might be said about the pottery industry. The woollen textile industry was soon almost to rival cotton in the technical and social changes experienced at home and in the quantities exported, but its new technology was introduced only at the very end of our period if we abstract from the numerous scribbling mills that were to be found along many West Riding rivers. Other industries in which important innovations occurred, such as steel or glass-making, and non-ferrous metal-smelting and working, were too small to catch the eye of many observers.

However we draw our limits, it is an impressive list to which have still to be added such other innovations or expressions of a new entre-preneurial spirit as the building of canals, the extension of shipping, shipbuilding, and commerce, innovations in the credit system and continuing investments and improvement in agriculture. Certainly, nothing comparable had ever been happening before in such a short span of time. There was undoubtedly a change in quality in the economy, but it is important to note that by the 1790s that had hardly as yet been transformed into a change in quantity.

Thus, spectacular though the increase in output might appear by earlier standards, even the fastest growing industries—cotton, iron, coal, steam-power—were later in the nineteenth century to experience decades in which the incremental growth alone greatly exceeded the total output of the 1790s.[40] Looked at in contemporaneous terms, large areas of the economy were advancing in this period, if they were advancing at all, at their leisurely traditional pace, as if Richard Arkwright had never been. It is doubtful, indeed, whether even the members of the two Houses of Parliament had any inkling as yet that they were living through a revolution, though they were grateful enough to accept the gifts of the new industrialism in the war in the form of mass-produced uniform cloth, the semi-automatic shaping of naval blocks, or the remarkable ease with which loans could be raised for impecunious continental allies. Foreigners and others, seeking to visit the sites of this new world, had to pinpoint the works on the map among many miles of uninteresting countryside, rather as we would today if we visited the star properties of the National Trust.

One reason why this disproportionately small leaven was able to activate the whole mass was that it was concentrated in significant, even crucial, ways. Above all, the British industrial revolution was a regional phenomenon. Let us look briefly at the main regions which saw significant innovatory changes in the period between the 1760s and 1790s.

The southernmost district affected by these innovations was Cornwall. The bases of this concentration were clearly the mineral resources, tin and copper, and the long traditions, including a unique system of law and company organization, based on them. Important changes began in the 1740s as the demand for copper, the more recently mined ore, rose and drove the miners to look for metal deeper underground. Newcomen pumps and large capital resources were needed, and since coal was expensive there, Cornwall became the first major market for Watt steam-engines in the 1770s and 1780s because these, although more complex and more costly than the existing Newcomen engines, used much less coal. Boulton and Watt, the steam-engine designers of Soho, cut their teeth on Cornwall. China Clay began to be mined in c.1755, but it was tin- and copper-mining and smelting which formed the basis of one of the most advanced engineering centres in the world to the 1840s, and of a complex industrial society exhibiting early developments of banking and risk-sharing to deal with the particular needs of local industry as well as a remarkable attempt to cartelize copper in the 1780s. Although fishing flourished, Cornwall quickly became dependent on imports for food. As early as 1748, the export of grain was prohibited, and, despite great improvements in methods of husbandry, there were threats of famine and increasingly large shortfalls from the 1790s on.[41] In the second half of the nineteenth century, mining declined sharply and Cornwall began to convert from a leading industrial region into a holiday resort area.[42]

Shropshire, also, was favoured by mineral resources, in this case coal and iron ore close together, with the Severn as a major traffic artery. It was there that iron was first successfully smelted with coke, and in the second half of the eighteenth century its leading firms, particularly the Coalbrookdale group and the enterprises of John Wilkinson, the 'iron king', were the undoubted technological leaders in iron making and using. Iron rails, iron boats, iron as constructional material in bridge building (Ironbridge, 1779), and the accurate boring of metal cylinders, are just some of the crucial innovations of those years, made in an industrial complex linked by means of rails, canals, canal inclines, and rivers which themselves constituted part of a new technology. On the basis of coal and iron, there were erected brickworks, potteries, glass and chemical works, armaments works, engineering plants: a roll-call of Shropshire Newcomen steam-engine makers leaves out few of the leading names of the age. Yet by 1815 the region was in decline. The giving out of mineral supplies and the shortage of limestone are only part of the answer, for the area still exported pig iron to other districts for some decades thereafter. A land-locked position with poor communications to the main markets, and the failure to build up large local iron-using industries, have variously been blamed. It is significant that an important feature of the years of decline was a relative fall in iron wages leading to the emigration of skilled men.[43]

Neighbouring South Staffordshire, the 'Black Country', was also based on coal (the famous 30-foot seam), iron and water transport, here supplemented by a long tradition of skilled metal working. It developed one of the earliest canal networks and here also, glass, chemical, engineering, and armaments works followed. Birmingham, as the commercial centre of the region, was ultimately to take on an industrial existence of its own, bringing new life to the district in the twentieth century. However, the real expansion of the district, as far as its heavy industry was concerned, occurred towards the end of the period only, and it became the leading ironmaking region in *c.*1810–30, declining rapidly, with strong signs of technical backwardness, in the 1880s.[44]

The sources of North Wales's industrial boom were more mixed: coal, slate, iron, lead, copper, water power all played a part, so did low wages and good harbours and a favourable geographical location in relation to South Lancashire. Few inventions were actually made in the region, but it was among the earliest to set up modern ironworks, copper-smelting and working plants, engine-building works, and cotton mills. Brick and lime works and an early canal system were other developments essentially based on coal. There were also woollen, linen, and rope-making industries, as well as local banks and shipping firms.[45] Yet somehow this early promise was never fulfilled. Copper began to give out in the 1820s, cotton-spinning declined in the 1830s, but it was the failure of coal output to expand which sealed the doom of North Wales as a major centre of industry: today, like Cornwall, it is mainly a holiday and recreation area. Perhaps the industries were too scattered, the valleys of the area too inaccessible to each other; perhaps, also, it lacked the critical mass to sustain by other means a a career begun by mineral resources.

It was in the uplands of Derbyshire that Arkwright set up his first cotton-spinning mills from 1771 on. There he found an area rich in lead ores as well as water power, and with a long tradition of domestic textile work to add to incomes on poor unhospitable soil. In addition to Arkwright, the other great innovators Lombe, Paul, Hargreaves, Cartwright, and Strutt had also set up in the area or nearby. Apart from its very obscurity, which ensured low wages as well as the absence of the machine-breaking tradition well known in other areas, this region was chosen in part because it was within reach of the framework-knitting centres downstream, which formed the early market for the cotton twist.[46] Its hour of glory, when most of the know-how was found there and men made pilgrimages to it to learn how to run water-powered cotton mills, was but short. Within fifteen years the main weight had shifted to Lancashire, and while local spinning and lead mining continued to flourish, the region soon became a backwater again.[47] It may be held that the area was never large enough, nor its industries comprehensive enough, to qualify for inclusion as an industrial region; or it may be held that it was only part of one, to include the adjacent lowlands in which framework-knitting, and before long, coal and iron, as well as cotton in the west, ensured continuous industrial survival.[48] Clearly, it was handicapped by extremely bad communications from the start, but it is for this area that the interesting claim has been made that it was the strain on engineering resources which caused its downfall. According to this view, the relatively few regional machine-builders were so fully engaged in the construction of complex knitting-frames, while the best of them were tempted away by the higher wages offered in Manchester, Sheffield, or Birmingham, that the area dropped behind the innovations introduced in Lancashire and could never catch up.[49]

Lancashire, or, to be more precise, the southern portion of the county together with adjacent parts of Cheshire and Derbyshire, is doubtless the most clearly defined, the classic industrial region. The role of cotton was so central to the process of industrialization, that in Rostow's scheme it has been termed the 'leading sector',[50] the implication being that its own expansion would stimulate, modernize, and expand other sectors, such as machine-building, coal-mining, the means of transport, the provision of credit, and others. Whatever explanative power may lie in this idea of linkages—and it has been criticized by some as well as eagerly adopted by others—it is evident that the forward and backward linkages derived from cotton benefited in the first place the Lancashire (and Clydeside) regions in a mutually reinforcing way, rather than the whole of the country.

Cotton, or cotton/linen textiles, were not the only industries of

Lancashire. Thus there was an old-established metalworking industry in the Warrington area, and before long a chemical industry developed in the St. Helens area on the basis of coal and salt. Glass works, potteries, copper works were also to be found there. The first modern English canals, the Sankey and the Duke of Bridgewater's Worsley Canal, both in Lancashire, were for coal rather than cotton. Nevertheless, most of the local drive to attract population, stimulate coal-mining, transport, engineering, and chemicals came directly from the cotton industry. Cotton was the motor, and in the first instance it was Lancashire, rather than England, that was the vehicle driven by it. The unique contribution of Lancashire to the history of steam-engine making,[51] let alone textile engineering, and to the development of the credit system,[52] are well known and it was the intensive local competition which helped to stimulate these regional advances in industrial technology and commercial organization, as well as scientific and social investigation.[53] As noted above, these industrial occupations should not be thought of as urban only: the villages were filled by weavers, miners, market gardeners, and others who were similarly part and parcel of the same industrial complex. In the nineteenth century cotton, and Lancashire with it, was to see its real expansion on the basis of steam-powered mills, but by that time the building of mining, engineering, metallurgy, and chemicals plants, among others, ensured the survival of the region as a major industrial area irrespective of the fate of cotton textiles as such.[54]

The West Riding of Yorkshire, across the Pennines from Lancashire, showed similar market-oriented enterprise among its textile manufacturers, although the more sophisticated spinning and preparatory techniques could be introduced only with a delay of about twenty years in the case of worsteds and even longer in the case of woollens. Thus large factories began to be built only in the 1790s though there were at least 115 fulling-mills in existence in the 1770s and 170 mechanically powered scribbling mills in 1787. In other respects, economic life in the two regions was comparable. In some areas, as in Rochdale and Saddleworth, the working of the two kinds of textiles overlapped, and Yorkshire developments were certainly influenced by the experience of the western county. In Yorkshire, too, fast streams and later coal provided the power,[55] transport, iron-making, and pioneer engineering enterprises were quickly in evidence, and a sophisticated commercial organization was built up,[56] though the financial organization was less exceptional, possibly because growth was slower and later, imposing less strain on local resources. The main difference was that the raw material was originally home-produced rather than imported by sea. The region was in fact a good deal farther from the sea than industrial Lancashire, making upstream traffic more costly, but woollens and worsted could be exported without difficulty downstream and later, when coal had to be transported, the railways were there to bridge the distance. Like Lancashire, the industrial complex became sufficiently varied to survive irrespective of any fluctuations in the fortunes of the woollen and worsted industries.

The industrial region around the rivers Tyne and Wear was clearly called into being by its coal. At first easily mined and close to navigable rivers, the local coal was still the most favourably located in relation to the London, the East Coast and the South Coast markets even when mining became more difficult. There was thus a strong economic incentive for the astonishing capital investments in pumps, deep mining equipment, and waggonways to keep up the coal supplies, which ultimately led to the most seminal innovation of the nineteenth century, the railways. On the basis of cheap coal and good transport there developed salt works, glass, soap, and chemicals industries, as well as shipbuilding, ironworks, and some steelmaking. Something of a prodigy among British industrial regions in the eighteenth century, the North-East has been characterized as stagnant and disappointing for a while thereafter[57]—possibly having the linkage effects of its coal supply weakened by largely exporting it—and it took a renewed upward turn only with the rise of iron and steel shipbuilding and armaments manufacture in the second half of the nineteenth century.

The history of the Clyde Valley as an industrial region began in the mid-eighteenth century with the spread of linen manufacture for the market. The next phase saw the astonishing development of the tobacco trade of the City of Glasgow, which led to little enough direct employment in the region, but helped to create the capital that furthered many other local industrial ventures,[58] as well as to the early growth of a sophisticated local banking system. Canals and tramroads to open up the nearby coalfield were the next step, and when the opportunity arose, the Glasgow port facilities and the pre-existing skills relating to (linen) textiles helped to make the area into the second major cotton region in our period. Mills, as in Lancashire, were built first in distant locations, in search of water power, and then moved to the cities when steam became available. South-West Scotland's advantage lay in high-quality fine cottons, for which the earlier specialization in linen weaving and tambouring had laid the foundation. Important ironworks and chemical works were also founded, and for a while Glasgow became the leading chemical centre in Britain.[59]

As in England, the countryside around the main cities, Glasgow and Paisley, filled up with domestic weavers and others dependent on the factories, but by the 1820s it was becoming clear that the region was technically dropping behind Lancashire beyond the point of recall possibly because it was below the minimum critical size.[60] At that moment, it was enabled to execute a second switch, by the discovery by J. B. Neilson (1828) of the efficacy of the hot blast in iron-smelting. Plentifully supplied with coal and the blackband ironstone, which could now be worked, the region quickly climbed to the position of the leading ironworking region, as well as before long the largest ship-builder, and a major engineering and armaments centre, while at least some of the textile tradition was maintained in the manufacture of thread, shawls, and other high-quality products.[61]

Lastly, the industrial concentration in London should not be forgotten, although the metropolitan region, unlike the others, did not owe its existence as a centre of population to commodity production. Apart from possessing the service and direct supply industries found in all cities, the taking in of each others' washing, sometimes technically more advanced than elsewhere because of its sheer size, like the porter brewing noted above, London also became the specialist location of the production of goods and services that were exported to other regions. These included printing, furniture, glass and other luxury-goods manufacture, shipbuilding, the processing of colonial goods, and the provision of banking, insurance, and commercial services.[62]

There is no uniformity about these regions, and indeed it would be surprising if there were, since their development was based on different combinations of various industries, settled on different traditions, natural resources, localities, and transport facilities. Nor is this necessarily a complete list. It might be argued, for example, that the beginnings of mechanical cotton spinning in Ulster,[63] or the modern ironworks in South Wales, together with the more traditional occupations existing there, made those regions significant enough to be included in this phase. Yet our list includes all the areas harbouring any of the major innovating activities, those that find their way into the textbooks (with the significant exception of those relating to agriculture) as either triggering or constituting the beginnings of the first industrial revolution. A detailed study of any of them reveals, as does the over-all view of all of them, to what extent the power of the early acceptance of new ideas, and the influence of the pioneer, were grounded on the existence of these relatively limited regions, providing as it were a system of walls within which the new ideas could reverberate and gain reinforcing strength, rather like the heat in the metal furnaces of the eighteenth century, instead of being diffused ineffectually across the length and breadth of a mostly unreceptive island.

Yet small is not always beautiful—or effectual. It should be noted that of the ten regions enumerated (of which two were doubtful cases), four declined soon after they had made their vital contribution (Cornwall, Shropshire, North Wales, and the Derbyshire uplands) and two more (Tyneside and Clydeside) had to get something like a second wind to survive as centres of progressive industry; only two clear cases (Lancashire and Yorkshire) and a third slightly doubtful one (the Black Country) survived unscathed. Three broad groups stand out among the causes of the decline of certain industrial regions. One is the exhaustion of minerals, or the discovery of cheaper alternative supplies of them. The second is a locational shift elsewhere, or a new development in transport, which renders the region less favourably located than rival areas. The third is a question of size. A small compass may be an ideal milieu for the first halting steps in an innovation, but beyond a certain point an industrial region has to be of a certain size to remain viable. All of our failures were, in a sense, victims of size and/or lack of alternatives. Even rivers and harbours, at one time attractive because of their limited size, may in time become fetters on further development. There might in principle also be a fourth cause, though it was not found in this sample: that is a decline in the area's main market(s), without the ability to switch to meet the alternative or substitute demand.

It was almost as though there had had to be larvae and pupae in this process, driving the evolution forward but not themselves surviving to see it come to its full fruition. This can also be viewed in a different way. An economy containing only one of those early four regions which did not survive, or indeed all four but no other, could most likely not have carried the process further: all the brilliant promise of our first phase, contained in such inventions as those of roller-spinning, of the factory, of the steam engine, might have led only to a half-way stage, perhaps carried forward in more favoured climes elsewhere while Britain, like Shropshire or North Wales, found herself being overtaken and left behind. In other words, it seems that the first industrial revolution, as it passed through its different phases, had to have bases with different endowments for each of them, and it was only because of the variety of resources in Britain, and the existence always of further untapped resources—engineering talent, unused water-power, trained textile workers—somewhere else at each stage, that the whole process could be, in one sense, completed here.[64] There had to be a certain minimum size and variety in the country that was to carry through single-handedly as it were, a complete industrial revolution; the process relied, in effect, on certain external economies in its spatial and historic sequence, expressed by the ability to shift its focus of growth, as it similarly relied on the internal economies of concentrating on limited areas. Industrialization did not merely spread outwards, like ripples in a pool, though it did that too, covering ever more areas. It also required different nourishment and a different soil at successive stages.

This soil, or nourishment, lay in the different endowments of different regions. Some of these were socially or historically conditioned: local skills, freedom from guild powers, a strong dose of Calvinism. But many consisted of natural resources: minerals, waterpower, location along transport routes. Their significance is put into much sharper focus by the regional phase approach.

These conclusions, derived from the early phase of industrialization, will be applied to the Continent of Europe below. In the process, they will have to be modified to take account of the far more complex relationships obtaining among the later arrivals.

The Later Phases

In the rhythm of British industrialization, the period 1790s-1820s constitutes the next phase. Stimulated, burdened, and distorted by twenty-two years of war in the first part of this period, the economy suffered a severe post-war crisis and the first modern boom and slump, associated with massed home and foreign investments, the crisis year being 1825. Throughout these shocks and set-backs, the expansion of industrialization went on apace.

In cotton, this phase saw the building up of an urban, steam-driven spinning industry, while the water-driven plants, and the outlying areas and single mills scattered over the Midlands stagnated or closed down. The Glasgow region reached its zenith and began to lose ground and so did Ulster: henceforth Lancashire was virtually to monopolize the industry. Power weaving was made economical and in the 1820s rapidly drove the handloom weavers out of the coarse and plain sections of the industry. At the same time, specialist machine builders emerged, to take over the workshops of individual mills and accelerate technical adaptations. The pattern of the industry for the rest of the century was set by 1830.

Ironmaking expanded by multiplying existing types of furnaces, the next important innovation, Neilson's hot blast, falling into the very end of this phase. In search of ever larger quantities of iron ore and coal, the industry hit first on South Wales and then on South Staffordshire as its main centres, bringing with it in each case a costly network of canals and tram-roads.[65] In steam-engine making, Watt's patent ran out in 1800 and engineering works were found in every major industrial region, including London.

Coal output expanded both in the former leading area, the North-East, and in other districts made accessible by canals. Among the fastest growers were the West Riding, Lancashire, the Erewash Valley,[66] Scotland, as well as Staffordshire and South Wales.[67] No outstanding technical innovation occurred within the industry itself, though there were many improvements, particularly relating to the lining of pit shafts and to ventilation. But the industry benefited from, where it did not directly stimulate, the extension of the canal and waggonway system, the building of powerful pumping and lifting engines, and, towards the end of the phase, the laying-down of the first rails for steam-driven traffic. All these helped coal-miners to tap previously inaccessible natural riches, either by going deeper underground or farther inland from the waterways.

For the woollen and worsted textiles this was the period of transformation into a power-driven factory industry. The pattern of cotton was largely repeated, in the sense that spinning was mechanized first, while hand-loom weavers were replaced by the power-loom only in the next phase.[68] Flax spinning was also mechanized in this period, suddenly giving Britain an unaccustomed price advantage over the formerly dominant producers on the Continent.

There were fewer spectacular innovations in those years, although some, like machine printing, were as revolutionary for their own industries as the cotton or iron inventions earlier. At their end the opening of the Stockton–Darlington Railway ushered in a new phase of economic history. There were, however, innumerable follow-through improvements, assisted by the emergence of specialist engineering and machine-building firms, which helped to pull the industrialized regions further ahead of the rest, and Britain further ahead of the Continent. Above all, the industrialized regions now thickened up as industries were attracted by the transport network, the local market, and repair facilities, the engineering talent and the enterprise and capital to be found there. Some regions, as we have noted, who could not manage these extensions, did not survive, but those that did were strengthened by this diversification.

One major new region emerged in this phase: South Wales. Some ironworks and coal-mines had been started in the first phase near the head of the valleys, where the minerals were found close together and were easily mined. But the full opening-out of this mineral field as of some others had to wait for the canal 'mania' of the 1790s.[69] At first the industrial–transport complexes were parallel rather than linked, the canals and associated tram-lines in each case conveying the iron and coal down the valleys to the ports of Swansea, Neath, Cardiff, and Newport respectively, but by the end of this phase some cross-connections had been built and the area had, in many respects, gelled into one. Copper-smelting and tin-plate making, both based on coal, were the other main export industries of the region.[70]

The beginnings of Ulster as an industrial region on the basis of the concentration of linen spinning, using in part the facilities of the earlier cotton industry[71] (thus reversing the sequence of the Clyde Valley) may also be put in this period, although it could not be said to have become a major industrial region until later in the nineteenth century. At the same time, three of the early starters, North Wales, Shropshire, and Upland Derbyshire, declined markedly.

The railway era which began with the opening of the Stockton–Darlington (1825) and Liverpool and Manchester (1830) railways, was the dominating innovation of the third phase, lasting to mid-century. Representing a massive investment and building effort, the railways also affected and frequently transformed practically every factor and product market in Britain. Thus they made London accessible to coalfields other than the north-eastern one, and similarly shifted the sources and routes of London's food supply. Labour markets widened as people found it easier to look for work farther afield, perhaps even outside their region, and coal could now be used to smelt minerals that were found some distance from it across country.[72]

Yet, in significant contrast to the European Continent, the railways did not materially alter the economic geography of Britain. That had been fixed by coal, and while the railways here and there extended the workable parts of a coalfield as in South-West Durham, the East Midlands, or the Scottish Lowlands, and in North Wales they 'helped to nip the Industrial Revolution in the bud'[73] they did not call into being a major industrial region that had not existed as such before. Only in the second half of the century were they instrumental in developing mineral areas, such as Tees-side and Furness, and in locating ports and seaside holiday resorts.

Needless to stress, the building-up of such a vast network of permanent way, with the appropriate lines of rails, rolling-stock, and other equipment, strained many of the supplying industries, as well as the markets for capital and for the particular type of physically strong male labour mostly employed. In 1847, the peak year, about 250,000 men, or 4 per cent of the occupied males, were employed in building railways in the United Kingdom; over the whole building phase of the 1830s and 1840s, up to one-fifth of the output of the engineering industry may have gone to British railways; in the peak year only, railway investment took 7% of the national income, though it was generally much less than that; and in terms of material, railways used up around 12% of brick production and 7% of iron production, the peak-year shares being 33% and 18% respectively.[74] Important in each of these respects, the railways did little more than absorb the growth potential of those years, though the strain was unequal over the highly cyclical period of building. There is no sense in which railways could be said to have helped to create British industrialism, or a significant share of it.

Apart from the railways, the most significant industrial changes were the development of the hot blast which turned the Scottish Lowlands into the major British ironworking region and laid the base for the third reincarnation of the Clydeside industrial region, and the conquest of weaving by the power-loom, which drove that process from the villages into the towns and the cities. There were, as before, innumerable piecemeal improvements which helped to raise output without transforming the industries concerned.

The mid-point of the century has often been taken as marking the end of this phase, and in some sense the end of the whole process of industrialization known as the Industrial Revolution in Britain. The Great Exhibition of London held in 1851, centred on the Crystal Palace which in its cast-iron columns and glass panes itself epitomized the mass-production capabilities of the new system, seemed to set the seal on its successful completion. In sheer quantity, the output of many commodities such as coal, iron, and textiles, had reached levels unprecedented, unparalleled elsewhere and unimaginable even a short while earlier. Older processes and producers abroad could frequently no longer compete in costs, no matter how low their wages were to be depressed. Britain was now the 'workshop of the world'. The power to solve technical problems had given British industrialists the self-confidence to look energetically for similar solutions whenever new problems arose in sectors which had so far remained traditional. And, at last, the system had begun to yield results in rising real incomes, in the sense of an expanding flow of goods and services, for even the least favoured of British citizens—though not necessarily for the citizens of Ireland.

Yet it is important to stress how limited still was the impact of the new industrialism in Britain in the mid-nineteenth century. It has been pointed out long ago that at that time only in some textile trades was true factory employment to be found among a majority of workers; it was among a minority in others, and it was exceptional, rather than normal, elsewhere.[75] In other words, employment even in the manufacturing and mining sectors, let alone in the services or agriculture, was still typically in the kind of workshops or working conditions, using the kind of technology, that had been familiar in 1750, a hundred years earlier. Among the major sectors of industry, building (including road, canal, and railway building), the production of most consumption goods including metal goods, furniture, clothing, watches and clocks, vehicles, and china, the final stages in food processing such as baking and meat preparation, and much mining and quarrying, had not yet gone through an 'industrial revolution' as commonly understood.[76] There had been no revolutions in technology there, manual skill or personal know-how were still predominant, there was no central motive power, no factory and no mass production.

It can thus be seen that the spotty, regional, occurrence of 'industrialisation' in the spatial sense was paralleled by a similar distribution among industries. These two phenomena were related, but they were not identical. Thus many of the most traditional forms of industrial employment were to be found predominantly in the heart of the industrialized regions, while in some cases, particularly where suitable minerals existed, units of the most advanced industry might be found in an otherwise unprogressive region. What they had in common was that they were both the result of the economic concentration of the new industrialism on limited areas only.

It should be stressed that these massive pre-'industrial' sectors, forming a veritable sea round the small islands of industrialization, were not necessarily those which had resisted the onset of the new age: many had been called into being by the factories themselves. Thus the growth of textile-spinning, one of the most 'revolutionary' of industrial occupations, called forth a greatly enlarged number of hand-loom weavers working within a domestic system, some of them, indeed, being former hand spinners cast adrift by the spinning machine who 'soon found full employ in the loom on machine yarn'.[77] The factory, in this case, had not replaced domestic work, but had given it a boost. The market mechanism which had brought this about operated though the drastic fall in real costs in the carding and spinning stages, which ensured reduced prices, and thus expanding markets, for the finished product, even though the unit cost of weaving had not been lowered at all and may have even been raised. This could be either because formerly part-time weavers were now full time[78] and carried a higher opportunity cost, or because less efficient people now turned to weaving, or, more generally, because weaving had to attract additional hands and therefore had to raise its incomes in relation to other incomes. The number of cotton hand-loom weavers, together with other auxiliary domestic workers attached to the cotton industry, rose from an estimated 90,000 in 1795 to 270,000 in 1811 and 300,000 in 1833.[79] When weaving became mechanized and pulled into the factories in its turn, lowering the real costs of woven fabrics still further, it was employment in the clothing industry which proliferated, in the same way and by the same mechanism, in the second half of the nineteenth century.

For the earlier phase, the dramatic impact of the new technology on the productivity of spinning may be illustrated by the following figures, showing operative hours necessary per 100 lb. of cotton.[80]

Indian hand spinner (18th century)	50 000 +
Crompton's mule (1780)	2000
Arkwright's rollers (1780s–1790s)	250–370
Power-assisted mule (*c.* 1795)	300
Roberts's automatic mule (*c.* 1825)	135

The productivity of labour had thus risen about 150-fold to the end of the century, and 300-fold by 1825. The fall in costs was less dramatic, since the new methods required more capital per worker. Nevertheless, the costs of capital-plus-labour fell rapidly enough.[81]

Table 1.1. Labour and Capital Costs, in £, per lb. of cotton

	40-hanks	*100-hanks*
1779	0.70	—
1784	0.45	—
1786	—	1.70
1796	—	0.775
1799	0.21	—
1806	—	0.21
1812	0.05	0.142
1830	0.028	0.111
1860	0.019	0.071
1882	0.014	0.052

Compared with a century earlier, the coarser yarn had fallen to 2% of its original cost, and the finer yarn to 3%. In both cases the greater part of the fall had occurred before 1812.

Weaving output began to increase in the following phase and for a while its technical gains exceeded those of spinning.[82]

Table 1.2. Annual Output per hand, in lbs.

	Spinning Cotton yarn	Weaving Cotton goods	Increase since 1819/21 Spinning	Weaving
1819/21	968	342		
1829/31	1546	521		
1844/6	2754	1681	X 2.8	X 4.9
1859/61	3671	3206		
1880/2	5520	4039	X 5.7	X 11.9

Similar developments took place in the iron industry, in which the production of iron and steel goods expanded on the basis of the lowered costs of pig or bar iron, and *mutatis mutandis* in other sectors. We shall find this mechanism of a technological differential between the stages of operation on the same product furthering the expansion of employment in the less developed sectors, to be of great significance in the study of the propagation of industrialism across Europe.

In fact, it would be quite erroneous to suppose that because no revolution in technology had occurred in certain sectors or industries and no change in organization was discernible in them they had been left unaffected by the transformations elsewhere. Industries and regions were profoundly affected by their environment, that is to say, the contemporary changes in other sectors of the economy, even though their own processes had been subject to no or to no significant changes.

Thus a visitor to the metalworking areas of Birmingham or Sheffield in the mid-nineteenth century would have found little to distinguish them superficially from the same industries a hundred years earlier.[83] The men worked as independent sub-contractors in their own or rented workshops using their own or hired equipment. A minute division of labour ensured quality and variety without any elaborate equipment or a great deal of artificial power: nearly all depended on the skill of the individual workman. Training was by apprenticeship within the craft, usually regulated in some way, and women and children might perform ancillary and lesser skilled tasks within a family or family-like setting. The link with the market was through a merchant-manufacturer, or putter-out, who provided the orders, sometimes also the raw materials, and saw to the finishing, packing, and dispatch; his position was constantly undermined in slumps by the 'little mester' who was willing to work for less, to depress wages, or employ unskilled labour, sometimes by lowering the quality of the product. These industries, it was clear, were still waiting for their industrial revolution.

Yet there were profound differences between their position then and that of a hundred years earlier, or that of similar districts on the Continent that were not equally within reach of the new industrial regions. Thus, on the technological plane, there might be no great changes in forging, casting, or grinding,[84] but there would be steam-engines in place of water-wheels, allowing a more concentrated location of the workshops, more regular working, and a closer link-up with the market.[85] Even in the workshop a variety of gadgets such as stamping, cutting, shaping machines too trifling to be noted by the historian, eased and speeded work. There might be gas light, water pipes, better grease to help inside the workshop; outside, the merchant-manufacturer would be aided by cheap printing to advertise his wares all round the world, and a railway and steamer service to dispatch his goods, should orders be forthcoming.

Railways also helped to introduce the Sheffield man to a wider labour market, and brought cheaper food to him: yet it should be noted that both railway lines supplying the city, the Manchester, Sheffield, and Lincolnshire, and the North Midland, had been built largely by outside captial.[86] The banking system as a whole was more appropriate to an advanced economy, and in a few years limited liability would become freely available for a world in which the typical Sheffield firm was increasingly becoming an anachronism. In this respect, also, Sheffield and places like it benefited by industrialization elsewhere.

Attitudes and outlook were also in part shaped by events elsewhere. Sheffield had a supply of newspapers, fed by telegraphic information, inconceivable a hundred years earlier, and constantly bringing news from the more advanced regions of the country. The internal structure of Sheffield industry made for trade unions of the eighteenth-century type, but local unionists were aware of a trade-union world outside, shaped by different forces, and could not remain uninfluenced by it. The Sheffield Outrages Enquiry of 1867 showed the extent and consequences of that particular anachronism.[87] Similarly, local Radicals absorbed the ideas of contemporary Chartism, though they tended to transform it into something quite different from the revolt of the 'fustion jackets and unshorn chins' erupting in other regions.[88] At the same time, the very attitudes that allowed Sheffield manufacturers to risk their capital by exporting to Australia, Latin America, or China derived from the success with which the industries that had been revolutionized had pioneered these markets earlier.

Thus, among the advantages of having advanced areas as not too distant neighbours were access to cheap supplies of raw materials such as iron, of machinery, and the lowering of the costs of all commodities, including food, that had to be brought in from a distance. Similarly, commercial and transport links with the region's own markets, including whatever markets existed in the advanced areas themselves, were immensely improved largely owing to the overspill effects of efforts of the advanced regions. They gave producers in cities like Sheffield a significant competitive advantage in third markets over other producing areas abroad, like those in Austria or Germany, that might themselves possess a not dissimilar productive capacity, but lacked the infrastructure and other facilities built up, for Sheffield, by its more advanced neighbours. Again, areas like

Sheffield could tap capital, technological aids, commercial information, the network of consuls, and the protection of the British navy,
all of which had been built up essentially for the use of the advanced
export regions of Britain.

Proximity to successfully 'revolutionised' regions also had its disadvantages. Labour might be drawn away to the growth area, though
this was not the case in our Sheffield example, and certainly higher
wages would have to be paid, though not necessarily identical wages,
for those employed in comparable non-export industries, such as
local transport and distribution, personal service, and even in such
crafts as printing, building, or engineering. High wages are not, of
course, a disadvantage except to export competitiveness. It is in fact
one of the more significant differences between the pioneer regions
in Britain and the latecomers that the latter, when their turn came,
found in existence either ready-made or easily adapted a factory
legislation, a trade-union movement inspired by the early industrializers, and a generally more enlightened public opinion within which
their labour policy had to operate. The sufferings of little children
(and less so, of women) of the early factory and mining period were
never to be repeated elsewhere to quite that extent or for that length
of time, precisely because they occurred later in an environment that
was enriched by the experiences of the first phases of British industrialization. Food prices might also be raised by the competing demand
of the powerful neighbour, and the price of other items in widespread
demand, which had themselves not benefited by a new technology,
such as horses, would be similarly affected.

Above all, it was possible for the region which had failed to keep
up with the technical advance of the leading regions, possibly because
it lacked the critical mass, or supplied a substitute which could not
adopt the new methods for technical reasons, to see its basic industry
wiped out altogether, and to become de-industrialized by the progress
elsewhere. In a buoyant environment, those made redundant by de-
industrialization could be absorbed in other sectors, though not without agonizing costs of adjustment. Thus the rural cotton weavers
round Manchester who were replaced by the power looms in city
weaving sheds did not revert to agriculture when the rationale of their
occupation collapsed, but were found alternative though often unsatisfactory employment in the Lancashire industrial complex.[89] But
it was not entirely unknown for a whole region to lose its industrial
character. In the United Kingdom, North Wales and the East Coast of
Ireland furnish the best examples.[90]

These experiences can be generalized. We are dealing with areas
between which factors of production, particularly labour, showed

some, but generally only weak, mobility. there was therefore, in the first half of the nineteenth century, a tendency for the higher wages which the higher output of the industrialized regions could finance, to pull up the wage level even in areas in which there had not yet occurred a revolution in production to make the payment of higher wages out of higher output possible. The tendency was weak at any one time, but powerful over a long period of half a century or more. The problem, to put the issue slightly differently, was how to distribute the benefits of higher productivity as social gain even among those industries which had not contributed to it, and this appeared very clearly as a regional industrial problem.

Its solution, in the British case, was achieved very largely because it was a slow, secular process. In part, the social gain was spread by lower prices of cotton goods, coal or iron manufacturers, to all consumers; in part, by transfers of capital, and the construction of public utilities which again spread some of the benefits; it was also solved in part by slight movements in the labour markets and adjustments in wages; and ultimately it might be solved by the spillover of an improved and more productive technology also into the relatively backward regions. But this last step could not always be taken, and where a measure of de-industrialization took place, it tended like industrialization itself, to be cumulative.

The mechanisms sketched here are not unfamiliar to economic theories dealing with foreign trade since the days of Adam Smith and Ricardo. But there is no standard economic analysis to deal with them because, having set up a problem, economists assume an instantaneous solution by a move towards equilibrium, whereas in fact that adjustment may take a whole historical period and form the stuff of economic history. We shall return to these issues and discuss them at length when we deal with the spread of industrialization across Europe;[91] what we wish to stress here is that there is no difference in principle between trading relations, and the consequences which follow from them as between countries and as between industrial regions, though the frontier may add many complications in detail.

Contact with an economically more advanced region may thus have its dangers as well as its advantages. In Great Britain (but not in most of Ireland) the advantages predominated. To this point also we shall return later. What is beyond doubt is that each region was profoundly affected by being contemporary with others at a different stage of development. Thus Sheffield in 1850 was not simply a century behind the advanced textile regions, set to catch them up by following the same path. Its path, and indeed its position, even within its pre-factory stage was profoundly different because it had advanced areas as contemporaries with which it was in commercial as well as in intellectual contact. Backward regions (or countries) do not merely take a different route because they are backward and therefore have a bigger jump to take than the more advanced regions when it was their turn, as has been convincingly argued by Alexander Gerschenkron.[92] Their experience is also different because they live in a different world from that inhabited by the advanced regions when they were at comparable stages of development.

It should be evident that similarly profound influences were exerted by the advanced industrial regions on those which had no industry at all but lived by exporting their agricultural surplus. There were first the new machines, such as threshing machines, iron ploughs, even steam ploughs which constituted a direct fall-out from the technical advances of the industrial regions. 'The proximity of the mines', it has been noted, 'made the Cornish farmers far more mechanically-minded than those in the purely agricultural districts of England',[93] but sooner or later machines were to find their way even into the backwoods of Lincolnshire and East Anglia. Where industrialists and mine owners took over land to feed their horses or employ members of the families of their workers, they were often known as agricultural improvers.[94]

Railways were rarely built into agricultural regions until late in the nineteenth century: where they were, as in East Anglia, they made losses. But although the railway map faithfully reflected the industrial geography of the country, thickening into networks in the advanced industrial regions, there were also long-distance lines linking these with each other and with London. Where they passed through agricultural areas they helped to move their product and spread the regional specialization, which was one of the most powerful upward drives in British agriculture.[95] Railways also released land formerly used for horses and brought fertilizers and town manure more cheaply to the farmer.[96] Very close to the urban centres, the symbiosis became one of market gardening and dairying, and remarkable numbers of animals were kept in the built-up areas of towns, in London, at least, largely as part of the breweries and distilleries economy.[97]

Industrialization, it is well known, also raised wages in agriculture, this being one of the ways by which its social benefits were spread, leading in turn to higher efficiency and a redistribution of factors to make those higher wages possible. But it would be, once again, to misunderstand the industrialization process to assume that all agricultural wages as such benefited. First, the process was a very slow and secular one;[98] and secondly, it was regional in nature. As Elizabeth Gilboy showed, it was those in or near the industrializing regions which alone benefited in the later eighteenth century, overtaking the previously superior southern and West Country wages. According to James Caird's famous table, these differentials had been confirmed and strengthened by 1851.[99] 'Who will work for 1s. 6d. or 2s. a day in a ditch when he can get 3s. 6d. or 5s. a day in a cotton work, and be drunk four days out of seven?'[100] may have been a rhetorical question showing remarkable ignorance of life in the mill, but it contained a grain of truth. Temporarily, canal and railway building would also drive up wages[101] and so, more powerfully, did proximity to London. Even within an industrial county 'the rate of wages is in proportion to the distance . . . from the seats of manufacturers . . . (because of) the immediate wages to be obtained at the manufactories'.[102] On the other hand, the kind of transhumance found in other countries, in which the first generation of factory workers still went back to the villages to bring in the harvest, was largely absent in Britain. Town workers helped indeed with the harvest, but only in the vicinity of their place of work. To return to one's home appears to require a peasant mentality, and apart from some marginal areas like mountainous Wales,[103] Britain conspicuously lacked a peasantry.

Thus industrialization, properly speaking, remained a local phenomenon even in the later stages of the industrial revolution. But the areas lagging behind in industrial development, and those specializing in agriculture, were profoundly affected by their contemporaneity with the changes in the advanced regions.

Some Preliminary Hypotheses

How far is this phase/regional approach to the British industrial revolution a valid one? Is anything gained by viewing the process in this light, rather than, as is common, as a single national process, with only marginal areas like Northern Scotland, Southern Ireland, and Central Wales excluded? Above all, is it anything but a trivial point to make that since industrialization was a slow process, it had to begin somewhere, with one or two sectors, and then spread so that at any one time some regions would be changed and others would lag behind?

To be valid, and to fit into the widely accepted concept of the British industrial revolution as a sequence of phases (if not stages),[104] the region must have an operative as well as a descriptive meaning. It must mean more than a number of industries side by side. It must as a minimum generate an interaction that would be absent if the component industries were not juxtaposed in this particular way.

Some of the evidence for just such interaction has already been presented, but all of it may conveniently be summarized here. Regions, to begin with, frequently had distinct technological traditions, affecting their path of progress. Thus in coal-mining, the Shropshire long-wall method contrasted with variants of the pillar-and-stall method in the North-East, and colliery railways developed in two systems that had almost nothing in common: the narrow-gauge Shropshire railway, with its peculiar-shaped waggons, and the broad-gauge Newcastle waggonway, with quite different vehicles. Other districts accepted one or the other, possibly with modifications.[105] Again, in the enquiry of 1842 it was found that some districts, but not others, employed women underground and even the serfdom of the Scottish mines was a phenomenon of the East of Scotland rather than the West,[106] while the Staffordshire butty system was not found elsewhere though a modified form existed in the North-East only.[107] Although expert 'viewers' from the north-East were brought into most districts from time to time to suggest improvements and thus helped to unify practice, yet in many details the practice between regions differed so much that migrating miners found it very difficult to adjust. Some of these differences were caused by geology: the special problems of the 30-foot seam in the Black Country, for example,[108] or the broken nature of the Welsh seams, but most had evolved from earlier traditions and then survived as independent factors. There was also a certain lag between regions: thus South Wales took over coal technology only after a considerable delay, and Lanarkshire may have been up to twenty years behind Lancashire in cotton technology.[109] As coalfields worked for different kinds of markets, the marketing/transport arrangements also differed widely.

Beyond mere technology, regions also developed a style of their own, including forms of industrial organization, and the levels of quality and markets aimed for. This seems to have played a major part in what is perhaps the most frequently discussed regional transfer within the British industrial revolution, the rise of the West Riding woollen and worsted industry at the expense of the West Country and East Anglia. There is no close agreement even on the timing of this transfer, and among the causes for the loss of competitive ability in the two southern areas are the lack of coal, the absence of sufficient water power (at least in East Anglia), and the need to import long wool for West Anglia's worsted spinners from elsewhere, since the local sheep produced mostly short-stapled wool. But since the days of Daniel Defoe and Josiah Tucker, it has also been widely accepted that among the major causes for this dramatic switch of the location of what was then Britain's premier industry was the style of organization: the southern regions had large capitalistic merchant-clothiers or putters-out, with a labour force reduced to little more than wage-earning status, whereas the Yorkshire 'manufacturers' were the weavers themselves, employing the spinners of their own or neighbouring families and organizing their own scribbling mills, an entirely competitive and flexible group who made contact with the export merchant only at the point of sale of the finished piece of cloth in the city cloth markets and cloth halls. Other, associated causes of Yorkshire's success are said to have been its concentration on cheaper ranges of goods, for which the market was growing, and its increasing ability to copy the well-established high-grade textiles from the south while holding down the price. There was also the violent opposition of the skilled labour force in the south to new machinery. Finally, the demonstration effect of nearby Lancashire, particularly in the hilly border regions where the two textiles overlapped, is also cited.[110] Most of these factors relate to traditional style rather than natural endowment.

In the older mining areas, like the Forest of Dean, the Derbyshire lead-mining district, and in the Stannaries of Cornwall regional practices and styles were enshrined in separate laws which survived in some cases into the modern period. The Cornish system of wage payments is, in its field, unique, but it is reflected in a similar system of payments for Cornish fishermen.[111] In South Wales, it has been suggested, the particular style of local industry derived from the abundance of raw materials there. Industrial organization could usefully be contrasted as between Shropshire and neighbouring Staffordshire, and probably arose from the sources of local capital and the role of large landowners.[112]

The organizations of industrialists were virtually exclusively regional. This reflected their consciousness based on their experience that their market, the competitive world within which they operated, and the effective boundary of their power was given by the regional, rather than the national dimension. Where a true cartel to limit output and control prices was to be formed, it was by nature regional, as in the case of the Newcastle 'Vend' or the Cornish Metal Company. Similarly, ironmasters met in regional groupings to attempt to organize their trade, though there were also some sporadic country-wide meetings from 1808 onward.[113] In textiles, the Worsted Committees, though regional, might be considered tied mainly by their industry, but the Manchester Committee for the Protection and Encouragement of Trade (1774) soon became a regional body, which was ultimately transformed, via the Manchester Commercial Society, into the Manchester Chamber of Commerce (1820). Similarly, the Birmingham Commercial Committee of 1783 'aimed at representing the general economic interests of the district'. By contrast, the nation-wide General Chamber of Manufactures, called into being by the fight against Pitt's Irish resolutions of 1785, soon fell apart because of the unbridgeable gulf between the interests of the new 'revolutionised' industries and the majority of traditional manufactures.[114] Meetings of industrialists as employers were conducted on a regional basis and black lists against trade-union activists were regional. The labour market, above all, was regional and was perhaps responsible more than any other single factor for making the region into the operative economic unit, just as the availability of a pool of experienced labour formed one of its most powerful external economies.

With very few exceptions, all internal migration in Britain in that period was migration into the industrialized regions, including London, or into the gaps left by such migrants.[115] Although there are some indications that the main industrial regions (with the very important exception of London) may have shown a higher rate of natural increase than the rest of the country,[116] it was migration which was the mechanism by which the most striking outward characteristic of the industrial regions was achieved, namely their rapid population increase. It is not always possible to obtain statistics for areas even approximately congruent with economic regions, but in the few cases where this can be done, the results show a remarkable divergence of the industrial regions from the surrounding areas.

Thus for England and Wales, population figures and changes were as follows:

Table 1.3.

	Estimated Population in 000s				Increase in %		
	1701	1751	1801	1831	1701-1751	1751-1801	1751-1831
Agricultural Counties, incl. Wales	1949	1960	2605	3691	1	33	88
Mixed Counties	1922	1930	2786	4043	0	44	109
Industrial–Commercial Counties	1955	2251	3765	6318	15	67	181
Of these, the five counties Durham, Lancs., Staffs., Warwicks., and West Riding only	811.8	1016.3	1904.6	3360.1	25	87	231

It is clear that the industrial regions began to pull away sharply only after the onset of industrialization. In Scotland, the population of the Central Belt rose from 464,000 to 984,000 between 1755 and 1821, or from 37% to 47% of the total (on 14% of the land surface). In the three cities of Glasgow, Paisley, and Greenock the population had increased twelvefold between the beginning of the eighteenth century and 1831.[117]

Immigrants came from agriculture or from occupations made redundant by the new industry.[118] They were attracted by higher wages, though often the differential was nominal rather than real, or, sometimes, simply by the prospect of work. Once there, they were likely to stay even if their original employment collapsed, having become part of the shifting labour force which kept the structural changes of mining and manufacturing going. In some twentieth-centuy countries at similar stages of economic development there is a labour influx into the cities, particularly the capital cities, far in advance of employment opportunities there, released by images of attractive city life. Such can hardly have been the case in the British Isles, judging by what we know of the industrial towns then. There may have been some misdirected migration to the capital cities London, Edinburgh, and Dublin, in misunderstanding of the employment opportunities to be found there; and Mayhew's reports[119] provide some proof of this, but on the whole the population growth of the British industrial regions reflects the growth in their employment closely enough.

Beside the mass migration to learn the skills of the new industrialization, there was the more select movement of those who had to teach them. In the transfer of technology between one region and another, which played as important a role as the transfer between countries which has received very much more attention, the movement of skilled personnel was often critical. As Archibold Buchanan brought Arkwright's methods to Scotland, English ironworkers helped to establish the Carron Works there.[120] Shropshire ironworkers stiffened the crews of Welsh blast-furnaces and rolling-mills, as Shropshire itself had been developed by migrants from Staffordshire. Similarly, Newcastle mine managers were invited to bring the technology of the collieries of Cumberland, Yorkshire, Warwickshire, Scotland, and other areas up to date.[121] Once established in a region, classes in Mechanics' Institutes, Technical Schools, and Colleges of Art tended to reinforce the skill and know-how advantages of the local industrial community. The advantage of possessing a local engineering capacity was evident. It is significant that of the 48,000 engine and machine makers enumerated by the Census of 1851, 14,000 were found in Lancashire and Cheshire, 6,000 in the West Riding, 6,500 in London, and major concentrations also in the West Midlands, the North-East of England, and West-Central Scotland. At the time, it took five to seven years to train an engineer, and in booms employers would have to refuse orders because this number could not be increased fast enough.[122]

There is also a sense in which the provision of capital was a local affair. Before the days of easy joint-stock company formation, most of the capital of typical firms would come from the active proprietors, their families, and their close friends. Capital was therefore rarely invested outside the region.[123] The base of the normal 'country bank' which would be expected to supply much of the circulating capital, generally by discounting bills of exchange, would also be regional,[124] often arising from the trading or agricultural sector, and from the declining industrial areas as well as from industry itself.

Yet an industrial region expanding vigorously in its industrial revolution would frequently require capital beyond its own powers of saving. This was particularly so where a costly infrastructure, consisting of roads and docks, normally financed from within the region, had to be built up at the same time. If industrialization had occurred, as it were, on a national base, it might well be that capital shortages would have been a serious brake on development, and would have slowed it by worsening the periodic crises which followed the speculative booms of that period. As it was, the industrializing regions could sustain longer capital deficit phases by drawing on the savings of the rest of the country.

The part played by the banking system, which had become national long before the economy as a whole, has often been described.[125] London as the central exchange, channelling funds from the surplus (savings) regions to the deficit (investing) regions by means of bills, fulfilled precisely this function of concentrating some of the country's surplus savings in the industrializing regions in the period of this growth. The differential in interest rates which provided the motive force for this flow was one aspect of the existence of regional capital markets, though data do not exist as yet to test how strongly these forces operated.[126] 'There is', Adam Smith stated magisterially but ambiguously, 'in every society or neighbourhood an ordinary or average rate both of wages and profit in every different employment of labour and stock.'[127] Although merchants, residing in London or other trading cities like Glasgow or Bristol[128] were often prepared to invest permanently in industry, particularly in their own line where they could judge the abilities of their active partners, on the whole these loans to industry were short term. Periods of expansion, financed by credits on this basis, were therefore followed by balance of payments crises and liquidations which bore a strongly regional/financial character. In the case of Scotland, where distances were sufficiently large, the banking system for legal reasons quite different, and observers still accustomed to treat the industrial region which dominated the Scottish economy in this respect as a separate country, the existence of these balance of payments crises accompanying the local liquidity crises following an overexpansion of regional credit was quite clear.[129] Elsewhere the sequence of events was similar, but rarely seen as such, though it was not entirely hidden from contemporary observers.[130] If data existed, the import and export trade of each major region in Britain would be as significant for an understanding of the progress of industrialization in Britain, as the trade pattern of European countries is for Europe.[131]

Lancashire, as might be expected, showed the regional nature of its capital market most clearly. Even outwardly, as long as it was a capital deficit region, it was distinguished from the rest of the country by using bills instead of coins and local bank notes. The latter, used almost exclusively within one region only, were found early on in other industrial regions, including Yorkshire and the West Country; but after the Bank of England set up branch banks in the 1820s there, they were largely limited to the agricultural regions of England.[132] Lancashire (with the adjoining parts of Cheshire and Derbyshire) switched straight to the notes of the Bank of England when the latter had established its branches in Manchester (1826) and Liverpool (1827), and to the cheque system of joint-stock branch banks thereafter.[133] By the 1830s, Lancashire, particularly Liverpool,[134] had become a capital-surplus region, the only one, apart from London, to invest on a large scale in railways outside its own district. Each of the banking systems of the Newcastle, South Wales, West Midland, and Yorkshire regions also showed distinctive features.[135] Since a run on one bank in a region would quickly endanger all the others there, they would help each other within this narrow circle in a crisis, just as they would normally take each other's notes and cheques.[136]

There was a regional element even in taxation. In the absence of a central bureaucracy, taxes on property were assessed and collected by local dignitaries and businessmen who could by successful manipulation of in-payments and transfers to London, accumulate large local funds which they could make use of for their own benefit for varying periods. The Land Tax, on the other hand, by its peculiar fixity in terms of regional and local distribution approximately in line with later seventeenth-century values, favoured the advancing northern industrial districts by not raising their share as their property values rose.[137]

Taxes were largely spent in London, in garrison and dockyard towns, and in country homes and watering places by those who drew the more or less merited 'pensions' from the state. Holders of the Funds would also not predominate in industrial regions.

A successful industrial region not only constituted an important trading partner with other parts of the country, and with regions abroad. It also developed a full economic life of its own, and became able to adjust changing comparative costs within its own borders.

Thus as city rents and wages rose in Leeds, the main finishing centre of the West Riding, wool-manufacturing moved out, giving way to engineering as well as shoemaking, service industries, and even linen: the share of firms associated with wool production in Leeds fell from 58% in 1728-59 to 14% in 1834. The share of production of other towns and villages also changed rapidly with changing technology and factor costs.[138] What was important was interdependent diversity,[139] in terms of backward and forward integration, service trades, infra-structure including a good transport system, and close linkage with markets and supplies to enable the region to react quickly to changing costs, prices, or fashions. Where these elements were present, the tendency would be for the region to pull ahead of the rest, and for regional inequality to increase cumulatively for very long periods.[140]

It remains to draw two types of conclusions that would aid the understanding of the expanded process of industrialization in Europe. The first can be stated very briefly. In view of the actual process on a regional, as well as an industrial basis, the national statistics which are normally used to illustrate economic growth cannot bear the enormous weight which is usually placed on them. This is so whether they are drawn up on the Markovitch principle of including both new and old industries, down to an estimate of domestic labour, or on the Bairoch principle of including only the new industries. In both cases, growth is diluted by the inclusion of large non-growing elements, and the latter method also neglects the relative rate of decline and replacement or survival of important sectors of the economy. Thus a moderate rate of growth overall as measured conventionally may hide either a moderate rate of widespread industrialization, or very fast and successful indus-trialization limited to some key areas—two very different processes. The extent of the distortion will depend on the proportion of a country actually included in the industrializing regions and sectors. In Britain, even the extremely fast growing, and successful, 'leading sector' of the cotton industry expanded from around 1% of national product in *c.* 1781-3 to 4-7% in 1800 and a maximum of 7-8% only in 1811-13.[141]

The other type of conclusion refers to the uniqueness of the British experience, many features of which we cannot expect to find repeated on the Continent. Britain, as has often been noted, had a favourable political and legal climate, it had a long tradition of industrial employ-ment and commercial enterprise, it had colonies[142] and a relatively high level of accumulated wealth, and it had been mercifully free from foreign invasions for many centuries. Apart from some marginal regions, there were no peasants in Britain and virtually no feudal privileges; instead, there was a wage-earning class used to working for money wages. Much may have been made by British economic historians of the benefits of canals in 'opening up' territories hitherto more than twenty miles from a navigable waterway, but compared, say, with the ironworking regions of Styria or the Urals, the whole of Britain was extremely accessible. Britain also had the advantages of a wealth of minerals, including coal, and of a soil and climate favourable to mixed agriculture.

Whatever may be the 'causes' of the industrial revolution, or the 'causes' of its first appearance in Britain, it is clear that when Europe became in some sense 'ripe' for it and science and technology stood ready for the next leap forward, several locations in Britain would enjoy important advantages over all but a very small number of favoured regions on the Continent. This was true, *mutatis mutandis*, also for the secondary industrial and the agricultural areas and closeness in development to the 'take-off point' makes a great deal of difference to the ease with which industrialization proceeds.

The leading sectors and regions in Great Britain were not faced, as those everywhere else were, with the rapid emergence of rivals which had to be met quickly on pain of de-industrialization. Instead, they developed slowly, organically, the speed dictated by the availability of supplies and market opportunities undisturbed by the emergence of more potent rivals abroad. No matter how stumbling and groping the way forward, everyone else was much farther behind. By 1790 the United Kingdom had reached an output of 15 kg. iron per head (if spread over the whole population), a level not reached by Europe until 1870; she used 2 kg. of raw cotton, which was reached by Europe only in 1885, and a maximum of 38-42% of the population was left in agriculture—the level reached by the Continent in the middle of the twentieth century only.[143] Thus, whatever the advances in any single region on the Continent, possession of a group of regions enjoying the external economies of their own existence gave the British as a whole quite exceptional advantages.

These advantages were temporarily increased even further by some of the consequences of the revolutionary and Napoleonic Wars. For while in Britain the disturbances were minimal, contacts with overseas suppliers and markets were maintained, and methods of mass production stimulated by some specific war demand for guns and uniforms, for example, the effects on the Continent were generally negative. Conscription, occupation, battles, actually lowered and disrupted production; even where output was stimulated, as in Belgium and parts of the Rhineland, these regions found themselves frequently geared to the wrong markets in post-war conditions. Moreover, the compulsory isolation enforced by war and the Contintental System allowed several British industries to race ahead technologically and create an unbridgeable competitive gap. When trade then began to flow again, it appeared to observers both in Britain and on the Continent as though the whole of the British economy were superior to European countries as a whole.

The peculiar position and attendant advantages of Britain should, indeed, be borne in mind. Yet this simplifying national picture is misleading. There were areas on the Continent not far behind the British: 'the history of the rapid acceptance of British industrial advances in the valley of the Meuse and Sambre is not vastly different from the history of their acceptance, say, in the valleys of South Wales'. The example of Belgium (and the Ruhr later) proves 'first that Western Europe was a single economic community within which circumstances might give rise to similar results; and secondly that industrial growth was essentially a local rather than a national affair. In this regard it is perhaps unnecessarily inexact to talk of England and the Continent rather than, say, of Lancashire and the Valley of the Sambre-Meuse. Each country was made up of a number of regional economies.'[144] It is time to turn to see the experience of the European Continent in this light and on the lines laid down by the British pioneers.

Part I

The Phase of Economic Integration. From the Eighteenth Century to the Crisis of the 1870s

Chapter 2

The Pre-Industrial Setting of Inner Europe

The Europe which had to accept and absorb the new industrialism and the many social changes associated with it, was not a stagnant, inert, or purely traditional continent. On the contrary, Europe was a continent made up of many variegated and contrasting economies, and was in the process of fundamental development and change, of which the French Revolution was only the most influential example. Many of these changes and developments were very similar to those which had preceded and, indeed, formed part of the industrial revolution in Britain. When, therefore, the continental communities had to face the challenge of British industrialization, expressed most dramatically by the flood of cheap mass-produced manufactures which poured into their markets in 1815 and threatened to kill off many of their traditional industries, they found no insuperable obstacles in following the same path. That process of first following and then transcending the British example is the essential subject-matter of this book.

The regions of Europe differed, however, very greatly in their preparedness for these changes, and in their ability to copy or bypass them. There was, as it were, an 'inner' Europe, situated in the north-western corner opposite the British Isles, which was closest in many important aspects to the social and economic structure that had produced the autonomous changes in Britain. Surrounding that core in descending circles there were other areas, increasingly less prepared, forming the *Gefälle*, or gradient, frequently described by German historians, which we shall notice in various aspects of economic and social life. This slope should not be imagined as solid territory within which everything had been first prepared and then changed over to modern industry in one steady sweep, like a country conquered by solid lumbering infantry. Rather it resembled a *Blitzkrieg* battlefield in a classic Guderian campaign, in which strategic strongholds had been captured far in advance while leaving much of the open intervening territory still in enemy hands. The industrial revolution jumped, as it were, from one industrial region to another, though in a general direction outward from the North-West, while the country in between remained to be industrialized, or at least modernized, much later, if at all.

Moreover, this conquest did not proceed indefinitely outward. At first it met a well-prepared soil on which it could maintain a rapid and successful thrust, shifting forward the frontiers of 'inner Europe'. But then there came a line where the process stopped, sometimes for generations, and, in some cases, until today. Beyond it, there were only scattered outposts, too weak to affect much the surrounding country as the more densely spaced industrial regions in Britain and in 'inner Europe' had been able to do.

No history that sets out to describe realistically how Europe was industrialized can leave out this manner in which the process occurred, and the interrelationships which it set up as it proceeded. Moreover, since it took place over a considerable period of time, such factors as market conditions or current technology were very different for the various regions as they reached appropriate and similar stages of development, and it was the interplay of these locational, temporal, and contemporaneous factors which explains much of the economic development of Modern Europe.

This and the next two chapters will deal with the industrialization of 'inner Europe', inside the barrier, and Chapter 5 with simultaneous developments in the 'periphery', the lands left outside, up to the turning point of the 1870s. We begin with the agricultural background.

Agrarian Society and Industrialization

Although we speak of feudal society and agrarian traditionalism, European agriculture, as far as we can tell, was never of one mould, and never entirely stable. Changes in population, in climatic conditions, in techniques and forms of organization, changes in markets and the political power of crown, nobility and gentry, kept the system in constant flux. By the later eighteenth century changes had become faster, and the differences between regions wider than ever.

It is not easy to impose order on the chaos of differing systems of tenure, of obligations, of payments, of technique, and of law which characterized European agriculture at the time. Nor is the task lightened by the fact that nowhere in economic life did legal or administrative fiction differ more widely from reality. For the land was difficult to supervise and control, and perhaps even to understand from the towns; customary relationships and unwritten conventions, in largely illiterate communities, were more significant than those rigidified on paper; and the exigencies or calamities of harvest failure, enemy occupation, epidemic, migration, or simple population rise could impose *ad hoc* solutions which could take a long time to find their way into the official or nominal structure.

One way of attempting to understand the reality of European agriculture is to begin with the recognition that, in addition to providing food and various raw materials, it had the purpose of providing large incomes for powerful classes in each society who offered little or no economic benefits in return. Human ingenuity and local historical conditions had built up a variety of rights, claims, obligations, or forms of ownership of land, all designed to transfer the largest possible share of income from the actual tiller of the soil to someone more powerful than he while leaving him just enough to carry on this process year after year. This transfer, according to circumstances, could be in the form of services, of payments in kind, or of cash, or of a mixture of them, the forms themselves, and the surrounding circumstances, being subject to significant changes, and carrying important implications. For our purposes, the most significant implication was the fact that important linkages existed between the form of agrarian tenure and preparedness for industrialization.

Probably the most favourable agrarian conditions for a least some types of industrial expansion existed in parts of the Netherlands. In a development which can be traced back to the sixteenth century, and which was closely connected with the enormous commercial and later industrial success of the Dutch provinces, the Dutch reacted to the pressure of population on food supply, not by crowding ever more people on the available land, thus lowering the marginal return on their labour, but by holding the numbers on the land fairly constant and making them more efficient by specialization, while allowing the rest of the population to enrich society by working in industry or commerce in the towns.[1]

It is not clear which came first, the commercial/industrial development or the agrarian adaptation, but it is worth noting that even in 1500, the parts of Holland considered here were among the more densely populated in Europe.[2] By the mid-seventeenth century, Holland was the most densely settled, most highly urbanised region in Western Europe, having attracted immigrants even from the other Dutch Provinces.

The success, as against the Malthusian model, had been achieved in part by higher efficiency on the land. In turn, this was based very largely on division of labour, the rural communites including specialist drainage workers, transport workers, peat-cutters, carpenters, and many others, as well as specialist farmers, all co-operating closely with the local towns. In part it was also the result of a great deal of investment in drainage, in farm buildings, in manure from the cities and in farm animals. It was also based on better technology, new crops, the concentration of market gardening and dairy farming near the towns,

and more intelligent planting. By the early nineteenth century, when
information is more reliable, the average yields over the seed corn
among the four main sorts of grain were 11.3 : 1 in the Netherlands
and Britain, 5.9 : 1 in France, Spain, and Italy, 5.4 : 1 in Germany
and Scandinavia, and only 4.4 : 1 in Eastern Europe[3]—a not untypical example of the European *'Gefälle'*. Variations within each
country, significantly, were just as wide. Thus in 1800-20, yields in
East Friesland were 12.0 : 1, but in the rest of Germany only 5.0 : 1,
while in France, towards the end of the eighteenth century, yields
were as low as 3 or 4: 1 in Roussilon or Limoges, but 11: 1 in
Flanders, and about 5:1 on the average.[4]

There was, however, another reason for the Dutch success: it was
that part of the food, particularly grain both for human and animal
consumption, was imported from the Baltic. The Dutch food ecology
could be sustained precisely only because it fitted into a European
exchange economy, just as the Dutch Golden Age of the seventeenth
century, with its financial, commercial, and industrial achievements,
could be sustained only because it had a large part of Europe as its
hinterland, because the Dutch concentrated in their lands the supplies
of colonial goods, financial services, and other luxury products for a
very large geographical region, even though the upper stratum to whom
they were accessible was only a narrow one at the time. The Dutch
economy in the Golden Age represented therefore, as it were, many
of the most profitable and privileged activities skimmed off from
much of the European Continent and decanted into the small vessel
of the maritime Provinces. It was both the desirability of this luxury
trade, and the narrowness of the stratum on which it was based, which
accounted for the vigour with which Holland's chief rivals, France
and Britain, fought her over the spoils, and the restrictive mercantilist
doctrine with which the struggle was justified. It should be noted that
the counterpart of this vital grain import into Holland, the grain supply
from the East, had equally profound, though less desirable consequences for the agricultural export regions.[5] It should be stressed, also,
that the grain deficit was limited largely to the Province of Holland.
Zeeland had a grain surplus for export, and many Dutch areas actually
exported butter and cheese.

Feudal obligations had, of course, been abolished in the advanced
areas well before this process started, though Gelderland in the East
and Overijssel, not affected by urban capitalism, kept some of theirs
until late in the eighteenth century. These districts, it has been correctly observed, were much more akin to the German Münsterland
across the border than to the other United Provinces.[6]

On drained land, the farmers were frequently tenants of urban companies which had financed the major schemes. Almost everywhere Dutch leases were favourable to improvements put in by tenants. Groningen had an unusual lease known as *Beklemrecht*, in which the rent was fixed in perpetuity and the tenant enjoyed absolute security and could dispose of the lease as he saw fit, except that he could not subdivide it, or diminish the value of the land. Alternatively, he would be compensated fully for any improvements made. There would also be a fine payable on change of ownership, and there could never be more than a single proprietor. The landlord would agree to such a lease in return for a large initial payment, and the tenant obtained what was in effect a safe holding in fee simple at less than the full purchase price. A lease of this kind not only encouraged investment and careful husbandry, but also limitation of population.[7]

Up to the end of the seventeenth century the system had favoured the expansion of output and of total population and had provided a prosperous market for local industries, but the equilibrium established by the Dutch agrarian system fitted the stagnating economy that supervened thereafter equally well.[8] The stable population equilibrium itself may have been the result of this early successful urbanization: it may well have been the case that, given the high mortality in European towns and their need to recruit population from the healthier countryside, the weight of Dutch towns had become so great within the economy that all that the population surplus from the countryside could do was to fill up the gaps without leading to an over-all increase.[9] This may be put differently: while the commercial and industrial hinterland of Dutch towns, on which their original growth depended, extended far into Europe, their population hinterland was limited to a much smaller region.[10]

The unique development of the western advanced regions of the Netherlands in the sixteenth and seventeenth centures was thus achieved, not by squeezing the peasants, but by letting the agrarian population share in the modest prosperity of the age. This striking success of one age may have contributed, by raising wages and taxes for administrative and welfare services, to stagnation in the next age,[11] but it laid the foundation for the successful modernization of the Dutch economy at the end of the nineteenth century in which an intelligent, well-equipped farming community played a major part.

If the agrarian history of the Dutch Netherlands can be encompassed in two, or perhaps three major regions, that of Belgium and France would have to be divided into so many separate regional histories, each quite different, that justice could not possibly be done to all. Despite all that has been written about him, one who knows him best has written that 'the French peasant never existed'.[12] We can therefore pick out only some important areas to illustrate themes rather than attempt a comprehensive account.

Flanders, north and south of the border, was a region of small, intensively tilled farms. Although without the close link-up with the local towns such as we have found further north, they had yet also turned early to a market economy, growing cash crops, including industrial crops like tobacco and flax,[13] some for long-distance export. The Flemish tradition was not to subdivide farms at death so that, in the absence of towns, the growing population turned to rural industry, mainly textiles based on flax—a typical 'proto-industrial' landscape. When that industry gave out, Flemish peasants came to be among the poorest and least progressive in Western Europe.[14] The long-standing tradition of *Pachters-regt*, under which the outgoing tenant was compensated for all unexhausted improvements, including manure and crops in the ground, encouraged intensive cultivation. In Eastern Belgium, in the industrial Walloon area, where much larger holdings had been the rule, as well as around Ghent, the growth of mining, metallurgy, and the textile industries after 1750 had, typically, called into being market gardening, dairy farming, and diversified agriculture to supply the non-agrarian population.[15]

The abolition of all seignoral claims, restrictions, and obligations without payment, decreed in 1793 during the French Revolution, made relatively little difference to Belgium when it became a part of France in 1795, though the confiscation of church lands and their sale to private persons gave a strong boost to capitalist agriculture in an area where church property had been particularly extensive. Over much of the rest of France, however, these burdens and restrictions had weighed heavily on the peasants and had been a major cause of the riots and rebellions that formed the rural background to the Revolution.

Apart from the northern regions, adjoining the frontier with Belgium and equally heavily industrialized, it was the area around Paris which had become the most market-oriented, and in which both large and small holdings coexisted in a capitalist milieu, working the land with up-to-date methods to supply the nearby urban population. Here the *laboureur*, the substantial peasant with his own plough team, had separated most clearly from the *manœuvrier*, who was driven down to wage labour, and he had become much like the *fermier* or large estate bailiff or the English farmer equivalent. These areas, together with the North-West, and Alsace-Lorraine, contained not only many of the most flourishing industrial centres of France, but also the farms with the highest yields per acre, the points of origin of the agricultural revolution which only gradually and often belatedly affected other regions.[16]

Yet elsewhere too agriculture had by no means been stagnant. Like the rest of western Europe, French peasants had been profoundly affected by the general price fall, especially of grains, to the 1720s, and their steady rise thereafter, exceeding the rise of other prices and accelerating to a peak in the war years around 1810, only to fall again in the years of peace that followed.[17]

Over much of the rest of northern France (north-west of a line from Bordeaux to Metz) and some areas to the south, the typical peasant was the *censier*, a man who enjoyed security of tenure as a copyholder, with the right to sell, lease, exchange, or even to give away his land, but only 'with the assent of the landlord, always with the obligation to pay, and often a great deal'.[18] In addition to the limited *cens*, there were superimposed *surcens*, amounting to more than the original *cens*, tithes, and other payments like the *Champart* and the *lods* and *rentes*, fines which became payable to the *seigneur* when land was bequeathed or sold, and there were additional taxes, dues, and obligations which did not allow the *censier* to benefit from the rising prices, and occasional famines, of the later eighteenth century. He it was who gained most from the Revolution, ending up in effect a secure freeholder on his plot, still sharing some rights in the common lands which were distributed only with extreme difficulty, despite government encouragement, over a period lasting in some cases more than a century.

The conditions of soil and climate, as well as market conditions, differed widely between the regions, but as the French economy developed and industrialized in the course of the nineteenth century, it would be true to say that all agrarian regions were in contact with some market, even if only that of a local town or a more distant market reached with difficulty. As first canals, and then railways began to link up the French economy, these contacts became much more effective, though the differences between regions accentuated according to the distance from a useful railway line or water-way.

The Census of 1851 showed some 3.8 million landowner-cultivators in France, of whom 1.8 million cultivated just their own land and over 850,000 leased some land in addition, or a total of 2.6 million owner-entrepreneurs. Over 1.1 million had to make up their incomes as owner-cultivators, by working elsewhere, and less than 60,000 owners worked their land through managers. As late as 1892, of 6.6 million employed on the land, one-half were proprietors and one-third were full owners. The French peasant had, by then, without doubt, developed a classic capitalist mentality: he was acquisitive, scrimping, and saving, hard-working, reacting rapidly to markets and prices. Certainly, plots were cultivated with care and devotion, particularly in the case of specialist crops like vineyards, and yields compared well with those of the rest of Europe, outside Britain, Holland, and the areas enumerated above. Yet historians, taking their cue from contemporary opinion, are practically unanimous in their view, which has become commonplace,[19] that the typical peasant held up progress in France not only on the land, but also in industry. For although he had reached a certain level of efficiency, he did not advance beyond it, since that would have needed capital, and whatever capital he amassed was used, not to invest in improvements in his own plot, but in buying more land. Much of French land was held under partible inheritance, but plots did not become smaller because the peasantry kept to smaller families, and on the whole did little more than reproduce itself: for every family with two sons, inheriting half a holding, there was another holding without heirs coming on the market. The law of succession was matched almost equally with an exceptionally easy system of land transfers by public notaries aided by a public land register.[20] The system, together with the mentality which it created, was thus alleged to have been the main cause of the French population stagnation at a time when the rest of Europe registered a rapid increase. Peasants stayed on the land, for non-pecuniary reasons, even if wages in the towns were higher. In the absence of a growth market in the villages, and of a cheap labour supply from the countryside, French industry was then alleged to have lacked the incentive and the conditions of growth in the nineteenth century.

The main system in operation beside that of peasant proprietorship was that of *métayage*, called *mégerie* in the south, or share-cropping. It was found in the southern regions mostly, and is sometimes referred to as the 'Mediterranean' system, since it also occurs in other regions outside France bordering the Mediterranean, including Southern and Central Italy and Spain.[21] It has had an even worse press than that of the peasant owner. Preferred by landlords and tenants both for reasons of prestige and status as well as for risk-sharing, it produced a feeling of insecurity in the tenant, which, aided by the knowledge that half the returns of any improvement would go to someone else, inhibited all permanent investments, all new technologies and new rotations, such as revolutionized northern agriculture. Nor could it develop its own, for in effect, it lacked an entrepreneur.

There were many variants, virtually all working against the interest of the tenant. Sometimes his share was only one-third, as in the *renterre* of North Burgundy. In other areas, the tenant had to provide all the seed, or pay all taxes, tithes, and other burdens. In Poitou, in addition to these disadvantages, he would receive less than half the grain, and was little more than a farm servant. In Berri, again, he was liable to make the agreed deliveries even if disease or some other disaster had decimated his stock. Leases like those of La Nièvre in which, to name yet another burden, the peasant had to keep a minimum number of adults on the farm were felt to be particularly oppressive if wages outside were higher than the marginal returns on the land, which was normally the case. In the South-West, where the landlords were urban bourgeois, elaborate contracts and a battle of wits to break them were the rule. Tenants were usually heavily in debt and often bankrupt.[22] *Métayage* created small, inefficient holdings and a poverty-stricken peasantry. No area dominated by *métayage* has seen a successful industrial 'take-off', and in France it was found in the poorest and most backward regions. Vineyard areas had *complant* leases, in which the *complanteur* was owner as long as there were vines, after which the land reverted to the landlord.[23]

Even within the southern climatic regions, there were important differences. Languedoc, not unlike Catalonia across the border, succeeded in matching the population increase of the eighteenth century with a rise in farm output, including cash crops like wine, alfalfa, and silk, and an industrial expansion, led by the woollen industry, in the towns.[24]

These traditional views have, however, recently had to yield to new insights. For one thing, it is now recognized that whereas some regions remained stagnant and backward—and indeed some remained so inaccessible to capitalism and industrialism that even in the mid-twentieth century, industrial firms settling in their midst had to recruit labour from outside, since the local agrarian surplus labour was disinterested[25]—at the other extreme there were regions which compared with the best of the more advanced British agriculture. New crops, new rotations, even farm machinery, were to be found in the North and around Paris as early as anywhere in Europe. Animals, on the whole, were larger and more productive in France even than in Britain,[26] and certainly exceeded the weight of those found in most other countries.

Above all, it has been recent statistical work, among which that of J. C. Toutain is outstanding,[27] which has shown that remarkable increases in the productivity and the output of French agriculture occurred both in the eighteenth and the nineteenth centuries, and has made necessary a revision of the traditional negative view of the French performance. The French peasant may have hoarded his capital and his labour, but outside certain limited regions, he was willing to learn, and he reacted to the market with greater efficiency than he has been given credit for in the past. As meat prices began to overtake grain prices by the mid-nineteenth century, peasants changed over to stock-raising fast enough. The number of cows rose from 9.9 million in 1840 to 13 million on the smaller territory of 1882. It is not clear whether it was this which forced labour to move to the towns and industries, or whether it was the attractions of higher wages in the town which depleted the farms and forced them to turn to pasturage:[28] if the latter, then it was not agriculture which had held back industry, but on the contrary, the lack of initiative in the towns which had forced agriculture into stagnation.

Overall, taking the progressive with the stagnant regions, real agricultural product per head grew in France in the first two-thirds of the century by about 0.6% per annum, and although it thereafter stagnated, this still compared well with the British performance of under −0.1% and −0.5% for the same periods; output per person actively employed in agriculture in France rose by about 0.7% in the first period but stagnated thereafter. Total output, measured in francs at current prices, rose from an average of 1,185 m.fr. in 1701-10, 2,601 m.fr. in 1781-90, and 3,413 m.fr. in 1803-12 to 8,712 m.fr. in 1895-1904 and 11,663 m.fr. in 1908-14.[29] Wheat production, a significant item in French agriculture, rose as follows,[30] comparing well with changes in the rest of Europe, when the stationary French population, compared with its rapid rise elsewhere, is borne in mind.

Table 2.1. Wheat Production (million bushel)

	France	Europe	France, %
1831-40	190	712	26.7
1881-7	290	1231	23.6
1909-14	318	2090	15.2
% increase, 1831/40 to 1909/14	68	194	

Real output per active male agriculturalist rose from 851 fr. in 1701-10 to 1,168 fr. in 1803-12 and 1,904 fr. in 1885-94. In absolute terms, however, French agricultural output per head was much below that of the British and fell further behind in the course of the century, labour productivity, on a common denominator, being only around 80% of the British in 1803-12 and about 65% in 1905-13.[31]

A more recent view is that while in the eighteenth century French agriculture was undercapitalized, and used too few animals and too little manure, in the nineteenth, its stimulus as a market is doubtful, but it did contribute capital, including capital for exports which brought orders for French industrialists. But within those totals, there were wide regional variations, the north-central areas (south of Paris) growing fastest, probably by adopting the rotations of the north.[32]

The regional agrarian differences of Germany are better documented

than those of France, mainly because the area which later became
Germany consisted of a large number of independent political entities
for which separate statistics were collected, and which were treated
as competing economies by contemporaries. Again, there were far
too many variants to be treated here in detail: only some typical
agrarian systems can be described.

Along the Rhine, the French had abolished feudal dues during their
years of occupation, and conditions approximated to those of the
classical French system. Much of Western Germany had, in fact, been
turned over to peasant occupation well before the end of the eighteenth century, stimulated by the markets of the towns and the potential freedom available to runaway serfs there.[33] Perhaps two-thirds of
the land was peasant-owned, but the remaining one-third, which was
demesne land, had also largely been leased to peasants, so that the
landlords' income consisted largely of money rent.[34] The commutation of feudal dues in these circumstances hardly interfered with the
progress of capitalistic agriculture. Thus in the Grand Duchy of Hesse,
the personal feudal dues, i.e. those not tied to any particular land
held by the peasants, but to them as persons, were made redeemable
in 1811 by payments spread over a period of years. Those due to the
sovereign, as large landowner, were easily converted into taxes; the
others took until the revolution of 1848 to settle in some cases. An
act of 1836 made all rent charges into which feudal dues had been,
or were to be, converted, redeemable on favourable terms. The state,
which happened to have some surplus funds at its disposal at the time,
paid off the feudal lords at 18 years' purchase, while it collected
from the peasants an annual sum which was actually less than the rent
payable before, but which still made the peasant into a full proprietor
in 49 years.[35] In Württemberg, it was an edict of 1817 which first
announced the abolition of personal serfdom. In 1821 practical
methods of implementation were laid down for the royal estates, but
it was not until 1836 that details were published for the ending of
labour services, feudal burdens, and dues elsewhere and the work of
commutation was completed in 1841 only. The remaining, rather more
significant dues, were abolished only in the revolution of 1848-9,
and actually commuted by 1852-3. Baden laid down its methods of
payment for emancipation in various acts in 1820-8, whereas in the
Dukedom of Nassau some burdens were ended by edicts of 1812 and
1826, with little effect, some further progress was made after an act
of 1841, but compulsory conversion came only in the revolutionary
years 1848-9. This relatively small territory showed an exceptional
variety of local terms and conditions of feudal dues and burdens.[36]

In the more barren uplands, small-scale peasant proprietorship was often the basis of industrial employment, as in the Sauerland, and indeed the Bergische Land and the County of Mark generally.[37] Those areas could therefore absorb an increasing population without necessarily leading to famine conditions, or enforced emigration. In some of the less industrialized regions with the same type of agrarian holding, such as Württemberg and other countries of the South-West, however, small proprietorship favoured relative over-population, and in the years of bad harvest of 1816–17 they became the main sources of German emigration to Eastern Europe, while in 1846–7 the refugees turned to overseas destinations.[38]

The pressure on land was shown by the fact that, where the law permitted, small holdings were divided into ever smaller ones, and even assarted land was divided into strips. In the Allgau, however, strips had been consolidated in the eighteenth century.[39] Bavaria and the Austrian lands adjacent to it, including Salzburg, Upper Austria, and the Tyrol, had less favourable conditions for the peasants. Estates survived as units of cultivation and were run by bailiffs (*Meier*) for the landlords, while the institution of the *Hofmark* gave the landlords judicial powers over the consolidated area of the estate and the surrounding country. Peasant burdens were high to the mid-nineteenth century, and few peasants owned their freeholds.[40]

In the North-West, conditions approximated to those of adjacent Holland. The Netherlands were, in fact, the main export market, first for hay, and after 1750, when relative prices changed, for cattle. Later still, cheese became the leading export. Large farms developed in this area, including the demesne farm which tended to slip into the hands of the *Meier* as of hereditary right. At the same time, as over most of northern Germany, there were also numerous groups of smallholders, allotment holders, and cottagers, known variously as *Brinksitzer, Kätner, Kossäten,* and *Häusler* (among others) who would make up their income by wage labour either with larger farmers or in the *Meierei.*[41]

Farther north, in Friesland and Schleswig-Holstein, the marsh peasants had achieved full freedom from feudal obligations well before the nineteenth century on large holdings of two hundred acres or more each, on the basis of animal husbandry and free wage labour. Serfdom was formally abolished in 1805, but on the central *Geest* lands, where the old strip field-system remained, and on the east (Baltic) coast, full emancipation had to wait for the revolution of the mid-century.[42]

Central Germany formed in many ways a transitional area between East and West. Large demesne holdings might exist, belonging to the nobility, the Church, the universities, or the municipalities, but they were surrounded by rented peasant farms on which the tenants had either hereditary leases or which they might even hold in fee simple. Some labour dues might be due to the estate, but the estate farm also provided paid jobs in peak periods. It seems likely that labour services, introduced generally in a state like Saxony only in 1735 and 1766, were enforced because of a labour shortage. The transitional or mixed nature of the system there may also be seen by the fact that while the landlords had judicial powers, as in the East, and even then not universally, the peasants were free, as in the West—though even here there were islands of servitude, as in parts of Hanover.[43]

The real distinction, the real *Gefälle*, was between the West as a whole, and eastern, East-Elbian Germany, the land of large estates worked directly by the squires, the home of oppressive feudalism. In some of these areas, especially Upland Saxony and Silesia, industrialization had made great inroads into the system. Thus in Saxony, where holdings could not be divided, and the number of peasant holdings thus remained constant, or actually fell, at a time of increasing population, new categories of settlers outside the estate economy, like *Gärtner* and *Häusler*, and even wage labourers without any land, supplied industrial labour-power in the villages outside the feudal system. Round Berlin, market gardening and dairy farming helped to feed the large city population.[44] But, as everywhere else in Europe, feudal agriculture was associated by the eighteenth and nineteenth centuries with industrial backwardness, and that part of Germany will be treated below with the other peripheral regions of Europe.[45]

Unlike the French population, the population growth was continuous in Germany over the whole of our period. In the eighteenth century there was still space for it to grow; but in the first half of the nineteenth century it increased faster than the capacity of industry to absorb it, while agriculture had come up against limitations of land. Thus while, in some sense, the German social problem was one of inadequately growing industry, it appeared as 'overpopulation' on the land.[46] Only in the East was there plenty of space, and it is therefore permissible to see in this expansive potential in the East, but not the West, an important influence on the actual course of economic development in these two regions.

The share of agricultural employment fell with industrialization, and the agricultural population grew only from around 7.0 million in 1800 to 8.7 million in 1850 and 9.7 million in 1900,[47] but its output both in terms of output per head, and per acre, rose remarkably fast. The main contributing factors were capital and technology. Throughout, the small-scale agriculture of the West showed much higher yields per acre than the East: in Prussia in the early nineteenth century for example, the Rhineland's yields stood at 175 while that of East Prussia was only 57 (Prussian average = 100),[48] but efficiency rose in all regions.

There were land-drainage schemes, particularly in Prussia, to make poor land more fertile, and transport improvements to make distant lands more accessible. New crops like potatoes, sugar beet, and clover and other grasses allowed better use of the land and of the fallow, together with improvements in crop rotations. Thus the potato, introduced into the Electoral Mark of Brandenburg on any scale only after the famine of 1771–2, registered a harvest of 5,200 t. in 1765, 19,000 t. in 1773, and 103,000 t. in 1801 and helped to mitigate later bad harvests, except for 1846 when it failed itself. Beet-sugar production rose from 25,000 cwt. in 1836–7 to 986,000 cwt. in 1850–1. Animal breeds were improved, the merino being introduced into Prussia in 1748 and into Saxony in 1765, and technical schools of agronomy, such as that in Württemberg in 1818, helped to spread the better methods of Britain and Holland. A. D. Thaer, the best-known scientific propagator of British methods, opened his school in 1806 and was later given a chair at the new University of Berlin.[49]

The 1830s to the 1870s, when industrial prices fell while agricultural prices rose in Germany, were the golden years. Agrarian production rose by 174% between 1800–10 and 1871–5, while population increased by only 66.5%, for Germany as a whole. These were the years when Justus von Liebig advanced and propagated new ideas about artificial fertilizers, in which Germany took the lead, while other methods spread from abroad.[50] The index of yield per acre shows the following changes between 1850 and 1912:[51]

Yield per acre, Index 1800 =100	1848–52	1908–12
Wheat	119	201
Rye	119	199
Barley	138	248
Oats	160	278

By the last quarter of the century, the most advanced areas in Germany reached yields per acre and per head equal to those of the leading regions in Britain, Holland, and Denmark, though the strong *Gefälle* to the east remained.

Nevertheless, unlike France, Germany was increasingly unable to feed herself. In other words, the food-supply zone of the German industrial economy reached out beyond the political frontiers, to Holland, Denmark, Austria, Russia, and ultimately even overseas with profound effects on the economic interrelations of Europe. Behind this generalization and others of its kind lurks a complex interplay of regional agrarian realities, sometimes favourable to industrialization at certain stages and at other times hostile, being themselves funda-

mentally affected by industries and industrial populations and sometimes even symbiotically connected with them. Within those shifting
limits, regional agrarian traditions contributed to delineate the particular map of the progress of European industrialization.

Traditional Industry: Urban Crafts and Guilds

In some sense, the medieval town represented an antithesis to the
feudal countryside: it had usually bought its freedom from feudal
obligations, it administered itself, it existed by industrial specialization, by trade over shorter or longer distances, by grasping the opportunities of change. Most historians have taken the towns to be a
powerful dissolving element in feudal society.

There were towns and cities that lived by trade, but the basis of
most was their industrial production. Industry, in turn, was organized
in guilds. Guilds, at first, were given or absorbed numerous functions
that favoured progress. They organized the training of apprentices,
preserved standards of skill and quality, guaranteed the integrity of
their members, found them a market and, at times, a raw material
supply, and, above all, freed them from feudal exactions and let them
share in the town government. They also provided rudimentary social
services such as subsistence for widows and orphans,[52] organized
religious services and secular entertainment and, if need be, helped to
furnish an urban militia or equip professional soldiers.

As the centuries passed, however, the system that had once been
progressive increasingly came to impose rigidity on the economy until
ultimately it became a fetter on progress. Thus, as components of
town councils, guilds obstructed immigration or the acceptance of
settlers as full citizens, often condemning their own town to stagnation while others advanced. By refusing to recognize masterships
acquired elsewhere, they inhibited the mobility even of qualified
craftsmen. They built up a vast body of minute regulations on qualities
and permitted sizes at a time when technical innovations and new
markets demanded change and adaptability. France registered about
300 new sets of rules between 1715 and 1789, or an average of four
a year: that for the Dauphiné in 1782 contained no fewer than 265
paragraphs.[53] Guilds also wasted much time and effort in demarcation
disputes between crafts,[54] and in true monopoly spirit, tried to prohibit altogether the use of new commodities which competed with
their products. Thus their ban on printed calicoes in France by
numerous ordinances between 1686 and 1759 led to immense sufferings, cruelties, conflicts, and deaths, and substantially handicapped
French industry when it finally attempted to turn to the cotton
manufacture.[55] Typical is the reaction of the Strasburg 'Council of

Fifteen' as late as the 1770s to a new cotton manufacturing firm which found it difficult to get established and therefore tried to sell some of its products locally: 'it would upset all order in trade if the manufacturer were to become merchant at the same time, and infringe the most sensible rules laying down who are allowed to trade in this city'.[56] In Brandenburg-Prussia, similarly, the guilds held up some modern manufacture, like frame-knitting in Magdeburg, by up to half a century, and prevented the introduction of new technology like the Dutch loom, in the latter part of the eighteenth century.[57]

Some positive features remained. The insistence on an apprenticeship led directly into systems of training skilled workers for such new industries as engineering and metal working. The limitation on numbers of journeymen and masters, where it was kept, prevented some of the worst forms of early capitalistic exploitation. Thus in Prussia, of 1,230,000 persons in the regulated trades, 820,000 or two-thirds, were estimated to have been masters, and only one-third journeymen and apprentices, and even in 1846-7, the masters, at 1,070,000 still outnumbered the rest, at 930,000. Only in the building trades did some 286,000 apprentices and journeymen greatly outnumber the 66,000 masters, and there clearly guild rules were harder to enforce.[58]

Towards the end of the eighteenth century the guilds were threatened from two directions. From one side, the absolutist state, jealous of its sovereignty, sought to limit the independence of the guilds and to bring them under its direct authority. As early as 1673, Colbert had attempted to bring the French guilds under royal control partly in order to use them for tax purposes, and although the law was largely ignored, it was inevitable that once the state had become interested in the guilds, it would seek to use them, and not always in the interests of their members. Thus an ordinance of 1736 tried to limit guilds to the large towns only, and another, of 1755, allowed any French subject, wherever qualified, to set up in any town outside Paris, Lyons, Rouen, and Lille. This provision, self-evident from the point of view of the mercantilist state, destroyed one of the basic principles of the guild system. Laws of 1762 (confirmed in 1765 and 1766) retained the rules on quality control in rural industry, but transferred their administration from the town to royal officials. Restrictions on the hosiery trade were dropped in 1745, on the wool trade in 1758, on calico-printing in 1759, and on wholesale trading in 1765. In 1766, Turgot tried to do away with the system altogether, and although his edict was repealed in the same year by Necker, the latter damaged the system further by 'rationalising' it over the country as a whole. Henceforth there were to be three categories of guilds: those which returned to the old system, but paid heavily to the king for the privilege; those which allowed anyone to become master by simply registering with the police; and the merchants, who were free. Unwillingness to pay the new fees and misunderstandings in practice further confused the principle,[59] which had virtually lapsed into anarchy even before the Revolution abolished all guilds in 1791.

In Belgium, the guild system ended in 1784 after a struggle. Spain reformed it in 1760-70, Northern Italy in 1770-87.[60] The Holy Roman Empire ushered in a new era with a law adopted at the Regensburg Reichstag in 1731. This explicitly strengthened the territorial political authority over the autonomous rights of the guilds, and attempted to hold the latter purely to their economic functions by drastically cutting or totally abolishing their social role, their political pretensions, and many of their trade practices and abuses. Above all, they were to lose their judicial powers and become subject to the jurisdiction of the territorial sovereign. Prussia accepted the Act in 1734-6, Saxony soon after, Baden in 1760, and Austria in 1770. Bavaria, which had anticipated the Imperial decree, adopted stricter rules in 1764. In the interest of favouring some particular industries which they wished to foster, the Prussian kings were not above whittling away certain rights and powers here and there. Frederick William I lifted some restrictions on the numbers of certain apprentices and journeymen in 1723, and in 1783 this was made applicable to all. Silk was removed from all guild restrictions, and so were cotton workers, wool-combers, button-makers, hat-makers, and watch-makers. In 1792 women and children were allowed to work in silk-ribbon making in the face of guild regulations. In Saxony, immigrant craftsmen and those introducing new 'manufactures' were free of all guild restrictions. In Bavaria, the sovereign bypassed all urban controls by granting *Hofschutz*, including the right to settle and carry on trade, to any manufacturer or worker he wanted to foster, thus creating a second parallel system of registration. In Austria, similar effects followed from the 'commercial trades' instituted in 1754: by 1776 there were 84 of them, and by 1785 they were freed from all guild membership.

Guild rules as a whole were abolished in the Rhineland in 1790-1, in Westphalia in 1808-10, and in Prussia (excluding those provinces then temporarily not under the Prussian crown) as part of the great reforms of 1806-10. The hesitancy to follow the French example of wholly abolishing guild powers found in other German states was due not so much to tenderness for the guilds, but rather to a desire to prevent the mobility of young men to escape military service. Prussia reintroduced non-compulsory guilds with wide but ambiguous powers, which included a prohibition of organization and of strikes among factory workers, in 1845.[61] They had survived, but much diminished in power. In Berlin, the proportion of non-guild masters had changed as follows:

	1826	*1845*
Bakers	5.1%	19.0%
Plasterers	0	65.4
Shoemakers	35.0	81.7
Plumbers	54.3	86.0
Tailors	59.5	35.2
Joiners	62.8	86.5

Saxon towns retained their rights over the industries of the country-side as late as 1858, and only the North German Confederation abolished those rights in 1869, Mecklenburg being, as so often, the last to cling to archaic forms.

The second, more lasting, threat came from the development of industry working for the market outside the control of the guilds altogether. Although some guilds like those of Prussia[62] were to emerge later as independent handicraft associations, and others hung on by making high-quality goods, leaving the villages to produce the cheaper grades, or even as in Zurich, monopolized the putting-out and sales of the country-made goods,[63] yet it is one of the commonplaces of economic history that they lost out to superior 'free' enterprise because of their inherent competitive inferiority, and would have done so irrespective of any state action, which in any case was often designed merely to deal with the consequences of their inferiority.

As town merchants sought out cheap country labour, free of any limitation as to numbers, wages, or conditions, the guild workers found their jobs disappearing, and their town, as the Troyes weavers complained in 1789, subject to *desœuvrement*.[64] This undermining proceeded at different speeds according to different conditions, with strong rights over their rural hinterland, the *Bannmeile*, as in Saxony, holding out a little longer. In Silesia, the linen industry had been started in the country as early as the sixteenth century to circumvent the guilds; around Aachen, it was only in the eighteenth century that the guild-controlled woollen industry languished while the fine-cloth maker of Montjoie flourished, and in nearby Mülheim the regulated silk industry declined, to expand in the free surrounding territories. In the Austrian Netherlands, the stagnating towns kept the luxury trades, but spinning, knitting, and lace-making had moved to the villages. In the go-ahead atmosphere of the Wupper valley, the newly established weavers' guild of 1738 was quite unable to hold up the expansion of the free village industrialist, and it was abolished again in 1783 after some rioting. By 1800 it was found that in Prussia, even in the under-developed East, one-third of all the craftsmen were 'free' in the villages; in the West it was as high as two-thirds, and for the country as a whole, around one-half.[65] In Bavaria, where the repulsion by restrictive town guilds was reinforced by the attraction of landlords who welcomed industrial workers into their *Hofmarken* as tax and rent payers, only 12% of the registered industrial population was found in the towns and 88% in the country in 1816; among the total industrial population, masters and journeymen together, the ratios were 25% and 75% respectively.[66] What has been called the 'Territorialisierung der Gewerbe'[67] could hardly go further.

Many of the urban handicraft centres of Europe became the locations of modern industry. This was because of their skills and traditions of industrial work, and not because of their guilds, but rather in spite of them. In Germany and Congress Poland, guilds would expel members and deprive them of all their accumulated rights if they went to work in a factory.[68] The guilds had to be bypassed or broken before modern industry could grow up on their ruins. Among early developers, as in Britain, Belgium, and much of France and Western Germany, they withered before the factories ever appeared; in Southern and Eastern Germany, where rulers could learn from the West what their next step might be, they had to be more deliberately curbed. But it would be hard to maintain that much impetus for progress came from them. The locus of the expansionary industrial force was to be found elsewhere, in rural industry.

Rural Industry and 'Proto-Industrialization'

Statistics which show that over most of Europe until the latter part of the nineteenth century persons working in agriculture greatly outnumber those employed in industry can be misleading. Many, perhaps most peasants' wives and daughters spun in their leisure hours, or made clothes;[69] peasant houses, barns, perhaps even fences and tools, were put up or made by men nominally in agrarian employment; roads were built by (often compulsory) peasant labour.

Again, there would always be craftsmen in the villages, providing goods for local consumption, and their numbers were rising with improving technology: wheelwrights, blacksmiths, carpenters.[70] Peasant crafts for wider sale were found particularly where long winters or local supplies of timber, stones, or other materials gave a comparative advantage. In some regions, at some periods, the share of industrial work increased. The transition may have been continuous in practice, though its recognition by the statistician or historian is abrupt. At some point the fuller or full-time industrial occupation became so significant that we call the population 'industrial .

Regions with concentrations of such people were found all over

Europe, though more frequently in Inner Europe than in the periphery, and they were of various types, just as we have found them to have been in Britain. We may group them broadly into those concentrated around a large city, those spread more widely in fertile regions, and those spread more widely on infertile and barren lands. Among them, there were again subgroups, according to whether they were based on textiles, on minerals and metal, on other industries, or a mixture of them.

Cities as poles of attraction for rural industry, to supply the city markets themselves, are limited to capital cities, Paris and Berlin, for example, in Inner Europe, and Vienna or St. Petersburg in the periphery. The rationale was the concentrated demand for certain products coupled with the high rents, costs, and wages which tended to drive any but luxury trades and those tied to the point of sale, into the cheaper countryside around.[71] In Berlin, as also in Dresden, Vienna, and other capitals, there was added to it the overspill from manufacturers encouraged by the Crown for mercantilist or prestige reasons or located there for reasons of patronage. In Berlin the silk industry (favoured as against the provincial rival in Krefeld) was the best-known example among several. Typically, the spinning and weaving of the pre-factory age were later replaced by dress-making and other similar domestic work as occupations for the poor as the formerly rural villages were engulfed in the growing city.[72] The surroundings of Paris had such industries as stone-quarrying, brewing, and printing.[73]

Normally, however, the role of the local town was not to act as the market, but as the seat of the putting-out merchant, the central entrepreneurial figure in this phase of development. For rural industry in Europe at the time was essentially industry for a distant market, organized on a capitalistic basis by firms which combined commercial and industrial functions, the purchase of raw materials and intermediate product at various stages, and the sale of these and of the end product, with the supervision, and sometimes management and control, over the acutal manufacturing process, though the latter might be carried on in the workers' own homes. This system of industrial production, which we also found to exist in Britain, lasted much longer as the predominant system on the Continent, from the end of the seventeenth century, if not earlier, to the mid-nineteenth.

The varieties of its manifestation were endless. The putter-out might be a large firm or a small one, working directly or through one or more levels of agents, selling directly to distant markets or through other merchants. He might leave more or less freedom to his workers, attach them to him by more or less permanent bonds, advance them more or less of the necessary capital. In some cases, he merely gave the orders, not taking possession of the product until it was ready for sale; in others, he owned the product as it passed through its various stages of manufacture; in others still, he also owned the tools and equipment, and possibly even the premises used by the producers. Much of this was in constant flux, affected by changing market conditions and changing technology. Thus the tendency for firms to become larger and to add to their roll of outworkers was counteracted by the opportunities for up-and-coming small firms to open up new lines. Similarly, the tendency for equipment to become costlier, as in the case of Dutch looms or knitting-frames, so that its ownership shifted increasingly from the worker to the putting-out merchant, was counteracted by the rise of new trades, such as dressmaking, which required practically no equipment at all. Throughout these changes, however, the logic of the system remained the same: on the one hand, capital and entrepreneurship able and willing to grasp the opportunities of distant markets, within the same country, elsewhere in Europe or overseas, and supply them on a large scale; and on the other hand, dispersed manufacture in the countryside enjoying low costs of production. Low costs, compared with the handicraft sector, were achieved mainly by low costs of living on the land, by the widespread use of 'inferior' labour, i.e. women and children, by the depression of real wages made possible by the agricultural part-incomes of the workers, and by an advanced division of labour.[74]

While there were few parts of Europe without some examples of this kind of employment, if only part time, strong concentrations were found in a few regions only. In some, they had arisen because the raw material was locally grown: thus Flanders became a producer of linens, and the Lyons silk industry, showing a mixed urban and rural location, had at any rate easy access to its raw material. There was a tendency for those domestic industrial regions which lay in rich farmlands not to convert later to factory industry, but to revert to agrarian specialization when the domestic workroom was replaced by the power-driven mill, as among the linen and woollen workers of Picardy and in Upper Normandy.[75] Wool from local sheep, timber from local woodlands, plentiful water-power, and metallic ores as well as coal were other locational determinants, but in their case the successful settlement of industrial plant was almost invariably accompanied by the third of our characteristics, poor agricultural land. The bulk of Europe's rural industries was to be found on inferior soil, or in areas not easily accessible.

In part, this had simple natural causes: timber, for charcoal used in glass-making, lime-burning or metal-smelting, for bark used in tanning, or as material for furniture-, toy- or musical instrument-making, was

an alternative product of the soil, generally found in uplands unsuitable for field cultivation.[76] Sheep, also, providing the raw material
for one of the main textile industries, were frequently concentrated
in upland grasslands without alternative uses. Even fast-flowing streams
for water-power were associated with hills rather than fertile plains.
As it happens, many of the key minerals, though by no means all,
were also found in hilly regions, frequently difficult of access.

Apart from natural resources, labour was the main factor of production, since capital requirements were negligible. It was labour
which tended to be cheap where there was no alternative employment
on the land and which, in varying measure, accentuated the pull of
industry towards the less fertile regions of Europe.

Possibly the most concentrated industrial region on the Continent
was the Sambre–Meuse area. Here as many as 15,000 out-working
nailmakers have been estimated to have existed by 1740 in the Liège
region and in 1730 240,000 firearms are said to have been made in
the city itself, there were coal-mines, and there were some very early
steam-engines. Adjacent Verviers was the centre of a flourishing
woollen industry, which continued over the border into Aachen.[77]

Across the Rhine, the Siegerland with its metal industries, and the
valley of the Wupper with its concentration of textiles, first linen,
later silk, 'siamoises' (cotton/silk mixture), as well as cottons and
woollens, formed another major industrial region which expanded
rapidly in the eighteenth century, largely in the form of rural employment. By the end of the century it had begun to reach a higher stage
of development. Wages there had risen to a point at which it became
wothwhile to transfer some of the work across the Rhine to Gladbach-
Rheydt in search of cheaper labour. The Lower Ruhr was also being
developed on the basis of coal and *Rasenerze*. Exports went down
the Rhine, but also to Bremen and Hamburg.[78]

Farther east, the Saxon uplands and Lusatia again flourished on
the basis both of textiles and of minerals. By 1799, there were 15,000
hand-spinners within four miles of Chemnitz having textiles as their
main employment, while Bautzen became the centre of a knitting
industry working for export. There was also calico-printing, lace-
making, and silk- and damask-working. Metals were worked in the
Erzgebirge, as well as glass and clock manufacture. Some of these
industries had been founded by immigrants, others could expand only
by attracting immigrant workers.[79] Other areas with concentrations
of textiles and minerals were to be found in Silesia (mainly linen and
coal) and in the French Nord (cottons, linens, woollens, and coal).

In these areas it seems that, on the whole, the causes of industrial
location and concentration were positive, manufacture having been

attracted by the availability of resources, combined sometimes with good communications, or, as was said for Berg, Mark, or the Netherlands, with government and a social system favourable to economic development. Only for Saxony has the doubt been raised whether the origins of its early industrialization were to be found among the natural resources, or whether a population pressing on limited land was forced in desperation to seek employment in the non-agrarian sectors.[80] It may not seem at first sight to be of great significance whether the concentrations of rural industry arose because of a demand pull or a supply push. Yet the dynamic and the accompanying social history may take a very different course according to which predominates.

A great deal of recent historic writing has come down on the side of the supply push, describing a mechanism of growth in which increases of demand, the successful opening-up of distant markets, also plays a part, but in which the supply of the principal factor of production, labour, grows independently and often faster owing to social changes inherent in the process itself, and therefore presses down wages and working conditions as industry expands. The process has been described as 'proto-industrialization' and has the merit that it combines in a symbiotic way changes in quantities, methods, and organization of production with changes in population and in social behaviour which were observed at that time. At its most ambitious, the description would lay bare the heart of the mechanism that led directly to the industrial revolution itself.

The term, not perhaps happily chosen since it seems to disregard earlier forms of industrialization, derives from the term 'proto-factory'[81] which, at least in the purely semantic sense, has more to recommend it. It first appeared in print in a seminal paper by F. F. Mendels,[82] which skilfully blended together industrial history against and in combination with the shifting agricultural and social background of the age. Curiously enough, its own preferred mechanism of change was later neglected and substituted by another, which this original paper seemed to hold in lesser regard.

Mendels set out to discuss the remarkable rise in rural industry before the factory, separate from the factory and not necessarily leading to factory industry. While using traditional technology, this industry was market-oriented and clearly related to the market opportunities developing in overseas areas, as well as in Europe itself because of rapidly rising population and rising incomes. The impetus from them, transmitted through merchant-entrepreneurs, was effective in promoting fundamental change precisely because it was concentrated in a few regions only. Since technology did not change, more output meant more labour, and one important way in which labour could be used for producing industrial goods without creating a labour shortage and raising wages was to use rural labour between harvests and other agricultural peak periods, when there was much disguised unemployment in the traditional European village. With industry and agriculture effectively dovetailed, a temporary equilibrium could be achieved. The process is thus based on the use of hitherto unexploited resources, an example of 'vent-for-surplus' development. It did, of course, also keep up the supply of harvest labour for agriculture.[83] When thereafter industry moved to the cities in the true industrial revolution factory stage, and took some of the labour with it, a shortage of labour at harvest times could clearly be seen to emerge, leading to rises in wages. In France this phase did not occur until the 1850s, in Belgium until the 1860s.[84] It is this mechanism of using agricultural labour in surplus for part of the year which later authors have largely ignored.

Mendels also described a second mechanism. Its symptom was the concentration of industrial employment, and therefore of an unusually large population per acre, in regions which were inherently infertile and therefore unable to feed it. Examples were the northern Low Countries, Saxony, Lusatia, and Northern Bohemia. Each of these had to rely on exports to meet basic food imports. In Flanders, studied closely by him, he noted a close correlation between the social behaviour of the 'proto-industrial' population and the relative prices of grain, brought in by that population, and linen, on which its wages depended, in other words, on its terms of trade. When the terms of trade moved in its favour, and its real piece wages therefore moved up, the number of marriages, and frequently the number of births, were observed to rise. However, when the terms moved against the industrial population, nuptuality and births did not decline. There was thus an asymmetry[85] or ratchet effect, leading to sharp increases in population in the proto-industrial areas and, in view of its dependence on imports, to a particular vulnerability to harvest failures, such as could be observed in Flanders in the 1840s.[86]

A substantial rise in population, evident over the whole of Europe from the early eighteenth century on if not earlier,[87] did indeed precede Industrial Revolution, and a close connection between it and the prelude to industrialization could indeed illuminate a crucial historic chain of causation. Moreover, the mechanism as described has the merit that it seeks to explain the rise of very similar proto-industries out of very different social, legal, and agrarian backgrounds. The causal link, however, was always the pressure of population on inadequate supplies of land.

This pressure could develop even in normally fertile regions, by a preceding population rise, or by shifts in social power. In some areas, for example those devastated by the Thirty Years War, population rise would bring positive, rising marginal returns at first, but after a while the classical sequence of falling marginal revenues in agriculture would set in. Since the pressure in this case arose from the side of labour, real wages would fall and rents would rise. In areas of primogeniture, a landless class of labourers would develop; in areas of partible inheritance, holdings would become smaller, and various types of less than full peasants would emerge, each with some land, but obliged to find part of their income from work outside their holdings: cottagers and *Kossäten, Büdner* and *haricotiers, Gärtner* and *manœuvriers*. Jobs might at first be available among large farmers or the manor estate, but as the supply increased, the terms of employment would deteriorate further. Estate owner could pay off their labour with tiny holdings of land, undermining further the position of the former smallholders.[88] The pressure was demographic and economic and would lead to similar results in widely varying agrarian systems.

In former times, the movement would have been halted and reversed either by Malthusian positive checks, such as famines and epidemics; by emigration, if free land were available elsewhere; or by preventive checks, that is to say a deliberate reduction in fertility. This may have occurred in Colyton in Devon with the decline of the New Draperies and even in Shepshed in Leicestershire as late as the nineteenth century.[89] Apart from delayed marriages, primitive methods of contraception, abortion, and infanticide were also widely practised.[90] Possibly these various methods were combined to form a social control of numbers, a 'homeostatic' system which kept population fluctuating around a tolerable level. Once proto-industrialization begins, the equilibrium is broken and there is no counteracting mechanism: population and domestic industry grow jointly, reinforcing each other's extension.

The initial pressure need not even have come from a population rise, as postulated above. A change in relative prices would change the opportunities of agrarian employment. Thus in the first half of the eighteenth century, as grain prices fell faster than meat prices, farming areas changed over to animal husbandry, and since pasture requires less labour than tillage, labour was set 'free' and driven to look for employment elsewhere. It is true that only in Britain, by means of enclosures, and in Holland, where capitalism had altered agriculture even earlier, could people be driven off the land altogether with such ease, to seek their income in town or industry. The various feudal or semi-feudal relationships elsewhere would still allow a peasant to be left without adequate income from the land, and forced to find other employment, even if he could not be deprived of his scraps of land and his rights within the village altogether. In mixed regions like Saxony, a class of people—servants, journeymen, farm labourers—had emerged even within a feudal framework who were completely mobile, and without any claims to land, and their numbers were growing.

Table 2.2. Electoral Saxony: Population without adequate rights to land[91] (% of Total Population)

	1550*	1750	1843
Gärtner, Häusler (minimal land, no rights)	4.6	30.4	46.8
Inwohner (no land whatever)			
Towns	5.1	16.3	17.6
Countryside	12.6	8.1	5.4
Total	22.3	54.8	69.8

* Without Upper Lusatia.

The effects of this enforced mobility would become more powerful by being localized, rather as the quirks of the English Poor-Law allowed the landlords and ratepayers of 'closed parishes' to concentrate their pauperism in neighbouring 'open parishes'. Thus the Austrian Waldviertel prevented land sales to outsiders so as not to lead to population increases, while Swiss towns, by excluding newcomers from the townships themselves and also the flat lands outside their gates over which they had control, drove this population to concentrate on the uplands, unprotected because hitherto considered valueless and incapable of sustaining any but a very thinly spaced population.[92]

At the same time in regions where soil or climatic and geographical conditions were unfavourable to agriculture, landlords and the authorities which they controlled positively invited settlement by encouraging industry or commercial employment as the only way of increasing their rent rolls and tax incomes. The penurious Prussian kings used various degrees of force to convert paupers, invalids, beggars, vagabonds, prisoners, soldiers' families, and even soldiers in off-seasons into domestic textile workers, to raise royal incomes.[93] Examples of landlord encouragement may be found in the Silesian–Bohemian frontier strip and as far east as the non-black soil regions of Central and Northern Russia. Making the somewhat heroic assumption that Russian serfs paying in labour services (*barshchina*) were agricultural, whereas those whose dues had been commuted to money payments (*obrok*) were in industrial or commercial employment, it has been argued that the very different distribution of payments between regions illustrates this preference.[94]

Regional variation in peasant payments in Russia
(Percentages Barshchina/Obrok)

	1765-7	1858
Black-Soil Region	75 : 25	73.1 : 26.9
Central Region	40.8 : 59.2	32.5 : 67.5
Yaroslavl	35.9 : 64.1	12.6 : 87.4

It is certain that most rural industry working for the market in Russia was found in the central rather than in the fertile provinces.

The infertile, or agriculturally disadvantaged region thus played a key role in European industrialization. It remains to be described how areas that were originally underpopulated became concentrations of population as well as industry and set up a growth dynamic that ended only with full industrialization, or else with hunger and mass emigration.

The link was provided by the family, which reacted to new forms of industrial employment by changing social attitudes, including those relating to marriage and fertility. The traditional family, on the land or in handicrafts, had sound economic reasons for limiting the number of its children. If more than one son survived in the country, the holding would have to be split, or all the sons except one would have to turn into landless labourers. In the towns, where the guilds generally limited the numbers of journeymen and apprentices, as well as controlling the entry of masters into the trade, the dilemma could be equally painful. Even as sole son and heir, prudence and social practice required one to wait for marriage until the farm or the workshop was vacant, and in all traditional societies the postponement of marriage is one of the most potent means of family limitation.

Once established, neither the peasant household nor the master craftsman's was a maximizing unit. Guild regulation and feudal exactions saw to it that output was kept within bounds, that accumulation did not take place, and that production-consumption balanced within the family household. Indeed, the distinction between production and consumption was by no means clear, and it would not have occurred to the members of the household to compare the contributions of each to them, even if they could have measured them.[95]

Into this traditional framework in reasonable equilibrium entered the outside proto-industrial employment with its own, quite different logic. The tensions between the two complete systems could then be seen to amount to a powerful engine for fundamental change.

In the early stages, filling in time between harvests, the members of the family could accept outside industrial work, perhaps as spinners or weavers, below true production and reproduction costs, for the opportunity costs of their labour was around zero and the capital used—mainly the house and the land—was treated as means of subsistence and not calculated in at all. At the same time, the rent which the family could pay was larger than that derived from the land alone, and in consequence it was soon pushed up to absorb part of the industrial income. Both landlord and putter-out did well out of the early proto-industrial family, but the family itself moved into a position of low-wage employment that would turn into a poverty trap when its allocation of land declined with rising population induced by the process itself.

Attracted by the low wages, merchants diverted more orders to the villages. Spare labour capacity was available not only in fertile regions between peak seasons, but also, and particularly, in infertile regions where agriculture by itself could not feed a family. Households drawn into this network soon found that with wage levels given and technology constant, their real income depended on the number of working to non-working members. While this was always so, to some extent, the earlier system had put up strong barriers against improving the ratio by having more children. Now, as capitalist entrepreneurs depressed wage rates to levels just acceptable to the more favourably placed families, other families were pushed to or below the margins of subsistence, and were thus strongly encouraged to raise their wage-earning potential within the same house and on the same holding by adding working hands to it. The labour of women was usually not physically heavy and could be continued until late stages of pregnancy. Children could begin to earn their bread from an early age. And so the birth-rate increased markedly among proto-industrial families. Despite the poverty and high rates of mortality, more survived, and the population began to grow.

As children turned into adolescents, they found that they could improve their position still more by pulling out of their own families and setting up as married couples: nothing stood in the way, a cottage could soon be rented, and the tendency of higher numbers of children per marriage was enhanced by earlier marriages, contributing a further impetus to population rise.[96] Once the process had begun, it was self-reinforcing, for the rising population itself contributed to keeping wages at or below subsistence, which in turn drove the households involved into yet faster increase. Moreover, the population increase has to be seen in relation to the land available. Both in the formerly agrarian, and in the barren marginal regions, the absolute quantity of land per family would fall as the absolute size of the population increased. The buffer available in their own plots, or in taking part in the harvest of larger holders in the area, was constantly reduced. Industrial payments and rents, initially calculated on the basis of a double source of incomes, thus became inadequate, and the reaction within the system could only be to produce still more wage-earning children and thus to turn the labour market still further against the worker. Times of falling real wages did not, therefore, lead to a fall in marriages: the system, as Mendels had noted, was asymmetrical. At the same time, the industrial households became ever more dependent on buying in food, and the industrial districts as a whole became increasingly food-importing economies. Workers became extremely vulnerable to rising food prices, and particularly to famines in bad harvest years, since in such times their poor communications might exclude them from farther supply areas, even had they been able to pay for the imports.

Yet from the social point of view the system had much to recommend it. Family life was close and satisfying, conforming to traditional views of the role of parents and children. Where some agriculture still survived, the agrarian rhythm combined with an indoor occupation seemed, in a European climate, to satisfy a deep human need better than full specialization. The economic status of the proto-industrial worker might be that of a wage earner, but he was in some sense still his own master, who still controlled (together with wife and children) the timing of his own work. In the industrial communities created, families of this kind had status, and could rely on mutual support. It was, in part at least, for precisely these reasons that proto-industrial workers left their villages and their industries with the greatest reluctance only, and only when in dire need. Rather like cotton hand-loom weavers and framework-knitters in England in somewhat similar circumstances, proto-industrial workmen on the Continent clung to their industries, in their locations, even when earnings were driven down well below subsistence and, as in the case of the Silesian weavers and Flemish textile workers, they left, or perished, only when faced by literal starvation.

What was essentially an industrial development thus had significant repercussions on population growth. It served to 'destabilise' a long-run equilibrium,[97] or rather to cut out a feed-back mechanism whereby formerly a divergence from the equilibrium had been slowed and reversed. The unchecked population growth in certain industrial regions then became one of the conditions favouring industrialization. Causal connections, as is so often the case, moved in both directions.[98]

How valid is this analysis? How accurately does it describe the realities of the growing export industries of Europe in the prelude to industrialization, and the causative socio-economic developments lying behind them? Was there such a thing as proto-industrialization, and did it form a kind of enclave within societies obeying its own economic, social, and demographic rules?

There can be no doubt of the correctness of one of the observed premisses, the close locational correlation between adverse agricultural endowment and rural industry. We have noted it before, and it has been widely supported by recent research. From the uplands around Verviers, providing for little more than animal husbandry, to the poor valleys of Upper Alsace, served by putters-out from Basle, and the even less hospitable uplands in Switzerland itself, supplied from Zurich and St. Gallen; from the slopes along the Wupper Valley, barely enough to provide potatoes and root crops, and grazing for a cow or a goat for the industrious textile workers, to the Saxon Erzgebirge and the Silesian Riesengebirge, it is the marginal, infertile regions which seemed to attract industry in the seventeenth and eighteenth centuries. Gloves around Grenoble, clocks in the Black Forest and in Switzerland, musical instruments, glass, iron goods, but above all textiles: as long as their technical processes permitted it, the expansion of their manufactures for the market will be found to a remarkable extent not to have taken place in the settled industrial towns, but among the cheap and often barely trained labour of less developed areas, frequently difficult of access and poorly provided with the amenities of life.[99] 'If the woollen manufacture of Verviers and Encival did not give them the means to subsist and pay their rent by spinning and preparing wool . . .' as one petition of 1750 put it in relation to one such area, 'they could not live there, or exist only in utter poverty on their well-nigh unproductive soil'. In what looks at first like a perverse relationship, it is precisely the regions which could not feed their population which registered the fastest population increase. It is surely a merit to have fastened on these relationships and attempted to bring them together in a single logical theorem.

In some cases, comparisons of similar areas show up the correlation in a particularly striking way. It may even have held for countries as a whole, as in the comparison between Holland and Belgium: thus the Dutch, despite their industrial traditions, their towns, and their rich farmers and burghers, failed to industrialize at the turn of the nineteenth century, whereas it was the poorer country, with its poor peasants and poorer communications, that industrialized first.[100] More impressive are local comparisons, particularly those based on the detailed study of Eastern Flanders, the area centred on Ghent. Here, within a fairly narrow compass and in a similar milieu, could be compared villages on poor sandy soil with those on richer lands and others in an intermediate position. In the eighteenth century, it was the infertile soil villages in which by-employment, and later full employment, in the linen industry became important, and it was in those regions that population increased rapidly as births to marriages ratios rose and the standard of living fell, whereas on rich agricultural land incomes were high, births to marriages ratios were low, and population actually fell after 1740. It was important for this particular region that the nearby city of Ghent which could normally be expected to act as a pole of attraction for suplus population could offer no employment, so that the people on the poor soil, in the Vieuxbourg region, had to turn to linen. Intermediate areas, with mixed quality soils, showed social consequences between these extremes. Similar comparisons could also be made between larger areas, for example the industrial regions of Overijssel and Twente in Holland, where population rose fast in the eighteenth century, and Sallaud and Friesland, which were still largely agricultural, where it did not; or between the inland areas of Flanders as a whole, which had sandy soils, subsistence agriculture, entrenched peasants with fragmented small-holdings, linen, poverty, and overpopulation cured in the end only by famine and enforced mass emigration, and the maritime areas of Flanders, where heavy soils made large capital-intensive farming more economic, and an area of rich farms and wage labourers became an agricultural export area where population remained stationary and incomes high.[101] Matching local correlations could be observed elsewhere: thus in Prussia, the fastest population growth between 1816 and 1849 occurred in the industrialized regions (*Regierungsbezirke*) of Trier, Düsseldorf, Cologne, and Arnsberg, where holdings were small and generally infertile, and the slowest in Münster, an area of large rich farms.[102]

The Flemish example has been widely quoted[103] and may be said to constitute the main base for the proto-industrial theorem. Yet it is not clear that its experience can be generalized over the rest of Europe, and several reservations, both theoretical and derived from observed facts, have been brought forward against accepting it as the only, or even the standard, type of dynamic rural industry in that period.

As far as the population link is concerned, the direct influence of high linen prices/wages, or for that matter low wages, on the birth-rate does not seem plausible. It would be at least seven, and possibly nine or ten years, from conception until a child became a bread-winner, and meanwhile it would burden the industrial family in precisely the most damaging way. Changes in marriages, leaving aside enforced marriages because of pregnancies, and the effect on numbers by the numbers of marriages in the immediately preceding period, would seem to be more plausible *a priori* causes. However, a test study carried out in the Prussian district of Hagen, a typical proto-industrial region depending mainly on iron and steel goods and the textile industry, found no correlation between marriages and the Mendels industrial goods/food price ratio. On the other hand, a correlation between marriage and birth-rates and food (rye) prices alone was found to have existed.[104] There was also a long-term rise in real wages, or, in other words, not all increases in income were converted into children. If, on the other hand, it is considered that in 1820–68, when these relations were tested, Hagen was already past the classical proto-industrial stage and half-way to full industrialization, which it would reach in the last quarter of the century, then a way out of the impasse of proto-industrialization, which the theorem does not admit, must have existed.[105] It should also be noted that Hagen in this period actually attracted immigrants[106] (and in short phases, when it lost population, lost it to the even more rapidly industrializing neighbouring Ruhr area), and that for Prussia as a whole, the provinces with the highest birth rates were the three eastern ones which had practically no industry at all.[107] Other studies of agrarian, urban, and rural industrial areas also found no correlation with the shape of the family structure.[108] Within the German orbit, population rise in this period would lead to falling incomes in the purely agricultural areas, while proto-industrialization would hold up incomes.[109] Altogether, the very concept of a measurable reaction of family behaviour to economic stimuli does not square well with the assumption of the non-market-oriented peasant household, the concept of the 'ganzes Haus'[110] stressed in the supporting literature.

A second line of criticism is that the theorem fails to distinguish between different social settings. In particular, areas with strong proto-industrialization in a framework of personal servitude, such as Silesia, Brandenburg, and Bohemia, should be distinguished in their origins and impact from those working in a free market economy.[111] Thus in eighteenth-century Silesia weavers preferred and were willing to pay more for a house without or with little land than one with more, because it bore fewer labour dues to the lord.

Perhaps most seriously, the concept fails to deal with what ought to be one of the most fundamental aims of enquiry: the way in which some of the regions affected were able to convert to full industrialization, while others de-industrialized and reverted back to agriculture. In other words, the question still to be debated is whether we are dealing with a transitional phenomenon, or with a dead end, and how far these alternatives were determined by inherent features.[112] It may well be that future studies will throw more light on this issue. Here we can turn only to alterntive explanations, those relating to the setting.

Where good agrarian alternatives existed which would become relatively more profitable on the basis of comparative advantages arising from stronger industrialization elsewhere, a reversal to agriculture, or de-industrialization of a positive kind, was likely. This tendency was reinforced if the initial rural industry had been relatively weak and dispersed and without a strong export market. The de-industrialization of parts of Bavaria and Central Germany, Eastern Westphalia, Lower Normandy, Brittany, and Languedoc might be explained in this way.[113] Behind it was ultimately the effective competition from more advanced regions, which in *c.* 1815-30 meant generally Great Britain, but later might be some continental centres as well.

There could also be, as it were, negative causes, a failure to adopt more modern methods under competition without an alternative. This might be because of poor location in terms of rising markets or developing means of <u>transport</u>, which seems to have been the case in the Silesian textile industry, or distance from coal, which may have been important in Flanders: where several causes coincided, survival was all the more difficult. Conversely, favourable location in relation to transport and markets or necessary raw materials, particularly coal and mineral ores, would favour the transformation to the full factory system. Rural industries provided a ready-made labour reservoir of workers possessing both industrial skills and some market orientation,[114] as well as a reservoir of skilled entrepreneurs. Despite the low fixed-capital component in most rural industry, the totals involved in circulating capital were very large in relation to initial fixed investments in factory-type industry.

At its peak, rural industry included some enormous enterprises. The Abbeville firm of van Robais employed 1,800 in central workshops, 10,000 in their homes, and in 1780, Puech of Carcassone and Montel of Bédarieux, some 1,000–1,500 each. In Silesia, Heymann of Breslau employed 71 in, 1,400 out in cottons, Sadebeck, a Reichenau employer, 6,000 spinners, 1,200 winders and shearers, 2,400 weavers. Wegely, in Berlin, in 1782 had 3,466 workers, Lange 3,534, and the royal Lagerhaus some 5,000. Von Leyen's Krefeld silk enterprise had 3,000 workers in 1768. Scheibler in Monschau (Montjoie) 4,000 in 1760, and Schüler, the leading calico-printer in Augsburg 3,500 at about the same time. The famous Calw woollen-mills employed in 1787, 168 in, 933 weavers and 3–4,000 spinners out. In Bohemia, economically part of Inner Europe, J. J. Leitenberger employed 5,000 in 1791 and J. M. Schmidt about 1,700 in 1775 and over 7,500 in 1838, of whom 7,000 were outworkers. The largest Austrian cotton firm, at Schwechat near Vienna, employed 23,549 spinners, and a total of 25,181 in 1785, and there were others nearby employing 13,711, 12,613, and 7,913 spinners, respectively. Probably the largest single firm of all was the Linz woollen manufactory, acquired by the Austrian state in 1754. In 1786, at its peak, it employed 34,935 workers, of whom 29,338 were domestic spinners. Of the latter, 16,820 lived in Bohemia, requiring an elaborate transport system to supply them. Even in Russia, a firm like Garélin employed 120 calico-printing tables, 900 looms, and 1,400 workers.[115]

It is clear that if conditions were favourable, firms of this kind would lack neither capital nor market connections to switch to mechanical forms of spinning or weaving. In point of fact, only some made the transition, and the rest declined in the face of competition on the part of machine-produced yarn. Taken as a whole, however, European industrialization owes a great deal to the preceding domestic industry and its prime mover, the capitalist putting-out merchant.

The Centralized Manufacture

In continental Europe as in Britain, rapid economic and technical change caused confusion in terminology. Manufacture or manufactory, the remaining major type of industrial organization, had several meanings, different at different times and places and sometimes even simultaneously. In each case, a large enterprise is to be understood—the 'proto-factory'. Three main variants may be distinguished: (a) the central workshops preparing and finishing the work of rural out-workers, large only because the firm is large but consisting of many independent small units grouped side by side, found mainly in textiles. Confusingly, this is sometimes called 'decentralised manufacture' or even 'putting-out factory'. (b) units having to be of fair size or requiring much capital for technical reasons, as in metallurgy, mining, or glass-making; (c) a grouping of workshops for which there is no economic or technical reason, but which has resulted from a royal monopoly or from the initiative of a territorial magnate. The boundaries between these are not clear, and the categories are not mutually exclusive.

Most of the large putting-out firms listed above, as well as many others, had taken to the practice of preparing and finishing their textiles on their own premises, by direct wage labour, in the towns rather than putting out that work also. The logic behind this was that it gave them better control over quality and finish, it protected their often valuable materials, such as dye-woods, from theft, it safeguarded any trade secrets, and is also gave them an opportunity of checking the quality of the fabrics sent in by the outworkers, before it was dispatched for sale. Where guild quality regulations, or excise duty, required inspection, such inspection was less burdensome if carried out in central premises.

The technology was still primitive: fabrics were trimmed by hand-shears, dyed in single vats, printed by hand-blocking on tables. But the units in which this work was performed could be quite large. Thus the Linz woollen manufactory, noted above, employed 102 dyers and finishers in 1786; the Schülers, the Augsburg calico-printers, employed 350 centrally, Calw had 168 centrally in 1787; the Berlin *Lagerhaus* in 1782 had 19 sorters, 92 scribblers, 60 nappers, 81 pre-parers, 14 dyers, 7 pressers, 4 burlers, 13 fullers and washers, and 2 in the machine-room, and probably some more, such as winders and warpers, or a minimum of 292, and probably over 400, out of a total workforce of 2,844 in central workshops. In Plauen (Electoral Saxony) it was the town itself which set up a calico-printing works, encouraging local weavers to take their cloths there rather than sending them to Nuremberg, Augsburg, Hamburg, or Bremen. There and in Chemnitz, calico-printers originally worked for the trade, but before long some began to put out work themselves, as the nodal points of rural industry.[116]

There were some trades other than textiles, as well as in some textile branches, in which technological or economic needs made larger units essential. As early as the seventeenth century, Dutch shipyards greatly exceeded all others in efficiency because of their extensive division of labour. Sugar refineries were plants with considerable capital, and in 1661 Amsterdam had 60 of them. There were at the time 600 industrial windmills, used for all kinds of purposes from timber-sawing, oil-pressing, and tobacco-pressing to paper-making, starch-making, and lead-milling.[117]

Dutch brickworks were calculated to have produced twice as much per head in the seventeenth century as the British during the indus-trial revolution. There was also the great pottery of Delft, a reflec-tion of burgher wealth and its status symbols. In the following century the potter's art rose to still higher levels with the introduction of chinese-type porcelain, first at Meissen in Saxony (1709), followed soon after by Vienna, Sèvres, Höchst, Nymphenberg, Berlin, and other capital cities or their suburbs. With their manual workers, artists, and royal bureaucrats, working under monopoly conditions, these were substantial enterprises. Thus about 1750, Meissen employed 378 and Berlin 400 people.[118]

There were also other luxury trades which tended to large enterprise: glass-making, clock-making, damask-weaving, armaments production, though many of these were royal or protected manufactures and should be considered under that heading. The large ironworks might also have a local monopoly or cartel organization. The Erzberg group of works produced 130,000 cwt. pig iron in 1783, beside the output of steel forges and plate forges. In Vordernberg, production was 185,500 cwt. in 1786. At Creusot, four blast-furnaces were producing 5,000 tons of iron a year, and Wendel's two furnaces at Hayange 900 tons.[119]

Possibly the most interesting examples of large manufactories put up by noblemen were to be found in the Czech lands. Conditions were propitious in the early eighteenth century, since politically and socially powerful grandees found themselves in control of large numbers of serfs, often on poor or upland soils, yet not far from markets and from the examples across the border in Saxony and Silesia. Moreover, there was state support to be had. Count Waldstein's woollen mill at Oberleutensdorf, set up in 1715, has often been described,[120] and one mill was actually founded on the initiative of Franz Stephen, husband of the Empress Maria Theresa, at Kladrub, in 1751.

These plants might be laid out in a grand, almost lordly style, the workshops being housed under a single substantial roof. The workers usually lived in special settlements or colonies nearby, as much under the control of their lords as in the villages. While the techniques were not originally dissimilar from those used in more humble enterprises, and factory discipline was feudal rather than capitalistic, and indeed the works were not always successful since their capacity was less able to adapt itself to the market than mercantile manufactories, yet they could benefit from some division of labour, and their very size and the influence of their owners gave them the opportunity of reaching more distant markets, while also gaining access to new technologies from the West. They also often managed to obtain privileges and even loans and subsidies from the state. Some of these works may therefore with some justification be considered forerunners within the relatively early industrialization of Bohemia and Moravia.

Elsewhere in Europe it was the sovereign who called into being or supported, though not necessarily with his own funds, enterprises which with varying justice have been called royal (imperial, or ducal) manufactures. The impetus was often mercantilist, and the example was set by France under Colbert. Among the methods used by Colbert to set up or keep going certain enterprises were tax relief, subsidies, and bounties, monopolies or protective duties, interest-free loans, royal orders for products, medals, and prizes, religious freedom for Protestants, compulsory purchase of land, legal advantages such as protection from creditors, tax-free salt, wine, or food, and exemption from the onerous duty of quartering soldiers. Other autocrats, such as the King of Prussia, might add a supply of labour (servile or of foreign immigrants), technical information, and exemption from conscription, to this list. In some manufactures the crown might itself take on shares, or take over ownership.

Few of the privileges were a direct burden on the royal exchequer, though about 3 million *livres* were paid out in direct subsidies under Colbert in his twenty-two years of power. Some of the enterprises he fostered were large manufactories, such as the Gobelins works, an older foundation but revitalized from 1667. In addition to tapestries, it also produced engravings, furniture, and jewellery to the highest artistic standards of the day, and purely as luxury goods. Another major company which owed its existence to Colbert's efforts was the Saint-Gobain glass works. Other favoured works were 'collective' units rather than a single works, such as the woollen industry of Sedan, Elbeuf, or Languedoc, or the arms factory at Saint-Étienne. Only the large centralized plants became immediate royal property, including Gobelins, Sèvres, the porcelain works, the soap works, and the gun factories, but the royal influence went much wider than luxury goods and armaments. It was part of Colbert's policy to encourage import substitution even in mass production trades. Over 400 establishments resulted from his efforts, including 300 in the textile industries and many others among paper, iron, and metal goods.[121] Many of these, in Colbert's time and after, were 'decentralised manufactures', forming the core of numbers of rural workers. Thus Messrs Bourdon and de la Rue, Elbeuf manufacturers, who received a privilege in 1690 for manufacturing Dutch and English style cloth at Pont l'Arche, 'were soon putting out work in neighbouring villages'.[122]

Another method of Colbert was to bring in foreign workers with skills not yet developed in France. These included Venetian glassworkers, shipwrights from Holland, gun founders from Nuremberg, tin-plate makers from Germany, metal miners and smiths from Sweden and Alsace. The Van Robais, weavers from Middelburg, were brought in in 1665, granted religious tolerance and 20,000 *livres* in grants and 80,000 *livres* in loans to set up a cloth factory in Abbeville, and theirs became one of the largest enterprises in France by the end of the eighteenth century.[123] Other Dutch specialists were brought into Caen, Carcassonne, Saptes, Guise, and other places, to establish textile industries and to Rochefort and La Rochelle to set up shipyards. At the same time, the revocation of the Edict of Nantes wrought havoc among some French key industries, and dispersed skilled Huguenot entrepreneurs across Europe to the territories of France's main rivals. As a result, the king in 1686 had to lend 500,000 *livres* to set up a company to improve the iron and steel manufacture, and more Belgians and even Dutch were brought in to repair the economic damage done by the expulsion of the native Protestants.[124]

When new techniques began to percolate through from Britain in the later eighteenth century, France still used the method of government support for their introduction. Thus John Holker and John Kay were supported in various ways by the authorities in their campaign to modernize the French cotton industry.[125] Again, the cotton firm of Hausmann and Hertzog, of Colmar, was given the privilege of a *manufacture royale* in 1775, and before long employed 12–13,000 outworkers.[126]

The Prussian royal enterprises were largely the work of the eighteenth century. Under Frederick the Great, royal ironworks were founded at Malapane and Kreuzberg in Upper Silesia in 1753-5, and two further works at the end of the century, in 1794-1801 at Gleiwitz and Königshütte. Malapane and Gleiwitz became technical pioneers for the whole of Germany. The first coke blast-furnace was started at Gleiwitz in 1796, and over 50 steam-engines were built there between 1808 and 1827.

In Berlin, royal manufactures included the arms factory at Spandau, the *Lagerhaus*, the largest woollen manufactory in Prussia, the china factory, the gold and silver works, and there was constant support for the silk industry. The Overseas Trading Company, the *Seehandlung*, which had been turned into an investment bank in the early nineteenth century, supported a wide range of industries, including paper, chemical, engineering, and iron and steel works, flax-spinning mills and grain as well as shipping and agricultural enterprises.[127] Some of these represented the transition from the 'manufactory' to the factory-type industry. Munich also had royal gold and silver, woollen, and leather manufactories.[128]

In spite of the strict Prussian regulations on guilds, urban status, and serfdom, a city like Berlin, and to a lesser extent other towns also, had room for a growing industrial population which did not fit into any of the established categories. In 1729, one in 9.7 inhabitants had been working in industry, and in 1801 this had grown to one in 4.2,[129] and many of these formed a new urban proletariat, unprotected by guilds and no longer tied to the soil. Perhaps the best-known example of a local industry bursting the bonds of guild restrictions without becoming fully rural, or turning to factory organization, was the silk industry of Lyons. Even at the end of the guild period, when nearly 35,000 of a city population of 143,000 were employed in it, the organization by 300 merchant putters-out, controlling workshop masters who in turn controlled members of their family and other workers, was clearly in defiance of all normal guild principles. By the early 1830s, high rents, high food prices, and over-crowding had driven many workers into the suburbs and the rural surroundings. The violence and brutality of the two rebellions of 1831 and 1834 dispersed the industry further into the countryside, without altering its essential workshop, putting-out character.[130]

Number of looms in the Lyons silk trade[131]

	Lyons	Suburbs	All Urban	Rural	Total	% Rural
1790	16000	500	16500	30	16530	0.2
1830	18000	11278	29278	8265	37543	22
1870		30000	90000		120000	75

We have described the three main forms of industrial organization in existence in Europe before the industrial revolution, the guilds, rural domestic industry, and the centralized manufacture, often enjoying privileged status; but new forms of employment and organization were constantly being created between the break-up of rural and guild traditions on the one hand, and market opportunities on the other. It was often these sectors, because they were not tied to traditions and obligations, together with the most adaptable of the older sectors, which provided the nucleus for the new industrial enterprises that were to transform the face of Europe.

Chapter 3

The Early Industrializers

Profound changes were affecting the economy of Europe in the historical phase preceding the industrial revolution. We have traced some of them in the last chapter. They include a transformation of industry in many regions, and in particular the rise of large 'manufactories' or 'proto-factories' and a rapid extension of domestic industry organized by putting-out merchants. They also include the emancipation of the serfs from many or all of their fixed obligations and the development of specialization, new techniques, and capitalist relations on the land. Guilds in the towns and serfdom in the country were subject to a ubiquitous, if irregular, process of attrition.

Behind these changes stood a great expansion of markets and a steady accumulation of new technology. New markets were found overseas, for the proto-industries; in the wealthy courts and among the armies and navies, for the manufactures; in the denser settled industrial and capital city regions, for the agriculturists; and among the growing population, a common feature of the whole of Europe, which provided the market opportunities for all kinds of goods and for labour. Other factors also played an important part. Absolutist states, highly centralized by current (if not by modern) standards, ordered armaments, altered tariffs and taxation systems, and sought to intervene directly in the productive industries, though not always with the results they intended. Better roads, docks, and waterways, whether built for commercial or strategic reasons, helped to open out some of the new markets. Financial and commercial institutions, banks and great merchant houses, innovated more efficient methods and made larger-scale trade and production possible. Great advances in science permitted not only better and more methodical observation of the world around the scientist, but also reacted back on industry, commerce, and transport with guide-lines for further progress.

It is not possible to say, though it might prove to be an interesting speculation, how the history of the Continent might have progressed had it been allowed to proceed along the lines set by its own quite significant advances sketched here.[1] But it was not to be; for the transformation of the British economy jerked it out of its existing paths, and instead of developing out of its own traditions, it had to react, adapt, and adopt. The complex story of these reactions in the leading economic regions of the Continent is the subject of the present chapter.

At first sight it is not at all clear what was distinctive about the British contribution. The Continent, as we have seen, had areas of its own which were advancing along a broad economic front. There had been significant progress in the fields of technology, organization, commerce, and finance. Output and wealth were rising for growing numbers. What was different in Britain? In other words, what did the 'industrial revolution' actually consist of?

No general agreement will be found in the large literature which exists on this question, though there is little dispute about the broad outlines. There would be scant value in adding to the theoretical discussion. Instead, our contribution is best made by examining what was actually transferred across the Channel, and what actually changed in the recipient areas.

The most obvious item to be transferred was the new technology. That, it should be stressed, was transferred whole: there was no adaptation. The steam-engines, spinning-mules, blast furnaces, or railway-systems installed on the Continent were exactly like the British ones, though in the early phases they might be ten or twenty years out of date by the time they were set up and, above all, they might be put in in a different sequence.[2] This was so even though the technical solutions developed in Britain had been answers to specific British problems and were appropriate to British factor endowments which might not always be those of the Continent: cheap coal, plentiful but low-grade iron ore, easy access to colonial cotton, plentiful water, certain types of skilled labour, and so on. Where factor endowments were different, British technology might not be accepted at all: thus the slow adoption of coke-smelting in ironworks in many French regions was clearly due to the fact that in their actual locations, small-scale charcoal furnaces were actually cheaper than the larger coke plants would have been. But no alternatives were developed: if local factor endowments were such that British technology could not be made to pay, the region remained agricultural or, if it had had some early industry, it de-industrialized. It was not until several generations later, towards the last quarter of the nineteenth century, that alternative technologies, not particularly suitable for British conditions, were to be developed.

The spread of British technology along these lines was possible because there were, in fact, several regions in Europe which had similar factor endowments, and had encountered economic and technical problems similar to those of the leading regions in Britain. They also had encountered a growing timber and therefore fuel shortage, they had access to coal, to iron, to European textile fibres such as flax or wool, or overseas fibres such as cotton, they met, further, a growing pressure of population on the land, and they could dispose of a working population not dissimilar in skills and possessing similar value systems. Much of this was true of North America also.

Regions with different but potentially equally rich endowments, did not develop rival technologies to make use of them. The rich timber lands of the north and east of Europe, the water power of many great rivers and mountains, let alone the oil of Romania, were not developed as alternatives to the British coal and iron technology. Instead these areas were frequently made subservient and colonized, confirming them in their backwardness and underlining their peripheral status against what Wallerstein[3] would call the all-powerful world system of industrialization of the British type.

Whatever may be said or surmized about other great cultural breakthroughs in the rise of man, it is clear that the origins of the new industrialized world were not polycentric. There was but a single source, as far as the bundle of key technologies was concerned. There was only one single process of European industrialization. The character of its expansion, moreover, serves to underline the significance of technical change within it.

Technology has its own logic which it imposes on its methods of practical application. Thus it was not only steam-engines or cotton-mules which were taken over complete on the Continent, but also factory organization or the layout of railway-lines. The farther we move away from sheer technical solutions involving inanimate matter, however, and the more we deal with the human component of industry, the less true to their model were the continental replicas. Even the skills of workmen might have other boundaries and groupings, and so had the authority of foremen or technicians. Labour contracts, or the status of workers, could vary more widely still, and there were serfs working in factories in Bohemia in the eighteenth century and Russia until the middle of the nineteenth, though even in this field some alignment and basic similarity became clearly necessary after a certain stage. The sources of capital, the social rights of entrepreneurship, and such legal conditions as patent laws or laws relating to the ownership or leasing of land might differ more widely still.

It was this tension between genetic similarity and particular difference which, as always, supplied much of the creativity of the European economy in this period. For while the technology accepted by Europe was the same, and in that sense other regions followed exactly in the footsteps of Lancashire or Clydeside, with the sole difference that they were some decades behind, they did so out of different traditions. They also did so, precisely because they came later, into a different world, a world made different by the coexistence of more advanced regions. These differences of timing and temporal coexistence, together with the differences in regional traditions and styles, form an important element in our account of European industrialization.

The Leading Industrial Regions

By common consent, the area which accepted earliest and with the greatest ease the gospel of industrialization emanating from Britain, and which came closest to the British model, was the Sambre–Meuse region, together with the Scheldt Valley of Belgium and northern France. To follow tradition, we shall consider the regions each side of the frontier separately.

The Belgian industrial belt contained early and successful examples of all the key industries of the industrial revolution period: coal, iron, engineering, cotton, and wool, together with some other industries based on coal and advanced technology, such as glass and chemicals. In each of these sectors it compared reasonably well in terms of timing and technology with any of the major British industrial regions, though not with all of them put together, that is to say, the whole British economy, although that is the somewhat incongruous way in which these comparisons are usually made.

The basis, as always, was coal. The coalfield is long and narrow, stretching in an approximately east–west direction, and dipping to the west. Coal was therefore worked first from the shallow seams in the east, where adit drainage into the valley bottoms was possible, but it was the western section, the *Borinage*, which was forced by its deeper mines to take the lead in technology. The first Newcomen pump was erected in the eastern part of the coalfield in 1720, well before most British fields; but there were only 10 of them in that part of the field by 1812, and only 13 in the Charleroi (East Hainaut) section, whereas the *Borinage*, which installed its first in 1737, ultimately made use of large numbers. Here as in other coalfields, Newcomen pumps survived well into the middle of the nineteenth century, since their main drawback, a high coal consumption, mattered little at pit heads where boilers could be fed by small or unsaleable coal. The first Boulton and Watt engine was erected as early as 1785 at Jemappes, but as in Britain, it took a long time to become popular on the coalfield. Winding-engines had to be of an advanced type, and the earliest were installed in the *Borinage*, where the depth of pits compared with that of the most advanced regions in Britain. By 1829, the average pit depth there was 167 metres (about 92 fathoms) and the lowest depth was 297 metres (163 fathoms), and 82 pits there used steam for winding, as against 55 using horse gins. The shallower pits elsewhere managed to go on longer with animal power, though by 1839, the Liège sector used 59 steam-engines, as against 29 hand-winches, and 5 horse-gins. In 1838, the average depth of pits in the whole of Belgium was 210 metres, and the lowest 437 metres; by 1866, 437 metres was the average and the deepest pit, west of Mons, was 1,065 metres (582 fathoms) deep.[4]

The output of the field reached 2.3 million tons in 1831 and over 5 million tons in 1846.[5] It has been pointed out that in 1811 the Belgian output of coal, if spread over the whole of the population, worked out at 450 kg. per capita, compared with 600 kg. for Great Britain, and a mere 40 kg. for France.[6] While such figures give a misleading impression, since Belgium was itself a part of France for which it supplied about half the coal, it emphasizes what a large part of the coal production of Western Europe was concentrated in that very small area in the first half of the nineteenth century. The eastern sector supplied very largely the industrial complex around Liège and Verviers as well as the Dutch market, and the central area, after the completion of the Charleroi–Brussels canal in 1832, supplied the growing market of the capital. But much of the output of the *Borinage* went to France, and much of the history of transport improvement in that area and in northern France is concerned with the means of taking that coal to Paris and other French departments. In 1814–30, Belgian coal also went to Holland, but was thereafter replaced by British coal. While exporting largely to the south, Belgian industry also drew coal, as well as pig iron, from Britain.[7] A glance at the map will show the logic of that sector of international trade.

There was also an old tradition of ironmaking, mostly by the bloomery method, using local timber and water-power. Liège was a major European centre of armaments production, and nails were made in the Ardennes nearby, and at Charleroi. Stimulated by the large French market to which the area belonged as an integral part in 1795–1814, several leading entrepreneurs turned to modern methods. In the Liège area, 25 rolling mills were installed in 1800–15, mostly water-powered. At Charleroi, Paul Huart-Chapel invented a reverberatory furnace for melting scrap in 1807, a modern rolling-mill was built at Acoz nearby in 1812,[8] and more rapid development followed in the 1820s, led by several local entrepreneurs and one Englishman, Thomas Bonehill. The first puddling-furnace was erected in 1821, and the first coke blast-furnace in 1827. By 1830 there were ten, and rolling-mills and steam-engines showed the active advance of those years to which several British technicians contributed. Works like Hannoret–Gendarme and Marcinelle became integrated concerns and in 1841 the amalgamated Marcinelle and Couillet works were stated to have become the largest ironworks on the Continent. In 1845 they produced 30,000 t. of rails. Total pig iron output rose from 29,000 t. in 1816 to 135–150,000 t. in 1835.[9] The last charcoal furnace was closed down in 1851.

This major advance of Belgian ironmaking was connected with railway building from 1834 on. The government, faced with massive industrial failures and widespread unemployment as a result of the loss of markets in Holland and the Dutch colonies, which were the consequence of Belgian independence from Holland declared in 1830, grasped that the country's economic role was to act as the advanced industrial region for a wider economic hinterland even if the latter was outside its borders. In building up rapidly a remarkably complete railway system it had thought mainly in terms of transport, from Antwerp to Germany, bypassing the Rhine mouths, and linking with France to the south, but the initiative soon paid off in production also. The Cockerill works, encouraged by the home railway market, for a time became the leading continental suppliers of locomotives to customers in most parts of Europe and the direct transmitters of the latest British technology in this field.

Cockerill's exemplified the pioneer role of the Belgian industrial region in the industrialization of Europe, as well as its indebtedness to Britain. William Cockerill had arrived in Belgium about 1798 to make textile machinery of English design for the woollen industry of Verviers. Finding himself limited by an exclusive contract to a major woollen manufacturer, J. F. Simonis, he let his son-in-law, James Hodson, set up another engineering works to equip other woollen mills. In 1807 the Cockerill works moved to Liège where, with his three sons, the founder created a plant making textile machinery for the whole of France and areas beyond, employing 2,000 people by 1812. John, one of the sons, transferred the works to Seraing in 1817 where it concentrated on iron-making (it had a coke blast-furnace by 1829) and heavy engineering. A Boulton and Watt engine had been imported from Britain in 1813, to be used as a model. The company built its first steam-engine in 1818, and by 1830 another 201 had been added. It was on this basis that the works could quickly switch to railway orders some years later.

Rather like the British in relation to Belgium, the Cockerill Brothers not only sent finished machinery abroad, but travelled themselves to advise on the industrialization of other countries, particularly Prussia. Their role as a major transmission centre of British technology should not, however, lead us to neglect other major engineering works in the same region. There had been attempts by local makers to copy British machines even before Cockerill's arrival. Later, Houget and Teston supplied woollen machinery to much of Europe, and the Phoenix works of Ghent were among the cotton machinery pioneers.[10] This trade was greatly aided by the still operative British prohibition on the export of machinery.

The woollen industry, centred on Verviers, near the eastern end of the coalfield, also had a long tradition. Straddling the frontier between the Austrian Netherlands and the Bishopric of Liège, the region's workmen often commuted between one country and another, and the manufacturers could originate their exports from whichever territory seemed more favourable from a tariff point of view. This predisposition to smuggle was fostered by the high tariffs against the imports of woollens maintained by both France and Holland, the nearest foreign markets, which had as a further consequence that most exports went into Germany, Poland, Russia, and the Baltic States. Official statistics show cloth exports to have gone to the extent of 86.5% to 'Germany' (some to be sent farther), 7.5% to Liège, and 5.5% to the United Provinces. There were also sales to Spain and later to North America, while imports of raw wool came mainly from Spain.[11] The region was thus a typical centre of export industry. From 1794 on, the frontiers of France were thrown open to the Verviers manufacturers, and although they came into competition with some of the traditional French manufacturing centres inside the Empire, the new opportunities were grasped with success.

Until the end of the eighteenth century no modern machinery was used in the industry. There were 27 fulling-mills of a traditional kind along the Vesdre and its tributaries. From 1765, the region began to dye its own products, Eupen specializing in dyeing in the piece, and Verviers in dyeing in the wool. Mechanization began in 1801, when the first spinning-machine was set up, over thirty years after its introduction in Britain. As there were around 25,000 hand-spinners in the vicinity of the urban centres, there was scope for rapid investment, and within the first decade, 118 frames were set up. At the same time, the flying-shuttle speeded the work of the weavers.[12] At the end of the French period, the industry suffered comparatively little, switching easily to exports to Germany, the Mediterranean countries, Italy, Russia, Scandinavia, and Holland. Though behind Britain in technology, the Verviers exporters could compete with British exports on the basis of lower wages. The following figures refer to the Verviers area. By then, there were 68 steam-engines of 513 HP in 185 mills.[13]

The cotton industry, by contrast, had no long local tradition, except

	Looms	Output pieces
1789	500	20000
1812	1190	47500
1834	2500	100000

in so far as, like the Clydeside industry, it settled amongst the skilled textile workers of the linen industry. Its location in Ghent was somewhat detached from the rest of the industrial region[14] and its introduction had something of a dramatic and romantic, not to say incongruous, aspect about it.

Like several other areas, Ghent began its interest in cotton goods by printing imported fabrics from the mid-1750s on. By 1799 there were at least nineteen printing firms in the city, some of them quite large and using the modern rollers. It was a merchant, rather than a manufacturer, Liévin Bauwens,[15] who decided to smuggle out of England in somewhat hair-raising circumstances, a set of cotton-mules, complete with steam-engine. Because of local unrest, he set up his first mill in 1800 at Passy, near Paris, but a second one was built in Ghent in 1801, and by 1806 there were ten mechanized mills in and around the city, mostly owned by Bauwens or members of his family, building their own machines. When the blockade of 1806 prevented the import of woven fabrics, looms were also set up, and by 1812 there were 3,600. The industry expanded with dizzying speed: by 1812 there were 103,000 mule-spindles in 25 mills, installed and active, and by 1815 there were 250,000, employing 4,671 spinners, beside 5,000 weavers and 2,257 printers. Bauwens, it should be noted, had made an equally dramatic exit by going bankrupt in 1811,[16] but the local industry was more than a flash in the pan. It was modernized between 1819–23, installed its first power-looms, made locally by English workmen or smuggled in, in 1821, and by 1830 it had 50 steam-engines. The local 'Phoenix' engineering works supplied many parts of Europe with cotton machinery.[17]

Linen developed in an entirely different way. It had been the traditional industry and proto-industry of the Flemish countryside, and its entrepreneurs seemed unwilling or unable to adopt, let alone initiate, improved techniques. When British makers succeeded in subjecting flax to a machine-spinning process, the Flemish industry collapsed in one of the most dramatic reversals of fortunes found in European economic history. The statistics relating to its main foreign market, the French, tell their own story.[18] (See Table 3.1.) The loss, it is important to stress, was in yarn exports rather than in woven fabrics, though in the Paris market, Irish and Scottish linens also were beginning to replace the Flemish. British spinners were, in fact, invading the Belgian market itself: imports of yarn from Britain to Belgium

Table 3.1. French Linen Imports (000 Tons)

	Yarn			Piece-goods		
	Britain	Belgium	Total (incl. others)	Britain	Belgium	Total (incl. others)
1832	30	685	835	—	2935	3170
1838	5295	405	5800	1395	3375	5180
1842	10695	545	11310	1820	2345	4395

amounted to a mere 12,000 pounds in 1833, but had increased over a hundredfold, to 1,305,000 pounds, in 1838. Some machine-spinning mills had been set up from 1837 onwards in Ghent and Liège, and the numbers of machine-spindles rose to 97,000 in 1846,[19] but this did not help the 220,000 rural hand-spinners. The not untypical attempt to solve the problem by keeping out yarn imports merely endangered the 57,000 weavers, as piece-goods exports continued their fall. Expecting, somewhat irrationally, the crisis to be temporary and unable to move to any other occupation, the Flemish spinners' suffering, when potato blight and bad harvests in 1845-6 destroyed their crops, forms one of the saddest, and best-known, chapters in European economic history.

Belgian coal- and machine-based superiority showed itself in various other industries, of which only a few can be mentioned here. Chemical bleaching led to the development of a chemical industry and to the innovation of the Solvay process later in the century. There were also paper-mills, sugar refineries, and tanneries, and the glass industry, benefiting from cheap fuel and cheap labour, drove British glass not only from most continental markets, but even invaded the British market itself by the middle of the century. By its end, 95% of Belgian glass made was exported.[20]

By the accidents of history, the political boundaries of the Spanish and later Austrian Netherlands, and of Belgium, before 1793 and after 1830, were so drawn that they included very little land apart from the broad, central industrial belt. Belgium was therefore commonly referred to in the nineteenth century as the most industrialized country in Europe after Great Britain.[21] If, by a similar accident, it had remained part of France, or part of Holland, the same region would have been subsumed under the heading of a relatively slowly industrializing 'economy'. Both descriptions, by concentrating on the political boundaries, are inapt and misleading. As we have seen, it would be more correct to describe the Belgian industrial region as the earliest to accept British technology and British methods, and, by transmitting it further, to make for a time much of Europe far outside its borders into its economic hinterland, deriving advantages from this relationship not unlike those of the Northern Netherlands some two hundred years earlier. Another way of looking at it would be to draw a distinction between Belgium and the rest of Inner Europe, and to see the Sambre-Meuse region as the first of the ever widening circles of industrialization, and the rest of Inner Europe as the second stage. Whichever way it is measured, Belgian industrialization had been achieved by 1860-70.

To what did the region owe its early start? Clearly, it benefited from an industrial and commercial tradition and a long acquaintance with capitalist relations, from rich national resources, including coal, iron, timber, and water-power as well as flax and wool, and from a splendid location, across the Channel from Britain and between the advanced areas of France, Germany, and Holland. These were evidently more than enough to outweigh the disadvantages of the Roman Catholic religion which had proved to be an obstacle to industrialization in other parts of Europe, and of a disastrous political history which punctuated the Belgian industrial revolution by a series of throw-backs and severe crises. However, there were compensations in being governed, first by a Dutch King who began to woo his reluctant southern subjects by economic concessions from about 1821 on, and, after 1830, by ruling groups who had fewer agrarian interests than any other in Europe, to obstruct their pursuit of commercial and industrial progress.[22] Both developed further an already efficient transport network, the Dutch by canals, the Brussels government by railway-building. In addition, the king poured money in the form of shareholdings and subsidies into all major firms, and in the Société Générale pour favoriser l'Industries Nationale developed the successful model of an industrial bank,[23] followed in 1835 by the Banque de Belgique and by the Société Nationale pour les Enterprises Industrielles et Commerciales, and before long by other banks in Belgium and most of Europe. This financial concentration helped to develop an early joint-stock system in Belgium and to attract French and British capital into the region in the 1830s and 1840s. In the second half of the century, Belgium herself became a major exporter of capital to Germany, Russia, and overseas. The post-1830 governments, pursuing their support for capital, kept all signs of labour emancipation down with remarkable single-mindedness, so that wages, already held down by a rapid population increase and the Flemish disaster, were kept down in relation to productivity well below those of the rest of Europe.[24] As its growth continued[25] and its competitive strength increased, Belgium turned from a protectionist into a relatively free-trade country, importing a growing share of its food consumption, as well as iron ore, wool, cotton, and even flax and sugar beet, and exporting a larger share of its output than any other country in Europe,[26] Britain included, though not necessarily a larger share than any other industrial region.

Across the frontier to the south, the Belgian industrial region spilled over into France, mainly to the two northernmost *départments*, Nord and Pas-de-Calais, but extended to adjacent *départements* also. These frontiers had been altered more frequently than almost any other in Europe and they had no economic resource significance. We are basically dealing with the same region.

The coal, continuing to dip towards the west, lies deeper than in Belgium. The area near the frontier, around Valenciennes, was developed in the eighteenth century, but even then large-scale enterprise was necessary. The Anzin coalmining company, started in 1757 on the coalfield opened up in 1717, was throughout this period one of the largest enterprises in France, liberally supplied with capital and privileges from Paris. The first Newcomen pump was set up in the coalfield in 1732. By 1830 the Nord produced 390,000 tons and in 1845 it produced 945,000 tons, or 22.4% of France's output. The coal was got at high cost, and could maintain itself against Belgian competition only by tariffs and obstruction of the water-ways to Belgium. The field was extended slightly after 1820, but the real breakthrough to open up the deeper pits in the west was possible only with the more advanced technology of the second half of the century.[27] In 1851 the first pit of the western extension, at Courrières in the Pas-de-Calais, was opened up: that area was to carry most of the expansion in the main wave of French industrialization. By 1913 the Pas-de-Calais alone produced 20½ million tons (or half the French total),[28] and the whole northern field some two-thirds. The region became France's 'Black Country'.[29]

Textiles formed the main traditional industrial occupation in the region. The woollen industry had been widespread in France in the eighteenth century, but there were local concentrations. The Champagne was one of the fastest-growing areas, increasing its share of French output from 12% to 16.5% in the course of the eighteenth century. Held back somewhat by poor transport early in the nineteenth century, Reims yet raised its production of worsteds fivefold between 1808 and 1848.[30] It was one of the earliest centres to use carding-machines built by Cockerill and by William Douglas, a Paris engineer, also of British origin,[31] and one of the first to drop hand-spinning altogether. Sedan had also become a major centre in the early nineteenth century, and the spinning of combed wool was established around Amiens in 1825. The first spinning machine had been introduced there in 1815, and by 1830 there were 170 in 19 mills. Roubaix, a woollen town in the eighteenth century which had turned to cotton, converted back to woollens in the 1830s: the number of its woollen spindles went up from nothing in 1830 to 105,000 in 1839. By 1843 63% of its woven output was in woollens.[32] These towns were spinning fine worsted yarn and the Nord *département* altogether had 220,000 spindles in 1843, but still nearly 420,000 cotton spindles. The first successful use of the power-loom was reported from Reims in 1844, though it took many years to become widespread.[33]

While the northern woollen industry spread in a broad band along the frontier, showing a very uneven record of mechanization, cotton was from the beginning under greater pressure from British competition to instal machine methods. Before 1800 the story is one of considerable efforts by French governments and entrepreneurs and a large number of British mechanics and experts, like Holker, O'Flanagan, Morgan, Brown, Hall, Wright, Jones, Garnett, Wood, Hill, Milne, Lecler (?Clark), Theakston, Flint, Foxlow, and Sykes, among others, to make a beginning, but their success was, at best, temporary and localized.[34]

The main cotton centres had at first been in Normandy, but the poorer peasants of a broad swathe of land from Picardy over (French) Flanders to the Nord were also ready to take up weaving, if a yarn supply could be organized. By 1810 there were 22 cotton-spinning mills in Lille, 13 in Roubaix, and 8 in Tourcoing, mostly using hand-driven jennies, but water-power and even steam came in among the pioneers before 1820. Around 1840, over half the French factory workers were concentrated on this belt: 100,000 in the Nord, 20–30,000 in Flanders, and 130,000 in Picardy, in addition to 150,000 in Normandy.[35] Normandy was working on the coarser counts, and finer spinning was almost entirely limited to Alsace, Paris, and the north, the triangle of Lille, Roubaix, and Tourcoing forming the main concentration. In 1833 the distribution of fine spinning was as follows:

Fine cotton spinning in France, 1833[36]

	No. Mills	Spindles (000)
Paris	3	25
Tourcoing, Lille, Roubaix	20	160
Rest of Northern France	8	125
Alsace	9	182

Possessing coal, the North was the most suitable region to supply mass-produced standard semi-finished manufactures, some of which could be finished elsewhere.[37]

The northern French departments were in all respects less well placed than their Belgian neighbours to produce iron, but the closing of the frontier in 1815 and tariff protection gave them their chance. There had been some ironmaking under the Empire,[38] but the region's expansion, aided by Belgian immigrants who came south to cross the tariff barrier, and by some British, may be dated from about 1820. In 1823-4, a Belgian named Renaux set up a modern iron refinery and forge, using steam-power and employing British workers on up-to-date equipment. It was 'a firm where English workmen processed Champagne pig iron by an English technique on equipment probably built in Paris by Englishmen and located at Raismes in order to take advantage of the cheap, abundant coal from Anzin pits'.[39] There other Belgians had set up three nailing firms around Valenciennes in which all but 37 of a total complement of 588 were Belgian in 1822. By 1835, the Nord *département* had 297 steam-engines, and together with four neighbouring ones (Seine-et-Oise, Seine-Inferieure, Aisne, Pas-de-Calais) had nearly half of the steam-engines in France.[40]

By then, the traditional self-financing of provincial textile centres had given way to some provision from Paris, particularly for heavy industry and for short-term discounts. The Banque de Lille opened in 1836, to be followed by a private bank in the following year and an industrial bank in Valenciennes. The Bank of France, which had maintained a branch in Lille in 1810-14, opened another in Valenciennes in 1846, in the same year in which the Caisse Commerciale du Nord began trading in Lille. The Société de Crédit Industriel et de Dépôts du Nord, linked with the Comptoir d'Escompte, opened there in 1866 with a capital of 20 million francs.[41]

On its eastern side, the Belgian industrial region spilled over into the Aachen district, where coal and woollen manufacture in such areas as Monschau and Eupen mirrored developments in Verviers, though Aachen itself, hampered by guild restrictions had fallen behind in the eighteenth century. Since it was in a competitive relationship with other Lower Rhine producers it has normally been considered a part of the Rhineland–Westphalian complex.

In the eighteenth century there were two major concentrations here, both on the right bank of the Rhine: the ironworking regions of the Siegerland, and the textiles concentrated mainly along the Wupper Valley. These were hilly districts with poor agricultural resources, but benefiting from the existence of rapid streams[42] and timber for fuel and power. Other advantages were the relative commercial freedom within the Duchy of Berg, and accessibility to the Rhine cities to provide markets and capital. They made the region one of the most industrialized and densely populated in Europe by the end of the eighteenth century.[43]

The Berg–Mark iron industry drew its ore from Nassau, to work it up in small charcoal bloomeries and charcoal furnaces into semi-manufactures, and in further water-driven hammer works into finished articles. Solingen and Remscheid, with their surrounding villages, made cutlery and arms, while wire-making, as well as scythes, sickles, tools, pins, and needles, had spread eastward into the Mark to Ennepe and the Lenne Valley. This was a typical 'export' industry, supplying much of Germany and beyond, though suffering from British competition in the first half of the nineteenth century.[44] As finishing branches they were among the most difficult to mechanize, but when the next stage arrived, in the second half of the nineteenth century, the district was among the technical leaders of Europe.[45]

Immediately adjacent was the textile area centred on the Wupper towns of Elberfeld and Barmen. Originally a transit station for sending textiles for finishing to Holland, it took over the finishing itself in due course, the 'Garnnahrung' or bleaching-guild monopoly dating from 1527.[46] By the eighteenth century the local merchants were drawing linen yarn from a wide fan of supply areas stretching from northern Westphalia to Brunswick and Hanover, putting it out to be woven to large numbers of urban and rural weavers, bleaching and finishing the fabric and funnelling its sales to North and South America as well as West Africa,[47] as part of the Atlantic economy and to Holland, Germany, and, in the case of yarn, to Britain. In the middle of the century, silk ribbon and fabrics, as well as the widespread 'Siamoises', half-cotton fabrics, were added. By the 1790s local manufacturers had begun to put out cottons across the Rhine to Gladbach-Rheydt in the search of cheaper labour.

This active, enterprising society, with its trading connections, its access to capital, and its labour skilled in several types of textiles,[48] was ideally suited to pick up the new technology from Britain. A local merchant, J. G. Brügelmann, who had visited England, managed to copy Arkwright's water-frame, probably with the help of English mechanics, and set up a water-powered mill at Ratingen, near Düsseldorf, in 1783, which he called Cromford after his model. His twelve-year monopoly and the usual difficulties experienced on the Continent in copying British technology made this an isolated example for a while, though Brügelmann himself took shares in two more spinning mills as well as in dyeing plants.[49] By 1799 there were 10 machine-spinning mills in Wuppertal, some driven by water and some by horses. J. H. Bockmühl's locally invented machine for making bootlaces was by then also water-driven.

At first, the changes wrought by the French Revolution affected the region favourably since it could capture some markets formerly supplied from France. When Napoleon drew his boundary along the Rhine, the manufacturers on the left bank of the river, in the old silk centre of Krefeld and in Gladbach-Rheydt found themselves inside the Empire and continued to flourish, but those on the right bank suffered severely by being excluded from the imperial markets.[50] Some migrated to the west. After the war the region, like others, found that the technological lead of Britain had widened considerably. Technical innovation was slow at first. A steam-driven cotton mill began to operate in Elberfeld in 1821, using a 6-HP engine. By 1834 there were ten engines, with 62 HP between them in Wuppertal industry, and there were 37,000 cotton-spindles installed on the east bank of the Rhine and 37,000 on the west bank,[51] but by the mid-century cotton spinning had disappeared in Elberfeld and Barmen, only 29,444 spindles remaining in Sonnborn.

Instead, the region took to weaving and finishing where the British technical lead was less pronounced. Power-loom weaving began in 1842. Employment in the administrative district of Düsseldorf will show the development.[52]

	1846	1861
Woollen and Worsted Spinning	5239	2342
Weaving: Woollens	5590	6189
Cottons	12469	13133
Silk and silk ribbons	18985	26634
Ribbons	3710	28969

By 1861, 60% of the workers in Barmen and Elberfeld were in true factories; there were one hundred and sixteen steam-engines in the two towns, and backward integration had become particularly strong. Engineering and chemicals gradually took over as textile employment declined. The dye-works of Friedrich Bayer and Friedrich Weskott opened in Barmen in 1863; lack of space induced them to move to Leverkusen in 1891.[53]

North of this district flowed the Ruhr across what was largely an agricultural region in the eighteenth century. Some small coal-mines were being worked by part-time peasants by means of levels. In 1780 the river had been made navigable and in due course metalled stone ways were laid from the pitheads to the river. The first horse-drawn tramroad of one-mile length followed in 1829. But coal output remained insignificant. There were also some minor charcoal ironworks in the district and some small engineering workshops, but the first puddling furnace was not started until 1826, and there was no coke blast-furnace until the Friedrich Wilhelm Ironworks in Mülheim blew in its first in 1848-9, some one hundred and forty years after the invention of the process.

The 'Ruhr' industrial region (most of which in fact lies a good deal north of the river) thus developed late, but then its development came with a rush. Within half a century it had become the most important industrial region on the Continent. At the base of its prosperity was its excellent coking coal, which could be raised with the technical means of the mid-nineteenth century, provided a market was available. The market, in turn, came with the building of railways, which simultaneously needed coal, set up a demand for iron, which also needed coal, and provided the means to carry the coal cheaply also to more distant users, or bring iron ores into the coalfield. Apart from the coal and some iron ores which quickly gave out, the Ruhr district was favoured by the nearby Rhine, as a means of transport, by early access to the important Cologne–Minden railway which reached the district in 1848-9, and by later links to the main canal network. It lacked labour and capital, both of which had to be imported. But there were ten engines, with 62 HP between them in Wuppertal in trial developments adjacent to the south, including entrepreneurial talent, local engineering and ironworking demands and skills, transport links, and the reservoir of a population used to industrial work. It was only in its later phases, from the 1880s, that recruitment to the Ruhr district had to come from farther afield, particularly the German East.[54] By starting late, the district also benefited by borrowed technology,[55] and avoided costly pioneer errors: thus its mines were from the beginning built on a large scale, so were the iron and steelworks, and vertical integration and cartelization came earlier to the Ruhr than anywhere else in Europe.

The first successful sinkings to the deep coal through the marl occurred only in the 1840s, after trials in the 1830s had been, typically, commercial failures. Coal output which had been a mere 388,000 tons in 1815 and 1.7 million tons in 1850, rose to 11.6 m.t. in 1870, 60.1 m.t. in 1900, and 114.2 m.t. in 1913. This last figure represented 60% of the German output, and more than 2.8 times the whole French output. Ironworks were established in two main foundation waves, the early 1850s and the early 1870s. Krupp's of Essen were the first on the Continent to work the Bessemer process in 1862, the Hörder Verein following in 1864 and the Bochumer Verein in 1865. The district later turned mainly to the Siemens–Martin furnace, the first one being installed at Krupp's in 1869. By 1913 the Ruhr produced 8.2 m.t. of pig iron, or 42.5% of Germany's total, and it had become the leading centre of steelmaking, heavy engineering, and armaments, besides producing chemicals, glass, textiles and several other important manufactured exports.[56]

Upstream from Rhineland–Westphalia, Alsace seems at first sight to have little in its favour as an industrial pioneer. There was no coal, no other raw material, little local wealth, and, above all, there were very poor communications to the sea, for, quite apart from technical problems, the Rhine was of little commercial use before the treaty of 1831, and many goods went overland to Le Havre instead. Coal prices in francs per metric quintal in 1826, were 3.60-4.00, and at times up to 5.50 in Alsace, compared with 1.27 in the Nord, 0.20-0.90 in the Loire field, and 0.60-0.80 in Britain. There were also restrictive guilds and misguided royal policies.[57] In its favour Alsace had clean water and water-power, low wages, access to Swiss capital, a textile tradition partly based on government favours, a frontier situation, which frequently proved conducive to early industrialization and in this case to a lively smuggling trade to Germany, and, as some would have it,[58] a Calvinist people surrounded by less businesslike Roman Catholics. It may also be that Alsace's isolation protected her for a critical period from English competition.

There was a small, old-established charcoal iron industry, but Alsace's industrialization was based on cotton, adding other textiles and backward linkages later. Alsace began with the printing of calicos (*indiennes*), a trade over which it increased its hold in the first half of the nineteenth century: 6 million metres were printed in 1806 in Mulhouse, rising to 43 million metres in 1847. Roller-printing was introduced at Wesserling in 1803, in Mulhouse in 1804, and by 1820 there was printing in two colours, by the 1830s in five or six colours. Weaving followed. The Sainte-Marie area had 6,000 looms in 1832, 15,000 in 1848-9, making 28,000 pieces in 1814, but 400,000 pieces in 1838. It was in 1821-2 that 'barns, cellars and even ground-floor rooms were converted into weaving sheds, to the great dissatisfaction of wine growers and farmers', recalling the situation of Lancashire in the 1790s. Some power-looms were introduced in the 1820s, and by 1846 there were 15,000 in Alsace, or a similar number as hand-looms.[59]

But it was in cotton spinning that Alsace pulled ahead most clearly from the rest, particularly by its early mechanization, and the skill in high quality cotton production. By 1834 Nicolas Koechlin and Hartmann span 300 and 320 counts. The first mechanical spinning-mill was set up in 1802 at Wesserling, driven by a water-wheel built by Scipion Périer of Chaillot. By 1812, there were 11, and the numbers of hand-spinners were declining rapidly. By 1828, there were 500,000 machine-spindles; by 1864, 706,000 self-acting mule-spindles, and by 1875, 1,315,000 of greatly increased efficiency. Among the industries to be stimulated by cotton was chemical manufacture. Haussmann, of Logelbach, first introduced Berthollet chlorine-bleaching in 1791, and several local innovations followed in 1818-20. In 1822 Mulhouse opened a school of chemistry.[60] Engineering became more important still. While at first heavily dependent on such English designs as those Dixon and Risler—Nicolas Schlumberger, indeed, was said to have brought his plans over from Manchester 'sown in his coat'—Alsace before long became a major export centre for textile machinery and other engineering products, including locomotives. Koechlin, of Mulhouse, made history by selling locomotives to the USA in 1869.[61] Among the more important local inventors was Josué Heilman, who developed a power-loom in 1826, and a wool-combing machine which revolutionized its industry in 1845-6.[62] It remains to be added that the growing local industrial complex also had ironworking, woollen, hatmaking, sugar refining, wallpaper, and other export industries. Like the Belgian region it had by the mid-century become a secondary centre extending British technology (and some of its own) to tertiary areas.

Higher up the Rhine valley still, the Swiss industrial region, stretching in a broad arc from Basle to Glarus, had also been built up in unpromising conditions, but enjoying some of the same advantages, among which were an early start in cotton printing and the art of spinning finer cotton than any other European district, including Lancashire.[63] Low wages gave a further competitive edge. Yet this northern Swiss industry was among the earliest to take to mechanization, the first machine-spinning mills being opened in Saint-Gallen in 1801 and Zurich in 1802. These were hand-driven 'mule-jennies', unable to stand up to British competition after the war, and for a while much yarn was imported, but by the 1830s the Swiss had changed to water-powered mules, and by the 1850s to self-actors. There were 660,000 spindles in the region in 1844, 1.15 million in 1856, and 2 million in 1872, making it the second largest industry in Europe after Lancashire.[64] Weaving also came under pressure from Britain, and after some early trials with power-looms around 1830, stifled by Luddism, they were put in in numbers from 1842 onward.[65]

In view of the handicaps, including an absence of resources other than water-power, and rising tariffs around the neighbouring traditional markets, the success of the Swiss entrepreneurs in maintaining and expanding major export industries, in raising wages, and in exporting capital and skills over the tariff walls to Alsace, Baden, Swabia, and Northern Italy is remarkable.[66] It was done partly by switching, like the British, to overseas markets, by putting out work to nearby low-wage districts like Vorarlberg, Swabia, or the Black Forest,[67] and by turning to sectors in which skill and inventiveness counted for much, and weight of material for little. These included a flourishing silk-twisting and weaving and ribbon-weaving industry, peaking about 1870 and then declining, but being replaced by chemicals and above all precision engineering, supplying a European market. Both developed from ancillaries to the textile industry. Between 1800 and 1850, the share of Swiss industrial employment in textiles fell from 75% to 27.5%, and in cotton alone, from 51.5% to 6.5%, but watches, metals, and machinery had risen from 5 to 20.5%. By 1860 Switzerland stood second in Europe in the 'modernity' of her industry, and she was the most specialized industrial country on the Continent, importing 20% of her food needs in 1850 and 85% in 1913. By then, she had the highest machinery export per capita in the world, and the highest total trade.[68] These ratios should be seen in relation to the small non-industrial sectors included with the main population belt in this small country: the Ruhr or Alsace as separate economies would have shown very similar figures, could they be obtained.

Saxony and Lusatia also had built up a powerful textile industry, as well as metallurgy and other specialisms, in the proto-industrial or 'manufacture' stage. Several of these had been producers of luxuries, such as silk, cotton printing, porcelain, gold and silver braid, musical instruments, and glass, but in the industrial revolution the emphasis was on mass production goods,[69] above all textiles, tobacco, railway engineering, and printing. Saxony had wool, flax, even some mulberry trees; several minerals, kaolin, and clay, some coal and iron, timber, and water-power. She also had an unfavourable agricultural soil and a long mountainous frontier with Austrian Bohemia whence came skilled refugees as well as plain linens to be finished. Leipzig, as the main market for sales of manufactures to Eastern Europe, provided commercial links and these were strengthened in the railway age when the city became a major junction. A further advantage of Saxony over other German areas appears to have been the positive attitude of the government which abstained from interfering in the industrialization process, curbed the baneful effects of guilds and town monopolies, and carried through the peasant emancipation speedily and relatively painlessly.[70] As an exporter of textiles, Saxony suffered from British competition after 1815, particularly in cottons. Although the jenny had spread quickly, in the 1790s, the cheaper imported British yarn drove out spinning. When British supplies were cut off, the first water-driven mules were set up in 1799, and by 1807 there were four mechanized spinning mills built with the aid of British mechanics. In 1831 there were 84, containing 361,200 spindles. These were all water-driven, and the first steam-engine was not put into a mill until that year; in 1860 there were 707,000 spindles and 14% of the looms were mechanical. By the mid-century, Saxony had become a major exporter not only of textiles, centred on Chemnitz, but also of textile machinery, steam-engines, and locomotives to other parts of Germany.

Steam-power in the country rose from 2,400 hp in 1846 to 46,000 hp in 1862.[71]

Until the spectacular rise of the Ruhr region, Saxony was the densest populated, most highly industrialized area of Germany. Her population grew faster than that of any other part of Germany, at a compound rate of 1.46% from 1834 to 1910, and in 1925 she was the most densely settled country in Europe, exceeding even Belgium and England, and with 61% of her population in industry, the most industrial. In one tabulation designed to show the modernity of the economic structure, the index (Germany = 100) for Saxony, stood at the top at 142, with Württemberg and Berlin. North-Rhine Westphalia, with Hildesheim, was rated at only 112.[72] As in the case of Belgium and Switzerland, the fact that political boundaries enclosed the industrial region pretty tightly with little agricultural acreage to dilute it, was responsible for the early favourable showing of Saxony in the statistics. What is significant is that despite the efforts of Prussia to keep out Saxon products in favour of her own, and in spite of the protectionist policies of the states to the south and east, Saxony, like Rhineland–Westphalia, was the industrial centre for a considerably wider area.

The development of the Silesian industrial region took a very different course. This had been the most advanced province of Austria, before it was taken by Frederick the Great in 1742 and incorporated into Prussia. Its strengths were then the domestic linen and woollen industries, but like Flanders, they failed to adjust to modern machine methods and died with similar agonies at about the same time. The region's handicaps, in addition to those suffered by Flanders, included the deliberate favouring of Berlin/Brandenburg at the expense of other provinces; the late survival of serf labour; and the lack of capital among aristocratic entrepreneurs.[73]

Coal mining and iron manufacture, by contrast, took fairly quickly to the new technologies. In 1740 there had been 12 charcoal blast-furnaces, 28 direct process furnaces, and 34 bloomeries in the Breslau district, and others were founded soon after, including the state-owned Malapane and Kreuzburg furnaces in 1753-4. At the Friedrichsgrube lead and silver mine, a steam-pump from Britain was installed in 1782, and by 1800 there were seven more. New collieries included the royal Königsgrube (1790) and Zabrze (1791) pits. Under the direction of John Baildon, a Scotsman, the first regular coke smelting-furnace on the Continent was put up nearby at Gleiwitz in 1796, and two more followed, complete with steam-driven bellows, at Königshütte in 1801.[74]

But all this precociousness was, as it were, skin-deep only. The coal output of the whole of Upper Silesia was only 41,000 t. in 1800, equivalent to a single colliery of the third rank in Newcastle at the time, and as late as 1867, one-third of the blast-furnaces still used charcoal. Real expansion, like that of the Ruhr region, came in the 1850s and 1870s. Coal output rose to 975,000 tons in 1850, 5.8 million tons in 1870, and 24.8 m.t. in 1900. Pig iron output was 247,000 t. in 1870. The first Siemens–Martin plant was put up in 1872. Even then, the region remained backward compared with the Ruhr. Though benefiting from its excellent coal, it was tied for too long to local iron ore and to antiquated techniques; it lacked good regional markets; it was cut off by the frontier from some of its natural labour reservoir; it failed to get adequate transport to central markets, and its organizational structure remained that of smaller firms, still dominated by local landowning families.[75]

Another region with great potential in the eighteenth century but falling behind in the nineteenth was Normandy. Its cotton industry suffered from the fact that it had concentrated on the coarser yarns which were those in which British machine-spindles dominated the market first. The region was excellently placed on the main trade route to Paris and with easy access to raw cotton, to British coal, and to Paris capital, but this accessibility may also have been a disadvantage in some respects, since it raised local wages and encouraged intensive concentration on meat and dairy farming.[76]

Cotton was the most important local industry, and at first developed well. In 1795 there were seven water-driven mills and there were twenty more in 1804. By 1810 there were 425,000 spindles in the region out of the French total of 1,540,000, or 27.6%.[77] Reduced because of the competition from British yarn, the region expanded its weaving, at first in the countryside, later by power-looms in the towns. There were 80,000 looms in 1865, and 57,000 in Seine-Inférieure alone in 1847; in that year there were also 7,800 power-looms in the Seine-Inférieure Department, or more than in Ghent eleven years later, but the local industry fell behind Alsace. The woollen industry, which was found, with some linen, mainly south of the Seine, with an early centre in Louviers and Elbeuf, mechanized more slowly still.[78] By the end of the century the region carried little industrial weight.

The last region to be examined here, that lying east of the French Massif Central, was another one of those that were based on both textiles and heavy industry. The chief textile manufacture was the silk industry of Lyons, originally a city trade but spreading increasingly into a wide band of rural surroundings.[79] Silk-ribbon weaving was concentrated in Saint-Étienne, a town in which textiles and metallurgy were of roughly equal importance, with 8,000 working in textiles in 1833 and 10,000 in metals, and in Saint-Jean Bonneford and villages around. There had also been an early cotton-mill in Lyons, and the fine muslin manufacture of Tarare was on the edge of the same region.[80] Silk throwing had been mechanized by a process that was widely known in Italy, France, and Britain by the eighteenth century. Weaving, aided in its patterned branches by the Jacquard loom perfected by 1806, had reached a technical plateau also, and there was no new technology in Britain to offset against the skill and tradition of the Lyonnais. Aided by easy access to the raw material from Southern France, Italy, and farther afield, and by the lowest interest rates in France,[81] the region dominated the world markets in finished silks and it was significant that, together with the cotton manufacturers of Alsace, the silk manufacturers were the most steadfast, and sometimes the only defenders of free trade in France in the generation before 1860. In the free-trade years which followed they managed to knock out several foreign competitors.[82]

The Upper Loire Valley was also one of the main centres of coal-mining and of the iron industry. Up to mid-century and the extension of the northern coalfield, it was much the most prolific field, producing 1.4 million tons in 1845 or one-third of the French total. As local coal was considered to be of superior quality it was exported not only to Lyons and Roanne, but even to Paris by lengthy water-ways, taking 6-8 months to get there.[83] The local ironworks also used the coal, and were thereby encouraged to adopt British methods relatively early. Puddling was introduced at Saint-Étienne about 1819-20 by iron-masters who had studied the process in Britain. The hot blast was introduced about 1830, crucible steelmaking around 1814 by William Jackson, a British expert, with fourteen workmen from Sheffield and Birmingham.[84] The district also had a flourishing secondary iron industry, including tools and arms, and was among the first to benefit from supplying the railways. It became the cradle of the French railway system. Marc Séguin built there the first major line in 1827, a one-track horse-drawn railway of a length of eleven miles, running from Saint-Étienne to the Rhône et Andrézieux. This was extended to Roanne in 1833. Meanwhile the first line to use locomotives, which ran for thirty-six miles across the heart of the region from Saint-Étienne to Lyons, also built by Séguin, with his brother, had been opened in 1832. The region has held its own as an industrial centre since then, the only one in the southern half of the country.

It remains to be noted that the largest cities, and in particular the two major capitals, Paris and Berlin, maintained their momentum as industrial regions in their own right. They attracted particularly industries requiring immediate access to markets, such as fashion goods and other consumer goods, but failed to hold them as soon as they turned to repetitive mass production, where high wages and high rents became a disadvantage. In that category, as in London, only engineering survived and Borsig (opening in 1837) in Berlin was for a time Germany's premier locomotive-builder, as Siemens (opening in 1847) dominated his industry, electrical engineering, in the second phase of the German industrial revolution. In 1840-5, Paris was responsible for 40% of French industrial production in volume, including major shares in cotton and engineering and in 1845 it had 161 locomotives out of 313 then in France. Its share of France's population rose from 4.8% in 1801 to 11.6% in 1901 and 17.2% in 1954. In 1959 it still had 67% of the French automobile industry, 60% of aircraft, 55% of electrical goods, and 44% of chemicals, beside the consumption goods.[85]

Some modern industry appeared also outside these regions, in smaller regional concentrations, like those of Saarland, built round its coal,[86] or the Wurttemberg textile industry, or Le Creusot, the most advanced French ironworks, situated on its Blanzy coalfield, or even in individual works, particularly those built on the site of some raw material. Yet, as in Britain, there seemed to be a minimum critical mass necessary for a progressive industry to maintain its momentum and keep up technically with the leaders. To all intents and purposes, we may take the small handful of regions enumerated here as the significant channels of entry of the process of industrialization into Inner Europe.

The Leading Industries

Before turning to a discourse of the significance of this regional development, it may help to clarify the process of industrialization further if we cast a brief glance at the progress and competitive inter-relation of the main industries concerned.[87] The task is not entirely straightforward. For one thing, available statistics are mostly on a national basis and lump together industrial regions and others, and products (say, pieces of cloth) produced by modern methods with those produced by traditional methods. For another, continental historians are inclined to greet the appearance of the first jenny or the first Newcomen pump as the start of industrialization, and to neglect the many failures of technologies transplanted from Britain and the long experimentation, often lasting ten or twenty years, before the foreign plant actually took firm root. The 'industrial revolution', by some definitions, is precisely the period between the first introduction of new techniques, and their predominance, together with an appropriate sound capital goods supply, within major productive sectors.[88]

Nowhere was the gap between Britain and the Continent wider than in the case of coal. As a consumption good, the domestic use of which rises with rising incomes and better housing, and as an industrial input measuring most accurately the consumption of energy and hence the progress of industrialization in the most general terms, coal became the symbol, as it was also to an important extent the cause, of the British lead.

Production figures are misleading to a certain extent, for coal is in part a substitute for wood and charcoal. Its output should be compared with that of the sum of all fuels, or their energy equivalent, to show its significant growth, but no usable statistics exist for such a comparison. Nevertheless, there is in most coalfields a distinct 'revolutionary' change between the shallow or level working with a handful of men requiring equipment costing a few pounds at most, and the deep mining, requiring pumps, complex raising equipment, a large complement of men, and therefore a large-scale organization. Thus the extension into deep mining is connected with the development of a market which, in turn, requires transport for a very bulky, cheap commodity, in the form of at least a horse-drawn rail system to the nearest water-way and in its absence, nothing less than a complete railway system. Steam engines, wire ropes, and railways were therefore the most characteristic contribution of the coal-mining industry to the general technical progress of Europe, and it was partly owing to this high-powered technology that coal-mining has never been counted among the raw material supply industries which mark the backward, dependent, or colonial economy, as logic would dictate, but, on the contrary, among the characteristic features of the industrialization process on the British model.

The deep-mining revolution had reached the North-East of England, and some scattered other regions, by 1740; by 1790 it had been passed by most of the major fields in Britain, only South Wales trailing a little. On the Continent only the Belgian field (with French Valenciennes) had passed that phase by 1790. The Saar reached it by the 1830s, but the main northern coalfield in France, the Ruhr field and Upper Silesia, despite earlier trials, only in the 1840s–1850s. This gap is shown in the output figures. In 1800, Britain probably produced five or six times as much coal as the rest of the world put together. By 1830–4, when better statistics exist, the British output was still more than three times that of the rest of Europe put together, and in 1850–4, a good deal more than twice (50 million tons against perhaps 22½ m.t.).[89] No matter how the supply of energy for wood and water (in which Britain was also still strongly represented) is calculated, the lead is enormous. It was only by the turn of the century that comparable, though not equal, figures were reached elsewhere.

Per Capita Figures compared as follows in 1860 (two major countries of Outer Europe being added for comparison).[90]

Table 3.2. Some European per Capita Figures, 1860

	Raw-Cotton Consumption kg.	Pig-Iron Production kg.	Coal Consumption kg.	Fixed Steam Installed HP	Railways*
United Kingdom	15.1	130	2480	24	44
Germany	1.5	13	400	5	21
Belgium	2.9	69	1310	21	30
France	2.5	26	390	5	18
Switzerland	5.6	6	c. 50	3	28
Austria–Hungary	1.2	9	190	2	10
Russia	0.5	4	c. 50	1	1

* Derived from the formula $\dfrac{V}{P + 3S}$ in which

V = Length of railway lines open, in km
P = Population, in millions
S = Area, in 10 000 square km.

The coal figures, it should be noted, are those for consumption of coal; the figure for Belgium, like that for fixed steam-power, is thus under-represented and was of the same order of magnitude as that of the United Kingdom while French production would be only around 230 kg. on the same basis. In terms of price, British coal would still compete everywhere it was admitted.[91] The permeation of modern industry in other regions, if spread over the total population, is still far behind Britain, but the much greater equality, among the leaders, of railway mileage should be noted.[92]

In steam-power, the gap in 1800 was probably of a similar order of magnitude as for coal, though no statistics exist. Apart, once more, from Belgium, even the advanced regions on the Continent still used about as much water-power as steam even by mid-century. Total (including mobile) steam-power per capita, in 1850 still showed the gap, but it had begun to be closed very rapidly by 1880:

Total Steam-Power per Thousand Population[93]

	1850	1880
Belgium	16	111
France	7.5	81
Germany	7.6	113
Great Britain	62	256

Engineering on the Continent was still entirely derivative in the early years of the century. Cockerill and others in Belgium, Manby and Wilson near Paris, and numerous other British *émigrés* built engines and machines from British models, blueprints, and memories. Native engineers, like Périer of Chaillot, were rare. By the 1820s, a generation of continental engineers had begun to set up important workshops, Koechlin and Schlumberger in Alsace, Egells in Berlin, Harkort at Wetter, Escher in Zurich. Some of the more original and inventive continental minds still tended to take their ideas to Britain, like König his printing-press, because of the capital, the enterprise, and the engineering skill available there, but by the mid-century, there were textile and locomotive works in areas like Belgium, Alsace, Paris, Berlin, and Saxony which could compete on an international scale.

The coke-smelting of iron, a key invention for Britain, was as long delayed as coal-mining technology. Cheap charcoal and a limited market for iron kept the continental industry backward and located in small units in often inaccessible places. Early experiments were indeed made, as by William Wilkinson at Le Creusot in 1785[94] and by John Baildon in Upper Silesia some years after, but the real breakthrough came only from 1819 at Saint-Étienne, Le Creusot, and Lorraine, from 1828 in Belgium, and after 1850 elsewhere. Yet even in 1870, Great Britain was still making half the world's pig iron. Puddling, the manufacture of the refined bar iron from pig iron derived from the blast-furnace by a modern coal-using method, spread fairly rapidly in several regions from about 1821 on, nearly forty years after its first introduction in Britain. Crucible steel was produced only in a few individual works, and continental steelmaking had to wait for the Bessemer revolution which began in the 1860s. By then the technical gap between Britain, the Ruhr, Belgium, and, soon after, Lorraine, had practically been closed.

In textiles, British technology differed in no important respect from that used on the Continent as late as the 1760s. Then a series of spinning inventions, together with machinery for carding and roving (generally made and sold on the Continent as a single set) transformed the cotton industry, and some thirty years later the worsted and soon after the woollen industry. The cost savings were such that competition by hand spinning became impossible overnight, though competition by the jenny, a small hand-machine constituting an intermediate technical stage, might continue provided wages were low enough. Power-weaving, however, invented in principle in 1785, and commercially effective in Britain in the 1820s, led to less striking reductions in costs, and hand-loom weavers might compete for decades before being driven out by accretions of technical superiority on the one hand, or starvation on the other.

The installation of textile machinery in the countries of Inner Europe occurred in two waves, before and after 1815. Some early examples of jennies, and even the more complex and more productive mules and water-frames had found their way across the Channel quickly enough to meet a spinning bottleneck which had become as evident there as in Britain.[95] They were to be found in northern France, Alsace, the Rhineland, Saxony, and Switzerland well before the end of the century, and in the early years of the new century increasing numbers were produced locally. When peace came, it was found that Britain had made such progress in the interim that few yarn producers could stand up to her competition. Cotton-spinning mills closed over a wide area, including Normandy, Picardy, even northern France, and the Rhineland. Only regions with a progressive group of entrepreneurs, and possibly some protection by distance, like Alsace, Switzerland, and Saxony managed to survive, in part. The relative success of Switzerland emerges from the table on p.108 above.

On the basis of cheap British or locally produced yarn, weaving, knitting and lace-making survived much better, even as an export industry,[96] over much of Northern France and Flanders, Paris, and the other textile regions, including some scattered centres in Southern Germany.[97] For a while hand-loom and power-loom were operated side by side, but by the time the British power-loom won through, in the 1840s, the leading continental centres were in a much better position to build or instal their own than they had been in the change-over period for mules thirty years earlier. The switch to power-looms took place in the 1850s and 1860s.

For wool, where a similar sequence occurred of mechanized spinning first, followed much later by mechanical looms, the power of survival on the Continent was greater, though some traditional regions, like the Languedoc, were unable to modernize and became de-industrialized altogether. This was in part due to the local availability of the raw material, and the greater varieties of fabrics made than in the cotton branch; but in part the reasons have to be looked for in the timing: the change-over occurred in a later phase, when continental engineers had acquired greater skill and experience.

In linen the change was the most dramatic. Probably the most widespread of the textile industries, conducted on a domestic basis over a broad sweep across the whole of the North European plain and much of the upland as well, it formed the largest export item for such regions as Flanders and indeed for the whole of Germany as well. Flax-spinning proved technically the most difficult among the natural fibres to mechanize successfully and although various shifts had occurred, the British, for example, having gradually replaced imports in the course of the eighteenth century by home production, many competing regions could co-exist. The breakthrough of machine-spinning in Britain in the 1830s based on the invention of Philippe de Girard, a Frenchman, suddenly altered this equilibrium, and British yarn invaded the traditional markets of others. Several of these regions, like Silesia and Flanders, were unable to compete not so much because the technology was beyond them, but because their proto-industrial structure could not absorb a change-over to a factory system. After a delay of around twenty years, such areas as Ghent, the French Nord, and the Rhineland did indeed accept modern flax-spinning and linen-weaving technology. Silk-weaving was not further mechanized, after the Jacquard attachment, until the 1870s, though a usable power-loom had been invented in 1835 by Josué Heilmann and Charles Webber in Alsace, and it remained narrowly based on a handful of areas like Lyons, parts of Switzerland, and Krefeld along the Lower Rhine.

Among other trades of significance only the chemical industry can be mentioned here. A number of key innovations here were based on the work of French scientists: Leblanc's process of deriving soda from sea salt (1789), and Berthollet's method of chlorine-bleaching above all. In Alsace, Koechlin developed the 'Adrianople' red dye in 1810-11. All these were used in textile manufacture and thus benefited mostly the British. It was thus no less than just that Perkins' discovery of coal-based dyes in 1856 should, after an interval, have mainly been used to expand chemicals production along the Rhine. While the chemical industry was at first located near the coal and the salt, it moved to the transport arteries, though still near the coal later in the nineteenth century, as it absorbed an ever larger assortment of raw materials.

The Role of the Region in Industrialization

In spite of the central role played by the Region in European industrialization, it has found remarkably little attention in the literature. What little generalized thinking there has been on its significance has been largely derived from present-day regional planning, that is to say the attempt to steer developments according to a pre-conceived pattern[98] rather than from the observation of what actually happened in the past.

Our discussion will concentrate on two interrelated questions. The first will be the extent to which the region as such has influenced developments, to what extent, in other words, local concentration has produced results different from those of a conceivable random distribution across the Continent. The second will examine some of the factors which favoured, in the actual European context of *c*. 1815–75, one region rather than another.

Basically, the methodology of this book is to study the supply factors, and over-all (though not necessarily localized) demand is taken for granted. The question, then, is this: given a demand and technical means derived from the British experience to meet it, why and how do the key industries cluster in a certain way?[99] A second implicit assumption is that Inner Europe, in general, was not too distant from Britain in income, savings, attitudes, techniques, and other key factors to be capable of imitative effort. We are, once more, dealing with a biologically similar, but individually different phenomenon. This would not necessarily be true of Outer Europe then, still less of industrializing countries today. The regionalism described here therefore belongs to a distinct and unique time and place, though no doubt there are features in it which recur in other circumstances. Finally, we also assume a minimum level of agricultural efficiency, either in the immediate vicinity, or within reach of a cheap water-borne trade, to sustain an industrial population. This might well be a limiting factor, in the sense that a region which cannot be fed cannot be industrialized, but could scarcely be included among the causative or determining factors.[100] Agriculture might also, with proto-industry, form the major recruiting ground for labour.[101] The correlation between the survival of feudalism and industrial backwardness is subsumed under our heading of the general readiness to absorb the British system, and will be discussed in its own context later.[102] It may, however, be argued that certain inheritance and ownership patterns tend to favour a more rapid transfer of an agricultural population to full-time industry.[103]

The region as a phenomenon of significance in European industrialization has, to begin with, a historic dimension. There were regional concentrations of industry and commerce before the actual phase of industrialization, and the location of these earlier conglomerations had an obvious relationship to the pattern that developed subsequently.[104] Moreover, that influence of the existing distribution is continuous at every stage in relation to the following one. Had the system been started *ab ovo*, it might well have shown a very different distribution and very different developments from those which existing investments, linkages, locations, and even technology forced upon it in fact.

It is remarkable how little this historical dimension is considered in modern location theory, except when concerning itself with the problems of the declining industrial regions. Then the patterning derived from some out-of-date technology or by-gone market conditions moves into the centre of the picture. Yet the history even of the profound and fundamental changes of the industrial revolution shows how far the burdens and the benefits derived from the past came to dominate the positive course of events.[105]

What modern location theory stresses in the explanation of regional conglomerations are above all transport, resource endowments (including power), markets, technology (production functions), and labour supply.[106] It is influenced by von Thünen and Alfred Weber, though Walter Isard succeeded very elegantly in the 1950s in combining that tradition with classical Anglo-Saxon substitution analysis,[107] and as such it tends not only to be ahistorical and static, but also fails to make a clear distinction between the causes for concentrations of industry in regions as such, and for the growth of particular industrial regions. There have also been attempts to find explanations in the behavioural field, and in an authority–dependence relationship.[108]

However, it is the merit of the small band of specialists active in this field to have established, beyond a doubt, the significance of regional patterning in modern economies. Some of their thinking also helps to illuminate the specific role of the region in the first phase of European industrialization. Among economists, it is particularly François Perroux who has incorporated the experience of that phase in his notion of a growth-point (*pôle de croissance*) at which a leading industry (*industrie motrice*) establishes a dominant and possibly monopolistic position, building up a complex of other industries and services around it, though this is not necessarily thought of as regional.[109] The regional approach has become accepted by economic historians also,[110] though perhaps in theory rather than in the way they actually write history. Certainly, attempts have been made to apply econometric studies of production functions to such regional coalfields as the Ruhr or the French coalfield in the Nord, as well as to the whole of the French Nord, and it is recognized that there may be competition between regions, as for example between the various cotton-goods producing regions of France in the nineteenth century.[111]

The key feature of the region, which justifies the concept instrumentally, is its relationship to the rest of European society, and above all its imports and exports. A region, like any other arbitrarily fixed component of the world economy, trades with the rest of the world, though that trade is not always easy to discern or to measure. If the region has a significance in the European industrialization process, it must be found above all in these trading relations.

Trade takes place because some factors are immobile,[112] and in the period discussed here neither capital nor labour moved with ease out of the region, though they moved easily enough within it. Seen purely formally, there is thus a gap or break in the declining curve of factor mobility outward from its given location, represented by the boundary of the region. Men will change employers, and bankers will provide loans within the region with a facility which they would not match in relationships with outside firms, and these were often the most powerful causes for contemporaries to see themselves as working within a region as the operative economic unit, even though other loyalties might pull elsewhere. At the same time, a region's trade, at least to other regions within the same country, unlike the trade relationships across the borders and between sovereign countries, was not complicated by varying exchange rates or differences in legal requirements. Before the French Revolution, it is true, several major European countries were carved up by internal customs barriers, but these did not normally coincide with operative economic regional boundaries.

As we saw in the British example, regional trade might lead to regional payments imbalances. Given a unified national banking system, in which economic activity went on within regions but financial activity was nation-wide as in the United States, it was possible to match these imbalances by a continuing flow of liquid assets.[113] In Europe in our phase this was not so (except within Belgium and, possibly, also within Switzerland) and as long as banks were regional there were therefore temporary strains, particularly during financial crises. The efforts to overcome them were among the most potent causes of the rise of central banking. The Banque de France instituted a drive for covering the whole country with sufficient regional branch banks in 1848, and the Bank of Prussia was, in effect, turned into a Central Bank in 1846, both of these developments occurring well ahead of the major industrialization spurts in the state which they served.

Each region thus has one or more important export industries.[114] Homer Hoyt, calling this the economic 'base', developed the concept of the export multiplier (since then called the 'activating interaction potential'), that is to say, the amount of employment in services and supplies, or the taking-in of each other's washing within the region, which the export industries would generate. Particularly when modified, as appropriate, by the import content of exports, the share of exports in total employment within the region was, in empirical studies in the mid-twentieth century, found to be remarkably small.[115] There is reason to believe that, given the much lower standards of living and comfort of the industrial population, the service sector was much smaller, and the export sector formed a larger component of the regional economy during industrialization than they do today.

Whatever the relative size, it provided the economic *raison d'être*

for the region. When it expanded, the region expanded, and if it con-
tracted the region would de-industrialize or become a depressed
area.[116] Not only the fortune but also the nature of the base industry
was of profound importance for the region. If it was of a kind not to
lead to technological and associated economic change, the region
would not industrialize at all:[117] that was, in essence, the position of
the regions for which the base industry was agriculture. Again, a heavy
industry base, with little female employment, would put a different
stamp on a region than a light industrial or service base providing
mixed employment. It is therefore not at all suprising to find that in
debates on economic policy, representatives of the local service industries will identify with the case of their base, even though it might
have nothing to do with them at first sight, on such issues as free trade
and protection.[118]

With the passage of time there have been changes in the meaning
and functions of economic regions. Thus it has been argued that in
France, economic regions had greater meaning in the eighteenth
century, and regional differences became more significant the farther
we go back in history, while in the nineteenth century, France may
be said to have become a single economy.[119] But this confuses regions
that live with little contact side by side as detached, but structurally
similar economies, with the nineteenth-century region which is linked
to the rest of the economy precisely because it has specialized functions within the whole, like an organ within the body. It need hardly
be said that the frequently expressed view of the advantage of poor
soil for industrial growth depends entirely on the existence of market
links with the rest of society. The notion of a 'functional' as distinct
from a 'homogeneous' region is also important here, stressing that
the region is a complex of interrelationships.[120]

The dual character of a region in flux in the period of industrialization is also brought out in the role ascribed to improved means of
transport, particularly railways. On the one hand, railways helped in
the formation and strengthening of the modern region by widening
the markets for its specialist exports and allowing it to drive out the
less specialized, less technically advanced localized manufacturers
elsewhere who had hitherto enjoyed the protection of distance. On
the other hand, they subjected the region itself to the competition of
other advanced regions, and effected a selection of the best endowed
among the regional complexes. This dual influence, the scale and substitution effect, was neatly illustrated by the two-phase impact of
railways on Dijon: at first they benefited local brewers and wine-
growers by extending their regional markets, but ultimately both
these groups suffered from even more effective producers of wine in

the South of France and of beer in Alsace and Lorraine, when rail communications finally linked these also to the city. The sequence was the same in the Champagne, and a similar effect has been ascribed to the Zollverein, and to establishment of free trade within Austria, which in this respect acted like a cheapening of transport costs.[121]

In the early, founding stage, the scale effect of industrialization was important. It accentuated the differences between regions, and above all, between the industrializing region and the rest. Although the region of more concentrated industrial activity had existed in the period of domestic industry, the factory, coke blast-furnace, and steam-engine gave it a more full-blooded reality. The growing gap might not show up at once in incomes, in which regional differences tend nowadays to be measured, for the massed factory proletariat might, for a while, have lower average incomes than the sparsely settled farmers and craftsmen might have had before,[122] but ultimately incomes also pulled apart, while other indicators, such as industrial structure, density of roads, railways, and other facilities and services showed growing dissimilarities from the start. There exist two contrasting views about the course which developments will then take. Some observers believe that once the process starts, it will grow cumulatively, success begetting success, while the regions which lost out in the first round are increasingly sucked dry by the winners and left further and further behind. Others believe that 'success' in this sense will bring its own nemesis, that the industrial zone will sooner or later choke in its own congestion, high rents and high wages, and labour turbulence, and will revert to a 'depressed area' or de-industrialize altogether, while others will come forward and even up the relative levels. These two models, which Gunnar Myrdal has neatly labelled the 'backwash effect' for the ever widening gap and the 'spread effect' for the positive influence on the surrounding economic regions,[123] have been of great concern to development economists and those considering the problems of the depressed regions of Europe.

In point of historical fact, detailed studies in the industrialized countries, particularly in the United States, with the use of the states and regional groupings of states as units for which good data exist, have shown a characteristic 'inverted U' form of development of regional differentiation. In the earlier phases of industrialization, the classic industrial revolution, the gap widens and the industrial regions pull away, especially in terms of income and capital per head and industrial structure, but after a certain period, and usually well into the twentieth century, the trend is reversed and the formerly backward regions begin to catch up.[124]

The causes for this differentiation are complex, and the 'inverted

U', in as far as it represents a common course, is the outcome of a balance of several opposing influences which vary over time. Among the most important of these are the external economies of the industrial complex, the factors of production of entrepreneurship, capital, and labour, natural resources, and the influence of government, apart from the region's own inner development.

External economies play a critical part in the early stages. Some of them are genuine savings that may come from economies of scale in maintaining stocks or labour reserves, in using specialist equipment or local know-how, in assembling buyers and sellers, and in spreading innovations quickly. Up to a point, local householders are a market as well as a source of labour. Social overhead capital, such as the transport system could be used more fully and gas and water supply more economically. These might be considered aspects of a 'vent for surplus' benefit, as regional growth allowed hitherto unused resources to be brought into use.[125] Others are based on the fact that in regions in which the middle classes were strongly entrenched, industrialists were enabled to externalize their costs at the expense of the community. Instead of providing workmen's houses, insurance, technical training, or fuel supplies, as had to be done in isolated communities, employers transferred the burdens to local authorities and thus shared them with others. The point of reductions in external costs need not, perhaps, be laboured. It is found in all standard books on regional analysis.[126] Nor need the costs of congestion, the pollution, and rising rents of the industrialized regions in their maturity detain us much; they fall, in any case, outside the period now being considered.[127]

How far did entrepreneurship contribute to the rise of one region rather than another, and possibly to its ultimate decline? This question is beset by pitfalls and ambiguities. In part, it depends on the role we are prepared to assign to entrepreneurship as such. How far are entrepreneurs the passive conductors of economic opportunities, and how far ever truly creative in the Schumpeterian sense? Thus if the market for coal is favourable, and if coal is known to exist, and collieries are therefore developed using well-tried technical means, can we ascribe much influence to 'entrepreneurship', or could we say that in a capitalist milieu, there are always plenty of people willing to take opportunities to make money, and the difference between the industrial region and the others is that these opportunities, given the actual market and technological conditions, existed in the one but not the other. The truly great towering Napoleon of business who shapes his opportunities even if, by the rules, they do not really exist, if there be any such, may affect the course of a single firm or even a small town, but scarcely create a whole region.

Between the automatic or passive reaction, and the Schumpeterian true innovator, we are left with special groups with a particular group behaviour of their own, who might without these personal character-istics not have developed a certain region, and who are numerous enough to have affected, as a group, the course of regional history.

The claim has been made for Calvinists, particularly in Alsace, but it can also be made for them in the Lower Rhine and the Berg region.[128] Again, the negative claim has been made that inbred, provincial, con-servative groups of French entrepreneurs were responsible for the industrial decline and stagnation of certain French industrial districts, or that the prevalence of aristocratic, basically landowning families in the Upper Silesian coalfield, contrasting with the self-made owners or paid managers of the Ruhr and the other coal districts, was in part re-sponsible for the failure of Upper Silesia to make use of all its oppor-tunities in the later nineteenth century.[129] Certainly, different regions have different styles,[130] particularly among the entrepreneurs, and while many aspects of these are derived from objective conditions, of the way minerals, sources of power, or means of transport, for ex-ample, are available, yet it may well be that the difference between the local industrialist or metropolitan banker, the Roman Catholic nobleman or the Calvinist merchant, may just have affected the fate of certain regions. As we move, with the second half of the nineteenth century, into the era of the joint-stock company with its own increas-ingly competitive recruitment into top management, the idiosyn-crasies of regional entrepreneurship seem less and less likely to have an independent effect of their own.

The role of capital is, again, ambiguous. In the early stages of in-dustrialization, capital is largely regional and it is conceivable that the development of regions may be held back by lack of access to funds. This certainly happened on certain occasions in peripheral Europe, but was much less likely in Inner Europe in our period. In part this was so because banks always stood ready to discount short-term paper, and fixed capital was on the whole still a relatively small item. In certain cases, as in Alsace, and the Lower Rhineland, capital was provided from outside the region, by such cities as Basle or Cologne, and Paris would help to finance the deeper coal-mines of the North and the privileged manufactures of various kinds. In the Netherlands it was Holland that had the capital, yet Belgium that developed.[131] There are strong arguments for the view that there was no over-all capital shortage in Germany in the first half of the century,[132] but if there had been, it should have affected all districts[133] and in any case it is not easy to determine. At one extreme, the fact that a certain entrepreneur failed to obtain capital is no proof that there was a general shortage, and at the other extreme, the fact that supply and demand balanced at a reasonable rate of interest is no proof that there was enough, for in imperfect local markets there may have been rationing by means other than interest rates, and at a very slight expansion in demand there might have been a severe shortage. Certainly, local capital was not mobile between regions,[134] and on theoretical grounds, as well as going by American experience, the existing variations in wage levels may be taken as consistent with variations in the availability of capital between regions.[135]

For large schemes of a public utility kind, particularly railways, capital shortage cannot have affected regional developments for more than a very brief period in any particular case, for here the capital market was much wider than the region. At the height of the railway boom, Europe was to all interests and purposes a single capital market.[136]

There is better information available about the labour market. It was one of the most obvious characteristics of the industrial region that its population grew much faster than that of its surrounding areas, that it became more urbanized, and that it carried, either from the start of building up the new industries or within a few decades thereafter, a much more densely settled population.[137] Clearly, industrial regions formed zones of net immigration, as well as possibly registering a higher natural increase than other areas. For this reason, figures of national population increases, and *a fortiori* of average national density per square mile, may be as misleading as average figures of national economic growth-rates.[138]

On the face of it, a large immigration would point to the existence of high wages, to attract the immigrants, and indeed it has been claimed that in a region like Saxony it was the high wage level which led to technical innovations. Conversely, low wages were a sign of technical backwardness and of falling behind. On the other hand, low wages often form a component of growth on industrialization models, to explain, for example, why Belgium found it so easy to industrialize and why Holland, with so many advantages, but the disadvantage of high wages, failed to do so.[139]

The issue is, once more, more complex than theory is willing to admit. The meaning 'high' and 'low' is not always clear. Wages might be high in the immigration zone, not for any given occupation, as compared with the same occupants elsewhere, but by offering jobs which always pay more than the jobs predominating in areas losing people, like agricultural districts. Moreover, migration often occurred, not for better pay, but for a job of any kind and non-pecuniary considerations, like unfreedom on the land, or the hope of rising in the town, might have played a part. Conversely, the low money wages of an area like Belgium might be for non-apprenticed trades, or might reflect lower costs of living. Cross-regional comparisons are difficult because of different job specifications, different hours and conditions, and differing costs of living, but some differences were large enough to outweigh any possible modifications by such factors. One such gap was that between British wages, and below them Dutch wages and the much lower wages paid elsewhere. But there were also some continental regions which paid distinctly lower wages than other comparable areas: thus Alsace, Switzerland, and Silesia paid lower textile wages than Normandy or Flanders.

Within a region, there were shifts and locational movements according to the ability to pay rents and to bear transport costs, and this would have a tendency first to fill the empty spaces within the regions until agriculture had disappeared, and then to push outwards, the outer ring being formed by those least able to bear high rents and most able to bear transport costs and/or distance from the central amenities.[140] This ideal scheme was, however, in practice overlaid by new means of transport like the Cologne–Minden railway which pulled the Ruhr district northward, new industries, and new mineral workings, particularly in the case of coal. The result was an industrial belt or zone as the core of a region.[141]

The settlement of new industries was a striking feature of the more successful of the industrial regions of Inner Europe. Several began their industrial revolution with more than one base industry, generally textiles and heavy industry, though these were side by side rather than strictly in the same location: the North of France, Belgium, Lyons–Saint-Étienne, Rhineland–Westphalia, Saxony. Others were added, like Ruhr coal, iron and steel, Wuppertal chemicals, and engineering almost everywhere. Few industries lasted in a given location without such blood transfusions, either from complementary industries or from extensions and innovations, and a one-industry region would be a candidate for de-industrialization.[142] The inability to create, or attract a major addition or alternative could itself be taken as a sign of weakness. There seemed to be, as in Britain, a minimum critical mass, related in part to external economies, like engineering, transport, or labour supply, but also to the inner dynamic of the industry itself. Enclaves did not, on the whole, grow.[143] To that extent decline, like growth, could be cumulative.

Resources could modify the picture. A good source of salt, potash, or iron ore could keep going, especially after being linked to the railway network, whether it gave rise to an agglomeration of other industries or not. The only exception is coal. Coal was the major location factor in Britain as in the majority of the continental industrial zones, and others survived only if they had reasonable access by water to a supply of good coal.

The timing, however, was different. In Britain, the expansion of coal-mining preceded, as well as accompanied industrialization; it was clearly a precondition as well as a beneficiary and accelerating factor once the industrialization process had begun. On the Continent, coal rarely came first, and it was the apparently favourable cost ratios of non-coal methods, such as using water-power for spinning-mills and bellows, and charcoal for metallurgy, which frequently held back some of the major continental centres and made them unable to compete with Britain on even terms. Yet the Continent also had a timber shortage, becoming acute in the first half of the nineteenth century.[144] Timber was available, as in Britain, from far away sources like the Baltic shores, Russia, and the Central European mountain ranges, timber indicating, as the inverse of the grain lands, the borders to which the economically more advanced population of Europe had pushed forward. Timber and charcoal were therefore available at ever increasing cost. The Continent also had more water-power, greater distances behind which local high-cost firms could shelter, less favourable coal deposits, and poorer overland and water-borne transport routes.

Thus coal as determinant developed late. Several of the French fields and Upper Silesia even then were too cut off to sustain a regional advance on a broad front. Apart from the Belgian field, the breakthrough had to wait for the railway–iron–coal block, in which each supported the rapid growth of the other two, in the 1840s and particularly the 1850s.[145] In the case of the Ruhr, the momentum, fed by good transport and an equally buoyant iron industry, would no doubt have been strong enough to carry the region forward even if it had not occupied the margins of a flourishing textile and metallurgical region and benefited by its engineering and chemical capactiy, and its market for coal. Coal also became the determinant of location in peripheral Europe, particularly Austria and Russia, up to the end of the century; those without it, like the Swiss, the Alsatians, and the North Italians, had to try and make do with water-power and with industries consuming relatively little power.

Some modern theory emphasizes the market as location factor.[146] To some extent, this is a question of transport since markets are normally scattered and favourable location therefore means access to many markets rather than a single one. There are two important exceptions to this. Where the industry produces an intermediate good, used only by one other industry, it will move close to its buyer—or vice-versa, depending on weights and raw material sources. The tendency will therefore be for this link to reinforce existing concentrations. The other exception is the capital city, forming a particularly concentrated market for certain industries, like luxury and fashion goods, printed matter, and, sometimes, military needs. Conversely, the dispersal of political power in Germany, creating many 'capitals', reinforced later by the dispersal of railway headquarters for the same reason, may be held responsible for the scatter of certain types of industry in that area in the nineteenth century.[147]

Governments affect location in various ways, not all intentional. Occasionally, for example when the Berlin government tried to draw industry to Brandenburg, they wanted specifically to influence location. At other times, as in the planning of railway-lines or the effects of war or preparations for war, the effects were a by-product of a strategy which had quite different objectives. Thus the French South-West and South lost by the Revolutionary and Napoleonic wars, whereas the North and East gained. This is best discussed as part of the total effect of government on industrialization, bearing in mind that laws and tariff barriers are less and less enforceable the farther east we go, down the *Gefälle* in Europe.[148] In the twentieth century, it is in part deliberate government action which ensures the narrowing of the gap between the industrialized regions and the poorer agrarian or de-industrialized parts of the country, but this may have happened marginally even in the nineteenth century by the effects of taxation, raised in the richer regions, while the expenditure on infrastructure was spread more evenly, as has been claimed for Austria.[149]

If the basic industry of a region declines and no substitute is found, the region declines also, and the local employment multiplier makes this a painful process for the local service industries as well as for those employed in the export sector. Sentiment, optimism, the relics of opportunities, and age keep people there who by economic logic should have emigrated, and the emigration of the young and active aggravates the regional problem. Social overhead capital is run increasingly uneconomically and expensively. Backwardness is also cumulative.[150]

In the twentieth century, the problems of the depressed areas as *Entleerungsgebiete*[151] have become a major aspect of social policy, but they existed in the period of industrialization also. In the first phase which we are considering now, they are essentially regions in which proto-industrialization or 'manufactures' flourished, but were then displaced by the new industries. Often they lost not only their markets to the newcomers, but also their capital and labour. In this respect, as Fribourg found, for example, it is a disadvantage to be too close to a growth region.[152] Major centres of industry then actually de-industrialize,[153] and the scatter of local industries which in the easier days before the factory had employed many people in small groups in town and country is similarly wiped out. Those formerly employed, part time or full time, in industry, return to agriculture, subside into unemployment, or emigrate, only a relic of handicraft industry or other local specialism bearing witness to the former activity.

The declining areas become such because, like the growth regions, they are, or were, connected with world markets. Though they would normally lose their capital and labour to neighbouring regions, the successful competitor may be a long way away: Languedoc wool lost its market in the Levant to Yorkshire exporters. Conversely, the easy success of some growth regions was due to the fact that they did not have to create new demands or new markets, but simply captured existing markets, with all their distribution facilities from displaced traditional makers. This displacement was generally a long-term process stretching, in the case of Flanders or Silesia for example, over half a century or more. The co-existence of old and new, the 'dual economy' of this type,[154] was as much a feature of industrialization as was the other 'dual economy', linking industry and agriculture, and the third type, linking factories in one stage of production with non-mechanized domestic work in another, such as mechanical spinning and hand-loom weaving, until the latter was also mechanized. In the fairly homogeneous, Inner Europe of our phase, differences in income between regions were much greater than average differences of income between countries,[155] and represented much the more significant economic reality of structural and trade interrelations and complementarity.

The Role of Transport

Industrialization means mass production, and mass production means access to mass markets. An industrial revolution, it has always been known, must be associated with a transport revolution to reach these markets. But the road, water-way, and railway network never reflected only economic needs. These means of transport also had military and political purposes, or might even be a form of conspicuous consumption.

We are on fairly safe ground in the negative case. We may take the absence of any metalled road whatever in the eastern provinces of Prussia in 1815 to be a sign of the absence of trade, or the poor communication system of Russia or Spain to be a sign of the absence of aggressive intent, for even Napoleon's armies were severely hampered there in their movements. But we cannot be sure positively what an existing means of transport signifies. Thus a French road might carry cotton goods to a sea-port, but it might also carry troops to the frontier, or the pomp and splendour of a royal procession. It will not be immediately obvious for which purpose it has been built, and the logic and timing of each purpose would be quite different. In this difference of timing and purpose between serving the industrializing economy and serving other ends, we are near the heart of one of the determining factors in the actual course of European industrialization.

The case of transport is a useful opportunity for pointing out that while the different states of Europe, and their separate regions, will be at very different stages of economic development, and therefore require very different transport networks appropriate to them, their rulers will all want to live up to the same contemporary standard of what is expected of an absolutist sovereign. They will all want armies, and similarly equipped armies, even though the productive apparatus to feed, clothe, arm, and pay them may be quite different. To allow them to march to the frontiers will require similar roads, but the additional uses to which these roads will be put, in the years of peace and behind the front lines in war, will be quite different. In some cases, as for example along the northern and eastern frontiers of France, they will carry traffic and yield high economic returns. In other areas, say along Austria's military frontier regions to the south east, they will be neglected and deserted.

Further, the building of these means of transport, always an expensive matter and a sizeable burden on the economy, will have very different economic functions and consequences, according to the level reached at the time of their building by the area in which they are located. This may be seen in the case of roads; it is less evident in the case of water-ways, which have few strategic or political purposes, but was overwhelmingly present in the case of the main new form of transport created during industrialization, the railways.

The word 'road' has stood for a variety of things in the past, from untreated ribbons of land left vacant between tilled ground, to wide metalled highways, for which bridges, embankments, cuttings, and even tunnels have been constructed at great cost. We are here concerned mainly with metalled, all-weather roads which could keep wheeled traffic moving much faster and over a longer part of the year, both for military and for economic purposes than untreated tracks. Since the days of the Romans, few of such roads have been built until the eighteenth century. They were found mostly in Britain and along the Atlantic seaboard of the Continent, and petered out towards the east. Clearly, there had been little need for them before growing commercial traffic led to a road-building boom in Britain and in central Belgium in mid-century, for people travelled on foot or on horseback and goods were conveyed by water if they had to move any distance. In earlier centuries the capital cost of building and maintaining roads could never have been justified by any conceivable weight of traffic.

In France, however, the road network that began to be built in the 1730s had the largely political purpose of helping to unify the kingdom. In 1716, the *Corps des Ingénieurs des Ponts et Chaussées* was set up, and their own technical school, the only one in Europe at the time, was established in 1747. This small professional group of engineers began to build up what was by far the finest road system on the Continent. By the end of the eighteenth century, France had 40,000 km. of roads of 12-20 metres in width, of which 4,000 km. were paved, and the budget of the *Ponts et Chaussées* had risen over the century from 700,000 *livres* to 15 million *livres*.[156]

That all this had little relevance to economic need was shown not only by the fact that while the network did thicken up in the industrial regions, to the north and east of Paris, roads largely ran indifferent to the local population and its activities, from Paris and other capitals to the frontiers,[157] but also by the fact which Arthur Young noted with some astonishment, that they were largely empty.[158] In the turmoil and neglect of the war years they quickly fell into a very bad state of disrepair.

Whether this kind of expenditure had much positive effect on industrialization may be doubted. On the positive side it helped to train an excellent cadre of technical specialists who were later to be active in the more useful work, and there was an evident benefit where strategic and economic needs coincided. But the funds used up, bearing in mind the French system of taxation which burdened mostly the productive classes, would almost certainly have been better spent elsewhere. This was still more certain in the case of the autocratic rulers of poorer countries with even less traffic to justify their attempt to imitate the pomp of France. Examples could be found in Spain, where 10,000 km. of carriage roads had been built by the end of the eighteenth century, Piedmont, or Prussia. Prussia had had no metalled road before 1775, and those built before 1800 were but isolated stretches, while thousands of tons of coal or iron ore in the Berg districts were still conveyed annually on the backs of men or horses, or on wheeled barrows. Russia did not begin her modern road-building until 1831.[159]

In the new century, road-building reflected economic needs more faithfully, and by and large, was undertaken by the public authorities only where commercial traffic justified it. Contemporary complaints, indeed, tended to suggest that it limped badly behind need. In France, Napoleon's decree of 1811, dividing roads into imperial, to be maintained from central funds, and departmental, to be the responsibility of local authorities, still led to some expenditure for strategic purposes, but after the restoration the repair and extension of the network began in earnest. In 1800–14 an annual 196 km. of new roads had been brought into use. This rose to 399 km. a year in 1814–30, 1,326 km. a year in 1831–47, and still a respectable 585 km. a year in 1848–60.[160] Equally important was the improvement of existing stretches. These figures show to what extent much of France had still been cut off from the rest of the country and from world markets at the beginning of the century, even though, especially for short-distance traffic, roads were still the main carriers: as late as 1829, two-thirds of the French traffic of 2,760 million ton/kilometres went by road.[161]

Belgium, using the turnpike principle like Britain, extended its road network by a quarter in 1814–30, and then doubled it to 1850. In Prussia, it was particularly the western advanced industrial provinces which insisted on better roads to carry their increased commerce. The government, somewhat reluctantly, increased the road-building budget from 420,000 thaler in 1821 to 3 million by 1841, and employed up to 15,000 workers (in part to alleviate unemployment) to increase the network from 3,162 km. in 1816 to 11,046 km. in 1846, or three-and-a-half times. Again, this showed the prevailing backwardness at the beginning of this period. In 1801 a commercial journey from Lennep to Silesia via Hamburg and back took 73 days, and in the 1820s, it was found that on urgent business it took nine days of hard riding from the industrial region of Berg to its port of Lübeck.[162] By contrast, the French stage coach could travel in favourable conditions 300 km. a day by 1830. Farther east, in the eastern provinces of Prussia, and still more so in Poland and Russia, all road-building efforts petered out. 'In general, the road system was most satisfactory where industrialization had proceeded farthest; the road map of Europe corresponded to that of the industrial revolution.'[163]

Canals and river improvements were, with very few exceptions, built for commercial purposes only. They represent very large lumps of expenditure and were thus almost invariably financed by public authorities, but were tied far more to pre-existing geographical possibilities than roads. In vew of these different opportunities it is not easy to compare fairly the performance of different regions in this field. The main use of the water-ways on the Continent as in Britain, was for the conveyance of bulky commodities, such as coal or grain, at very low speeds and at very low cost.

There were essentially two types of canal built in this period, though

the types shade into each other and some canals would fit both categories. The first is the canal linking two river systems, each with its
own complex water-borne tradè. The second is the canal for a specific
traffic, such as exports from a coal district, or imports into a large city.

It is the former in which we may occasionally find a government's
grandiose plans, rather than a genuine traffic need as the main driving
force. Ambition here frequently ran ahead of capacity, and water-
ways were cut between the upper reaches of rivers, or with such.poor
supplies of water and narrow guages, that they were of little use and
carried little traffic when they were completed. The Canal du Midi,
built in the seventeenth century, was of this kind, as also the Briare
canal between the Loire and Seine systems completed in 1642, but
made useful only in 1724, and the Orleans canal, completed for the
same purpose in 1692. Others cut in the nineteenth century were
those from the Rhône to the Rhine, the so-called 'Canal Monsieur',
finished in 1832, which carried coal to Alsace,[164] from the Saône to
the Yonne, the Burgundy, the Marne to the Rhine, and Marne–Aisne
canals.[165] At the same time, there were several such canals in the
Netherlands which certainly were of central commercial importance.
Holland had 500 km. of new canals by the 1660s.[166] Belgium had
1,600 km. of navigable waterway by 1830, of which 450 km. were
canals, and the Maastricht–Antwerp canal, linking the Meuse to the
Scheldt, was completed in 1856, while Liège was linked to Maastricht
by the Meuse lateral canal.

Of the other type, the Saint-Quentin canal (1803-10) with its
associated canalized Oise and the lateral (i.e. parallel to the river)
Oise canal, completed in 1836, to bring northern coal to Paris,[167] and
the Dortmund–Ems canal (1899) opening a route for heavy goods
traffic to the sea in a northward direction, were outstanding examples.

In France, the Restoration government was left with several half-
finished schemes and grandiose plans. Its main building efforts derived
from the comprehensive national plans drawn up in 1820 by F. L.
Becquey, Director-General of the *Ponts et Chaussées*, which envisaged
a total of 10,000 km. of new canals. The Bourbons added 930 km.
to the 1200 km. in existence and the Orleans Monarchy another
2,000 km. of water-ways, including river improvements. The schemes
were financed by the government which raised loans for the purpose
from the money market.

In Germany, Prussia was the main canal-builder, most of her canals
being of the river-connecting type, forming East–West links between
the SE–NW-flowing rivers. The Oder–Spree Canal of 1669 linked the
Upper Oder and Silesia ultimately with Hamburg. There were also
the Plauen and Finow canals (1745), linking the Elbe with the Oder,

the Fehrbellin Canal (1766), the Bromberg Canal (1774), linking the Oder with the Vistula, and the Klodnitz Canal of 1806 which linked the Upper Silesian coalfield with the Oder. Other canals affecting the Brandenburg area were the Oranienburg canal (1831-8), the Berlin-Spandau ship canal (1849-58), and the Landwehr and Louisenstadt Canal (1845-50). Berlin thus had excellent water-way communications, and had access to cheaper coal (from Britain) than many other parts of Germany. Altogether, Prussia built 790 km. of water-ways, of which about 600 km. were river improvements, in 1796-1836.[168] Annual investment rose from an average of 2.3 million thaler in the 1820s to 4.2 million th. in the 1840s.

In the West, the Ruhr had been made navigable by 1780 and for a while became the busiest river in Germany, its peak being reached around 1860 when it had 338 ships and carried almost one million tons, nearly all coal. The other main rivers were hampered by innumerable tolls. From Dresden to Hamburg in 1812-14 a transit time of one week on the Elbe was lengthened to four, because of the tolls, and traffic often preferred the route to Holland by road. For the Rhine, the Congress of Vienna had decreed free transit, actually achieved by treaty in 1831 and secured in 1868, but only for the Riparian states. The Scheldt was opened in 1833 and secured by Treaty in 1839.[169] The Dortmund-Ems canal, as noted above, was opened in 1899, its westward connection to the Rhine, the Rhine-Herne Canal, in 1914, and the eastward extensions in 1915 (Ems-Weser), 1916 (Weser-Elbe), and 1938 (Magdeburg).

Here, also, the timing is of significance. In Britain, canals had been a part of the industrial revolution, particularly used for conveying coal. Their strength was the short, local link, from colliery, quarry, or iron-works to the market or the sea, while the through routes, given the geography of the country, were of less significance: no useful quantity of coal, for example, ever reached London by canal. As soon as the railways were established, most of the canal system became redundant and fell into disuse, though there were significant local exceptions.

In the countries of Inner Europe, apart from the Netherlands, canals were frequently built ahead of industrialization, carrying inadequate traffic over poorly provided and maintained routes, in part, at least, built for commercial-strategic reasons by governments which had little idea of the course of industrialization. Canals, therefore, like railways thereafter, became political objectives on a regional basis.[170] The industrial revolution was accompanied by railway, not canal building as in Britain, and it was only after the mass traffic had been created, in part by the railways, that canals once more became worthwhile on a larger and more generous scale.[171] This was partly so because of the favourable conditions of the northern European plain, containing much flat, well-watered country, but in part it was the timing of industrialization which had reversed the order.

In the case of railways, the timing differential stood out much more clearly. Since railways satisfied many different objectives, such as the transport of goods, the conveyance of passengers, the movement of armies, of particular significance to Russia after the Crimean War, but a matter not neglected in France or Germany, or were sheer prestige objects and status symbols, they did not fit neatly into the industrialization timetable like the machine-spinning of cotton and the coke-smelting of iron. Moreover, the British example had shown clearly enough that railways prompted the production of coal, iron, and engineering goods; they could form profitable investments and become a gold mine for speculators and promoters. Above all, the building or absence of a line could make or break a district or a region, once the building of the national network had started, so that loud and powerful voices were raised by lobbyists for the building of lines to particular spots the sums of which would have greatly exceeded the lines needed for the country as a whole. However, the agitation helped to give a district upward lift to the planning.

Thus railways, once they had proved profitable, spread astonishingly quickly across the Continent. The first public line to run with locomotives is usually held to be the Stockton–Darlington, opened in 1825, but this was simply a coal line which additionally allowed private outside persons to put their coaches on the track. The first properly designed and built public railway, the Liverpool and Manchester, was opened in 1830. France opened her first in 1832, Germany and Belgium following in 1835, Russia in 1837, Austria in 1838, Italy and Holland in 1839, Denmark and Switzerland in 1847, and Spain in 1848[172] These, admittedly, might be pioneer lines, with no or only limited follow-ups. Yet as we have seen,[173] railway mileage was distributed much more evenly across Europe than other economic indicators. By 1870, in round figures, lines open for traffic (in thousand kilometres) were as follows:[174]

Austria–Hungary	10.1
Belgium	3
France	17.5
Germany	19.5 (1871 territory)
Italy	6
Spain	5.5
Holland	1.4
Switzerland	1.4
United Kingdom	24.5

Inner Europe (given the size of countries) still had the advantage, led by Britain and Belgium, and there was here a network going down to small capillaries tapping minor towns, collieries, or single large works, whereas peripheral Europe had, by and large, not got beyond main lines to major cities and abroad. Yet railways had, by any reckonning, become a massive fact there also. Railways therefore arrived on the scene at very different stages in the development of regions. They arrived in Britain (and the north-eastern states of the USA) at the end of the industrialization process; indeed they had to, since there had to be iron-making, steam-engine making, and coal capacity, as well as capital in the monetary sense, to build them, as there had to have been a long development process for the innovation itself which stretched over decades and centuries, mainly evolving within the colliery districts of Britain. In Inner Europe (and parts of the USA), by contrast, they arrived with the industrial revolution, and formed an integral part of that process. In Outer Europe they arrived ahead of it.

Thus in Britain, simplifying a little,[175] it could be said that the traffic existed before the lines were built; in Inner Europe they were being built as the traffic grew to justify them; and in Peripheral Europe the early lines of this period were completed without adequate traffic to justify them. It follows that in Britain, as well as in parts of the USA, railway companies could be financed by private capital seeking profitable investment. In Inner Europe, and other parts of the USA, private capital required a government guarantee of interest, or subsidies in different forms, before building most lines, for they were balanced on the knife-edge between profitability or a wait for various periods before traffic caught up with construction, though some systems, like that tapping the French North, were as well placed as British lines. Only the first pioneer lines in those areas needed foreign, mostly British, capital, before the local communities could supply their own. In peripheral Europe not only was a government guarantee necessary, but even with it, there was not enough native capital, and capital therefore was foreign, frequently lent to the government, as the only known reliable agency, rather than to the railway company. Finally, going even farther outward, to such areas as Turkey, the foreign investor additionally made sure he could control the government, or at least its tax-raising activities, before venturing his capital, for there the railways had arrived before even a modern state structure had evolved.

Behind this Gerschenkron-type sequence of substitution of private capital, by private state-aided, foreign state-aided, and foreign state-controlling capital, there lies the more significant reaction of railway building on the industrialization process, and the economic progress of the societies concerned. In Britain, railways merely boosted an industrialization process in full swing, helping ultimately to export capital, capital goods, and facilities to provide cheap food and raw materials by means of lines laid overseas. In Inner Europe, railways helped to stamp ironworks and coal-mines out of the ground, to provide a major part of the dynamic for industrialization, directly as well as indirectly by their effects on all markets. But in the periphery they had no such effect over many long decades. There iron, rails, locomotives, engineering specialists, as well as capital, were imported. Native industries, far from being stimulated, were swamped by the cheaper foreign imports made possible thereby. The countries fell into debt and had to meet increasing servicing charges, worsening their balance of payments, without necessarily possessing an asset which as yet was yielding a social, let alone a financial, return. For them, railways became a status symbol they could not yet afford and which threatened to ruin them. Ultimately, however, when industrialization began, after varying intervals they would have an economically beneficial effect also.

Here we are concerned with Inner Europe only. In spite of basic technological similarities, and the laying-down of networks in which an observer, at the end of the process, would have been hard put to it to discern any national idiosyncrasies, the building itself was strongly influenced by governments and their policies. Belgium, as a young state with a most uncertain industrial future following its independence from Holland and exclusion from Dutch markets, decided as early as 1834 to create a national system, in the form of a cross of a north–south and an east–west route centred on Malines, together with some branches, ensuring convenient communications between Britain, France, Germany, and Holland. That original system was practically completed in 1844 by the state, issuing bonds in Britain and at home, but from 1842 on, private companies were licensed, at first mostly British, using British contractors and engineers, but later there was also some French capital to join the Belgian. By 1850 about 150 km. of private lines were open, and in 1870 about 2,100 km., out of a total network of over 3,000 km. The state subsequently began to buy up some of the private lines, and after 1880 many light railways were built, half-way between railways and tramways, peculiarly apt for a country of closely grouped small towns rather than large cities, to give Belgium (if measured as a country, not a region) the densest railway network in Europe.

In France, as we have seen, there was an early line in the St. Étienne coal district, and local lines were built in Paris, the Mulhouse–Tann branch (1830), and Strasburg–Basle (1841), and a line from Ales to Beaucaire. Some 427 km. of track were open in 1840. As for the major building, it had to wait for a national plan, designed by A. B. V. Legrand, another director of the *Ponts et Chaussées*, in 1841 and passed as law in 1842, though some major parts of it, including Paris–Rouen and Paris–Orleans, were set in motion before that date, basing themselves on the outline 1833 plan. According to this Act, the state was to lay down the exact lines, to buy the land (aided by local authorities in the original provisions, repealed later), and to build the permanent way, but could lease the lines to private companies who were to provide the equipment, including the rails, and the rolling-stock and keep the track in good condition.

When the crisis of 1847 struck and halted progress only the sections that were likely to be the most profitable (to Calais, to the north, and around Paris and Marseilles) had been built, to the extent of a little over 3,000 km. Half the private shares were then allegedly in British hands.[176] Building was resumed in the Second Empire, under a government that was eager to develop the railways, and by 1857 the planned network of 1842 was largely complete and in the hands of six large companies, each of which controlled a segment of the country around its trunk-line, in the form of a triangle with the apex in Paris, with a single transverse line, Bordeaux–Marseille in the south. The next stage was the building-out of local lines inside these territories.

Funds for the original lines in the 1840s depended largely on the co-operation of the Paris Haute Banque. In the 1850s, financiers con-trolled the developments more directly, and the battle between the Rothschilds, representing the older banks, and the Pereire Brothers, with their Crédit Mobilier, representing a rival group, for railway con-cessions both inside France and in other European countries,[177] has fascinated many observers at the time and since. While several of the trunk-lines could be kept profitable, this was less certain in the case of the branches, and to encourage their building the goverment under-took under the Franqueville conventions of 1859, supplemented by others in 1863–9, to guarantee the interest of the capital for the latter, the 'new' network. This served to make railways already burdened by their *lignes électorales* even more strongly subject to politically inspired decisions. By 1870 the main French network, including a few smaller private lines, was completed.

The war interrupted the work of construction and removed a government that had stood particularly close to the great financiers and concessionarires.[178] In 1878 the Freycinet plan envisaged a 'third' network, beside the original and the 'new', of about 9,000 km., beside proposing that some of the smaller and non-viable lines should be bought up by the state. New conventions of 1883 regulated the financing of the plan. The private companies were to build the third network lines, with the help of state subsidies, and in addition they were to receive interest guarantees on the whole of their capital, including that used for the first network which had not hitherto had that privilege. By 1903, over 1,000 million francs had been paid over to them under the scheme, while the state, by exchange, controlled the unprofitable south-western line and took over the bankrupt western line in 1909. The network meanwhile grew from 22,000 km. in 1880 to 39,500 km. in 1914.

In the German States, governments also took a hand in railway planning and finance. A short suburban line had been completed in 1835 between Nuremberg and Fürth, and there was also the Berlin-Potsdam railway. The important Leipzig-Dresden line in Saxony was opened (115 km.) in 1839, and the Magdeburg-Leipzig line in 1840. The main building programme began in the 1840s. Prussia was not at first eager to support the new means of transport, but granted the concession of the Cologne-Minden railway, as the first stage in linking the eastern and western parts of the country in 1836. In 1842, the Prussian government, taking a more positive attitude, began to plan lines and to subsidize or guarantee the interest of those built in areas in which traffic did not yet justify their building, like the Berlin-Köthen and Berlin-Stettin railways. The first Prussian state railway, running through the Saar coalfield, was begun in 1847. By 1875 57% of the lines were in private hands, 26% were nationalized, and 17% were private lines under state administration. From 1879 on, Prussia began to nationalize all her private lines, a process all but completed in 1914.

Several of the southern and western states were more eager to support early railway building than was Prussia. Baden had a state system of which the first stretch, Heidelberg-Karlsruhe, was open in 1843. Württemberg decided on state lines in 1845, Hanover in 1842, and Bavaria in 1844. Saxony and Hesse-Kassel had mixed public and private systems. Altogether, German building got off to a much more rapid start than that of the French in the 1840s, though the ton-miles moved remained well below the French until 1870. The various German countries between them had 4,822 km. open in 1850, 11,026 km. in 1860, and 33,865 km. in 1880. It became clear from about 1844 onward that, aided by the workings of the Zollverein and the lack of congruence between State frontiers and economic needs in most cases, the various lines were coalescing into a system in the northern half of Germany. The Southern states used railways consciously as an expression of their independent statehood and designed systems centred on their own capital cities with little regard for through traffic.[179] The Baden railways indeed had been started on a wider guage and were converted to standard only after 1853.

The sequence of interactions between the building of the railways and the acceleration of economic growth and change in the industrial structure was much the same over the whole of this area, though the timing differed. Belgium was slightly ahead, followed by the French North, Alsace, Upper Loire-Rhone, Rhineland-Westphalia, and Saxony, with the lesser industrial areas and the countryside between following in their wake.

The earliest railways were built to carry existing traffic: they arose out of the interaction between the new technology from Britain and the needs of large concentrations of population at a relatively advanced stage of economic development on the Continent. Those early lines were of three types: city-suburban, such as Paris, Berlin, and Nuremberg, mainly for passengers; those within the industrial regions, such as some of the Belgian lines, the French North, Leipzig-Dresden or Dortmund-Elberfeld, carrying mainly bulk goods; and strategic lines over longer distances, such as Paris-Lyons-Mediterranean (P-L-M), Cologne-Minden, and parts of the Belgian 'cross'. While the first two types were built to deal with actual traffic bottlenecks,[180] this was less evident in the last type, which therefore frequently required government support in one form or another.

Although still relatively small, this early building programme greatly exceeded the capacity of the economies concerned. There was a massive influx of capital from Britain into Belgium and France, though to only a minor degree into Germany where there seem to have been sufficient local savings; by the 1850s the French were already exporting railway capital themselves to the European periphery. More significantly, railway building was accompanied by an equally decisive import of material in the first stages, principally iron, rails, coal, and locomotives, mainly from Britain but also from Belgium and even from the USA. Thus of the 51 locomotives used in Prussia to 1841, only one, and that an unsatisfactory one, was built in Germany, but 40% of the 124 installed in 1842-5, and 93% of the 270 bought in 1850-3 were home-built. Borsig built his first locomotive in Berlin in 1841; by 1858, he had built his thousandth. Henschel at Kassel built his first locomotive in 1848, his two-thousandth in 1886. Most of the rails laid in Germany in 1835-45 were imported and even up to the 1860s, German rails were still largely made from imported pig iron. The Leipzig-Dresden railway required 2½ times the annual iron production of Saxony, and amounted to an equivalent of 30% of the current annual iron output of Prussia. In France, also, imports of pig iron and of rails, from Britain and Belgium, rose in the 1830s and early 1840s,[181] and most of the locomotives were foreign, largely British. Details for 1843 give the following distribution of locomotives owned by the early lines:

	Foreign-built	French-built
Beaucaire	16	—
Montpellier	6	—
Paris–St. Germain	38	12
Paris–Versailles	12	3
Paris–Orleans (1845)	38	11

On the Paris–Rouen line, an essentially British company, the locomotives were built in the Company's workshop at Sotteville, staffed entirely by British craftsmen.[182]

Starting from this base, a mutually reinforcing growth pattern emerged. The striking reductions in transport costs achieved by the railways gave a strong boost to industry, particularly bulky productions, which in turn provided income for railways and incentives to build more. The carriage of coal and iron in particular was cheapened, allowing new markets to be won, and large modern works to be set up depending on wide markets to supplement the antiquated small charcoal plants that had hitherto been protected by distance and transport costs. Among the best markets for iron and engineering products were the railways themselves.[183] In view of the less developed iron and engineering industry at the start of this process, and the relatively larger railway programme, boosted in part for political reasons beyond what was economically justifiable,[184] the impact of railways on the growth of those key industries was much greater than in the Anglo-Saxon countries.

In Belgium, the growth of coke ironmaking in the 1830s and 1840s was directly related to railway demand, for both home and foreign lines. On a low estimate, the demand for rails alone was 26.1% of the total iron output in Germany, in 1840–63, rising to 54.2% in the peak years 1854–9. In the 1860s and 1870s, it may have amounted to one half. In 1846 35.7% of all Prussian steam horsepower was in locomotives; in 1875 it was 74.0%. Around 1860, German rail exports began to exceed imports. It was a classic case of import substitution leading to backward linkages, and forming a main ingredient in the rise of German heavy industry to its first great boom in 1871–3.[185] A similar close relationship emerged in Austria.

In France, rails represented 13.7% of bar-iron output in 1845, (over one-third in the peak years 1847, 1856, and 1863) and 26–27% of bar-iron plus steel output in 1865–85. 83% of the steel made to 1873 was used on rails, 35% in 1885–95, and still 20% after 1895. Again, import substitution soon turned into exports. By 1854, the French output had risen to 500 locomotives a year, and capital export from France was matched by locomotive exports. But even peripheral countries soon had their own railway workshops in which locomotives were first repaired, then built: by the end of the century they existed in Austria/Hungary, Russia, Switzerland, Italy, Sweden, Holland, and other countries.[186]

The impact on labour and capital should also not be forgotten. German railway building alone, leaving out of account the manning of the lines, employed 178,500 in 1846 and peaked at 541,000 in 1875 and 320,000 in 1879. French capital investment in railways averaged 151 million francs a year in 1845-52, with peak periods of investment in 1853-67 (averaging 393 m.fr. a year), 1880-5 (483 m.fr.), and 1907-14 (415 m.fr.). In the 1850s and 1860s this represented over 13% of gross domestic capital formation. In Prussia, new railway shares issued in 1845-9 represented the equivalent of one-third of the national budget each year. Before long, the total invested was to exceed the national debt. In the 1850s and 1860s, the annual figures were between 15% and 25% of total capital formation.[187] The role of the German railways as 'leading sector' finds support in the fact that while the social product grew by 2.6% per annum in 1852-1913, railway traffic grew by 6.6%[188]

The significance of these figures is not merely one of quantity, but also of kind. In a country like Germany, with little experience of investment outside government papers, railway shares created a market for shares and helped the remarkable increase in joint-stock company formation in the 1850s-1870s. Since these railways had high returns, they encouraged further investments. They also helped to establish steamer lines, to unify regional and later national labour markets, to develop postal and telegraph traffic, and to extend export markets as well as encouraging the movement of emigrants. Not least, they also contributed to making the growth-path one of exuberant booms followed by destructive slumps.

National Developments

The bulk of this chapter has concentrated on structural changes in economic regions and economic sectors. The role of the political entity, except in the case of Belgium, Switzerland, and, to some extent, Saxony, has been largely ignored. Governments and states mattered greatly in the process of industrialization, even before the 1870s, and some of their influence will be discussed below.[189] But since most history is written in terms of states, there is less need to go over familiar ground than might otherwise be the case. A summary of some of the specific national aspects of the growth path in France and Germany follows, to complete the picture.

In France, the main interest lies in a comparison with Britain on the one hand, and Germany on the other. Different and to some extent conflicting statistical series exist for total output, industrial output, and national income,[190] but they all seem to agree that France, starting from a fairly equal level with Britain at the end of the eighteenth century or the beginning of the nineteenth,[191] had slipped badly behind at the end of the nineteenth, particularly in the development of her 'modern' industry. Similarly, Germany, starting from a position well behind her, had caught France up and far overtaken her by *c.* 1900. As we have seen, and as is widely acknowledged, such over-all figures have little meaning, as they average out very different regional developments according to weights which depend on the exogenous datum of the way the frontier runs, but some of the explanations offered are of interest. We shall examine particularly those which take account of the differences in timing, meaning thereby that similar stages in development were reached by different economies at different points in European history, and had to be played out against a very different background.

Several historians who are impressed by the fact that French average incomes were never much below the British, despite the country's poor showing in terms of coal or iron output, have suggested that French developments should not be characterized as slower than the British, but different. An extreme version of this has been to use the Gerschenkron model as basis for the argument that it was France that was the pioneer, starting her industrialization by the mid-eighteenth century and proceeding with relatively little social cost thereafter, and it was Britain, as the follower, which had to turn to hasty methods of catching up at great cost to the generations which lived through the industrial revolution.[192] The British sequence, far from being the model, would then be an aberration. A slightly weaker version argues that both countries were contemporaneous, but pursuing different paths, the French emphasizing agriculture, consumer goods (in which they had a high productivity), and smaller, more scattered firms, as against the British concentration on coal, iron, heavy engineering, and textile yarns.[193] With emphasis on the rapidly growing population in Britain, compared with its near stagnation in France, one could also take the view that the enormous British effort merely kept a larger population at the level at which the French managed to keep their stationary one without trouble.

Lévy-Leboyer's characterization of the French form of industrialization as being 'upstream',[194] takes account of British coexistence.

For it was precisely because Britain had achieved an unchallengeable superiority in capital and intermediate goods that France and other followers had to concentrate on consumer goods and on those using more of the relatively cheaper factor of production, labour, while Britain, as the pioneer, could impress her comparative advantage in capital-intensive industries upon the rest of the world. Among the disadvantages suffered by France in comparison with her neighbour across the Channel and frequently listed in the literature, there are several which we have already taken account of in our regional analysis: lack of adequate and favourably sited coal, the scatter of iron deposits, and a geographical configuration which created detached economic provinces with little contact between them.[195] Others, such as the effect of peasant agriculture,[196] and the alleged weaknesses of French entrepreneurship, we have discussed above. Yet others include the slow population growth, combined with a slow urban growth, with the absence therefore of promising new markets; the heavy weight of the large old-fashioned industries holding back the few new industries and responsible for the characteristic 'dual economy' structure of France; and the ambiguous attitudes among the traditional ruling élite to industrialization.[197] There is also the 'false dawn' effect of favourable terms of trade over the first two-thirds of the century, with a consequent lack of incentive to expand exports, and the oft-quoted failure of the banks, which disposed over a great deal of capital, but invested it outside productive industry except for one or two large firms, and railways.[198] This implies a particularly unfortunate timing sequence, investible funds having accumulated before industrial opportunities, teaching their owners to trust other objectives and to continue with them even when industry emerged, in exact contrast to the German capital market in which savers and banks grew up, in the 1850s, when railway and industrial companies were normal targets for investment.

Yet even if we ignored the flourishing regions of France which contradict these pessimistic premisses and confined ourselves to an average covering the whole country, there was by no means uniform slow growth over the century. On the contrary, there were spells of remarkably fast expansion,[199] as fast as any shown by the allegedly 'successful' industrializers like Britain, Belgium, or Germany. These were the 1830s, the 1850s, and after a long period of stagnation beginning in the 1860s and continued by the after-effects of the defeat of 1870 and the world-wide depression, the remarkable 'second industrial revolution', the period of growth especially in steel, engineering, and textiles from the mid-1890s to the First World War, which brought France right back among the leaders in the modern sectors.

Such sustained fast growth could not have taken place in several lengthy phases, had the negative elements been so pervasive. The standard analysis forgets the many positive factors operating in France: ordered government, economic freedom, and governments favourable to bourgeois enrichment, the best system of higher technological education in the world, a large internal market, a high standard of living and a high propensity to save, a long industrial tradition and the existence of various specialist skills, some coal and iron, good ports both on the Atlantic and the Mediterranean, and some good rivers, among others.

In view of these ambiguities, it is not surprising that there is"no agreement on the onset of industrialization in France." According to Dunham, the period from 1815 to 1848 marks 'the infancy and the beginning of the adolescence of the Industrial Revolution', maturity not being attained until after 1860. Leuillot would date the 'pre-industrial revolution' from the crisis of 1825 rather than 1830. Rostow put the 'take-off' period at 1830–60. Marczewski, while admitting that the 1830s (and 1890s) saw particularly fast rates of growth, saw no take-off at all in the nineteenth century, though there might have been one in the eighteenth. Lévy-Leboyer could also see no definable revolution, while Crouzet put it into the period 1845–75. A number of others, including Claude Fohlen, agreed that the real acceleration came after 1840.[200]

Germany, by contrast, has received good marks in the literature, for good performance in the industrialization stakes. Perhaps the main reason for this view is that the German course, unlike the French, followed closely the British model, being concentrated in a relatively brief and clearly marked period of years, and being based on the classical sectors of coal, iron, engineering, and, to a lesser extent, textiles. The changed emphasis between this and the British case, in which textiles were 'leading', could be explained by the Hoffmann and Gerschenkron models according to which latecomers would put greater weight on capital goods. There has therefore been less controversy about timing. The two great foundation periods of the 1850s and early 1870s fitted the classical model so well that Rostow's 'take-off' designations for 1850–73 has been widely accepted, though Hoffman opted for 1830-5–1855-60 and Tilly would include the 1840s for the 'first burst of heavy industrial growth'. The only available set of statistics also show the early 1870s and the years from the mid-1890s to 1913 to have been periods of fast growth in national income.[201] In the phase to the mid-1870s, Germany changed from a relatively backward economy by comparison with other western regions into a powerful industrial nation.

Among the causes for this 'success', the availability of capital through the joint-stock banks founded in the 1850s has already been mentioned, and there was probably plenty of capital even before 1850.[202] Other favourable factors included good supplies of grain, flax, and wool to the mid-century and good coal thereafter, an excellent technical and general education system, and the early building-up of the railway system.[203] Curiously enough, commerce is also mentioned, and in particular, the successful sale of corn and wool to Britain at a critical time so that industrialization in Germany went ahead without balance of payments problems.[204] Yet there was no German 'commerce': there were some thirty-nine States, each with their own trade balance. One more sophisticated analysis admits a division into two Germanies, eastern agrarian and western industrial, connected with each other only indirectly by trade via Great Britain,[205] but in fact there were many German economies with complex trading relationships.

This splitting-up into several markets, even under the Zollverein, for purposes of railway planning, subsidization, education, and other matters, must be considered among the adverse factors plaguing German industrialization. Another adverse factor frequently mentioned was British competition,[206] allowed to enter German markets much more easily than was possible under the unitary administration of a country like France. Imports entered via the free cities like Frankfurt or Hamburg, and profited from inter-state rivalries. To these must be added the survival of guild rights, despite their formal abolition, the survival of restrictive relations in agriculture, the absence of large cities, and the rapid population rise, which at least in the first half of the century could be matched neither with enough land, except in the East, nor with enough industrial capital, and therefore led to a severe Malthusian crisis in mid-century.[207] Such an enumeration would, on balance, hardly show any advantage over France.

How much, in fact, of the German 'success' was a reflection of the dramatic opening-up of the Ruhr, together with that of the Saar and Upper Silesia (as of every other hitherto inaccessible coalfield in those years) aided later by the incorporation of the iron ore of Lorraine, and the cotton and potash of Alsace? What would the textbooks tell us now of benefits of the German educational system or the ruthless efficiency of German industrialists, who now figure so largely in historical explanations, if the coal had existed, not along the Ruhr but, say, in Holland or Normandy instead? Where was the vaunted German predilection for size and capital goods before the railway when the most prominent industry was a small-scale, and still lagging, textile industry?[208]

Perhaps these are unfair questions, for German technical education and entrepreneurship were real enough, though they were caused by, as well as reacting back on, the industrial possibilities open at the time. But they point to the fact that large countries like France or Germany were patchwork quilts of very different economic regions,[209] each of these regional economies reacting to its opportunites in the light of its available resources in the widest sense. Frontiers imposed a grid on this pattern of living economic organs, a grid that might change with wars, conquests, and treaties but still had relatively little influence on economic growth. To impose an artificial unity on the groups of regions that found themselves inside one of the grids, rather than to observe their similarities across the borders, and their interrelationships extending across a large part of the European Continent, obscures, rather than illuminates history in this period.

Chapter 4
Paths of Transmission

So far we have stressed the new technology in the process of European industrialization. Industrialization, for us, up to this point, has meant the imitation and absorption, at first or second hand, of the technology pioneered in Britain. This is because in some important sense the acceptance of the new technology in certain key industries did appear to be critical: without it, no industrialization as we understand it, could take place, but once it was accepted successfully on a wide enough base, nothing seemed to be able to prevent the region concerned from 'taking off'.[1]

In part the logic behind this sequence was that in our period the technological gap to be bridged, the new tricks to be learnt, were not yet very large, and it was not too difficult to make the jump in the advanced areas of Inner Europe where the other economic and social requirements were very largely present already. Thus there were several regions with a good-sized industrial population, used to handling textiles or metal goods and to work for wages, there were entrepreneurs, there were savings looking for investment opportunities, there were governments obeying the rule of law more or less faithfully and being favourably inclined towards the rise of industry,[2] there were transport routes and trading relationships, and many other prerequisites. As for the technology, the construction of cotton-spinning mules was not beyond the comprehension of cabinet-makers and clockmakers of the traditional kind, nor were coke blast-furnaces totally strange to men who had been brought up to operate blast-furnaces with charcoal fuel. Moreover, by modern standards, commerce and transport still proceeded in a fairly leisurely way. It was not always necessary to adopt the most up-to-date method at once. Hand-jennies competed for a while with frames, water-power with steam-engines, according to local prices and factor supplies, and British goods, even if cheaper, might take some time to seek out and dominate distant and out-of-the-way markets.

This is not to say that similar relationships would hold at other times and places. On the contrary, it is clear that they would not.[3] Even in the nineteenth century, there were parts of Europe where, for example, there was no free labour, where no savings existed, no industrial traditions, possibly not even markets or means of transport. As, almost inevitably, the chance to absorb the new technology reached them later than the favoured areas of Inner Europe, that technology had, itself, become more complex and costly and therefore harder to imitate even by well-prepared societies. *A fortiori* today, when technology is incomparably more demanding, while populations who wish to adopt it, frequently lack virtually all social and economic prerequisites, an emphasis on technology as the major trigger of industrialization would be wholly misplaced. Examples are not lacking of attempts to try just that, to import a complete works with its expert managers and its carefully tooled spare parts into a backward economy, only to see the imported industrial venture wither and die, or remain as a foreign enclave, without much direct influence on the host economy.

It would be just as mistaken to argue back from these failed experiments of today that technology could not have been an effective trigger in early nineteenth-century Europe. In the advanced parts of Inner Europe, capitalist relations, capital, labour, and much else, did not have to be introduced. They were there already and capable of absorbing the new technology if suitably packaged. Once it came, it brought lower prices, wider markets, greater incentives to further investments, forward and backward linkages using mostly existing resources but also creating new ones, and all the rest.

Nevertheless, the process was not simple, nor did it necessarily move along the same path in each case. It is the purpose of this chapter to explore some of the paths used, concentrating again, though not exclusively, on the first phase, the transfer of the industrialization process to the advanced regions of Inner Europe.[4]

The Transfer of Technology

A great deal of interest has been shown, particularly among historians of the recipient countries, in the transfer of technology, and above all the transfer to the pioneers of each country or region. Apart from two major general works[5] there are numerous specialist studies, and it is in fact virtually impossible to pick up any book on industrialization without finding examples of this transfer, generally from Britain, but occasionally also from the first generation of disciples, in Belgium, France, Switzerland, or the German states. It is an integral part of the history of each country, and there would be little point in piling case upon case here also. We shall, instead, confine ourselves to some general observations, using individual cases merely as examples.

The transfer of technology was not, of course, a new phenomenon.

Italian technology in the Renaissance, later German, Dutch, and French technology flowed down the *Gefälle* from whatever were the leading regions in any given phase to areas just below them. The Huguenot exodus, it was noted above, fertilized many Protestant industrial and commercial regions of Europe. In all these movements Britain had been the recipient until the later eighteenth century when it was found that in one industry after another, and not only, significantly, in the lead industries of the industrial revolution, she ceased to be the disciple and became the pioneer.

But the new technology now emerging from Britain opened up a gap between her and the rest that extended not only over a broader front, but was also becoming wider than in any earlier example. In a generally mercantilist age it was clear that technical know-how was a major economic asset, and legislation was passed in Britain prohibiting the export of machinery and blueprints as well as the emigration of skilled artisans. An earlier law, relating to textiles, dated from 1695, but the main first operative acts were passed in 1781-6. They were first relaxed in 1824, when artisans were again permitted to emigrate, and in 1825 a licensing system made the other regulations more flexible. All of them were repealed in 1843.[6]

Whatever the economic logic behind these regulations, their enforcement exceeded the administrative capacity of the day. They had a certain nuisance value, but the traffic in machinery, designs, and experts soon learnt to adjust itself to them and was not seriously incommoded. Several transfer mechanisms developed. Apart from the scientific literature which could be legally obtained in Britain, foreigners learnt of the new processes by sending industrial spies, by coming to work in Britain for a time (the two categories are not always easy to separate), by smuggling out machines or drawings, and by hiring British experts at all levels: managers, engineers, or skilled workers. In all these the initiative was taken by the Continent. There were also numerous cases in which skilled British nationals decided to seek their fortunes abroad, by emigrating first and finding sponsors afterwards. These included some of the most prominent, including John Holker, who attempted to introduce some early cotton technology into France, and William Cockerill. Once the new equipment or process had got abroad, it could either be installed in a competitive firm and made to work, or used as an exhibition model, or erected in technical schools and colleges for the instruction of native technicians.[7] Usually several of these methods were combined.

There was still some traffic the other way: British firms continued to receive ideas, innovations, and skilled ingenious immigrants from the Continent.[8] These, however, tended to be individuals who sought to establish themselves, or their innovations, where they believed the greatest chance of acceptance to lie, rather than the transfer of accepted methods. All this changed rapidly in the 1860s: by then innovations might originate equally well in several leading economies, severally or (as in the case of the internal combustion-engine) jointly.

Meanwhile some areas were receiving their technological aid and advice not directly from Britain, but from other countries, at second hand as it were. This serves to underline the role of the early industrializers of Inner Europe not merely as victims of the superior British onslaught, but as playing a key role in the interrelationships between all parts of the Continent at different stages of development. The Cockerills and others sallied forth from Belgium to install machinery in Germany and Russia, for example; Belgians helped to develop the northern French coalfield, as also (with Frenchmen) the minerals of the Ruhr. Styrian steelworkers instructed French and Württenbergers, as those of the Harz had instructed the County of Mark; the Swiss and the Saxons taught many of their neighbours and while Bohemia learnt from Holland, Belgium, and Germany, and Italy learnt from Alsace, Switzerland, and Germany, there was no western country which did not send some technicians or key machinery to Russia.[9]

Yet by far the most important transfer was that from Britain to the leading regions on the Continent. No numerical or statistical data are available, nor would such data have much meaning, for the significant fact was not how many British mechanics actually went abroad to set up workshops or train up local personnel, nor how many actual British mules or Newcomen engines were assembled there, but that they were everywhere the first to be assembled there. There is no single important industry in any of the major continental regions that did not have British pioneers as entrepreneurs, mechanics, machine builders, skilled foremen and workmen, or suppliers of capital (and usually several of these combined) to set them going, Thus in France, British technical aid in modernizing the cotton industry ran from 1738 until well into the nineteenth century, and its details would fill a small volume; woollen, flax and jute machinery similarly waited for British initiative, though there were some significant French inventions in those fields. The indebtedness of the main French coalfields, ironworks, and engineering establishments is even greater, and in engineering in particular, the British furnished not only the trigger, but stayed there to build up the majority of French works in existence in the first phase of industrialization, which in turn became the instruments for transforming the rest of the economy. Names such as Manby and Wilson, Steels, Radcliffe, John Collier, John Jackson, Allcard, and Buddicom are only the best known in a long list, and all the first generation of French engineering-works founders had some of their training in Britain, including Constantin Perier, Ignace de Wendel, F. C. L. Albert, and Dufaud of Grossouvre. In iron-working, 'Joseph Bessy brought no less than forty-two English families to the district of Saint-Étienne, and it is known that English foremen and many English workmen were used for many years by all the leading forgers (*sic*) of France.'[10] The early making of railway equipment, and railway building, was similarly wholly borrowed from Britain, though, once more, individual discoveries and inventions were also made by Frenchmen and others.

Repetition of this kind of list for each country would be tedious. Suffice it to say that the direct British influence on Belgian technology was a good deal stronger than that on the leading French regions, including the Paris region, while that on the main German centres was weaker, partly because their development was longer delayed, and some of their technology came indirectly via the other continental centres. The Swiss, also, took the technology of their leading industries, cotton and engineering, from Britain, though again not without adding some inventions of their own.

We have seen[11] that continental industry followed the path of the British in modernization with some considerable delay only. This delay varied as between industries and sectors; it was much extended during the wars and the blockade of the French revolutionary and Napoleonic wars, and sometimes lengthened even further in the years of peace that followed. It was only in the 1860s that the gap began to be closed. The Bessemer process, for example, first announced in 1856 and finally proved successfully in practice in Britain in 1859-60 reached all major continental centres within less than ten years.

There were several reasons for this lag, but among them the purely technical figured very largely. The first trial of a new machine or a new process, even when using British equipment or British specialists, almost invariably failed, even though it might have been operating in Britain for a generation or more—the extreme example, perhaps, is coke-smelting, started up at Le Creusot by William Wilkinson, a leading British ironmaster in 1785, about seventy-five years after the first successful experiments and over forty years after its widespread adoption in Britain; it failed, and it was over thirty years before it was tried again in France, even in areas where costs were favourable. Textile machinery failed with monotonous regularity at first trial, and again many years might elapse before another trial would be attempted, and a further delay would occur before the new had firmly taken root. Behind every failure to pursue the innovation with vigour might be uncertainties about markets, or less than wholly favourable factor prices, but there can be no doubt about the repeated early failures on purely technical grounds of machinery and processes long since established in Britain.

A good example was the Boulton and Watt steam-engine, diffusion of which was more rapid than most since the innovation was rather spectacular and therefore widely known as well as likely to be bought as a prestige object. Yet even here it has been possible to identify a three-phase sequence of delay in its acceptance abroad. In the first phase, a single engine would be bought, with no noticeable effects on its region. In the second, after several had been installed, there would be a more sustained interest, and the attempt be made to build engines locally, possible with British help. Only in the third was enough knowledge assimilated locally for successful engine building. In France, that stage could be said to have been reached by 1815, or, say, thirty-five years after Britain; in Belgium and 'Germany' (apparently Upper Silesia, Berlin, and the Rhineland) in 1820; and in 'Russia' which may be taken to mean a small region around St. Petersburg, in 1825.[12] The delay in absorbing the new technology fully and being able to do without foreign help altogether would vary, other things being equal, with the general developmental gap. Inner Europe was able to emancipate itself in a few decades; in countries like Russia, where there was no native groundwork to build on, foreign machinery-makers had monopolies or nearly so, and dependence on them continued for generations.[13]

Part of the delay in our example of the Boulton and Watt engine was possibly caused by lack of demand, and as long as there were imported engines, supplied directly by Britain, the technological learning problem did not arise. But some of the delay, especially the attempts to copy in stage two, was caused by technical problems of imitation. Wherein lay the difficulty?

Several observers have pointed to the manual skill and practical experience as the most obvious lack in the imitating regions.[14] That is the kind of skill which cannot be learnt out of books, nor even absorbed in a brief visit of inspection: the final filing of machine parts, the recognition, in a moving piece of equipment, where the tension is too great or the play too loose, the almost instinctive knowledge when the wind is right for blowing in a furnace, or when the molten metal is ready for tapping. Even a skilled and experienced man might be lost abroad, for details which he had taken for granted at home, such as quality of ores or metals, or measurements, might be different and he would lack experience to deal with them, and the collaboration of other specialists might be missing.

This particular delay was therefore limited to a particular and unique phase in technological history in a particular environment. It belonged to the phase when new methods were complex enough to exceed the experience and reach of a single craftsman, and needed the collaboration of capital goods and of other skills, but had not yet reached the level (achieved when later industrializers came to that stage) when the technology could be systematized and transmitted in the abstract, without the personal experience of human agents, and when a viable and flexible engineering industry could produce a replica of any model put before it. Such an industry, in turn, could arise only as the result of the development of mechanization, and that point was to be reached in several regions in the 1860s. By then, technology could often be diffused faster across national boundaries than within them.[15] Here, then, lay the key role of a mature engineering industry and of a systematic applied science and technology in the process of imitative industrialization. They play a part different from that required in the pioneer country, but a fundamental part none the less. In that particular phase of European industrialization they made the difference between some disjointed beginnings, and a regional industrial revolution.

Population Increase and Migration of Labour

The industrialization of Europe, like that of Britain, took place against a background of a population increase at a rate for which there seems to be no historical parallel. Certainly, if we were to extrapolate backwards the growth-rates observed after 1650 or 1750, we would quickly reach an impossibly small population for the Contintent. Unless, therefore, large numbers of the pre-industrial population were wiped out by repeated disasters rather than by occasional ones for which there is some evidence, the rate of population growth accompanying industrialization represented something new in European history.

The following table represents a fair consensus of current estimates of the population of Europe (in millions).[16]

		Approx. annual rate of increase, %
c. 1650:	100	—
c. 1750:	156*	0.44
1800:	205	0.54
1850:	275	0.59
1870:	320	0.76
1900:	414	0.86
1913:	481	1.16

* Including Asiatic Russia.

The rate of growth was not only high, it was also rising over the critical period, while a high and rising rate of emigration was maintained at the same time. These rates were of the order of magnitude familiar in under-developed countries today, but considerably higher than those obtaining at the time in the non-European world outside the areas of European settlement.[17]

It is tempting to bring the population increase into some relationship with the transformation of the European economy. It can be done without difficulty, by treating population increase either as cause or as effect, or as both, if we limit ourselves to a single country. Applied to Europe as a whole, however, the problem is that the increase seems to have occurred everywhere, including regions of very different ecological conditions and at very different stages in their industrial evolution. Thus increases of around 30–50% between *c.* 1750 and 1800 were registered for Great Britain, France, Belgium, and Holland, among the most advanced countries of their day; they were found in Ireland and Germany plus Austria, which were agrarian economies with some advanced sectors; they occurred in Hungary, Norway, and Sweden, which were basically food and raw material producers; and, finally, they were not dissimilar in Russia, the most backward region in Europe. Even the countries outside those limits, Finland (with rates higher than the 'norm'), and Italy, Portugal, and Spain (lower than the norm) were not too far away, given the uncertainties of the statistics.[18]

One explanation which might embrace all these different milieux might be that there was a secular decline in the virulence of certain killer diseases.[19] While this would be a wholly exogenous and accidental factor from the point of view of industrialization, it could be combined with greater social control, to contain the spread of epidemics, and to level out the ill effects of poor harvests which had been among the most significant causes of death by weakening the resistance to diseases among the undernourished population. This appears to be the view of M. W. Flinn and possibly also of H. J. Habakkuk, who stressed in particular the success of Europe in cutting out the declining phases of the see-saw by which population had been kept stable, and thus setting up a movement going one way only.[20]

Explanations of this kind assume that the falling death-rate was the decisive variable, and that the population rise was a consequence of changes in the economy and in society. It has, however, also been argued that the operative variable was a rising birth-rate, caused by earlier marriages and/or a decline in contraceptive measures, and theories are not lacking which see the population change as a cause, rather than a consequence, of economic change.[21]

Clearly, if purely biological explanations are to be ruled out, and social and economic factors brought into the picture, then no single mechanism can have been operative for the whole of Europe. Demographic movements belong to the numerous social tendencies the effect of which differ greatly, according to which stage in economic development society has reached—as those who have observed the present medical revolution, which has led to a slowing-down of population increase in the West, but a population explosion in poorer countries , have good reason to know. The apparently similar over-all rates of population increase in nineteenth-century Europe[22] hide great variations among economic regions and the stage of development they reached in relation to the rest of the European economy,[23] and, the national figures are, as ever, averages which may be misleading. Where one type of economy predominates, such as peasant proprietorship with a small urban sector, balanced by the capital city which, typically, cannot reproduce itself but absorbs much of the nation's national increase, total growth will be low, and that was the position of Holland in the eighteenth century and France in the nineteenth. The French experience caused much comment, and gave rise to many theories relating to national character, but in fact there were other important regions with similar demographic characteristics, like the German Münsterland; there were also regions whose population stagnation, though superficially similar, had quite different causes, such as Ireland.[24]

There have been purely agrarian societies which have been among the fastest growers in Europe.[25] Typically, their populations expand without coming up against a natural barrier either because empty land allows them to expand extensively, or because new techniques allow more intensive cultivation. There might be reduction of the fallow, the substitution of labour-intensive crops, or switching from animal husbandry to tillage. Proto-industrial development, as we have seen above,[26] can absorb much labour in a rural setting without burdening the agrarian sector unduly,[27] while modern factory industry, collected in ever larger conurbations and supplied by improved means of transport from an ever increasing hinterland, can absorb additional population to a practically unlimited extent. It should also be stressed that a high rate of growth is compatible with both high and low birth- and death-rates: thus the Italian North and the Italian South had very similar rates of increase in 1895, 9.5 as against 8.2. But the North achieved it with a death-rate of 23.7 and a birth-rate of 33.2, while the South had rates of 29.0 and 37.2 respectively.[28]

The complex reality behind a national average may best be illustrated by the case of Prussia/Germany. Most German lands had registered a fast rise after 1650, making up for the devastating losses of the Thirty Years War in less than three generations, the approximate figures being:

1620 : 16 million
1650 : 10 million
1740 : 18 million

Prussia grew at about the average rate and between 1740 and 1805 expanded further from 3.2 million to 5.7 million (on the extended territory of 1748), or by 8.9‰ a year. But in the eastern provinces both birth- and death-rates were higher than in the central provinces, and these in turn were higher than in the industrial and small-farm western provinces. Prussia as a whole gained by the imigration of some 300,000 settlers in this second phase, who with their descendents amounted to one-third of the total population at the end of the reign of Frederick the Great (1786) and thus gave the country a higher than average growth-rate. Württemberg, a typical agrarian, small-farm land, grew at about the average rate, while Saxony, heavily industrialized, grew at a rate below the average.[29] In 1816–19, with its death-rate at 29.4‰ and a birth-rate of 44.3‰, Prussia had the demographic structure of a typical under-developed country. The natural growth figure remained high until about 1870, then declined steadily in what was again the typical demographic transition.[30] However, even this figure hides the fact that the Prussian agricultural East had high birth-, death- and natural reproduction-rates, the West had lower birth- and death-rates, but high reproduction-rates, whilst Saxony had lower increases and the agricultural South-West of Germany also grew more slowly. The Prussian East still had empty spaces, but much of the rest of Germany (except for the industrial regions) was fully settled at existing technology, and the continuing rise of population thus came up against a Malthusian over-population barrier. The crisis came, as in Ireland and Holland, with the potato blight and the bad harvests of 1845–7, and led to massive emigration from the small-farm areas of Germany. In Württemberg, Baden, and Hesse, the population actually declined in absolute numbers.[31] It was only the subsequent industrialization, especially of the Ruhr-Rhineland area, as well as the continuing growth of Berlin, which allowed Germany as a whole to escape the Irish fate. Similar regional variations in population increase may be observed elsewhere, e.g. in France and Sweden.[32]

It is against the background of a rising population, expanding everywhere even if at differing rates, but finding economies very differently equipped to receive them, that the major migration movements have to be seen. They were one important way of adjusting the labour factor to the other more immobile factors, such as land and regional industry, over Europe as a whole. There was the usual friction, varying with distance,[33] and misleading Adam Smith into his famous dictum that men were of all 'sorts of luggage the most difficult to be transported';[34] but the frontier was, at most, a minor obstacle to such movements. In the eighteenth century, when labour was considered an asset by mercantilist absolute rulers, they aided these migrations by widely publicised concessions to immigrants, but the crowned heads of Russia and Austria, Prussia or Saxony would have had little success had they not operated with the economic logic of empty lands or idle resources, waiting to absorb the surplus population from other parts of Europe.

It is not always easy to distinguish between the move of individual experts, and the move of large enough numbers of them to qualify as labour migration. The flood of Huguenots, and of the stream of skilled workers, with their families, attracted by Frederick the Great into Prussia, helped to spread new industry, but also amounted to a significant shift in the labour-supply curve. Many of those 300,000 who moved to Prussia were agricultural settlers, filling the empty and depopulated north-eastern provinces. Russia, under the Empress Catherine II, attracted Germans, Romanians, Bulgars, Czechs. To Hungary came Croats, Serbs, Slovaks, even Germans, to the number of 100,000. Poland received Little and White Russians, Jews, Lithuanians, Germans. Among the chief losers were parts of Germany and Switzerland whose emigrants included many mercenaries, and the Slavonic fringe areas. Saxony was the main loser of skilled industrial workers (apart from France which had expelled her protestants) to Silesia, other parts of Prussia, and Austria. Many skilled emigrants also left Bohemia in the eighteenth century.[35]

The character of migration changed in the first half of the nineteenth century. There were few empty territories left, apart from the eastern fringes of Russia,[36] to attract mass migrants, and rulers who wanted to build up advanced levels of industry had to import prototypes of machines rather than skilled handicraft workers. Migration was therefore less spectacular and it extended over shorter distances. Men moved into the industrial territories, like Alsace, the French North, Saxony, the Rhineland, or the textile towns of Northern Italy, and they flocked into the capital cities.[37] But this could not absorb the total population increase which began to build up in the countryside, and the food crisis of the mid-forties exploded the accumulated pressure in a wave of hunger and overseas emigration from South-West Germany, Ireland, Scotland, and, a little later, from Scandinavia. Two and a half millions left Germany between 1815 and 1870.[38] From 1861–90, Germans and citizens of Austria–Hungary emigrated in large numbers to Russia as well as to North and South America.[39]

The mechanism was a disequilibrium between a population increase which seemed to draw its power from technical means developed outside these backward economies, and the inability of those economies to absorb the resulting additional people at existing prices (determined by the advanced economy), techniques, and home capital supplies. A similar imbalance developed in the periphery of Europe in the next phase, beginning in the 1890s. Though the world was a different place by then, the same safety-valve, emigration, was still open until 1914, though not after 1920.[40] In Inner Europe, meanwhile, competitive modern industry had been built up, eager to absorb much of the increased population and to draw it from a wide area into the industrial regions. The most dramatic of these movements was that to the Ruhr. There had been some moderate immigration there in the growth phase to 1873, mostly from nearby areas. The explosive growth beginning in the 1880s exceeded the capacity of even the regional population, and coincided with a phase of development in which the landless agricultural workers and others in East Elbia felt their exploitation and deprivation of civic rights harder than before because of improvements elsewhere in Germany. Whereas in mid-century it was Western Germany that appeared over-populated, towards its end it was the eastern provinces. A mass migration set in by German-speaking as well as Slavonic-speaking, Polish and Masuric workers, joined by others from the Habsburg Empire. At least 230–240,000 East Prussians arrived, together with 58,000 Masures and 200–250,000 Poles. In the cities to be settled last, the proportion of eastern migrants was particularly high. Thus in Gelsenkirchen in 1907, 61.4% were immigrants, of whom 32.9% were from a distance and 67.3% of these (or 22% of the total) from Eastern Germany. One in three of the schoolchildren there spoke Polish in 1890.[41] In the last years before the war there was increased long-distance migration also into the industrial regions of Saxony and Upper Silesia, where 'distance was more important than national frontiers'.[42]

The Export of Capital

Whereas the mass migration of labour across Europe reached its peak in the eighteenth century, to be reduced in scope in the first half of the nineteenth and to re-emerge in a different form in the second half, capital exports in the modern sense on a large scale made their beginning only in the nineteenth century with the onset of industrialization. Before that, typical foreign loans were in the form of trading ventures or government papers: a large proportion even of the British public debt was held by the Dutch up to 1780.[43]

The characteristic form in the period of industrialization was the fixed investment in public utilities, principally railways, but also in docks, tramways, and gas, water and electricity works, but investment in industrial and mining enterprises, in government stock, banking and insurance companies, and even in estates and plantations was not unknown. There were two developments very largely responsible for this new phenomenon. The first was the set of technical innovations which made large initial investments in fixed capital, and further investments to keep it going, necessary, and profitable. The second was the unevenness of development, the coexistence of similar demands among countries in different stages of development, while the capital to meet them was available in the more advanced regions only.

Capital was the quintessence of property ownership in the rising economic system, and claims on capital were the most generalized form of that property, and the most mobile. If adequate profits beckoned, then irrespective of the level reached by the society concerned, or its form of government, capital would flow there as easily across frontiers as within them. Europe was a set of interconnecting vessels, and 'capital export is a means of levelling out national rates of profit'.[44] This image of liquid levelling out, here used by a critic, was widespread also among the staunchest defenders of the system: 'The Turks', rhapsodized the *Times*, 'have a fine territory, and no money, energy, or skill; we have all three, and they pour into Turkey as naturally as water finds its own level.'[45]

In the case of railways, as we have seen, it was largely the quest for political prestige and strategic advantage that prompted governments to support the building of lines ahead of demand, and they, together with docks and other associated works, formed one main target for productive investments abroad. Another was the public utility. The motive was basically the 'demonstration effect', that most potent mechanism released by the contemporaneousness of different societies. Here, as in the case of many other consumer goods, the facility might be outwardly similar as in the advanced economy and make similar profits, though used and afforded by a much smaller section of the community. Thus around the mid-nineteenth century, British gas companies supplied Amsterdam, Rotterdam, Ghent, Cologne, Tours, and Karlsruhe, as well as Rome, Constantinople, and Christiania. British-owned gas companies with seats abroad supplied additionally about twenty towns in France, Germany, and Austria at the same time.[46] A third target for investment was the development of national resources such as minerals. These products might well then be produced for export, at least in the first instance, and investment would thus partake of the character of a colonial relationship.

In the later eighteenth century, when loans had largely gone to governments, they had been negotiated through solid banking-houses in Amsterdam, London, and certain German and Swiss cities. Since the subscribers came from a small and well-informed wealthy class, they took great care to lend to sound governments only. When the uneven development of industrialization opened up the possibility of foreign investment in the kind of productive enterprises with which we are mostly concerned here, the existing banks were overwhelmed by the quantity and variety of purpose of these capital flows, and new types of banks and company structures arose to fill the gaps.[47] But once these mechanisms of channelling capital abroad were set up, they could easily take on a life of their own. The floating of loans was highly profitable to the promoters, irrespective of the merits of the issue, and their eager offer of funds met the inexhaustible demand from spendthrift, incompetent, and corrupt governments overseas, but also in the Balkan peninsula, including the Turkish Empire.[48] In the lending to governments which now developed and accompanied the lending for productive purposes, papers were taken up by groups that were far more numerous, and more gullible, and it was an altogether very different traffic, for different purposes, from that of intra-European government loans of the eighteenth and earlier nineteenth centuries. One of the significant factors was now frequently the weakness of the recipient governments. Working on the 'principle that the fruits of capitalism invested in so-called backward countries must, if native agencies provide inadequate security, be protected by European-constituted agencies',[49] political intervention ensued, and led to conflicts which belong to a later chapter.[50]

The first important capital flows derived from industrialization related to railways. At the beginning it was the British who financed railways abroad, in America as well as in Europe. The first important French railways, including the lines to Le Havre and Dieppe, to Orleans and the West, the Nord, and several Ardennes lines, owed much of their capital to the British, and so did the first Belgian network of the 1830s, built by the government, and the second of the 1840s, built almost exclusively by British private companies, as well as the early Dutch railways. The peak of this development was reached in the crisis of 1847–8, when allegedly half the French railway capital was in British hands,[51] but, significantly, British interests then turned away towards overseas areas, keeping some stakes only in the peripheral areas like Russia, Italy, and Turkey. Inner Europe was left to the other early industrializers in a manner that reflected both geographical logic and the rising competitive powers of the Continent.

France had received not only British capital for her early railways, but was also the recipient of more traditional foreign capital wherever she had heavy local concentrations of industry: Geneva invested in Lyons, Bâle in Alsace, and Belgium in the Nord.[52] From the mid-century, however, the flow reversed. Massive quantities of French capital flowed outwards while meanwhile also building up a railway system, urban developments, and other costly capital projects at home. The story of the battle over railway, banking, and other concessions, between the older Haute Banque, led by the Paris Rothschilds, and the newer investment banks, led by the Péreire Brothers of the Crédit Mobilier (1852–67), has often been told.[53] Indeed, fierce battles for concessions, control, and strategic advantage, as well as for income and interest guarantees involving the political authority in each country, were an essential part of the build-up of economic assets which had such strong political links, but the end result was that a modern transport network was created, covering the whole of the Continent, in which French investments[54] loom almost unbelievably large. The well-known map in Cameron's study shows the German Empire, Holland, and the Scandinavian kingdoms as the only countries in which French capital played no significant part. French capital did, however, go into the Ruhr mining and other works.[55]

The question whether Frenchmen invested too much abroad, in the sense of weakening the industry of their own country, has been raised from time to time,[56] as in the parallel British case. The particular role of France as the financier of Europe in the period *c.*1850–1914 may indeed be a reflection of the different course taken by 'French' industrialization, concentrated as it was in a few peripheral and poorly integrated regions, and badly balanced between a relatively high income yet a dearth of 'modern' capital-intensive industries. Yet, before the 1870s at least, such an approach would have made little sense to the investors looking for maximum economic returns, and guided by banks that might have their seats in Paris, London, or Frankfurt, but were in every other sense international.

Belgium, the recipient of generous supplies of capital from Britain, France,[57] and King William I of Holland also turned into a capital exporter herself without much delay. Her investment at first spilled over the frontiers into the heavy industries and railways of the neighbouring French North and the German Rhineland, but also found its way into Spain, Italy, Poland, and Russia, for similar purposes.[58] Swiss investment, as we have seen, went mainly into the industries of France as well as South-Western Germany and Northern Italy.[59]

Germany, by contrast, was relatively self-contained during the period of industrialization. There had been some tradition of support for industrial concentrations by banking-houses from a distance, as in the case of Berg and Mark industries financed from Cologne.[60] Foreign capital also flowed into Rhenish–Westphalian mining and metallurgy in periods of rapid early growth. But German railways were mainly financed within Germany and, up to the 1870s at least, little German capital flowed outward to foreign railways apart from Austria and Russia. At the critical time of the 'take-off', German investment banks developed to channel the plentifully available savings into industry, some building on native inspiration, like the Schaaffhausensche Bankverein (1848), and others, like the Darmstädter (1853) and the Berlin Discontongesellschaft (1851, reorganized 1856), influenced by the Crédit Mobilier. This form of banking became a characteristic feature of German industrialization, aiding both its speed of progress and its early tendency to form cartels and suppress competition.[61]

With the rise of German economic power there also came an expansion in capital exports. By 1914, there were major German holdings in Austria-Hungary, the Balkans, Russia, and Turkey (as well as overseas), and Germany, catching up the two leading capital exporters, Britain and France, overall had taken second position in Europe. A recent revised estimate put the relative position of foreign-owned capital in Europe and in the world as follows in Table 4.2 (milliard francs).[62]

Table 4.2.

	In Europe	Total	% in Europe
France	4.7	9.05	51.9
Germany	2.55	5.8	44.0
UK	1.05	20.0	5.2
USA	0.7	3.5	20.0
All other	3.0	7.1	—
	12.0	45.45	26.4

After the watershed of the 1870s, foreign capital played a diminishing role inside Inner Europe itself, but it spilled over into the peripheral countries, in a second wave-like movement. The gap in technology and incomes being larger there, foreign capital carried a more significant weight in industrialization, and remained longer before being repatriated. Scandinavia, Austria, and Italy[63] occupy an intermediate position here, Russia, and beyond her, Turkey, forming the extremes. In a clear reflexion of the way in which industrialization advanced across the Continent, the peripheral countries, while still heavily dependent on capital from the more advanced creditor nations, themselves began to send capital abroad for the development of their own peripheral neighbours who were even less developed. Thus Austria invested in the Balkans, Italy exported capital to the Balkans and to

Anatolian Turkey, and even Russia invested in Turkey and in her Asiatic neighbours.[64]

Foreign capital played a particularly significant part in the industrialization of Russia. This is not surprising if we recall that 'Russia', as a political entity, included some concentrated and potentially rich, but late developing industrial regions, weighed down by a vast and extremely poor and backward agrarian sector, as well as by high transport costs caused by huge distances and severe seasonal variations in the weather. There was thus need for an expensive infrastructure, beyond the means of the local economy, if any development were to take place, and there were all the assets of a large and powerful state to guarantee the interest on investments in relatively small sectors of it.

Foreign investment in Russia occurred in two main waves. The first was largely concerned with railway capital and (after earlier beginnings) reached its peak in the 1860s. The lines constructed then had their main justification in strategic and prestige reasons, they remained economic enclaves, and foreign investors required government privileges, interest guarantees, and/or direct Russian government participation in debenture capital before they would venture their capital. There was some investment in other industry also, the activities of Ludwig Knoop, selling Lancashire cotton machinery to new mills against part payment in shares being perhaps the most remarkable.[65]

The second wave began in the 1890s, strongly encouraged by the Prime Minister, Count Vitte, and continued, with interruptions, until the early years of the First World War. In these years the share of foreign capital in total company capital actually increased. It was much more comprehensive, covering, beside railways, also mining, metallurgy, and engineering, oil, textiles, public utilities, as well as banks and other financial institutions. Although there was some direct investment, foreigners still preferred shares or debentures guaranteed by the state, or investment through banks which also had a state guarantee. In 1914, they held 46.6% of the public debt, and in 1916, 45% of the capital of the ten largest joint-stock banks.[66] For 1916–17, the share of foreign capital (without counting indirect bank capital) has been estimated at 90% in mining, 50% in chemicals, 42% in metal-smelting and processing, and 2.8% in textiles.[67]

The French, who held much the largest share of Russian government paper, also led in industiral holdings, with 32.6%, followed by Britain (22.6%), Germany (19.7%), and Belgium (14.3%). Originally, Germany had held the lion's share, but in 1886–7 Germany attempted to exert pressure on the Russian government by a drive against her foreign credit and, in a well-known episode, Russian political attachment switched, with her funds, to France.[68] While capital (unlike other items) still moved as freely across Europe after the 1870s as before, it had now become entangled with higher diplomacy.

The Role of Government

Much has been written not least by government agencies themselves, about the contribution of governments in the first phase of industrialization c.1815–1870s, but little of it will bear close examination. The issue which has roused considerable emotions in the past, has turned out to be more complex than was at one time believed.

The State's most positive contributions were often rendered by small, inconspicuous actions, such as the holding of industrial exhibitions or the founding of technical colleges, like the Berlin Gewerbeschule of 1821, though it should be remembered that Britain had the poorest public provision of schooling in the West, which did not become universal until the 1870s, and the best industrial record, while the record of countries with good schools, like Prussia and Scandinavia, was far less impressive. The state also helped by providing a framework of law, 'internal peace and external security' (including the suppression of trade-union and democratic movements), within which private investment was encouraged.[69]

Among the other beneficial lines of action, the abolition or repeal of damaging restrictions by which earlier rulers had held up the drive to industrialization were of particular significance. The bulk of these regulations, on guilds, privileges, or standards, had been positive when first enacted, but, being designed to hold and stabilize certain achievements, proved unable to absorb rapid and fundamental changes. The abolition of these, as well as of internal tolls and staple rights,[70] and of restrictions on acquiring certain types of property or entering certain occupations, worked in the same direction. Tariff protection is an entirely different matter, and will be discussed in the next section, but it is worth noting here that in many cases imports of raw materials and semi-manufactures were taxed as highly as those of finished goods, and that taxes on exports were also quite common. Both these were likely to have had negative effects on industrialization.

The introduction of unified and internally more consistent commercial legislation, particularly that contained in the Code Napoléon, symbolized this positive contribution of governments to economic progress. To this must be added the unification movements of Germany and Italy which created large internally free markets. These, it is important to stress, had quite different basic aims, the economic benefits being incidental by-products. Even the German Zollverein, which turned out to be a step on the way to a large unified Empire had originally purely administrative and fiscal objectives,[71] and it was some time before its potential for the aggrandizement of Prussia was discovered. Italian unification did not, at first, lead to industrialization. In general, however industrialization in Inner Europe was distinctly favoured and eased by the fact that so many of the contemporary political movements happened to work in the same direction, as part of the secular movement of bourgeois emancipation which accompanied the spread of capitalism. By the same token, the cost was heavy when the two movements began to pull in different directions after the 1870s. Even in this favourable period before the watershed, however, the spirit of nationalism had not always positive effects: it destroyed the larger economic unity of the Netherlands, which had made excellent economic sense, for the sake of Belgian independence in 1830.[72] It was typically ironic for movements of this kind that the Belgians, who had clamoured for protection when under Dutch rule and had made Dutch-imposed free trade (or rather, the compromise of moderate protection) a major complaint, themselves turned to that free trade which they had so bitterly opposed before, a few years later, when their economic efficiency had become more evident.

Inevitably, railways loom large in the state's role in industrialization, since at the least, all lines had to have concessions to get compulsory rights of purchase and some guarantee against duplication, and many had to have privileges and subsidies of one kind or another in addition. The record here is mixed. It is best in Belgium, where an early plan was made and carried out in the 1830s, followed by private licensing in the 1840s. Belgium was a railway builder's paradise, and the ease with which the secondary system was constructed by private capital makes it scarcely credible that there would have been any problem had the state kept out of the more obvious primary system also. Certainly, the state charged commercial rates for its infrastructure.[73] In France the issue is more clear-cut. The log-rolling of politicians delayed the start of serious building by some crucial years, to 1842. The system of finance, as evolved over the century, seemed to guarantee the maximum costs to the State with the maximum secure benefits to shareholders, as well as the greatest possible diversion of lines for political reasons (*'lignes électorales'*) against economic sense. Inevitably, lines were built first where they were wanted even under the French system, but sections of the planned network which tapped regions without adequate traffic tied up valuable capital that could have done better elsewhere and meanwhile had to be serviced out of taxes.[74] Against this, the false decisions of a free system like the contemporary British one seem a very small price to pay.

In Germany, the matter has been studied in some detail. The judgement appears to be that under political direction, lines were often wrongly located from the point of view of the later complete network. As late as 1830, Prussian officialdom quashed the idea of a steam railway in the Ruhr, and the first important line in the area, the Cologne–Minden, was a model of bad planning. Farther east, the Prussian railways ran parallel to the Saxon frontier for long stretches, in order to try and freeze out the more successful rival industries across the border. Under state direction, lines followed the wrong freight-rate policy, and they lacked safety and security. While some of their capital came from the government, it was largely raised from the middle classes in the first place, who would presumably have found the money directly for the railways themselves.[75] In the European periphery, state insistence on building lines 'too early' diverted resources, and burdened the economy and the budget by interest and amortization payments for many years, out of other incomes, which these societies could ill afford,[76] until, possibly much later, they got over the hump of industrialization.

It was the direct support for certain manufactures that has frequently been claimed as the main contribution of governments to industrialization but in retrospect it turned out to have been the least useful. The principle goes back to Colbert, who burdened France with a great array of uneconomic enterprises, many set up merely for prestige reasons or to pander to the luxuries of the Court, but forming a steady drain on the taxpayer. Some potentially able entrepreneurs were trained by the system to ignore costs and markets, and to concentrate on the skills of extracting subsidies from officials rather than on mastering new technologies. Above all, the system stifled initiative, a key factor in the then phase of economic development. The French system was duly adopted by other rulers who could afford it even less, including those of Spain, Russia, Austria and the Austrian Netherlands, Scandinavia and the German and Italian states:[77] the smaller the Court, the greater the chance of corruption and favouritism to add to the waste. Some industries of future significance emerged from the system, but at enormous cost to the taxpaying classes, precisely those who were eager to invest their money themselves. The only countries which did not copy Colbert were Britain and Holland, the most successful economies of the eighteenth century.

Such judgements do not come easily to the twentieth century, which relies so much on the state apparatus to counteract a large range of harmful effects of private enterprise in industry. In the late eighteenth and most of the nineteenth century, matters were very different. Private enterprise was small, flexible, variegated, and responsible in the sense that managers administered their own property. The state apparatus was weak, incompetent, corrupt, or representative of certain sectional interests rather than being administered by a 'neutral' civil service. In every country there were powerful political forces opposing industrialization altogether.[78] Moreover, measures pretended for the national interest were in fact commonly favouring one sector at the expense of greatly harming another.[79] It really did occur that the Duchy of Berg gave its pioneer cotton spinner a twelve year monopoly, thus preventing other mills from being set up; that Spain taxed coal in the 1840s making its ironworks revert to charcoal; that the Austrian tax system favoured small firms and inhibited enterprise, that Prussian officials held back the modernization of the Ruhr and opposed machinery elsewhere, and that it proved impossible to secure the freedom of the Rhine navigation decreed by the Vienna Congress over many years because of political squabbles, until the railways forced a major reappraisal.[80] Industries did best, it has often been observed, where states were too small[81] to have mercantilist ambitions: Switzerland, one of the most successful early industrializers in spite of all the odds, had practically no government until 1848. Within Germany, Saxony, the most successful industrializer, had ceased early on to 'encourage' industry.[82]

France herself suffered much from her Colbertian heritage, even in the nineteenth century. Only twenty to twenty-five persons decided on basic economic questions, complained one of the Péreires, and they were often wrong, they favoured vested interests, or copied foreign methods unsuitable to French markets or factor prices. The most thorough-going study of the French economy in the first half of the century came to the conclusion that the French state, 'opposed progress': 'what was necessary, in sum, was to neutralise the State'.[83] Even in Napoleon's day, when France had supreme political power, economic direction to make France the industrial supplier of Europe led either to the strengthening of industry in the periphery, as in Belgium or the Rhineland, at the expense of the French heartland, or it drove the industrialists excluded from the French markets to push the French out of other markets in exchange.[84] Napoleon's plan to plant 32,000 hectares of sugar-beet in 1811 must stand as proxy for all such efforts:

There was not enough seed, in some places none at all, no account was taken of the nature of the soil, the order to plant sugar-beet came too late in the season, the farmers did not know what kind of beet to sow and did not dare to weed the crop for fear of not recognizing it. . .Transport facilities to the factories were lacking. and the farmers were often stranded with their beet, or else it arrived rotten at the factories. There were too few factories to deal with the harvest. The yield of sugar was only 2% of the weight of beets, and its taste was disagreeable. In the end the area planted in the whole Empire in 1811 was only 6,785 hectares.[85]

The efforts of Prussia, and particularly of Frederick the Great, have had a better press than the French. The foundations of this were laid by nationalistic German historians who set out to read back into an earlier Prussia the economic successes of the Empire after 1871, and it has not always proved easy to be sufficiently critical of them.[86] Thus on the much-praised and much-discussed programme of support for industry. Frederick spent 60,000 thaler a year, compared with 12–13 million thaler a year on his army, and 22 million on his palace at Potsdam. Moreover two-thirds of that tiny industrial support went on the pet silk industry which had no significance for economic progress. To support these schemes, the Prussian king deliberately disadvantaged the western provinces and in some respects treated them worse than foreign countries; he attempted to freeze out Saxony, and kill the Leipzig Fair. Yet Saxony and the Rhineland flourished, and Berlin-Brandenburg did not.[87]

In the nineteenth century the record was better. The Prussian *Seehandlung* under Rother's control in particular, has been praised as an active industrial bank. Yet even that supported mostly schemes favouring the nobility and was viewed with misgivings by many industrialists; most of the units which it backed failed to make ends meet, and in 1845 it was formally excluded from further participation by industry.[88] By contrast, the handling of private-enterprise banks by Prussian officialdom has been widely judged to have been obtuse, ham-fisted, and inimical to progress.[89]

It may be granted that the successor countries, having a longer leap to take, and having to copy rather than innovate, provided logically greater scope for governmental action than Britain as pioneer.[90] Bureaucracies, after all, are better at following well-trodden paths than at taking risks by striking out on their own. But while they had the advantage of hindsight and of avoiding the mistakes made by the pioneer, such as pursuing dead-end lines or starting at the wrong scale,[91] they equally frequently forgot that they were not the pioneer, and that circumstances, factor prices, and markets in their case, were different. Moreover, we have looked at the best Civil Services, the French and the Prussian. Others had a worse record. What is often forgotten is that the occasional good done by the state, in subsidizing a successful mill here or equipping an industrial spy there, has to be set against the enormous costs and the diversion of resources[92] of its useless or harmful forms of intervention.

Altogether, the role of the state in industrialization has often been overrated.[93] Its most useful contributions were generally made unconsciously, while pursuing other aims such as power or a taxable surplus; its most negative actions were frequently those that were intended to aid industrialization.

Trade and Industrialization

We have left one range of governmental activity on one side for separate treatment: that relating to foreign trade. In our phase of history, it was the most hotly debated of all economic policy issues.

There has been much misunderstanding, and much mystification, on the function and significance of trade. A great deal of trade goes on, between villages, between towns and between regions, and it differs in no fundamental respect from 'foreign' trade. The trade so widely and earnestly discussed and captured in the official statistics is thus an arbitrarily separated-out part of a complex exchange network. It may therefore give us a one-sided and distorted picture of an economy and its trading; its structure depends essentially on where the frontier is.[94] Now frontiers shifted a good deal in our period, and disappeared altogether within Germany and within Italy after the unification of these countries. Thereupon, what were formerly, say, Saxon 'exports' to Prussia suddenly disappeared from all trade statistics, though nothing might have changed in reality.

There is a second source of misunderstanding, of particular danger to those trained in modern economics. Neo-classical theory teaches that 'at the margin' things can easily be exchanged for each other: a country short of some pig iron, say, can easily sell some of its own products somewhere, and buy pig iron from a willing seller at market prices. While this is true at the margin, theory very often fails to note that it is not necessarily true where the bulk is concerned. A shortfall of some iron is a very different matter from lacking an iron industry altogether, as far as the industrialization of a region or a country is concerned. As we proceed from the margin to cover more and more of a supply, sooner or later quantity changes into quality, and what was merely one of many objects of exchange may become a determinant of the nature and structure of an economy.

This may be put differently. In some trade relationships, goods of nearly identical nature are exchanged: Marshall termed them 'cross trades': 'The exportation of goods that are very nearly alike in opposite directions on the same line of travel.'[95] Experts will know the difference between them, and some consumers will feel deprived if they fail to obtain precisely the quality and style they wish from the other country and are fobbed off with the home product instead. Nevertheless, it could not be maintained that to cut off the trade in those commodities will inflict serious hardship, or make a noticeable difference to real national income. Other goods are less perfect substitutes: woollen against cotton goods, perhaps. To deprive a population of one or the other by interrupting trade would cause greater hardship to consumers; to make at home the goods formerly imported, would raise their unit costs considerably. Yet these losses would still be quite tolerable. So we may go on, differentiating more and more, until we reach the extreme case of an economy exporting, say, manufactured goods and importing in exchange tropical products which it could not produce at any cost, or minerals which it lacks altogether. In that case, the failure to export, or to buy by other means the goods lacking at home would have far-reaching consequences. We are often misled by the fact that logically we can imagine a continuum of substitutability, into thinking that because goods may be and often are in fact substituted at the margin without difficulty, there are no structural effects of trade anywhere. In the spectrum, green runs imperceptibly into blue, and we should be of little use to a painter if we assured him that there was no significant difference between blue and green.

The trade of towns with towns, of industrial regions with industrial regions, of industrial regions with their agricultural hinterlands, and of country with country, is made up of some items that can easily be foregone, and others which are vital for the well-being and progress of the people concerned. This has always been felt instinctively by politicians and industrialists, though it has often implicitly been denied by economists. There is an empirical base to Mercantilist policies to be found in this kind of consideration.

Lucien Febvre captured some of this distinction in his famous introduction to the history of the Seville trade, though the dividing-line ran differently from that of the nineteenth century.[96] There was nothing in common, he thought, between: 'The coastal trade of bulk goods, useful but in no way precious . . . the barter, the modest purchase, the short-haul transport to which it gave rise', and the precious metals from the West, raising a bourgeois class and altering the power-structure of Europe. 'Beside so many great things what is the importance of this local trade, this potluck trade of the sound and its barges, dragging prudently their fat stomachs under foggy skies?'

To some extent the difference between marginal and fundamental trade is a question of time. Substitution may be difficult in the very short run, but it becomes progressively easier, the more time there is for adjustment. For a large enough adjustment, the time span necessary may be that required for what we call industrialization: such 'adjustments' are the stuff history is made of, and are of a different order from the weekly changes in import and export orders following marginal shifts.

Economies in the midst of an industrial revolution, or existing in a continent in which others are at different and changing stages of industrialization, find their trading relationships changing significantly in the process. It is our object to find out how they are modified and what role was played by trade in European industrialization. Economics is of limited help here, for while there exists a vast literature on the economics of foreign trade, it does not appear that these specific relationships have been of much interest to economists. It is not too difficult, however, to derive them from existing international and interregional trade theory.

One root of that theory goes back to Ricardo. In his famous example of the trade between England and Portugal in which England was better at making cloth and Portugal better at growing wine he showed that trade would take place and would benefit both countries. He showed further that this would continue to be so even if one of them was better than the other at providing both commodities, provided that *relative* costs of production within each country were different. This 'comparative cost' doctrine has since then been incorporated in all international trade theories.

Ricardo also introduced the assumption, which again became common to all classical models, that it was the peculiar nature of trade across frontiers that factors, particularly labour, would move within countries but not from one to the other, though it should be noted that Josiah Tucker, writing forty years before Ricardo, had made it a part of his explanation that the best labour *would* move from the poorer to the richer economy. Both Ricardo and Tucker drew attention to better technology as an element in price differences giving rise to trade, a point which has often been neglected since, and both also allowed for differences in natural endowments. They also both came up against the problem that the total price level was higher in the more advanced countries—a problem that was to resurface many times later, at least among those economists who paid some attention to reality, without finding a solution. Tucker, being more realistic than most, concluded rather lamely that the poorer country would indeed always undersell the richer one, if transport were possible.[97] Finally, all the classics, including Adam Smith who as usual hedged his statement with numerous qualifications and exceptions, took it as one of their assumptions that there would be a common wage level within each country.[98]

With Ricardo, therefore, many of the important bricks which entered into all later theories had been assembled, at least for a world in which gold and silver permitted the direct comparison of prices everywhere. Several additions and refinements were made to this classical approach in the course of the next century.

James Mill returned to the bothersome issue of the differing price level, using, significantly, a regional example (London–Wales) as well as a national one (England–Poland) for his illustration. While he also had no explanation for its existence, except for the circular one that the general price level in Wales was lower because more, and more important, commodities enjoyed a price advantage in Wales than those which enjoyed a price advantage in London, he explained its survival also by the costs of transport which prevented a total levelling of prices.[99] James Stuart Mill refined the comparative cost doctrine, and in particular, returned to the view that comparative advantages would cause industries, and labour, to migrate. Such migration would be easy within the country, less easy to neighbouring countries like France, Germany, or Switzerland, and very difficult to Russia, Turkey, or India. Ultimately, (anticipating twentieth-century thought) trade would cause internal shifts to the point at which internal price ratios would have been equalized in each country, except for costs of transport. On the troublesome issue of the price levels, the younger Mill had it both ways. Prices would be higher in an advanced country like England, because English goods were in greater demand abroad than the typical bulky imports were here; but in fact there was no price difference, as Nassau Senior alleged. British prices merely seemed to be higher, because in England it was food and services that were costlier, and they loomed large in people's consciousness; manufactures were cheaper.[100]

In a contemporary contribution which was largely ignored, Longfield argued that on the assumption that wages had to be the same in all industries and that international trade made prices the same everywhere, the export industries would be those in which the productivity of labour was relatively highest and the wage levels of different countries would be proportional to their average labour productivity. There were certain similarities to this also in Nassau Senior's approach.[101]

Marshall added little to the theory, and dealt with the price level problem by apparently assuming, in somewhat obscure passages, that though it existed, it was always in process of being solved by changes in factors and prices.[102] Taussig, however, extended classical theory in several directions. He explained how comparative costs would work if one of the two countries, being more productive, also paid higher wages in all industries: the richer country (USA) could still sell its export commodity (wheat), because labour was more efficiently used, while the poorer (Germany) was better at something else (linen production) because, although it used its labour less effectively, it paid lower wages. On the tricky issues of the price level, Taussig also made advances. Differential prices, apart from transport costs, were impossible in goods that entered trade, which he called 'international' goods. Goods not traded, however, so-called 'domestic' goods, could be variously at above or below the prices charged elsewhere, depending on relative wage costs and the relative efficiency at which labour was used in their production. The more advanced country did not necessarily have higher prices, according to Taussig, nor was the dearer country always the more efficient. Within each country, however, wages would have to be levelled out, so that if, e.g. better terms of trade or other successes allowed the export industries to pay higher wages, these would have to extend to the domestic industries also, with variable consequences, except for non-competing groups. Taussig also noted the significance of the ratios of internal factor costs: thus in the USA, where immigration caused unskilled labour to be relatively worse paid than skilled labour, industries employing unskilled labour would have an advantage, while countries with low interest rates, like England, would have advantages in capital-intensive industries. Finally, he was realistic enough to notice that cost curves were not horizontal within countries. Even in its less advantaged lines, a country would have regions or units that were well placed, so that rarely would 100% of a necessary supply have to come from abroad.[103]

Thus the classical structure still stood reasonably secure when it was shaken by a different approach from Sweden. This was initiated by Heckscher in a seminal article of 1919 and worked out by Ohlin in a book published in 1933 which stressed even in its title that the theory applied to inter-regional as well as to international trade.[104] Their argument was complex. What is of significance for us was the attempt to account simultaneously for differences in techniques used, and different factor endowment and powers, as between countries. Heckscher argued that, in the initial position, each country will concentrate on the commodities which use its own most plentifully available factors, and buy in those in which the use of its scarcest factor is most pronounced. If some factors are mobile and others are not, the mobile ones will be moved to combine most productively with the others. Ultimately, 'differences in comparative costs are bound to disappear as trade expands'.[105]

Ohlin developed this as one aspect of location theory, special only because frontiers were involved. 'Neighbouring districts may be regarded as belonging to the same sub-region if natural or transfer resources are similar, if labour and capital move easily between them, or if goods move freely between them but with greater difficulty to another group of districts. In each case the grouping is affected in a manner appropriate to the problem in hand.'[106] The unity of the monetary system would make little difference to location, but would affect the monetary adjustment. Trade, between regions as well as between countries, would continue until factors are proportional, but they cannot be equal because some factors cannot be moved. Mobility of goods, or trade, thus compensates to some extent for the immobility of factors.[107] 'Frictions' can delay, but will not ultimately prevent, the attainment of such equilibrium. In addition to such minor frictions, Ohlin had to admit several major disturbing elements in practice. With most of these we need not concern ourselves here,[108] but of interest is the recognition that the successful use of the 'abundant' factor may make it more abundant and intensify the international unevenness of factor supplies: thus the success of the chemical industry in Germany attracts more technical labour to it and leads more young men to study chemistry; or that successful investment brings out more local savings. Ohlin also briefly touched on the price level problem and observed that, 'Other things being equal, home market prices will be low in regions where the factors of production important in home market industries are cheap', whereas in places like Alaska, all will be dear except the oil, which is cheap. International wage differences could be explained, apart from differences in skills etc., by the fact that labour was combined with different factors. But Ohlin found that there were substantial price differences between countries, not only in 'non-competing home market goods', but among 'international goods' also. Apart from tariffs, explanation must be sought in transport costs and in marketing. On empirical as well as on theoretical grounds, Ohlin thus agreed with Cassell in thinking the purchasing-power parity theory untenable. Price levels were made up of many commodities, each with its own elasticities, and foreign-exchange rates, the only possible links, depended on foreign-exchange markets with their own pushes and pulls.[109]

Ohlin's work, beside some seminal ideas on location theory, contains a wealth of data relating to international and inter-regional economic links, but the qualifications and restrictions which they interpose make it impossible to test the basic theory. It has to be accepted on its plausibility and internal consistency alone. Nor have later attempts to test it been much more successful. Moroney and Walker, for example, in a paper outstanding for the brilliant summary of the discussion to date, do indeed find Heckscher–Ohlin proven, but the result is marred by the fact that nearly half their own tests were negative, and by their rather typical a-historical approach: 'Perhaps the initial endowment of natural resources', they conclude,[110] 'may be more important than relative abundance of material capital or labour in determining the *initial structure* [italics in original] of comparative advantage. After the initial structure is established, however, relative endowments of material capital and labour are important in influencing the pattern of industrial growth'. As new resources are discovered and labour and capital migrate "the concept of 'initial endowment' loses meaning". Quite so: but when do we find this initial endowment? In what year does history begin? Ohlin, at least, knew that the locational specialization at any time depended in part on the past.[111] Other studies, such as those of MacDougal and Kravis,[112] found the Heckscher–Ohlin assumptions confirmed at least to the extent of finding particularly high labour productivity in each country's export industries. Both were however equally compatible with the classical theories.

In recent years, the Heckscher–Ohlin theorem has been greatly extended and refined by Lerner, Tinbergen, Samuelson, and many others, and similarly, Viner and his disciples have kept the classical tradition alive. We cannot pursue them here further, except perhaps to note that Haberler has attempted to combine both, by seeing them as special cases of a general equilibrium approach, in which dynamic growth, changes in technology and in factor supplies are also included.[113] What is of significance for our present purposes is that, apart from occasional asides,[114] and one useful largely pragmatic approach, economic theory continues to ignore the relationship which was by far the most important and dynamic in nineteenth-century Europe: the trade implications of the industrial revolution, as a process which took place most unevenly at different stages and differing speeds as between regions, sectors, and countries.

The exception to this generalization originated in the dissatisfaction, found particularly in American business schools, with the failure of economic theory to explain many of the major observable phenomena in international trade. By focusing on the technological gap which is always found to subsist for a significant, even if not indefinite period between the more and the less developed country, a number of economists have developed the doctrine of the 'product life cycle'. This may explain why a new product would develop first in the richest economy, despite its high costs, how it would then be taken over by other developed countries, and might ultimately be produced in less-developed areas because of their cost advantages, being in due course perhaps even re-imported into the originating country.[115] Hufbauer has gone one step further to distinguish between 'technological gap trade', exporting downwards to less developed markets, and 'low wage trade', exporting up the gradient on the basis of lower wages. This approach has also been used to explain why poor and technologically more backward countries would tend to concentrate on the production of lower-quality variants of a commodity in the international division of labour. Though it is geared to the experience of the USA in the second half of the twentieth century rather than Europe in the nineteenth, and concentrates on new products rather than new processes, it will be clear that this approach offers some vital ingredients towards an explanation of the role of trade during the industrialization of Europe.

There is in addition one major study which has put differential industrialization, the European–North American reality into the centre of the picture, using countries as units. The massive two-volume work of Dupriez and his collaborators[116] however, is in essence concerned neither with trade nor with industrialization as such but with the price-level phenomenon which, as we saw, so troubled the classics. Nevertheless, it has the merit of recognizing that Europe industrialized in a differential process in which some late starters managed to catch up and even overtake the leaders by successfully adopting their technology and then extending its principles. It also is concerned, as we are, with long-term developments rather than short-term equilibria, and with secular and fundamental change rather than with trade cycles, payments imbalances, and movements in exchange rates.[117]

It should be said at the outset that one of the main questions which the study apparently set out to answer, the cause of the higher price level in advanced countries, still remains unresolved, except for the statement that while traded 'international' goods must have the same prices everywhere, prices will fan out upwards from them in advanced countries, and downwards in backward countries.[118] No explanation is provided for that phenomenon, unless it were the observation that since wages are higher in the richer country, e.g. in the USA in relation to Europe, personal services, including margins in retail shops, will be costlier;[119] by the same token, however, manufactures containing high technology and little labour will be cheaper.

In the process of pursuing this question, the authors develop a number of most valuable insights. Their picture is one of a wide gap in prices and wages between the advanced country and the backward economy, narrowing as the backward economy catches up, with wages more or less keeping in step with the rising labour productivity achieved, until complete alignment obtains, and this, in turn, reflects the growing provision with capital, and therefore the growing relative scarcity of labour, in the advancing and catching-up country.[120] Prices and trade play an important part in this process. For it is relative prices, dictated by world prices, or the prices of the advanced and/or dominant economy, which transmit the commands to structural changes within the industrializing economy, while these changes, in turn, will affect relative prices, and the export potential of the country. With improved transport, more and more commodities are brought into international traffic, until technology and, with it, relative and absolute prices tend to equality.[121] Natural resources will still cause some differences to persist, but with advancing technology natural endowments progressively lose their significance.[122]

The model is precisely adapted to the industrialization period in Europe. Its assumptions are that the economies are not too dissimilar, so that adaptation and eventual catching-up are possible. In two of their detailed case studies, Germany in relation to Britain, and industrial Europe (Britain, Belgium, Germany) in relation to the USA, the model can be made to fit remarkably well, despite numerous minor problems. In the third case-study, the Congo in relation to Belgium, the cultural, social and economic differences were so large when contacts between the two economies began, that different conditions were created.

The accent is on prices, but the underlying reality is the change and adaptation of technology. The process of alignment occurs because the follower adopts the technology of the leader. In every phase the better technology will drive out the inferior one, and this is the mechanism by which real costs are progressively lowered. If prices between countries at different stages are equalized, as in the case of German and British textile prices in the first half of the nineteenth century, this was a 'false' equality, achieved because higher wages were matched by better technology, and vice versa.[123] There are even hints, though unfortunately little more than hints, of the key relationship between trade, technology, and the diffusion of technical progress. There is recognition that, if better technology is to compensate the advanced economy for its higher wages, that better technology will not occur equally in all sectors, though the higher wages will: 'in the country with high money wages, prices of goods are more or less higher than those of the country with low money wages, according to whether more or less possibility exists of differentiating productive techniques'.[124] It is these differences in the price relatives, it must be clear, which make trade possible and aid in the spread of technology.

Let us start with two assumptions. The first is that culturally, socially, and economically the countries of Inner Europe and Great Britain were not very far apart.[125] The second is that competition, helped possibly by trade unions, will equalize wages in any economic region (bearing in mind internal differences due to skill, etc.) and, because of relatively high factor mobility, will also keep wages fairly in step within each country. Between countries, however, real wages and standards of living will be roughly proportional to productivity.[126] In our period, the main element in the upward surge of productivity, and in its differentiation between countries, was the process of industrialization, spreading outward from Britain

There are indications that British wages were above continental ones, except for the Dutch, even in the eighteenth century.[127] Certainly, when the clouds of war had lifted in 1815, they were found to be so, the differences becoming wider the farther east one went.[128] Behind this difference lay differences in average productivity, based on technology.[129] But the technology of industrialization, as we have seen, proceeded very unevenly. It was enormously effective in the spinning of cotton, the spinning of worsted yarn, or the making of pig and bar iron, for example: in those sectors there was no possible wage level to which a continental competitor could sink to achieve the same prices with traditional methods. There were other industries in which differences in labour productivity were about equal to differences in wages. But where they were less, and in particular, in the extreme case where Britain used the same techniques as the Continent since no new technology had yet been created, as in weaving before the power-loom became economical, in embroidery, dressmaking, or hand-smithing, the Continent enjoyed the full price advantage of its lower wages. This was well known to contemporaries.[130] British costs and prices compared with those of any given continental country thus fanned out about the average given by the standard of living/wage ratio: well below in new technology areas, in accordance with the cheapening effect of the technology, well above where techniques were still similar. At the margin there were goods which the Continent could not yet make at any cost, such as machinery.

There were, of course, other influences still operating on regional price differences: natural resources, like coal; the relative cheapness of capital in Britain and other advanced regions; traditional or arcane skills; or tariffs, subsidies, and other political measures, among others. But increasingly, and before long overwhelmingly, the price differences were based on differences in productive techniques. In Europe in the phase of its initial industrialization, the comparative costs of Ricardian theory, and the relative scarcities of the Heckscher–Ohlin theory, came to be based first and foremost on the technologies of the industrial revolution.

Britain's trading partners in Inner Europe faced in two directions: to the more advanced economy on the one hand, and to less advanced neighbours on the other. They were able to buy yarn, pig iron, and machinery from Britain at prices they could not match, but their weaving and finishing of textiles, their working of iron could well stand up to Britain, not only at home but even in third markets. Towards their more backward neighbours, they stood in the position of the industrial supplier. Rhineland–Westphalia, Saxony, or Bohemia had no difficulty in selling their finished textiles to the less advanced regions of Germany and Austria, and farther away to Russia and overseas. As first Belgium, later the leading regions of France, Germany, and Switzerland, in turn industrialized, they took on increasingly the role of the leader, turning the next rank of economies, Poland, Austria, and Italy, and ultimately even Russia, into the intermediate type. Meanwhile, the early economies in the West, principally Britain but increasingly also France, Switzerland, and Belgium, finding themselves technically caught up and even overtaken, and also possibly adversely affected by a lag of wages among the latecomers in relation to their productivity,[131] were increasingly forced to abandon exports to Inner Europe altogether and to find markets in Russia and overseas.[132] This, however, was not inherent in the model. What was central to it, was that at every stage, for every economy concerned, no matter how badly it might compare with the leaders, there was still a wide open world available, in the European periphery and beyond, in other continents, which was technically more backward still.[133]

Geography also played an important part here. For with the given means of transport and border control of our period, immediate neighbours had an immense advantage in transport costs and smuggling possibilities.[134] British cloth, for example, would have had to have very much lower costs of production to compete with, say, Bohemia in Hungary, or with smuggled Saxon wares in Russia. Even Mirabeau noted that 'few countries are as favourably placed as Prussia for having manufacturers, since it borders along its whole length on a barbarous country [sc. Poland] where they do not exist'.[135] To which Otto Hinze's view might be added that 'from the trade point of view, Poland was then for Prussia what the colonies were for England: a large market for exports and for the supply of cheap raw materials'.[136] In effect, British manufactures had access essentially only to coastal lands, or lands adjoining the broad rivers, like the Rhine, Elbe, or Oder. The secondary and tertiary industrializers thus enjoyed significant protection of distance for their markets,[137] while themselves, in this particular phase of transport technology, still being accessible to British-made industrial inputs; they would find better transport networks in existence when they were ready to deliver high-technology exports in their turn.

These trading relationships between the more and less industrialized nations have for well over a century been consistently misinterpreted as an 'exchange of food and raw materials' against 'manufactured goods'. As it happens, the coverage is not dissimilar, but it is false. It remains false also when converted according to Colin Clark's scheme into 'primary' and 'secondary' industry products, even when these are falsely identified in turn, as by Fourastié, with high technical progress = low price rise for secondary industry, average technical progress = higher price rise for agriculture, and least technical progress = fastest price rise for the tertiary, or service sector.[138] Each of these equalities is wrong, and the identification as a whole is wrong.

The exchange pattern is one of high modern technology content to low (or none). Thus coal, which is plainly a primary or raw material, has always belonged to the export list of the most advanced European economies, and thus has upset innumerable statistical tables; classified as a high-technology product, it fits without difficulty. So does Cornish copper. By contrast, embroidery work or the painting of musical boxes, though undoubtedly industrial, would never be mistaken in the nineteenth century as a likely export item of the more advanced economy. Nevertheless, the similarity is well observed and, for many purposes, the traditional classification may stand as proxy for the correct one.

We see, similarly, that the French belief in France's 'upstream' industrialization[139] is well observed, though wrongly classified. France concentrated on weaving and finishing, not because it was nearest to the consumer, but because the technical gap against Britain was least. Again, much speculation about the French concentration on high-quality mass goods or low-quality goods has been misdirected.[140] The specialisms have little to do with national character, but depend on the relative level of technology of which the less advanced country is capable, given its wage levels and other costs. The belief that while Britain began with textiles, later comers began with metal (capital) goods, does however rest on more solid foundations. These were that the whole of European technology, including that of the pioneer countries, changed over time to become more capital-intensive in a technical, even if not necessarily in the value sense, according to the Hoffmann model so that the later arrivals faced a different technological world in which metals played a larger part.[141]

Perhaps the limitation of this model should be stressed once again. It can apply only to Europe, in a certain phase of development, and can apply in its purest form only where the cost or efficiency differences of a new technology are so large as to blot out all other possible comparative advantages. The less clear-cut these differences, the more other factors, like costs of capital or rents or tariffs, will enter into the calculation.

Within these limits, the emphasis on technology offers us an explanation for the temporary stability of the foreign-trade pattern: at any given time it may be found to be in equilibrium. At the same time, like every good model, it also offers a dynamic explanation, drawing attention to the major factor in long-term change. Before turning from stability to change, or put differently, from the logic of how industrialization affected trade to the logic of how trade affected the process of industrialization, some concrete examples are in order.

Unfortunately, it is not at all easy to show our mechanism working in practice. First, because the needed statistics are either non-existent or unreliable, and even the British series, which is probably the most trustworthy, requires time-consuming recalculation, with the chance of introducing new errors, to arrive at actual values traded. Secondly, even where they measure accurately the movement across a frontier, this may indicate neither origin nor destination. Thus much of the trade to the Netherlands was destined for Germany, and much of what was dispatched to Germany was destined for Poland or Russia, or was smuggled to various destinations from Frankfurt. Even Kutz's well-known study of Anglo-German trade limits itself to sea-borne trade and simply omits all the traffic across Holland and Belgium. Thirdly, as always, frontiers do not necessarily define the operative economic regions: thus, around 1800, the links of Bohemia, in the Czech lands, were mostly with foreign countries north and west, while the links of Moravia and Silesia were inward, to the Danubian provinces and further south and east.[142] In any case, an enormous range of statistics would be required to provide comprehensive pictures of all the inter-relationships. Here only some samples can be given in which, generally, the information was provided by those who knew the reality behind the statistics.

Even eighteenth-century Europe had known the kind of trade in which the more advanced countries exported mostly manufactured products, while the less developed economies returned food, raw materials, and agricultural products such as hemp, hides, or skins.[143] With the British industrial revolution from about the 1780s–1790s[144] the technological gap became large enough to become the major component in comparative cost differences. After the interruption of the war it was at its height in our period 1815–1870s. Lévy-Leboyer summarized the position regarding textiles around 1840 as shown in Table 4.3 (simplified from the original).[145]

To Europe (except for the Mediterranean areas) which represented just under a third of exports, yarn had become the predominant export in cotton and linen, though not in wool. Piece-goods could not be sold there as easily as to the less developed world, to which Britain sent woven fabrics almost exclusively: trading relationships as between these two broad regions were therefore of a very different kind. The Mediterranean was in an intermediate position. It will also be noticed that by then, more than half the textile exports, and around two-thirds of cotton exports by themselves, went to countries outside Europe.

Table 4.3. British Textile Exports. Annual Averages 1837–42 (£00)

	Cotton		Wool		Linen		Silk	Total	= %	% in the form of yarn (ex. silk)
	Piece-goods	Yarn	Piece-goods	Yarn	Piece-goods	Yarn				
Europe except Mediterranean	2115	5076	1355	340	555	850	99	10 390	32	61
Mediterranean	3635	733	585	5	400	20	19	5397	16	14
Overseas	10 000	886	3510	30	2200	–	622	17 248	52	5.5
Totals	15 750	6695	5450	375	3155	870	740	33 035	100	

British yarn imports, to feed the local finishing industries, can be traced in this period also in particular markets, such as Germany, Russia, France, Switzerland, and Belgium. Within Germany, 79% of all yarn imports went to the three fastest industrializers: the Rhineland, Saxony, (kingdom and province), and Brandenburg.[146] Other leading British exports were pig iron and bar iron, though these were influenced by railway building as well as by the mechanism discussed here, and machinery, especially steam-engines and cotton machinery. In the 1840s, Platt's of Oldham exported half the cotton machinery they made: machinery for over one hundred entire cotton factories was exported.[147] The typical relationship then was that 'British industry sent machinery and intermediate goods to French industry which returned finished manufactured goods to British consumers.'[148]

France, Belgium, and Germany were, at first, recipients of the cheaply made semi-manufactures from Britain as well as of machinery and locomotives, but at the same time acted as 'advanced' economies to those farther out in the periphery. In due course the mantle of this intermediary position, or 'Mittlerstellung', in Hassinger's apt phrase, passed to Italy and Austria: the high-technology import–low-technology export, facing 'uphill', existed in their case at the same time as the opposite relationship 'downhill' to the outer periphery, the Austro-Hungarian Monarchy having its own internal trade relationships of a similar kind between its two component parts as well as the external ones.[149] At the end of the line, at least until the early twentieth century, stood Russia, receiving high-technology goods from all parts of Europe,[150] although in her case, there were differences in structure which distorted the model in certain respects. Thus cotton-spinning mills were set up in the central provinces very early and maintained themselves by abysmally low wages and protection by distance from the sea.

The trade of Germany (taking the states that were later to form the Reich as a whole) conformed to the normal pattern, but had certain interesting features of its own. In the period 1815– *c*.1850, when Germany's leading industries began to 'take off' into high-technology methods, she imported yarn from Britain, iron from Britain and Belgium, machinery mainly from Britain, as well as British coal. Using the water-ways, British coal could penetrate beyond Berlin, iron even to Silesia. There were important movements within Germany as well, Saxon yarn in particular enjoying a wide sale.[151] By contrast, German weaving and stocking-knitting enjoyed an easy superiority: in 1836–60, the values of cotton yarn imported into the Zollverein exceeded the values of woven cotton goods imported by a factor varying between 19 and 72, i.e. yarn imports were between 19 and 72 times as large.[152] Exports to the west consisted to a large extent of Baltic grain, two sides of the triangular trade with Britain (grain, timber from the eastern provinces to Britain; manufactures from Britain to the western provinces) complementing the west–east trade of manufactures within Germany.[153] For a brief time, in the 1830s–1840s, there were also large exports of wool to Britain, until Australia and other overseas territories took over that market. To the east and the south-east and even the Mediterranean, however, Germany exported manufactures, including linen goods up to 1830, as well as clothing and metal goods.[154] This 'Mittler' position changed remarkably quickly with industrialization, and the most striking change in the trade figures from 1850 to 1914 is the way in which high-technology semi-manufactures and machinery switch from the import balance to occupy an ever larger share of the export side.[155]

The actual trade statistics, even when they have been worked over by modern scholars to remove their most obvious imperfections leave much to be desired. They do reflect these changes, but they are often also overlaid with other movements, including tariff and frontier alterations. The statistics of German trade with France before and after the French Revolution and Napoleonic periods reflect well enough two countries that were, taking their very mixed regions all in all, at about the same stage of development.[156] (See Table 4.4.)

The collapse of the French transit trade in colonial goods is evident, but the export of French drinks reflects in part the chequered tariff policies. There is a rough balance among most items, but the table has weaknesses. Thus the distinction between 'manufactured' and 'industrial' (more traditionally made) goods is not clear, and the conflation of raw materials and semi-manufacturers in 1833 blurs the single most important dividing-line.

The statistics of German trade with Russia show clearly its one-sided nature in the same period. The averages of the percentages of the years 1827–33 inclusive for the most important trade items were as shown in Table 4.5.[157]

Table 4.4.

% of Total Trade Values	Average 1787–9		Average 1819–21			1833	
	F→G	G→F	F→G	G→F		F→G	G→F
Colonial goods	61.1	–	0.3	–		6.3	–
Drink	10.7	–	28.3	–		15.9	–
Food	–	24.9	–	20.8		–	8.7
Manufactured products	18.6	18.2	40.1	9.8	Textiles	37.8	15.2
Industrial products	2.1	12.0	13.9	19.1	Other manufacturers	8.2	8.2
Industrial raw materials	5.2	29.0	8.3	36.0	RM and semi-manufactures	9.2	15.2
Metals	–	15.1	–	9.8			
All others	2.3	0.8	8.6	4.5		22.6	52.7
Totals	100	100	100	100		100	100

F→G: French exports to Germany.   G→F: German exports to France.

Table 4.5.

German exports to Russia		*Russian exports to Germany*	
Colonial products	22.6%	Hemp and linseed oil and linseed	16.7%
Silk goods	20.1	Grain	15.5%
Cotton yarn	12.0	Tallow	14.0
Cotton goods	3.5	Flax and hemp	12.0
Woollen goods	5.7	Timber and products	8.7*
Silk	4.4	Potash	6.1
All others	(31.7)	Copper	2.8
		All others	(24.2)

* Average of 6 Years only.

Some of the German exports, above all the colonial products but also some of the textiles, were not German productions, but re-exports, telling us nothing about their country of origin: the silks came in part from Switzerland and France, the cotton yarn probably largely from Britain.[158] On the other hand, the surprisingly large share of imports made up by silk goods—not, at first sight, a typical Russian consumer good—shows in a flash how marginal the whole of foreign trade was in a backward economy like Russia, if the consumption of the tiny class of wealthy noblemen could loom so large in the trade statistics. Unlike the more advanced western economies, trade as yet hardly affected the mass of the inert Russian colossus.

As for relations with a more advanced economy, the key was Anglo-German trade. Here, in contrast with her trade with Russia, the main exports of Germany were those arising from the more primitive sectors. The leading items include some of the types of goods imported from Russia. Their shares (averages of the years 1827–33) were as follows:[159]

Wool	53.4%
Grain	21.9
Timber	9.0
Skins and hides	3.9
Seeds	2.9
Flax and hemp	2.6
All others	(6.3)

British exports to Germany also showed some of the expected features.[160]

Table 4.6. Percentages of German imports from Britain

	Averages: 1814/15	1827/8	1832/3
Cotton goods	42.0	35.7	30.1
Cotton yarn	17.0	27.8	34.7
Woollen goods	6.9	13.5	14.7
Woollen yarn	—	negl.	2.8
Iron and steel	0.3	1.0	1.6
Iron and steel goods	2.0	1.5	1.6
Machinery	—	0.2	0.2
Refined sugar	21.9	13.6	6.5

Others require comment. Cotton and woollen fabrics still loom large; but some of them are for re-export, and most are for the non-industrialised regions of Germany. Sugar was being successfully replaced in Germany by home-grown beet-sugar. Machinery and iron and steel, despite their intrinsic importance, amounted to very little in the total trade balance: the railway age was still to come. But it is the cotton yarn (with the woollen following, as expected, with some delay) which may be puzzling: the item is large enough and it grows quite steadily, yet its dynamic does not dominate quite as much as one might have assumed. The reason is that it was precisely this type of commodity for which falls in costs of production were most drastic so that large increases in quantities imported depending on price elasticities, might result in no change in recorded values at all. Between 1814 and 1846, British exports rose by 4.3% p.a. in volume terms, but by only 1.1% in value terms.[161] It is precisely these improvements in the terms of trade, aided by the relative rise in the price of grain, before long the major German export, which helped Germany to benefit so much from its British connection.

As industrialization proceeded, the German intermediary position gradually tilted towards the role of the industrial economy.[162] For a while it held the balance: thus semi-manufactures, in the circumstances of the day a key indicator, registered a 135% increase in export volume in 1836-8 to 1854-6 for the Zollverein, against an 128% increase in import volume.[163] Cotton yarn sent out, as a proportion of home supplies, rose from a low of 25% in 1835 to 44% in 1853, 88% in 1874, and then stayed mostly over 90%. At the same time exports hovered around one-sixth of total production. The two faces of Germany, to the west and the east, are well delineated in the trade of Hamburg, which kept particularly detailed trade statistics. According to them,

Vis-a-vis Britain, Germany takes on the position of a supplier of food and raw materials and a buyer of manufactures (*Fertigwaren*). This is so particularly for Hamburg's transit trade, and for the German agrarian coastal regions in the immediate vicinity of the city. But Germany as a whole is *industrially inferior* (italics in original). Commerce with the rest of the trading partners shows quite a different structure . . . In their regard, Hamburg represents, as a port, the *superior industrial country* which buys food and raw materials and sells manufactured goods.

In Bremen, by contrast, where there was little trading with Britain, Germany appeared wholly as the advanced economy, exchanging her manufactures mainly for colonial produce.[164]

This account, while it neglects the export ports of the backward parts of Germany, like Dantzig, correctly grasps the growth of the industrialized sectors as those enjoying comparative advantages. The following rough estimates, referring to the whole of Germany, show some of the changes. The two-way movement of coal, determined by the quality and location, and the declining dependence on imported cotton yarn, out of phase with the still rising dependence on imported pig iron for railway building, should be particularly noted.[165]

Table 4.7. Germany: Imports and exports expressed as % of home production

	Imports, averages		Exports, averages	
	1836/8	1854/6	1836/8	1854/6
Grain	1	6	6	9
Cotton yarn	200	88	25	8
Cotton goods	3	1	19	19
Woollen yarn	1	19	1	2
Woollen goods	5	3	21	29
Pig iron	5	38	1	1
Bar iron and steel	13	6	3	2
Coal	4	9	16	13

Finally, summary statistics for the Zollverein alone in 1860 show the striking geographical division of the trade pattern (in %).[166]

Table 4.8.

	Food	Raw Materials	Semi-Manufactures	Finished Goods
Imports from:				
Eastern Europe	42	46	5	7
Western Europe and North Sea	23	c.33	34	c.10
Baltic	34	30	31	4
Exports to:				
Eastern Europe	12	17	22	49
Western Europe and North Sea	c.14	c.13	6	c.67
Baltic	38	31	12	19

The particular trade 'uphill' and 'downhill' described by our model and evident from the statistics was not merely a passive or permissive element in the successful industrialization of Germany. The British connection, as well as the links with the agrarian German States, with Russia, Poland, Austria, and the Balkans, were among the most important propelling forces in that movement. Apart from the obvious point that without the British industrial revolution, there would not have been any industrialization on the Continent either, Germany received directly, in the normal course of trade, machinery which could be copied and which exerted its demonstration effects, and cheap semi-manufactures with which it could capture markets by cheapening the finished goods into which they entered. With those often came specialists and sometimes also finance. The learning process was here of particular significance. We have seen in how many cases British technology failed to take root at first go, and right up to 1850 and 1860, continental centres frequently failed to achieve British productivity and economy even when using apparently similar equipment.[167] Whether the causes lay in lack of skill, poorer external economies, more expensive capital or supplies, it was the example of British success which kept continental pioneers and experimenters going until they reached similar proficiency. Thus the sector in which Germany enjoyed an advantage, such as weaving, was stimulated and expanded, and sooner or later mechanization spread on the basis of the machinery and methods imported from the advanced country.[168] As soon as Germany did adopt British technology in full in any sector, that sector would undersell the British as long as German wages overall and in detail had not yet caught up with British levels, which was not to happen before 1914. At the same time any modification to suit continental prices or conditions, any deviation from 'slavish imitation', was also likely to capture markets.[169]

Modern economic theory has had no difficulty in identifying the mechanisms by which one trading partner benefits by the technological progress of its powerful neighbour. Sir John Hicks, reducing the relationship to its barest essentials, has shown that it is most likely to happen when the advance, resulting in a real cost reduction, occurs in the export industries.[170] This is inherently plausible, and we have briefly adverted to the possibility of the innovating country gaining no advantage, and even sustaining a loss of income, in certain extreme imaginable cases, leaving all the benefits to its trading partners by improving their terms of trade,[171] —provided they are close enough in income and structure to benefit from it. It has also been shown that this advantage will accrue even if the backward economy starts out as a simple raw material producer, provided it has a real enough comparative cost advantage in its export commodity to begin with. Canada, the American North-West, Denmark, and Sweden, among others, have been used as examples.[172]

The danger of this relationship may well be greater to the advanced country. Hicks showed the disadvantages suffered by one country if its trading partner goes in for technical advance which is import-substituting, rather than export-biased.[173] Britain was equipping her rivals while they were in a better position than herself, paying lower wages, to make use of the new technology. We have seen how she was driven out of European markets, while imports *from* the industrialized countries formed the most rapidly growing item in her own trade balance.[174] This threat would have existed even if she kept in step with further technological advances, and there were several powerful reasons to divert her from doing so, including the ease with which she was able to redirect her trade to colonize the rest of the world, while her rivals colonized their own backward regions at home.

The benefits of the British connection for Germany (which here must stand proxy for all such connections in Inner Europe) are now widely recognized.[175] Yet throughout the period since then, beginning with Friedrich List, the opposite view has widely prevailed. The dominant impression created has been that of a poor disunited and exploited Germany, overrun by cheap British imports which threatened her economic existence as a prosperous nation, surviving the onslaught only by dint of heroic effort, by protection, and the power of the Zollverein to force more equal trade treaties on her trading partners. How has this view, which could be found *mutatis mutandis* to have been held by citizens of other economies also, succeeded in obtaining such a long and persistent hold?

In part, it was created by the Prussian myth-makers, for whom the Zollverein had to fit into the purposeful march of the German nation to heroic greatness, against the intrigues of her enemies. In part, the view suited the protectionist book, and protection tends to enjoy a good press since the benefits of any particular tariff are highly concentrated, while the benefits of free trade are widely diffused and felt less keenly. There are occasions when some of the victims of a tariff are also concentrated, such as the users of iron suffering from a tariff on pig iron, but they can be, and were in Germany, bought off by even bigger tariffs on the manufactured product than on the raw material.

There was, however, a further reason, important for creating the atmosphere in which the other causes could flourish. At the very beginning of our period, in 1815–17, Europe was indeed flooded by what seemed impossibly cheap British manufactures, which killed off many apparently promising continental plants in two or three traumatic seasons,[176] leaving a scar on the psyche of Europe which took nearly two generations to heal. But this damage was done precisely because trade had been interrupted, and not because of the existence of trade. In the twenty years of war, not only had British technology raced ahead without giving the Continent a chance of keeping in touch,[177] so that continental industrialists had been induced to invest in the wrong technology; they had also been induced to invest in the wrong sectors. They were attempting to compete rather than to be complementary, to concentrate on their weakness rather than their strength. It took much time, much learning, and painful readjustment to get back to a relationship in which Germany and others parts of continental Europe benefited and developed with the help of trade with the advanced economy. Nor did it help the long-term development of the image of that period that it also ended with a trauma, the inrush of American grain, which could not be requited by manufactures, thus leading to a secular deflation in Europe, the Great Depression.[178]

Not all trading with an advanced neighbour is of advantage. It turned out to be less and less so, we shall find, as we move outwards towards the European periphery. But for Inner Europe, it was a major channel of transmission of the process of industrialization.

The Differential of Contemporaneousness

We have had occasion to refer several times to the very different consequences that may arise when the same historic phenomenon reaches more or less simultaneously economies which are themselves at very different stages in their development. This differential was one of the most potent factors in European economic history (as it still is in

today's economic world); it has also been a fertile source of misunderstanding. We have termed it, somewhat clumsily, the 'differential
of contemporaneousness'[179] and it deserves some words of further
explanation.

If we move across the face of Europe in any given period, we find
many differences of culture, religious belief, social attitudes, and so
on, and they change over time. They will always affect the way in
which economic or technological changes were received, and they did
so undoubtedly in our period. However, they were increasingly put in
the shade by the progress of industrialization itself which came to
dominate the reaction of a society as it came to dominate so much
else. There was some convergence: Saxony began to look increasingly
like the West Riding, and the French Nord like the Scottish Lowlands.
At the same time there was also an increasing gulf opening up between
those areas which had adopted the new industrialism, and those which
had yet to follow suit.

At the beginning of our period the differences in national income
between countries were not yet strongly marked and even the richest
was still very poor by later standards. Recent calculations, in terms
of the somewhat doubtful 1960 US dollar, show a hardly discernible
'Gefälle' in GNP per head in Europe in 1800-60.[180]

Table 4.9.

	1800	1830	1860
Early industrialized countries*	(209)	298	454
Later „ „ *	(219)	(252)	328
Nordic countries*	(193)	(210)	273
Russia, Romania, Bulgaria	(170)	(171)	180
Mediterranean countries*	(203)	(259)	(309)

* Belgium, France, Switzerland, United Kingdom.
* Austria-Hungary, Germany, Netherlands.
* Denmark, Finland, Norway, Sweden.
* Greece, Italy, Portugal, Serbia, Spain.

These estimates are too uncertain to give any confidence even as to
the ranking order in 1800, except possibly for Russia, and they are
still doubtful in 1830, but they begin to pull apart beyond any doubt
by 1860. At the beginning of the century, the differences do not get
much larger even if we try to go behind the averages to individual
countries. In 1830, the lowest (Russia 170, Finland 188) still showed
incomes no less than half the highest (United Kingdom 360, Holland
347). By 1860, the ratio between the extremes had opened out to
3½ : 1,[181] but most countries were still grouped around the middle.
Since the poorer countries were growing more slowly, however, the

gaps measured in years necessary to catch up were beginning to widen alarmingly.

The similar nominal income of 1800 hid, however, a series of different structures which were mainly responsible for the differences in the subsequent growth-rates. Freedom for private capitalists in the West, in Britain, Holland, or France, contrasted with bleakest serfdom and a status society in Russia. In high-technology goods, the differences were striking even at the beginning of the century, and widened in many cases still further as the century progressed. A few key indicators for some representative countries may help to provide a picture:[182]

Table 4.10.

	Raw-cotton consumption per capita, kg., in 5 year averages			Pig-iron production per capita, kg., in 5 year averages			Coal consumption per capita, kg., in 5 year averages		
	1810	1860	1910	1810	1860	1910	1810	1860	1910
Belgium	—	2.9	9.4	c.10	69	250	—	1310	3270
France	0.3	2.7	6.0	c.4	25	100	c.40	390	1450
Germany	—	1.4	6.8	2	14	200	—	400	3190
Italy	—	0.2	5.4	—	2	8	—	—	270
Russia	—	0.5	3.0	—	5	31	—	—	300
Spain	—	1.4	4.4	—	3	21	—	—	330
Sweden	—	1.5	3.6	c.30	47	110	—	c.90	910
Switzerland	—	5.3	6.3	—	—	—	—	—	—
United Kingdom	2.1	15.1	19.8	c.20	130	210	600	2450	4040

Again, it is striking how quickly the leading countries move away from the backward ones, if the gap is calculated in terms of the years it would take the backward country to catch up at its current rate of progress.[183] Thus if we take the United Kingdom in 1790 as base, her iron production per head would be reached by the Continent of Europe only in 1870, eighty years later, her raw-cotton consumption only in 1885, or ninety-five years later, and her low proportion of the population in agriculture only in the middle of the twentieth century.[184] This latter ratio draws attention to the fact that British industrialization was played out against a backward world, the British economy specializing into a kind of role in the world economy which was no longer open to the later comers.[185] It may also be argued that there is little meaning in a continental 'average', and some regions were much closer behind Britain. But the different circumstances in relation to their surroundings, in which industrialization took place first in Britain, then among the early followers, and then among the later ones, profoundly affected their actual history. There are thus two ways of looking at this same phenomenon. We can emphasize that the same technology, or the same body of ideas, or even the same market conditions, affect parts of Europe simultaneously, which are very differently equipped to deal with them; or we can emphasize that economies industrializing in sequence each do so in a very different European and world environment. They each illustrate different aspects of European history, and both are needed for its full understanding.

Alexander Gerschenkron drew attention to the consequences of economic 'backwardness'. He showed that countries which are apparently engaged in the same process of industrialization but at different historical times, follow quite different paths, according to their degree of backwardness. Their catching-up was not a repetition of the first, but an 'orderly system of graduated deviations from that industrialization.'[186] Countries that are backward have been more deeply scarred by mercantilism; having a greater gap to overcome when they arrive at the 'take-off' or 'big spurt' point, they then grow faster, they go in more for heavy or high-technology industry, and they are constrained to adopt different methods of finance. Thus in Britain, industry was largely self-financed, while in Germany, as an example of the second generation, only banks could amass large enough sums to finance the big spurt. In Russia and other countries further behind still, it had to be the state. With these different sources of finance, also came different types of control and organization, the later methods favouring the larger firms. These later alternatives, such as high technology from abroad in place of native skilled labour, and bank or government capital in place of entrepreneurial savings, may be considered to be substitutes by the latecomers for missing factors.[187]

In spite of the obvious weakness that Gerschenkron views states as the only units worth considering, though they contain territories at very different stages of backwardness, and in spite of some criticism in detail, his approach has stood up well to detailed scrutiny,[188] and is now widely accepted. It certainly has changed the framework within which comparative industrialization is now studied. Yet its basis is strictly limited. It merely looks backward into each country's own history, neglecting, except implicitly, its contemporaries at each stage. It uses, as it were, one dimension only, lacking the second dimension of the impact of contemporary events.

We have already drawn attention to the profoundly different impact and consequences of the railways spreading across Europe according to the varying stages of development reached by different economies. These differences apply both to the history of the railways themselves, and, perhaps even more fundamentally, to the host societies. A very similar story could be told about canals and other public works.[189] Similarly, we have noted the differential effects of population growth which simultaneously affected all of Europe, but spelled either Malthusian disaster or proto-industrial impoverishment or rapid economic progress according to the stage reached in the development of the factors of production in the region. The effects of this differential have been of great consequence in many other areas of economic life as well, They have often been observed singly but their similarity in principle has not received adequate attention.

Thus the new agricultural techniques, as they were diffused across Europe from the eighteenth century on, had very different consequences in areas of capitalist farming and in the serf-worked latifundia of the European East. Conversely, the emancipation of the serfs, though nominally often similar, yet led to a very different agrarian and social structure as between East-Elbian Germany and the farmers of the German South-West.[190] Perhaps more significant still is the role of timber, unduly neglected in British (if not in American) historiography. It can be argued that the timber resources, at least of the temperate climate zone of Europe, had been gradually diminished by population growth and economic advance as part of the movement by which agricultural settlement gradually filled all the empty spaces of the Continent. Holland exhausted her resources first, but was able to import freely from less developed regions. When Britain reached the stage of exhaustion in turn, her economy was too large to continue such purchases with impunity and began to turn the terms of trade against herself. The successful quest for alternatives as building material (iron) and as fuel (coal) then turned out to be at the heart of her industrial revolution. Her technology then flooded other economies which had not yet wholly exhausted their own timber, but were the nearer to that exhaustion, the more advanced they were: some timber was left in Germany and France, more in Austria, more still in Russia and Scandinavia. Differences in the subsequent timber economy of these regions reflect the differential timing of industrialization in terms of their own historical development.[191]

Legislation permitting the easy formation of joint-stock companies spread quickly across Europe in the 1850s, and their contribution to overspeculation and widespread bankruptcies in the less sophisticated European economies has often been commented on. In banking, the backward economies, using the experience of the pioneers, could bypass some of the difficulties of the latter by enjoying the benefits of more efficient banks, ahead, as it were, of their own stage of growth and more appropriate to more advanced economies. At the same time, however, banks and particularly central banks were internationally meshed into the same system, and those in the less advanced areas, and their economies, had to absorb shocks transmitted by the advanced world of a nature to which they were not yet properly fitted.

On balance, the transmission of these trade and crisis cycles emanating from more advanced economies could not but be damaging to the less developed ones.[192]

There is one phenomenon in which the differentiation of reactions according to the stage of development reached has received some attention. This is the massive influx of grain from overseas into Europe in the 1870s, itself in part a consequence of the transport revolution. While Kindleberger was particularly interested in the 'group reaction' of countries to each other,[193] it is clear that the graduated response, such as acceptance of cheap grain and conversion of grain into input for animal husbandry in Britain, Denmark, and Holland; sealing off of the home market by tariffs in France and Germany; or expansion of output to maintain export revenue while prices were falling, as in Hungary or Russia, closely reflected the stage of each economy. It may also be argued that the response to the preceding period of free trade was similarly graduated.[194]

Ideas cross frontiers with greater speed even than commodities, and military simultaneity has always been painfully obvious. The Russian army, still not unlike other European armies at the time of Leipzig or Waterloo, had to attempt to meet Western armies on equal terms at the time of the Crimean War while the economic gap had widened to make this practically impossible. Here was a country producing 5 kilograms of iron a head taking on countries producing 25 and 130 respectively. By 1914, Russian armies had to appear equal to the German ones facing them, since they were contemporaries, but in terms of Russia's economy they were quite anachronistic, and this was quickly reflected in supplies, transport, spares, skill with machinery, and so on.[195] Again, Italy and even Austria thought it their due to join the imperialist adventures at the end of the nineteenth century without an economic or even a shipping base to justify this, because as contemporary 'Great Powers' this was expected of them, not least by their own populations. Italy also proceeded to create a mercantile fleet for the same reason, which, like many a railway, lived on national prestige and subsidies rather than on a solid fare.[196]

Ideas were equally compelling. In Russian conditions without an adequate bourgeois class, state enterprises might well have been sensible in the nineteenth century, but 'however backward Russia's political structure was in comparison to that of Western Europe, the impact of the Zeitgeist upon it was irresistible'.[197] The Zeitgeist drove rebellious young men also to Socialism, a doctrine evolved in France in the 1830s and 1840s, and spreading quickly across Europe in the crisis of 1848 and its aftermath. Conceived as the appropriate philosophy for proletarians, Socialism reached Britain when a 'proletarian' class already existed, and was absorbed into its armoury with little impact: British workers did not need to be told that they had class interests. In France and Germany, socialist ideas grew up simultaneously with a substantial working class, and permeated their trade unions and political parties from the beginning. In Italy, trade unions created ahead of their time influenced the whole of their subsequent history. As for Austria, 'The economic backwardness of the country [Austria] disappears, one might say, hourly', Victor Adler confided to Friedrich Engels in 1892, 'and we have the advantage that our proletariat is spiritually ahead of the economic development, thanks to the neighbourhood of Germany.'[198]

Farther east still lay Russia, where Marxist ideas arrived before there existed the mass proletariat to whom they were to apply. The resulting anachronism, leading to the establishment of a dictatorship, not by the proletariat, but over the proletariat and over everyone else, was arguably a disaster not only for Russia, but more also for Socialism in the West. It was probably the most fateful of all the consequences of the differential of contemporaneousness emerging in the nineteenth century.

Chapter 5

Peripheral Europe in the Early Phase

Our discussion so far has been almost exclusively concerned with an arbitrarily defined 'Inner Europe', the scene of the first implantations of industrialization. Outer or peripheral Europe has been largely ignored, except as a somewhat passive recipient of new industrial product from the centre, and as a possible supplier of food and raw materials, absorber of surplus labour, and scene of capital investment from the advanced regions.

This picture must now be rectified in several ways. To begin with, the frontiers as drawn here, including Belgium, France, Switzerland, and the German lands except for East Elbia, owe not a little to the convenience of using national statistics and are debatable on any definition. Thus Bohemia, Moravia, Silesia, and Upper and Lower Austria with Vienna come very close to the areas included, and in this respect the frontiers of the German Confederation as established in 1815 would have formed a more sensible, though still inaccurate, eastern dividing-line for a realistic apportionment. The Lombard plain to the South, and Catalonia to the South-West, had almost equally strong claims for inclusion. At the same time, large parts of France and of Germany were in no sense industrialized or distinguishable from similar areas in the periphery, yet have had to be included in our definition of 'Inner Europe'.

A different problem concerns the Netherlands. In terms of modern industry, she has certainly been excluded with justice; but her income per head, the quantity of her finance and trading capital available, and the sophistication of its use made her a more advanced 'economy' than most regions of Germany. The question how to classify her must turn on purpose: the rise of industrialization, as defined here, occurred in the Netherlands well after the 1870s, and she is therefore, in spite of her unique earlier role in the history of Europe and her position in the nineteenth-century capital market, counted among the later industrializers.

Beyond the actual location of a frontier, the very concept of such a dividing-line does some violence to the facts. Rather than treat Europe as consisting of a high plateau, falling away to less favoured lowlands, it would be better to 'conceive Europe in this regard as a graduated unit',[1] but one in which peaks rose at various points, rather than one forming a constant slope to the east or the south. Tom Kemp has aptly phrased the relationship:

The advanced areas of nineteenth-century Europe had as their core the coalfields of northern France, Belgium and Western Germany; from here the influence of industrialisation fanned out along convenient lines of communication, including the sea, to other parts of these countries, with some outposts still further to the south and east, including administrative centres, sea and river ports and mineral deposits as the main nodal points. Thus the division between the advancing industrial and mainly agrarian regions cut right across the state frontiers and, once established, retained considerable influence down to the present day.[2]

The contrast between advanced region and less developed hinterland was real enough, but it existed in many places, and with varying slopes, rather than as a single line traceable on a map, dividing two internally homogeneous territories.

The periphery was thus affected by what went on in Inner Europe, but it also had its own development, imposing its own logic on its economic history. Some of the interrelations between these two major influences and their consequences will form the subject matter of the present chapter.

Agriculture: Emancipation, Markets, and Dynamics

Agriculture provided the largest source of employment, and the single most important source of income and wealth, in the periphery of Europe. In part, it represented the traditional self-supply. Increasingly, it also came to represent a specialist role in an international division of labour in which Inner Europe specialized in manufactured products and became dependent on imports of food and agricultural raw materials.

In Eastern Europe, the outstanding developments were the emancipation of the peasants from sefdom and the extension of the market economy on the land. Both were directly influenced by the industrialization of the West whence came market opportunities, new technologies, and liberal ideas, all of which favoured capitalistic relations in agriculture. However, these connections were neither uniform nor simple, and it is worth remembering that in some areas at least, serfdom itself or its intensification were the results of the opportunities provided by western markets, and in that sense justified the term 'capitalist' serfdom.[3]

In the Baltic lands the differentiation can be traced back to the fifteenth and sixteenth centuries. Before then, the development of cities, of trade, and of a rent-paying peasantry in the East was not dissimilar from the contemporary West. Thereafter, rising grain prices in the western price revolution, the decline of the Hansa and of their cities and their replacement by the Dutch and the English, form an interlocking complex with the rise of seigneurial power over peasant and burgher in the Baltic hinterlands in which causes and effects cannot here be disentangled. What is clear is that it led to the atrophy of nascent capitalist centres and to the re-emergence of a 'second' feudalism at the base of which were profitable grain sales to the West on the part of the feudal lord. It was to achieve this grain surplus that the lord had to deprive the peasant of his freedom and of all his land other than that needed for his subsistence, and to impose ever growing labour services on him for the lord's own quasi-commercial large-scale farming enterprise.[4]

After the upheavals of the Thirty Years War, timber and grain shipments through the sound took a strong upward turn, while prices fell, European prices converged, and servile conditions were extended and made harsher. The '*Gesindeordnung*' was passed in Saxony in 1650, in Russia the serf was tied to the land in 1646 and 1649 and his sale with the land permitted in 1682. All over Eastern and Northern Europe, from Bohemia to Prussia and Denmark, laws to deprive the peasant of his land and his freedom were passed or tightened.[5]

Moves towards a loosening of these particular chains began with the Enlightenment. The eastern portions of the North European plain form a geographical continuum, and the absence of natural frontiers has meant wide swings in political power and frequent major shifts in political boundary lines. The underlying economic realities and agricultural methods in particular, changed only slowly with soil, climate, and distance as one moved eastward, but the actual process of emancipation, being politically determined, showed strong variation in detail if general similarity in principle. Over the whole of the European east and south-east, emancipation occurred at a time when the landowning class was firmly in control and it was undertaken in a form which maximized the benefits to the large landowners, subject only to the need for sheer survival of the peasantry as a source of labour for the landlord and of taxation and army recruitment for the state.

The Prussian provinces were distinguished by the fact that, from an early date, they were combined under the same crown with some advanced industrial regions: first Silesia, and later the flourishing commercial mining and industrial centres of the Rhineland. But as Prussia expanded outward from its Brandenburg core, the traditional rulers, the Crown and the feudal landlord classes on whose support it relied, never relaxed their grip and by pyramiding their power, first within Prussia and then by virtue of the Prussian hegemony within the whole of Germany, managed to extend it over a very different economy from the one which provided their own base. The German Reich which emerged in 1871 had the muscles and sinews of western industry, but a brain still controlled by eastern agrarians, and this proved to be a menacing combination indeed for the whole of Europe.

For our purposes it is important to stress that with all the accretions of power which derived from her industrial provinces, Prussia let her agricultural transformation be dominated by her eastern landlords with very little reference to the West, except perhaps for the crisis year of 1807. At that time of defeat and humiliation, the Reform Act granted the free disposal of land, and freedom of choice of occupation to everyone, together with the end of hereditary villeinage. But any hopes the peasant might have had to reach the status of, say, the French or the Westphalian peasantry were quickly dashed. In the eighteenth century, the Prussian rulers had managed to end completely the landlord practice of driving peasants off their land (*Bauernlegen*)—a practice continuing in Mecklenburg until the nineteenth century—and they had emancipated their own serfs, but they had been powerless against the landowning class, the *Junkers*.[6] On some estates there had been commutation to wage labour, and the Dutch settlers of the eighteenth century, moving in the opposite direction to the grain, were always free. After 1807, the Junkers quickly regained their nerve and, far from conceding anything, made enormous gains from the change.

The ending of feudal obligations was a mutual process: the lord was freed from his obligations towards his serfs, and the latter were freed from their feudal obligations and legal dependence on their lords. But in practice it was treated as a one-way transaction, the lords having made the grant and therefore requiring to be heavily compensated. By the edict of 1811, the peasants were to be granted the freehold of their holdings on payment of one-third of their land to the Junker in the case of hereditary land, and one-half in the case of non-hereditary holdings. Even this edict was further whittled down by a later one of 1816, which restricted its provisions to the richer peasants who were of long standing, and greatly enlarged the scope of the Junker to dictate more onerous terms. The large majority of the peasants remained in limbo, neither serf nor independent, and could be burdened by increased fines and dues and even evicted from their houses. In 1821, they also lost the usufruct of the commons. Moreover, the Junkers retained their extensive and, for western minds, almost inconceivable juridical and political power over the villagers while eastern towns stagnated.

As a result, (and including purchases from impoverished holders), some two and a half million additional acres fell to the Junkers.[7] This represented 6% of the land, and 20-25% of the *additional* land of 1800–61. They also had the benefit of a helpless and expanding labour supply. The post-1815 years were depressed for agriculture and many estates changed hands, but from the 1830s, growing export markets, above all to Britain, ensured the prosperity of the *Gutswirtschaft*, the large estate economy. It should be stressed that the Junkers relied on an extensive type of agriculture, and although technically superior to the methods used farther east, its yield ratios and yields per acre were very low compared with the peasant farms of Western Germany. However, based on its low input costs of cheap land and cheap labour, and an ever improving transport, East-Elbian Germany was able to withstand even the final emancipation of the peasants resulting from the 1848 revolution without losing its expansionary momentum. The crisis came only in the 1870s with a combination of cheap American and Russian grain, benefiting in their turn from cheapened means of transport, with rising standards in the West which turned away from rye and the other coarser grains produced in Prussia, and with the flight of labour to better conditions in the western provinces of the Empire. The reaction of the Junker class to that crisis was to use their political power to force Germany into a new economic policy from 1879 onward.[8]

The large estate, worked by servile peasants who had only minimal holdings themselves, also predominated in the Baltic states or provinces of Lithuania, Latvia, and Estonia.[9] Conditions were similar in (Congress) Poland except that, until the railway age and even beyond, estate farming for export was limited to lands with access to the major rivers. Elsewhere, and over most of southern Poland (i.e. Austrian Galicia) the inaccessibility of a market for grain forced landlords to convert their harvest into spirits, or to collect a 'rent' from their poverty-stricken peasants that was based not on the returns from their lands, but on their opportunities of working in forests, towns, or in transport undertakings.[10] In Poland, which had been the chief source of grain exports in the seventeenth century, the imposition of the second serfdom actually led, not only to a deterioration of the position of the peasant, but to an actual decline in agricultural yields, as well as to urban stagnation.[11] Poland was thus an example of an economy in which linkage to the market of an advanced area led to retrogression and the discouragement of technical improvements by means of the imposition of a particular kind of feudalism.[12]

In the 1860s, once more for political reasons, the emancipation of the Polish serfs was conducted differently from that of the rest of the Tsar's dominions. The terms of 1864 were made far more favourable for the peasants as a method of striking at the continuously rebellious

Polish nobility, and a large proportion of the land was made over into peasant proprietorship. The ultimate result cannot have been entirely what the Russian government intended. A rapid increase in rural population, raising the numbers employed in agriculture in Congress Poland from 3.4 million in 1857 to 6.9 million in 1906 overcrowded the land and created a landless proletariat prepared to flock into the towns and help the expansion of Polish industry which was much more rapid than that in Russia proper. At the same time, Poland also took the lead in agricultural technology.[13]

There was no abrupt transition to the north-western Russian provinces: climate, soil, conditions of serfdom, and estate organization were similar and changed only gradually as one penetrated the depth of Russia. Three major agricultural areas could be distinguished in the Empire: the fertile 'black soil' belt, including much of the Ukraine, in which the servile dues were rendered mostly (over 70% overall) in the form of labour, the *barshchina*; the less fertile regions, mainly north of this belt, in which the lords did much better by charging a money rent, the *obrok* (60% overall) which was paid very often not out of the proceeds of the poor soil, but out of industrial or commercial earnings and might also be paid in kind; and the new lands of the south-eastern steppes and elsewhere where there were few serfs, but those mostly on a *barshchina* system.[14]

The systems however were mixed nearly everywhere, even if in different proportions. In *obrok* regions, most land was distributed to the peasants, though even there the lord might run a large estate farm under *barshchina*. In fertile regions, the proportions were reversed: the peasants held little plots, and mostly laboured on the lord's estates. Methods there tended to be appallingly backward and wasteful of labour since, as under Polish feudalism, the decision-making landlord or his agent did not consider the peasant's time or labour as a cost. In terms of yield and peasant real incomes, the Russian figures were far below those of the rest of Europe, though they were rising.[15]

As in Prussia, peasant emancipation followed national humiliation, in this case the Crimean War. Again as in Prussia, it was carried through by and in the interests of the landlords under the constraint that the ruler insisted on preserving a viable peasant class able to pay taxes and fill the ranks of his army. The provisions of the Emancipation Edict of 1861 were more complex because of the variable conditions in different parts of the Empire, but they also started from the assumption that the peasant had to make over some of his land, or pay in other ways, for obtaining his freedom from serfdom.

There is no space here for the intricacies of detail. State peasants (i.e. those formerly owned by the Tsar or various official agencies), comprising 47% of the total, did better than those on private estates. On the latter, 30,000 nobles kept ownership of 95 million *dessyatins* of land, while the 20 million emancipated peasants received very little more between them, some 116 million *dessyatins*. On fertile soils, matters were so arranged that landlords received the maximal land allocation, peasants the minimal. On average, peasants here lost 23.3% of their holdings. In the infertile regions, where the soil itself was of little value, it was the peasants' monetary contribution that was maximized. A government commission later found that the average peasant's contribution there, on a full holding, amounted to 200-270% of the annual income of the land allotted to him. The landlords, in other words, drew a 'rent' not merely on the land, but also on the peasant's non-agricultural labour. In the Polish provinces, as noted above, the peasants lost no land, and did much better altogether: their average of 5.7 *dessyatins* compares well with the three-quarters of the private peasants that received under four and the typical three *dessyatins* in the fertile south. About 2.6 million male serfs, or 4 million adults altogether, were left entirely without land.[16]

Peasants who were willing to accept only one-quarter of their due holdings, received it free. Some 640,000 had chosen this method by the end of 1877, which was popular where there was plenty of land to be leased.[17] The others found it in general impossible to raise their redemption purchase sum, and so the state advanced up to 80% of the money to the landlords, receiving it back from the peasants over forty-nine yearly payments that were added to the tax obligations. The remaining 20% had to be raised by the peasants themselves, often by borrowing from village usurers. Altogether some 870 million roubles were paid over by the state to the landlords, plus perhaps another 200 millions paid directly by the peasants.[18]

Encouraged by the building out of the railway network at the same time, some landlords used these sums to develop their estates by introducing modern methods, particularly in the fertile belt and along the transport routes. But most of them used their compensation payments merely to pay off mortgages[19] or to increase their consumption. The growing exports of grain were achieved in part by raising production, and output of cereal grains rose as follows:

(Quarters per head):-		
	1864-6	2.21
	1883-7	2.68
	1900-05	2.81

But in part they were achieved by cutting the peasant's consumption, particularly of meat. The share of wheat consumed by the home market was growing in those years, particularly after 1890, but the share of the harvest of other grains exported remained the same.[20]

There was one other major respect in which Russia failed to follow the 'Prussian solution'. It would clearly have overtaxed the state's police and administrative resources to grant the right of movement and disposal of property to individuals. Instead, peasants remained compulsorily members of the village community, the *Mir*, which exercized primitive police powers, held the land which it periodically redistributed among its members, and was responsible for tax payments. The peasant could buy out his share, and become truly independent, only on the most onerous terms, and there was strict control even over those who went temporarily into the cities to work in industry. Unlike East-Elbian Prussia after 1848, the Russian land system after emancipation provided little aid to industrialization, though it was accompanied by some useful administrative reforms.[21]

In the Austrian Empire, regions and provinces were subject to different laws and customs, and emancipation proceeded unevenly. Joseph II, the enlightened autocrat, had decreed an end to personal serfdom in 1781, but this made little difference economically, and the stricter limitations imposed, regarding the number of days per week which the peasant could be forced to work for his lord (the *Robot*), did not reduce the extent of exploitation either since they were regularly broken. Such limitations were enacted for (Austrian) Silesia in 1771, Lower Austria (1772), Bohemia (1775), Styria and Corinthia (1778), Carniola (1782), Galicia (1782), and Bukovina (1783). Some progress was made in the next three-quarters of a century in commuting labour *Robots* to money payments, though conscription, introduced in 1770, was frequently felt to be a greater hardship than the traditional exploitation. Maria Theresa's promising 'Raab system' of 1775, for turning serfs into peasant proprietors did not go beyond Crown and city lands in Bohemia.[22] In Hungary, the *Urbarial* patent of 1767 (applied to the Banat in 1780) attempted to prevent further encroachment on the peasant's land, but it was often ignored, and it excluded common pastures from its scope. A rapidly rising population (from 3.1 million in 1767 to 6.6 million in 1849) created land hunger and worsened the bargaining power of the peasant.[23]

Peasant emancipation in the Austrian Empire accompanied the revolution of 1848, a year of landlord weakness, and was confirmed by the Patent of 1853. At the time, 38.6 million days Hand-'Robot', 29.4 million days Team-'Robot', and a whole host of other burdens and duties had still remained.[24] In Hungary, the peasants paid nothing for their emancipation, landlords being compensated by a niggardly state, but many details were not settled until 1867, when the nobility was firmly back in the saddle. In the Austrian half of the Empire, peasants received much of their land, paying over one part of its value, amortized over forty years to the landlords in compensation. Total compensation to landlords rose to 520 million gulden, of which the Austrian share was 290 million. Larger farmers, who had existed under the old system, survived; only smaller farmers found their holdings unviable after the loss of the common, and sank down to become landless labourers. In Hungary a system not unlike the Russian emerged, the peasants paying 'rent' in kind and in the form of labour services. Sixty-four per cent of the peasants emerged with little or no land. The Hungarian nobility, which retained undisputed political power and could thus after 1867 shape economic policy in its own interests, was increasingly able to introduce more modern methods and thus extend the export of Hungarian grain, wine, and other agrarian products to Austria and areas further west in the years that followed.[25]

In Wallachia, the need to attract immigrants induced the ruler to abolish personal serfdom as early as 1746, but in Moldavia whence the population had not fled, there was only a redefinition of personal serfdom (*recinia*) in 1749. There was also limitation of the number of days' labour that the lords could demand. However, a strong reaction, something like a 'second serfdom', set in in the early nineteenth century, becoming worse after Turkey allowed the ports to be opened in 1829 and under the so-called 'Organic Regulation' of 1831. Within its apparently fixed provisions, the *Boyars* were able to use their juridical powers to enlarge the burden of the peasants' forced labour, and the process continued even after the Emancipation Act of 1864 which left about half the peasants without sufficient land, and most of them under the obligation to work off the purchase price by still more corvée labour. As pasture gave way to arable, and more Romanian grain began to reach world markets, there was an even stronger incentive to divert more of the peasant's working week for the lord's benefit. Here the peasant's position was further undermined by his land-hunger arising from population increase.[26] Under Turkish rule, peasants had been enserfed to the state rather than to their landlords, who had therefore a status akin to that of officials. After liberation, much of the land in Serbia, Bulgaria, and Greece therefore came into peasant proprietorship rather than into the hands of noble owners.[27]

Serfdom, in all its multifarious forms, was thus associated in parts of peripheral Europe from the eighteenth century both with developing modern industry elsewhere and with its absence at home. Estates worked by unfree labour were quite capable of switching from a static self-supply to an expanding external market demand until such times as the simultaneous transmission of liberal ideas, not to mention the arrival of revolutionary armies, made its survival untenable. The resulting reformed system was not necessarily 'capitalistic', though it was at least in part market-oriented, but it was certainly more open to later capitalistic penetration. There would be little value in disputing whether the survival of servile relations on the land inhibited industrialization, or whether it was the absence of modern industry which allowed servile relations to persist, since evidently both mutually reinforced each other.[28] What is clear is that the existence of a servile system, with its superstructure of feudal laws, political control, and appropriate attitudes to technological innovation, acted as one barrier to the spread of industrialization into certain regions, but not an insuperable one. Its temporary strengthening and eventual demise were not independent of the rise of industrial revolutions in the West, and, in turn, its late survival impressed certain characteristics on the local industrial system when the latter finally arose on its ruins.

A brief glance at the remaining important peripheral areas will complete the picture. In the Italian and Iberian peninsulas serfdom in the Russian sense had been abolished long before the eighteenth century, and its relics were ended by the Napoleonic administrations, though oppressive conditions for the peasantry, reminiscent of serfdom, certainly remained, particularly in Southern Italy, Portugal, and parts of Spain. Southern Italy had escaped the Napoleonic reform of 1808 and 1812 by delaying action until the nobility was back in power. The partition of the commons also benefited the richer landholders only. In contrast with Northern Italy, where conditions encouraged progressive capitalistic agriculture, the grain export boom from the south merely exhausted the soil.[29] In Spain, regional contrasts were equally marked. Peasants had secure holdings in the original Castilian territories in the north, as well as in the Basque lands and in industrializing Catalonia, where a modest quitrent, the *censo*, allowed the peasant to improve, inherit, mortgage, or sell his land, provided he paid suitable fines within his enfiteusis contract (freedom of action in return for fines). In the north-west, in Galicia and Asturias, the *foro* contract was binding for three generations and then renewable at higher rents: the Act of 1763, freezing these rents, led to a system of subletting which eventually impoverished the peasant and drove him into proto-industry. The greatest contrast was with the southern dry inland areas, particularly Andalusia, where large latifundia operated by exploiting a part-time landless labour force at starvation wages.[30]

While Spain as a whole was capable of raising an increasing output of grain, fruit, and especially wine in the course of the nineteenth century, the stagnating and unprogressive agricultural areas were incapable of aiding industrialization. The land could furnish neither labour nor capital, nor yet an expanding market to industry, except in the most favoured areas, the northern Italian plain and Catalonia.[31]

In strong contrast was the experience of the Scandinavian countries. Starting from a similar base, the dissolution of the feudal knot was achieved there in political conditions much more favourable to the peasantry than in Eastern Europe, by the Acts of 1786 in Denmark and 1789 in Sweden. The result was a relatively independent peasantry which was capable of adopting modern and market-oriented methods and greatly increasing output, both sustaining the industrializing sectors at home and providing some foreign exchange during the critical decades of the early 'spurt'.[32]

Industrial Centres

Before the industrial revolution, as we have seen, the gaps between different parts of Europe were much smaller than they were to become later and some industrial activity not unlike that in Inner Europe was to be found almost everywhere. There were also some significant differences. Apart from industries depending on locally found raw materials, there were few which supplied an external market, least of all a market in the advanced regions of Europe. Typically, there were peasant handicrafts supplying local needs, urban craftsmen, again geared to local markets, with possibly strong regional styling which might find markets farther afield, and a small luxury and/or armaments industry, fostered and subsidized by the local ruler. As a rule, these regions were on balance importers of finished manufactured products.

The Czech lands, as noted several times, came closest to the more advanced industrial regions of Inner Europe. A vigorous textile industry had developed in the eighteenth century, partly in the form of 'manufacture' but mainly as proto-industry with an export market as wide as those of neighbouring Saxony and Silesia. In linen, in particular, high quality and low wages assured not only European sales but even induced some British and other foreign capital and enterprise to develop them. Fifty-one per cent of the product of the industry was exported in 1796. There was also a woollen and a cotton industry, employing rural spinners and weavers, and urban finishing workshops. Many workers were still serfs, and so were even the putters-out, who could be obliged by their feudal lord to sell their wares at certain times and places, or to certain buyers only. There were large enterprises among them employing several thousand workers 'inside' and out, and the calico-printing works, especially those in Prague, also contained some advanced technology by the later eighteenth century. By the 1880s Bohemia employment in cotton exceeded that of Saxony, and in 1840 Austria as a whole contained more cotton-spindles than the Zollverein. By the 1830s some cotton-machinery engineering and also some ironworking began in the Czech lands, largely under British or German technical supervision, and from the 1840s on Bohemian ironworks delivered some of the materials for Austrian railways. Mechanization also started in Bohemian textiles in 1830–50, particularly cotton-spinning and printing, which employed 140,000, while the woollen industry trailed twenty years behind, and linen even further: some 400,000 linen hand-spinners, mostly in poor areas, opposed mechanization, and by the end of those decades shared the fate of their Flemish colleagues as soon as British machine-spun linen yarn reached Austria.[33]

Another important early industry was the milling of beet-sugar. After some abortive early beginnings, the industry restarted in 1831, and by 1870 had reached full mechanized maturity, as had another important regional industry, brewing.[34] Some traditional mining and timber-working concentrations were also found in Slovakia.[35]

While a part of the Czech lands thus approximated to the advanced western regions, other regions of Austria bore a much stronger similarity to the more stagnant East.

Against the undeniable advance of several, in contemporary [*c*.1850] terms, highly industrialised regions like Bohemia, Moravia, Silesia, Lower Austria and Styria, there was the contrast of the inactive stagnation, backwardness and traditionalism of the under-developed regions in the Alpine lands, and above all the provinces in the South-East and East of the Empire.[36]

Vienna and the surrounding province of Lower Austria formed another early industrial concentration, and so did Linz in Upper Austria with the headquarters of what was in the late eighteenth century the largest woollen manufactory in Europe, and the longest horse railway. Rather typically, that line, extending 130 km. in 1832 to Budweis and 200 km. (124 miles), including a branch to Gmünd, by 1836, had opted for horse traction after the success of the locomotive had become obvious, thus standing, like Austria herself, between progress and backwardness. Yet another concentration was formed by the iron and ironworking industry around the ore mountain in Styria. There were in Lower Austria in 1790 109 privileged 'manufactures', employing over 222,000 workers, of which 57 (with 18,300, plus close on 87,000 outworking spinners) were employed in textiles. Budapest was less industrialized, but as in Switzerland and Sweden in a different context, its own specialism had called into being by the 1840s at least one engineering firm that was leading in Europe: it constructed grain-mill rollers.[37]

That extraordinary patchwork quilt of nations and economies, the Habsburg Empire, could not only show examples of economic development from the most backward to almost the most advanced in Europe, it was also progressing even before the 1870s with reasonable speed.

In the mid-eighteenth century, only drastic mercantilist policies had been able to create certain key industries, even if not actually to make them competitive. The Pope was asked to reduce the number of the realm's feast days so that it could compete on more even terms with the Protestant countries, and he complied, 24 holidays being abolished in 1753 and another 20 in 1771.[38] By 1852 Austria came third in cotton spindlage and cotton consumption in Europe, after Britain and France, but ahead of Russia and well ahead of Germany, her iron output was respectable, so was the mileage of her railways, and her foreign trade showed a fairly balanced proportion of manufactures both in imports and exports.[39]

Eastern Germany, as well as Austria and the Czech lands, had some examples of serfs forced to work in what were quite modern types of industry in the eighteenth century, both in Silesia and in the older Prussian provinces; soldiers, prisoners, paupers, and orphans were from time to time similarly conscripted.[40] However, the classical examples of quite substantial industries subsisting under serfdom were to be found in the vast expanses of Russia.

They flourished best where there was a resource advantage, above all in the ironworks of the Urals region. Based on good ores and plentiful charcoal and water-power, the eighteenth-century Russian iron industry was not among the technical leaders, but it relied on a quite sophisticated transport system, including overland carriage, rivers, and canals, to cover the enormous distance to the Baltic ports which might require two navigational seasons to reach. There had been a flourishing iron industry around Tula in the seventeenth century, but starting practically from scratch in the Urals at the beginning of the century, the Russian industry had quickly overtaken the British as well as the Swedish, which had attempted to uphold prices by restricting sales,[41] the French and the German. By 1780, at the time of the British 'take-off', it produced nearly treble the British quantity of pig iron, according to one recent estimate.[42]

Table 5.1. Pig-Iron Production, 000 tons.

	Russia	(of which Urals)	Great Britain
1700	2.5	—	12
1720	10	(2)	17
1740	25	(12.5)	17
1760	60	(40)	27
1780	110	—	40
1790	130	—	80
1800	162	(130)	156

The quality and sheer extent of these supplies, derived from an area of over two hundred square miles, was sufficient to overcome the disadvantages of distance, which added 200% to the cost, and of the backward technology compared with Britain and even Sweden. Serf labour does not appear to have been an insuperable handicap at that stage. It clearly became so later with its rigid technology, high overheads, and conscripted part-time workers, when Britain pulled away, despite the handicap of poorer ores, by using coke and greatly improved technology. The Russian industry flourished, for a time, because of the West, and then declined once more because conditions in the West had changed. When the new demand for railway iron arose, it could not supply it.[43.]

There was also a local copper-mining industry, and other serfs might be used on estates in distilling, sugar refining, or traditional handicrafts.[44] There were state serfs in imperial mines and forests, and nobles' serfs working in industrial plants set up by their owners, but perhaps the best-known examples of servile industrial employment were the so-called 'possessional' factories. They were based on an edict of 1721 which made it possible to assign large numbers of serfs, sometimes entire villages, to certain factories. They would then belong to the factory, not to the owner, and would have to be bought and sold with the enterprise. The factories were than taken over by private merchants who were not serf-owners themselves, but quantity, quality, prices, and sales of the goods made were controlled by the bureaucracy. Altogether, the possessional factory formed a prime example of an institution developed for one purpose, misapplied to another, and it is not surprising that such workshops (they were not 'factories' in the modern sense) were soon found to be corrupt and inefficient. They were also a thorn in the flesh of nobles who used their own serfs, not much more efficiently, in their own factories, and an edict of 1762 prohibited the purchase of peasant villages. The phenomenon of the 'possessional factory' thereupon rapidly declined.[45]

It is not difficult to point to some centres of excellence in Russia towards the end of the eighteenth century, particularly where the government had taken a hand. After all, the purchasing power of the strong government of a large country which had not yet lost contact with western standards of income and output was large in contemporary terms.[46] There is a record of an early Watt-type engine built by a Russian in 1790 and an engine-building shop was set up in 1792 in St. Petersburg by one Charles Baird. Other foundries, engineering works, and gunworks followed, and in the Napoleonic Wars Russian artillery was technically among the best to be found. Again, the Russian government was among the first, in 1797, to order modern minting machinery installation from Boulton and Watt, and early examples of textile machinery and even construction can also be found. In 1802, an agricultural-machinery factory was set up by an Englishman.[47] Yet almost all of this was concentrated in a tiny corner of a very large territory, chiefly for non-commercial purposes, and it left most of the country quite untouched.

While most peasant villages, if not households, worked on some coarse textiles, mostly linen, some concentrations of the textile industry had begun to form in the eighteenth century, in the central provinces in and around Moscow. After 1820, a relatively modern factory industry developed in that region, able to supply most of the Russian Empire even if not capable of competing on even terms abroad. By the mid-century, Russian cotton production exceeded that of the Zollverein, over 60% of the cotton yarn used was home-produced and Russian machinery imports had risen ninefold between 1820 and 1840: Russia took 24% of the total British machinery exports in 1848. In linen, it is true, the export of fabrics had declined sharply by the mid-century, the export of raw flax had increased, and the Russian industry had thus become the typical loser in the race for technical progress, but there were some very modern mills also. The relative and temporary success of cotton-spinning showed the power of a simple, but almost up-to-date technology when combined with cheap labour and the protection of distance.[48]

In the Ukraine, 85% of all the sugar was alleged to have been produced in steam-driven factories by 1860, but in iron making progress was more chequered. The existing iron districts had no good coking-coal nearby, and despite some early experiments, the industry had stagnated. In 1870 the whole of Russia produced only 350,000 tons of pig iron, or little more than double the figure of 1800. Most of this was produced by charcoal, and used water-power, as at the beginning of the century.[49]

The total number of 'factories' had risen from 2,322 in 1812 with 119,000 workers, to 14,388, with 565,000 workers. Only 50% were free at the first date, compared with 87% in 1860. Including mines, ironworks, and other large enterprises, the total rises to 862,000, of whom 40% were serfs.[50] Although the industrial sector of the economy had thus freed itself from the trammells of serfdom before the Emancipation Edict, it would be wrong to imagine all, or even a substantial number of these workers to be employed in factories in the modern sense. Average employment per enterprise was only 39, and most of those were in workshops using very little fixed capital.

In the national statistics, Russian industry made a poor showing when the totals of its industrial regions were divided among the whole population on a per capita basis. Such a procedure under-stated the

Russian position in a certain sense, since St. Petersburg, the Moscow region, and above all Poland, where German, Jewish, and Polish enterprise had created major textile and engineering industries, a more settled industrial proletariat, and a society where lower interest rates and denser traffic showed a high stage of capitalist development, were not nearly as far out of line with the West as the average might suggest.[51] The contrast was greater in the two types of agrarian hinterland, the Russian serf village compared with, say, a village in Bavaria, Flanders, or Normandy.

The Iberian peninsula had some mining in traditional and newer concentrations, and royal manufactures for silk, tapestries, fine glass, and porcelain on which the government wasted enormous resources before allowing them to collapse.[52] There were also various fits and starts of genuine industrialization, of which perhaps the most hopeful was the brief efflorescence of cotton-spinning and weaving, as well as some ironworking and other industries established in South-Eastern Spain in the middle of the nineteenth century.[53] But it had one major industrial region which could stand comparison with the classical regions of Inner Europe: Catalonia. The eighteenth century saw a rapid population increase there accompanied by an agricultural revolution which allowed the Catalans to fill up their empty lands, irrigate hitherto infertile areas, and expand the cultivation of old and new cash crops. Above all, however, the cotton industry developed in what was as early as 1770 called 'a little England in the heart of Spain',[54] and by 1792, two-thirds of Catalan exports to the colonies were manufactures, much of the remainder consisting of spirits which had also undergone a process of industrial production. Catalonia was favoured by paying much lower taxes than the central parts of Spain, and cotton received protection in 1770 and 1779. By the end of the century cotton had become the leading sector. In 1805 there were 91 cotton mills in Barcelona, employing an alleged 10,000 workers, plus another 20,000 in rural areas, not counting hand-spinners, the total allegedly reaching 100,000. There was a large hat-making industry, a considerable woollen industry, a gun foundry, glass works, soap works, and much else. Coal was imported from Britain.

The war and the post-war crises destroyed much of this, particularly cotton. Catalonia's problem was that foreign markets were inaccessible, and the Spanish home market too poor: its main protected market, the South-American colonies, was lost and the homeward supply of capital dried up. There was renewed growth on a broader base from 1830 on, with capital repatriated from the colonies. In 1832 the Bonaplata mill in Barcelona installed its first Watt engine to be used for spinning, and by 1861 99% of spindles were mechanical and so were 45% of looms, but by then Catalonia had lost contact with the industrial leaders.[55]

In Italy, Piedmont and Liguria, and to a lesser extent Lombardy, had developed some modern industry and had begun to attract some of the attributes of industrial regions. At its base were the textiles, cotton and silk. But there was also some engineering, and very little mining and primitive iron-smelting. Some of the early and surprisingly advanced industries of Naples and also of Calabria failed to develop later.[56]

Further Theses on Economic Backwardness

It is time to return to some of the problems on contemporaneousness in nineteenth-century Europe. We have seen that the technology and the forms of organization transferred from the pioneeer regions to others created a different economic history rather than a repeat performance, precisely because the more backward regions were later, and found themselves in a world made different by the existence of the leaders themselves. These differences were evident in the transfer from the primary economy of Britain to the first followers. In the transfer into more backward regions still, the very technology and the very institutions themselves were frequently changed also. This transformation is often misunderstood, for things might carry the same name, but behind that common name might hide a very different reality.

We may start once more with railways, the universal carriers and status symbols. We have seen that only the advanced centres could, by the mid-nineteenth century, derive economic benefits from their construction: elsewhere they remained enclaves and frequently a heavy financial burden on the government and economy. But even when built, their functions were often quite different. In advanced regions they carried a dense, regular passenger traffic, mixed merchandise, as well as heavy bulk freight like coal, ore, or grain. Branches reached out to towns, mines, and ports to feed the main arteries. The cost savings derived from the new means of transport were enough to allow it to make charges which would cover expenses and leave a margin for profit. None of this was necessarily true in the periphery, where railways were built ahead of time, out of harmony with the economic stage of development of the surrounding territory.

There was some economic justification where a railway opened out a food or raw material supply zone, such as fertile wheat lands. The greater benefit of this development, it is true, tended to go to some advanced region elsewhere,[57] while the penetrated region was driven to specialize in a subordinate monoculture. In favourable cases, however, this might be the start of a more diversified growth of an expanded market economy. The railways of Hungary after 1867 and of

Southern Russia at about the same time were cases in point. In the late 1890s 23.3% of railway freight carried by the whole Russian network consisted of farm produce, and another 10% of processed foodstuffs, plus 13.5% of forestry products: over much of Russia the ratios were 70–90%.[58] There were no inward cargoes from the ports; nobles and officials travelled free, among the poor even long-distance seasonal harvest migrants walked.[59] Between the 1860s and the 1890s, freight per mile carried more than doubled, despite the accretion of less and less vital lines, giving an inkling of earlier under use, while the share of products other than grain and timber rose from 61% to 76% of the total. Even then, the 9.7 km. of railway per 1000 square kilometres in European Russia in 1895 (for Asiatic Russia it was 0.6 km.) compared with 106 km. for Britain and 80 km. for Germany,[60] and clearly had no role yet in any but long-distance traffic. In the words of one British traveller of 1895: 'On that journey one came into contact with the different stages of progressive civilization . . . the slow train on the mainline; the slower train on the branch line; the *Troika* to the noble country mansion; the sleigh and bullock to the peasant's home.'[61] Apart from the grain lands and the capital cities, the Russian railways of the first thirty to forty years were merely strategic; as another British visitor commented in 1854: 'Russian railroads are meant for Russian soldiers.'[62]

It was for similar reasons, and because of the absence of feeders, that Austrian railways failed to carry much even of the limited traffic there was. Even the relatively sensible Vienna–Brno northern railway could not attract enough traffic to become profitable, and for the others the chances were even smaller. They had been built only because there was money in it for the projectors and because the state willed it so and made the means available. Part of the state's objective was to level up the backward provinces, i.e. those with even less potential traffic. In Hungary, only around ten per cent of the lines had an industrial purpose: the rest was to tap the agricultural exports. By comparison even with Austria, Hungary had far less double track, and far less rolling-stock per track mile.[63] In Italy, likewise, railways brought no engineering orders to a country without iron or engineering capacity, and they had to be subsidized, for the traffic for them did not yet exist.[64]

In Spain the system was so obviously strategic, running from Madrid to various points on the periphery, that quite important cities *en route* were bypassed, as if the railway builders had no interest in their traffic; this followed the practice of earlier Spanish highways that were an 'alien line' across the country and even of such canals as existed.[65] In the words of one Spanish railway engineer in 1864, communications 'are of little use if there are no products to transport . . . Railways help to encourage the growth of industrial production; but where the latter does not exist they do not improvise [*sic*] it, as is shown by experience.' To which George Stephenson, prospecting the country in 1845, added: 'I have been a whole month in the country, but I have not seen during the whole of that time enough people of the right sort to fill a single train.'[66] In Sweden, railways built for the timber trade ultimately helped in economic development, but Ireland after 1850 has been described as 'an underdeveloped economy with a highly developed transport system'.[67] Worst of all was the system in the Balkans, for here the lines did not even obey the wishes of the territorial governments, but were part of a strategic battle of the Great Powers conducted at second hand. Even the most important Greek railway, the Athens–Piraeus–Pelopponese line, could raise only one quarter as much revenue per mile as the most rural and unprofitable French line, the Western. Turkey here furnishes the extreme example.[68]

It need hardly be stressed that for technical, no less than financial reasons the peripheral railways bore only a remote resemblance even in appearance to their models in the centre. Single-track, badly built, badly maintained, ramshackle, slow, unreliable, and always a little out of date, they were the poor relations of the European network as well as being, until such time as their surrounding societies caught up, more like foreign bodies than integral parts of their economies.

The obligation on peripheral Europe to accept mechanisms because their contemporary advanced neighbours had introduced them was particularly strong where the economic relationships of countries were closest despite their unequal development. Railways were one such field: central banking was another. Though protected by a nominally 'autonomous' metallic standard which did not automatically subordinate the weaker contemporaries to the pulls and pushes of the advanced economies as a 'managed' currency might have done, the peripheral countries had still, above all as debtors and future borrowers, to trim their sails to the wind from London or Paris. This was clear in the case of those who had tied their currencies to the bi-metallic franc, which included, at different times, Belgium, Switzerland, Italy, Romania, and several other states. It was also true of those who were aligned with 'neutral' gold, the system centred on London.

It would be quite wrong to believe that the Central or Official Banks (let alone other banks) of the peripheral regions were in any sense comparable with the Bank of England, the Banque de France, or the Reichsbank, in their functions, actions, or significance, despite the similarity of their name. Thus the Norges Bank of Trondheim, Norway, founded 1814, had no contact with or interest in industry or commerce, being a bank for official purposes: the Spanish Central Bank, the 'Bank of San Fernando' (1829), saw it as its duty to channel funds to the Treasury, and its successor, the Bank of Spain (1874), did not accept industrial assets as security until 1891. Worst of all, the Central Banks of the Balkan States were totally hamstrung by their overriding obligation to the foreign creditors to keep their countries linked to the gold standard.[69] Nothing could be further from the objectives of such institutions than to act as clearing-houses, let alone as sources, for commercial or industrial capital. By contrast, some peripheral late-comers used the central bank and the banking system deliberately to push forward industrialization, in part by mobilizing foreign credit: Russia furnished a good example.[70] In neither case could there be a parallel with contemporary advanced countries, or even with those countries when they in their turn had been at a similar stage of development.

Among the most misleading parallels is the comparison of urbanization between the periphery and the centre. In today's world the contrasts are well known. The large, and particularly the capital cities of countries in the Third World have reached a size and a growth-rate equal to or even greater than those in the West; but there is nothing in common, except the name of the city, between the vast shanty-towns of the unemployed, the broken-down public services compensated for by cheap exploitable labour, the concentrations of disease and hopelessness on the one hand,[71] and the centres of the highest standard of living yet achieved by man in the developed regions on the other.

Contrasts were almost as great, though of a different kind, in the nineteenth century, though they are frequently neglected even by the best of urban historians, beginning with A. F. Weber. Only with Max Weber, concentrating however on the classical and the medieval city, is there the beginning of an analysis of the differences.[72] This is not merely the distinction between capital city or administrative centre, industrial city or commercial port city, all of which might be found in the same country. The real differences of function and role derive from different stages of economic development, even of cities that were contemporary, were of similar size, and had nominally similar status.

Thus Berlin, the second German city after Vienna, was basically a garrison town. Of its 141,000 inhabitants in 1780, 33,000 were soldiers and their dependents, 13,000 officials, 10,000 servants—a total of 56,000 state employees of an absolute ruler, and their families. This bias changed only slowly in the course of the nineteenth century, and was still instrumental in determining the Berlin street system and the railway layout of Prussia. Small wonder that in 1793, 'en tout,

Berlin a l'air d'un grand quartier-général, d'un metropole militaire'.[73]
At a lower level, Halle had 3-4,000 military inhabitants; Magdeburg, 5-6,000 among 20,000 civilians; and Stettin, 4-5,000 among 13,000 civilians.[74]

St. Petersburg, a city containing 148,500 males and only 69,400 females in 1789, had among its 218,000 inhabitants 55,600 soldiers and members of their families. The rest, as in Berlin, were mostly officials, courtiers, or luxury-goods producers. Moscow in the early nineteenth century, likened by Max Weber, perhaps unfairly, to a 'large oriental city at the time of Diocletian', was 'a fortress and a seat of government, a centre for the church, and a commercial crossroads'. It was 'dimly lit, poorly policed and chronically short of water'.

In 1817 it had 4,341 street lamps, compared with London's 50,000. But there were 6 cathedrals, 21 monasteries, and 274 churches in 1819. It also had 1,000 watchmen, plus some constables, under the command of the military governor.[75]

Apart from those two cities, and Odessa later in the century, it is doubtful if other urban agglomerations in Russia could be described as towns and cities until the very end of the century. They were in economic and architectural structure very large villages, acting as (usually open-air) market centres for the surrounding countryside and, even if containing some industry, showing no other signs of urbanization. It should be stressed that until the emancipation, Russian towns had no free citizens in the European sense. Their inhabitants belonged to the rigidly limited merchant class unless they were nobles and officials, or their serfs.[76]

Southern Italy, by contrast, had numerous ancient towns, architecturally urban without a doubt, though with different economic functions from the cities of Inner Europe. Unlike the cities elsewhere, but similar to Holland, the Italian urban population had stagnated since the sixteenth and seventeenth centuries.[77] Naples, the fourth city in Europe in 1780, had among its 4-500,000 inhabitants some 100,000 beggars and homeless, an army of 20,000, and allegedly 30,000 lawyers. In 1860 there were still 400,000 people, and still no industrial or commercial centre. Instead, there was 'a malignant growth, and antheap of scurrying human beings, of whom two-thirds eked out their existence under unhealthy and humiliating conditions and without security'. Above this base, 'more mob than people', the middle class depended less on commerce than on 'the junk trade, occasional and most likely dubious commissions, lawyers' services of all varieties and courtiers' services of all kinds'. At the top was the nobility, alienated from the land and living beyond its means. Permeating it all was the *Camorra* 'with its own code of honour, taxes, courts and penalties, inflicting its own death sentences but inhibiting the actions of the legal courts'.[78] A close parallel might be found in arid Spain, with the un-productive, parasitic capital of Madrid on the one hand, and the 'essentially oversized farm villages' of Andalusia[79] on the other.

Such cities were far more akin to oriental conditions than to their contemporaries in Europe. There are European parallels evoked by the description of the Indian city as: 'Something of a military encampment of warriors and retainers living on the surplus and therefore creating a demand for services and manufactured goods, mostly of a luxury or semi-luxury type for the needs of the ruling class.'[80]

These cities, despite the similarity of their outward trappings, with their town halls, squares, mayors, and city police, were not only different from those of the West: they were also, on balance, a strongly negative influence on industrialization. Whereas in Inner Europe the city frequently provided capital, labour, mass markets, transport advantages, enterprise, and competition, and soon became almost symbolic for the industrializing region, the peripheral city, particularly the capital or administrative centre that was generally the fastest growing, was its very antithesis. There the landed classes spent their money wastefully, instead of improving their estates or the land and thus laying the foundation for economic progress.[81] The army of lackeys withdrew labour from useful work, as did the garrisons, and the commodity demand generated was precisely of a kind to inhibit industrial progress and strengthen the guild-ridden, expense-no-object, luxury crafts. Such cities overburdened the transport system—Madrid, indeed, killed off the agriculture of a whole region in order to keep itself going in its artificial location,[82] diverted enterprise and ambition, misdirected intelligence, as in the case of the Neapolitan lawyers, and drew attention away from local resources.

These tendencies, it should be noted, were strengthened, at least for a lengthy crucial period, by the very advances of Inner Europe. The demonstration effect here had largely negative consequences. Railways were laid to royal palaces, gas or water mains supplied a narrow layer of privileged classes, the new techniques were, and had to be because of the pressure of contemporaries, used to equip the army at greater expense than ever: innovations intended for mass markets were misused for a narrow luxury market and either diverted resources, or led to burdensome capital imports, while appearing to prove that the new-fangled notions do not pay. Above all, the city became the gate of entry to new technology manufactures from abroad, spreading outward from Naples, Madrid, Budapest, or St. Petersburg, to kill off native industry as unfashionable. There are exceptions, like St. Petersburg, but it is characteristic of most peripheral states that when industry finally does take root it is well away from the centres of conspicuous consumption. Meanwhile, in backward regions, even their apparently progressive aspects, like their large cities, may be converted into regressive liabilities by the advance of their contemporaries.

It is possible to see these phenomena as special cases of the Myrdal 'backwash' or snowball hypothesis, namely the assumption that once an economy pulls away, its advantages mount, and so do the disadvantages of those who fail to make an early start, so that the gap always widens. We have noted the hypothesis in Chapter 3 above in relation to regions, but it may be applied to larger economies and even to whole countries.[83] Once the gap has opened, the laggard is disadvantaged at every turn. Agricultural areas, like East Prussia, lose whatever industry they had and may then even have to suffer a loss of incomes in order to be able to sell their foodstuffs in international competition, as well as being subjected to severe price fluctuations, as seems to have happened in Russia for a while. Some of their best labour emigrates; railways serve only to bring in cheap manufactures from advanced regions to kill off home industries; foreign capital, as in Turkey, only helps to drag them down, and even if some modern units are started, they are handicapped by the absence or backwardness of ancillary industry, the problem of the growing minimum critical size for take-off.[84]

The Gerschenkron 'backwardness' theory illuminates the same handicap of the latecomer. For the 'deviations from the English paradigm', the 'big spurt', the need for substitutes, for bank and later government capital, the early concentration of industry in large units, are by definition second bests, because the conditions for the best, or model path, no longer exist. The handicaps are only in part due to the mere effluxion of time: they are largely due to the fact that the world has changed, that contemporaries are much richer, have advanced further, and thus themselves constitute a bigger obstacle[85] against which to set the better techniques and short cuts now available to the new industrializers, which the pioneers lacked at a similar stage.

Finally, governments of countries that have fallen behind are put under pressure to catch up, but find their avenues blocked: almost any measure that succeeds among the fortunate advanced countries, fails in their case, and there seems to be a phase when they can do no right. They tend to misconstrue their role as followers by wanting to copy the leaders exactly. Thus road and canal investments in Spain were largely wasted while, at the end of the nineteenth century, state support for the 'military-industrial complex' of Italy left the whole of her heavy industries, as well as her shipping, totally dependent on government support and without an incentive to become competitive.[86]

On the one hand, it could be argued that the sudden introduction

of free trade on unification damaged parts of Italy by exposing them
to the chill blast of foreign competition without adequate preparation.
Elsewhere, however, as among Russian industrialists or Hungarian large
landowners, tariff protection meant a continuation of easy-going incompetence or out-of-date methods. The tariff on Spanish grain levied
after 1825 forced the industrialized coastal regions to buy expensively
transported grain from inland rather than cheap grain imported by
sea, and severely damaged their feeble attempts to develop their industries. Action which did not hold up the industrialization of Germany
after 1879, proved near fatal in Spain. The Austrian attempt to assist
the 'spurt' in Bosnia–Hercegovina left the province worse off then
before. Similarly, the Spanish agrarian reforms, precisely because they
were attempted in a backward country, had results the exact opposite
of those intended. In Naples the attempt to encourage cotton-growing
by taxing raw cotton imports merely killed off the native cotton-
spinning industry.[87] Taxes in a country like Servia lay lightly on the
peasants, but heavy on the towns, whence any move for industrial
advance had to come; in Austria, they discriminated against the large
firm, which carried much of the progress of industry, but in Italy, the
system was geared to the industrial north, and Naples and Sicily were
damaged by it, even though the accusation that it was deliberately intended to favour the North may not have been true. In Russia, the
high taxation to balance the budget and thereby attract foreign investments may well have done more harm than good by inhibiting the
alternative, namely savings within the country.[88] Finally, when the
latecomer attempted foreign investment or imperialist adventures, he
found the best venues already taken, and his own inexperience an
additional adverse factor. Italy's costly, economically absurd, and
strategically pointless building of the railway from Antivary to Vir
Pazar in the Balkans in 1905-9[89] was mere farce compared with the
high drama of similar adventures on the part of Britain, France. or
Germany.

All these are examples of actions and measures which had been
positive and progressive on some occasions, but turned out to be negative and harmful to progress in the cases cited. The difference lay in
the stage of development reached by the economy concerned, and the
levels reached by contemporaries elsewhere. The peripheral countries
had relatively few links with each other, most of their trade being with
Inner Europe.[90] But both the advanced economies of Inner Europe and
the peripheral countries, found their relationship with the rest of
Europe, and the relative time-scale of overwhelming importance.

Of course, there were differences also among the backward regions.
The role of much of the periphery has been to turn into suppliers of

grain and other foodstuffs for the industrial core, and countries such as Russia and Hungary had begun to build up import earnings and some internal progress on such a base. The Balkans appeared later still on the scene as potential suppliers, around the turn of the twentieth century, but although their internal productive conditions were not dissimilar, they failed to repeat even the limited success of their models, backward though the latter were by western standards. The reason, it has been argued,[91] was that the economic system of Europe had meanwhile become less 'sympathetic' to such an export drive than it had been for Baltic, Russian, or Hungarian exports before the 1880s. The climate had changed, and we are in a new phase, the subject of the second part of this book.

Part II

The Phase of Economic Disintegration
the 1870s to 1945

Chapter 6

The Industrialization of the Periphery to 1914

A change came about in the character of the European economy in the 1870s. It is not possible to put an exact date to it: it never is in the case of movements of this kind. Its first signs became visible in the middle of the decade, the trigger often being the depression following the great investment boom of 1870-3, and the process was completed well before 1914. The change referred to is the growth, and ultimately the overwhelming influence, of the state and its role in the economic life of Europe.

The historic forces which brought about this development were closely connected with those involved in industrialization; the rise of the state, and ultimately the nation state as directing agent, is thus not accidental. The interrelations are too numerous and too complex to be dealt with here in any detail, but among them were the rise of a bourgeois class, of cities, and of new industries, each of which demanded the creation of new social and economic policies which in the last resort could originate only with the sovereign state. The ideals of nationalism, in many ways as significant in the revolutions in this period as were the shifting constellations of social class, had similar roots in part: the growth of literacy, of a literate class, and of a bourgeois class asserting its 'popular' right against dynastic and feudal privileges. Its spread into contemporaneous societies which were not yet in a comparably mature economic stage of development was to have the expected unbalancing results.

Above all, it was the progress of technology, at the heart of industrialization, which both enabled and compelled the state to take on ever increasing functions. Cheaper paper, printing, and other means of communication; better methods of transport and of guarding customs frontiers; more technological warfare requiring supporting industries; a greater share of foreign trade in national income, made possible by cheaper transport; a more urgent need for literate workers in industry; these and many other like developments pulled and pushed the often reluctant liberal–bourgeois governments into widening powers and responsibilities. As is the way of things, such growth, particularly the numerical expansion of the civil service, soon developed a momentum of its own and the state everywhere shed its reluctance to intervene in the economy. Among its most important new spheres of action was the attempted steerage and control over industry and, in particular, economic growth and the process of industrialization itself.

In the early phases of this growth, in the first three quarters of the nineteenth century, the expansion of state power was more often than not favourable to the new industry. We have noted above how often the state did more harm than good by maintaining the relics of mercantilist policies, and what damage might be done by the actions of backward states, misguidedly and anachronistically attempting to copy the leaders. By contrast, the great triumphs of nationalist-state building, the unification of Germany and Italy, clearly had positive effects on the industrialization of their societies—just as the application of the same principles to societies farther east at a different stage of development was to have disastrous consequences. Again, one of the few traditional functions of political authorities which had positive effects, public education, expanded in these decades, meeting new demands and using new means created by the industrialization process itself.

After the mid-1870s, however, the two developments, industrialization and the competing assertions of authority by the leading European states, came into conflict more often than they ran in harness. These conflicts, which increasingly affected the history of Europe, will be discussed in Chapters 7 and 8. Here we are concerned with the regions and countries of Europe which failed to make their breakthrough, or have their 'spurt', in the phase of integration, and whose industrialization therefore had to be carried through against a background of increasingly effective and increasingly destructive economic nationalism. It hardly needs to be stressed that these later, 'third-wave'[1] industrializers were not merely victims of this growing nationalism and its associated expansion of the role of the state, but themselves very strongly contributed to it.

The Gerschenkron model, according to which the state plays a larger role in industrialization among the later comers because the gap in technology and capital provision is by then so great that only the accumulated powers of the state can bridge it, unduly limits the causes and effects of this phenomenon. It sees it merely vertically as it were, in relation to a country's own history, and not laterally, in relation to its contemporaneous world. The fact was that all countries, including those well past their big spurt, showed an expanding role of the state, giving rise to the later concept of 'organised capitalism',[2] and affecting the conditions into which the later comers had to insert themselves. It is this fact, also, which justifies our treatment in this chapter in the conventional way, country by country. Development increasingly depended on positive government action, including action by social policies of various kinds to level up the backward regions,[3] though, as we shall see, this 'national' chapter organization does great violence to a development which was still dominated by regional differentials.

Being later, the European periphery does not merely have to allow greater scope to governments; its path is different also in other respects. Obviously, as stressed earlier, its later appearance on the scene means that the gap to be bridged is much wider. This may be dramatized by the calculation, whatever its degree of accuracy, that in the days of British industrialization, early in the nineteenth century, the capital per worker required was the equivalent of 4-5 months' wages; some decades later, 6-8 months' wages were necessary in France; whereas at the end of the century, when Hungary started, the load had risen to 3½ years' wages per worker.[4] This, in turn, has certain significant consequences, many of which have been stressed by Alexander Gerschenkron in his concept of backwardness. There is also now not merely a single model to be followed, that of Great Britain, but a choice of models, offering more or less apt alternatives.

But there are in addition the relationships with the rest of contemporary Europe which demand attention. We have seen them to be of critical importance in the more advanced regions, too, in this phase, but in the periphery they are of a fundamentally different nature. Some of the key differences may be enumerated here. First, industrialization finds less preparation, it appears to be less naturally arising from the antecedent development, and to be much more an import from without than a growth from within. Secondly, the main pressure is not so much on imitative action to preserve and modernize industry, but on complementary reaction to specialize in supplying raw materials, food, and other products by traditional methods. There is some similarity to the fate of the areas immediately surrounding the industrialized regions, but because of the greater distance from the advanced centres, and the greater extent of the territories concerned, it takes on a different guise. Agriculture or mining are therefore strongly stimulated and grow with the expansion of services such as commerce and transport, while industry stagnates for a time or even declines. This may well lead to the demotion of the peripheral area to 'colonial' status, in the sense of depending on foreign capital, seeing the natives degraded, and the gap between the local élite and the mass of the peasantry widened, but it need not do so. In the Scandinavian countries the same premisses led to very different results. Where the economy is small and flexible enough, as in Denmark, it can be best understood as an adapting part of Inner Europe, something like, say, Lincolnshire in England, rather than as an independent unit of the periphery.[5]

The variety of responses and adaptations is great, and will best be explained by actual examples.

The Habsburg Empire

Perhaps no other country bears clearer witness to the inappropriateness of the political frontier for the study of industrialization than does the Habsburg Monarchy. Straddling the dividing-line between Inner and peripheral Europe, the strong *Gefälle* within the country may be taken to symbolize the *Gefälle* of the Continent as a whole.[6] Since economic regions corresponded, even if very imperfectly, with some of the main national divisions which plagued the last decades of Austria–Hungary, they have received a good deal more attention in the literature than is customary in more homogeneous states.

In 1911–13, regional differences in incomes per head were as given in the following table (Kronen per head).[7]

Table 6.1.

Austria		Hungary*	
Alpine Lands†	790	Hungary of post-World War I	
Czech Lands‡	630	Boundaries	340
Galicia	250	Slovak lands	310
South Tirol, Trieste, Istria	450	Transylvania	270
Slovenia, Dalmatia	300	Croatia, Banat	310
Bukovina	300		
Average	520		

† The Later Republic of Austria.
‡ Bohemia, Moravia, Silesia.
* On a different base and should probably be raised somewhat for comparison.

The *Gefälle* was equally clear in terms of literacy. The percentage of illiterates in 1910 compared as follows:[8]

Vorarlberg	0.8%		
Lower Austria	2.4	Hungary proper	33.3
Bohemia	2.1		
Galicia	40.4		
Bukovina	53.9		
Dalmatia	62.8		

Hungary, with her fairly regular shape on the map, was clearly much more homogeneous, as well as more backward. The Austrian part of the Empire, sometimes referred to as Cisleithania, was stretched round a large part of the circumference of the Hungarian possessions, fitting rather like a brake-shoe around a wheel. Its two extremities (Bukovina and Galicia in the north, the Italian and South Slav provinces in the south) were the poorest, the central block much the most advanced region in the monarchy.

For some purposes, such as assessing its economic weight in the world, it is useful to consider the Empire as a whole, but since the two halves were administered in economic matters either separately or in part even differently after the Compromise of 1867, it is more appropriate to treat them separately, as 'Austria' (Cisleithania) and 'Hungary' (Transleithania). Certainly, in view of the Customs Union between the two partners operating from 1867, a large proportion of the economic literature of the day deals with the relationship and antagonisms between the two economies.

Taken by itself, Austria ranked with the leading industrializers of Inner Europe until well into the second half of the nineteenth century. This has often been forgotten, but has rightly been emphasized once more in the recent literature. According to Bairoch's composite index of industrialization, Austria was still level with Germany to 1860, with Sweden to 1880, and she was always ahead of Russia. On his calculation of GNP at constant prices, the Alpine parts of Austria exceeded France in 1860 and were still equal with her in 1913. In terms of horse-power in industry per head, Austria was well behind France and Germany, but had 3½ times the installation of Russia; the Czech lands alone, however, had overtaken France by 1880 and were well ahead by 1900. Around 1850, the cotton industry was still well ahead of the combined German ones, being third in Europe in terms of spindles in use and raw cotton consumed. Austria had among the largest and best-used railway networks in Europe, and in terms of track length per square mile or per inhabitant she was among the leaders from the 1870s. Her iron and coal production were well behind, though still a great deal higher than that of Russia, measured on a per capita basis, but as late as 1851 the per capita pig iron production still exceeded that of Germany. As a proportion of the European total, Austria produced 7.7% of the pig iron and 11.7% of the coal and lignite in 1908–12. The proportions employed in agriculture were not dissimilar from those of Germany or France in mid-century, but thereafter the structural conversion to industrial employment fell considerably behind. Finally, the degree of urbanization was comparable with that of Germany earlier on, though this also moved faster in Germany thereafter.[9]

Compared with most of Europe, the record is good and, until the mid-century, could stand comparison with Germany. Thereafter, Germany pulled away, but that comparison is hardly fair since there was no other country in Europe to match that unique German growth phase. Nevertheless, it is precisely because of the earlier similarity, and the similarity of culture and historical tradition, that the Austrian performance is generally deemed to have been a failure, and the question is frequently asked: why did Austria not match the German spurt after 1850? Some types of answer can be dismissed at once, since they refer to the period when development ran parallel, and could not therefore have been causes of the differences: the mercantilist and bureaucratic traditions, or the belated survival of servile conditions on the land. More explanatory power may lie in the suggestion that the critical years in which Austria fell behind, 1851-66, were marked by several wars on the part of Austria and the damaging deflationary policies to deal with their consequences, while Germany stayed neutral.[10] Wars are not necessarily hostile to industrialization and Germany waged her own wars in 1864-70, but there is a clear difference in the defeats suffered by Austria compared with the victories achieved by Prussia/ Germany.

The German spurt, it should be noted, was concentrated less in the older industrial regions such as Saxony or Silesia, or in the older industries, such as textiles. It was carried by heavy industry, centred on the Ruhr coalfield and the associated iron fields and heavy industry based on them, all well placed on transport routes to important markets. A Germany without those marvellous coal supplies at a time when coal was still the only major source of heat and power would scarcely have needed an explanation for its success: it is almost inconceivable that it could have pulled ahead of Austria at the then stage of technology.

Austrian rates of growth were, in fact, quite high; at 0.98% per annum per capita in 1860-1910, in Bairoch's figures, the growth-rate of GNP for the whole Monarchy was just above the European Average of 0.96%. Another calculation, based on the growth of real per capita assets, puts the annual per capita income growth at *c.* 2% in 1873-95/7 and again at 2% in the years to 1913, and a third rates it at 2.2% per annum for 1860-1913, among the highest in Europe. The industrial product (value added) per capita grew at a rate of 3.05% a year over 1841-1911, and 4.09% a year in the peak period 1865-85, according to Gross, and coal consumption by 10.4% a year in 1851-73 and 3.83% a year in 1871-1913. Coal output, in fact rose from 843,000 t. in 1851 to 30 million t. in 1913, the Hungarian figures being 110,000 t. and 5.8 million t. respectively.[11] The output of pig iron grew at an annual rate of 4% in 1851-73, 8.3% in 1891-1901, and 11.4% in 1901-11.

There is considerable disagreement as to when the real 'spurt' or 'take-off' occurred. N. Gross, basing himself largely on the coal consumption data, sees significant growth in the 1850s and 1860s, parallel with the German spurt; others point to the great investment boom, affecting particularly the infrastructure, of 1867-73; there are some who see the 'breakthrough' occurring in the 1880s and 1890s; others still are impressed by the accelerating economic growth on a broad front which helped to transform the Austrian economy, as it did most European countries, from the mid-1890s to 1914.[12] What is generally agreed is that, by the end of the period, there was no doubt that Austria was over the hump and had joined the ranks of the industrialized nations, and the conviction is also spreading that its path across that phase did not follow the model of Great Britain, Belgium, or Germany with their recognizable 'industrial revolutions'.

Within Austria, the new industrialism was highly localized, as in other advanced countries. In the German-speaking areas of what later became the Republic, industry was to be found around Vienna and in a belt reaching from the old ironworking areas of Styria to the textile regions of Upper Austria, with a small concentration in the far West, in Vorarlberg. However, the most industrialized regions were to be found in the Czech lands, where coal and iron ore were added to the traditional textile and engineering industries, with the heaviest concentrations around Prague, Brno, and along the northern frontier with Germany. By 1914 this was, in fact, one of the major industrial regions of Europe, with an industrial structure very similar to Germany's, containing 56% of Austrian industrial output, including 85% of her coal and lignite, over 50% of her pig-iron produce, 75% of cotton, 80% of woollen textiles, and 75% of her chemicals.[13] It has been calculated that taking the Monarchy as a whole, 11¼ million out of a total of 52 millions lived in industrialized regions in 1914.[14]

Austria's position within the European economy is best illustrated, as always, by her commodity and capital import and export figures. Her foreign-trade relations, with both her advanced and her backward neighbours, were strikingly similar to those of Germany with a lag of twenty to thirty years, Germany now representing the 'advanced' trading partner. In the 1850s and 1860s, between one-quarter and one-third of the Monarchy's trade was with the Zollverein. A major part of imports from the Zollverein consisted of cotton yarn, machinery, iron goods and textiles, exports being dominated by wool, timber, livestock, and grain. However, neither country conformed purely to one type or the other, and in particular, the provinces adjoining the Zollverein were the most advanced of Austria, while Bavaria, which formed a large part of the Zollverein border with Austria, was among the least industrial. Thus Austria also sent some steel, glass, linen and other manufactures north, while drawing agricultural commodities thence. To the south (including Italy) and east, Austria–Hungary exported largely finished manufactures in return for agrarian and primary products.[15]

This intermediate position, importing semi-manufactures and machinery from advanced Europe, and sending finished manufactures to the less advanced regions while importing food and raw materials, remained essentially the Austrian role until 1914,[16] though as the waves of industrialism lapped ever farther east, Austria took over increasingly the role of machine- and railway-equipment builder and supplier of high technology herself, as Germany had done before her. It may well have been that 'the shadow of German development loomed continuously over the efforts of the Monarchy to industrialize', but in fact, her lower wages allowed her to export finished manufactures, whereever her technology was up to date, to such markets as Germany and Switzerland. Some industry migrated even within the Monarchy to seek out lower wages.[17]

In capital movements, Austria also occupied an intermediary position in the European economy. Her banking system, based on Vienna, developed relatively early in relation to her industrial growth, largely on the basis of state loans. Even here, however, the first major investment bank, the Creditanstalt of 1855, was founded largely by foreign (French and German) capital, on the Crédit Mobilier model. Others followed soon after, the first Czech establishment, the Böhmische Eskompte Bank, opening its doors in 1863. Like the German banks, the Austrian firms took a direct part in the launching and management of industry, the Creditanstalt, for example, participating in 43 industrial firms in its total of 59 participations,[18] and like them, they contributed to the early formation of cartels. Austria has been described as the most cartelized economy after the German.[19]

Railways in particular depended on foreign, mostly French capital, and outside funds (including British, German, Swiss, Belgian, and even American capital) also found their way into other large enterprises. But the railways, sold to private enterprises or built by them in the first place in an earlier phase, began to be renationalized after the Act of 1881, and by the outbreak of war some 19,000 km. of the existing 23,000 km. of track were in the hands of the state.[20] In other fields, too, the balance of foreign investment began to swing round: by 1900 Austrian capital exports amounted to 80% of her capital imports and by 1913 Austria had clearly become a net exporter of capital, her annual balance of claims on capital account showing a figure of 597 million kronen against 246 million kronen in obligations, or a surplus of 350 million kronen. Total exported capital per head then stood at 180 francs (compared with 1,250 fr. for France and 450 fr. for Germany), and imported stood at 220 francs.[21]

The main target of Austrian investment was Hungary: of Hungary's 548 million kronen annual interest payments due abroad in 1913, 373 million went to the Austrian part of the Empire.[22] Austrian financiers and industrialists owned the lion's share of Hungarian railway capital, of which 70% came from abroad, as well as of her national debt, of which 55% was held abroad in 1914, and that part of her industrial and mining enterprises held in the form of joint stock. But later attempts by Hungary to subsidize industry by favourable railway rates and by concessions of various kinds added a further stimulus to Austrian firms to set up branches there. However, the share of foreign investment in Hungarian companies was falling, indicating the rapid strides which Hungary was making. From 60% in the boom years of 1867-73 it fell steadily to a mere 25.6% in 1900-13. According to another calculation, the Austrian share in Hungarian industrial joint-stock capital fell from 58% in 1880 to 27% in 1900.[23]

Hungary was still a largely agrarian country, with an economic and social structure showing many typical features of Eastern Europe. Her compulsory association with the advanced economy of Austria inside the free-trade zone of the Empire provided a textbook example of the effects of such a 'colonial' relationship without barriers. There is a long-standing, and still continuing debate, whether such association worked to the benefit, or the detriment, of Hungary—and, indeed, Austria.[24] In the nature of things, it can never be fully settled, because, if for no other reason, there can be no agreement as to what would constitute a 'better' development. There seems, however, to be a wide, and plausible consensus that the favourable market for her produce and the massive injections of capital provided by Austria gave Hungary a higher income than she would have had on her own, but held back her industrial growth. Behind a tariff wall, she would have been poorer but perhaps farther along the road to industrialization.

Certainly the contrasts between Hungary as largely agricultural, with a considerable commercial sector, some mining but little industry, in other words typically Eastern European, and Austria with a relatively developed industrial sector, or typically advanced, were stark enough. In 1841, there were only eleven steam-engines in the whole of Hungary, and in 1863 the horsepower used in industry and mining was a mere 8,601 HP. It grew rapidly thereafter, but even in 1898 the total was only 262,000 HP in industry (or 307,000 HP including mining), compared with 1.2 million HP in Austria and 3.9 million in Germany. Industrial employment in 1900 covered only 13.4% of the active population, compared with 23.3% in Austria and 37.5% in Germany,[25] and such industries as there were, were heavily concentrated on food processing, such as sugar refining and grain milling, beside the more traditional consumer goods in Budapest. No less than 41% of industrial output derived from food, against only 5% from textiles, but 26% in iron, metals, and engineering. By 1870 Budapest was the second largest milling centre in the world, after Minneapolis, but in 1900 27.5% of employment in larger enterprises was still in Budapest and in 1910, containing 4.8% of the country's population, the capital had 16.3% of its industrial employment and 23.6% of its commercial employment.[26]

Austria totally dominated Hungary's foreign trade, and this interdependence was still on the increase in the period 1884-1913, for which statistics exist. Hungary sent in those years about three-quarters of her exports to Austria, and drew a similar proportion from her: over half her exports were agricultural products, while between 80% and 90% of her imports were manufactures. By contrast, trade with Hungary represented only 30-40% of Austrian foreign trade.[27] In spite of this greater vulnerability, the advantages seemed to accrue increasingly to Hungary. The terms of trade turned strongly in Hungary's favour, and this, in turn, was not unconnected with being able to speak with a single voice, that of her large export-oriented landowners,[28] whereas Austria's interests were divided between industrialists and agrarians who were yet further disunited by the nationalities problem. Thus in a period when ever higher tariff barriers were being built up, agricultural protection, benefiting Hungary at the expense of the Austrian consumer, was applied more consistently than industrial protection, which aided Austria at the expense of the Hungarian; and while the Monarchy was persuaded to enter into tariff wars against Romania and Serbia at different times, in the interests of Hungarian producers but at great cost to Austrian industrial exports, Hungary heavily subsidized certain sections of her budding industry in order to protect them successfully against Austria.

Hungary became, in fact, one of the most rapidly growing economies in Europe. Her agriculture successfully switched from stock breeding to grain production and she became one of the world's leading grain exporters, although after 1900, in view of the rising tariffs elsewhere, almost all of these exports went to Austria. Hungarian agrarian output in 1911-13 stood at the following index figures (1864/6 = 100):

Wheat	285
Barley	250
Oats	219
Maize	362
Rye	118
Sugar-Beet	2165[29]

Total agricultural output, aided by the extension of the railway network, grew at the remarkable rate of 1.8%-2.2% per annum, and in view of the predominance of large estates which could afford to introduce modern methods, even though they did so but slowly, there was always sufficient labour set free to allow a rapid expansion of industry.[30]

Between 1880 and 1900, Hungarian output of coal rose 3.6-fold, iron ore 3.7-fold, steel 10.5-fold, and the number of railway wagons 11.5-fold. The railway network, which had in 1850 been one-fifth of that of Austria, whether measured per capita or per square mile, had in 1896–7 almost caught up in terms of area and exceeded the Austrian on a per capita basis.[31] After 1900 production rose even faster. The average annual rise of industrial output was a remarkable 7.3% in 1901–13 (compared with 4% in Austria) and total product per capita rose, at constant 1938–9 prices, from 425 Pengö in 1899–1901 to 500 Pengö in 1911–13 within the later (Trianon) Hungarian boundaries. Total product per person employed rose from 973 to 1,164 Pengö in the same period.[32] Parts of the new heavy industry were modern, well equipped, and highly productive, and, in the milling-equipment building firm of Ganz, Budapest had at least one modern enterprise of world stature.[33] Hungary was by no means industrialized by 1914, but the signs were set fair, even within the free-trade area which included the advanced regions of Austria.

Italy

Like Austria–Hungary, Italy was on the margin of Inner Europe with strongly marked regional differences representing in miniature the whole of the European *Gefälle*. These differences were greatly accentuated during industrialization: 'Italy', stated the Italian Labour Party in 1893, 'is a country in which a gap of almost a century separates one region from another and in which successive historical and contradictory epochs can be met within one nation.'[34] Before 1914 the industrial revolution with its modern industries had taken hold in one area only, the three north-western regions of the industrial 'triangle' having its points at Genoa, Milan, and Turin.

Italy had a long urban and craft-industrial tradition, she had good access to sea communications, a good climate almost uniquely in Europe suitable for growing the mulberry tree, the base of raw-silk production, and she had some scattered iron-ore deposits, in Lombardy and elsewhere. In the North, at least, there had been an early development of capitalist agriculture. On the other hand, internal communications were poor except in the Po Valley, and Italy lacks a solid coalfield. Her entry into the modern era had therefore to wait until the railways could deliver coal from abroad, and her industries could become competitive only when hydro-electric power became usable on a large scale, which was in the early years of this century. There was water-power in plenty in the Alps, and it was in the lower reaches of the Alpine Valleys that the first stirrings of water-driven industry were to be found.[35]

Before 1860, the only major export industry was silk-doubling and throwing. Silk yarn is the product of secondary industry, and according to that classification it ought to have been out of character for the backward economy to export such products to France and Britain. However, the technology used was primitive, the mills were small and scattered, and the yarn was the typical product of an older technology in which it is appropriate for the backward economy to specialize. In other textiles, it is worthy of note, Italy tended to make progress in weaving first, in the normal sequences for backward countries in the process of catching up.[36] There was also a small and out-of-date cotton-spinning industry.

Count Cavour who guided Italian economic policy after the unification of most of the country in 1860, and the urban intellectuals and rural landowners who supported him, had as their ideal a free-trade Europe in which railways would open out Italy as a supplier of agrarian products and consumer of the manufactures of others.[37] The aim was what one might call the Danish model and it may have been encouraged by the fact that, until 1857 at least, the terms of trade with industrial suppliers like Britain turned clearly and typically in Italy's favour as technical progress lowered the costs of production of manufactures.[38] Unification was certainly followed by an early expansion of the railway system. In 1859 there were only 1,798 km. in use in the whole peninsula, of which 919 km. were in Piedmont and 522 km. in Lombardy and Venetia, but only 98 km. in the whole Kingdom of Naples. In 1861–76, an average of 376 km. a year were added, 290 km. a year in 1877–85, and 302 km. a year in 1886–1905. By 1913 there were 19,000 km. and Italy was therefore in the same bracket as Austria or Hungary.[39] There were, however, few linkage effects at first, since Italy had to import all the iron and all the components except for the sleepers. Because of the losses, typical for an economy at that stage, made by the railways, the state had to buy back the Roman railway line in 1875 and gradually also the bulk of the others. The railways helped to set up some early engineering capacity by 1880, and they contributed to the boom of 1900–13, absorbing in the peak years 23–24% of the steel production.[40]

Output in the key modern industries was abysmally low in 1861 by comparison with such countries as France and Britain:[41]

	UK	France	Italy
Pig-Iron Output (000 t.)	4219	1065	25
Cotton Spindles Installed (million)	34	6.8	0.45
Steam-Engines Installed (000 HP)	2450	1120	50

Over-all growth-rates were well below those of the European average, and Italy lost ground. According to Bairoch's figure, GNP per capita grew in 1860–1910 at 0.39% a year compared with the European average of 0.96%, and the Italian GNP per capita was above the European average in 1830 and around it in 1860, but 20% below it in 1913.[42] Yet both those indices would be misleading. Modern Italian industry underwent a remarkable spurt in the last two decades of peace, and at least in the north-western quarter[43] a modern industrial society had been created, though national averages were inevitably depressed by the dead weight of the underdeveloped South.

The first twenty years 1860–80 were difficult years, when some traditional industries wilted under foreign competition, the standard of living fell as government expenditure and interest payments to foreign lenders rose, and agricultural export prices took a bad knock.[44] The 1880s were dominated by civic and house constructions. There followed a slump to 1895, and thereafter, both traditional industries and the industries of the 'second wave' of new industries registered remarkable progress. Cotton spindles rose to 2.1 million in 1900 and 4.6 million in 1914, of which no fewer than 3.5 million were ring spindles and in their wake, power-loom weaving expanded likewise, to 115,000 looms in 1912. Italy began to export cotton goods to areas farther down the gradient, such as Turkey and the Balkan countries. In silk also, weaving was added to throwing in the 1890s. Steel output rose from 200,000 t. in 1895 to 933,000 t. in 1913. Among the new industries, electrical engineering, aided by branches of the world's leading firms, Thomson–Houston, Siemens, and Brown Bovery,[45] and including the electrification of some of the nationalized railways, deserves special mention. Italy was also among the European pioneers of motor-car manufacture, being practically self-sufficient, there were promising starts in light engineering, including bicycles and typewriters, and G. B. Pirelli had opened his rubber factory in 1872. The annual industrial growth-rate in the final spurt of 1897–1913 has been variously estimated at 4.3%–5.4%, but electricity production rose by 15.0% a year, chemicals by 12.9%, iron and steel by 10.7%, and engineering by 7.5%.[46]

One reason frequently given for this remarkable spurt was the direct intervention by a number of large banks on the German model. After the bank crash of 1893 German bank capital began to flow in, and ultimately there were four major banking groups, of which two were German in origin, one Franco-Italian, and one Italian,[47] which provided not only the capital, but also much of the drive and the entrepreneurship. Hydro-electric power and the remittance by emigrants, which were a significant item in the balance of payments, also played a part.

Lastly, there was active government intervention. By promising large subsidies, the state encouraged native railway-engineering works (1882); it stood behind the Terni steelworks (1886), and by appropriate subsidies it also called a shaky shipbuilding industry into being (Act of 1885).

Italian tariff policy has come in for major debate. A low tariff of 1878 was followed by a stiffer one in 1887. Paul Bairoch has argued that it was this protection which created the condition for the industrial boom, whereas Gerschenkron maintained that the wrong industries, particularly iron and steel which required much imported coal, were being protected, and if policies had been more appropriate to Italian conditions, the spurt would have been much faster still.[48] In point of fact, however, it can be shown that 'effective' protection for industry was insignificant in spite of the high nominal rates, and that it would have made little difference, had an alternative tariff policy been introduced.[49]

The South was scarcely affected by these developments, and in many respects it bore a greater resemblance to the nearby African coast than to the advanced North.[50] In the 1870s the South, on 41% of the land, produced 53% of wheat and 32% of potatoes, but had only 17% of the industrial workers and 16% of the steam-boilers. Around 1900 it had 25.9% of the population, but only 12.1% of the taxable property. According to another calculation, 25.6% of the population in the mainland South had only 9.8% of the country's employment in firms of over 10 employees.[51] It could not form a market for the northern industrial goods, just as the North could not employ all its surplus labour. The result was one of the largest waves of emigrants ever to leave Europe. From an annual rate of *c*.150,000 in the 1880s it rose to 353,000 in 1900 and averaged 679,000 in 1909-13. Most of them were from the non-industrialized regions of Italy, the South and the Veneto. Over the period of 1891-1910 as a whole, the rate was the second highest in Europe, exceeded only by the Irish: 0.77% of the total population left every year; in the final years, it was up to 2%.[52] These movements, also, were consequences of the uneven industrialization of Europe.

Scandinavia and Holland

Around the mid-century the Scandinavian countries, Denmark, Sweden, and Norway, appeared to occupy a position very similar to that of the peripheral states in the south and east of Europe. Mainly agricultural, with scarcely any modern industry, poor, and dependent, they seemed destined to being opened up by foreign capital in order to become 'colonised' as suppliers of food and raw materials to the advanced areas of Inner Europe.

However, while their history, too, cannot be understood except as part of the European economy, close economic attachment to more powerful and more advanced nations does not seem in their case to have hampered either their growth in prosperity or their industrializ-ation. Though dangerously specialized in one or two primary com-modities—Denmark providing food, Sweden iron ore and timber, and Norway timber and fish—their heavy dependence on the British and later also the German markets, whence they initially also drew most of their manufactures, led not so much to a colonial relationship as to their becoming part of the metropolitan economies to all intents and purposes.[53] As in the case of the eastern and southern periphery, their economic spurts were heavily financed from abroad, and like them, foreign capital was channelled in mostly via government loans and found its way chiefly into railways, other infrastructure invest-ment, and primary production, particularly mining. Even Denmark, which had started out around 1870 as a creditor on capital account, having benefited by the conversion of the sound tolls in 1857 and the Sleswig–Holstein settlement in 1864, ended heavily in debt by 1914.[54] However, for them as for the USA and Belgium earlier, using other people's capital turned out to be an advantage rather than a disad-vantage and the expansionary boom was in each case export-led.

Between them, the three northern countries belonged to the fastest growing economies in Europe in the latter part of the century, both in terms of output and income. In Paul Bairoch's tabulation they appear as in the following table.[55]

Table 6.2. Per Capita GNP at constant prices (1960 US $)

	1830	1860	1913	Growth Rate 1830–1914, % p.a.
Denmark	(208)	294	862	1.73
Norway	(280)	401	749	1.19
Sweden	(194)	225	680	1.52
Netherlands	(347)	452	754	0.94
Finland	(188)	(241)	(520)	(1.23)
European Average	240	310	534	0.97

Moreover, though their late arrival implied a fast spurt and a wide gap, they managed to achieve industrialization with fewer sacrifices by their workpeople. The exploitation of children in factories lasted for a brief period only, and they avoided altogether being saddled with the soul-destroying slums of the soot-blackened industrial cities of Inner Europe. Those advantages arose in part precisely because these countries entered their grown path in the phase of the 'third wave' or second industrial revolution, with its cleaner hydro-electric power, its consumer-goods industries, and its social conscience and organizational lessons learnt in the first.

They were not particularly favoured by resource endowment. Norway and Sweden, it is true, had some resources of a kind also possessed by Finland and Russia, but their large spread on the map should not deceive us as to the relatively small extent of their cultivable land; agricultural land was more plentiful in Denmark, but she lacked any other resources whatever.

% of Land Use, 1901[56]

	Arable	Permanent Grass	Forest	Other and Unused
Denmark	69	6	8	17
Norway	2	1	22	75
Sweden	9	3	52	36

There was, in fact, serious overpopulation on the land in mid-century before industrialization could absorb the additional hands. It led, as in so many other countries, to massive emigration, particularly in the 1880s and 1890s, and again in the early years of the century. In 1871–1910 Norway still belonged to the highest emigrant regions in Europe, and Sweden and Denmark to the middle range.[57] The success of the northern countries must be sought in such factors as favourable location in terms of sea transport, early commercial and banking development, and human capital in the form of an active, healthy, law-abiding, and enterprising population enjoying the advantages of a relatively good education and early emancipation from serfdom. Sweden was the archetype of the 'impoverished sophisticate'.[58] Once again, a free peasant-based economy proved to be far more flexible and progressive than one based on large landed estates.

The Danish transformation was in many ways the most remarkable, since it was based on agriculture, under conditions of climate and soil that were in no way particularly favoured. It is generally agreed that the flexibility which allowed Denmark to achieve this development rested on her middle farmers who held 55% of the land in 1895 in holdings of *c*.50–200 acres. Denmark is the classic case of a country which opted for free trade, deciding to benefit from, rather than shut out, the cheap food which arrived in large quantities from the New World in the 1870s. Within a generation the Danish economy had switched from exporting grain to exporting meat and dairy products, while importing grain, used in part as cheap feed. It secured foreign markets in a highly competitive world by technical innovation, rising yields, and quality control. These in turn rested on co-operation, particularly co-operative dairies (the first in 1882), abattoirs (1887), and egg-packing stations (1891), as well as co-operative purchasing societies, and on education, of which agricultural colleges and the famous Folk High Schools were the most remarkable components.[59]

Once more, the division into 'primary' and 'secondary' sector is misleading: trading relations of advanced countries should show strength in high-technology, rather than simply secondary sectors, and Denmark's industrialization was largely achieved by high-technology agriculture. In industrial employment, which rose from 25% in 1845 to 29.5% of the total in 1901, some examples of modern industry were in this period superimposed on the traditional crafts. Employment in firms of over twenty-one workers rose from 77,300 in 1897 to 118,400 in 1913 and included one world-famous shipyard. Characteristically, textiles employed only 6% of those employed in industry at the beginning of the century, whereas food processing employed over 17%, using 28% of the horse-power. Clothing still employed over 20%, and metals and machinery were creeping up to that figure before World War I.[60] Industrial output grew at 4–5% p.a. (in 1890–7 at 7.2%) and virtually all of it was for the home market. In 1855–72, and again in 1906–14, much of it was concentrated in the capital, Copenhagen, which in 1914 contained 43.5% of those employed in large firms.[61]

Sweden had been a net importer of food since at least 1685, and by 1914 she imported half her wheat and 29% of all her grain, even though nearly half the population was still working on the land, five-sixths of them as peasants. Her traditional exports were iron as well as copper. In the nineteenth century her ironmaking fell behind technically, using the Lancashire process from *c*.1820 into the 1890s. Yet output of bar iron rose tenfold between 1815 and 1910, and modern steelmaking began with an open-hearth works in 1868, using imported coal, and the 'basic' process was introduced in 1890. Possibly Sweden was held back technologically by her surfeit of timber, though her restrictive and monopolistic policies on iron production, which lasted until 1859, were at least in part dictated by the need to husband charcoal supplies round the furnaces. It was the plentiful supply of water-power that allowed Swedish steelmaking as well as other industries to expand later without coming up against limitations of energy sources.[62]

The timber export boom ran from *c*.1840–1900, at its peak accounting for 40–45% of exports. It was largely induced by demand from Britain. In part it depended on the railway, and it was significant for the backward state of the economy that the country's first railway, built in 1849, was still worked by horse. The first short stretch of steam railway was opened only in 1856. Sawmilling and, later, pulp production helped the modernization of Swedish industry in the last third of the century. The real spectacular growth in industry occurred from 1893 on. Coal consumption rose from an average of 1.5 million t. in 1886–90 to 5.25 m.t. in 1911–15, while simultaneously the installation of hydro-electric power rose from 150,000 kw. to 550,000 kw.[63]

It is significant that while in the boom of 1871–4 when the first 'industrial breakthrough' occurred and in 1887–9 exports, and particularly exports of manufactures, rose faster than manufacturing output, this was no longer so in the 1890s and the early twentieth century.[64] The home market had now become of greater significance and Sweden, in close parallel to Switzerland, entered the international division of labour by concentrating in her exports on a small range, largely of sophisticated engineering products, requiring high skill and ingenuity and advanced technology. There also began a closer co-operation with the other Scandinavian countries.[65]

Norway had two assets of significance in this phase, her easy access to the sea, and her timber resources, to which were added later, as in Sweden, her wealth of hydro-power. The exploitation of the timber, again, as in Sweden and Finland, had to wait for the repeal of the British preferential duties for Canada in 1842, and by the 1870s sawmills and soon also pulp and paper-mills were the main agents for introducing modern engineering and modern industrial methods into the country.

About one-third of the timber industry and nearly all the railways were foreign-financed, but Norway's shipping was essentially native. This quite remarkable asset developed out of the traditional fishing industry, which continued to supply one of Norway's main exports. Norwegian crews sailing either old-fashioned sailing ships or second-hand steamships, kept one of the largest fleets in the world afloat on the basis of skill, low wages, and specialization on particular types of run. Shipping, whaling, and fishing provided 60% of Norway's exports in 1865–85, and 55% in 1895–1915.[66]

In Norway, even more than in her two neighbours, the remarkable expansion after 1870 was export-led, rather than based on the home market—a consequence of the high degree of integration with Inner Europe. The population was small, agriculture remained stagnant and largely self-sufficient, and it was often easier to transport goods from abroad than from another part of the country.[67] When hydro-electric technology reached the point of commercial feasibility around the turn of the century, foreign capital combined with local skills and facilities to set up some of the largest and most up-to-date power, smelting, and nitrogen plants in Europe.[68] Hydro-electric installations were enlarged from 200,000 kw. in 1908 to 400,000 kw. in 1912. Thus Norway, perhaps even more than the others, was spared the agony of the interim stage of coal-based urbanization.

Holland was yet another small country which was closely integrated with Inner Europe and set off on her phase of industrialization in the great secular boom to 1913. Like Denmark, she drew the maximum benefit of this integration by maintaining a free-trade policy, but she was distinguished in two major respects from the Scandinavians. First, she did not 'take-off' in mid-century from the position of a poor backwoods economy, but, as the tabulation on p. 233 above shows, had carried over from her days of glory in the seventeenth century a level of per capita incomes that was among the highest in Europe. Secondly, her specialist role in Europe was not that of supplier of food or raw materials, but of commercial services, including transit trade from her colonies, and financial services. Over much of the nineteenth century, Holland had by far the highest absolute figures of international trade per capita in Europe. To this service sector corresponded the relatively high incomes and wages, which were, over most of the nineteenth century, an adverse factor in Holland's industrialization.[69] There was, however, also a continuing tradition of specialist food production not dissimilar from the Danish model.

In 1815–30 Holland built some major canals, but in railway building, as in the installation of steam-engines, it had fallen far behind Belgium, which was then the European leader.[70] Employment and output in the key textile industries actually declined, and the Dutch have frequently been criticized, mostly by other Dutch, for living simply on their past glory—a failing with which the Britain of the later twentieth century is not entirely unfamiliar. *De oude tijden komen wederum* ('the old days will come again') seemed to be the operative sentiment.[71]

Yet many of the traditional industries, such as sugar refining, survived and expanded. Shipbuilding began to be modernized by 1850, and in some regions there was also a healthy growth of textiles on a mechanized basis after 1850. Holland could be described as a country which had no leading sector, but experienced a less painful balanced growth which has for that reason often been misunderstood. Among the industries which expanded then were sugar refining, tobacco curing, shipbuilding, engineering, and metals.[72] The Dutch transition was certainly eased by the colonies, for apart from providing goods for the traditional transit trade, the weaker and less competitive industries such as textiles and metal goods could still find sales in the exclusive colonial markets.[73]

The Dutch 'spurt' of the more conventional kind occurred in the years between 1890 and World War I against a background of free trade and agricultural crisis and readjustment. What was significant then was not only the switch to engineering and modern food-processing, but also the growth of large firms. As a proportion of all larger industrial units, large firms increased from 15.2% of employment in 1889 to 29.2% in 1909. There also occurred a distinct upward 'kink' of investment as against the growth of incomes around 1890, exemplified by the following figures:

Index 1876=100	*1891*	*1910*
Net Imports of Machinery and Tools	150	390
Net Imports of Iron and Iron Goods	139	400
Employment in Engineering	140	540
Additional Steam-Engine Capacity Installed in the year	160	390

In each branch the real growth took place after 1890.[74] As in the case of the Scandinavian countries, the relatively high proportion of employment in engineering was significant for the future.

The Russian Empire

We now turn from those countries and regions which were without doubt launched on an industrializing career by 1914 to those whose take-off was doubtful, as well as to those who were still taxi-ing to the runway. Russia belongs to the doubtful group. She has been fortunate in her economic historians who have celebrated her pre-1914 achievements and are in dispute, at most, only as to when exactly the process began. Yet, compared with the rest of Europe, all the Russian statistics remained dismally low. This was not only because her industrial zones were thinner on the ground, more diluted by hinterland areas, and thus less able to influence the national averages, but also because the agricultural sector was by far the poorest, most backward, and worst equipped, her illiteracy rate the highest, while several of the leading regions themselves still showed features of backwardness no longer met with in Inner Europe or among the second echelon of followers. Russia's role in the international division of labour was still that of the food producer starving himself to eke out an exportable surplus.

In per capita terms, weighed down by her vast poverty-stricken peasantry, Russia cut a very poor figure. Thus the per capita GNP in 1913 in the area later to become the USSR amounted to only 326 US $ of 1960, the fourth lowest, compared with an average of 534 for Europe as a whole. Similarly, the horse-power used in industry in 1907, 14.7 per 1,000 inhabitants, corresponded to the British figure of the early 1830s and the German figure for the 1860s, a lag of seventy and forty years respectively.[75] In absolute terms the record was better. Russia's consumption of raw cotton among the five leading nations had risen from 7.8% in 1890 to 12% in 1913, and her pig-iron production from 3.7% to 6.5%. Yet even so, her coal and pig-iron production was still below that of France, herself a laggard among the western countries diluted by a large agrarian sector, with a population only one-quarter the size of Russia's. Worse still was the position of engineering. Russia imported 35% of her electro-technical goods, 54% of her farm machinery, and 100% of her motor cars, rubber, and aluminium. Two-thirds of the machinery used in her industries had been made abroad.[76]

Among the most successful aspects of the Russian drive to industrialization in this phase was the extension of the railway network, the building-up of industry in the traditional areas of Petersburg, Poland, and the central provinces around Moscow, and the development of two new modern industrial regions based on national resources, Baku oil and Donetz coal with Krivoi Rog iron ore.

The early railways, as we have seen, were built essentially for strategic or prestige purposes and had few positive economic linkages. An important component of the later building programme, the Trans-Siberian Railway and its main branches begun in 1891, also had mainly political and military rather than economic objectives. Nevertheless, it could be said that in the second phase railways 'led to the introduction of modern technical and organisational methods in the country and paved the way for the rapid rise of international trade in the 1870's, based largely on the export of grain'.[77] While the opening-up of the export potential was the main achievement of the second phase, the third phase of the fast spurt beginning in the 1890s was to a not insignificant extent anchored in the iron and steel and engineering capacity called into being by the railway building itself. While in 1870–9 only 41% of Russian iron and steel needs were met from internal sources, the accelerating building programme was matched by growing iron and steel capacity: John Hughes's pioneer South Russia ironworks survived only because of railway orders. In 1893–9 the railways were said to have used 37% of the national pig-iron output, or not far short of the total output of 1890, but only a third of the enlarged make of 1900. By then, only 27% of the pig-iron consumption had to be imported. Here was a classic case of import substitution.[78]

The first peak of building occurred in 1869–73, when 1,884 km. a year were laid, but in the second peak, 1894–1903, the average for ten years was over 2,000 km. a year, about a third of which was built in Asia. By the end of the period Russia had the largest network in Europe, even though it was still small by comparison with the USA, and among the lowest in terms of mileage per acre or per head of population.[79] Railways now reached the cotton-growing Central Asiatic provinces as well as the Urals and the minerals of Siberia. The early lines had been generally built by (foreign) private companies under state guarantee, but the state also owned about 730 miles of railways by 1870, it shortly after took control over the Great Russian Railway Company, and after 1878 built and operated many more. It was through the railways that the state exerted its most direct influence on the Russian economy, particularly by channelling foreign funds into home development.[80]

Of the traditional industries, the record of cotton-spinning and weaving was undoubtedly the most successful in international comparative terms. Firmly based on earlier foundations laid in the three main industrial regions, Moscow–Central, Petersburg–Baltic, and Lodz in Poland, it expanded further, relying increasingly on raw-cotton growth within the Empire. It became a large-scale factory industry, the leading one among the textile and other mills which emerged in the last quarter of the century, accounting for 61% of textile production in 1887 and 45% in 1897,[81] and it was to increase particularly rapidly in the 1890s. Apart from the woollen and linen industry, large-scale production was also extended in the sugar refineries, in engineering and armaments production, and in some other industries.

Basically, Russia bore the character of a backward economy which had its modern industry implanted ready-made from abroad in a social system which did not provide a favourable soil for it. One consequence was that there was relatively little to be found between the large mill at one extreme, and *Kustar* or handicraft production at the other. The Kronholm cotton mill, founded among many others by Ludwig Knoop, was reputedly the largest in the world with its 12,000 workers, 475,000 spindles, and 3,700 looms on its site along the River Narva some 75 miles from St. Petersburg.[82] Technology was behind the most advanced in the West, and labour, in general, was footloose, unskilled, and unreliable by western standards as the rapid expansion brought ever new waves of peasants into the cities. In both respects there was a clear tendency to catch up and for a more stable work-force to develop, as in the West.[83]

Among the leading regions, the central area around Moscow employed in 1900 31.1% of the manpower in manufacturing, including 40.4% of factory labour, 60% of the spindles, and 74% of the looms to be found in Russia. Beside textiles, it also had engineering and specialized metallurgy. By 1914 its share had risen to 42.6% of the factory labour and 35.9% of total production. Yet even in the most concentrated areas of this industrial region factories were still thin on the ground, sitting sometimes in isolated spots, surrounded by the barracks of the living quarters, miles from other centres of population.

St. Petersburg tended to fall behind in the textile trades in this period, but increased its engineering, particularly railway, shipbuilding, and armaments capacity. Riga and Talinn had similar specialisms. Industry here was not spread over a broad region, but concentrated in the few large cities, and foreign capital and entrepreneurship played a particularly important part. Poland had textiles as well as coal and metals, and exported mainly manufactures to the rest of Russia in return for raw materials and agricultural production. Its growth slowed down after 1890, when that of the rest of the Empire accelerated, because of deliberate tariff and other forms of discrimination by the Russian government. Nevertheless, its total industrial output has been estimated to have risen from 11 million roubles in 1850 to 171 million in 1880 and 860 million in 1913.[84]

The most dramatic spurts occurred in the case of the heavy industries in the South. The iron industry in the older districts, the Urals and the central provinces, had been left behind by progress in other countries and Russian pig-iron production had fallen from 4% to 2% of the world's total between 1860 and 1880. The new impetus came from the rich ore field at Krivoi-Rog discovered in 1882. John Hughes's works at Yusovka (Stalino, Donetsk) was set up in 1871 and was in full production by 1874. Coal at Lugansk was proved in 1873. There were some years of uncertainty, but the industry was stabilized by the completion of the Donets railway, linking the Donets coal to the ore field over a distance of 200 miles by 1886. There followed a rush of investment; by 1898 there were 17 large smelting-works, 29 blast-furnaces and another 12 in the process of being built. These were modern units approximating to contemporary western technology. By 1913 the Donets produced 87% of the Russian coal, 74% of the pig iron, and 63% of the steel, excluding Poland.[85]

The rise of the Caucasian oil field was equally dramatic, though there were fewer linkages since the capital was largely foreign, the location was peripheral, and the product was mainly for export. The first modern plant was put up by Robert Nobel, a Swede, in the 1870s and other refineries as well as a fleet of tank steamers soon followed. The Trans-Caucasian Railway further helped the transport problem. Output rose from 2 million poods in 1870 to 631 million in 1900, when Russia produced one-third of the world's total, and then stagnated, the Russian share falling to one-sixth by 1913.[86]

These heavy industries, together with railway and other engineering and the cotton manufacture, were at the centre of the Russian industrialization drive. Some statistics may illustrate the tempo. (See Table 6.3) This may be compared with the general index of value added in manufacture at constant prices, which increased as follows[87] (1900 = 100):

1860	13.9
1890	50.7
1900	100.0
1913	163.6

Table 6.3. Production in Russia (million poods)[88]

	1860-4	1887	1900	1913
Pig Iron	18.1	36	177	283
Coal	21.8	276	986	2215
Iron and Steel	—	35	163	246
Oil	—	155	631	561
Cotton (imports)	—	11.5	16	26

Population, meanwhile, had increased from 74 million in 1861 to 133 million in 1901 and 161 million in 1911.

The growth of Russian industrial output and industry occurred in brief spurts, followed by some years of stagnation and recovery. The first boom lasted *c*.1867-73. It was the great spurt of the 1890s which is held by several observers to have constituted the critical breakthrough, to be followed by a second, though slower spurt in the years before the war. The spurt of the 1890s is associated with railway investment and the reign of Count Vitte, who set out with the deliberate aim of attracting foreign capital, mainly by maintaining orthodox financial policies to inspire confidence abroad, and of channelling these funds into railway and other investment projects. Whatever the cause of the trigger, the expansion was remarkable by any standards. The number of workers in large industrial enterprises rose from 1,425,000 in 1890 to 2,373,000 in 1900, and the value of their output from 1,500 million roubles to over 3,400 million.[89] It became the classical Gerschenkron spurt, showing a growth of industrial production of 8% p.a., a model for others who were far enough backward to require government finance to help them over the hump.[90] In the later boom of 1907-14, Russia was, according to the same view, past that stage, and it was now the banks that undertook most of the financing of major industrial projects and a more prosperous peasantry, rather than the government, that provided the market. Industrial output rose at 6.25% per annum compared with a rate of 5.72% for 1895-1913 or, by another calculation, of 5% per annum for 1860-1913.[91]

However, the matter was more complex than this, for while it is true that the role of the government declined, that of foreign capital remained dominant, partly exercised via banks that were themselves foreign owned or controlled. The importance of outside, as distinct from internal, ploughed-back funds remained high and with it the tendency towards large enterprises in cartelized industries. In 1914 41.4% of the factory work force was employed in units employing 1,000 workers each or over.[92]

The efforts of a government of what was by far the largest European country, concentrated on a few centres, were bound to achieve some result, no matter how limited when spread over the population as a whole on a per capita basis. Russia was helped also by possessing some of the key resources and by her political power which made her friendship valuable and induced friendly foreign governments to encourage their citizens to invest in Russian bonds. Yet quite apart from the low absolute levels achieved, there were many signs that Russia was still a dependent economy, not yet among the industrial leaders. There was the continuing reliance on foreign capital as well as on foreign engineering and machinery for complex or advanced technology; the primitive conditions surrounding even the most advanced work; the failure to exploit many of the natural resources which later investigation showed to have existed; the unregenerate technical backwardness of some industries; the heavy concentration on food processing and consumer goods.[93] Perhaps the verdict must be that her industrial revolution was but a 'partial' or 'incomplete' one, applicable to some sectors and regions, but not to the whole of Russia.[94]

The Outer Periphery: Iberia and the Balkan Peninsula

The remaining parts of Europe, the Iberian and Balkan peninsulas, did not get beyond the beginning of the industrialization process, except in very limited sectors and regions. Spain, as we noted in Chapter 5 above, possessed in Catalonia a region which was up among the leaders in the cotton industry towards the end of the eighteenth century, and other industries also developed at the time. Spain's mineral riches led to mining developments in the nineteenth century, and an early railway system of trunk lines was built up from the 1860s mainly by French capital, extending to 480 km. in 1865 and 6,400 km. in 1877. There were scattered examples of coke-smelting in Asturias in 1852 and 1859, and for a time the South-East also developed a promising industrial complex. Yet, except for the important Catalonian region, which itself was falling increasingly behind the European leaders, these beginnings had died down again by 1890, and Spain showed some of the most clear-cut cases of downward regional multipliers in action.[95] In 1900 over half the population still worked the land, and as late as 1960 the figure was 41.3%.[96]

There was some progress in the latter part of the nineteenth century, as in all other parts of Europe. It was to be found in a few areas only, in Catalonia and the Basque country mainly. Cotton consumption per capita in 1900-9 was higher than in Austria-Hungary and only just below that of Italy. Coal production rose from 455,000 tons a year in 1861-70 to 3,621,000 t. in 1911-13, and additional imports, mainly from Britain as return cargo for the ore shipments, rose from just over half a million tons to 2.7 million tons in the same period. Similarly, pig-iron production rose from a derisory 45,000 tons in 1861–5 to 412,000 tons in 1911–13. But for a country supplying much of Europe with iron ore this was a poor record, and the many non-ferrous metal mines remained enclaves, exploited by foreign capital after the Mining Concessions Act of 1868 for the purpose of exporting the raw material for manufacture abroad. Of the rich Basque iron ores, 81% were exported in 1881–1913, and only 8% worked up at home.[97]

Perhaps the relative stagnation of the peninsula can best be illustrated by Paul Bairoch's figures of gross national product per head. Measured in US $ of 1960, both Spain (263) and Portugal (250) were in 1830 still estimated to have figured above the European average of 240. By 1913, using the same measurement, Spain's average had grown to 367 and Portugal's to 292, but the European figure had by then reached 534. Only the Balkan states emerging from war and Turkish rule, were still poorer.[98]

Many of the 'modern' industries of Spain were not really competitive in world markets, but existed, like those of Holland, only because of their privileged position in the Spanish colonies. The loss of the bulk of the colonies by 1825, and of most of the remainder at the end of the century, was a heavy blow, leading to decline rather than creative adjustment to competition. Yet in other respects conditions appeared favourable to economic growth. There had been land reforms and some social and political gains by the bourgeoisie in Spain by the 1830s, the peninsula had good sea communications, the credit of the government on the international money market was good at times, there were rich mineral resources, including coal, and while the educational level was among the lowest in Europe, a strong government had at least founded a corps of road and canal builders on the French model (1799) together with a school for them thus providing a core of technically trained persons.[99]

The failure of Spain and Portugal to free themselves from colonial and peripheral status in the economic sense derives from a variety of causes. Their geography was favourable in the well-endowed and easily accessible coastal strips, but the inland areas were arid, difficult of access, and often without mineral or other raw materials. It is being increasingly recognized that Spain, in spite of her past imperial glories, always had been a poor country, and its inland areas such as Castile, had no traditions on which to build successful industrialization.[100]

Iberian agriculture formed an unfavourable base for economic progress. Peasants were poverty-stricken and ignorant, except along the coasts, and the latifundia were even less helpful. Yields were among the poorest in Europe, only just above Eastern Europe. The decision by the Spanish government to raise high tariff barriers in 1891 and

1906, levying ultimately a duty of 110% on foreign grain, led to an extension of grain cultivation and held up industrialization. The home market was always poor and resistant to change. Shortage of capital, lack of confidence, and repeated political upheavals combined to keep interest rates high. The chief exports were ores, fruit, wine, wool, and cork, demonstrating that Spain's comparative advantages were entirely those of national endowment rather than skills, enterprise, or capital.[101] After restrictions were eased in the 1870s, emigration eased some of the pressure on resources. In Portugal, significantly, it was the more progressive northern wine-growing region, rather than the stagnant agricultural south, which furnished most of the emigrants. On a comparable base, Portuguese emigration, as a proportion of the total home population, was the fifth highest in Europe in 1819–1910, at 5.47% a year, and Spain came eighth, at 3.84%.[102]

The Balkan countries were, without doubt, those least affected by industrialization in Europe by 1914. With the lowest incomes per head and the highest proportion of the population active in agriculture, with few towns and those mostly agrarian, with economies scarcely differentiated beyond the peasant craft and food-processing industries, most of the progress of the nineteenth century seemed to have passed them by.[103]

Such signs of modernity as existed, were largely the work of foreign capital, or, in a few cases, the result of deliberate government policy. Each had some length of railway, mostly conceived as part of a Balkan system to Constantinople rather than serving the local needs, the ports were built out, mainly by foreign capital, to export food and raw materials, and the most important 'modern' industry, oil production and refining at Ploesti, was 95% controlled by foreign capital. The client status of the Balkan countries was emphasized by the fact that the international treaties that had created them had, with the exception of Romania, deprived them of the power to raise tariffs. A large part of the foreign earnings and of the state budget of each country was by 1914 devoted to interest payments to foreign-asset holders.[104]

These influences were not without effect in the last two decades before the war. Starting from very low levels, the real output of manufacturing had annual growth-rates of 7% in Romania, 14.3% in Bulgaria, and 12.5% in Serbia in 1900–10. In Greece shipping registered a remarkable growth, in Romania it was oil and grain export, in Serbia mining as well as food processing, including the rise of the plum-based trades. Not only capital, but also skilled labour and management were attracted from abroad.[105] Much of this, however, was still at a primitive stage and formed only a small part of national income. Above all, it served the purposes of the advanced regions of expanding Inner

Europe and, if anything, helped to widen rather than narrow the gap. Even in 1914, the Balkans seemed destined to remain in the periphery for a long time yet.

The Second Generation of Industrializers

The countries and economies of the European periphery considered in this chapter exhibited great differences in experience in the period 1870–1914. Several of them industrialized easily, others partially, and others still had hardly made a beginning by 1914. Among the majority of them, the partial industrialization had a strongly regional element. In Russia there was rapid progress in parts of Poland, parts of the Baltic region, Moscow, and, above all, in parts of the Ukraine. In Austria, the industrialized regions were relatively limited enclaves in the north-west and around Lower Austria and Styria. Italy showed progress mostly in the North, Spain in the coastal regions of the north and of Catalonia. One might add to this that even in the European 'core' industrialization had not penetrated everywhere. The north-east of Germany, the centre and south-western quarter of France, Southern Ireland, and the Scottish Highlands, for example, were scarcely more advanced than many peripheral areas.

This seemed to be not merely a matter of timing, the result of observation at an arbitrarily chosen moment, so that, had we chosen a later moment, industrialization would have advanced much further into the virgin territories. On the contrary, there seemed to be a more substantial barrier around these regions holding back the tide, sometimes for many decades, sometimes overcome only after long and costly policies by very powerful governments, and in some cases persisting even until today. Certainly, their reaction was very different from the eager adaptation with which the early industrializers welcomed the innovations reaching them from Britain.

The mixed results, even within the same countries or provinces, should warn us against any easy single explanation of the relative liability to succumb to or enjoy an immunity against the disease of industrialism as it swept across Europe. Few regions were wholly suitable for it, few were wholly immune. In explanation of the causes of backwardness, we are driven to a reversal of the reasons considered responsible for early development. As in the case of the successful regions, we have here a set of relatively fixed factors, like resources, themselves changing in value, interacting with transport, with market needs, with factor mobility, and the luck of historical timing affecting them. The equipment and traditions built up over the preceding periods, clearly a key factor, straddle both these categories.[106] Together they might just tip the balance one way or the other, or indeed make the beam swing right over.

As always, resources are of major significance, particularly in the early stages of industrialization. Much of peripheral land lacks coal, including most of Spain, Italy, and the major concentrations of population in Russia. There is high-grade iron ore, but that of Italy is limited, that of Russia very distant.[107] The agricultural resources, mainly land and climate, are also among the poorest, making for a poor, backward, dispirited population in much of the periphery. A large part of Spain and Southern Italy are in this category, despite the frequent illusion that the latter could once more be the granary of Europe. The northern half of European Russia has very poor soil and extremes of climate, while the south-eastern Steppe land suffers frequent droughts.[108]

Russia, it is true, also has the fertile 'black soil' belt, but communications to it are poor. It was almost invariably communications and transport, rather than resources in or on the ground, that formed the true resources problem of peripheral Europe, even though there was an historical dimension to it, so that ultimately the new means of transport could unlock the riches of Donetz, Krivoi Rog, or even the Ural and Trans-Ural regions. At the current stage of development of transport technology, however, there was no way of developing most of inland Russia, most of the Habsburg Monarchy, or even the inland regions of Spain or Sicily: the failure to sustain the early spurt in the Urals, with their boundless treasure of iron ore and timber, was eloquent proof.

Twentieth-century man finds it difficult sometimes to envisage the full weight of the barriers of inaccessibility that existed in the eighteenth and nineteenth centuries. In Russia, the rivers froze in winter and the northern ports were closed, while in the summer the roads were appalling and there was not enough traffic on most of them to justify repair. The export of grain employed a vast army of oxen— themselves consuming a precious part of their load, while in 1815 it was estimated that there were 400,000 *burlaki* or boatmen, hauling vessels on the Volga. From the Urals, the 1,000-mile trip might take two seasons, wintering on the way. Even from Donetz or Krivoi Rog to Moscow there were 600 miles to be covered against the flow of the rivers.[109] In the Ukraine in the eighteenth century, grain was left to rot on the fields in a good year since there was nothing that could be done with it.[110] Clearly, these were not ideal conditions for the introduction of a progressive agriculture.

Spain was a country of 'rugged mountains, treacherous gorges, swift, unpredictable streams, and harsh weather [which] hindered the flow of commodities and knowledge of prices'.[111] Here also, poor roads hampered traffic, and absence of traffic inhibited road building.[112] Such transport as there was, on the backs of pack animals, was extremely costly. In Sicily, too, grain was carried to the sea-shore on mules, as there were no roads, and out to the boats by lighters, as there were no harbours. Much of the Southern Italian mainland was equally inaccessible.[113]

Austria–Hungary was attempting to develop the port of Trieste, but much of the country was land-locked, and the rivers rarely flowed in the right direction. In Hungary, in 1866, it cost 12–20 Kreutzer to carry the same quantity of goods 10–15 miles to the river, as it would cost 41–43 Kreutzer to transport 300 miles by river steamer, and in the late 1870s, transport cost of cotton yarn per *Zollzentner* to Bohemia was 1.65–2 fl. from Vienna, but only 1.40–1.50 fl. from Manchester. Transport to the Balkans was more costly still.[114] It is significant that even today, with all our new means of transport, difficulty of access is still considered a major reason for regional backwardness.[115] At the time, the problems were generally those of internal links. The edges or coasts had good communications but this could, in turn, be a source of weakness. The linkages frequently went outward, and germs of development remained enclaves which failed to kindle other districts nearby for lack of communication.[116]

In such territories serfdom and feudal relics lingered on much longer, and while such conditions have been shown to be compatible with some types of large-scale agriculture and industry, they were serious fetters precisely for the kind of competitive, risk-taking, flexible, and capital-intensive industry that was spreading outward from Inner Europe. In fact, as must be obvious from the poor soil, severe climate, and lack of opportunity of many of those regions, agriculture was generally low-yield, technically backward, and unenterprising; most people still worked on the land, but the farm population failed to offer a prosperous home market to potential industrialists.[117]

Urban development was frequently backward, sometimes, as in Eastern Europe, the result of direct action by feudal lords who feared the tendency of towns to attract away their estate labour and who wanted to keep all the profits of the grain trade in their own hands.[118] Spain and above all Central and Southern Italy did not lack towns, though, as we have seen above,[119] they were not centres of progress but guild-dominated, stagnating, and either too poor to offer markets to native industrialists or too rich to wish to buy from them. There was thus all-round poverty, and lack of demand:[120] 'The Croatian noble buys mostly foreign products, a bourgeoisie in effect did not exist, and the peasant, forming the large majority of the population, spends what little cash he has, on absolute necessities only and cannot possibly buy manufactured goods.'[121] There might be the possibility of exports, and there were examples of export-led developments as in

Switzerland or Catalonia, but it was obviously harder, in a world made uncertain by tariffs and competing industrializers, to build up an industrial complex without the solid foundations of a home market. Poverty also meant lack of capital and banking facilities, and while foreign capital did come in, it was made available for public works, mines, and large industrial units, leaving certain gaps always to be filled from native sources.[122] The complement of this was an almost permanent labour surplus[123] which kept down wages without necessarily favouring the industrialist.

Observers repeatedly stressed the adverse social milieu in the peripheral countries, as they had in the case of France, noted above.[124] Hungarian aristocrats and Russian landowners spent too much time on conspicuous consumption in the cities, Italian entrepreneurs were unwilling to take risks, Spanish society was too rigid, there was social resistance to change, and the educational system developed all the wrong qualities for industrial progress. Conversely, the bourgeois class was too small and too weak or it was alien and disadvantaged.[125] Inventors and technicians of genius were frozen out or 'were operating in an economic void'.[126] Similarly, labour was alleged to be inferior, unstable, unskilled, and uncommitted to industry. Certainly, the illiteracy figures of countries like Russia or Italy were extremely high even at the end of the century, and there was a '*Gefälle*' of literacy across Europe as there was of national incomes.[127]

As in the case of France, these intangibles have frequently been played down by other observers. When conditions are ripe, it is said, enterprise, market consciousness, and a capitalist spirit manifest themselves soon enough.[128] It is certainly true that some labour, no matter how 'inferior' and classified as traditionalist at home, yet had the enterprise to take the enormous risks involved in emigration into unknown societies with unknown languages.[129] Long-distance migration across the Atlantic was a particular feature of societies close to industrial take-off or in close contact with industrialized economies, but not quite there themselves: the phase when an increase of population had occurred, but there was not yet an increase of productive capital to match it. This phase applied to Ireland, Germany, and Scandinavia c.1845–85; it applied to the periphery from the 1880s on. Italians, Hungarians, Slovaks, Jews from Poland and Russia, and peasants from the Balkans then flocked to North America, Italians, Spaniards, and Portugese to Latin-American destinations.[130]

In reality, the matter was more complex. No doubt each society had potential leaders, entrepreneurs, inventors, or mechanics, but there was no simple cause and effect relationship between the Sombartian capitalist 'spirit' and the growth of industry, one being the cause, the other the effect. Rather, as in so many economic developments, they were mutually reinforcing, mutually cause and effect, with time (and the progress of the rest of Europe) as chief variable. Thus some exceptional spirit might found one enterprise, this would allow other activists to come forward, they would extend modern industry, which would in turn help to change social attitudes and encourage more enterprise, and so on. An industrializing economy would thus show the growth of both spirit and reality jointly, rather than one following the other. To look for a first cause in this process may be a search for the philosopher's stone, or at best a search for the trigger at a time when both the capitalist spirit and the examples of modern industry were insignificant in extent. It is in any case the progress, not the tiny spark at the beginning, in which we are interested. What matters is the ever changing surrounding circumstances, markets, resources, technology, political action, appropriate to each phase, which allow the process to go on, or inhibit it. These circumstances rarely all work in the same direction, and in peripheral Europe they were particularly close to an even balance. Thus the frequently asked question why Scandinavia developed so successfully and Iberia did not cannot be answered in terms of a single factor. Both started from a similar position in the mid-nineteenth century: a great imperial past, but a poverty-stricken, largely agricultural present, rich local resources exploited by foreign capital for foreign markets, dependence on the advanced economies, extreme climate, and poor transport facilities, and so on. But the differences were also multifaceted. On the one hand, differences in the mental and political climate: education and health in the North were among the best in Europe, there was a Protestant Church, a relatively democratic and uncorrupt government, and better internal peace. But there were also different transport opportunities in the North, different raw materials, boundless water-power, a different (even if also inhospitable) climate, and a different agrarian structure, and the list of potential variables could be extended at will.[131] It was their sum, or rather, as they were all interacting and reinforcing each other, their product, that made for 'success' or 'failure'.

Governments, also, were among the operative variables. We have seen above[132] that in backward countries, their actions, no matter how well-meaning, could easily worsen the backwardness, and it would not be hard to show how in successful industrializers the state could do no wrong even though, on the face of it, almost all its actions seemed misguided. Thus in Italy or France, positive government action merely aided the advanced regions but made the plight of the South still worse,[133] whereas in Russia, the all-pervasive, oppressive Hicksian state apparatus could, as Gerschenkron emphasized,[134] become the engine of growth at the appropriate 'spurt' moment.

Even wars had their differential impacts according to the relative level of economic development reached. The great French wars, as we have seen, served to emphasize the lead of the British over the continental industrialists, just as the two world wars of the twentieth century served to widen the lead of the Americans over the Europeans. Russia was propelled forward by two lost wars, the Crimean and the Japanese, because the defeats weakened the traditionalist forces that had stood in the way of all progress,[135] but in her third major war, the system collapsed altogether in 1917. The German wars of unification are also held to have helped her advance, or at least had no marked adverse effect. In the case of Austria, Spain, or the Balkans, however, heavy government expenditure on armament is held to have had purely negative effects,[136] diverting savings to the government or enforcing deflationary policies which had like effects. Of more significance still was that wars, themselves, took on quite different characters, with significantly varying consequences, according to the stage of industrial development reached by their participants.

Chapter 7

The Rise of Neo-Mercantilism 1870s to 1914

Up to the 1870s, as we have seen, the major steps towards the industrialization of Europe were taken within a political framework favourable to them, such as the rise of Liberalism and the creation of large
internal markets by the unification of Germany and Italy and the
post-1848 reforms of Austria. Moreover, much progress occurred by
ignoring political frontiers altogether.

This was increasingly less true in the decades which followed. In a
simultaneous movement, the political authority became progressively
more powerful, until by 1914 it could be said to have a dominant role
in the economy of each country, particularly in regard to industrialization, while at the same time its influence on economic progress
ceased to be a purely positive one. Specifically, governmental actions
increasingly came to disrupt the relatively easy and free intercourse of
commodities as well as factors of production between nations on which
the successful industrialization of Europe had so largely depended.

In the tangle of causation of this development, at last three strands
can be discerned, all interconnected yet best treated separately for
purposes of exposition. The first is the rise of nationalism as a political force and the drive towards the conversion of the political unit,
the European state, from its dynastic origins to an expression of
national unity and popular or democratic control. The theme forms
the core of European history in this phase and by its very vastness has to
be excluded from treatment here.[1] Its link with the industrialization
process is fundamental: the classes carrying it forward or adversely
affected by it fought out the revolutions of the period and their settlements, from the Code Napoléon as a consequence of the French
Revolution to the ending of feudal conditions on the land as a consequence of the revolutions of 1848. Conversely, the literacy required
by new urban living and factory employment created the teachers and
writers who did so much to propagate the national idea. The unevenness of the development of the nation state in this modern sense was
as marked as that of the progress of industrialization, and, in this phase,
what had once been a favourable influence turned into its opposite.
Thus the Russian government deliberately tried to hold back and

damage Polish industrialization as a reaction to the threat posed by incipient Polish nationalism, while in Austria–Hungary beneficial reforms were repeatedly held back by the obsession of politicians with their national, anti-dynastic cause. The massive damage inflicted on the populations of the Danubian areas by that obsession is, however, a feature of the post-war years and will be treated in Chapter 8 below.

A second strand is the growing technical need for state intervention of a new kind in economic matters, and above all a growing technological competence to discharge these functions. Mine inspection and safety at sea, sanitary intervention in the massed proletarian quarters of new cities and protection of children in factories, education for workers' children and police forces to hold them in check, are examples of a whole new apparatus of control developed by central and local authorities in response to the changes brought about by industrialization. The same changes also provided the means to carry it out. Cheap print and paper for forms by the million, telegraphs and postal services, railways with regular timetables, and higher output all round to be taxed for the maintenance of an ever growing civil service, are a sample of these. We should here also include the efficiency principle, transferred from the industrial sphere to state employment in place of the former nepotism. Among the technical improvements of the century most neglected by historians was the improvement in the ability to collect taxes. The Zollverein, like the Prussian tax law of 1818 on which it was based, was originally first and foremost an improved method for collecting customs dues,[2] just as the prohibitive Russian tariff system in the first half of the century reflected the inability of the Russian state to prevent smuggling, and its later reduction pointed to a growing efficiency in execution.

Over much of Europe, frontiers gelled into economically meaningful barriers only in our period:[3] even in apparently unitary states like *ancien régime* France, let alone Prussia or Austria, the operative economic frontiers had been *within* the country, between provinces and towns, rather than around it. Today, a standard work on regional economics can treat it as axiomatic that political boundaries are firmer and harder to change than economic ones; that they are fortified by more aspects of social life, including customs, laws, language, community feeling, security, fate, and history, while the economic region is distinguished only by price; and that regions near political frontiers often wither, since they have no (internal) hinterland and they are far from the political centre.[4] In the period of European industrialization, normally the opposite was the case, all these aspects, including even language but excluding law, worked more strongly towards a regional than a state identification, and on some important matters, such as inheritance or the ownership of minerals underground, even the law might show decisive regional variations. In particular, it was often the frontier regions that were the most progressive and most successful early industrializers, partly precisely because they were at the frontier.[5] The change-over largely occurred in our period.

Thirdly, the growing clash between economic need and nationalist demand found some of its inspiration in the industrialization process itself, and particularly in its uneven incidence. By the 1870s, the advanced industrial regions of Europe were surrounded by agrarian or underdeveloped regions, some of which shared the same political territory within state boundaries, others being outside and subject to other governments. Since men's attitudes to free trade and protection were always coloured by what they promised themselves from these policies, and thus depended on the competitive position of the industry or region concerned—however elaborate the economic or political theory with which this was rationalized—it is the interplay and dialectic of the regions which explain the shifts and changes of tariff policies, and particularly the return to protection as the standard European attitude.

Finally, this study is concerned with long-term secular trends and therefore normally ignores short-term cycles. However, like the consequences of the crisis following 1815, the watershed of the 1870s was influenced in a significant way by short-term disequilibria: one was the ending of the remarkable boom, especially in capital goods, of the early 1870s, leading directly into the devastating crisis later in the decade which proved to be the onset of the Great Depression lasting around twenty years. It is fashionable nowadays to declare that the Great Depression did not really exist,[6] but myths can have powerful policy consequences: there can be no doubt the 'the Great Depression marked the decisive turning point in the nineteenth-century history of the relationship between the State and the economy'.[7]

Coincidentally, bad harvests in Europe and the rapid lowering of transport costs by rail and improved steamship permitted a flooding of European markets by North American grain in the later 1870s which led to a permanent change in the world's grain trade, though the United States surplus itself soon began to shrink. An agrarian crisis was therefore added to the industrial crisis, and it is not difficult to see connections between the two. The most persuasive model is that of Paul Bairoch.[8] According to him, it was the large sales of American cereals, cotton, and other primary goods to Europe, while the USA were preventing return exports of manufactured goods by high tariffs and did not invest abroad, either, which plunged Europe into a deflationary spiral of a classical kind.

Thus both industrialists and agrarians, in some countries jointly, were persuaded to press for tariffs. These constituted the most widespread form of neo-mercantilism in this period, and we shall begin with them.

Tariffs and Trade Policies

The shock of British competition after 1815, accompanied by the bad harvest and famines of 1816–17, had led to the immediate imposition of a high tariff in many countries, but thereafter reaction was mixed, and changes tended in a downward direction from the mid-1840s onward. The lead was taken by Britain, certain of dominating the markets for manufactures, but protectionist in the agrarian field. The hesitant dismantling of the near prohibitive Corn Laws of 1815 was abruptly terminated by near free trade in corn in 1846 and the abolition of the Navigation Acts in 1849. The budgets in 1853 and 1860 completed the march towards the classic free-trade policy, the remaining customs dues being for revenue purposes only. The example of the economically most successful country necessarily influenced governments and public opinion elsewhere.

Prussia introduced a low tariff in 1818, adopted in principle also by the Zollverein from 1834. Some rates for manufactured goods were raised in 1844 and 1846, as the rise of industry began to dispute the hegemony of the agrarians, but absolute levels were still low. Austria under Metternich was mainly prohibitive, but following the revolution of 1848 Bruck drove protection downward in 1850, partly with the political objective of reaching a level at which Austria could force her way into the Zollverein in order to take over leadership in Germany. The treaty of 1853 between them which contained a most-favoured-nations clause was intended as a step in that direction—and was for that reason seen as a challenge by Prussia.

Following the general, though not universal, rule that the more backward the country, the higher its protection, Russia's 'Kankrin' tariff of 1823 was among the highest. However, fiscal motivations were stronger there than the desire to protect Russian industry which, as yet, hardly existed. The tariff was modified in 1849–57. Spain also, having lost most of her colonies, moved from a rigid mercantilism to protectionism in 1825.

In the West, the smaller countries tended towards modified or complete free trade. Leading among them was Holland, still mainly a trading and carrying rather than manufacturing economy, Switzerland in 1850–1, following her unification, Denmark, Norway, Portugal, and the German free cities. Belgium, protectionist at first, became almost free trade in 1849–53 when she realized she could undersell most others and needed cheap food, and Sweden followed in 1859. Piedmont under Cavour, dominated by landowners, saw herself as a natural agricultural foil for the industrialized nations like Britain and therefore encouraged the international division of labour by free trade in the 1850s, a policy at first followed also by united Italy after 1860.[9]

The key role was played by France, still by far the most important single economy on the Continent to mid-century and beyond. Strictly protectionist and not very dependent on foreign trade, the only voices for lower tariffs she had before 1848 were those of the successful exporters, like Alsace cotton and Lyons silk manufactures, Parisian fashion-goods producers, or Bordeaux wine merchants. Under the Second Empire, when some industrial successes at home and railway and banking investment abroad raised French self-confidence, the tight grip of the protectionist system was loosened. In 1853 Napoleon III lowered import duties on grain and cattle, on iron and coal, and reduced shipping preferences.[10] Other concessions followed in 1855, and in 1860 he concluded a far-reaching commercial agreement with Britain, the Cobden–Chevalier treaty.

Its significance extended far beyond the two countries concerned. Partly political in concept, to reduce the diplomatic strain between them, it provided for some concession by Britain, for instance not to tax or prohibit coal exports, to favour French wines and spirits while leaving some Portuguese preference, and to ease trade to the colonies, but there was little that free-trade Britain could specifically offer. The main concessions were made by France, which undertook to observe an upper limit of tariff rates of 25–30%, but in fact reduced actual rates below them over a wide range of goods. Much of French industry was strongly opposed to suffering the full force of British competition with but a thin armour of moderate *ad valorem* duties to protect them, and a total of 40 million francs was set aside for loans on favourable terms to industries which had to make the most drastic adjustments, of which around 9 million francs went to metallurgy and 16 m.fr. to textiles. Opinion has been divided to this day as to whether the sudden exposure to the cold blast of world prices served to spur French industry to modernize and advance, or whether it inhibited and slowed down the growth of native industry by encouraging manufactured imports.[11]

The treaty's main significance, however, lay not in the encouragement of trade between these two countries alone, but in the fact that it became a model for a whole series of similar trade treaties among the Western European nations and also some others. Within three years both partners had made similar treaties with the Zollverein and with Belgium, and before long Italy, Austria, Switzerland, the Netherlands, and the Scandinavian and the Mediterranean countries were drawn into the expanding network. According to one calculation, between 1861–70 Italy had concluded 24 such treaties, Belgium and France 19 each, Germany 18, Austria–Hungary 14, and Great Britain, having relatively little to offer, 8. Russia, also, enacted a fairly liberal tariff in 1868. The USA, however, held aloof.[12] As a rule, there were most-favoured-nation clauses and the upper limits of tariff rates were fixed by treaty and could therefore not be raised unilaterally: change thus could be downward, but not upward. Although tariff rates on imports from countries outside the circle of the participants could be, and occasionally were, raised without restriction, the charmed circle grew and with lowered rates a free-trade world seemed to be in the making in capitalist Europe. By 1873, for example, Germany had enacted the ultimate repeal of the remaining duties on iron, and was thus, with several of the smaller countries, on the way to join free-trade Britain. As another example, free Rhine navigation to the sea for everyone was guaranteed by treaty in 1868. The Cobdenite spirit seemed to have won through to set the scene for an unfettered development of the European productive forces.

At this point, the optimism of contemporaries was shattered by the crisis and slump, which turned out to be more serious than the usual cyclical downturn and marked the onset of a major, long-term disequilibrium leading to years of unemployment, stagnating, and massive losses. In the scramble for remedies and for scapegoats, free-trade policies came in for early attention. The sequence of events was different in each country but the general tendency was clear: salvation by tariff protection for whichever home interest was powerful enough to be able to secure it.

The German turn-around here was typical. The large East-Elbian landowners, much the most powerful social class in Prussia and therefore in Germany as a whole, were exporters, mainly to Britain, and passionate free traders in consequence. So were the trading interests and the free cities, as well as the more successful manufacturers. Other contemporaries understood Germany's intermediate position in the technological productivity chain and advocated tariffs only against Britain, but not against other markets where German manufacturers could compete without aid.[13] Again, users of intermediate products like pig or bar iron wanted cheap supplies. In these circumstances, the weaker industrialists were unable to hold up the widening of trade that was the consequence of ever lower tariff barriers.

All this changed abruptly in the later 1870s. Threatened by American and Russian grain in both British and German markets, the Junkers discovered the merits of protection with astonishing rapidity in 1876–9.

Similarly, the capital goods industry, counting its losses, found it easy to blame foreign imports. An alliance between 'rye and iron' was quickly concluded. The speed with which these groups managed to reverse policy and reintroduce protection in 1879 when the ink was hardly dry on the last repeal of the iron duties owes something to the specific conditions of Germany at the time. One was the skill with which the large landlords persuaded the bulk of the small farmers, who had nothing to gain and cheap feeding grains to lose by protection, to make common cause with them; and the other, the support of Bismarck, both for party political reasons in his Reichstag strategy, and for reasons of greater financial independence from the *Länder* that made up the Empire, since tariff revenues were among the few independent sources of income of the *Reich*.[14] However, the rate of progress was not very dissimilar elsewhere.

Early German rates were moderate, amounting to around 10–15% by value on industrial goods and 5–7% on agricultural goods, but they soon rose in the tariffs of 1885 and 1887, by which time corn tariffs had gone up fivefold.[15] In France also, agricultural protection was raised in 1885 and again in 1887, and the comprehensive Méline tariff of 1892 constituted a new high in protection and destroyed a whole network of treaties. In Russia, the decision of 1877 to levy duty in gold rather than paper roubles was equivalent to an increase of 30–33% in the rate of duty, and further increases occurred in 1881 (of 10%) and in 1885 (of 20%), partly in response to the rising grain duties in Germany and France. There was a further increase of 20% in 1890, and the new Mendeleyev tariff of 1891 had an additional upward tendency, though some rates actually came down, and its general objective was fiscal and monetary as much as protective. It was by incompetence rather than design that some rates, meant to be fiscal, turned out to be prohibitive, and that in other cases semi-manufactures were taxed more highly than finished goods.[16] The new Austro–Hungarian tariff of 1878 was still moderate, though double the earlier ones. Other increases followed in 1882 and 1887. Finally, among the larger countries, the change-over was most drastic in Italy, which had begun her existence with a conscious free-trade policy, supported by landed interests and city traders alike. Rising manufacturing interests, and agrarians threatened by cheap grain imports, spurred on by the wish to retaliate against the tariffs of others, formed an alliance for protection in the late 1870s here also. The Tariff Act of 1878 had low rates and was still largely fiscal, but the new general tariff of 1887, coming into effect in 1888, was clearly protective, and so was the still higher tariff of 1894.[17]

It should be noted that the commercial treaties of the free-trade interlude were commonly renewed, but on a different basis: they still retained the most-favoured-nation clause, ensuring a kind of 'fairness' among all contractual partners, but they no longer contained a guarantee of an upper limit. At the same time the 'general' tariff, i.e. the rates applicable to countries with which no treaty existed, had a strongly rising tendency, increasing the penalties of failing to come to terms. The norm, clearly, had switched back to protection from the brief liberal interlude, which had lasted less than twenty years. Between 1875 and 1895 duties on manufactured articles in Europe as a whole had been at least doubled.[18]

In 1891 Caprivi, the new German Chancellor, attempted to reverse the process by simultaneous mutual reductions. In a series of treaties signed in that year and coming into effect in 1892, Austria–Hungary, Switzerland, Italy, and Belgium joined Germany in a most-favoured-nations system at generally lower tariff rates to last for twelve years so as to allow industrial planning and adjustment. Serbia and Romania joined in 1893 and in 1894 Russia concluded a trade treaty with Germany, to run the same period as the 'Central-European' system, to the end of 1903.[19]

What is significant, however, is not so much the temporary success of the Caprivi policy, as the power of the opposition he aroused in Germany and the speed with which he was driven from office. Moreover, when the treaties came up for renewal, rates of protection resumed their upward drift. The eastern emerging countries also opted for high tariffs, Bulgaria instituting high rates in 1883 and raising them in 1897 and 1904, Romania enacted high industrial tariffs in 1893 and 1906, and Serbia raised a tariff against Austria-Hungary, her main trading partner, in 1906. Only Switzerland, Holland, Belgium besides free-trade Britain, still retained moderate, mainly fiscal, customs duties in the last years to 1914. In 1914, average levels of tariffs on industrial products have been calculated as follows (%):[20]

United Kingdom	0
Holland	4
Switzerland, Belgium	9
Germany	13
Denmark	14
Austria-Hungary, Italy	18
France, Sweden	20
Russia	38
Spain	41

Agricultural tariffs were particularly high in the larger countries, Germany, France, Austria-Hungary, and Italy.

It is no coincidence that it was the smaller, more successful, and unitary economies which held out best against the ever higher wave of protectionism, for protection was much furthered by the division of interest within the state itself. Typically, political frontiers had no relevance to economic reality and included regions, industries, and interests of various kinds, cutting many of them in half. Within the international division of labour there would be some regional industrial concentrations which could stand up to foreign competition and, indeed, export to the world, while others, and almost inevitably the majority, could not. As soon as improved transport, rising productive efficiency abroad, and their own cohesion had reached an operative level, the agitation of the latter for protection, for preferences, subsidies, or quotas, would begin.

Whether, or how soon, they succeeded, depended on the current power constellation. Two factors, one general and the other specific, helped the rapid spread of protectionism from the late 1870s onward. One was the fact that the industry requesting aid was usually concentrated, its main interest engaged, local deputies and representatives fully mobilized, and resources set aside for propaganda and agitation. The interests that would be most harmed by protection and preference, however, which were normally the general public, were diffuse, unorganized, without funds, and only marginally interested—unless, indeed, the commodity to be protected formed the main input of another organized industrial interest.[21] In the latter case the quest for protection was occasionally frustrated, but more often than not, the victim industry was bought off by being offered equal or even higher tariffs, and this was one of the most powerful mechanisms giving the protective spiral its upward twist.

The specific factor was the switch to protectionism by the agrarian interest. The latter, particularly the large landowners, still possessed everywhere (with the possible and significant exceptions of Britain and Holland) more political power than their economic contribution warranted, for obvious historic reasons. It was for this reason that the influx of cheap American, Indian, and later Russian and other grain, which made agrarian interests in the industrialized countries protectionist, exerted a more powerful influence on European economic policy than other market changes.

We have noted that once the process started there was some economic logic why it should continue to spread. The upward push was, however, immensely strengthened by the very fact that it had also acquired a political dimension. As soon as politicians, with their own methods and priorities, entered as a major factor, several new upward twists were immediately imported to the spiral. The horse-trading and system of mutual obligation, local patriotism, and xenophobia, the bluster and the wish to dominate, the link-up with international diplomacy and the sytem of alliances, which were the hallmarks of political activity at the time,[22] almost always tended to push tariff rates and preferences up, rather than down.

One peak of this dominance of the political over economic rationality was reached in the tariff wars which were as much a culmination of the methods of economic diplomacy, as military wars were of political diplomacy. The most destructive of these was the Franco-Italian conflict which lasted from 1887–96 or in effect to 1898. It arose from the Italian attempt to aid its own industries, particularly its silk industry, and was conducted by levying rates on the goods of the other country that were higher even than the general tariff applying to countries with which no treaty existed. Trade shrank drastically, to the benefit of other suppliers, notably Germany, and Italy, as the weaker partner, suffered more than France.[23]

France also waged a tariff war against Spain in 1882–5 and against Switzerland in 1893–5; there was a German–Canadian tariff war in 1897–1910, and Austria and Romania conducted a tariff war which lasted, on and off, from 1882–98. This began with a tariff on Romanian grain, levied by Austria in the interest of the Hungarian landowners, and also led to widespread supplanting of Austrian manufactured export to Romania by Germany. A similar development occurred in Serbia about twenty years later, c.1906–14 in the so-called 'pig war'.[24]

Antagonistic protectionist policies could also lead to wider economic and even diplomatic conflicts. A good example of this was provided by Germany and Russia in the 1870s and 1880s. Russia was essentially a grain exporter, for whom Germany formed an important market, but she also sent spirits, cattle, and agrarian-based raw materials and semi-manufactures. The tariff of 1879 failed to keep out Russian grain, since Russian exporters were prepared to go down ever lower in price, and the sharply rising German tariff rates, particularly for rye, severely damaged Russian interests without reducing the imports which had been the objective of the German agrarians. At the same time, rising Russian tariffs in the 1880s hit German heavy industry particularly hard, since Russian policy was designed in part to disadvantage the Polish industries which had been purchasers of German products. The need for a loan from Germany in 1884 obliged Russia to end her specifically anti-German policies, but the respite was only temporary, and in the end, these economic antagonisms contributed materially to the diplomatic breach between the two countries which drove Russia into the arms of France. The tariff conflict was not ended until 1894.[25] Here were examples of a 'political' logic so dominant that it will press on even when clearly harming the country's own economic interests, which were originally, and allegedly, the main motive for action.

The internal disharmonies, or unevenness of development, behind much of the protectionist-aggressive drive of this period emerged most clearly where an administrative frontier coincided largely with an economic one: this was the case in Austria–Hungary. The divide, fortified in 1867, separated the agrarian Hungarian component[26] from the mixed Austrian one, in which industrial interests were increasingly gaining the upper hand. Whoever conducted the Empire's economic policy had therefore to take account of interests which were complementary within the country but conflicting without, and there was the additional complication that the links with the natural trading partners of each half led across the territory of the other, the market for Hungarian grain and cattle lying in Germany and farther west, and the market for Austrian manufactures in the Balkans, and both could be harmed by transit policies open to each of them.

To some extent it was the German decision to keep out grain by high tariffs and cattle by allegedly veterinary regulations, which forced Austria–Hungary to keep out Romanian and Russian imports in turn, transmitting the pressure eastward. But it has also been alleged that it was Hungarian single-minded unity, compared with the diverse economic and centrifugal nationalist interests preventing any forceful policy on the part of Austria, which ensured that in the last decades of the Dual Monarchy, Austro–Hungarian policies increasingly favoured the agrarians, sacrificing some of the industrial interests in the process. In particular, it was the need to favour Hungarian agrarian interests which lost Austria her natural Balkan markets to the German competitor.[27]

Similar internal conflicts, though not highlighted by a political frontier, can be discerned also in Italy,[28] but the classic case is that of Imperial Germany. We have seen how, in highly typical fashion, her protectionist system had been built up on a common interest base of industry and the land, as soon as the land had switched sides as a result of the influx of cheap grain from overseas. However, in the following decades German industry made very fast progress. By the turn of the century, German manufacturers were by far the most efficient on the Continent, and by 1914 in Europe as a whole. Their exports were increasing by leaps and bounds, and they had little to fear from foreign competition. At the same time, the grain tariffs were becoming ever more burdensome as world prices fell farther below artificially high German prices. Also, the protective system became ever more absurd as the better-off population refused to eat the rye from East Elbia which therefore had to be exported and replaced by imports of wheat. Wage costs for manufactures, and feed costs for farmers, were kept up needlessly in the interests of a tiny class of eastern Prussian landowners.[29]

A purely industrial society, like Britain or Belgium, might have moved towards free trade, but the German agrarians obtained ever tighter limitations and preferences, if only at the cost of propitiating the industrialists with corresponding 'benefits' also. In order to persuade the many varying groups that the selfish interests of the narrow Junker class represented the national interest as a whole, a whole ideology had to be developed, clarified particularly in the controversy of *Agrarstaat versus Industriestaat*, which arose in the 1890s.

Agrarians like Adolf Wagner, Max Sering, and Karl Oldenberg favoured agricultural tariffs as part of an attempt to halt the further growth of industrial society. They opposed the vision of ever larger, physically inferior populations crowded into industrial towns, though, incongruously, they also deplored the smaller families of urban dwellers. They also criticized the isolation of urban and industrial living and, in wide-ranging essays characterized by passion rather than by evidence, they asserted that agrarian society had deeper moral and Germanic values than the immoral city and commercial life with its Jewish value system. Against them, liberals and Christians like Lujo Brentano, Friedrich Naumann, Albert Schäffle, and Max Weber pleaded for freer trade and an openness towards the world since it would allow incomes to rise and social programmes to be instituted.[30] The emphasis on a social conscience on the part of the liberals allowed the agrarians to put through their *Sammlungspolitik* under von Miquel, which rallied the industrialists to the agrarian cause, for common privileges and an imperialist drive and against social democracy. Thus under Bülow's Chancellorship duties could be raised still further.

It was part of the agrarians' case that Germany would do better to pursue a policy of autarky, in which a balance between industry and agriculture would produce all the essentials at home and which would not weaken the country militarily by dependence on imports. In the hands of some, this desirable policy was transmuted into an alleged actual trend by the doctrine of the falling ratio of foreign trade. The theory stated that growing industrialization everywhere would align countries with each other and allow them to expand their import-substitution industries at the expense of foreign trade. A more modern, though equally erroneous, version pointed to the growing share in total expenditure of services which could not be traded.[31] Some professed to see a maximum ratio of trade to income around 1875, with the United Kingdom at 30% (exports plus imports as a proportion of GNP), Germany 25%, France 16%, and USA 8%.[32] In the event, both the data and the prognostication were wrong. Trade, as part of the world gross product, rose from 3% in 1800 to over 33% in 1913, or by 24.1% in real terms per decade, and the rise continued after 1875. Several different estimates agree that world trade increased tenfold between 1850 and 1913. For some leading countries, exports alone, as a % of GNP, between the average for 1870/80 and 1910, moved as indicated in the following table:

Table 7.1.

	1870/80	1910	1913
Germany	16.9	14.6	
Denmark	20.7	26.7	
France	12.6	15.3	
Italy	10.2	11.0	
Norway	14.6	18.3	
UK	17.0	17.5	
Sweden	15.8	17.3	
(All Europe)	(11.7)	(13.2)	(14.0)

Only the German ratio had declined.[33] Between 1914 and 1945 the ratio did, indeed, fall as a result of the strong efforts of governments to bring it down, but since then it has risen to new heights. What the economists of the turn of the century had forgotten was the effect of factor movements and the increase in trade between countries of high incomes based not so much on factor endowments as on skill, fashion, technological specialization, and cumulative advantages of scale.[34]

The debate may have been more articulate in Germany than elsewhere, but fundamentally the issues were often the same. Protectionists, in the end, had other priorities than the greater prosperity and international co-operation claimed by free traders. These included the strategic benefits of autarky, the racial or moral superiority of one kind of occupation over another, and social conservatism. Many of these ideals have stood the test of time as little as the dubious data on which they were built. It is very hard indeed to find in them anything beyond special pleading of a class, usually large landowners but sometimes also manufacturers, who believed that they were more worthy of support than other individuals. This belief they had in common with all citizens; the difference was that, precisely at this time, they had the muscle to enforce it.

The Grain Trade

The influx of cheap grain from the 1870s had an important share, as we have seen, in ending the era of free trade and making policies of rising protectionism more palatable. Its significance, in fact, goes deeper still. It contributed to a fundamental shift in the European balance, and in particular the balance between the industrialized regions and their hinterland, and the balance between the expanding heartland on the one hand, and the periphery on the other.[35] It is therefore among the few developments outside Europe which have to be admitted into a study that tries to keep rigidly within the confines of one continent.

In one way, the crisis arose because the increase in the European population and in the production of cereals to feed it, which had kept, and continued to keep in the long term, a remarkably well-attuned common tempo, had got temporarily out of phase. In the third quarter of the century, the rising market had offered European farmers who responded to it high returns, which encouraged high investment.[36] But it also encouraged rising production overseas, particularly in North America, kept out at first by high transport costs, though some cereals from there had been coming into Europe from the time of the Civil War years when the grain surplus of the northern states could no longer be sold in the South.[37] A rapid drop in the costs of transport then threw large quantities, too suddenly for easy adjustment, on to a temporarily weakened European market.

It is ironic that the large wheat supply which reached European shores in the late 1870s from the United States with such momentous consequences was essentially a flash in the pan. American surpluses available for export thereafter declined, partly because of the growing urban market at home, and in part because production itself stagnated. Thus exports from the USA rose spectacularly from an annual average of 46 million bushels in 1869–71 to their peak of 166 m.b. in 1878–80, only to drop back to 123 m.b. in 1881–6, though there was a final rise to 146 m.b. in 1890–2. Production itself did not reach its peak of 442 m.b. of 1878–80 again until 1890–2.[38] By contrast, Indian exports had an upward tendency from 14 m.b. in 1880–1 to a peak of 58 m.b. in 1891–2, only to fall back to 28 m.b. in 1892–3, and Russian exports of wheat rose more substantially and steadily from an average of 266 m.b. in 1869–73 to 591 m.b. in 1889–93. Similarly, while rail freight Chicago–New York fell from 1/4½d. to 7½d. per bushel between 1869–71 and 1890–2, and ocean freight to Liverpool from New York from 6.78d. to 3.04d., freights from Odessa fell more spectacularly from 1/2½d.–1/3¼d. (1872) to 3d. (1892), and in India the railway rate per bushel fell from 1/2½d. (1873) to 7⅜d. (1886) from Jubbulpore to Bombay, and the ocean freight from Bombay from 1/7d. to 5¾d. in the same years.[39] Altogether, wheat transport costs dropped to insignificance between 1850 and 1913.[40] Maize exports from the USA, it should be noted, reached their peak in 1880, at 98 m.b., and then declined; the export of other grain was negligible by comparison.[41]

As overseas output grew, largely by extension of the cultivated area, Europe responded by similar extensions in the less-populated eastern regions and by remarkable increases in yields. The result was a spectacular growth in world output, above all in wheat, the main cereal entering into international trade. It rose from an average of 1,794 m.b. in 1871-80 to 3,731 m.b. in 1909-14,[42] or by over 100%, and the increase was particularly marked in the countries with poor yields to begin with, but which were now turning into exporters.[43] By contrast, output in France, Denmark, or Holland rose very little, and in the United Kingdom and Belgium it actually declined. Among the fastest growers were the following regions.[44]

Table 7.2. Output of wheat, in million bushels

	Av. 1831-40	Av. 1871-80	Av. 1909-14
Russia	110	224	792
Austria-Hungary	65	109	231
Romania	15	24	88
(USA)	(78)	(338)	(694)
(Canada)	(6)	(24)	(197)

Falling costs of production and transport led to a drastic drop in prices, which in turn meant that only those producers who could lower their own costs, or buttress their own protective system, could survive. World prices of wheat, for example, taking British prices as the standard, fell by nearly two-thirds from an index of 244 (1900 = 100) in the peak of 1873 to a trough of 84 in 1894; and even the decadal averages fell from 212 in 1871-80 to 106.5 in 1889-99, and while they rose again to 123 in 1909-14,[45] wheat prices then fell more sharply and rose more slowly than the general price level. Inside the producer countries, prices might fall further still. Thus while export prices of Russian grain fell by just over a third from 1871-5 to 1891-5, internal produce selling-prices fell to 52.5% and rye prices by well over half.[46] By contrast, prices of meat, eggs, and dairy produce held up much better, leading to a massive switch to these products in such areas as Britain, Denmark, Holland, the peasant regions of Germany, and Italy.

This influx of cheap grain into the core areas of Europe was met by very divergent reactions according to the stage of development reached in various countries—a classic case of the differential of contemporaneousness, as noted in Chapter 4 above.[47] It was also, as we have seen, instrumental in many key countries in changing the direction of economic policy which, in turn, led to corresponding action by other countries, thus turning Europe protectionist once more. This may be put differently. As soon as any region began to specialize in industry (even in the proto-industrial phase), it would induce a complementary specialization towards food and perhaps also raw material supply in its hinterland or other supplying area. Industrialization, since it proceeded regionally, led to a widespread intensification of such geographical specialization and the trade generated thereby, in an upward spiral of greater output and cost-reducing efficiency. As long as this development developed inside political frontiers, it was allowed to proceed unhindered and was, indeed, encouraged by the state. Gradually, however, the industrialized regions expanded beyond the power of their immediate hinterland to feed and supply them, and brought areas ever farther away into symbiotic relationship with themselves. Increasingly these would be outside the frontiers, just as economic logic dictated. The process was exactly the same as before, but it had by this extension become vulnerable to political interference, and where there were special interests powerful enough, they could use, or abuse, their power to attempt to inhibit the growth process for their own particular ends.

Not every government was prepared to allow this process, which had been considered highly beneficial up to that point, to be disrupted. Where agrarian interests had become too weak politically, as in Britain and Belgium, the policy of maximizing the benefits from the international division of labour prevailed, and cheap food and cheap feeding stuffs were as welcome as cheap raw cotton had been before. Where there was a predominantly peasant agriculture, as in Denmark, the reaction was the same, using the grain as input for supplying in part the same ultimate industrial markets. On the other side of Europe, Russia and the Balkans reacted by expanding and favouring all their food exports, while at the same time taxing agriculture in an attempt to foster industrial growth also. The sharpest turn-around occurred in the countries in the middle, possessing powerful or at least promising industries, yet agricultural regions significant enough to refuse to become victims of the march of progress. It was there, in Germany, Italy, and France, who were becoming food importers in spite of all efforts to halt this process, that the attempts to disrupt the natural economic interconnections with the rest of the world were strongest. Austria–Hungary, with a foot in each camp, managed by this position to absorb some of the shocks generated, while suffering more severely from others. In Spain, a grain-export country to 1869, there was no industry, and no flexible agriculture to benefit from the prohibitive duties of over 100% imposed in 1891 and 1906 as a reaction to imported grain. They merely helped to keep up home prices, impoverish the population, and delay industrialization as Spain turned into an importer of grain and other cereals.[48]

Space forbids a discussion of more than a few of the detailed consequences generated by this change in policy. To simplify matters, we may take it, as a rough approximation, that most of the extra-European grain was absorbed by Britain, the first economy to be tied up indissolubly with outside supply areas, though in point of fact some of that grain found its way into Europe, while Britain also took some Russian and Romanian supplies.[49] That overseas supply may be looked upon as a regulator which held down prices even if it did not enter in large quantities itself. The interest therefore focuses on developments internal to the Continent.

Germany was undoubtedly successful in delaying the decline of her East-Elbian estate economy, and she certainly succeeded in raising her grain prices, which had always been well below world levels, to well above them.[50] She thus became, with France, Italy, and Spain, a high-price food area, while east and west of them, for different reasons, food prices settled at a low level. She did not, however, succeed in preventing the process of increasing economic interdependence, though this had been a major argument among protectionists. Her dependence on imported food increased at a comparable rate with the British, though with an appropriate lag and at much higher prices. Germany turned from an exporter to a net importer of rye in 1843 (regularly from 1852), barley in 1867, oats from 1872 (after a period of balance 1859-71), and wheat in 1873. The total excess of grain imports over exports rose from 1.95 million tons in 1880-5 to 6.8 m.t. in 1913. While the British share of world grain imports fell between 1866-75 and 1909-13 from 50% to 33%, the German share rose from 18% to 24% in the same period.[51]

The balance of these imports came largely from the east. Russia, opened up by railways and steamships, and liberated from serfdom, was here the chief potential supplier since, given its own large production and consumption and its very low production costs, a small excess would weigh heavily in world markets. As a matter of fact, there was never more than a small surplus forthcoming, in the early decades because of low productivity, and later increasingly because of rising home consumption. In 1875-9 Russia exported the equivalent of only 15% of her consumption, and in 1910-13 only 22%, compared with 31% and 89% for the Danubian states, 150% and 228% for the West North Central United States, 20% and 122% for Argentina, and 100% for Canada in the latter year only.[52] From the 1890s, internal consumption here, as in the USA, took a sharp upward turn, rising from 68.1 million quintals per annum in 1893-7 to 136.8 million quintals in 1913, leaving for export a shrinking proportion, 24.3% instead of 33.7%, and an absolute quantity rising only very slowly, from 34.6 to 43.9 million quintals, if the statistics are to be believed.[53]

At that level, this figure was still much the most important contribution to European consumption, representing over one-third of the imports of the food-deficit countries of advanced Europe, and of course a much higher proportion of the continental deficit. Of world exports, Russia also had the largest single share in 1910–13, at 22.8%.[54] Nevertheless, the rise of Russian home consumption was significant and portentous. Between 1884–8 and 1909–13, Russia's share of world markets had fallen, by another calculation, in the case of wheat from 35.3 to 22.3%, in maize from 15.0 to 11.2%, in rye from 68.7 to 27.3%, and only in barley had it risen from 43.6 to 67.1%.[55] The story of the United States was beginning to repeat itself, *mutatis mutandis*. Industrial development spread from its centres outward, mopping up increasing shares of an increasing harvest, and thus competing with industrial regions in the west, the former customers, who now had to go farther afield.

The world was still large, and new granaries were still being brought into use. On the list of the chief wheat exporters in 1910–13, second place was held by Argentina (13.7%), third by Canada (12.6%), fifth and sixth by the USA and India (8% each), and eighth by Australia (6.8%).[56] Much of the surplus of all these countries went to Britain. The Continent also made use of its remaining peripheral areas. Since Italy and Spain had by then become grain import areas, the chief remaining sources were Hungary and the Balkans. The share of the 'Danubian countries' in world exports between 1884–8 and 1909–13 had fallen, in the case of wheat, from 18.6 to 15.8%, for maize from 30.9 to 23.9%, for barley from 26.2 to 12.2%, and it had risen, for rye, from 14.0 to 20.3%.[57] These totals, however, hid very unequal developments. In Austria–Hungary, it was the Hungarian kingdom which had large surpluses of grain as well as of cattle and horses, finding markets in Austria as well as Germany. The tariffs and restrictions built up from 1879 onward, which shifted the burden to the east, at first harmed the suppliers into the Dual Monarchy more than it harmed the exporters out of it.[58] The protected home market offered a secure, high-price outlet for Hungarian producers, many of whom were large landowners with plentiful resources and an abysmally low output and yield record, which could be raised substantially with existing techniques. As a result, Hungary registered some astonishing output increases. Between 1864–6 and 1911–13, output of wheat rose by 185%, barley by 150%, oats by 119%, rye by 18%, maize by 262%, and potatoes by 652%. Livestock showed similar increases. Nevertheless, so great was the buoyancy of the Austrian market that it absorbed all the increase and more: Hungarian wheat exports outside the Empire fell from 23% in 1882–6 to a mere ½% in 1912–13.[59] The American process had begun to operate here, too.

The gap was filled largely by Romania, perhaps the purest example of a crash development based on a suddenly opening foreign market, foreign investment, large estates, and merciless exploitation of the peasant. Its wheat output rose from 7 million quintals in 1860 to 30.2 m.q. in 1910, and its maize output from 6.8 m.q. in 1865 to 28.1 m.q., and while maize exports were at their peak in 1890–4, wheat exports continued to grow from an average of 334,000 tons a year in 1880–4 to 1,722,000 tons in 1905–6. By 1910–13 at an export of 1,450,000 tons, she stood fourth in the world, supplying 8.3% of world exports.[60] The other Balkan countries also showed remarkable increases in output, but at much lower absolute levels.[61]

A Rising World Economy

The system of tariffs, preferences, and subsidies instituted after the late 1870s looked superficially very much like the similar system dismantled by the liberal interlude in the 1860s. In method and means it was indeed similar, but the objectives and the whole framework of policy had changed in a fundamental sense. Whereas the mercantilist body of doctrine to which much of the pre-1860 structure owed its existence was essentially premissed on a static world, holding on to or increasing the share of a constant total, the politicians of the post-1879 era seemed to be attempting to hold up, or at least divert, an irresistible flood. It was change and increase which forced the hands of governments, not loss and stagnation.

Tariffs and preferences were not, of course, the only means used, nor their objectives the only current ones, though they were the most obvious weapons and the most hallowed by tradition. Before going on to discuss some of the other methods and their implications, it will be worthwhile to cast a brief glance also at the flood they were designed to stem or divert.

The logic of the industrialization process continued its own pressures, irrespective of changes in government policies. Industries and industrial regions and employment expanded, filling the gaps in the core countries and beginning to affect the periphery. Specialization, improved technology, rising output were features of this process as before, while some new aspects emerged, such as polycentric technology, larger firms, and the beginnings of cartels and monopolistic arrangements of a new kind. As the era of mass consumption dawned, and several of the major industrial regions began to draw level, interregional and thus international trade began to shift from the exchange of different commodities, to similar commodities, differentiated only by quality, style, design, or finish. This was an international division of a labour of a new kind, superimposed on the old one. It meshed the

European, and indeed the world, economy into an ever tighter network, as Cobden had predicted, as everyone became ever more dependent on everyone else.

Nor could governments exclude themselves from this process. Many vital economic, social, and cultural questions demanded an international solution for which governments were the obvious means that came to hand. Postal matters were a typical example. After a first conference in 1863, in Paris, a Union was founded in Berne in 1874 and the World Postal Union in 1878.[62] Co-operation arose out of obvious practical needs, and once an international agreement had been reached it required a permanent secretariat, and once that was established, it was in the interest of every country to join: the members, inevitably, had to be governments rather than private firms. Altogether, by 1910, there had been 9 collective international agreements on postal matters, 10 on telegraphs, 5 on underwater cables, 1 on wireless, 7 on railway-goods transport, 3 on the technical unification of railways, 2 on the Danube, 1 on the Suez Canal, besides 3 on the law of the sea and the Safety at Sea Conference of 1913.

Another important area for international conferences and lasting agreements and supervisory institutions was the attempt to prevent the spread of epidemic diseases, both human and plant, like phylloxera. There were 7 conferences on copyright, 1 on bills of exchange, 6 on coinage, 12 on sugar. There were also agreements on fishing, on labour protection, on anti-slavery and white slavery, on fighting 'anarchism', on prisoners of war, and on hospital ships in times of war. At the first Hague Conference in 1899, 26 countries were represented in an attempt to find means of international arbitration, and the Hague Court was set up in 1907. Altogether, 12 such collective international agreements have been counted in the period 1815-51, 45 in 1852-80 and 129 in 1881-1910.[63] Needless to say, international agreements and permanent organizations among private societies and semi-official bodies like Chambers of Commerce, were more numerous still.

Foreign investments, one of the most powerful means of pulling the international economy together, were largely private ventures, but in many of them governments inevitably got involved and forced into co-operation: Russian railways, Balkan ports, Romanian oil, or Italian investment banks. The foreign consortia that helped to build up the Russian and Italian armaments industries were also not without at least the tacit agreement of their respective governments, as were the link-ups negotiated between Ruhr coal and Lorraine ore.[64]

One of the most significant results of the growing interlinking of the European (and much of the world) economy by trade and investment was the development of a well-integrated monetary system.

Typically, it had not been planned or designed, nor was it ever officially recognized, but its evident utility, at least for the economically stronger nations, won it general acceptance. The gold standard, as it evolved, was based on the British Central Bank system, and although the Bank of England itself was nominally still a private institution, this had become something of a fiction, and elsewhere Central Banks stood certainly under official control or tutelage.

The Bank of England had returned to a gold standard in 1821, after the period of the suspension of cash payments. At that time, a variety of other systems or none was in operation in the rest of Europe, and it was the needless transaction costs suffered because of that lack of co-ordination, as well as the power and influence of the western Great Powers as markets and sources of capital, which led other countries to align their currencies with London or Paris as soon as they were able to, and ultimately, in effect, with London only. Germany went over to a Central-Bank-directed gold standard in 1870 and 1873, the Scandinavian countries followed in 1872, Holland in 1875 and 1877, Austria–Hungary in principle in 1879 though in practice only in 1897. The Latin Monetary Union of 1865, nominally on a bi-metallic standard, had by that time also gone over to gold, so that the whole of Europe was covered.

Potentially, a single European monetary system could be used for purposes of disruption and for browbeating of the weak by the strong, and it helped to transmit cycles of prosperity and depression across the frontiers.[65] For the time being, however, it facilitated commerce and finance. Moreover, the authorities in different countries were obliged by it to take account of each other's needs and plans.

The relative freedom of movement of capital was matched also by the freedom of movement of labour. The first (and probably last) period of 'travel without passport' benefited not only the middle classes on pleasure bent, but also those looking for work and existence abroad.

This was the period of the greatest trans-Atlantic migration. We have noted above that it was in the years when population increase had already taken place but industrial employment had not (yet) been created to absorb it, that an apparent 'over-population' appeared which sought salvation in emigration. In the period from the 1870s to 1914 it could certainly be argued that the progress in the core had disrupted former employment opportunities in the periphery, and that cheap grain from overseas had closed openings in agriculture, so that emigration was the only possible solution.[66] Something similar had happened in Ireland and South-Western Germany in the 1840s and 1850s, and in the Scandinavian countries soon after; it was now happening, on a larger scale, in Italy, the rural parts of Austria–Hungary, the

Balkans, and among the Jews in the Russian Pale, handicraftsmen and small traders overwhelmed by factory industry.

The main targets were overseas: North and South America, as well as the other Dominions for the British, and North Africa for the French. The fact that some 40% returned,[67] underlined the close linkage, in place of the former burning of bridges, which characterized that emigration phase. Important shifts also took place within Europe. Five million emigrated overseas from Italy in 1901–14, but also 3½ million to other European countries and the Mediterranean shore. In 1901–10, around 60,000 Italians a year migrated to each of Germany, Switzerland, and France. Other migration, in part seasonal, brought Hungarian workers to Austria, and workers from all parts of the Dual Monarchy, as well as from Russian Poland, to Germany, a movement of labour westward and northward as a counter-stream to the movement of capital eastward and southward.[68]

Bearing in mind the increases in trade and traffic, in the international migration of capital and labour, in international agreement and co-operation on a technical, economic, cultural, and scientific basis, and noting the ease of movement and economic interdependence which lay behind them, one might be forgiven for believing that the Cobdenite ideal was about to become reality. War, in view of this linking of interest, might be thought to have become the 'great illusion'.[69]

Alas, it was not to be. The apparent schizophrenia which led governments to encourage international economic co-operation while attempting to break it, in the assumed national self-interest, by means of tariff and other barriers, hid the gradual ascendency of the national over the internationalist. Although the logic of the first was largely political–strategic, and of the second largely economic, both motives had become intricately mixed well before 1914. All social groups, after all, seek cohesion, power, influence, and allies. Neither capital owners nor workers and trade unionists are by nature nationalist, let alone patriotic, and both appeal traditionally to their international ideals. 'It is the *trading spirit* which cannot co-exist with war', as Kant observed in 1797 'and it takes hold sooner or later of every nation'.[70] Yet the rising state power was too convenient a focus to be ignored. As one group after another was obliged or induced to see in it its centre of loyalty, that process itself served to divide the world more thoroughly. In the end, every Socialist party outside Russia, flying in the face of its programme and perhaps even to its surprise, supported the war of its own government in 1914.

Warfare by Economic Means

Tariffs are not, in themselves, causes of war: it is possible for nations to live peaceably side by side while taxing or inhibiting trade between themselves. Nevertheless, they establish or reinforce a certain rationale, particularly in the context of the post-liberal interlude in Europe. This new rationale was many-sided, but among its important aspects were the decision that states or national communities are more important than individuals, that defence (and offensive power) is more important than opulence, and that it behoves politicians to tell their peoples what is good for them. In the end, true liberalism is indivisible and its defeat on one front endangers all the others. It cannot be said that this new line met with much resistance: on the contrary, it proved to be both popular, and an excellent text for demagogy. It also provided one, not unimportant, component in the complex of conflicts which erupted into the First World War and, after diversion into largely economic warfare once more, ended in the even greater conflagration of the Second World War.

Among the clearest signs of the new trend was the attempt to interfere with the labour market for nationalist reasons—a revival of a mercantilist practice, but in nastier modern terms. Nothing was more natural, for example, than that Polish peasants and agricultural labourers should move into Eastern Prussian villages, to take the place of those who had left for better jobs in Berlin and in the western industrial regions, or that Polish workers should cross the frontier into German Upper Silesia. It was a classic case of matching labour with capital and increasing total output and welfare. It was the way in which the USA had become prosperous.

However, it was thought to weaken German's strategic eastern frontier. In consequence, the Prussian government closed the Silesian border in 1886 and began to expel all non-Prussian Poles, in a move which, quite apart from its inhumanity, also inhibited the future development of the coalfield. The agrarians, however, were too powerful to allow themselves to be harmed in this way, and thus in 1890 the foreign Poles were re-admitted to work, provided they went home for a certain period every year (*Karenz-zeit*); it was a cat-and-mouse game which suited the needs of agriculture, as the workers did not have to be maintained in the winter, though it was of less use to industry. In spite of these obstacles, such was the power of economic logic that some one million had come in by 1913, of whom 783,000 were seasonal: 437,000 in agriculture and 346,000 in industry. The conflict between political imperatives and economic interests had, by then, created an atmosphere of embittered national hostility.[71]

This was further fanned by a parallel drive to 'Germanise' eastern landownership. Strict rules about Polish landownership and subsidies for German schools may have put some money into the pockets of the Junkers, but the 21,000 new small farms created in order to keep the soil in German hands had little long-term effects, apart from further poisoning the atmosphere.[72]

Other countries moved in the same direction, though with less system. Thus Italians found increasing difficulties in France and Switzerland where employment might have helped to solve the problems of Southern over-population which the Northern Italian labour market was not large enough to absorb. Some of the older liberal attitude remained: overseas countries still welcomed immigrants, and Britain became a haven for persecuted eastern Jews, but the grip of the frontier was tightening here, too. After the war, even the USA began to restrict immigration, devising a rationing system in 1924 which particularly discriminated against the countries of the later wave of immigration from Southern and Eastern Europe. Other overseas governments followed suit, and by the 1930s, when the Hitler persecutions began, there was no country left in the whole wide world to accept immigrants as such.[73] The cold shoulder to foreign nationals had become standard and needed no explanation or justification: these were required only for the fortunate exceptions. Thus one of the prime movers of nineteenth-century growth had been extinguished.

Discrimination against the foreigner became the order of the day: higher harbour dues for foreign ships, veterinary laws to keep out foreign cattle, or laws to limit the numbers or drive out altogether foreign directors of joint-stock companies, though their money was still welcome. The Russian railways received their indispensable financial aid only if they ordered at least half their material from inland makers, and in turn Russian ironworks were subsidized to supply those makers. Germany developed a system of using railways to favour home industries as well as German ports and ships for emigrants in transit. The Hungarians similarly used their railways to favour their own producers. One new development was that discrimination could now be exercised, not in favour of subjects of the dynastic state as such, but of certain nationalities within them. Thus the Russians attempted to inhibit the further development of Polish industry, while the Hungarians discriminated against citizens of the Austrian half. The Hungarian 'Tulip' movement of 1906 even set out to boycott all Austrian goods.[74] In the Austro-Hungarian Monarchy, indeed, the differential effects of every economic action on different provinces, which in unitary states would have been taken for granted or become subject to modification according to their own inherent logic, were used to fan the flames of strident national hostility and to disrupt the development of the country's economy altogether.

The mutual interaction of economic and political logic to turn potential progress into disruption and ultimate destruction was to be seen most clearly, perhaps, and most fatally in the relationship with overseas territories in what came to be known as 'the' age of Imperialism. The penetration of overseas territories by European traders, investors, and settlers was by nature a highly competitive and individualist process. There was, in one sense, no particular reason to welcome rivals from one's own country or frown on those from another. But equally naturally, that kind of activity would lean on government aid from an early date: home governments were asked to protect expatriate Europeans diplomatically or by force of arms, to browbeat local governments, to provide monopolies and then protect those monopolies, to sanction land occupation by land 'grants' and slavery by a system of laws, and so forth.

A movement which contained many progressive elements thus became entangled into systems which were bound to exaggerate the negative sides, the oppression and exclusion, as well as channelling potential conflicts into particular directions which made them more dangerous. Students of Imperialism have often noted that there seemed to be little economic benefit derived from the colonies which European countries acquired in this period at so much cost and risk to peace. Their trading potential was often insignificant and their investment or settlement potential even less. Imperialism, they concluded, can have had no economic motivation. Other observers have argued that there must have been some hidden economic gains, for colonies certainly brought no political benefits: they engendered antagonisms and led to dangerous conflicts and rivalry with other European states, they burdened budgets with naval and military expenditures, and they killed off the liberalism of the middle classes[75] and the internationalism of the working classes.

The puzzle is a complex one, and other factors, such as the mystique of alternative societies, the missionary zeal of some Christian leaders, the provision of jobs for upper-class youths, and the ambitions of generals and admirals have also to be taken into account. Yet the answer does not lie along one or other line, but in the interaction among them. Imperial conflicts were but one, though possibly the most dangerous, of the tensions engendered by the contradiction between an economic logic that would unify Europe (and, increasingly, the world) and a political logic, that would divide her by ever more rigid and effective barriers. Gunnar Myrdal mistook the evidence when he stated that there were no conflicts between national and international integration before 1914, and that they arose only after that date.[76] These conflicts had begun, on a new level, in the 1870s; they had been brewing increasingly since then; and in 1914 they contributed to the explosion.

Chapter 8

War and the Inter-war Years

The First World War was largely a European conflict. Some overseas countries took part, including the colonies of the belligerents and the United States which entered late, but they did not alter the essential logic of the war. The costs and sufferings were also largely European, and the war ended the period of European dominance over the progress of world capitalism: one of its most decisive consequences was a drastic shift of economic power and dynamic elsewhere.

It was followed by a sequence of trade cycles which only superficially resembled the regular booms and slumps of the preceding decades of peace. There was, it is true, a post-war boom of 1920 followed by a recession, a rise after 1925 to a peak in 1929, a collapse to 1932 and a renewed rise to 1937, to give place once more to a decline interrupted by rearmament. However, the depression years of 1929–32 were so destructive, and the upturn thereafter so weak, that their impact must be granted a decisive traumatic effect on the whole of European development thereafter, like the years 1815–17 and the late 1870s. Certainly they contributed largely to the destruction of the political fabric of Europe including the ushering in of the Nazi government in Germany, and the outbreak of the Second World War in 1939.

How far the depth and extent of that second 'Great Depression' were due to the war has been a widely debated issue, linked to differences in view as to the nature of that depression itself. Some views have attributed its virulence to the basic dislocations of the 1920s, particularly the disequilibrium between the producers of manufactures and the primary producers that was the direct consequences of the war; others have seen it as starting intrinsically no different from other recessions but being aggravated by a particular reaction of the leading governments, which was indirectly derivable from the war; and others still saw both war and Great Depression as symptoms of a fundamental malaise, perhaps the last death throes of world capitalism.

It is not the object of this study to enter into that important and still active discussion, but to draw attention to a more fundamental way in which the war contributed to the subsequent economic disorganization. This was the manner in which states and governments took over control of economic affairs and became overwhelmingly the decisive elements in the economic fate of individuals, societies, and continents. While much of the critical phase of European industrialization had taken place, as it were, outside the purview of contemporary governments, the industrialization of the remaining periphery, as well as economic life in the industrialized core states had now come to be wholly dominated by the massive power and influence of politicians. States took on the guise of individuals, made decisions, were apportioned guilt or innocence, charted progress or retardation, interfered with the value of money and the rate of investment, and closed or opened channels of trade. The economic world of Europe had become, as a result of the decisive shift of power which occurred in the war, a world of states as almost the only units that mattered.

Moreover, the political units that had now become decisive were imbued by a strong spirit of nationalism. The victorious powers together with some neutrals and with Germany had been nation states even before the war, and the peace settlement, nominally based on President Woodrow Wilson's 14 Points which had called for a Europe organized in nations, attempted to reshape the remainder of Europe on the same principles. However, the nationalism that dominated now was not the democratic nationalism of the French Revolution, opposing the people to unrepresentative dynastic rulers as part of a supranational movement of liberation. The link between the nation state and democracy had by 1919 become, in Gerschenkron's terms, an 'anachronism' and nationalism often became 'the vehicle of deadly attacks on democracy in many countries'.[1] The enemy now was not national oppression: it was other nations.

European politics thus came to be complicated even more than before 1914, by the superimposition of 'national' interests on the traditional power diplomacy.[2] Further, since the peace settlement had included other principles beside that of nationality, such as the principle of punishing the losers and rewarding their potential enemies, as many grievances were created as had been met by the new boundaries; in truth, nationalities were so mixed in some regions that with the best will in the world, no frontiers could have been drawn so as to satisfy all parties. Moreover, new states had emerged which lacked experience and self-assurance, and in a competitive world in which in the absence of special international action the worse policy always drives out the bad, their pattern of behaviour quickly transmitted itself to the rest of Europe. The 'curse of inflated nationalism', or 'the drug of nationalism',[3] composed of ingredients derived from the First World War, almost at once laid the foundations for the Second.

Economic nationalism, it is true, added a new motive to the drive to industrialization within the remaining periphery of Europe. But, in a line of progression which leads directly to the present countries of the 'Third World', it was the governmental economic decisions which were

the major political influence responsible for the fact that many features of the policies, concepts and methods of economic development planning in such countries either do not make economic sense or would make economic sense only in certain specific and rather exceptional economic circumstances the actual presence of which no one has felt it necessary to establish by empirical economic research.[4]

It is therefore not possible to disentangle entirely the two themes of this chapter, the drive to industrialization among the remaining agrarian countries of Europe, and the changes in inter-regional and international economic relations between all countries in this period.

The Economic Consequences of the War

The war caused immense losses in human lives and human health, in material and productive power, and, not least, in the psychological security of the peoples of Europe. Exact calculations do not exist, and estimates are particularly unreliable in the case of Russia, but it is generally agreed that the losses in lives outside Russia amounted to nearly 7 million military casualties, 5 million 'civilian' casualties, and a birth deficiency of another 12 million, or a total of 12-24 million according to definition. Another 7 million were permanently disabled, and 15 million wounded. For Russia, counting in the period of the civil war that was a continuation of the conflict, deaths have been estimated at 16 million plus 10 million inhibited births, a similar total of 26 million people. Including the later victims of border conflicts and massacres following the war and the influenza deaths, total losses were 50-60 million, half of them in Russia.[5] For several belligerent countries, and leaving the frustrated births out of account, this amounted to 3-4% of the total population in actual deaths, or 10% of the male work-force, with much more serious consequences for the sex imbalance for the age groups in which human reproduction as well as labour productivity is highest. Another way of putting this is to note that Europe lost the equivalent of the whole of the expected population increase of 1914-19. For some countries the losses were much higher: thus Serbia lost 20% of her pre-war population and the French population was in 1919 still 1.1 million smaller than in 1914 despite the accession of Alsace-Lorraine.

Material losses are even harder to estimate since there are many possible definitions: direct destruction, loss of output, losses of capital and labour force, both actual and in the form of frustrated increases, and so on. One estimate put the direct government expenditure at $260 milliard, another includes an element for lives lost and comes to $338 milliard. The USA bore 17.4% of this, most of the rest being borne by Europe.[6] Another way would be to calculate how much sooner the European output of, say, 1929, would have been reached, had the war not interrupted the previous growth-rate. On that basis, on one calculation, Europe could have reached the 1929 level in 1921, an 8-year delay, and on another the delay in food production was 5.2 years, in industrial production 4.5 years, and in raw material 1.25 years.[7] There were enormous differences as between countries and parts of Europe.

However, such calculations leave out the indirect effects, both psychological and real, which followed from the dislocations and altered relationships arising from the war and the peace settlements. They are too numerous and varied to be treated here in any detail or comprehensiveness. Our account will deal, rather briefly, with five of the more important ones.

The most obvious was the relative decline of Europe as a producer compared with the rest of the world: thus Europe had 43% of the world's production in 1913, compared with only 34% in 1923, and 59% of the trade in 1913, but only 50% in 1924.[8] The main beneficiaries were the USA and Japan for manufactures, the USA as an international creditor, while Latin America and the British dominions gained as sources of primary products. However, the expansion of capacity called forth by the war and the post-war shortages proved a mixed blessing for the latter, for the ability and eagerness of Europe to make good the shortfall in the production of such commodities as wheat and sugar in the 1920s was one of the main causes of the massive world economic disequilibrium between primary world manufacturing producers which aggravated the Great Depression of the 1930s. It will be discussed further in the last section of this chapter.

A second consequence was the gap which opened up between the reduced production capacity of the belligerents, estimated at a lag of ten years of growth,[9] on the one hand, and the expectations of wage and salary earners, used to decades of improvement, on the other. Enlarged trade-union power and disappointed expectations led a shift in the distribution of incomes to wage-earners, and the resulting divergence between incomes paid out and the capital formation on which they ought to have been based led to particularly acute problems in Germany, which had to import its capital, and Britain, but existed elsewhere also.

Thirdly, the war, like all other major wars, was financed largely by

borrowing. In consequence, the national debt of the major belligerents
rose spectacularly:[10]

	1914	1919	expansion factor
France (milliard fr.)	33.5	216	6
Germany (milliard Mk.)	5	156	31
Great Britain (million £)	650	7.400	11
Italy (milliard lire)	15	94	6
USA (milliard $)	1	25	25

Only part of this came out of savings, and strong inflationary pressure
was generated by the credit creation of the remainder. The note cir-
culation increased over elevenfold in Britain and Germany and over
fivefold in France and Italy, and although prices rose only 2–3-fold
among the main belligerents, this was partly due to price and other
controls. What was left behind after the armistice was a suppressed
inflation which threatened everywhere to break its banks.

After the brief period of disarray in Central and Eastern Europe,
and boom in the West after the war, there were two ways open to
governments of handling the inflation. One was a deliberate policy to
halt and possibly even reverse the price rise, and then stabilize the
currency once more in relation to gold, either at the old point or at a
new, lower one. This could lead to high social costs, in terms of unemployment and the reduction in government social expenditure, and
was attempted only by governments certain of the internal stability
of their political system.

The other alternative was to go on borrowing until inflation got out
of hand and the internal currency practically lost its function as a
measure of value and medium of exchange. In that case, a wholly new
currency had to be introduced in the end, usually with outside help.
In the chaos of their post-war adjustment, Austrian prices rose 14,000-
fold, and Hungary's 23,000-fold. Both countries were ultimately helped
to stabilize by loans supervised by the League of Nations, Austria in
1922 and Hungary in 1924. Polish prices rose 2½ million-fold, and
Russian inflation, with its peak in December 1922 after five years of
civil war, drove prices up 4,000 million-fold. In 1922 the new rouble
(Chervonetz) was introduced and currency was stabilized in 1924, at
50 thousand million roubles for one new one.[11]

The most spectacular inflation occurred in Germany, where in the
course of 1923 prices rose to one million million times the pre-war
level. Though in part engineered by the government as a form of pro-
test against the reparations and, in particular, the occupation of the
Ruhr which followed the default on them, the inflation in its later
stages had got completely out of control. The currency was then

stabilized at 4.2 million million marks to the dollar, the new currency, the 'Rentenmark', gaining credibility in part because it was nominally backed by fixed property in Germany, but largely because its issue was limited and the German budget was, in fact, balanced from 1924 on.[12]

Given the enormous disruptions of normal economic activities and the impossible burdens placed on some governments, particularly those of the former Central Powers and of the Russian and Austrian successor states, and given also that there was an over-all shortage of gold for the ex-belligerents in Europe[13] so that the whole basis of the monetary system had to be thought out anew, a return to something like normalcy in monetary matters was, in fact, accomplished with remarkable success. Within their limits, statesmen and their advisers could be counted on to pull in the right direction. As early as 1920 an international conference at Brussels considered methods of bringing supply and demand of resources together, and pressed for monetary stability. The Genoa Conference of 1922 made more direct recommendations which led to the establishment of a Gold Exchange Standard, under which poorer countries could base their currencies, not on holding costly gold reserves themselves, but on holding interest-bearing assets of countries on the gold standard. International stabilization loans were concrete examples of that common sense.

Yet this was only one half of a story of political schizophrenia. It was not merely that loans to Central European countries brought with them power and economic influence and helped to keep Communism at bay, and that the gold exchange standard was a method of strengthening the control of the Bank of England over the European economy (while at the same time weakening its base at home), so that none of these measures was in any sense altruistic. What was more significant was that under the logic of the system, economic nationalism and a furtherance of the international community were incompatible. What governments had learnt was that unilateral manipulation of their currency had added a new weapon to their armoury in the battle of making gains at the expense of others.

Nowhere was the schizophrenia of those years more evident than in the fourth issue to be discussed here, the inter-Allied loans, the post-war aid from the USA, and the German reparations, all questions, basically, of inter-governmental payments. Immediately after the war, large areas of Central and Eastern Europe were in danger of starvation, either because of continuing fighting or, as in the case of the rump of Austria that had been left after the break-up of the Austro-Hungarian Empire, because frontiers now cut off the food supply from traditional sources. In view of the over-all shortages of food and fuel, no inter-regional help could be expected, and there were fears of epidemics and revolution that could spread over the whole area and beyond. Hungary and Bavaria did, indeed, have short-lived Soviet governments and there was political instability after the revolutions in Berlin, Vienna, the Baltic countries, Poland, and elsewhere. Only the USA were in a position to help, and substantial aid was sent from early 1919 onward. It is clear now that in the mixture of motives behind the American Relief Administration the political was very much stronger than the humanitarian, though when government aid was sharply curtailed after a few months, privately financed relief contributed another $500 million. The US government had sent food worth some $1,250 million, of which less than 10% was an outright gift. Ex-enemies had to pay cash, but for ex-Allies the deliveries were added to the accumulating inter-Allied debt,[14] further complicating that troublesome issue.

The total lent by the USA to the Allies in War and Reconstruction Loans in 1917–21 was around $12 milliard, but America was not the only lender. Britain had lent a somewhat smaller sum to the remaining Allies, including Russia, and France, though she was mainly a recipient of credit, had herself lent 15 milliard francs, or around $3 milliard. Italy, Belgium, and Russia were the remaining large recipients. These debts which altogether came to $26½ milliard had arisen largely because of deliveries in kind, expenditure by armed forces, and other aid in the heat of war. Now in the peace years, they remained as cold figures in the books, to be bargained over by the politicians. Britain, who was owed more by the other Allies than she owed to the United States was willing to forgo her advantage and cancel all payments, but the USA would not accept this, nor would she allow the continental ex-Allies to repay their share out of their reparations receipts from Germany. She was still less impressed with the argument that in view of the much greater sacrifice in lives and property made by the other Allies she might consider her financial sacrifice a fair equivalent. Such repayments as were attempted were not made easier by the very high tariffs maintained by the USA, and the fact that she was absorbing an ever larger share of the world's gold, so that she could not easily be paid either in commodities or in gold.

Arguments over these repayments led to much bitterness, as well as to serious crises and dislocations in a by no means stable financial world. Nor were there any benefits to set against these drawbacks. For, while the USA ultimately received $2.6 milliard out of her claim of $12 milliard before all claims and payments disappeared in the moratoria and repudiations of the early 1930s,[15] she had contributed all of it and more in the first place, largely in loans to Germany.

It may be argued that the hands of the American negotiators in this sorry performance were tied by a public opinion which insisted on its pound of flesh, and this was certainly so in the other segment of this circular relationship, the German reparations. In the jingoist fever of the early months after the armistice it was easy to whip up popular support for the idea that Germany should pay for all the damage caused by the war, and informed opinion could point to the success of the indemnity payment exacted by Germany from France after 1870, a capital injection which was considered to have helped German industrialization. The economic problems of the transfer of large sums were scarcely understood by anyone at the time.

Some repair work, payments for occupation costs, and deliveries in kind made a beginning, and by May 1921, Germany had delivered in reparations much of her merchant tonnage (2.2 million g.t.), 5,000 locomotives, 136,000 railway waggons and carriages, 24 million t. coal, agricultural livestock and machinery, and much else. The totals were valued by the Allies at 2.6 milliard gold marks, plus 2.5 milliard for Saar coal and public property, and by the Germans they were valued at 37 milliard gold marks.[16] Clearly, neither side had made an effort at a serious valuation.

It was at that point that the Allies had finally agreed on the total sum they were going to demand: 132 milliard gold marks. Whether such a sum was justified, and could have been raised by Germany, had she wanted to raise it, has for long been a matter of bitter debate.[17] Certain it is that the Allies would have been quite unwilling to accept the goods and services in which alone such payments could have been transferred, since they would have spread ruin among their own industry to the advantage of the Germans. Meanwhile the wrangling over the impossible demand contributed to the economic chaos in Central Europe, particularly in Germany herself, and served to undermine the moderate governments there and to strengthen the political extremists, with ultimately destructive consequences for all.

The sum having been decided on, the dreary farce of the annual 'payments' began as soon as the financial chaos of hyper-inflation, to which reparation demands had contributed, had been mastered in 1923. Under the Dawes plan of 1924 Germany was to pay annual sums rising from 1 milliard marks in 1924-5 to 2.5 milliard marks by 1928-9. The first year's instalment was largely paid out of an initial dollar loan, and the later ones were in fact financed by American investments in Germany, which were transferred as 'reparations' to the Allies and passed, in turn, as interest and repayment of the inter-Allied loans back to the United States.[18]

In this merry-go-round two aspects were notable. The first was that Germany received far more in foreign loans than she paid in reparations,[19] and that this capital helped to re-equip her industries and infrastructure, particularly in 1926-9, to become much more efficient and competitive than those of the victor nations receiving the reparations. By contrast most of the other recipients of American capital used it largely to stop up temporary holes and derived little long-term benefits from it.[20] The other was that while, in the circular flow, the reparations and loan repayments were contractual, the third segment, the American lending to Europe, was not and could be stopped at any time. It was so stopped in 1928, first in order to finance the stock market speculation in New York and later because there were no surplus funds available in the crisis after 1929. In the early 1930s there was even some repatriation of capital to the USA.[21]

In view of this dependence on a continuous stream of new American capital to 1928, the disruption caused by its falling away thereafter helped materially to worsen, if it did not trigger, the Great Depression. Germany was in difficulties at once and in her search for a remedy hit upon a savage deflation in 1930, which multiplied her unemployment and strengthened political extremism. In 1931 she drew British funds to herself which brought down the pound sterling in turn. As far as reparations were concerned, they were reorganized by the so-called Young 'plan' of 1929, which in effect meant a reduction in the annual rate of payments, to 1,708 million gold marks in 1930-1 rising to 2,429 million g.m. in 1965-6, though the details hardly mattered since payments were suspended by the Hoover moratorium of 1931 and never resumed.[22] As in the case of the inter-Allied debt repayments, it is not possible to say whether Europe suffered more by the immediate disruptive damages caused by the reparations policy, or by its ultimate contribution to Depression and War. The only certainty is that there was nowhere a beneficiary.

The fifth and last issue to be noted here relates to the particular policies pursued by the new states which had been carved out of the old Russian, Turkish, and Austrian Empires with additions from Germany, and which now stretched in an irregular band from Finland in the north to Greece in the south.

Altogether there were now 38 independent economic units in Europe instead of 26, 27 currencies instead of 14, and the frontiers had been lengthened by 12,500 miles. In the former Austrian lands, in particular, economic relationships of a fundamental nature, some of them going back over centuries, were thereby destroyed. Thus in the textile industry, the spinning and finishing mills were now in Austria, the looms in Czechoslovakia; Austrian tanneries lost the sources of their hides and tanning materials; the Alpine ironworks lost their coal, Czech industries lost their markets, Hungarian flour mills both sources of grain and markets. The Hungarian irrigation and flood system was now separated by the frontiers from its control points; frontiers separated workers from their factories, cattle from their grazing grounds, towns from their traditional food supply, sugar-beet factories from their fields. Worst of all, the railway system had no relation to the new political geography: centred on Vienna, it failed to connect different parts of Czechoslovakia with each other, some of the sidings near the frontiers were left without purpose, and in some areas, they crossed frontiers several times back and forth. Much of East–Central Europe became cut off from its former sea outlets, while Trieste and Fiume decayed.[23]

In those circumstances, one might have expected sustained action by the governments concerned to minimize the economic costs of their new-found national freedom and to do their utmost, at least in the short term, to abate the desperate hunger, unemployment, and loss of resources[24] in their countries. The very opposite was the case. Each of the agrarian countries wanted to cut itself off from the former sources of their manufactured supplies, now in Czechoslovakia and (rump) Austria, as completely as possible, in order to speed its own industrialization. In this, they went particularly for certain strategic industries, 'almost regardless of the size of the country, its location, or its available skills',[25] while opposing as far as lay in their power, foreign capital and foreign technical and managerial personnel. What they sought, in fact, was total import substitution in place of comparative advantage, each duplicating the work of the other, and each too small and too poor to carry out even a fraction of its ambitions. As a result, Austria and Czechoslovakia were forced to sell their manufactures in the West and overseas, drawing their food supplies from equally far afield, while neighbouring farmers had no markets.[26]

Firms with branches elsewhere, banks with head offices in Vienna, so-called 'war stocks' of materials, even individuals of a minority nationality became immediate objects of confiscation and despoliation, known as 'nostrification'. In the ensuing wrangle over compensation and counter-claims, trains were unloaded at the frontiers and goods trans-shipped, at great expense, for no country trusted another to return its rolling-stock, and this at a time when Hungary had only 27% of her locomotives left in repair and running, Romania 29%, Bulgaria 37%, and Czechoslovakia 62%. Romania had, in fact, carried off a large quantity of rolling-stock, to be left rotting in its sidings as it could not be repaired there, while transport languished.[27]

In most cases, these ambitions were backed not merely by traditional tariff policies, but by total trade prohibitions. At a conference in Pontorose the Central European countries had undertaken to end these, but in fact many continued to the end of the decade, then to be

swallowed up in the reinforced protectionist measures of the Depression. 'If the nations were disarmed in a military sense', as one
observer noted, 'they were left free, especially in Central and South-
Eastern Europe, to continue the conflict in the economic field'.[28] As
in the case of real war, each country was prepared to take considerable
economic suffering upon itself in the hope of inflicting even worse
suffering upon its neighbours and 'gave national prestige precedence
over wealth'.[29] Economic policy was thus nourished by natural hatreds
and continued to nourish them, preparing the ground for the next war.

Though the case of the Austrian successor states was the most obvious and most damaging, similar hatreds and self-inflicted economic
harm aroused by feelings of nationalism were generated in Upper Silesia
and Tessin, the Baltic states, South Tyrol, Germany's western frontier,
and, last but not least, the Turkish–Greek demarcation line.[30] The
economic damage done by the post-war settlement was probably at
least as great as that done by the war itself.

The European Periphery and Industrialization

The countries forming the belt between Germany and Russia, with the
exception of Czechoslovakia and Austria, belonged to that part of
Europe which had not yet become industrialized before 1914. We have
seen that some of their desperate post-war measures were designed
specifically to create, in each and every one of them, an industrial
base as part of their quest for national 'independence'.

It may be noted in passing that this approach was not that of the
earlier industrializers, though it has much in common with the mercantilism of the seventeenth and eighteenth centuries. Neither Britain
in the eighteenth century, nor Germany or France in the nineteenth,
even when they did seek to foster certain industries by tariffs or subsidies, set out with the intention of creating a complete industrial
complex by government intervention, though they were much larger
countries for which such an aim would not have been wholly unreason-
able. Instead, they supported this or that specific industry directly,
or levied a general tariff, both clearly designed to foster what was
already there rather than create anything new for which a natural base
was lacking.

If the plans of the agrarian fringe thus lacked a certain realism, they
were also unfortunate in their timing. Inasmuch as the simultaneous
developments in the rest of Europe mattered, and they mattered overwhelmingly for such small and dependent economies, they had turned
decisively against the would-be newcomers. Not only was the technological and scientific gap widening with every year that passed, as a
simple function of time, but Europe had ceased to be the open society

that had enabled industrialization to take place smoothly in one region after another in the nineteenth century. The easy way in which a new-comer had been able to insert himself into markets, by advantages of location, resources, skills, wage costs within common technologies, or superior advanced technology, had been largely closed: competitive success would be followed, not by an expansion of the market, but by rising tariffs, quotas, and exclusions.[31]

The preference for import substitution rather than comparative advantage was thus not without logic[32] though, as we have seen, it was initially adopted for quite the wrong reasons. However, the result of that choice was inevitably high-cost, inefficient, technically backward industries pushing inferior goods which could survive only by constant protection and official support and therefore generated massive cor-ruption. The symptoms will be recognized as belonging also to Third World industrialization of post-World War II, to which may be added the high proportion of capital in the major industries owned by the government.[33] Set in the midst of poor, basically agrarian countries, these pampered industries placed an intolerable burden on the peasan-try and on the state budget alike, and removed what little chance there had been of success as specialist primary producers.

It will not come as a surprise to note that in these circumstances, over-all economic progress was slow and those countries remained among the poorest in Europe. On Paul Bairoch's figures, per capita GNP (in 1960 US $) was as given in the following table.[34]

Table 8.1.

	1913	1938
Baltic countries	—	501
Bulgaria	263	420
Finland	520	913
Greece	322	590
Hungary	372	451
Poland	—	372
Romania	—	343
Yugoslavia	284	329
All Europe	534	671

Finland, it will be noted, was successfully lifting herself out of this group, though still on the basis of primary products.[35] Next to Greece, Hungary did relatively best among the remaining countries, her per capita income (1938 = 100) rising from 80 in 1926 to 106 in 1939. The Bulgarian income, from a lower level, also rose from 81 to 111, but the Yugoslav figure rose only from 97 to 106, the Romanian fell from 102 to 100 (1938), and for Czechoslovakia and Poland the index changes between 1929 and 1938 were 102 falling to 100, and 97 rising to 100, respectively.[36]

The industries which did make their appearance were textiles, intended as import substitutes but using much imported raw material, and timber, leather and food processing, using local materials. There was next to no iron and steel made, and machinery and engineering amounted to only 2.4% of the small industrial output in Bulgaria in the 1930s, 7% in Poland, 10.2% in Romania, and 14.15% in Hungary.[37] What there was, was patchy: there were railways with little traffic and output elsewhere stagnating for lack of transport, Budapest cornered half the Hungarian industry and in Poland, where inefficient power-stations generated electricity at twenty different voltages, the consumption ranged from 1000 KWL per capita in Silesia to 16 KWL in some eastern provinces in 1938.[38] Above all, the region desperately lacked capital. While Romania and Yugoslavia were still saddled with inter-Allied debts, all the countries needed injections of foreign investments, but these in turn presupposed a settled budget and balanced foreign payments, which were difficult to achieve without and ahead of foreign loans. In the end, all these countries became beholden to foreign investors, governmental and private, and were saddled with annual service charges, but little enough of those funds from abroad were used purposefully to raise economic efficiency on a long-term basis.[39]

In view of these efforts, it might seem surprising at first sight that the proportion of the actual population employed in industry and commerce remained low, and that the manpower in agriculture declined but little as a proportion, and even grew in absolute terms. The numbers employed in industry as a percentage of *total* population changed as follows:[40]

	1920	1938
Poland	1.4	2.4
Hungary	2.8	4.4
Romania	1.0	1.9
Yugoslavia	1.4	1.9
Bulgaria	(0.4)	1.7

By contrast, the agricultural population comprised 68% of the population in Poland, 70% in Hungary, 79% in the Baltic countries, and 81% in the Balkan countries. In absolute terms, the farm population rose from 17.3 million in 1921 to 20.2 million in 1935 in Poland, and from 3.4 million (1920) to 4.3 million (1935) in Bulgaria. Only in Hungary was there a notable drop in the proportion in that period.[41]

Behind this phenomenon hides the basic dilemma and tragedy of that region in the inter-war period. Thwarted in their drive to industrialization, its people also found their agrarian export markets closing against them, so that a rapidly rising population was driven back on its land, where, in the face of rising productivity, a 'surplus population' remained bottled up: the pre-war safety valve of overseas emigration had now largely been closed.

The wave of populism and democracy which swept over the region after the war, short-lived though it was, had led in many countries to a substantial redistribution of land from the large estates. Some 60 million acres in 12 European countries, amounting to 11% of the land there, were redistributed altogether, and about one-half of this actually went to smallholders, to settle new families or increase the holdings of existing ones. Only Poland and Hungary retained large estates, while in Bosnia and Dalmatia the reduction in the size of holding was the result of dissolving the Zadruga, the extended family holding. Whatever the intentions behind these moves, which were related to the temporary accession of power of peasant parties, the 'Green International', they had the consequence of reducing output at least for a time, but above all of making the population cling to the land.[42]

The area was still one of a high birth-rate, high death-rate, high infant mortality, but also a rapid rate of population increase. Population (in millions) changed as follows:[43]

	1920	1940
Poland	26.7	33.5
Hungary	7.9	9.2
Romania	15.5	20.1
Yugoslavia	11.8	15.8
Bulgaria	4.8	6.3

The result was over-population on the land. The concept of 'over-population' in this region between the wars has been much debated, and estimates of numbers involved differ, depending in part on definitions.[44] But the basic notion is that output does not go up with the extra hands on the farm, and would not be reduced if they left: additional human beings merely create greater poverty. On this basis, up to 30 million out of 100 million were surplus in the region. Productivity and yields actually went up in this period, though they were still very low by the standards of Western Europe or even Czechoslovakia and Austria. In terms of yields per acre they were higher than in the overseas grain lands, but in terms of output per person, very much lower.[45] But there was little point in producing more as there was no market and higher output only served to increase the proportion of the surplus population and to turn the terms of trade even further against the farms,[46] falling prices for food being one of the chief characteristics of this period. Thus specialization in the kind of cereal economy for which this region had proved to be suitable before 1914 had become unprofitable because of supplies from better endowed regions overseas; specialization in manufactures was thwarted by poverty and backwardness.

Regions reaching that stage earlier had, if migration in the cities was closed, the escape of emigration elsewhere. In view of the size of the population surplus in Eastern Europe between the wars, relief by emigration would have had to be on a massive scale—at least as high as the peak pre-war figures,[47] but it was an aspect of the disintegration of the world economy of this period that that option was no longer open. The USA decided on a quota system in 1924 which limited the annual immigration to 2% of the population of each national origin settled in 1890, when most of the migrants of Eastern and Southern Europe had not arrived yet: the total annual quota for that region was only 20,000. Other overseas countries also became restrictive and France, looking for replacements for her lost manpower in the early 1920s, attracted mostly migrants from the Latin countries.[48] Annual overseas emigration changed as shown in the following table.[49]

Table 8.2.

In 000s	Average 1911-14	Average 1925-7
Austria	414 ⎫	4 ⎫
Hungary	409 ⎬ 1240	3 ⎬
Russia	414 ⎭	⎬ 157
Poland, Romania	— ⎫	150 ⎭
Czechoslovakia, Yugoslavia	— ⎬	
Italy	1461	119
Spain	731	48
Portugal	253	25

The Iberian peninsula, the other major area of the periphery in 1914, exported wine, fruit, metals, and other primary products rather than cereals, but its relative position was similar. According to Paul Bairoch's calculations, Spain ($337 of 1960 in 1938) and Portugal ($351) were, with Romania and Yugoslavia, the poorest countries in Europe.[50] Yet Spain had seen some progress. She had benefited from her neutrality during the war, particularly in terms of shipping, banking, and staple industries, and from some imaginative hydro-electric and irrigation schemes in the 1920s, and both industrial and agricultural output had risen by around 50% between 1913 and 1929. The growing of oranges had become an efficient and capital-intensive sector of agriculture. Then the crisis struck, and as a specialized producer the throttling of international trade hit Spain particularly hard. Between 1929 and 1935, the output of iron ore fell by 39%, of pyrites by 49%, of lead by 56%, and of tin by 23%. All these were commodities for export.

But coal output (-3%) stayed at more or less the same level and a high tariff allowed food and textile output and consumption to be isolated from the world depression. In the civil war of 1936–9 the economy took several steps backward. In Portugal, it was Salazar's dictatorship which, by savage orthodox deflation from 1927 onward inhibited all economic growth.[51]

The only country to industrialize successfully in this period was Soviet Russia and her industrialization took place in almost complete economic isolation from the rest of Europe. It is not possible to treat Soviet industrialization as if it were simply another manifestation of the same socio-technical change that emanated from Britain in the eighteenth century and then spread to the rest of Europe, for behind the Soviet drive was a fierce new ideology, and an entirely different system of property and therefore of class relations. In the critical years Soviet industry and much of the rest of economic life were totally planned and controlled by government agencies, the profit motive had been cut out, and the price mechanism driven back to a subordinate role. All major means of production were owned by the community and their managers and controllers were salaried functionaries. Powers of coercion, normally reserved only for the armed forces at most, were applied through the whole of economic life and since government was so closely identified with economic successes and failures, these became issues of a far more political character than in any other European industrialization process up to that time. Moreover, the members of the ruling élite considered themselves to be the pioneers of a new social system, more advanced than that operating in the industrialized countries of the West and superior to it, so that they were convinced that the West would ultimately follow in their footsteps. This gave them much drive and self-confidence, as well as a motivation not available in the West, by which to persuade millions of workers, peasants, and managers to perform, at least for a certain period, prodigies of effort for which they could not for the time being receive any tangible reward. Whether the Bolshevik rulers of Soviet Russia also thereby succeeded in creating a new man with different value systems and a different psychology may be debatable, but there can be no doubt that the industrialization process was carried through within a different socio-economic framework.

Some close observers, like Gerschenkron and Von Laue,[52] have seen in many of the essentials of Russian development not so much the planned 'Socialist' economy but merely the logical outcome of the tasks facing the late starter, and this applies particularly to the central role played by government. Indeed, there has not been an example of industrialization carried out after that date in which the government has not played that role and it is hard to imagine any other way in this late stage of world industrialization outside very small countries which might be industrialized on the initiative of multinationals. More to the point, perhaps, was the fact that many of the actual tasks facing the Soviet government, the need to accumulate capital and train up skilled teams out of a poor and unprepared population, the problems of matching primary- and manufactured-goods production and consumption, capital and output, savings and investment, and not least, the problem of how to induce a dispersed peasantry to conform to the plans prepared for them, were not very different from those faced elsewhere and have, indeed, been used as models since. One overriding difference should, however, also be noted. The Soviet economy suffered at no time from over-production. The problem has always been how to produce more, to fill still unmet demands.[53]

Russia had, as noted in chapter 6 above, laid some substantial foundations for industrialization before 1913, but between 10–25% of these, in Poland, Finland, and the Baltic states, were lost to Soviet control,[54] and much of the rest was destroyed in the war and the civil wars that followed. By 1920, industrial output was down to 20% of pre-war, output of so-called large-scale production falling to as low at 12.8% while handicraft production suffered less and fell only to 44.1%. Manufactured consumer goods sold to the public had fallen even further, to 12.5% of the 1912 figure, and for some key commodities production had virtually ceased: thus only 1.6% of the pre-war iron ore was being produced, 2.4% of the pig iron, 4.0% of the steel, and 5.0% of the cotton. Foreign trade had fallen to one-tenth of one per cent in 1919 and was still only 8% of the pre-war level in 1921. As for agriculture, the sown area had dropped in 1921 to 70% of the figure for 1909–13, the gross yield of crops to 44%, and there had been sharp declines in the livestock. National income per head had fallen to less than 40% of the pre-war figure. The numbers employed as industrial workers dropped to about one-half and the population of Moscow and Petrograd to 42%.[55]

It is not easy to evaluate such figures, as also similar statistics for the destruction of the stock of capital, in terms of the potential of the economy for future growth and industrialization. Clearly, Soviet Russia started from a much better base than an economy which would show a similar output by using all its existing resources at full strength. Thus there were skilled workers and engineers, an infrastructure which needed relatively little input to restore it, and there was commercial and managerial experience. It was therefore generally understood that the recovery to the pre-war level of production which was reached in 1926 for agriculture and 1927–8 in the case of industry,[56] was a relatively easier process than any advance beyond that point would be.

At the same time, the recovery from such depths of destruction, with no foreign aid other than some famine relief in 1921, required a sustained effort which occupied most of the decade of the 1920s and set up enormous social and political strains in a population which had suffered one disaster after another and yet had repeatedly to be disappointed in its expectations. The upheavals of the preceding years had cost Russia a delay of fifteen years' growth.[57] In spite of the repeated claim of the Soviet leadership that its historic role was to shape its own destiny, it is clear that its actual policies were in large measure shaped by these severe economic constraints, at least until the great decisions of 1928-9, and in their more candid moments Lenin and other leaders admitted that it was so.[58]

The economic policy of 1917-28 falls into two clearly defined periods: 'War Communism' to 1921 and the 'New Economic Policy', or NEP, thereafter. In 1917-21 the young Soviet government was fighting on several fronts, cut off largely from the raw material supply areas and from the rest of the world, its industrial labour force depleted by being drafted into proletarian battalions, and it was therefore in no position to think of anything but survival. The nationalization of the land was an empty formality at the time, direct control of production an obvious necessity, and the virtual abolition of money emerged out of the rampant inflation. Such other measures as an egalitarian distribution system and the nationalization of industry might have been *ad hoc* solutions to immediate problems, but also suited the Bolshevik government's book. At first only those concerns had been nationalized which had refused to recognize workers' control, later there followed the banks, the state (but not the private) railways, and the merchant marine, in June 1918 certain specified key industries, and in January 1919 all larger firms to a total of 3,668. By the end of 1920 all concerns employing over 5 workers plus machinery or 10 workers without machinery were nationalized, making a total of some 37,000 concerns.[59]

There was, however, no way of regimenting the peasants. They refused to supply the towns without adequate returns, and requisitioning parties were met with violence, passive resistance, and the slaughter of animals.[60] It could not be in the government's interest to encourage further anarchy and destruction, and rebellions in the countryside in 1921 as well as the Kronstadt revolt of sailors, once among the revolutionary élite, convinced Lenin that the next phase of recuperation and recovery had to compromise with ideology in order to provide effective incentives at the grass roots. There had to be growth at all costs.

Under the New Economic Policy the government maintained firm control over the commanding heights of key industries, foreign trade, banking, and some central planning agencies, above all GOELRO, the electrification commission, which then turned into GOSPLAN, the central economic planning commission. But outside these, and above all on the land, a substantial degree of freedom was restored. In place of compulsory deliveries, peasants were required to pay a tax in kind, later in money; 75% of retail trade and 20% of wholesale trade returned to private hands. Even many productive concerns were leased back to private entrepreneurs, who made contracts among each other rather than obey allocations from above.[61] By 1923-4 only 38.5% of GNP was produced by the Socialist sector, 51.0% (but 98.5% in agriculture) being the result of small commodity production and 8.9% of private capitalism.[62]

Improvement in output was immediate and sustained. Despite inevitable difficulties, such as the 'scissors' crisis of 1923 when agricultural output had risen faster than industrial so that the commodity terms of trade turned against the peasant,[63] every year brought the country closer to normalization. By 1928, though Russia was still the poorest country in Europe, a point had clearly been reached where 'take-off' into industrialization could begin and for the first time in European history this was to be a planned, organized process. A fierce debate broke out as to the basic industrialization strategy to be pursued:[64] it was the last such debate to be held in the Soviet Union, for at the end of it Stalin had taken over, and his personal dictatorship branded any independent ideas as culpable treason.

Against those who urged a more moderate pace of industrialization, based on a relatively prosperous agrarian sector not unlike the western models, Stalin's plan called for a dramatically high rate of growth, faster than anything that had been achieved before. This was to happen under conditions of only minimal contacts with the advanced world, and with a much faster rate of growth of capital goods than consumer goods (though in the original versions the latter were to do better than turned out in practice): both of these conditions having strong military security connotations. Such a plan, implying massive transfers of labour from agriculture to industry and a savings ratio of at least 20% against a maximum of 10% known among countries at a similar stage of development hitherto,[65] could not be financed out of the still small industrial sector, even if the industrial workers were to continue to be starved. It had to come out of the pockets of the peasant, and here lay its gravest danger.

In the Russian village, Bolshevik ideology had been at constant loggerheads with facts since the Revolution. Ideology demanded favouring the small peasant and maintaining a benevolent neutrality towards the middle peasant, but both these were poor deliverers of

grain. In oft-quoted figures, it was pointed out that the former delivered only 11.2% of his output and the latter only 20%, whereas the
hated large peasant (still a poor man by western standards, but in
Russia unloved as the 'Kulak', or fist) delivered 47%.[66] Similarly, in
the constant exhortations by the government to master techniques
and increase output, the Kulak proved to be top of the form, but for
ideological reasons had to receive nothing but kicks for his pains. It
was clear that if the terms of trade were once more to be turned against
the peasantry, and if it had to give up the labour needed for the great
construction schemes, it would react, as before, by throttling supplies
to the towns. Something of this had in fact happened in 1928–9 as the
NEP was wound down and heavier taxes and severe discrimination were
visited on private peasants in general and on Kulaks in particular.[67]

Stalin claimed to have found the answer to this dilemma by collectivization, the dissolution of individual peasant holdings and their
merger in large units worked collectively in return for a share of the
total proceeds, calculated as a form of wage. That option had been
urged on the peasantry since the Revolution, but with minimal results.
Now Stalin claimed that there were moves in that direction from below,
though there are indications that he engineered those himself.[68] The
onset of the first Five-Year Plan that was to start industrialization on
the Stalin model thus also saw the massive drive to collectivization
in 1930.

Coupled as it was with an intensified campaign against the Kulaks,
it proved to be economically a most costly, and socially and politically
a most disastrous decision of the Soviet government. For in addition
to the vast economic destruction, and the human suffering which cost,
in dead and unborn, perhaps 10 million people and the uprooting of
5 million, it also barbarized Soviet society, for its inevitable occasional
economic failures were treated as treason and sabotage, and purges
and judicial murders came to dominate public life in an atmosphere of
hysteria and paranoia in the 1930s.

From the beginning, the drive to collectivize agriculture was a political party matter. Activists descended on the villages to force everyone into 'Kolkhoses' or collective farms, and within a matter of weeks
the proportion of peasant households enrolled had risen from 4% to
57%. Since most of these were involuntary, and there was no clarity
about the disposable property, the process was one of chaos and
destruction, which frightened even Stalin and the leadership. They
back-pedalled sharply, and in a few further weeks, by June 1930, the
proportions enrolled were down to 23%, and were allowed to rise only
gradually thereafter, stabilizing at 18½ million households, or a little
over 90% of the total by 1936.[69]

However, the damage had been done. There followed, first, a mass slaughter of animals, as peasants preferred to get an immediate benefit rather than hand their property over to the community, the number of cattle fell by a third, sheep and goats by one half, and horses by one quarter, and it took the rest of the decade to make up the losses. Even then, food deliveries to the towns were down by 20% while a similar gross agricultural output in 1936-9 had to feed a population some 13% larger.[70] Secondly, there was the war on the Kulaks. They had not been guilty of breaking any of the existing laws, but they stood in the way of collectivization, and the whole of their number, some 800,000 families, together with other peasants who were not politically reliable and others still who became victims of personal vendettas, were liquidated. Some were sentenced, many were deported to help build up Socialism at the frontier, and the remainder were deprived of their property also, but allowed to stay in villages on the worst land. Looting, destruction, and other forms of local lawlessness necessarily accompanied the process. The third consequence, a result of the other two, was the famine of 1933, claiming further millions as victims, while exports, which might have eased the path of industrialization, fell away to almost nothing.[71] Only the enlarged freedom of Kolkhos members to keep some animals and cultivate some private plots allowed agricultural output to rise gradually again thereafter, and rationing was ended by 1936.

Against these failures and sacrifices, there have to be set some remarkable achievements. Industrialization took place within the framework of a set of Five-Year Plans. The first, for 1928-32, saw a massive increase of labour and capital inputs with a corresponding increase in output but without an increase in productivity; in the second, for 1933-7, productivity increases and quality improvements became much more marked; the third, which stood under the shadow of war production, was interrupted by the German invasion in 1941. It has proved to be a very difficult matter to establish the actual growth rates of those years and estimates vary from 5-15% though the large majority of observers would put the rate of industrial growth at well over 10% a year. These are rates never before achieved, and equalled since then only by Japan. GNP rose at a lesser rate, while consumption probably rose at little more than 1-2% p.a.[72] The figures that follow in Table 8.3. may illustrate the kind of results achieved, in terms of actual output.[73]

The successes in human terms were equally impressive. Higher education expanded in line with all capital inputs, and a whole generation of peasants was integrated into modern industry and modern urban living. The establishment of fine educational, welfare, and social facilities should be set against the low rate of growth of consumer goods, and against the poor records of western societies at a similar stage of development. There can be no doubt about the enthusiasm and sense of mission and achievement of many of the pioneers who opened up and built completely new industrial complexes, like those of Magnitogorsk.

Table 8.3.

	1928	1940
Coal, in tons	35.5	165.9
Oil, in tons	11.6	31.1
Electricity, milliard kWh	5.0	48.3
Steel, in tons	4.3	18.3
Cement, in tons	1.5	5.7
Animal fertilizers, in tons	0.1	3.2
Metal-cutting machine tools, thousand units	2.0	58.4
Steam locomotives, units	479	914
Motor vehicles, thousands	0.8	145
Cotton cloth, m. linear metres	2678	3954
Woollen cloth, m. linear metres	87	120
Leather footwear, m. pairs	58	211
Clocks and watches, millions	0.9	2.8

By the end of the decade somewhat over half the population was still engaged in agriculture, but one-third of Soviet citizens now lived in cities and towns, and Soviet Russia was fast becoming a mechanized society. An industrial revolution in the western sense had been passed through in one decade. When the Germans struck, in 1941, they took on an economy which in absolute, even if not in per capita terms, had output figures comparable with their own.

The Break-up of the European Economy

The economic development of Europe in the inter-war years falls easily into two phases, with the financial crisis of 1929–31 as the turning-point. Before it, governments attempted at least half-heartedly, to restore in general terms the relatively stable conditions and free inter-change of goods that had obtained before the war while keeping up most of the individual restrictions for particular reasons. After it, all was swamped by a tide of tariffs, quotas, and outright prohibitions.

In the post-1920 slump it was not only the East–Central European states which were found to have imposed prohibitions on imports or higher tariffs. Thus Italy raised its tariffs in 1921, Spain in 1922, while both maintained some prohibitions, and France not only kept her quantitative import restrictions, but further added to them in 1920 and 1922. Poland reimposed import restrictions in 1925. According to League of Nations calculations[74] about as many countries had raised as had lowered their tariffs between 1913 and 1925. Tariff levels, in per cent:-

	1913	1925	Difference		1913	1925	Difference
Spain	33	44	+ 11	Austria	18	12	− 6
Hungary	18	23	+ 5	France	18	12	− 6
Switzerland	7	11	+ 4	Sweden	16	13	− 3
UK	0	4	+ 4	Denmark	9	6	− 3
Belgium	6	8	+ 2				

Nor had there been any great relaxation of exchange controls: in the mid-twenties they were still to be found in France, Italy, Spain, Greece, and most of the countries of East–Central Europe. Similarly, many physical controls are kept on.[75]

It is not at first sight clear why the worst features of pre-war economic nationalism were continued. The 1920s were relatively prosperous and the chastening experiences of the war itself, together with the determination not to have a repetition of it, expressed in the formation of the League of Nations, might have led one to expect a deliberate effort to return to a more open and interdependent European economy. International meetings and conventions did, indeed, urge greater liberality and collaboration, but, except for minor details, when the delegates returned home they became once more part of a milieu which refused to look beyond any immediate and any purely selfish results. The curious view had taken hold, as a League of Nations publication complained,[76] that any reduction in protection was damaging to the country making it, and could be granted as a concession to others only in return for a suitable quid pro quo. The lessons of the war years, it seems, had merely served to widen the range of means known to governments for interrupting trade and other forms of economic collaboration.

Thus the resolutions at Genoa in 1922 to avoid 'frequent (tariff) modifications for the purpose of economic warfare' and to keep to the most-favoured-nation clause found some echo, at least until 1930, and in 1924 some agreement on ending some customs-forms chicanery and on the mutual recognition of certain decisions in foreign courts of law was reached. Against this, a conference held in 1929 failed to agree to end discrimination and fiscal disabilities placed on foreigners, and the proposals of the Geneva Conference of 1927 to end all quantitative restrictions and prohibitions on trade were never ratified. The World Economic Conference of 1927 had many brave words to say on reducing tariffs, discrimination, subsidies, dumping, restrictions, and privileges for home companies as against foreign ones. This may possibly have led to a stabilization, but certainly not to a reduction of these practices.[77] It represented the high point of post-war international effort to improve the position rather than the attempt to prevent its deterioration, which became the preoccupation of the 1930s.

There was one respect in which the disorganization of markets, characteristic for the 1930s, and leading to protectionist policies, made an early and ominous showing in the 1920s, and that was the relative fall in food and primary-production prices. In the war years, European shortfalls had led to expanded production overseas, but as production recovered in the mid-1920s in Europe, markets began to be overstocked and prices fell. In other cases, war-induced demand for raw materials had disappeared again in the 1920s, with similar results.[78]

Thus the world's wheat stocks were 9.3 million tons after the 1923 harvest, and 21.3 million tons after 1929, and such commodities as sugar, produced both in Europe and overseas, showed a similar tendency. Total world agricultural commodities showed the following changes (1923–5 = 100)

	Stocks	Prices
1927	146	81
1929	193	64
1932	262	24

At that point, the standard reactions of such countries as Germany, Austria, or Czechoslovakia was to put up tariffs to keep out imports and keep home returns for farmers high.[79] This hit the food exporters of Central and Eastern Europe who found their balance of payments turn adverse and thus took appropriate defensive, i.e. protective measures themselves. A vicious spiral had begun.

In extent, these movements were mild compared with the collapse of food and raw-material markets in the depressed 1930s.[80] It was then that plunging prices led to poverty, in spite of high output among primary producers, and to unemployment because of the favourable terms of trade among manufacturing producer-countries. It is not our purpose here to investigate how this disequilibrium came about nor how, paradoxically, it continued, since the same measures would have benefited both,[81] but merely to note its consequences for economic relations in Europe.

The primary producers in Eastern and Southern Europe were also international debtors, and they suffered doubly by the price fall in the 1930s,[82] for the fixed burden of their annual payments became heavier in terms of the quantities of their own exports to transfer them: yet the more they tried to export, the sharper they drove down their prices. However, industrialized countries like Germany, Austria, and Britain, also showed adverse payments balances for a variety of financial and economic causes briefly alluded to in the first section of this chapter, so that they also had to try to cut imports and expand exports. It may seem paradoxical that all countries should show adverse balances at the same time, since the deficit of one country must be the surplus of another, but it was part of the mechanism of the Depression that the surplus countries did not allow that surplus to raise their home prices, encourage imports, and cause further unemployment, but instead they simply accumulated gold. In the desperate struggles to right the balance, acquire foreign currency, yet minimize the damage to home employment, the reaction of each country was to find equilibrium by diminishing trade. Thus world and European trade slumped, the barriers rose, and the world became disarticulated.[83]

Many methods were used for hampering trade, superseding the traditional tariff which quite lost in significance, though the catastrophically high Hawley–Smoot tariff imposed by the USA in 1930 led to some moves of retaliation.

Taking 1913 = 100 tariff levels in some leading countries rose as shown in Table 8.4.[84]

Table 8.4.

	1927	1931
Germany	122	244
France	97.5	160
Italy	112	195
Switzerland	160	252
Romania	140	207
Hungary*	131	197
Czechoslovakia*	137	220
Austria*	77	158
Spain	132	185
Bulgaria	296	420

* Comparison is with pre-war Austria–Hungary.

In 1930–2 there was an orgy of physical limitations on the entry of foreign goods such as quotas and restrictions.[85] By 1937, the following proportions (by value) of imports were subject to quota restrictions or licences:[86]

France	58%
Switzerland	52%
Netherlands	26%
Belgium	24%
Ireland	17%
Norway	12%
UK	8%

But these methods were largely superseded by two other linked methods, increasingly dominant and largely responsible for breaking up the traditional European and world economy. One was the manipulation of the currency, and the other the formation of bilateral agreements and of blocs.

Currency manipulation for the purpose of correcting trade balances was frequently forced on governments since, as we have seen, it was in the financial or payments mechanism, which had to deal with capital repayments and reparations as well as current trade that the pressure was first felt. Countries had learnt in the 1920s to snatch temporary advantages by comparative devaluation, and this method of protecting the home product and favouring exports was applied even by the major currencies, the pound sterling in 1931, the dollar in 1933, and in the end the franc and its gold bloc in 1936.

For weaker currencies under pressure that method would have availed little and might have been counter-productive unless supported by other action. Thus Hungary coupled with it special exchange facilities and in Romania imports from certain countries were controlled by having to be paid through a certain account only. These actions led to retaliation, and within a short period all the weaker economies had imposed some form of exchange control, while the creditor nations blocked their credits to them as a response to the interruption of their debt servicing.[87] By far the most complex system was developed in Germany where extremely drastic steps were called for, first by the severe strain on capital accounts, and later under the Nazi government by the re-employment and rearmament drive. Basically, the system consisted of blocking the accounts of foreign creditors and allowing them to be spent only on German goods or at a heavy discount elsewhere. A battery of Effektenmarks, Registermarks, Askimarks, and other forms of currency allowed the German authorities to tailor the amount of discount to the differing economic strength of their trading partner, discriminating against those who needed the German market most. The mark had ceased to be an international currency, and at the same time the government had acquired complete control over foreign transactions.[88]

It has since been held that of all forms of protection, exchange depreciation was the least helpful to the countries that tried it, and the most harmful to the rest.[89] Be that as it may, the device of applying particular pressure to those trading partners who could resist least because they had a favourable trade balance was applied even more consistently in bilaterial trade agreements. Linked with clearing systems, they became a device for balancing the trade of each pair of countries, thus turning the complex, sensitive, and economical system of intra-European trade into the atavism of a barter economy by the late 1930s. Germany's relations with the countries of Eastern and South-Eastern Europe became one of bartering their food and raw materials against

German manufactures. For long seen as a mere political device for attaching these countries to German's plans of conquest, this barter system is recognized now as economically beneficial to both parties in the circumstances of the day, and as having been forced on the eastern countries by the sanctions imposed on them by their western creditors as the result of their bankruptcy.[90] The device was used in other parts of Europe also, for example in the relations between Britain and the Scandinavian countries. There were 170 Clearing Agreements in Europe in 1937 and 70–75% of the trade of Europe was bartered.[91]

In addition, 'blocs' of adjacent or politically linked countries developed, giving preference to each other to the exclusion of outsiders. The British Empire became such a community after the Ottawa Agreement of 1932, and France, Holland, Belgium and Italy had comparable relations with their colonies. The attempts of others, such as the Scandinavians, Holland with Belgium and Luxemburg, or Germany with Austria, to form similar associations were usually vetoed by either France or Britain, but the repeated attempts by the western powers to encourage such collaboration among the Danubian countries foundered on the latter's inability to agree.[92]

The result of all this was a substantial fall in trade, both in absolute terms and as a proportion of output: the law of the diminishing proportion of trade, formulated at the end of the previous century, seemed to have begun to operate at last. What was particularly noticeable was that owing to the changing terms of trade, it was the *value* of primary products which fell drastically and was matched by the volume of manufactures in that decline; while the prices of the latter held up much better. World index figures were as follows:[93]

	1926–9 (1913 = 100)		1937 (1929 = 100)	
	Production	Trade	Production	Trade
Foodstuffs	} 125	118	108	93.5
Raw materials			116	108
Manufactures	139	125	120	87

In the worst years of the slump, trade in raw materials in terms of gold values, had been down to 35 (1929 = 100) in 1938 and 1934. Of 49 primary-producer countries, 24 registered falls of between 60 and 70% between 1928/9 and 1932/3.[94] The countries of Central and South-Eastern Europe were particularly hard hit: thus Romania's export of cattle dropped by 42% in quantity between 1929 and 1934, but by 73% in realized value.[95]

Even in the worst years of the 1930s, some efforts still continued on an international level to reverse this process or at least mitigate its consequences. The Stresa Conference of 1932 attempted to raise grain prices and sales for the Danubian countries in Europe. The more ambitious World Economic Conference held in London in 1933 started with the correct assumption that tariff reduction and exchange stability could be achieved, if at all, only if they were made internationally and simultaneously by many countries, but that conference failed also, largely because the USA were not yet prepared to forgo the advantages of floating the dollar. In the following year, the USA passed the Reciprocal Tariff Agreements Act which led to substantial tariff reductions with a number of trading partners, and the Tripartite Agreement of 1936 achieved a measure of exchange stability between the three main currencies that were still free, the US dollar, the pound sterling, and the French franc. As late as 1938 attempts were still being made by various governments to reduce tariffs and increase trade. Nor were ingenuity and originality lacking: 'proposals for embryonic international monetary funds were legion'.[96]

Yet they were swimming against the stream. Some, perhaps the majority of statesmen knew that it would be of advantage to prevent the break-up of Europe, but the dynamics of the system did not allow them to act. Some theoretical justification for the drive towards autarky in conditions of high unemployment of resources[97] was later found by Keynes and some of the Keynesians, on the grounds that protection would prevent a downward multiplier at home and save more in terms of employment, than was lost by foregoing cheaper imports. They thus argued that governments had been instinctively right in choosing to cut themselves off from the adverse effects of foreign unemployment and price falls. But this seemed, pragmatically, a weak argument even then, since the recovery of the 1930s was the weakest on record, the 'boom' of 1937 still showed mass unemployment, and some of the best-protected economies like the USA made the worst recovery.[98] Even the theoretical justification, never better than promoting the second best, is now once more in doubt.

Barriers to foreign trade, it is now seen, also had their multiplier, like free imports. By 'Tariff, currency depreciation or foreign exchange control, a country may worsen the welfare of its partners by more than its own gain. Beggar-thy-neighbour (*sic*) tactics may lead to retaliation, so that each country ends up in a worse position from having pursued its own gain.[99] That the 'national interest' was often 'far removed from the maximisation of social welfare'[100] has since been shown to be the case in detailed investigations and econometric tests. Tariffs did not correlate with recovery , while they clearly depressed income levels.[101] Moreover, they greatly increased fluctuations and insecurity.[102] Worst of all, the climate of blocs and autarky, of economic nationalism, and of gaining benefits by hurting others, the division of Europe into economically warring nations using politics to control that economy and vice versa, was part of the milieu out of which the Second World War arose, and was probably bound to arise.[103] Because of this background, its outbreak was certainly felt to be less of a break with the preceding years of nominal peace than the outbreak of the war in 1914 that had been destined to lead to continuous conflict, economic and military, for thirty-one years.

Epilogue

Chapter 9

Reintegration into Two Europes

On the face of it, there were many striking similarities between the First and Second World War. In both, the latecomer nations, those who had arrived too late to share in the colonial scramble of the pre-1914 days or who for other reasons resented their disproportionately limited political power in view of their economic strength, led on both occasions by Germany, met the sated powers who were attempting to preserve the status quo, led by Britain, France, Russia, and (after some delay) the United States. In both, economic potential and stamina played the decisive role in the long run, in spite of early military gains snatched by one side or the other, and both wars were conducted with economic as well as military means.

Yet the basic differences were equally striking. Apart from the adhesion of Japan, fighting virtually her own war in the Far East, and Italy to the Axis side, what was most fundamentally new in the war of 1939-45 was that it was in part ideological, and not purely national, and that it was preceded by the internal transformation into fascist dictatorships of the revisionist states, as well as of others, in Europe. In turn, that transformation reflected the social tensions of the age which were partly derived directly from the First World War itself, and in part from the Depression, implying an indirect link with that war. In other words, among the major differences was precisely that it was the second round in what looked to many, not without justification, as the same continuing conflict.

The feeling of 'never again!' which animated those who made the peace after 1945 was, therefore, much stronger than after 1918 and it was strengthened further by the explosion of the nuclear bombs which brought the war against Japan to an abrupt end. For they had made it clear that there was now a new military technology available which would ensure that there would be no victor in a future world conflict, and that little would remain of European civilization after such a holocaust.

The reinforced determination to have done with World Wars for good led to two types of consequences. One derived from the conviction, held particularly in Eastern Europe, that both wars were the result of German aggression, and that the best guarantee of peace was the permanent weakening of Germany. Linked as it was with the Soviet insistence on regaining the territories that Russia lost after 1917, and on pushing the frontier of Soviet power well to the West, as well as with the centuries-old struggle between German and Slav, the crushing defeat of Germany was followed this time by a *de facto* peace settlement in which much of what had been eastern Germany went to Poland and Russia, while the remainder of Germany, in a manner which was not planned but which in retrospect seems inevitable, was divided between the Federal Republic, becoming part of western society, and the German Democratic Republic (GDR) adhering to the Soviet or Socialist camp, each retaining control over part of Berlin. For different reasons, and by a chemistry which is still not clearly understood, neither part became revanchist and (from the standpoint of 1979) both seem unlikely to become so in the foreseeable future.

Neither of the other two aggressor states, Japan and Italy, was similarly dismembered, though they lost all their colonial possessions and, again for different reasons, they also ceased to pose a threat to peace. The sting had therefore been taken out of that part of the world order which had, by its unbalance between economic potential and political power, consistently caused unrest and twice actually provoked major wars.

The other consequence was a highly critical attitude towards the failures of the inter-war years and a determination not to repeat the mistakes made then. While keeping within a similar world framework of advanced welfare capitalism dominated by Europe and North America, the statesmen who determined the peace settlement consciously and deliberately set about their task of formulating an international political and economic order which carefully dealt with all the sources of conflict. instability, and grievance that had bedevilled the 1920s and 1930s. The institutions created from 1944 onwards, at first by the Allies and then by a growing share of the world community, strongly bore that mark of being designed to overcome one or other of the pre-war problems and on the whole they succeeded beyond all expectation.

Not that the world remained without conflict. For the strong position of the Soviet Union among the victor nations implied that the western hegemony would now be challenged by a rival Marxist-Communist would-be world system, which first had a single focus in Moscow, later developed a second one in Peking, and before long had other minor foci and variants, just like the sytem which if faced. The conflict was carried out on a world-wide basis, but as far as Europe was concerned, it split the Continent in two yet, curiously, helped to consolidate each half, and sped its economic development and integration.

It thus reversed the centrifugal tendency of the years to 1945. In this way, political drives and economic interests came once again to be moving in the same direction, with benefits for both though, for the time being, moving perilously along two parallel lines instead of one. It is within this framework that the last remaining areas of the Continent are now being industrialized.

The Effects of War and the Economic Recovery

The Second World War lasted somewhat longer than the First—just under six years compared with somewhat over four—and it was more costly and destructive both in terms of human lives and material property. The total and direct loss of life in Europe alone was 42 million, or more than three times the 1914–18 figure, and of this total, 25 millions of the dead had been citizens of the USSR, and 7 million were Germans. Military deaths were estimated at 16 million, and civilian at 26 million.[1] Unlike the First World War, the majority of those latter died because of deliberate inhuman treatment meted out to them, whereas the victims of disease were comparatively few in number. The number of wounded has been estimated at 35 million.

Germany occupied most of the Continent in 1940–4 and ruthlessly exploited it. Some 104 billion marks ($42 billion) were diverted from other countries to Germany in levies and credits, adding 14% to German GDP in those years, but causing hardship, destruction, malnutrition, and starvation elsewhere. France was depressed to below one half of her pre-war standard of living, Yugoslavia to one third. Yugoslavia, the scene of partisan fighting, lost one half of her railway tracks, nearly all her motor cars, one half of her deep-sea vessels, 45% of telephone and telegraph networks, 40–50% of agricultural machinery and equipment, 60% of her horses, 53% of her cattle, 70% of her ironmaking capacity. In Poland 65% of industrial properties were destroyed, one-third of the railway lines, 80% of rolling-stock, and 58–82% of livestock; there were also 9 million people to be resettled. In Hungary, the losses were of a similar order; in Russia, where the main fighting took place, they were much more grievous, 1,700 towns and cities were devastated there as well as 70,000 villages, 84,000 schools, 60% of transport installations and 70% of industrial. All told, Russia lost 25% of her immediate pre-war capital stock, Austria 16%, Germany 13%, France 8%, and Britain 3% plus an equivalent of 15% in foreign assets, making a total of 18%. In terms of 1938 national income, capital losses ranged as follows:-

Romania	29%	Hungary	194%
Bulgaria	33%	Poland	350%
Czechoslovakia	115%	Yugoslavia	274%

Germany suffered most *after* the war: by 1945 her income was down to under 25% of the pre-war per capita figure, to 29% in 1946 and 40% in 1947 and even in 1948 reached only 66–70%. Ten million houses were destroyed in Europe, plus six million that remained un-built. Human misery is perhaps most clearly expressed in the figure of 30 million 'displaced persons' roaming across Europe at the war's end, and 10 million Germans expelled and transferred westward by October 1946. Even as late as 1946, 140 million people (excluding the USSR) were still on a diet of an average of under 2000 calories a day, and only Britain, Denmark, Sweden, and Switzerland enjoyed over 2,500.[2] Finally, the total costs of waging war have been estimated at $730 billion, of which $560 billion represented the European theatre of hostilities, compared with $270 billion for World War I. The largest part of the cost, 37%, was borne by the USA, 25% each by Britain and the Dominions on the one hand and by Germany on the other, and 7% each by the USSR and Japan.[3]

Yet, whatever the hardships of the actual war years, and the human tragedies caused by death and injury, such figures of losses tend to exaggerate the permanent economic costs of the war. Some countries which suffered great diminution in their capital stock, such as Britain and Germany, yet benefited by the expansion of high-technology engineering and chemical industries in war time which laid the foundations of modern industry in the post-war years.[4] The need for ever increasing war production and for protecting plants from air attack had brought new industries to hitherto backward regions, and millions of workers, many, it is true, very much against their will, were being made acquainted with modern techniques and works routines. Though rails and bridges were damaged, the permanent way, the canals, harbours, or coal pits remained, and it was not too difficult to restore them. Human skills, spare parts, even stocks, could be brought into play again more quickly than had been anticipated. It also helped that the lessons of the post-1918 years had not been forgotten.

Little was heard of reparations this time, though Russia exacted some $15–20 billion, mainly from East Germany, but also from Austria, Hungary, and Romania. Western Germany, while she had to bear the occupation costs until 1953, was meanwhile relieved of payments on her pre-war debts, and paid after that date on a much scaled-down basis. The debts of others were also largely cancelled, for one reason or another, and only the United Kingdom, felt to be in the early post-war years the only potential economic rival to the USA, was left with substantial debts to pay off, and the loss of much of her overseas capital.[5]

Above all, relief and pump-priming action, mainly by the USA, was provided much more rapidly and more substantially than after 1918. The reasons for this were only in part humanitarian. They derived more urgently from the recognition of a conflict with the Soviet Union and her emerging ring of allies and the belief, held rightly or wrongly in the USA, that poverty and economic chaos fostered Communism. Early aid was thus a key weapon in the emerging 'cold war'. This, also, was a lesson learnt from the experience after 1918.

Even during the War, the American Lease-Lend programme had made some $43.6 billion worth of material and services available to the Allies, mainly the United Kingdom and the Soviet Union, in effect in the form of outright grants, except where simultaneous return services ('reverse Lease-Lend') could be made available. At its end, a massive first-aid action by the United Nations Relief and Rehabilitation Administration (UNRRA) distributed mainly American funds to the tune of $3 billion by the end of 1946 to Eastern, Central, and Southern Europe to avert suffering and starvation. There was also the loan to Britain jointly provided by the USA and Canada.[6]

However, the most effective and dramatic form of aid was the so-called Marshall Plan, conceived in 1947 at the height of the Cold-War tension, and passed in 1948. In part, this has to be seen as simply a material-aid measure. Over $13 billion worth of American goods and services which otherwise could not have been afforded by the sixteen European states that made use of it, plus $10.5 billion in counterpart funds, were made available. Much of it was turned into capital equipment, into vital raw materials or seeds, or was simply used to allow local populations to survive until they could pay their own way again. Although never more than marginal in terms of total European national incomes, Marshall Aid represented a shot in the arm at a critical time, having a far greater effect than can be measured in dollars.[7] In particular, by making the key foreign currency available it allowed recovery to proceed without the pressure on the foreign exchanges which would normally require deflationary policies and halt progress. The rebuilding of the European economies could thus proceed unhindered until European exports could pay for all the imports required. It also contained a great deal of direct aid towards modernizing Europe's technology.

However, American aid was offered on conditions, and since the Soviet Union and her allies found these unacceptable they had to refuse the aid and thus seriously slow down their own rates of recovery. Among the conditions was the obligation to engage in collaborative action, at first within the European Recovery Programme itself and later within the other agencies built upon it. It is within this framework that Europe's drive towards economic reintegration was to take place. It will be described in the following section.

Thus Europe climbed out of the economic set-back of the war with astonishing ease. By 1947 Austria, Germany, France, Italy, and the Netherlands, among the western countries, had still not reached their pre-war levels of industrial production, and all except the United Kingdom and the neutrals, Switzerland and Sweden, were below it in agricultural output. By 1949 they had all exceeded their industrial output, some by a wide margin, and by 1951 it had become clear that economic growth at an unprecedented rate was taking place, at least among the industrialized nations: the lag of Spain, Portugal, and Ireland in agricultural output had become very marked by then. Some details are provided in Table 9.1.[8]

Table 9.l.

	Index of Industrial Production (1937–8 = 100)			Index of Agricultural Production (1934–8 = 100)		
	1947	1949	1951	1946/7	1948/9	1950/1
Austria	56	123	166	70	74	98
Belgium	106	122	143	84	93	111
Denmark	123	142	162	97	97	126
Finland	117	142	177	75	106	115
France	92	118	134	82	95	108
Ireland	122	151	176	100	96	106
Italy	86	101	138	85	97	109
Netherlands	95	126	145	87	104	123
Norway	115	140	158	98	101	118
Portugal	112	112	125	99	95	102
Spain	127	120	147	88	80	86
Sweden	141	157	171	104	109	113
Switzerland	–	–	–	107	112	120
United Kingdom	115	137	155	117	122	130

Once this growth started, there seemed to be no stopping it. Moreover, although there were some fluctuations, there were no recessions, let alone depressions, there was at worst a temporary slowing-down of growth from time to time, until the crisis brought in from outside by the action of the oil-producers in the 1970s. The secular boom was based solidly on heavy investment, on the acceptance of new technology, on full employment of labour and capital, on labour mobility and flexibility, and on a rising division of labour and scale economies exemplified by a sustained export boom, foreign trade throughout growing much faster than output.[9] By 1953 Europe was in equilibrium on international account, and from 1963 on European Central Banks were even in a position from time to time to support the US dollar.

Starting from the reasonably normal year of 1950, per capita real output rose by an annual compound rate of 4% to 1970, compared with only 1% in 1913–50 for Western Europe, the Eastern rates being marginally higher. Once again, only a statistical table can fully expose the details.[10]

Table 9.2.

	Annual average compound growth rate of real output per capita			
	1913–50	1950–70	1950–73	1970–6
Austria	0.2	4.9	4.90	3.8
Belgium	0.7	3.3	3.64	3.3
Denmark	1.1	3.3	3.34	1.5
Finland	1.3	4.3	4.45	3.4
France	1.0	4.2	4.35	3.2
Germany (W.)	0.8	5.3	5.02	2.0
Greece	0.2	5.9	6.18	4.1
Ireland	0.7	2.8	3.02	1.8
Italy	0.8	5.0	4.69	2.2
Netherlands	0.9	3.6	3.67	2.7
Norway	1.8	3.2	3.31	4.0
Portugal	0.9	4.8	5.27	3.5
Spain	−0.3	5.4	5.21	4.2
Sweden	2.5	3.3	3.04	2.1
Switzerland	1.6	3.0	2.94	−0.2
UK	0.8	2.2	2.31	1.8
Av. Western Europe	1.0	4.0 }	4.35	2.4
Av. Eastern Europe	1.2	4.3 }		

It will be noted that there were three groups of countries here. The majority grew at a rate of 4–6% a year; the Scandinavians and Swiss showing much higher growth-rates up to 1950 and starting from a high absolute level, then growing at a little over 3% only in 1950–70; and the United Kingdom growing much more slowly at just over 2% and holding down the dependent Irish rate also. Total output, of course, grew at a considerably higher rate, 4.4% a year in 1950–60 and 5.2% in 1960–70 in Western Europe and 8.6% and 4.9% in Eastern Europe. Average non-agricultural employment grew by 1.6% p.a. in 1950–70 in the West and 3.0% in the East; average population by 0.8% p.a. in the West and by 1.0% in the East.[11]

Actual standards of living rose by lesser proportions, particularly in the East, mainly because the proportion of national income devoted to capital formation was rising; there were also considerable variations in the resources devoted to armaments. Moreover, in the early years an unusual amount had to be devoted to the backlog of repair and maintenance accumulated in the war years. Nevertheless, such economic growth brought remarkable prosperity which spread to virtually the whole population because the general labour shortage, even for unskilled labour, drove up all wages, and it brought with it also expectations of further increases. However, it also brought with it new social problems that were problems of surplus rather than of deficiency, including those of congestion and pollution and, not least, it led ultimately to the appearance of an energy crisis.

Economic Reintegration and the Completion of Industrialization in the West

While the Second World War had engendered an exceptional amount of national hatreds, it had also left in its wake, paradoxically, a fellow-feeling of common suffering. In one way, all the ordinary citizens of Europe had become victims of the failures of the economic and political order, and national hatreds had been one of the main agencies responsible for this.

It has often been remarked that among the main architects of the post-war drive to the unification of 'Europe' (by which is often meant that small part of the Continent first brought together in the Common Market) were men who had found the hatreds across the frontiers to be of particular absurdity and personal poignancy: Robert Schumann, the French leader who had been a German officer in the First World War, Alcide de Gasperi, the Italian who had once been a member of the Vienna Diet, and Konrad Adenauer, the Rhinelander with a tendency to prefer his western neighbours to the Prussians. The ideals of European unity had become a fervent hope among some in the Resistance movement, as it had among dreamers and idealists in various epochs in the past. Yet, when it came (restricted though it was to the western portion of the Continent), it is significant how limited its impact was in the purely *political* sphere: states fully retained their sovereignty and freedom of action, as shown by France when she left the North Atlantic Treaty Organization (NATO) in 1965; the planned European Defence Community of 1952 was a total failure and Euratom (of 1957) a partial one, and even in 1979 the interest in the newly constituted European Parliament was, at best, lukewarm. Where the concept gripped and became truly operative was in the economic sphere. Thus the Common Market has even survived the French boycott of 1965.[12]

It began, appropriately enough, in the realm of coal and steel. The frontier dividing Lorraine iron ore from Ruhr and Saar coal had been one of the most harmful to economic logic—even if the territories dividing them, Alsace-Lorraine, had not changed masters four times in seventy-five years.[13] Under the 'Schumann Plan', the European Coal and Steel Community (ECSC) was launched in 1950 and got going in 1951 among the six countries that were later to form the Common Market:

France, West Germany, Italy, Belgium, Holland, and Luxemburg. Although conceived by its founders as only the first step towards wider collaboration—and, it may be added, opposed by French steelmakers and by almost all coal producers—it was a down-to-earth bread and butter organization. When its transitional period ended in February 1958, it had abolished all duties, restrictions, direct and indirect discrimination for the five commodities covered, coal, coke, iron ore, steel, and scrap among the six countries. Trade in iron and steel (though not in coal and coke) had multiplied, output had nearly doubled, and the Community was as active in aiding investment and modernization in steel, the expanding sector, as it was in compensating and retraining redundant coal miners in the contracting sector.[14]

Directly out of that practical experience arose the will to extend internal freedom of trade to the whole of economic life. Based on the Spaak Report, the Treaty of Rome was signed in 1957 to inaugurate the European Economic Community (EEC) of the Six, or Common Market. Over a total transitional period of twelve years (later foreshortened) these six countries were to form a customs union of completely free trade within, and a common tariff without. It was clear from the beginning that in modern conditions, a customs union, in order to be effective, required a great many other common actions beyond mere tariff rates, to buttress it, though only experience could show what they would be. A Social Fund to aid poorer regions, and an Investment Bank were planned from the beginning, and turned out to have had rather limited practical utility; a common currency or even co-ordinated financial policies are still not in sight; against this, social provisions, the treatment of monopolies, and tax regulations have been aligned to a considerable degree. Freedom of mobility of labour, and rather less so of capital, were among the targets of the early stages.

It has never been clear whether the EEC should be looked upon as a step towards a more integrated Europe as a whole or whether, by abolishing tariffs within its part of Europe only, it has distorted trade more than ever and made the ultimate liberalization of the Continent more difficult.[15] Certainly, the Common Agricultural Policy, much the most costly and positive of its activities, recalls all the worst features of inter-war protectionism: a totally artifical and monopolistic market, artificially high prices to be paid by consumers, leading to overproduction, the slowing-down of the restructuring of the economy, and the deprivation of outside countries with lower costs of a vital market for them. Less crass examples could be quoted from other spheres. Yet the Six have also shown, by various forms of association and the acceptance of new members, that they see themselves not as an exclusive club, but as the nucleus of a much larger free trade area.

Be that as it may, the EEC has become the overwhelming economic fact in Western Europe in the post-war years. This is mainly due to the successful economic growth of its members, which was well on its way before the Treaty of Rome, but has continued under it and has made it an industrial and economic power of the same order of magnitude as the two superpowers , the USA and the USSR. By the late 1970s, it had become the world's largest trader. Under its shadow, the United Kingdom formed a looser organization, the European Free Trade Association (EFTA) in 1959 with six of the smaller nations, later also joined by Finland, but she was ultimately driven to seek full membership of the EEC which was accepted, together with that of Ireland and Denmark, in 1973. Other adhesions are anticipated at the time of writing. Greece was 'associated' in 1961, Turkey in 1963, Malta in 1970, and Cyprus in 1972. The Yaounde Conventions of 1963 and 1969 continued the privileged association of most of the former colonies and dependencies of the original Six with the EEC, and in February 1975 the Lome convention gave 46 African, Caribbean, and Pacific (ACP) states similar privileges. The generalized system of preferences (GSP) for all developing countries, introduced in 1971, was, however, of relatively limited value.[16]

This expansion has taken place within a European and world milieu which was itself liberalizing and expansionary. Within Europe, we have seen that the OEEC (which became the Organization for Economic Cooperation and Development, OECD, to include also the USA and Canada, in 1961) turned into an instrument, not only for allocating Marshall Aid, but for easing trade and payments between the members. The European Payments Union (EPU) became, in effect, a form of mutual credit among the European states to permit the expansion of trade on limited national reserves; full convertibility in 1958 was a symptom of growing economic strength as well as of balanced payments.

Among international organizations, the International Monetary Fund (IMF) agreed in Bretton Woods in 1944 and the General Agreement on Tariffs and Trade (GATT) proved to be of the greatest significance. The IMF was deliberately designed to prevent the kind of competitive devaluation and restrictionism that bedevilled pre-war economic relations, by providing a credit pool, contributed to by all nations, orginally of $7 billion, to be drawn on by deficit nations in accordance with certain rules. At first inevitably simply a means of drawing on US dollars, the resources of the IMF have since been repeatedly enlarged, and while it cannot rectify a fundamental disequilibrium, it has proved able to tide countries over even large temporary balance of payments deficits. In return, it exacts abstention from certain discriminatory policies.

GATT secured the support of thirty-seven of the major western trading nations, conducting some 80 per cent of the world's trade, for a concerted attempt to remove restrictions on trade which would falter if conducted by smaller groups of countries. While the 'Dillon Round' and the 'Kennedy Round' attempted actually to lower tariff rates, the most significant contribution of the Agreement was to maintain a code of conduct, to abolish discrimination, reinstate a firm most-favoured-nation principle (except for Customs Unions), and create an atmosphere of mutual trust.[17]

As always, it was not clear how far expanding trade helped a high growth-rate:[18] certainly, exports rose much faster than output in the major countries, permitting the description of 'export-led growth', particularly among the fastest growers, and disproving finally the belief in the falling export quota which appeared to have been supported by the experience of the inter-war years. It is difficult to deny the more liberal policies of the period a share in this upward movement. Trade among the EEC countries increased fastest of all, but the buoyant EEC economies also provided a growing market for outsiders.

Whereas in 1913–50, the annual compound growth-rates in exports exceeded 1% for very few countries and for Western Europe as a whole averaged only 0.1%, in the post-war years they were generally 7% a year or more, except for the United Kingdom, and for some countries the rate reached double figures. Exports rose much faster than output in every single country, and in some cases were over twice as fast. Table 9.3. provides some details:[19]

Table 9.3.

	Annual Compound Growth-rates, at Constant Prices (commodities only): 1950/2 to 1967/9		In relation to GNP (GNP growth rate =1)		Exports f.o.b. as % of GNP, 1976
	Exports	Imports	Exports	Imports	
Austria	11.0	10.6	2.2	2.1	20.9
Belgium	8.6	8.3	2.5	2.4	48.1
Denmark	6.8	8.1	1.7	2.0	23.7
Finland	7.1	7.2	1.6	1.6	22.5
France	7.3	8.7	1.5	1.7	16.1
Germany (W.)	12.0	12.6	1.9	2.0	22.9
Greece	9.4	8.5	1.6	1.4	11.4
Ireland	6.7	4.8	2.7	1.9	41.6
Italy	13.1	11.1	2.4	2.1	19.4
Netherlands	9.3	8.8	1.9	1.8	44.9
Norway	7.3	7.8	1.8	1.9	25.3
Portugal	7.0	8.1	1.4	1.6	11.3
Spain	8.0	13.8	1.3	2.3	8.3
Sweden	6.8	6.7	1.7	1.6	24.8
United Kingdom	3.1	4.4	1.1	1.6	21.0
Switzerland	–	–	–	–	26.4

The freedom of movement of capital, it should be noted, was restored to a much smaller extent than that of commodities, even within the EEC, where Articles 67–73 of the Treaty of Rome provided the framework. These Articles were unusually vague, both as regards the timetable and the means to be taken, and this may reflect the suspicions voiced in the Spaak Report on which the Treaty was based. Freedom for capital exports and imports might not only endanger the balance of payments, it argued, but also permit speculative attacks, avoid taxation at home or exchange control abroad, and permit capital to move from the less to the more developed areas.[20] Although growing economic strength made many of these fears groundless, there has, in fact, been very little movement of capital among the EEC members, and still less among other European states. The only substantial capital transfer came from the USA, as well as from some of the international bodies. Short-term capital movements, particularly through the Euro-dollar markets, were much more significant. It may well be that restrictions were deliberately kept as a weapon in domestic policy and to protect privileged borrowers at home, such as governments and local authorities.

Here was one respect in which the nineteenth-century freedoms were not restored. By contrast, labour mobility was granted more generously, particularly within the EEC: this may well have been aided by an early appearance of labour shortage as against the mass unemployment of the inter-war years. The EEC found quickly that to give reality to this freedom, social security payments for families left at home, as well as housing and other policies had to be co-ordinated also. Conversely, the obligation to comply with strict housing regulations which foreign workers cannot easily afford has given Germany, a major immigrant country, the means of curtailing their stay. Workers from Greece and Turkey, as associated states, and from Spain and Portugal, by special treaty, were given privileges similar to those granted to workers from full member countries. Together with workers from Yugoslavia and from Italy, where successful economic growth at home led to a reverse movement in the early 1960s, these formed the main areas of labour supply. Britain, France, and the Netherlands also received substantial numbers from their colonial and associated territories outside Europe. The OEEC had as early as 1953 adopted the rule that home workers had preference over foreigners only for the first few weeks of a job opening, and thereafter other members' workers had equal access. Sweden and Switzerland concluded separate treaties with their potential supply countries.[21]

In the immediate post-war years, most immigrants went overseas: in 1946–54, over 6 million went to the USA, Canada, Australia, Israel,

Argentina, Venezuela, and Brazil alone. In 1950–65 the main migration occurred within Europe, the total of foreign workers rising to 7–8 million in the mid-sixties. Most of these were short-term visitors, though a strong minority became permanent settlers, particularly in France. In relation to the home working-force, the largest numbers of foreign workers were found in Switzerland (32.3% in 1964), Luxemburg (21.7%), and Belgium (9.8%).[22]

Movements of capital and labour across frontiers are substitutes for each other (and, within limits, for movements of commodities). Labour migration which reached almost, though not quite, the proportions of the pre-1914 years, thus took the place of the mobility of capital. It seemed a more appropriate way for linking the European economy in an age where capital equipment was far more complex and more dependent on ancillary services, and more fitting for an age of economic liberalism built on strong states in contrast with the laissez-faire liberalism of the nineteenth century.

As the upsurge of industrial output permitted Western Europe to complete her industrialization, two types of area remained to be transformed: some complete states, and backward regions within countries which had industrialized before. Among the former were Spain, Portugal, Greece, and, doubtfully, the Republic of Ireland.[23] Among the latter, the most significant were the Italian South and the South-West and Massif Central of France, but there were many others of lesser extent.

The highly restrictive common agricultural policy (CAP) of the EEC continued earlier traditions in the three larger Common Market countries, France, Germany, and Italy, and, reinforced as it was, by Commonwealth preferences and protection in the United Kingdom, created most difficult conditions for the development of the mediterranean countries listed here as food suppliers. Thus the share of agricultural imports in total imports among the EEC countries fell from 52.6% in 1951 to 17% in 1961. All the advanced areas of Europe showed a remarkable increase in agricultural yields and even faster increases per head at home, based on mechanization, on the widespread use of chemical fertilizers and pesticides, and on the enlargement of the typical farm size so that the degree of self-supply rose at the same time as the proportion of the population engaged in agriculture fell, and their average income (including non-monetary benefits) came to approximate to that of those in non-agrarian employment.[24] EEC costs were far above world prices, but the CAP saw to it that the costs were borne by consumers and foreign suppliers, *not* the farmers, and the system encouraged surpluses which occasionally threatened even markets outside the EEC. By 1970–1 the EEC was self-supporting or virtually so in wheat, potatoes, milk, wine, vegetables, pork, and poultry and had a dangerous surplus of sugar and butter; the only major food-stuffs of which it supplied under 90% of its needs were fats (41%), oats (88%), and beef and veal (89%). The accession of Britain, Denmark, and Ireland shifted some of these items in detail, reducing its self-supply of wheat (to 86%), sugar (86%), and butter (83%), but increasing its capacity in oats (91%), beef and veal (94%), and pork (105%). The associated overseas territories provided colonial foods. Moreover, it became abundantly clear that the income elasticity for food consumption was well below unit with rising prosperity: the proportion of consumer expenditure spent on food fell between 1960 and 1970 from 47.3% to 42.2% in Italy, and from 35–42% to 30–33% among the other five.[25]

Thus, inasmuch as industrializing countries require markets for their agrarian products in the advanced regions at the time of their trans-formation, the EEC CAP and similar policies in Britain were unpro-pitious. Nevertheless, the over-all buoyancy of the industrialized west and its markets had a substantial net positive effect on them.

A glance at the table on p. 315 will show that the three southern countries, Spain, Portugal, and Greece, were among the fastest growers in Europe, only Ireland being held back by its dependence on the stag-nating British economy; but Ireland's growth also began to accelerate towards the end of the period. The following statistics exhibit also the rapid rise of employment in the non-agrarian sectors, as well as the extent of the leeway still to be made up in comparison with the ad-vanced parts of Europe.[26]

Table 9.4.

	Per capita GDP in 1960 US $		Growth of Non-Agricultural Employment % p.a.	% Employment in Agriculture		% of GDP arising in Agriculture
	1960	1973	1950–70	1964	1974	1973
Greece	718	1769	2.3	50.0	35.2	16.1
Ireland	919	1474	0.4	33.3	24.3	18.0
Portugal	514	1247	1.1	38.7	28.2	14.6
Spain	529	1179	2.5	35.3	23.1	11.9
All Europe	1157*	2077*		—	—	—
Western Europe	—	—	1.6	13.9†	8.9†	

* Incl. USSR   † Extended EEC of the Nine.

Other indices, such as educational provisions or the proportion of capital goods produced at home, would also show these countries near the bottom of any European table, yet the differences seemed to be of degree, not of kind. In each country, the drive to industrialization has been put smoothly into gear, with possibly lower social costs and the benefits of later technology, than faced the earlier industrializers though each of the four countries started at a different level and has proceeded at a different speed.

Spain, as we noted in chapter 8 above, had made considerable progress when she received a sharp set-back by the Civil War: in several sectors, production did not reach its pre-1936 level again until 1950. In the war years, though spared the losses of the fully belligerent, Spain suffered losses of markets and the absence of vital deliveries particularly of capital goods from the advanced areas of Europe. In the 1950s she was still subject to the boycott of most international world and European associations and her entrepreneurs were stifled by protection and tight, if incompetent, state control. The needs of the Cold War then loosened this isolation. From 1953 on, the USA sent aid, mostly in the form of agricultural surplus commodities, to the tune of $100-150 a year; in 1955 Spain joined the Agricultural Committee of OEEC and became a full member of the organization in 1959, in 1958 she joined IMF and the World Bank, and in 1963, after some tough bargaining, she also became a member of GATT.[27] By then there had been some technical progress, especially in agriculture and in the infrastructure, particularly with regard to electricity supply and road and rail transport.[28]

The breakthrough came with the new course in internal economic policy in 1959. The package decided on then included reductions in tariffs, regulations, and internal government controls; encouragement of integration with the rest of Europe, including foreign capital imports; and a deliberate policy for economic growth. Despite a temporary crisis in 1959-61, and balance of payments deficits in the 1960s (reversed in the 1970s with the help of the tourist trade and emigrant remittances), there can be no doubt of over-all success. Spain truly industrialized in the 1960s. In a Europe in which each economy advanced, Spain rose in that decade in the production of electricity from 12th to 10th place, in steel from 13th to 9th, and in cement from 7th to 6th. The index of industrial production as a whole (1929 = 100) rose from 320 in 1959, at a compound rate of 10.79% p.a. to 988 in 1970. The population employed in agriculture fell from 50.5% in 1940 to 41.7% in 1960 and 22.2% in 1975, that in industry rose correspondingly from 22% to 24.7% and 36.8%.[29] Although much of this was achieved only with the aid of foreign capital, Spain now has an adequate steel, engineering, motor-vehicle, and capital-goods industry on which further 'self-sustained' progress can be based.

Portugal's position in the table is not too dissimilar from that of Spain, and her recent progress equally fast, but the structure of her economy is different. The heavy capital-goods base is lacking, exports still largely consist of food, drink, and industrial raw materials, and there is a suspiciously large 'services' employment sector among petty traders and others.[30] Portugal, like Spain, has kept out of both World Wars but has lately seen great political changes, including the loss of her overseas colonies; she is, among the groups considered here, the farthest away from industrialization.

The recent progress of Greece has perhaps been the most remarkable of all. Traditionally a country of agricultural producers, traders, and shippers, her industry has made up fast for lost time in recent years: the compound growth-rate of industrial output in 1962–75 was no less than 9.4% a year, and in the same period, the share of manufactures in exports rose from 11% to 50%, in each case about one-third representing industrial raw materials and semi-manufactures. Much of this is due to foreign capital, of which $1.8 milliard flowed in in 1953–71, and which contributes 70% of exports, as well as largely to imports. At the same time her shipping tonnage, another large foreign currency earner, rose from 13.8 m. Gross Register Tons in 1962 to 48.3 m. GRT in 1975.[31] Although still a poor country, particularly in her agricultural sector, Greece is now well on the way to becoming an industrialized economy.

The Republic of Ireland is politically an independent country, but has never fully withdrawn from her links with the British economy. With free labour mobility and (until 1979) in effect a common currency, her trading relations with the rest of the British Isles are as close as those of any other comparable part of the United Kingdom, if the statistics allowed us to separate out the details of British regional trade. In recent years her successful policy of attracting European industries to her duty-free enclaves, and the benefits derived from the EEC CAP, have speeded her progress, and it may well be that greater detachment from British stagnation will allow her to catch up faster in future. Nevertheless, as far as the past is concerned, her problems were more akin to those of the major non-industrialized *regions* inside advanced countries, like the Italian South, Corsica, and the French South-West. Above all, her problem was to see her most active labour drained to the metropolitan areas with little benefit beyond the regular remittances.

Since the war, these problem regions have received increased attention, both from their own government and from the Social Funds and other agencies of the EEC. The extent of the problem can be gauged from the fact that differences within countries were greater than the differences between advanced European states. Thus around 1960, average incomes were $820 in the Italian North, $360 in the South; in France, the index was 166 for Paris, 38 for Corsica.[32] The persistence of these differences in spite of substantial government action points to strong geographical reasons, rather than failure of past policies. Evidence from social enquiries stresses the tenacity of social relations and cultural traditions once appropriate to the regional economies, but now hampering their development as important factors in perpetuating the gap.[33] Given a sufficient effort from the centre, as the *Cassa per il Mazzogiorno*, started in 1951, and a battery of related preferences have shown in Southern Italy,[34] all these regions can be developed, but frequently only at the cost of slowing down the progress of the country as a whole.

Industrialization and Integration in Eastern Europe

The countries in this group have 'Socialist' economies, which at this stage in their development may be taken to mean that the major means of production are collectively owned and that economic life is to a large extent controlled by central planning agencies rather than by the market. Their policies are closely modelled on those of the Soviet Union though two of them, Yugoslavia and Albania, are no longer in the Soviet political orbit.

In Eastern Europe the drive to economic integration was, if anything, even more directly linked to the conflict across the Iron Curtain than in the West, as the lesser economy always finds its relation with the greater impinges more on its existence than vice versa. It was at one of the hottest points in the Cold War, in 1949, that the Council for Mutual Economic Assistance (CMEA) commonly known as COMECON, was formed between Russia and five of her Eastern European allies; Albania joined soon after, the German Democratic Republic (GDR) was admitted in 1950, and only Yugoslavia remained outside.

Paradoxically, precisely because the member states had planned economies, COMECON involved a good deal less co-ordination of economic planning than the EEC and, arguably, less co-operation even than was presupposed by the much looser OEEC. Since economic decisions in the East are made by the political authorities, any transfer of some of them to an outside body would constitute an immediate infringement of political sovereignty. It is a problem also known, to a much smaller extent, in the West, but there were historical reasons why it should be felt more acutely in Eastern Europe. It is worth reminding ourselves that in the early post-war years, Eastern Europe was less monolithic than it was to become later. While Communists were everywhere in the government, they ruled only with the aid of shifting and uncertain alliances wth other groups, different in each country. The hatreds engendered by the war, particularly between the Slavs and the Germans and their allies, the Hungarians and Romanians, were still a mordant reality. In these circumstances, the merging of these proud nations in a common Eastern European Community was quite unthinkable. Later, when a move might have been possible, the pattern was set.

Moreover, the dominant Stalinist doctrine envisaged for each country a growth path that was to be as close a replica as possible of the Soviet experience. There was to be not a single Socialist Eastern Europe, but a group of similar states. Early action certainly followed that model. Industry, or its larger firms, was nationalized quickly. Poland had taken over 86.3% of industry in 1946, Czechoslovakia 65% in 1946, followed by all works with over 50 employees in 1948; in Yugoslavia 88% of larger properties were state-owned, the rest, including trading agencies and foreign property, following in 1948; in Bulgaria, the state's share rose from 20% to 84% in 1947 plus 9% to co-operative hands; in Romania, it was 90% in 1948; in Hungary, the large majority; in Albania, 53% of output arose in the state sector of industry and another 31% in the co-operative sector in 1946; and the Russian sector of Germany, that was to become the GDR, nationalized in 1946 all Nazi property, all monopolies, as well as the land, the minerals, the power-stations, and other major enterprises. Moreover, the remaining large agricultural estates, as well as ex-German and formerly Hungarian property, were redistributed everywhere, so that the whole of the region became one essentially of small peasant holdings. Agricultural co-operation was encouraged, with a rather larger share in private plots than in the Soviet Union, but state farms remained a small minority except in Romania where they covered 21.6% of agricultural acreage in 1950 and 29.4% in 1960, Czechoslovakia (10.7% and 15.5%), and Poland (8.9% and 11.5%).[35]

These countries were poor by Western standards, having been in addition most grievously damaged and impoverished in the war. They did not start from the same base: Czechoslovakia and the GDR were highly industrialized countries; Poland had gained advanced industrial regions from Germany, particularly in Silesia, in addition to some of her own, and the Soviet Union, though poorer than the first two, and consisting largely of backward and poverty-striken agricultural or primary-producing provinces, also had some powerful industrial centres. By contrast, Hungary outside Budapest, Romania, Yugoslavia, and Bulgaria were among the least industrialized regions of Europe. Nevertheless, the intention was that all were to develop equally as quickly as possible to Stalin's pattern: all were to have iron and steel works, and put most of their efforts on capital-goods industries; consumer goods were to follow more slowly later. All this was subject to national five- or six-year plans which, after some initial trial years, were to work to a common date of 1955, except for Bulgaria.

This was the very antithesis of an international division of labour, and in consequence very little trade developed between these countries, despite their close political and (after the Warsaw Pact of 1955) military-political collaboration. In its first few years, COMECON was dormant, for there was little for it to do. In 1955-6 there began some co-operation in railway management and nuclear research, and specialist commissions were set up, of which there were 21 by 1966, as well as an exchange of technical information: 26,000 Soviet technical specialists were sent out to the other countries in 1957-64. There was some multilateral clearing from 1957, centred at first on the USSR State Bank, but it involved only 2-3% of trade and, as no balances could be carried beyond the end of the year, there was no credit involved. Joint ventures were largely bilateral, like the development of certain mineral deposits, or the Hungary–Soviet agreement of 1964, according to which the Hungarians would make rear axles, differentials, and drive shafts and the Soviet Union would make the front axles, with drive shaft and buffer springs for buses for both countries. Truly common action was rare. It included the 'friendship' crude-oil pipeline from Russia to Poland, the GDR, Czechoslovakia, and Hungary, the coaxial TV cable from Moscow westward, the Danube power-station supported by four countries, and the more general production allocation of the type that awarded all heavy rolling-mill building to the USSR and Czechoslovakia, light rolling-mills to the GDR and Poland, wire-drawing equipment to the GDR and Hungary, oil-drilling and refining equipment to the USSR and Romania, and excavating machines to the GDR, Czechoslovakia, and the USSR.[36] But such collaboration was largely limited to engineering products.

In the absence of a common plan, trade was basically bilateral, generally also with bilateral clearing. Moreover, in the absence of an agreed or uniform pricing system, it was essentially barter, conducted on the 'import first principle', exchanging what was short at home against what was surplus, rather than trading on the principles of comparative costs in order to increase total efficiency. Indeed, since prices were artificial, interest rates variable and often notional, and turnover taxes were levied at different rates, prices gave no clue as to where production was cheapest. Inasmuch as prices were used, they were taken from the West: this could be done for machinery, but became impossible in the case of such commodities as fresh food. Some attempts were made to introduce effective pricing and accounting in the liberalizing years of the mid-sixties, but they remained ineffective.[37] Thus trade as a proportion of national income remained much lower than in Western countries, and trade within COMECON as a proportion of total trade did not rise, though it was much higher than the trade links of the Soviet Union with her partners had been before the war. Towards the end of the period, trade with the complementary economies of the West tended to gain relatively to that of the parallel economies within the COMECON.[38] As a co-ordinator of economic planning and development, the role of COMECON has so far been minimal.

Yet it would be wrong to minimize its positive contribution to the industrialization of Eastern Europe. A comparison with the inter-war years will at once show up the difference in the atmosphere and background of mutual aid instead of bitter hostility, and between post-war growth, labour and material shortages, and social improvements on the one hand and pre-war stagnation, unemployment, and over-production, disfigured by attempts to solve economic problems at the expense of the poorest members of the community, on the other. The Soviet Communist model, like the Western one, was one of regional industrialization, and a catching-up with the advanced economies of the West. Trade, as in the West, grew faster than output,[39] and the tendency of a falling export ratio was reversed here, too.

Given the low starting-points of these countries in terms of industrial strength and the virtual absence of any outside aid, their economic achievements were truly astounding, possibly exceeding even the growth-rates of the West. In view of the differences in measurements and various technical problems, direct comparisons are even more difficult to make than between countries within the same social system: thus the East, at similar levels of total national income, tends to provide more social services, while an apparently similar flow of consumer goods will be worth less in real incomes because of minimal, troublesome distribution facilities which throw much of the cost of distribution on the consumer, and because of irregular and unpredictable supply, and lack of choice. Paul Bairoch's figures provide one comparison, and they are here reproduced together with growth-rates which, measuring like with like, are more meaningful than absolute levels.[40] (See Table 9.5.)

As might be expected in countries following the Soviet model, these over-all figures hide wide sectoral differences. In particular, the growth of the heavy and capital-goods industries was much more rapid than the increase in the production of consumer goods. The forced pace of the building-up of a heavy industrial base in each country was often costly and wasteful, needlessly duplicating units at uneconomical sizes, building ahead of experience and erecting works irrespective of calculations of comparative costs.[41] But within its set limits, it was successful. By 1962, COMECON countries were responsible for 30% of the world's industrial but only for 22% of its agricultural output and they therefore belonged to the industrialized part of the world.[42]

These countries are now clearly over the hump: they are either indus-trialized, or well on the way to industrialization.

Table 9.5.

	Per Capita GNP at constant prices (US $ of 1960)			Per Capita GDP Annual growth %
	1950	1973	Annual growth 1950-73,%	1973-6
Bulgaria	423	1755	6.38	7.3*
Czechoslovakia	785	2438	5.05	4.2
GDR	571	2445	6.53	5.3
Hungary	560	1851	5.34	4.6
Poland	556	1842	5.35	4.8
Romania	319	1360	6.51	(9.9)
USSR	585	1887	5.22	3.2
Yugoslavia	339	1182	5.58	4.5
All Europe	749	2077	4.53	—

* 1973-5.

According to their own statistical sources, some of the sectoral dif-ferences in the early key growth years were as indicated in Table 9.6.[43]

Table 9.6.

	Cumulative Annual Growth-Rates, 1950/2 to 1967/9 %				Output Index 1965 (1951 = 1)		Annual Growth-Rate 1951-64 %	
	Total Manu-facturing	Metal-using	Chemicals and Rubber	Textiles and Light Industry	All Industry	Engi-neering	Gross Product	
							Industry	Agri-culture
Albania	—	—	—	—	—	—	15.9	5.2
Bulgaria	12.5	19.9	21.8	10.2	6.9	16.6	13.7	5.4
Czechoslovakia	8.3	11.4	12.7	6.1	3.6	6.3	9.0	1.4
GDR	8.3	10.7	9.3	6.4	3.9	5.6	9.8	7.2
Hungary	8.1	9.5	15.4	6.3	3.9	5.4	9.8	2.6
Poland	10.3	16.6	15.1	8.3	5.1	14.2	11.6	2.2
Romania	11.8	27.1	21.3	10.0	6.5	12.5	13.3	4.3
USSR	9.6	14.0	13.1	6.9	4.6	7.6	10.8	4.2
Yugoslavia	—	—	—	—	—	—	10.5	6.2

The pattern, forced by central decision, was very different from that in the West, where industrialization generally began with consumer industries which required less capital and could build some on pre-existing skills. Here the growth of textiles, a typical consumer product, fell greatly behind the expansion of the capital goods sector. On the Eastern model, the transition years could be traversed more quickly, but at a greater temporary loss in consumer welfare. The basic indus-tries on which all further industrialization depends were created, in some cases practically out of nothing, with astonishing rapidity, and countries which before the war possessed at best some rudimentary beginnings of capital-goods industries became exporters by the mid-sixties. In 1964, engineering products formed 47% of the total exports of Czechoslovakia and the GDR but also 33% of Polish and Hungarian exports, 24% of Bulgarian, 21% of Russian, and 18% of Romanian.[44] In all of them, the leading imports came to be industrial raw materials and at times even grain. Some of them seem to have jumped over several stages of development familiar in the West, at the cost, however, of severe selective neglect. Thus housing, road and rail infrastructure, provisions of telephones and shopping facilities, but above all consumer goods as a whole had to take second place to achieve the set targets.[45] The same impression is conveyed by other statistics. Thus, by comparison with the West, these countries maintained very high investment rate, of around 25% of GNP, Czechoslovakia and the GDR investing at the lower rate of around 20%. But their real wages rose much less than their output, only doubling, at most, between 1950 and 1963.[46] It is scarcely conceivable that a market economy could have maintained such a balance, at any rate without a massive political repression of protests, and there have indeed been a number of riots and rebellions, almost always triggered by issues of real wages. It remains to be seen whether the planned economies, having laid their industrial basis by means of 'half-enforced and half-spontaneous industrialization'[47] can now switch back to convert the productive apparatus to its true function, the production of consumer goods and services. By the 1960s, the industrial structure had become very like the Western one.

Agricultural output, it will be observed, though growing at much lower rates than industry, still showed a very respectable growth. This was all the more notable since the forced industrialization depended on a massive switch of labour out of agriculture. For Eastern Europe as a whole, non-agricultural employment rose by a compound annual 3 per cent over 1950–70. Agricultural employment, however, fell substantially, as shown in Table 9.7.[48]

Table 9.7. Agricultural employment in mid-year, 000

	1950	1970	Drop, %
Bulgaria	2982	1782	−40.2
Czechoslovakia	2250	1314	−41.6
GDR	2069	1199	−42.0
Hungary	2121	1479	−30.3
Poland	7113	6131	−13.8
Romania	6914	6229	−9.9
USSR	32 800	32 000	−2.4
Yugoslavia	5676	(4680)	−17.5
All Eastern Europe	61 925	54 814	−11.5

If the majority of pre-war observers were right, there was much dis-guised unemployment on the land in these countries, and a certain proportion of the labour force could be withdrawn without ill effects on output. Yet, considering that it was likely to be the younger and more enterprising who left for industry and the towns, the figures clearly bespeak also a major transformation in techniques. Here, in a final table, are some of the key statistics:[49]

Table 9.8.

	% of GNP						% of Employment			
	Agriculture			Industry, incl. Construction			Agriculture		Industry, incl. Construction	
	1950	1967	1976	1950	1967	1976	1950	1967	1950	1967
Bulgaria	39.4	15.6	21.3	23.7	52.0	58.9	82.1	41.8	9.9	35.7
Czechoslovakia	23.9	12.4	8.4	41.5	52.7	80.2	36.9	19.1	33.9	46.0
GDR	11.3	8.7	9.6	41.5	58.6	69.0	22.9	15.6	45.5	46.9
Hungary	29.7	20.6	15.7	31.5	43.1	59.1	49.8	30.0	25.0	39.8
Poland	36.9	24.2	15.5	26.5	42.4	64.4	53.5	39.9	25.6	34.2
Romania	31.3	22.0	18.3	23.3	44.0	63.1	74.3	53.8	14.2	27.1
USSR			16.5			63.7	46.0	30.0	26.0	36.0
Yugoslavia	27.6	22.6	16.7	28.6	40.6	50.5	78.3	56.7	12.5	25.0

The changes were particularly striking in the most backward econ-omies, in Bulgaria, Romania, and Yugoslavia, and there is here, as also in the tendency for the least industrialized countries to grow fastest, a catching-up process at work. The intention to make the 'Socialist' countries as near as possible equal to each other was, of course, inherent in the critical post-war decision to make each country a mini-replica of the Soviet model, containing a complete range of industries and being as nearly as possible self-sufficient. It implied the rejection of the idea of a supra-national economy to which each region would contrib-ute what it was best fitted for, with the corollary that the nation state, as economic entity at least, would wither away in favour of the wider Socialist community. No doubt the fierce, because so often thwarted, nationalism of that part of Europe had its share in this decision, as well as Stalin's inflexible views as to the right path to Socialism.

It is noteworthy that the pursuit of geographical equality was less single-minded within the boundaries of states, though constant lip service was paid to it. Regional differences are greater within the Soviet Union than almost anywhere else in Europe, and are in part associated with national territories, though there are good geographical and historical reasons also. In Yugoslavia, another federal state in which economic region and nationality might broadly coincide, the levelling-up of the more backward regions was a major part of the economic development programme, but in spite of deliberate efforts to carry it out, the differences have in fact widened instead of narrowed.[50]

Other countries had developed in an equally lopsided manner. In Hungary, Budapest contained 62.3% of all industrial workers in 1938, while in Czechoslovakia the Slovak part had only 7% of the country's industry in 1937 and only 45% per capita income of Bohemia in 1945. In Poland, in spite of much levelling-up, the value of the 'product of Socialised industries' varied in 1967 between 11,200 zloty per capita in the North-Eastern Region and 40,200 zloty in the Southern, though with agricultural output added in, the differences narrowed to 44,100: 25,600.[51] On economic grounds, new industries even in planned economies would generally tend to be located where some industries exist already, since less has to be spent on infrastructure—the familiar dual economy problem—or they would be near raw materials or markets[52] and any deliberate redistribution from those locations involves an economic cost which may be very much larger than any possible social gain. The planned Eastern European economies remain ambivalent on this issue, but it does not look as though they would industrialize their backward regions inside the advanced economies any faster than the West.

Further Outlook and Some Conclusions

Whatever the exact definition of 'industrialization'—and this book has deliberately avoided attempting it—it is clear that it is being completed in Europe, as the last gaps are being closed, the last areas of resistance mopped up. A process which began only two hundred years ago in a few remote counties of Britain has now covered a complete continent.

After a break of some decades, conditions seem again propitious for this kind of economic advance, and we seem to have come full circle to a framework akin to that of the nineteenth century which favoured industrial progress. Appearances, however, are misleading and history does not move in circles: rather its mode of progress is dialectical, the return to more open economic relationships across the frontiers in this case taking place under different conditions, among which a much advanced technology, and an overwhelmingly important role played by governments are outstanding. Yet the basic equation holds: a European economy moves forward more easily and with greater returns for its citizens than one chopped up into non-communicating parts.

Alas, the price that had to be paid for this is that there are now two Europes, not one. Economic relations between them, at the time of writing, are good, and the relatively small amount of trade done between them is limited not so much by deliberate politically inspired obstruction as by the fact that the Eastern economies were so constructed as to need relatively little trade altogether. Movement of capital across the 'Iron Curtain' is extremely limited, and movement of labour practically impossible, but each of the two halves is large and varied enough to find economic bases for development within its own territory without being hampered by the lack of access to the other for a long time to come. There are the neutrals, above all Finland, Austria, and Yugoslavia, who maintain important links with both. Altogether, there are no possible economic causes for war between them in the foreseeable future, though there are few hopes of greater integration either.

Lessons that may be learnt from this story have to be applied with extreme caution. Lessons for later comers who might wish to follow in the European path, in particular, are largely negative. For while it is obvious that the technical means, the machines, power-stations, or metalled roads, may be copied with usually only minor modifications, this account of European industrialization has shown, above all, that the process is never repeated in identical fashion. On the contrary, the timing is all-important. The path chosen, the opportunities open, the sequences and speed depend on the phasing of the arrival of a region on the threshold of industrialization, and on the actions and potentials of the contemporaneous world. In turn, its arrival at the threshold at one time rather than another was in Europe linked to its resources, its 'location', and its historical tradition up to that point. While this was true for each region, it is also true for Europe as a whole: among other reasons, Europe was unique *because* it was the pioneer.

The differences arising from the differences in the timing are all-pervasive, but one aspect deserves special emphasis, and that is the role of government. The political rulers who found, in the early phases of European industrialization, that some of their provinces were beginning to industrialize, lacked the knowledge and the power, as frequently they also lacked the desire, to help the process along. Today's governments possess all three, and are driven by the expectations of their people to use them, and this is true of dictatorial governments, who form the large majority in the non-industrialized world, as much as of those with a genuine democratic base.

The classical European type of industrialization was driven forward by thousands of individual decisions, no decision-taker being required to know whither the economy as a whole was going. Industrialization by central direction is deliberate and is therefore looking for lessons; but the lessons must be applied with genuine historical understanding.

There is one further lesson that is often required of historical accounts: an essay in prediction. What can we learn from the European past that will help us shape our destiny in a more desirable way in the future? Alas, here also, the historian must counsel caution. For, in the last resort, industrialization is but a means, not an end. Fraught with sacrifices among those who live through it, the product of some of the finest examples of human ingenuity, initiative, and enterprise, industrialization yet offers no satisfaction, only opportunities. It only enlarges the possibilities of human development though to an unprecedented degree. It is for future generations, with very little guidance from the past, to use or misuse the opportunities provided by the industrialization process of the last two hundred years.

Notes

PREFACE

1 Peter Mathias (1972), pp. 503, 508; and Chapter 4 below.
2 Alexander Gerschenkron (1966b), p. 358.
3 Joel Mokyr (1977), 989; Alexander Gerschenkron (1977), pp. 347-58.
4 e.g. Jacob Viner (1953) pp. 42-51.
5 S. Pollard (1973) 636-48, also idem (1974) 3-16, 58-62.
6 W. W. Rostow (1960a).
7 E. A Wrigley (1961); (1962); and (1972) 225-59.
8 e.g. Simon Kuznets (1951) 27-8; (1972) 75-101.
9 Herbert Spencer (1902), ii, 568-642.
10 Peter Mathias (1972), p. 510. See also the excellent discussion of these issues in C. P. Kindleberger (1967), Chapter 15: 'History and Economic Growth: Search for a Method'.
11 I am indebted for this and related points to fruitful discussions with Professor Friedrich Rapp of the Technical University, Berlin.

CHAPTER 1

1 A. Toynbee (1884); Paul Mantoux (1961); T. S. Ashton (1948); Phyliss Deane (1965); Peter Mathias (1969).
2 D. C. Coleman (1977), pp. 1-3.
3 François Crouzet (1967), esp. pp. 146-55. It has also been argued that the chances of Britain and France were similar, and Britain 'took off' first by 'stochastic selection'. N. F. R. Crafts (1977), 429-41.
4 'Access to co-operant or complementary factors of production and access to the market . . . are essential to the concept of economic resource'. P. T. Bauer and B. S. Yamey (1957), p. 43. Cf. also W. N. Parker (1972). His hypothetical question as to what would have happened if oil rather than coal had been easily available in Britain might be answered not only by the surmise that the techno-logical sequence of inventions would have been different—oil-fired boilers and the transport of oil having different requirements from those based on coal, but that, if oil had been found in regions outside the coalfield, industrial location, the growth of cities etc. would have been equally drastically affected.
5 E. A. Wrigley (1972), 247; E. L. Jones (1974), p. 8.
6 J. Aikin (1795), p. 96.
7 S. Timmins (1967), p. 213.
8 W. Minchinton (1954), 69-90; H. Hamilton (1963), p. 218; C. N. Parkinson, (1952).
9 T. J. Raybould (1973), p. 56; W. H. B. Court (1938), p. 12; T. C. Barker and J. R. Harris (1954); T. C. Barker (1960); Joseph Priestley (1831; 1967), pp. 7-19, 233-41.

10 E. L. Jones (1977), p. 492; D. Defoe (1962), ii, 33. By 1828, on a generous calculation, the counties containing the woollen and worsted industries produced no more than 25 per cent of the home-grown wool between them. John James (1857; 1968), p. 424.

11 e.g. 'In those counties where the soil is proper for carrying on agriculture, the disposition of the people is always inclined to rural affairs; while, in other parts, where the soil is sterile and unproductive, the genius of the people is turned to manufacture and trade . . . While the inhabitants of the favoured soil raise corn for the support of the community, those who are not blessed in this way, manufacture goods for the comfort and convenience of the happy agriculturalist and in this manner both equally promote the public good . . . thereby making good the old proverb, that a barren soil is an excellent whetstone to promote industry.' Robert Brown (1799), p. 226, Appx. p. 16. It is interesting to note that the woollen areas that were particularly praised by Defoe in the 1720s as containing both flourishing industry and agriculture began their relative industrial decline soon after, op. cit., e.g. i, 62, 283, 285.

12 Jones (1977); idem (1965) 1-18; idem (1974) p. 429; idem (1968a), (1968b); A. H. John (1961), 187-8. Also see Joel Mokyr (1976b), 372, 379, 392.

13 See Chapter 2 below. Also Jones (1977), 492-9.

14 Joan Thirsk (1961), 70-88; idem (1973), 63-4. Some of these products may have been "Z" goods in the well-known definition by S. Hyman and S. Resnick (1969).

15 Richard Ippolito (1975).

16 See also P. K. O'Brien (1977), 174. Later, in the nineteenth century, there would be Malthusian pressure in the fringe areas, such as the Scottish Highlands, and above all Ireland. T. C. Smout (1969), pp. 351 ff; L. M. Cullen and T. C. Smout (1977b), p. 14; M. W. Flinn (1977); R. D. Collison Black (1972), 194-6; L. M. Cullen (1968b), 79 ff.

17 G. H. Tupling (1927), pp. 167, 189, 215; A. P. Wadsworth and J. de L. Mann (1931; 1965), pp. 274, 308, 311, 321; Louis W. Moffit, (1925), pp. 16, 67; David Hey (?1977), pp. 26-7; E. J. Buckatzsch (1950), 303-6; P. F. W. Large (1978), pp. 4-5; J. D. Marshall (1958), pp. 39-41; J. James (1857), pp. 252, 283, 590; J. D. Chambers (1932), p. 95; idem (1953), 319-43; idem (n.d.), p. 4; A. H. Dodd (1933), pp. 27, 335; L. M. Cullen (1968a), p. 6; W. H. Crawford (1977); N. B. Harte (1973b); Defoe (1962), ii, 222-4, 270; Witt Bowden (1925); 1965), pp. 173-4.

18 S. D. Chapman (1973), 128-33.

19 E. H. Hagen (1958).

20 L. Moffit (1925), pp. 233, 244-5; A. E. Musson (1978), pp. 50-1, 71; Smout (1969), p. 372; E. A. Wrigley (1967), 44-70.

21 For the remarkable concentration of engineering talent in Shropshire, see Barrie Trinder (1977), p. 164, and for Lancashire, footnote 51 below.

22 e.g. Defoe (1962), i, 72, 115, 218, 271, 279-80, ii, 33, 248, 337, 365, 401, Also A. Slaven (1975), pp. 84-6; B. A. Holderness (1976), pp. 85-9.

23 W. H. B. Court (1938), p. 194.

24 Musson (1978), pp. 57-8; Mokyr (1976b), pp. 375-6; C. H. Lee, (1971), p. 8.

25 N. B. Harte (1973b); Defoe (1962), ii, 362-5; H. Hamilton (1963), pp. 137-63; L. M. Cullen (1972), pp. 60-4; A. J. Durie (1977); W. H. Crawford (1977), pp. 24-32; E. R. R. Green (1949).

26 R. G. Wilson (1971), pp. 42 ff.; Phyllis Deane (1957), 107-23; R. G. Wilson (1973). See also D. C. Coleman (1973) and (1969), 417-29.

27 Musson (1978), p. 50; Joan Thirsk (1973); S. D. Chapman (1972), 7-50; J. D. Chambers, pp. 4, 13-14, and idem (1932), pp. 104 ff. and (1929), 296-329.

28 S. R. H. Jones (1978), 356-61; Smout (1969), pp. 372, 387-8; J. R. Kellett (1958); W. G. Hoskins (1935; 1968) p. 51; E. F. Heckscher (1955), ii, 301-25.

29 Peter Mathias (1959); Dorothy George (1925), p. 198.

30 L. Weatherill (1971); Simeon Shaw (1827); G. I. H. Lloyd (1968); P. F. W. Large (1978); A. Birch and M. W. Flinn (1954); J. R. Harris (1978), pp. 201-2; S. Timmins (1967); W. H. B. Court (1938); David Hey (?1977); Marie Rowlands (?1977), pp. 29-31; T. J. Raybould (1973), p. 26; C. H. Lee (1971), p. 18. W. B. Honey (1949); Llewellyn F. W. Jewett (1865); John Thomas (1971).

31 John Whyman (?1977); John Lowerson (?1977); J. V. Beckett (?1977); Defoe (1962), i, 43, 217, ii, 291, 296, 316, 371; W. G. Hoskins (1935), pp. 51, 81; A. H. Dodd (1933), p. 110; E. L. Jones (1977), p. 498 and (1974b), pp. 424-5; R. H. Campbell (1971), p. 3.

32 John Prest (1960).

33 For Lancashire, see Wadsworth and Mann (1931), pp. 316-20; Tupling (1927), pp. 167, 178, 215, 227-9; Aikin (1795), pp. 20, 23, 203-4, 235-46; John Holt (1795), pp. 13, 169-72, 179-82, 209-13; A. B. Reach (1972), esp. pp. 66, 110, 118-21; George W. Daniels (1920), pp. 137-9. For Yorkshire, see *ParlP*, 1806, iii, p. 268; Ev. James Ellis, p. 8, Joseph Cooper, p. 33, James Walker, p. 182, (Sir) James Graham, pp. 444-7; R. Brown (1973), pp. 77-8, 225-8, Appx. pp. 12-18; W. B. Crump (1931), pp. 6, 72, 77 ff; H. Heaton (1920; 1965), pp. 290-3; J. James (1857), p. 267; Defoe (1962), ii 193-203; J. Aikin (1795), p. 93; W. H. Long (1969), pp. 50-4. For other areas, see Witt Bowden (1925), p. 116; A. H. Dodd (1933), pp. 47, 330; Adam Murray (1813), pp. 132, 149-50, 167; John Rowe (1953), pp. 225-31; B. Trinder (1977) p. 60; P. F. W. Large (1978); D. G. Hey (1970) and (?1977) p. 26; J. D. Marshall (1958), pp. 70-1.

34 The idea was certainly present among the large early cotton-mill owners. Chambers (n. d.), p. 62.

35 e.g. F. Singleton (1970), p. 82; T. M. Devine (1979).

36 *Vale of Trent* p. 38; R. A. E. Wells (1977), pp. 1-2; W. H. Long (1969), p. 52; A. Murray (1813), pp. 97-9; A. H. Dodd (1933), p. 6; Defoe (1962), ii, 199-200, 211; J. Aikin (1795), pp. 44-5, 303, 362, 398, 574; John Holt (1795), p. 184; L. Moffit (1925), pp. 84-5; Marie Rowlands (?1977), p. 34.

37 L. M. Cullen (1968a), p. 206; W. H. Crawford (1977), p. 32.

38 J. D. Marshall uses that expression to describe the fate of Furness (1958), p. xiv.

39 See e.g. the table in L. A. Clarkson (1971), pp. 88-9.

40

	Coal (m. tons)	Pig Iron (000 tons)	Raw Cotton Retained Imports (m. lb.)	Wool Clip and Retained Imports (m. lb.)	Steam-Power Installed (000 HP)
1800	12.0	180	56	(108)	20 (max.)
1850	56.0	2250	588	183	300
1860	80.0	3830	1084	251	-
1870	110.4	5960	1075	320	977
1880	147.0		1373	358	-

Sources: S. Pollard 'A New Estimate of Coalmining Output in Great Britain, 1750-1850' *EcHR* (forthcoming); P. J. Riden (1977); B. R. Mitchell and P. Deane (1962); A. E. Musson (1976).

41 J. Rowe (1953), pp. 42-3, 211, 231.

42 Michael Havinden (?1977).

43 A. Raistrick (1953); B. Trinder (1977); W. H. B. Court (1938), p. 191; C. H. Lee (1971), p. 16; Alan Birch (1967), pp. 146-8; C. K. Hyde (1977).

44 P. F. W. Large (1978), p. 1; Henry Johnson (1967); John James (1967); T. J. Raybould (1973); W. H. B. Court (1938); A. Birch (1967), pp. 148-57; B. L. C. Johnson and M. J. Wise (1950); W. K. V. Gale (1950).

45 J. R. Harris (1964); A. H. Dodd (1933).

46 S. D. Chapman (1972), pp. 22, 26; R. A. Church (1966), pp. 1-5; J. D. Chambers (1932), pp. 35 ff.; idem, pp. 16-17.

47 S. D. Chapman (1967); George Unwin (1924); J. Aikin (1795), p. 498.

48 John Heath (?1977).

49 S. D. Chapman (1967), pp. 31-2, 172. A similar point has been made about the West Riding in the 1790s: D. T. Jenkins (1973), p. 254.

50 W. W. Rostow (1960b) chapter 11; also R. M. Hartwell (1971), p. 170; E. J. Hobsbawm (1968).

51 A. E. Musson and E. Robinson (1969), pp. 393-458.

52 T. S. Ashton (1953); Seymour Shapiro (1967). See also note 133 below.

53 Wadsworth and Mann (1931); G. H. Tupling (1927); G. W. Daniels (1920) *passim*; J. Aikin (1795), pp. 3-4; A. E. Musson and E. Robinson (1969), pp. 89-118; D. A. Farnie (1979), p. 209 and *passim*.

54 L. W. Moffit (1925), p. 130 and *passim*; John Holt (1795), pp. 208-9.

55 Water-power survived in the higher and remoter reaches of the valleys well into the nineteenth century, while steam was being installed lower down: M. T. Wild (1972), pp. 208-9.

56 R. G. Wilson (1973); D. T. Jenkins (1973); L. Moffit (1925), pp. 218-20; R. G. Wilson (1971), pp. 6-7, 54-5, 90-9; A. E. Musson (1978), p. 86; K. G. Ponting (1971), pp. 35-6; E. Lipson (1921; 1965), pp. 242-8; J. James (1857), p. 283 and *passim*, 326, 591 *passim*; H. Heaton (1965), p. 259 and *passim*; W. B. Crump (1931); F. Singleton (1970), p. 38; J. Aikin (1795), pp. 554, 567, 574; R. A. E. Wells (1977), pp. 4, 9-10.

57 Defoe (1962), ii, 251; D. J. Rowe (?1977); idem (1971); N. McCord and D. J. Rowe (1977); Edward Hughes (1952); J. H. Clapham (1967), p. 50; N. McCord (1980).

58 T. M. Devine (1976).

59 A. and N. L. Clow (1952); Bruce Lehman (1977), pp. 125-9.

60 A. Slaven (1975), p. 106.

61 Birch (1967), pp. 171-7; A. Slaven (1975); Smout (1969), pp. 393-4, 404-9, 421-30; R. H. Campbell (1971), p. 97 and *passim*; H. Hamilton (1963), p. 160 and *passim*; W. Bowden (1925), pp. 114-16; John Butt (1977); T. M. Devine (1977).

62 Wrigley (1967); P. G. Hall (1962).

63 J. J. Monaghan (1942-3), 1-17; L. M. Cullen (1972), pp. 92-3; D. Dickson (1977).

64 In another sense, there can be no meaning to 'completion' in a continuous process and Britain ran out of luck around 1870, lacking what was required to sustain the next phase in a leading position.

65 A. Birch (1967); P. J. Riden (1977).

66 John Heath (?1977).

67 S. Pollard, 'A New Estimate'.

68 D. T. Jenkins (1975).

69 Forty-four new canal schemes were approved in the four years 1791–4, costing an estimated £6.7 million. T. C. Barker and C. I. Savage (1974), pp. 42; Charles Hadfield (1959); idem (1960).

70 W. E. Minchinton (1969); idem (1957); A. H. John (1950); idem (1972), pp. 513–21.

71 Cullen, p. 106; Green (1949); J. M. Goldstrom (1969).

72 Barker and Savage (1974), chapter 3; Michael Robbins (1962); P. S. Bagwell (1974).

73 A. H. Dodd (1933), p. 119.

74 Barker and Savage (1974), pp. 70, 78–9; G. R. Hawke (1970); Wray Vamplew (1969), 33–65; B. R. Mitchell (1964), 315–36.

75 J. H. Clapham (1936), ii, 22–5.

76 Raphael Samuel (1977); also A. E. Musson (1978), pp. 107–8.

77 W. Radcliffe (1828), p. 62.

78 R. H. Campbell (1971), p. 103.

79 S. D. Chapman (1972), p. 60.

80 Ibid., pp. 20–1.

81 Thomas Ellison (1886; 1968), pp. 55, 61.

82 T. Ellison (1886), pp. 68–9. These figures are the averages for the whole trade. See also V. A. Gattrell (1977), pp. 95 ff.; M. Blaug (1961), 358–81; T. S. Ashton (1962), p. 249; D. A. Farnie (1979), p. 199.

83 G. I. H. Lloyd (1968); S. Pollard (1959); A. E. Musson (1978), pp. 107–8; Marie Rowlands (?1977); S. Timmins (1967); Conrad Gill (1952), i, p. 99.

84 As early as 1786, James Watt and James Keir had argued before the House of Lords that the Birmingham metal-goods trade enjoyed a competitive advantage over those of Europe and America by being able to draw on the products of su-- perior machinery, such as cast-iron forge hammers, rollers of mixed steel and iron, and slitters. W. H. B. Court (1938), p. 249.

85 For the profound difference made by apparently extraneous changes of this kind, see John Prest (1960), p. 96 and *passim*.

86 Sheffield in 1836 owned only 5 per cent of the North Midland Railway's capital. M. C. Reed (1975), p. 164.

87 S. Pollard (1954) and (1971).

88 John L. Baxter (1977).

89 Duncan Bythell (1969); E. P. Thompson (1963), pp. 270–1; R. H. Campbell (1971), p. 186.

90 A. H. Dodd (1933); L. M. Cullen (1972), pp. 119–29.

91 Chapter 4 below.

92 See p. 213 below.

93 J. Rowe (1953), p. 254. For Yorkshire, see R. Brown (1793), p. 61; for Essex, John Booker (1974), pp. 28–33.

94 Chambers (n. d.), p. 62.

95 For the Scottish example, see R. H. Campbell (1971), pp. 155–60. Also W. N. Parker (1971), p. 76.

96 A. H. Dodd (1933), p. 48; R. Brown (1973), pp. 150, 225; A. Murray (1813), pp. 149–150.

97 Peter Mathias (1967), 80–93.

98 Some modern theory has begun to recognize that time lags, and some rise in the agricultural sector, play a part in development: e.g. Lloyd F. Reynolds (1969), p. 93.

99 'An examination of (the) table shows very clearly that the higher wage of

the Northern Counties is altogether due to the proximity of manufacturing and mining enterprise. . . the line is distinctly drawn at the point where coal ceases to be found.' James Caird (1968), p. 511; E. Gilboy (1934), pp. 219-27. Also J. Aikin (1795), p. 551; A. Murray (1813), p. 167; R. Brown (1793), p. 203, Appx. p. 52; A. H. Dodd (1933), p. 340; F. Singleton (1970), p. 86; E. H. Hunt (1973). For rent differentials see Arthur Young (1771), iii, 425.

100 Caird, p. 213.

101 E. L. Jones (1974), pp. 213-18.

102 John Holt (1795), pp. 179, 205.

103 A. H. Dodd (1933), pp. 330-1. But see T. C. Barker (1978), p. 90.

104 In treating British industrialization in phases, no hard and fast division is implied, but an observed sequence in which one or other development deserves emphasis at different periods, and in which each phase is seen as evolving out of the preceding one. Perhaps the main difference as against the 'stage' theory is that there is no implication that other economies would pass through a recognizably similar sequence of phases, even though their industrialized character at the end was not dissimilar from that of Britain.

105 M. J. T. Lewis (1970); B. Trinder (1973), pp. 11-12, 120.

106 Smout (1969), p. 433. *Children's Employment Commission (Mines), First Report ParlP*, 1842, pp. 24-30, 35-7. The districts employing women and girls underground were Lancashire, the West Riding, the East of Scotland, and South Wales.

107 A. J. Taylor (1960), pp. 215-35.

108 Henry Johnson (1967), p. 21; T. J. Raybould (1973), p. 20; M. Dunn (1844).

109 A. Slaven (1975), p. 87; Campbell (1971), p. 190; A. H. John (1950), p.165.

110 J. H. Clapham (1910), 195-210; J. K. Edwards (1954), 31-41; M. F. Lloyd-Pritchard (1951), 371-7; E. L. Jones (1974b), pp. 426-9; J. de L. Mann (1971), pp. 116-25, 187-90, 219; W. G. Hoskins (1968), pp. 51-3, 74-6; S. D. Chapman (1978), p. xxi; *Woollen Manufactures* 1806, Report pp. 3, 8; E. Lipson (1921), pp. 248-51; K. G. Ponting (1971), p. 123; idem (1970), pp. 43-4; R. G. Wilson (1971), pp. 7, 132-3; and idem (1973); L. Moffit (1925), pp. 153-4; Jennifer Tann (1973), pp. 218-20; H. Heaton (1965), p. 259; Defoe (1962), ii, 204-7; W. Bowden (1925), p. 124; J. Aikin (1795), p. 574; Charles Wilson (1965), pp. 294-5; F. Atkinson (1956).

111 J. Rowe (1953), pp. 10-17, 265-6; G. R. Lewis (1908).

112 A. H. John (1950), p. 137 and *passim*, 165; B. Trinder (1977), p. 211.

113 P. M. Sweezy (1938); G. C. Allen (1923), 74-85; H. Hamilton (1967); Birch (1967), chapter 6.

114 A. Redford (1934), esp. pp. 2-11, 69; W. Bowden (1925), p. 166 and *passim*.

115 A. Redford (1964). See also Everett S. Lee (1966), 47-57; Michael Anderson (1971), pp. 34-8; D. F. McDonald (1937).

116 P. Deane and W. A. Cole (1969), Table 26, p. 115.

117 Ibid. Table 24, p. 103; A. Slaven (1975), p. 135 and *passim*; T. C. Smout (1969), pp. 261, 392.

118 J. Mokyr (1976b), pp. 391-2; G. H. Tupling (1927), pp. 215-18; A. H. Dodd (1933), pp. 381, 386.

119 Henry Mayhew (1967); E. P. Thompson and Eileen Yeo (1971).

120 R. H. Campbell (1961), pp. 30-1, 35-6, 48, 78-9; idem (1971), pp. 39-42, 65; Smout (1969), pp. 252-5, 387.

121 B. Trinder (1973), pp. 311–17, 335–6; A. H. John (1950), pp. 58–65.

122 The Census was notoriously unreliable in detail in its classification, but there is no reason to assume a particular regional bias. See Musson (1978), p. 118; Keith Burgess (1975), p. 11.

123 S. D. Chapman (1973), p. 136; S. Shapiro (1967), pp. 150–1; Wadsworth and Mann (1931), p. 211 *passim*; F. Crouzet (1972), p. 51.

124 W. G. Hoskins (1968), p. 49; L. S. Pressnell (1956), pp. 333, 342; S. Shapiro (1967), p. 152.

125 Pressnell (1956), pp. 81, 99–105; S. Shapiro (1967), pp. 93–101; T. S. Ashton (1970), pp. 81–7.

126 Pressnell (1956), pp. 223, 254, 556.

127 *Wealth of Nations* (Everyman ed. 1970), i, 48.

128 A. H. John (1950), p. 166, but also see pp. 48–9; J. de L. Mann (1964), pp. xxiii–xxiv; T. M. Devine (1976), 1–13; Crouzet (1972), pp. 169–70.

129 At the time of the 1772 crisis it was estimated that English investments in Scotland totalled £500,000. H. Hamilton (1953); idem (1956); A. Slaven (1975), p. 49 and *passim*; Smout (1969), p. 243; R. H. Campbell (1971), pp. 57, 65–74, 133–44; Defoe (1962), ii, 376; idem (1706 a and b) quoted in Smout, p. 243.

130 E. A. G. Robinson (1969b); Pressnell (1956), pp. 25, 357; John Holt (1795), p. 198. Ireland has also often been treated as a separate economy with its own imports, exports, and balance of payments, Dublin performing a part analogous to London: e.g. L. M. Cullen (1968a), pp. 181–5; idem (1972), pp. 128–9 (1967), 14–16; R. D. Collison Black (1972), pp. 198–9.

131 C. H. Lee (1971), p. 5; E.A. G. Robinson (1969a), introduction, p. xvii.

132 Pressnell (1956), pp. 152–5; R. O. Roberts (1958), 230–45.

133 T. S. Ashton (1953); A. Redford (1934), p. 159; Pressnell (1956), pp. 19, 172–4; B. L. Anderson (1969), pp. 72–3; S. D. Chapman (1979), 50–69.

134 For Liverpool's particular capital structure, especially later in the nineteenth century see A. G. Kenwood (1978) 214–37; also J. R. Killick and W. A. Thomas (1970), 96–111; S. A. Broadbridge (1969), 184–211; idem (1970); M. C. Reed (1975).

135 Pressnell (1956), pp. 152–3, 246, 250, 301; T. M. Hodges (1948), 84–90; B. L. Anderson and P. L. Cottrell (1975), 598–615; G. Jackson (1972), p. 209 and *passim*; John (1950), pp. 48–9.

136 Pressnell (1956), pp. 280–1, 457, 472.

137 L. Moffit (1925), p. 127; L. S. Pressnell (1953), 378–97.

138 G. W. Rimmer (1967), 130–57; R. G. Wilson (1971), p. 133; H. Heaton (1965), pp. 273–4, 288–9; W. B. Crump (1931), p. 16; J. James (1857), pp. 369–70, 388, 409.

139 e.g. John Jones (1967), pp. 72–4; C. H. Lee (1971), pp. 17–18; L. H. Klaassen, P. W. Klein, and J. H. P. Paelinck (1974), *Themes: Relations between Regions*, pp. 95–8; E. L. Jones 'Constraints' (1974b), p. 428. Grenville Withers' evidence in *ParlP*, 1839, XLII, p. 671.

140 G. Myrdal (1971), pp. 22–5. For further discussion on this point see pp. 186–8 below.

141 Tihomir J. Markovitch (1965); Paul Bairoch (1976b); Barry Supple (1972), p. 31; S. D. Chapman (1972a), pp. 64–6; N. F. R. Crafts (1978), 613–14; P. Mathias (1972), p. 498.

142 R. Davis (1962–3), 290.

143 P. Bairoch (1976b), p. 188, also idem (1965), 1100 *passim*. Yet total GNP was not very different from much of Europe: the difference was structural, limited

to a few key sectors which did not yet show up noticeably in national figures: (1976b), pp. 154-6 and idem (1976a), 279, 286.

144 E. A. Wrigley (1962), 15-16. It will be clear how much this author, in common with many others, has profited from Wrigley's seminal paper.

CHAPTER 2

1 Jan de Vries, in a classic study, described the two alternatives as the 'peasant model' leading to poverty, food shortages, and possible Malthusian consequences, and the 'specialisation model' adopted in effect by the Dutch. Jan de Vries (1974), pp. 4-10 and idem (1975). See also Rudolf Häpke (1928); H. K. Roessingh (1970), 105-29.

2 Not quite among the densest. These included a significant proportion of regions which were among the first to industrialize successfully later, and also some which failed to do so: Norfolk, Kent, Île de France, Normandy, Jülich and Berg, the Po Valley. De Vries (1974), p. 81.

3 B. H. Slicher van Bath (1967), 43, 94; also idem (1963), Table III, pp. 330-3. Some Dutch returns were as high as seventeenfold and even twenty-eight-fold in the case of wheat.

4 Slicher van Bath (1967), p. 97; Henri Sée (1942), ii, 197.

5 See Chapter 5 below.

6 E. Baasch (1927), p. 36.

7 Emile de Laveleye (1881), pp. 469-70. Similar leases were also found in Brittany, the Channel Islands, Portugal, and, with some significant differences, in Lombardy.

8 J. G. van Dillen (1974), pp. 201-2.

9 De Vries (1974), pp. 80, 113-18.

10 That region included adjacent areas of Germany whence Amsterdam and Rotterdam attracted many poor German immigrants. J. A. van Houtte (1977), pp. 231-2.

11 Charles Wilson (1969), p. 23; Joel Mokyr (1976a), p. 198.

12 Pierre Goubert (1974), p. 378.

13 Laveleye (1881), pp. 449-59.

14 See below, p. 111. Also J. A. Van Houtte (1968), p. 101; A. S. Milward and S. B. Saul (1973), p. 448; G. Jacquemyns (1929).

15 Herman van der Wee (1978), p. 136.

16 Michel Morineau (1970); J. P. Cooper (1978), 24-5.

17 P. Léon (1970), pp. 20-1, 345. The total agrarian price rise between 1730-40 and 1801-10 has been estimated as follows:

England	+ 250%
North Italy	+ 205%
Germany	+210%
France	+ 163%
Netherlands	+ 265%
Austria	+ 269%

Ibid., p. 196.

18 F. Braudel and E. Labrousse (197)), p. 130. There were still around one million near serfs 'mainmortables' at the time of the Revolution, mainly in Savoy, Burgundy, and Franche-Comté. Jerome Blum (1978), p. 35.

19 e.g. Alexander Gerschenkron (1977), p. 266.

20 T. E. Cliffe-Leslie (1881), p. 304. But see P. Hohenberg (1972), 233, for the view that transaction costs for land sales were high and E. v. d. Walle (1979), pp. 128, 136–7, for a critique of the population stagnation theory. It is a fallacy often found in the literature that partible inheritance itself creates small holdings. It is population increase, coupled with, and possibly caused by, such a system of inheritance, which does so. H. J. Habakkuk (1955) 3; Lutz B. Berkner (1976), 71–95; L. Berkner and F. F. Mendels (1978), 209–23.

21 M. Boserup (1963), pp. 209–15.

22 Braudel and Labrousse (1970), pp. 142–4; L. de Lavergne (1877), p. 307; F. F. Mendels (1978), 789.

23 Sée (1942), p. 180.

24 Emmanuel Le Roy Ladurie (1974), esp. pp. 144, 303–11.

25 C. P. Kindleberger (1964), p. 235.

26 Patrick O'Brian and Caglar Keyder (1978), p. 120 and *passim*.

27 J. C. Toutain (1961).

28 Martin Gerard (1966), pp. 109–28; A. Armengaud (1951), 172–8; G. W. Grantham (1975), 293–326; R. Price (1975), p. 78; Newell (1972).

29 J. Marczewski (1965), cxxxviii and cxl; O'Brian and Keyder (1978), p. 92; Toutain (1961), Part II, p. 64.

30 Cited in W. W. Rostow (1978), pp. 147, 164–5. However, some of these figures rest on very dubious foundations.

31 O'Brian and Keyder (1978), p. 91; Toutain (1961), Part II, p. 207.

32 Braudel and Labrousse (1970), pp. 155–6; Hohenberg (1972); W. H. Newell (1973), 697–731. But see J. Pautard (1965), who believed that the north grew fastest (pp. 67–8).

33 Herbert Kisch (1972), 301–2.

34 Friedrich Lütge (1963), p. 191 and *passim*. This is the best short up-to-date account of the regional differentiation of German agriculture in our period.

35 R. B. D. Morier (1881), pp. 394–441.

36 H. Winkel (1968), pp. 41–57; E. Schremmer (1963), pp. 15, 103.

37 G. Hohorst (1977) pp. 180–1, 190; G. Huck and J. Reulecke (1978), p. 65.

38 H. Haushofer (1972), p. 119. Significantly, population rise was much slower where feudal dues had not yet been commuted, as in the Münsterland, Bavaria, and Austria. Wolfgang Köllmann (1976), p. 12.

39 W. Abel (1967), pp. 301–2, 305.

40 J. A. Faber (1974), 190; Abel (1967), p. 328.

41 Lütge (1963), pp. 190–1; Haushofer (1972), p. 43.

42 Haushofer (1972), p. 47; Milward and Saul (1973), p. 77.

43 Lütge (1963), pp. 188–9; idem (1934), esp. pp. 186–7, 197–201; S. Sugenheim (1966), pp. 444 ff.

44 Karlheinz Blaschke (1967), esp. pp. 180–95; Horst Krüger (1958), p. 34; Ingrid Thienel (1973); Haushofer (1972), pp. 217–18.

45 See Chapter 5 below.

46 Köllmann (1976), pp. 12–14; idem (1974), pp. 107, 216; Wolfgang von Hippel (1976), pp. 274–5.

47 Friedrich-Wilhelm Henning (1975), p. 169.

48 Haushofer (1972), p. 47.

49 The best brief account is Ernst Klein (1973); also see W. Abel (1972), p. 32; idem (1967), p. 295; Günther Franz (1976), pp. 276–320.

50 Folke Dovring (1966), pp. 654–6; Helling (1977), esp. pp. 9, 16, 26.

51 Günther Franz (1976), pp. 309 and 518.

52 Childless couples could have apprentices to make up the family and allow the widow to run the shop, should the husband die. Michael Mitterauer (1976), pp. 79-80.

53 Eli F. Heckscher (1955), i, 216.

54 Sée (1942), p. 257.

55 Ibid, *passim*, pp. 157, 172-4.

56 Georges Livet (1974), p. 397. For Mulhouse's prohibition of cotton spinning in the city in 1754, see Robert Lévy (1912), pp. 10-11.

57 Krüger (1958), p. 34 and *passim*. To the restrictiveness of towns was added the ban by the Junkers on industrial work by their serfs in the countryside, so as to keep up the labour supply to their agricultural estates. The Electoral Mark thus became one of the few regions of Europe in which the proportion of the town population in the total fell, and in which industry regressed in the eighteenth century. Ibid, pp. 30-1.

58 K. H. Kaufhold (1976), pp. 322-5.

59 Heckscher (1955), i, 137 *passim*, 214-9; E. M. Saint-Léon (1922), esp. pp. 532, 569-596.

60 P. Léon (1970), p. 286; J. C. La Force (1965), chapter 6; S. B. Clough (1964), p. 15.

61 Wolfram Fischer (1972b), 296-314; Jürgen Bergmann (1971a), pp. 257-60; R. Forberger (1958), pp. 61, 214-15, 267-8; Hugo Wendel (1920); Eckart Schremmer (1970), pp. 240, 243; Ilja Mieck (1965), p. 57; R. Koselleck (1975), pp. 597-9; H. Freudenberger und G. Mensch (1975), p. 77; T. S. Hamerow (1966), pp. 22-4, 29.

62 Bergmann (1971a), pp. 266-8.

63 Alfred Hoffmann (1975), p. 31; Rudolf Braun (1967), 555; Henri Sée (1923), 47-53.

64 Sée (1923), p. 52.

65 Herbert Kisch (1959), 543, 557; idem (1972), pp. 350-2, 355-7, 406; W. Fischer (1972b), 322-3; H. Kellenbenz (1974), pp. 58-9; M. Garden, 'Rappel du système économique pré-industriel', in Pierre Léon (ed.), *Histoire économique et sociale du monde*, (6 vols. Paris, 1978), iii, 13 ff.

66 Eckart Schremmer (1972), 23-4.

67 Eckart Schremmer (1975), p. 17; idem (1970), pp. 345 ff.

68 W. Dlugoborski (1973), p. 29.

69 In Germany it has been estimated that in the early eighteenth century perhaps one-third of the villages had industrial employment and a hundred years later it was around two-thirds. Henning (1975), p. 157.

70 F. Braudel (1973), p. 379.

71 K.-H. Schmidt (1974), esp. pp. 721-6.

72 Otto Büsch (1971b), pp. 94, 98; I. Thienel (1973), pp. 26-7, 241-50; H. Krüger (1958), pp. 160-3, 212, 308-11.

73 J. Bastie (1971), pp. 470-5; M. Lévy-Leboyer (1964), p. 116 and *passim*.

74 For some general considerations see J. Mokyr (1976b), pp. 372-4; Frédéric Mauro (1955), 117-20; E. L. Jones (1977), pp. 494-5.

75 Sée (1923), pp. 49-51.

76 Haushofer (1972), p. 50; Kellenbenz (1974), p. 62; Schremmer (1970), pp. 494-8; also see W. Fischer (1962), p. 325.

77 Kellenbenz (1974), p. 56; J. A. van Houtte (1977), p. 264; Laurent Dechesne (1926).

78 H. Kisch (1972), *passim*; Bruno Juske (1949).
79 Blaschke (1967), esp p. 148 and *passim*, 231; Forberger (1958), pp. 54, 65.
80 Blaschke (1958), p. 187; H. Kresewetter (1980).
81 F. Redlich und H. Freudenberger (1964), 372-401.
82 Franklin F. Mendels (1972), 241-61.
83 Hla Myint (1971), pp. 120, 124-8; E. J. T. Collins (1974), p. 62; René Gendarme (1954), p. 51.
84 Mendels (1972), pp. 242, 254.
85 See also Mendels' report on his thesis (1971), 271.
86 J. Mokyr (1976a), pp. 239-52; G. Jacquemyns (1929), 11-472.
87 See Chapter 4 below.
88 Peter Kriedte (1977a), pp. 41-4. This is much the best collection of essays on the subject of proto-industrialization. The unpublished dissertation by Rudolf Boch (1977) also provides a thoughtful and critical introduction.
89 David Levine (1976), pp. 249-51.
90 E. A. Wrigley (1969), pp. 112-24; idem (1972), 255-6.
91 Blaschke (1967), pp. 190-1.
92 Kriedte (1977a), pp. 47-8.
93 Krüger (1958), p. 201; K. Hinze (1963), p. 144.
94 Kriedte (1977a), p. 53. In Russian conditions of weak urbanisation and a very restricted burgher class, putting-out entrepreneurs sometimes came from the peasant or even the landlord class. Ibid, p. 73.
95 This part of the analysis owes much to Chayanov's view of the peasant family: A. V. Chayanov (1966). Also see Daniel Thorner (1962), 287-300. The analysis assumes that the nuclear family household was normal in Europe: e.g. Peter Laslett (1965), pp. 93-5. That belief has now been strongly challenged: F. F. Mendels (1978).
96 The preceding paragraphs are largely based on Hans Medick (1977a and b). Also idem (1976) and (1976b), Peter Laslett (1976), and David Levine (1976).
97 Hans Medick (1976), p. 261; David Levine (1976), p. 253.
98 Peter Laslett (1976), p. 26.
99 Rudolf Braun (1960); E. V. Tarlé (1910); Abel (1972), pp. 50-1; Huck and Reulecke (1978), pp. 65, 68, 169; E. L. Jones (1968), 64-6; W. O. Henderson (1967a), p. 120; E. Schremmer (1972), pp. 18-21; A. Hoffmann (1971), 66 *passim*; F. W. Henning (1975), pp. 165-8; H. Kellenbenz (1974), pp. 47, 61, 71-6; J. A. van Houtte (1977), p. 258; G. Livet (1970), p. 317; Joel Mokyr (1976a), pp. 138-47; A. Klima (1974), 50; Pierre Lebrun (1948), p. 441.
100 Mokyr (1976a), pp. 24-5; E. A. Wrigley (1972), p. 250.
101 P. Deprez (1965), 608-30; F. F. Mendels (1971), p. 270 and (1975), 179-204.
102 Köllmann (1974), p. 217. For Ireland, see Almquist (1979).
103 e.g. E. A. Wrigley (1969), pp. 137-8.
104 Hohorst (1977), pp. 214-17. For Ireland, see Almquist (1979).
105 Hohorst pp. 222-4; also Wrigley (1969), pp. 162-3.
106 This was common. It means not only that population increases there are not simply the results of the alleged social effects but also that the picture of these areas as repulsive poverty traps in comparison with rural areas cannot always have been true: e.g. Wolfram Fischer (1973), 161-3.
107 Köllmann (1974), pp. 62-9; high birth-rates were connected with high death-rates, both regionally and in short-term fluctuations.
108 M. Mitterauer (1976), pp. 63-4.

109 Hohorst (1977), p. 350.

110 Otto Brunner (1956), pp. 33–61.

111 Johannes Ziekursch (1915), p. 139; Will-Erich Peuckert (1931), p. 46 and, in general, Boch (1977).

112 Mendels (1972), p. 246.

113 Haushofer (1972), pp. 51–3; Eckart Schremmer (1976), 76–8; Jürgen Schlumbohm (1977), p. 293, and Peter Kriedte (1977b), pp. 297–8; Alfred Hoffmann (1975), pp. 35–6; Pankraz Fried (1975), pp. 185–6; Köllmann (1974), pp. 77, 108; Henderson (1976a), p. 119; Sée (1923).

114 Joel Mokyr stresses this aspect, treating the products of rural industry as 'Z-goods' in the terminology of modern development theory. That sector can yield labour for a long time without raising wages, in a modified version of the 'labour surplus' economy, while profits in the modern sector remain high and make accumulation possible as long as it competes largely with the backward sector only. However, this syphoning-off of labour need not take place within the same region, but could occur in a neighbouring territory. Joel Mokyr (1976a), pp. 133 ff. Also D. M. Bensusan-Butt (1960); A. N. Argavala and J. P. Singh (1963); S. Hymer and S. Resnick (1969), 493–506.

115 Braudel and Labrousse (1970), ii, p. 252; Hinze (1963), pp. 144–5; Krüger (1958), p. 200; W. Troeltsch (1897); A. Klima (1974), p. 55; W. Zorn (1961), 422–47; V. K. Yatsounski (1965), p. 370.

116 Zorn (1961), pp. 435, 438; P. Léon (1970), p. 287; Forberger (1958), pp. 170–6.

117 U. P. Ritter (1961), pp. 240–1; Jan de Vries (1976), pp. 93–5; Violet Barbour (1966), pp. 65–70; R. W. Unger (1978).

118 Zorn (1961), p. 444; Forberger (1958), pp. 126–7: Krüger (1958), p. 268.

119 Forberger (1958), pp. 61, 126–7; Zorn (1961), p. 440; F. Braudel (1973), pp. 414–16; Herman Freudenberger (1968), pp. 422–33; Claude Fohlen (1973), p. 54.

120 H. Freudenberger (1963); also see idem (1966), 167–89; and Freudenberger and Mensch (1975); also J. Schlumbohm (1977), pp. 200–1; A. Klima (1962), p. 478. Somewhat confusingly, Freudenberger and Mensch offer two contradictory definitions of a 'proto-factory', see pp. 52–3 and 68.

121 P. Léon (1970), pp. 112–13; J. Lough (1969), 222–47; Charles W. Cole (1939).

122 Charles W. Cole (1943), p. 119.

123 It may be worth noting that in 1711 the Abbeville management was still Protestant. The manager was Dutch, the two under-managers English and Genevan, and seven out of the ten foremen were Dutch. Germain Martin (1971), pp. 68–75, 413.

124 Ibid., pp. 216 ff.; C. W. Cole (1939), p. 119 and *passim*; W. C. Scoville (1960).

125 A. Rémond (1946).

126 G. Livet (1970), p. 319.

127 U. P. Ritter (1961), pp. 76–89; Krüger (1958), pp. 206–8, 236.

128 Schremmer (1970), p. 643.

129 Krüger (1958), pp. 262, also p. 75.

130 Robert J. Bezucha (1974), chapter 1; E. Pariset (1902); Maurice Garden (1970); Braudel and Labrousse (1970), ii, p. 252; Pierre Cayez (1980).

131 Bezucha (1974), p. 25.

CHAPTER 3

1 D. S. Landes (1969a), p. 138.

2 François Crouzet (1972), pp. 104-4, 121-3; M. Lévy-Leboyer (1964); also see pp. 174-5 below.

3 Immanuel Wallerstein (1974).

4 Jan Dhont and Marinetta Bruwier (1973), p. 331 ff.; N. Caulier-Mathy (1971); N. J. G. Pounds and W. N. Parker (1957), pp. 131-3.

5 B. R. Mitchell (1976 ed.), Table E1.

6 Jan Craeybeckx (1970a), p. 197.

7 J. H. Clapham (1928), p. 57.

8 In 1811 output of iron per head was 10-11 kg. in Belgium, compared with 4 kg. in France and 20 kg. in Britain. Craeybeckx, p. 197.

9 Dhont and Bruwier (1973), pp. 338 *passim*; Milward and Saul (1973), pp. 443-4; J. Mokyr (1974), 368; Paul Schöller (1948), 579 ff.

10 Milward and Saul (1973), pp. 444-5; P. Lebrun (1948), pp. 241-2.

11 Lebrun (1948), pp. 81, 130-8, 155; L. Dechesne (1926), esp. chapters 8 and 10.

12 Lebrun (1948), pp. 202 ff., 246 ff., 271, 375-6.

13 J. Mokyr (1976a), pp. 44-50; Lévy-Leboyer (1964), p. 98.

14 By 1861 87.5 per cent of steam-power was in Hainaut and Liège, only 12.5 per cent in East and West Flanders, among these four provinces. Laveleye (1881), p. 447.

15 A. Desprechins (1954); Fernand Leleux (1969).

16 J. Dhont (1969), pp. 15-52.

17 Dhont and Bruwier (1973), pp. 347-50; Lévy-Leboyer (1964), pp. 59, 87; Mokyr (1974), p. 366; F. -X. van Houtte (1949), pp. 101, 131, 161, 170.

18 Lévy-Leboyer (1964), p. 108.

19 Henri Pirenne (1948), vii, pp. 126-9.

20 A calculation of 1868 showed Belgian glass-making costs to be lower than the British in 10 out of 11 cost items, only coal being cheaper in Britain. T. C. Barker (1977), p. 118, also pp. 191-2; R. Chambon (1955); Craeybeckx (1970a), p. 199.

21 Statistics representing this kind of thinking have recently been put together with great skill by Paul Bairoch. Limiting ourselves to the countries of Inner Europe, and converting to a per capita basis, the results are as follows:-

Per Capita indicators of industrial power in certain European countries, c.1860

	Pig iron	Raw cotton consumption	Coal and brown coal	Fixed Steam per	Railway network,
	kg.	kg.	kg.	1000 inh	km.
UK	131.6	15.1	2697	24.3	0.583
Germany	13.3	1.5	422	5.5	0.322
Belgium	71.3	3.0	2030	21.1	0.368
France	25.8	2.5	240	4.9	0.251
Switzerland	5.6	5.6	16	4.0	0.436

Paul Bairoch (1976b), pp. 171, 270-3. Also see E. A. Wrigley (1962), *passim*.

22 P. Lebrun (1972), pp. 141-86.

23 Ch. Terlinden (1922), 1–39; R. Demoulin (1938), Chapter 3, 4 and 5; Rondo Cameron (1967c), pp. 129–50; Bertrand Gille (1973), iii, 266–7.

24 Low wages as a factor favouring growth, particularly compared with Holland, have been stressed by Joel Mokyr (1976a), pp. 166 ff.; and (1974), pp. 376 ff.

25 Some representative Belgian annual growth-rates, 1850–75:

Coal (tons)	3.8%
Pig iron (tons)	6.8%
Steel (tons)	17.9%
Glass (value)	6.6%
Steam-power installed	9.0%
Railways (in place)	8.4%

Cameron (1967c), p. 148.

26 Pireene (1948), pp. 165–6, 363–6; Milward and Saul (1973), pp. 450–2.

27 See the map in Marcel Gillet (1969), p. 181. Also Pounds and Parker (1957), pp. 91–4, 141, 144.

28 J. Lestocquoy (1946), pp. 322–5; Lévy-Leboyer (1964), pp. 303–19; Marcel Gillet (1973); M. Wolf (1972), 289–316; René Gendarme (1954); Pounds and Parker (1957), pp. 147–51;

29 Braudel and Labrousse (1976), 578. Also see C. P. Kindleberger (1964), p. 261; M. Gillet (1969).

30 Tihomir J. Markovitch (1976), 648–9, 653; A. L. Dunham (1955), p. 285.

31 For Douglas, see Charles Ballot (1923), pp. 178 ff.

32 B. Gille (1970, p. 38; Lévy-Leboyer (1964), p. 129; Claude Fohlen (1956), pp. 175 ff.

33 Dunham (1955), p. 284 and *passim*; Lévy-Leboyer (1964), pp. 166, 168.

34 Ballot (1923), pp. 42 ff.; Philippe Guignet (1979); Charles Engrand (1979).

35 Lévy-Leboyer (1964), p. 73; R. Gendarme (1954), map on p. 64; Pierre Deyon (1979), 83–95.

36 Lévy-Leboyer (1964), p. 95. The total number of spindles in the Nord in 1849 had risen to 550,000, with some more in Picardy. Clapham (1928), p. 66.

37 Colin Heywood (1977), p. 24; C. Fohlen (1956), pp. 228 ff.

38 K. Lestocquoy (1948), p. 100.

39 R. G. Geiger (1974), p. 213. Also Pounds and Parker (1957), pp. 170–7.

40 Ibid., pp. 216–17; R. Gendarme (1954), map on p. 60.

41 Gille (1970), pp. 35–43; Guy Palmade (1972), p. 137; M. Gillet (1969), p. 199; R. Gendarme (1954), pp. 178–83.

42 Around 1860, 37 streams beside the Wupper had water-wheels in the Kreise Remscheid and Lennep. In 1836, according to one report, there were 381 mills, grinding works, and forges driven by water-power in an area of 10½ square miles. Hermann Ringel (1966), p. 5.

43 In 1804, of 10,230 families in Kreis Lennep, 6,761 (66%) depended on industry and transport, and only 2,469 (24%) on agriculture. The rest were described as officials, paupers, etc. Ibid., p. 34. Jülich and Berg's industrial exports of 8,234,000 thaler in 1773–4 were divided as follows:

Cotton and linen	3392	)5315	(64.5%)
Woollen	1923		
Iron	1942	)2827	(34.3%)
Brass	855		

Wolfgang Zorn (1961), p. 424.

44 Norman J. G. Pounds (1968), pp. 22–3, 38–9; Bruno Kuske (1931), pp. 34, 49, idem (1949), pp. 2–3, 127–8; W. O Henderson (1967), pp. 26–7; Fritz

Schulte (1959); Guy Thuillier (1961), 878.; Gerd Hohorst (1977), pp. 193–7; Pounds and Parker (1957), pp. 46–50.

45 Ringel (1966), pp. 73–6.

46 Walter Dietz (1957).

47 Herbert Kisch (1972), p. 337; Walter Dietz (1977).

48 Herbert Kisch (1959), pp. 555–6; J. Reulecke (1980); Max Barkhausen (1974), 212–73. The privileges of the Barmen and Elberfeld guild of weavers were abolished in 1783.

49 Dietz (1957), pp. 118–19; G. Huck and J. Reulecke (1978), pp. 148–52; Kisch (1972), pp. 399–400; but see Joachim Kermann (1972), p. 200.

50 J. Reulecke (1977), pp. 51–4; Heinrich Brauns (1906), pp. 2–4; H. Kisch (1962–3), 304–27; Pierre Benaerts (1933), pp. 21–2.

51 Reulecke (1977), p. 56; Ringel (1966), p. 64; Wolfgang Hoth (1975), p. 226.

52 Ringel (1966), pp. 156–7; also Hoth (1975), pp. 167 ff.

53 Reulecke (1977), pp. 66–9.

54 W. Köllmann (1974), pp. 250–60; H. G. Steinberg (1967), pp. 49–51; W. Brepohl (1948).

55 The first steam-engine in a Ruhr colliery, at the Vollmond pit near Bochum, put up in 1799, was British. Wooden tubbing was introduced in 1853 by Saxon and Belgian engineers, cast-iron tubbing in 1855 in Mulvany's 'Hibernia' colliery. Paul Wiel (1970), pp. 151–2.

56 There is a large literature. Among the most useful works are Paul Wiel (1970) and idem (1963); Pounds (1968); Steinberg (1967) and idem (1965), 175–244.

57 An estimate of 1826 put the share of Alsace in the upstream Rhine traffic at 1/20. Paul Leuillot (1959), ii, 265, 294–8. The Rhone–Rhine canal, finished after many difficulties in 1832, did not even lower the price of coal as much as had been hoped. Lévy-Leboyer (1964), p. 321.

58 Palmade (1972), p. 98; E. Juillard (1968), p. 39. Also, in general, Robert Lévy (1912), pp. 14 ff., 20 ff., 210 ff.

59 G. Livet (1970), pp. 318–19; Lévy-Leboyer (1964), pp. 75–8, 87, 94; Robert Lévy (1912), pp. 7–9; Serge Chassagne (1979); Pierre Caspard (1979).

60 Leuillot (1959), pp. 357 ff., 378–80, 402; F. L'Houillier (1970), p. 404; Roger Price (1978), p. 103; C. Fohlen (1956), pp. 208–20; Robert Lévy (1912).

61 Leuillot (1959), pp. 347–9; L'Houillier (1970), pp. 407–8; Claude Fohlen (1970), p. 207.

62 Dunham (1955), pp. 270, 276–82.

63 S. D. Chapman (1972a), p. 21; W. E. Rappard (1914), p. 43 and *passim*; Anne-Marié Piuz (1972), pp. 533–41; J.-F. Bergier (1974), pp. 61 ff.

64 Milward and Saul (1973), pp. 455–6; B. M. Biucchi (1973), iv/2, p. 647; Lévy-Leboyer (1964), p. 180; W. Bodmer (1960), pp. 280–3, 338–9; Rappard (1914), p. 199; J. -F. Bergier (1974), pp. 88 ff., 110.

65 Béatrice Veyrassat-Herren (1972), p. 492; W. Bodmer (1960), pp. 291–5.

66 Wolfram Fischer (1972b), p. 379; Bodmer (1960), p. 327.

67 Veyrassat-Herren (1972), p. 488.

68 Ibid., pp. 483–4; Paul Bairoch (1976b), pp. 137, 174, 275–81; Chapman (1972a), p. 21; Albert Hauser (1961), pp. 194–5; J. F. Bergier (1974), pp. 130–1, 144–5.

69 Rudolf Forberger (1958), p. 36; Frank B. Tipton (1976), p. 30.

70 Helmut Zwahr (1978), pp. 30, 37; Tipton (1976), pp. 14, 31–6.

71 Forberger (1958), pp. 290-1; Martin Kitchen (1978), p. 26; Horst Blumberg (1965), pp. 25, 28, 55; Tipton (1976), p. 35; Günter Kirchhain (1973), pp. 39-42, 237.

72 Knut Borchardt (1976), p. 232; also see Wolfram Fischer (1973), p. 164; Walther G. Hoffmann (1963), p. 97; Karlheinz Blaschke (1965), pp. 69-70; H. Kiesewetter (1980).

73 Kurt Hinze (1963), pp. 80-1; Peuckert (1931), pp. 84 ff.; Comte de Mirabeau (1788), ii, 54 ff.; Kisch (1959); Horst Krüger (1958), pp. 58, 61; Hermann Fechner (1907), pp. 674 ff., 725, 735.

74 W. O. Henderson (1967b), chapter 1: 'Reden in Silesia, 1779-1802'; idem (1956), pp. 196, 201-2; Krüger (1958), p. 45; Fechner (1907), pp. 587, 613, 625; N. J. G. Pounds (1958), pp. 31-71, 97-9.

75 Toni Pierenkemper (1979); *Der Steinkohlenbergbau in Schlesien* (1947); Hans Marchand (1939), p. 81; Dr Voltz (1913); Borchardt (1976), p. 231; Lawrence Schofer, (1975), pp. 7-8.

76 Markovitch (1976), p. 651; Bertrand Gille (1970) pp. 25 ff.; Pierre Chaunu (1972), pp. 285-99; Lévy-Leboyer (1964), p. 88.

77 Another calculation puts the French total at only just over 1 million in 1810: Lévy-Leboyer (1964), pp. 28-9, 59; Ch. Ballot (1923), pp. 107 ff., 121.

78 Lévy-Leboyer (1964), pp. 69, 93; J. Vidalenc (1970), p. 417; Ch. Ballot (1923), pp. 171, 213; C. Fohlen (1956), pp. 193-203.

79 pp. 82-3 above.

80 Lévy-Leboyer (1964), pp. 133, 142; Guy Palmade (1972), p. 61; C. Fohlen (1956), pp. 186-8.

81 Gille (1970), p. 54.

82 Barrie M. Ratcliffe (1978), pp. 77-8; Louis Gueneau (1923), pp. 49-50; A. L. Dunham (1971), pp. 17, 263-7.

83 Lévy-Leboyer (1964), pp. 305, 314-21; Claude Fohlen (1970), p. 208; Pounds and Parker (1957), 86-8.

84 Dunham (1955), pp. 119 ff.; Gerd H. Hardach (1969), p. 70; Bertrand Gille (1968), p. 94; E. A. Wrigley (1962), pp. 47-8. Also see F. Caron (1979), pp. 428-30.

85 R. Price (1975), p. 128; Lévy-Leboyer (1964), pp. 51, 95, 384; Kindleberger (1964), p. 256; J. F. Gravier (1964), p. 152; Claude Fohlen (1966), p. 143. For Berlin, see O. Büsch (1971b); L. Baar (1966); Ingrid Thienel (1973); Stefi Jersch-Wenzel (1971a); Max Krause (1902); J.-F. Gravier (1947), esp. pp. 134-5, 139-44.

86 E. Klein (1974), pp. 753-74; idem (1970); Henderson (1967b), chapter 4: 'The State coalmines of the Saar, 1740-1870'; Ernst Jüngst (1931), p. 468; Henderson (1956), pp. 203-5; Peter Borscheid (1978).

87 'Modern industrialization is . . . largely the rise in the share of the new industries, the first of which were ushered in by the Industrial Revolution in England in the second half of the eighteenth century with mechanised cotton textiles . . . iron and steam power.' S. Kuznets (1965), p. 195.

88 The following paragraphs owe much to Milward and Saul (1973), pp. 89 ff. and 185 ff., and D. S. Landes (1969a), pp. 211 ff.

89 B. R. Mitchell (1976).

90 Bairoch (1976b), Table 54, p. 173.

91 In the 1870s it could still compete in South Russia and at the end of the century in Berlin. R. Fremdling (1975), pp. 61-3.

92 See pp. 129-30 below.

93 Landes (1969a), p. 221. The figures are based on Mulhall and particularly those for 1850 should be read as broad estimates only.

94 Gabriel Jars had apparently suceeded in smelting with a mixture of coke and charcoal in 1769. Pierre Léon (1961), p. 28.

95 Hans Mottek (1964), ii, p. 98 *passim*; Kirchhain (1973), *passim*.

96 C. Heywood (1977), Table 3.

97 e.g. Hans Mauersberg (1966), pp. 76-80, 100-2; P. Benaerts (1932), p. 385.

98 'Regional economy is a science of decision. It presupposes the determination of aims, the use of means and the choice of the most effective instruments to achieve those aims.' J. R. Boudeville, quoted in J. R. Meyer (1968), p. 44.

99 J. Mokyr (1976b), p. 390; idem (1976a), p. 208.

100 Chapter 1, p. 31 above. Also see Krüger (1958), p. 55; Kisch (1972), p. 369; B. Kuske (1949), pp. 12, 108-9; 118-19; Alfred Hoffmann (1975), p. 32; Joseph Harrison (1978), p. 7; A. Pred (1962), pp. 44 ff.

101 Lloyd F. Reynolds (1969), 89-103; E. L. Jones and S. F. Woolf (1974b), pp. 13-15.

102 Chapter 5 below.

103 H. J. Habakkuk (1955).

104 E. Schremmer (1978), 205-33; Paul B. Huber (1979), pp. 27-53; Wolfgang Zorn has developed the interesting notion of dividing the influence, as existing in 1820, into 'structure', the historically transmitted stable element, and 'Standort', or location, as the mobile element, affected by capital and entrepreneurship (1966), p. 353.

105 W. Dlugoborski (1973a), p. 4; E. A. G. Robinson (1969b), pp. 5-6; G. Hohorst (1977), pp. 330-1; Wolfram Fischer (1973), p. 159; Karl-Georg Faber (1968), pp. 396-7, 401. In fairness, it should be admitted that Salter takes into account historical endowment as a 'gift of the past', akin to a 'gift of nature'. W. E. G. Salter (1960), Chapter 4.

106 G. H. Borts and J. L. Stein (1968), pp. 159-97; F. Voigt, K. Otto, G. Leuterburg, H. Frerich (1968), pp. 391-2; Erich Maschke (1967), 77; K. Hinze (1963), p. 64; Sigurd Klatt (1959), p. 259; Fritz Voigt *et al.* (1969); some indication of the geographers' approach will be found in Nicholas Sánches-Albornoz (1974), 725-6.

107 W. Alonso (1968), pp. 337-66; L. H. Klaassen, P. W. Klein, and J. H. P. Pealinck (1974), pp. 99-110; Börenter (1970).

108 J. Friedman (1972); A. Pred (1967).

109 François Perroux (1965); idem (1961, 1969), Part II, chapter 2; idem (1950); also F. Voigt *et al.* (1969), p. 30; Niles M. Hansen (1965-6), pp. 3-14; Braudel and Labrousse (1976), iii/2, p. 578; J. R. Lasuen (1969); Friedrich Buttler (1975), esp. p. 30. Centre Européen (1968) discussion on p. 77; A Kuklinski and R. Petrella (1972); T. Hermansen (1972), pp. 1-67; Institut d'économie régionale (1968), p. 243. Also see B. Balassa (1962), chapter 9; Reinhard Spree (1978), p. 29. For a critical view, see M. Blaug (1964); Stuart Holland (1976), pp. 6-7.

110 e.g. W. W. Rostow (1978); p. 385: 'The coming of industrialization to the United States poses sharply a problem to be observed in a good many other nations . . . that is, the uneven regional pace of modernization within national societies . . . Especially in early stages of growth, some (regions) may be only slightly affected and left as quasi-traditional backwaters while growth proceeds rapidly in regional industrial enclaves.' Also see, e.g. W. Köllmann (1975); Fremdling, Pierenkemper, and Tilly (1979), pp. 9-26.

111 Carl-Ludwig Holtfrerich (1973); Marcel Gillet (1973); M. Wolf (1972); Michael S. Smith (1978), 142.

112 A. Gerschenkron (1970), p. 98; Stuart Holland (1976), pp. 24-5.

113 J. Ingram (1968); Douglass C. North (1966), pp. 114-17.

114 These may be services as well as industries producing commodities, as for example in port conurbations. Capital cities supplied some 'services' which the rest of the economy might not wish to have, like certain types of government activities, but had to pay for as if they were export services from the capital.

115 J. R. Meyer (1968), p. 33; C. L. Leven (1968); C. M. Tiebout (1968), p. 90; Harvey S. Perloff *et al.* (1960), p. 93; Walter Isard (1960), pp. 182-90, 270-1; Horst Siebert (1970), pp. 4 ff.; E. A. G. Robinson (1969b), p. 16; Harry W. Richardson (1969), chapter 1; Buttler (1975), pp. 113-18.

116 Again, capital cities might form the exception to this rule as far as their productive industries are concerned. They can keep on generating incomes without providing market services for the rest of society by means of taxes, *rentier* incomes, and the like.

117 Cf. the seminal article by Douglass North (1955), 243-58. Also M. L. Greenhut (1966), 461-80; Klaus Megerle (1979), pp. 105-30.

118 Ratcliffe (1978), p. 130; Heinrich Best (1979).

119 Pierre Chaunu (1964), 174. See also J. R. Meyer (1968), p. 25; Michael S. Smith (1978), pp. 139-40.

120 Klaassen, Klein, and Paelinck (1974), pp. 94-5. Also K.-G. Faber (1968), p. 405; F. Voigt (1969), p. 11.

121 W. Isard (1956), pp. 236-8; Robert Laurent (1970a); L. Baar (1966), pp. 37, 40-2; Herbert Matis (1972), p. 29; also Frank Tipton (1976), pp. 4, 147; Institut d'Economie Régionale de Sud-Ouest (1968), pp. 236-8; Michael S. Smith (1978), p. 140; Michel Han (1977), p. 177; F. Caron (1979), pp. 421-3; A. Pred (1962), pp. 32 ff.

122 K. Borchardt (1968), p. 128. Certainly Saxony, the most industrialized state, consumed less meat than the German average in 1835-65. Frank Tipton (1976), p. 38.

123 Gunnar Myrdal (1971), pp. 27 ff.; Horst Matzerath (1978) pp. 31-2, 77-9; G. Hohorst (1977), pp. 331-2; H. Matis (1972), p. 29; E. Ames and N. Rosenberg (1971), pp. 413 ff.

124 J. G. Williamson (1965); W. W. Rostow (1978), p. 439; 7th International Congress of Economic History, Edinburgh, 1978, Theme A4, esp. pp. 170 (F. Hodne and O. Gjolberg), 172 (J. G. Williamson), 177 (Paul Bairoch), 201 (L. Jörberg and T. Bengttson), 497 (C. P. Kindleberger); F. Voigt *et al.* (1969), p. 23; K. Borchardt (1976), p. 231; H. S. Perloff *et al.* (1960), pp. 51, 591 ff.; R. A. Easterlin (1960a), pp. 141-203; C. A. Roberts (1979), pp. 101-12.

125 Frank Tipton (1976), p. 12; Richard E. Caves (1965), 95-115.

126 e.g. Isard (1956) p. 17; H. S. Perloff *et al.* (1960), pp. 81-3; F. Voigt *et al.* (1960), pp. 30-1; F. Voigt (1968), 'Federal Republic', pp. 393-4; F. Buttler (1975), pp. 17 ff. Lord Kaldor has added an interesting rider to the acceleration principle. If faster growth leads to greater efficiency in the growth region, but labour is paid no more than elsewhere, labour (as in Leontief's model of the USA), will in fact get a lower efficiency wage, the returns to capital will be greater and the region will derive a cumulative advantage. N. Kaldor (1970), 337-47; also Harry W. Richardson (1973), pp. 30-3.

127 e.g. Voigt (1968), p. 397; Hansen (1965-6), pp. 5-6; H. W. Richardson (1969), p. 55.

128 Matzerath (1978), pp. 77-8; Wolfgang Zorn (1972), p. 385; J. Reulecke (1977), p. 53. But see Kindleberger (1964), p. 95, and Gendarme (1954), pp. 178-83.

129 The lengthy debate on this subject was initiated by D. S. Landes in his paper on 'French Entrepreneurship' (1949), 45-61; see also J. C. Sawyer (1951) and D. S. Landes (1951); S. B. Clough (1946); Michael S. Smith (1978), p. 141; Pierenkemper (1979); Bruno Kuske (1931), p. 39; Gras and Livet (1977), *passim*.

130 Thomas P. Hughes (1974), 126-30; also his unpublished paper 'Regional Technological Style'.

131 J. G. van Dillen (1974), p. 207.

132 See note 202 (this chapter).

133 Richard Tilly (1968), p. 490.

134 Jean Bouvier (1970), p. 343; Knut Borchardt (1972), p. 226; B. Gille (1970); L. Bergeron (1980).

135 G. H. Borts (1960), 319-47; Mokyr (1976b), pp. 380-2.

136 See chapter 4 below.

137 E. Klein (1973), p. 48; H. Krüger (1958), p. 33; Pierre Léon (1970), pp. 216, 225.

138 E. A. Wrigley (1962), p. 156.

139 E. A. G. Robinson (1969), p. 10; Jörberg and Bengttson (see note 123 this chapter), pp. 205-6; D. Saalfeld (1974), pp. 419 ff.; H. Krüger (1958), p. 317; Mokyr (1976a), pp. 166 ff.; R. Forberger (1958), p. 69; Z.-W. Sneller (1929), 196.

140 J. H. von Thünen (1842, 1966); Heinz Haushofer (1972), pp. 153 ff.; International Economic History Association (1978), pp. 352-3; Bruno Kuske (1931), p. 37; Gendarme (1954), pp. 55 ff.; W. Isard (1956), pp. 7-10; P. Benaerts (1933), p. 525.

141 Knut Borchardt (1968), p. 127; F. Voigt (1968), p. 397; Gendarme (1954), p. 157; Pierenkemper (1979) and Peter Borscheid (1979). In Saxony and in the French Nord, it can clearly be shown, some districts inside the region actually lost population in these shifts: Blaschke (1965), pp. 76-7.

142 Douglass North (1955), p. 254; Gendarme (1954), p. 66 *passim*.

143 Gunnar Myrdal (1956), p. 100; International Economic History Association (1978), Maczak, p. 10.

144 Krüger (1958), p. 43; G. Martin (1971), p. 303; Hans Mauersberg (1964), p. 186; H. Winkel (1968), pp. 32-3; Jean Vial (1967), i, 14, 16, 60-2.

145 Borchardt (1976), p. 231; Mokyr (1974), p. 327; R. Price (1975), p. 120; Lévy-Leboyer (1964), pp. 301, 314; E. A. Wrigley (1962), pp. 3-8, 24, 95 ff., 134 ff.; Pounds and Parker (1957), p. 141.

146 e.g. H. S. Perloff *et al*. (1960).

147 E. Maschke (1967), p. 77; L. Baar (1966), p. 73; Otto Büsch (1971b); pp. 102-3; P. Benaerts (1933), p. 518.

148 See chapter 4 below.

149 H. Matis (1972), p. 30.

150 S. Groenman (1968), pp. 18-19; discussion, p. 84.

151 F. Voigt *et al*. (1969), pp. 8, 29.

152 Jean Valarché (1969); A. Gerschenkron (1977), pp. 45-6; Pavel Hapák (1978), pp. 321-4; Marc Auffret, Michel Hau, M. Lévy-Leboyer, in *7th International Economic History Conference* (1978), p. 227.

153 Borchardt (1976), p. 231; Pankraz Fried (1975); Kindleberger (1964), p. 227; W. O. Henderson (1967a), p. 86.

154 Institut d'Économie Régionale (1968), p. 244.

155 F. Crouzet (1972), p. 108; Stuart Holland (1976), pp. 76 ff.

156 P. Léon (1970), pp. 154-5.

157 See map in ibid., p. 156.

158 L. Girard (1966), p. 218; J. A. Houtte (1965), p. 104.
159 R. Price (1975), p. 8.
160 P. Léon (1970), p. 155; Ringel (1966), p. 38.
161 Lévy-Leboyer (1964), p. 290.
162 Milward and Saul (1973), p. 441; W. O. Henderson (1967b), pp. 47–50; R. Koselleck (1967), pp. 630; Ringel (1966), pp. 41, 48–53; Paul Thimme (1931); U. P. Ritter (1961), pp. 145–8; Paul Schöller (1948), p. 562.
163 L. Girard (1966), p. 220.
164 Despite its importance, it was unusable for an average of 160 days in the years 1839–40, Lévy-Leboyer (1964), p. 321. Also cf. R. Price (1975), p. 17; P. Leuillot (1959), ii, 228–36.
165 A. L. Dunham (1955), chapter 3; J. H. Clapham (1928), chapter 5.
166 Jan de Vries (1976), p. 173.
167 See the map in M. Gillet (1973), p. 399.
168 W. O. Henderson (1965), p. 197; U. P. Ritter (1961), p. 141; Wolfgang Zorn (1964), p. 102; Otto Most (1967), p. 42; Richard H. Tilly (1978), p. 413.
169 P. Wiel (1970), pp. 348–9; E. F. Heckscher (1955), i, 68–70; G. Livet (1970), p. 326; E. Juillard (1968), pp. 32, 137; maps in F. Lütge (1968), pp. 150–1; J. F. E. Bläsing (1973), pp. 36–72; P. Benaerts (1933), p. 296.
170 e.g. Kindleberger (1964), p. 20.
171 R. Fremdling (1975), pp. 73–4.
172 Paul Bairoch (1967b), p. 28.
173 Above p. 108.
174 Clapham (1928), p. 339.
175 Traffic existed in and between the industrial regions. Agricultural regions were still liable to bankrupt the lines laid through them, and the same was true of the Continent, and is still true today. See the maps on pp. 17 and 24 in Hans Dieter Ockenfels (1969).
176 Anne-Marie James (1965) p. 123. But see chapter 4, note 51 below.
177 See chapter 4 below.
178 L. Girard (1952).
179 See map in H. Kellenbenz (1976), 371; W. Zorn (1972), pp. 282–3; P. Benaerts (1933), pp. 297–305.
180 Fremdling (1975), pp. 108–9, 162–4. In France, up to 50 per cent of the final price of metal goods was made up of transport costs, and coal doubled its price in 48 km. by road, 100 km. by water. R. Price (1975), pp. 109, 120.
181 Fremdling (1975), pp. 76, 80–2; Lévy-Leboyer (1964), pp. 323, 389, 407; M. Kitchen (1978), pp. 51–2; Hans Mauersberg (1964), p. 190; C. P. Kindleberger (1975a), 273–4.
182 Lévy-Leboyer (1964), pp. 383–4.
183 In Prussia, coal represented 1% of railway ton-kilometres carried in 1850 and 30% in 1870, Fremdling (1975), pp. 70–2, 90. Also see Mitchell and Deane (1962), Table G2; R. Price (1975), p. 133; Lévy-Leboyer (1964), pp. 296, 364; Fohlen (1966), p. 148; Kindleberger (1964), p. 28.
184 Hans Mottek (1964), ii, p. 151 *passim*.
185 Milward and Saul (1973), pp. 443–4; Fremdling (1975), pp. 78–82; idem, (1979), pp. 207–11; Richard Tilly (1967), pp. 152–3; idem (1976), ii. 567; Otto Büsch (1971b), p. 91; L. Baar (1966), p. 29.
186 Monique Pinson (1965), pp. 27, 135, Tables 5, 14; Anne-Marie James (1965); S. B. Saul (1972), pp. 48–9; François Caron (1970a), pp. 330, 336; Gerd H. Hardach (1969), p. 19; Jean Vial (1967), pp. 235–8.

187 Fremdling (1975), pp. 98-9; Caron (1970a), pp. 316-17; J. Marczewski (1963), p. 130; Koselleck (1967), p. 618; R. Tilly (1978), p. 414; M. Lévy-Leboyer (1978), pp. 239, 250; idem (1964), p. 704.

188 Richard Tilly (1976), pp. 566-7.

189 Chapter 4 below. By contrast, concentration on 'national' territories which have not even such attributes of statehood as customs barriers or separate currencies, as units in which to study industrialization is likely to be particularly misleading. Michael Hechter (1971-2), 96-117, is a good example.

190 Three modern series have been constructed for this period. F. Crouzet (1970b), 56-99, and reprinted in R. Cameron (1970a); idem (1972b), 271-88; M. Lévy-Leboyer (1968a); Jean Marczewsky (1965). A further partial series has been constructed by Paul Bairoch for his comparative European study. *Commerce extérieur,* also his (1965) and (1976a). Also see T. J. Markovitch (1965) issued with Marczewski's study, and J. Marczewski (1961); Monique Pinson (1965), p. 14; O'Brien and Keyder (1978); François Perroux (1955).

191 e.g. Ralph Davis (1973), chapters 17 and 18. This premiss is sometimes disputed. Kindleberger (1975a), p. 256; Heckscher (1955), i. 197.

192 Richard Roehl (1976), 233-81; a similar line of thought may be found in J. Marczewski (1963), p. 129, and T. J. Markovitch (1976).

193 O'Brien and Keyder (1978), also Lévy-Leboyer (1968b), 281-98; J. Marczewski (1965). For some figures, see R. Price (1975), p. 96.

194 Lévy-Leboyer (1964), *passim,* esp. pp. 169-74; F. Crouzet (1972), p. 121.

195 P. Leuillot (1957), 246; Marcel Gillet (1974), pp. 319-25; J. H. Clapham (1928), p. 56; Jan de Vries (1976), pp. 250-1; Lévy-Leboyer (1964), pp. 300-1, 796; Henderson (1967a), pp. 5-6; Kindleberger (1964), pp. 26-7; F. Crouzet (1972), pp. 113-16; Claude Fohlen (1973), iv/1, 52-4; Pounds and Parker (1957), p. 141.

196 M. Lévy-Leboyer (1971). It is possible to hold the opposite view, that French agriculture was held back by a failure of urban demand to grow, Vernon W. Ruttan (1978), 714-28.

197 Dennis Sherman (1977), 717-36; idem (1974); Rondo Cameron (1970), 1418-33; M. Lévy-Leboyer (1968a); Pierre Léon (1960), pp. 164, 180; Henderson (1967a), pp. 94-5; Kindleberger (1964), pp. 80-1, 261; Claude Fohlen (1973), pp. 202-3; T. K. Markovitch (1970) and François Crouzet (1970a); M. Lévy-Leboyer (1978), p. 266. Also see Note 153 of this chapter.

198 Kindleberger (1964), p. 39; Rondo Cameron (1967b), p. 117; Claude Fohlen (1973), pp. 221-3; Jean Bouvier (1970a), pp. 355-6; F. Crouzet (1972), p. 118. Investment as a proportion of national income had a declining tendency in the second half of the nineteenth century, Lévy-Leboyer (1978), pp. 233-4, 239, and (1964), p. 705 and *passim.*

199 Kindleberger (1964), p. 9.

200 A. L. Dunham (1955), p. 433; J. Marczewski (1963), p. 129; Claude Fohlen (1973), pp. 9-18, discussion following Fohlen's 'Charbon' (1966), pp. 149-50; P. Leuillot (1957), p. 247; M. Lévy-Leboyer (1971), p. 793; F. Caron in Pierre Léon (1978), ii, 488-91.

201 W. G. Hoffmann and J. H. Müller (1959) and W. G. Hoffmann, Franz Grumbach, and Helmut Hesse (1965); E. Maschke (1967), p. 73; R. Tilly (1978), p. 386; Paul Jostock (1955), pp. 82 ff.

202 Richard Tilly (1967a), pp. 158-9; Alexander Gerschenkron (1966b), p. 12; Ernst Klein (1967), p. 100 and *passim*; Kindleberger (1975a), p. 270; U. P. Ritter (1961), pp. 128-9; Knut Borchardt (1972), pp. 217 ff.; H. Winkel (1968), pp. 12-13, 19; Ekkehard Eistert and Johannes Ringel (1971). Some capital shortage,

however, was evident in the de-industrializing regions: Wolfgang Köllman (1974) p. 37, Richard Tilly (1967a), pp. 169 ff.

203 e.g. Richard Tilly (1967a), pp. 152–3; Paul Bairoch (1976b), p. 244; W. O. Henderson (1967a), pp. 29–30; Kindleberger (1975a), p. 266.

204 Paul Bairoch (1976b), pp. 239–40.

205 Rolf Horst Dumke (1979). Also his thesis (1976).

206 Köllmann (1974), pp. 37, 212; Henderson (1967a), p. 13.

207 e.g. Wilhelm Abel (1972), pp. 68–9; Ernst Klein (1973), p. 7; Kindleberger (1975a), p. 257.

208 Blumberg (1965), p. 23. Also cf. *Wrigley* (1962), p. 86.

209 e.g. Krüger (1958), p. 112; W. Zorn (1972), pp. 379–86; Fremdling (1979), p. 277.

CHAPTER 4

1 Rondo Cameron (1972), p. 526.

2 Tom Kemp (1969), p. 4; Clough and Livi (1956), p. 339.

3 e.g. William Parker (1971), p. 141; R. Solo (1971); J. Murphy (1967), pp. 21–2; Neil W. Chamberlain (1967), p. 163; Adelmann and Morris (1979), p. 175.

4 Industrialization leads to many other changes beside the technological: factory and company organizations, management problems, trade unions, social problems, to mention but a few. All of them have their own intrinsic interest, but derive largely from local traditions, the transfer being minimal. They are not discussed further here, except in so far as their problems had wider ramifications.

5 W. O. Henderson (1954); Werner Kroker (1971).

6 David J. Jeremy (1977); Arthur Redford (1934), pp. 131–2. Belgium attempted similar legislation in 1814. Robert Demoulins (1938), p. 194. Saxony, Prussia, Austria, the Palatinate, and others prohibited the emigration of skilled workers. Kurt Hinze (1963), pp. 201–4.

7 Peter Mathias (1975), pp. 100 ff.; I. Mieck (1965), pp. 87 ff.; U. P. Ritter (1961), pp. 52 ff.

8 Margaret T. Hodgen (1952), pp. 189, 194; W. O. Henderson (1967a), p. 8; Paul Bairoch (1976b), p. 141. French chemistry was particularly important, e.g. Jacques Godechot (1972) pp. 361–2; Hans-Joachim Braun (1975), pp. 71–85; Lilley (1973), pp. 229–33.

9 Among the vast literature, see, e.g., U. P. Ritter (1961), p. 75; I. Mieck (1965), p. 108; F. Delaisi (1929), p. 42; Gerd H. Hardach (1969), pp. 69–70; Wolfgang Zorn (1964), p. 104; Roger Portal (1966), p. 818; N. J. G. Pounds (1968), pp. 76–8; R. Forberger (1958), pp. 45–51; Aubin and Zorn (1976), pp. 546–7, 964, 969; Bernard Michel (1965), 1003; A. Klima (1977), 572–3; Freudenberger and Mensch (1975), p. 32; Pierre Léon (1970), p. 114; R. E. Geiger (1974), pp. 45–51; Herbert Matis (1972), p. 73 and *passim*; Gerhard Adelmann (1969), p. 96; H. Krüger (1958), p. 40; Monique Pinson (1965), pp. 37–8; W. Zorn (1972), p. 381; Pierre Vilar (1972), p. 427; Paul Guichonnet (1972), p. 551; Fremdling (1979), p. 227; D. M. Smith (1968), p. 383; Crisp (1976), p. 62; Schulze-Gävernitz (1899), pp. 81–95; Léon (1978), iii, 551–2; Wrigley (1962) p. 20; W. Fischer (1962), pp. 118, 215.

10 A. L. Dunham (1955), p. 129.

11 Chapter 3 above. Also J. J. Murphy (1967), pp. 10–11; Paul Bairoch (1976b), p. 27.

12 Jennifer Tann and M. J. Breckin (1978).

13 P. H. Clendenning (1977); R. Munting (1978); W. O. Henderson (1967a), pp. 211-3; P. I. Lyashchenko (1949), p. 424.

14 Peter Mathias (1975), esp. pp. 106. 112; idem (1972), pp. 504-5, and W. Fischer in discussion, p. 511; J. R. Harris (1978), esp. pp. 227-8. But see I. Svennilson (1964); N. Rosenberg (1976), p. 198.

15 J. J. Murphy (1967), p. 10.

16 Walter F. Willcox (1969b), p. 63, also pp. 640-4; S. Kuznets (1966), pp. 35-8; Paul Bairoch (1976b), pp. 23-4; Léon (1978), iii, p. 169, iv, p. 67.

17 Bairoch (1976b), p. 18; UN, *The World Population Situation in 1970* (NY 1971), p. 4. quoted in Hohorst (1977), p. 87.

18 B. R. Mitchell, in *Fontana Economic History* (1973), iv/2, Population Table 1. See also Milward and Saul (1973), Table 4, p. 119, though the reference for that in the essay by Glass and Grebenik in the CEHE vi/1, seems to be in error. P. Léon (1970), pp. 41-2, 215, 232; E. A. Wrigley (1969), p. 153; Carlo M. Cipolla (1972), pp. 101, 103; Marcel Reinhard, André Armengaud, Jacques Dupâquier (1968), chapters 12 and 13, p. 681; Nadal (1973), p. 533; Armengaud, (1973), pp. 29-30, 38 ff.; Blum (1961), pp. 278-9.

19 This seems to be favoured, e.g., by J. D. Chambers (1972), esp. pp. 100-6.

20 M. W. Flinn (1974), pp. 285-318; H. J. Habakkuk (1971).

21 e.g. D. B. Grigg (1976), pp. 135-76; Easterlin (1967), p. 99.

22 Good summary tables will be found in D. V. Glass and E. Grebenik (1966), pp. 61-2.

23 So do those of the eighteenth century. For the telling regional differences in Italy, see Reinhard, Armengaud, and Dupâquier (1968), p. 222; for the German coalfield, Wrigley (1962), pp. 10-11.

24 Jacques Dupâquier (1978), pp. 143-55; Köllmann in discussion to his 'Demographische Konsequenzen der Industrialisierung in Preussen', in Léon, Crouzet, Gascon (1972), pp. 282-3.

25 Folke Dovring (1966), pp. 604-6.

26 Above, chapter 2.

27 Thus in Saxony, while total population rose from 1,018,000 to 1,856,000 or by 82 per cent between 1750 and 1843, the classic age of proto-industry, the population classified as 'Bauern' remained constant at 250,000. Blaschke (1967), pp. 190-1.

28 Reinhard, Armengaud, and Dupâquier (1968), p. 385.

29 Wilhelm Abel (1962), pp. 274, 303; idem (1972), pp. 10, 31; Ernst Klein (1973), p. 5; G. Hohorst (1977), p. 126.

30 Lawrence Schofer (1975), p. 19; Hohorst (1977), pp. 131, 149; Schissler (1978), pp. 174-9; W. R. Lee (1979a) and (1979b).

31 Peter Borscheid (1978), p. 174; Ernst Klein (1973), pp. 45-7; M. Bergmann (1967); Walter Achilles (1975), p. 121; Wrigley (1969), pp. 155-6; W. Köllmann (1974), p. 106; idem (1976), p. 14; idem (1972); F. Burgdörfer (1969), ii, 316-17; V. Hippel (1976); Benaerts (1933), p. 557.

32 P. Léon (1970), p. 216; S. Helmfried (1974).

33 P. Borscheid (1978), p. 167; Edgar M. Hoover (1969), p. 354; G. K. Zipf (1946).

34 *Wealth of Nations* (Everyman ed.), i, 67.

35 P. Léon (1970), pp. 226-7, 378-9; E. Klein (1973), p. 6; W. Köllmann (1976), pp. 27-8; Blaschke (1967), pp. 113-16; Krüger (1958), pp. 52, 121, 159; H. Haushofer (1972), p. 124; H. Fechner (1907), pp. 125-7; Stefi Jersch-Wenzel

(1971a); Wladyslaw Rusinski (1973), p. 84; Hermann Freudenberger (1966), p. 171; T. S. Hamerow (1966), p. 83; Forberger (1958), pp. 38–45; L. Baar (1966), p. 14; Werner Conze (1969), pp. 75, 81; K. Hinze (1963), pp. 33 ff;. 83 ff., 129–30, 204–6, 237–9; H. Kisch (1959), p.545; Bergier (1968), pp. 9–10.

36 Peter I. Lyashchenko (1949), pp. 420, 587; V. V. Obelensky-Ossinsky (1969), pp. 556 ff.

37 Gino Luzzatto (1969), p. 206; Geiger (1974), p. 214; I. Mieck (1965), p. 17; Klaus Goebel (1977), pp. 102–3; Hartmut Sander (1977); I. Thienel (1973), pp. 96–100; Paul Leuillot (1959), ii, 11–15.

38 Paul Bairoch (1976b), pp. 111–14; Henderson (1967a) p. 43; Haushofer (1972), p. 125, Lawrence Schofer (1975), p. 19; Köllmann (1976), pp. 27–9; idem (1972).

39 Immigration into Russia

		From Germany	From Austria
(000)	1861–90	1046	700
	1891–1915	325	132

Obolensky-Ossinsky (1969), p. 569.

40 See chapters 7 and 8 below.

41 H. G. Steinberg (1976b), pp. 49–51; Lothar Baar, in *Econ. Hist. Assoc.* (1978), p. 94; Köllmann (1976), pp. 17–27; idem (1974), pp. 171–3; N. J. G. Pounds (1968), pp. 128–30; P. Wiel (1970), pp. 69 ff.; Milward and Saul (1973), p. 149.

42 W. Dlugoborski (1973), pp. 43–4, 49; idem (1975), p. 126; Lawrence Schofer (1975), pp. 24–5; Karlheinz Blaschke (1965), p. 72; *Econ. Hist. Assoc.* (1968), Theme B.9. pp. 450–5.

43 Alice Carter (1953), pp. 159–61, 322–40.

44 Rudolf Hilferding (1968 ed.), p. 427.

45 London *Times*, 20 Feb. 1857, quoted in Donald C. Blaisdell (1966), p. 45.

46 Leland Hamilton Jenks (1971), pp. 185–6.

47 David Landes (1969b), pp. 112–27.

48 The classic study is still L. H. Jenks (1971).

49 Blaisdell (1966), p. 234.

50 Chapter 7 below.

51 Such estimates have recently been held to be 'absurd'. Platt (1980), p. 7; Henderson (1967a), p. 114; Monique Pinson (1965), p. 123; Lévy-Leboyer (1964), pp. 623, 678; H. Pirenne (1948), vii, 95; F. Crouzet (1972), p. 118; L. H. Jenks (1971), pp. 140–53; Bläsing (1973), p. 86.

52 B. Gille (1970), p. 90; C. P. Kindleberger (1964), p. 56.

53 The classic study is Rondo Cameron (1961). See also, among others, Gino Luzzatto (1969), pp. 206–9, H. Matis (1972), pp. 106–15, 165–7; Kindleberger (1964), pp. 43, 266–71; Alexander Gerschenkron (1966b), pp. 12 ff.; Anne-Marie James (1965), pp. 144–6; E. Juillard (1968), p. 93; Guy Palmade (1972), p. 175; Eduard März (1968), pp. 31 ff.; B. Gille (1970), pp. 125 ff., 164 ff.; François Caron (1970a), pp. 337–8; Rondo Cameron (1967b); L. H. Jenks (1971), pp. 170 ff., 240–5; Henderson (1967a), pp. 145–8.

54 It should perhaps be added that the Crédit Mobilier group itself was Franco-British and in part cosmopolitan. Jenks (1971), p. 176.

55 Rondo Cameron (1956), pp. 281–321; and (1961), chapter 12; F. Delaisi (1929), p. 85; C. P. Kindleberger (1975a), 277; Wrigley (1962), p. 20; Benaerts (1933), pp. 350–68.

56 e.g. Jean Bouvier (1970a).

57 R. Cameron (1967c), p. 145; Lévy-Leboyer (1964), p. 616 *passim*; Léon

(1978), iii, p. 503.

58 Kindleberger (1964), p. 56; H. Winkel (1968), p. 11; Kindleberger (1975a), p. 277; Lévy-Leboyer (1964), p. 624; Pirenne (1948), vii, p. 366; R. Cameron (1967c), pp. 130, 141; idem (1961), chapter 11; Wrigley (1962), pp. 17-19.

59 H. Winkel (1968), p. 10; Wolfgang Zorn (1972), p. 390.

60 W. Zorn (1964), p. 106; H. Winkel (1968), p. 4; E. Juillard (1968), p. 93.

61 Richard Tilly (1967a), pp. 159-62; also idem (1966); Jacob Riessner (1911), Ekkehard Eistert (1970); Wilhelm Hagemann (1931); Rondo Cameron (1956b), pp. 113-30; Rudolf Hilferding (1968), pp. 414-18; K. Borchardt (1972), pp. 222-3; Gille (1973), pp. 285-7.

62 Paul Bairoch (1976b), p. 104, also p. 101, and M. Kitchen (1978), p. 228; Guy Palmade (1972), p. 175; H. Feis (1930); but see Platt (1980) for a plea of downward revision. Against all this, the assertion that 'history provides not one case of a country which has received substantial foreign investment (in which the capital remained effectively foreign and was not accompanied by colonists) which is today generally conceded to be developed' must appear puzzling. André Gunnar Frank (1975), p. 9; K. W. Hardach (1967), p. 19.

63 Edvard Bull (1960), pp. 264, 267; Karl-Gustav Hildebrand (1960), pp. 277, 284; G. Myrdal (1964), p. 98; Cameron (1961), chapter 14; R. A. Webster (1975); Kenneth Berrill (1963), pp. 295-6.

64 H. Matis (1972), p. 168; R. A. Webster (1975), pp. 126 ff.; R. Quested (1977); Lyashchenko (1949), p. 641; Waltershausen (1931), p. 593.

65 Lyashchenko (1949), pp. 413, 491; Henderson (1967a), pp. 211-13, 223-4.

66 Olga Crisp (1967a), pp. 225-9; idem (1976), p. 203; R. Portal (1966), p. 859; Kenneth Berrill (1963), p. 297; Lyashchenko (1949), pp. 534, 556, 649, 700-13, 737; Gregory (1979), pp. 381-5; M. Falkus (1979), pp. 13-14; Milward and Saul (1977), p. 493; von Laue (1963); Sontag (1968); Kahan (1978), p. 273; Kaser (1978), pp. 471-5.

67 Lyashchenko (1949), p. 716.

68 Kindleberger (1975a), p. 486; Olga Crisp (1953-4), pp. 162-3; Müller-Link (1977), pp. 275, 301, 322-38.

69 F. C. Lane (1975), p. 15; also B. Supple (1973), iii, p. 308; W. Dlugoborski (1980); E. Schremmer (1978), pp. 206-7.

70 Wolfgang Zorn (1972), p. 381; idem (1964), p. 100; P. Borscheid, *Textilarbeiterschaft*, p. 198; I. Mieck (1965), pp. 19-20; E. Heckscher (1955), i, pp. 73, 77, 82, 462-3. However, the abolition of the internal customs barrier between Austria and Hungary in 1850 seems to have made little difference. Thoms. F. Huertas (1977), pp. 19-25; Lévy (1912), pp. 14-18; 205; W. Fischer (1962), pp. 34 ff., 68 ff., 196 ff.; Supple (1973), iii, p. 338; Benaerts (1933), pp. 121-2; Fink (1968), p. 8; Brusatti (1973), pp. 32, 112.

71 Rolf H. Dumke (1978).

72 H. R. C. Wright (1955).

73 Pierre Lebrun (1972), p. 169.

74 Maurice Lévy (1952), pp. 145 ff.

75 R. Fremdling (1975), esp. pp. 114 ff., 124-61; H. G. Sternberg (1967), pp. 186-8; H. Kellenbenz (1976), p. 372; Richard Tilly (1966), pp. 484-97.

76 e.g. Lyashchenko (1949), pp. 334, 556, 585; Henderson (1967a), pp. 224-6.

77 Alec Nove (1972), pp. 86-7; P. Léon (1970), p. 111; K. Hinze (1963); R. Forberger (1958); I. Mieck (1965), p. 150; P. Léon (1960), p. 180; F. B. Tipton

(1976), p. 146; G. Martin (1971); Charles Ballot (1923); E. Heckscher (1955), i, pp. 172-3; Vilar (1958-9), pp. 113-16; Enciso and Merino (1979);   La Force (1965), esp. chapters 3 and 4.

78 Ernst Klein (1976), pp. 112-13; Alexander Gerschenkron (1966a), 711; Otto Büsch (1971b), p. 14 and idem (1962).

79 R. Portal (1966), p. 824; Kindleberger (1964), pp. 20, 279; B. M. Ratcliffe (1978), pp. 80-1, 88; Francesco Vito (1969), p. 213; Müller-Link (1977), pp. 85-7; La Force (1965), p. 167.

80 Jordi Nadal (1972), 204; Wolfram Fischer (1972), p. 300; idem (1962), pp. 41-5, 67-72; R. Tilly (1966), pp. 137-8; E. Juillard (1968), pp. 32, 137; Freudenberger (1967). For other examples see Herr (1958), p. 127; Ringrose (1970), pp. 138-9.

81 Of course, this is largely an illusion, arising from observing states that consisted largely of a single industrial region without a hinterland to weigh it down. Small states which were, as it were, only hinterland, performed particularly badly, e.g. Portugal or the Balkan states. Explanations of the success of small states are therefore generally misguided as well as being implausible. S. Kuznets (1960), pp. 27 ff.

82 Anne-Marie Piuz (1972), p. 540; H. Kisch (1959), p. 555; Max Barkhausen (1974); Bruno Kuske (1949), p. 176; Kindleberger (1975a), p. 628; H. G. Sternberg (1967), p. 93; Fritz Schulte (1959); Milward and Saul (1973), p. 464; F. B. Tipton (1976), pp. 31-2. For a contrary view, see Paul Bairoch (1976b), pp. 312-13.

83 Lévy-Leboyer (1964), pp. 701, 710, 714; C. Heywood (1977), pp. 26-7.

84 Eli F. Heckscher (1921), pp. 297-301; Léon (1978), iii, p. 361. In a curious parallel, the Hungarian Governments of 1867-1914 also devoted a large share of their industrial subsidies to enterprises in the more advanced, peripheral, but non-Magyar parts of Hungary.

85 B. H. Slicher van Bath (1963), p. 277.

86 e.g. W. O. Henderson (1963) and (1967b).

87 Max Barkhausen (1974), pp. 239, 258-9; Hermann Kellenbenz (1963), p. 20; H. Krüger (1958), pp. 68, 83, 94, 112-16, 126-7; H. Fechner (1907), pp. 725-35.

88 Krüger (1958), p. 97; U. P. Ritter (1961), pp. 78 ff., 107-12; Wolfram Fischer (1963), p. 92. For Austria, cf. H. Matis (1972), pp. 110-11.

89 H. Winkel (1968), p. 14; M. Kitchen (1978), p. 91; Richard Tilly (1967a), pp. 157, 169; idem (1968), pp. 484 ff.; I. Mieck (1965), pp. 164-200; R. Koselleck (1967), p. 613; U. P. Ritter (1961), pp. 128-30.

90 Wolfram Fischer (1972), p. 291; idem (1977), p. 216; K. Hinze (1963), p. 3.

91 Paul H. Cootner (1963).

92 e.g. J. Harrison (1978), p. 42; Lampe (1975), p. 83.

93 e.g. T. Kemp (1978), p. 89.

94 It is only by neglecting this point that some economists have made such heavy weather of the obvious theorem that the smaller the country, the larger the share of income devoted to foreign trade. Cf. S. Kuznets (1960); idem (1951), pp. 33-4; Horst Siebert (1970), p. 35; Maizels (1963), pp. 69-71.

95 Alfred Marshall (1923), p. 128, also p. 125.

96 David Ricardo (1817, Sraffa ed., Vol. i, 1970), pp. 134-8; Josiah Tucker (1776), Tract 1: 'Whether a Rich Country can stand a Competition with a poor Country (of equal natural advantages) in raising Provisions, and Cheapness of Manufactures?' p. 30 and *passim*; Gottfried Haberler (1950), p. 228.

97 Tucker (1776), p. 18.

98 According to Adam Smith, however, it was not the richer country necessarily, but the country in which incomes were growing fastest, that would have the highest wages. (1970), i, p. 62; also 48, 66.

99 James Mill (1965), pp. 174-6.

100 John Stuart Mill (1965), pp. 21, 574-5, 584-9, 604-5, 609-10. Fenoaltea's criticism of Ricardian doctrine on the grounds that it ignored the nineteenth-century reality of factor flows must therefore end with John Stuart Mill—if it was not anticipated by Tucker. S. Fenoaltea (1973), p. 740.

101 M. Longfield (1931), pp. 55-6; also see R. E. Caves (1967), p. 15 and *passim*, much the best recent summary of the debate.

102 Marshall (1923), p. 157.

103 F. W. Taussig (1927), pp. 24-5, 34-79.

104 Eli Heckscher (1950), pp. 272-300; Bertil Ohlin (1968).

105 Heckscher (1950), p. 286.

106 Ohlin (1968), pp. 160-1.

107 Ibid., pp. 24-9, 35.

108 Ibid., pp. 49 onwards.

109 Ibid., pp. 112, 171-3, 179, 188-92, 290-1.

110 J. R. Moroney and J. M. Walker (1968), p. 269.

111 Ohlin (1968), pp. 92, 155.

112 G. D. A. MacDougal (1951) and (1952); I. B. Kravis (1956).

113 Gottfried Haberler (1970), pp. 2 ff.; R. E. Caves (1967), pp. 29-30. Also see C. P. Kindleberger, *Econ. Hist. Ass.*, 1978, Theme B, 10, pp. 495 ff.

114 Harry G. Johnson (1971), pp. 149-52.

115 J. Cornwall, (1977), pp. 186-190; L. T. Wells (1972); R. Vernon (1966); I. B. Kravis (1956b); M. Posner (1961); Hufbauer (1966), pp. 29-32, and chapter 6.

116 Léon H. Dupriez, N. Bárdos Feltoronyi, G. Szapary, and Jean-Philippe Peemans (1966, 1970).

117 Léon H. Dupriez (1966b), p. 22.

118 Ibid., p. 11, also p. 17.

119 Ibid., p. 9; Georges Szapary (1966), pp. 277, 299-301, 389, 418-19.

120 Dupriez (1966b), pp. 7-8, 18, 25, 34, N. Bárdos Feltoronyi (1966), pp. 77, 113, 217, Szapary (1966), pp. 269, 285.

121 Dupriez (1966b), pp. 18, 30, 33, Feltoronyi (1966), pp. 237 ff., Szapary (1966), pp. 291, 301-2.

122 Feltoronyi (1966), pp. 52-3; Jean-Phillipe Peemans (1970), ii, p. 7.

123 Dupriez (1966b), p. 15, Feltoronyi (1966), pp. 93, 240, 244.

124 Szapary (1966), p. 301, also Peemans (1970), ii, p. 6, and F. Crouzet (1972), p. 121.

125 e.g. Milward and Saul (1973), p. 39.

126 It is theoretically possible to envisage an increase in productivity, and a share of the commodity export so large that the adverse terms of trade actually lead to a reduction in incomes following a rise in productivity. This may have happened temporarily in Lancashire, little children being exploited so that foreigners could get cheaper cotton yarn, and in Saxony. But it was highly exceptional. E. R. Caves (1967), p. 152; J. S. Mill (1965), Book III, chapter 18, Sec. 5; Jagdish Bhagwati (1958), pp. 201-5; Murray Kemp (1955), pp. 467-8.

127 E. A. Wrigley (1972), p. 240.

128 e.g. Lévy-Leboyer (1964), pp. 65, 91; W. Abel (1972), p. 9; Mokyr (1976a), pp. 101-2; L. Girard (1966), p. 282; Crouzet (1972), p. 119.

129 This was in contrast to the proto-industrial phase, in which the industrial regions, having no advantage in technology, actually tended to have lower wages than other areas. Forberger (1958), p. 235; Lévy-Leboyer (1964), pp. 112–13.

130 e. g. Arthur Redford (1934), pp. 129–30. and Dr Ure in 1836, quoted in V. A. C. Gattrell (1977), 119; Wittschewski (1892), p. 419; Lotz (1892), pp. 45, 59.

131 There are good grounds for assuming that lower wages gave an edge to industrializing economies. J. Mokyr (1974), pp. 376–80; also his (1976a), p. 46, and (1976b), p. 392; S. B. Saul (1972), p. 42.

132 Pirenne (1948), vii, 366; Veyrassat-Herren (1972), p. 488; Kindleberger (1964), p. 272; Paul Bairoch (1976b), p. 213; Redford (1934), p. 96; J.D.Chapman (1972a), p. 52; Werner Schlote (n. d.), pp. 82, 86, 92.

133 G. Myrdal (1964), p. 257.

134 Martin Kutz (1974), pp. 189–91, 212; Bodo von Borries (1970), pp. 11–12; Schulze-Gävernitz (1899), p. 121.

135 *De la monarchie prussienne*, ii, 27.

136 Quoted in Krüger (1958), p. 56. See also p. 94.

137 W. Zorn (1972), pp. 381–2; R. Munting (1978).

138 *Le Grand Espoir du XIX Siécle* (Paris, 1963), chapters 1 and 2. Szapari converts this to a classification according to relative labour costs (1966), pp. 296–300.

139 Lévy-Leboyer (1964), pp. 49, 56–7, 95, 157–9, 169–71, 174–5, 288–92, 410; Jürgen Schlumbohm (1977b), p. 279; F. Crouzet (1972), p. 122.

140 H. Matis (1972), p. 90; G. C. Allen (1929), pp. 409, 443; V. K. Yatsunsky (1960), p. 299; Leuillot (1948), ii, 389; Lévy-Leboyer (1964), pp. 114–15, 180–1; Tom Kemp (1969), pp. 23–4.

141 Fritz Voigt *et al.* (1969), pp. 16–17; W. G. Hoffmann (1958); idem (1965), p. 154; S. Klatt (1959), pp. 245–7; T. Kemp (1969), p. 26.

142 Herbert Hassinger (1964), p. 98; A. Redford (1934), pp. 94–5; Martin Kutz (1969), 179; Bowring (1840), Appx. VI–XVIII. Also, more generally, Kutz (1974), pp. 9–38; von Borries (1970), pp. 7–14, 22–33, 185–92.

143 e.g. Pierre Léon (1974), 407–32; idem (1970), pp. 178–82; W. S. Unger (1959), 210–14; Mirabeau (1788), ii, 67, 76; H. Krüger (1958), p. 56; W. Zorn (1961), p. 444; and footnote 136. this chapter, above.

144 F. B. Tipton (1976), p. 33; W. E. Rappard (1914), p. 126; H. Krüger (1958), p. 47.

145 Lévy-Leboyer (1964), p. 180. Also see Kindleberger (1964), p. 273.

146 Ernst Klein (1967), p. 90; Olga Crisp (1972), p. 442; R. Portal 'Industrialization' (1966), p. 807; W. Bodmer (1960), pp. 291, 295; Milward and Saul (1973), p. 445; A. Marshall (1923), p. 121; Lévy-Leboyer (1964), pp. 105–8. See also John James (1957), p. 419; Bowring (1840), pp. 18, 34–5, 55.

147 John Foster (1974), p. 229.

148 This was said of *c.*1854–1905. O'Brien and Keyder (1978), p. 162.

149 Herbert Hassinger (1964), pp. 112–13; idem (1964b), pp. 82–3; T. P. Huertas (1977), pp. 14–15; H. Matis (1972), pp. 89, 175, 375–80; R. A. Webster (1975), pp. 43, 50, 93; J. J. Murphy (1967), p. 13; Aubin and Zorn (1976), p. 599; Bernard Michel (1965), p. 989; Peez (1892), p. 187; Van Houtte (1949), p. 262; Schöller (1948).

150 Olga Crisp (1972), pp. 442, 450; Henderson (1967a), pp. 210–11; R. Portal (1966), p. 814; Lyashchenko (1949), p. 510; S. Strumilin (1969), p. 158; Schulze-Gävernitz (1899), p. 565.

151 N. J. G. Pounds (1968), pp. 68–9, 96–7; Borscheid (1978), pp. 72–3;

H. Matis (1972), p. 88; R. Fremdling (1975), p. 76 and *passim*; Schlumbohm (1977b), pp. 282 ff.; Voltz (1913), p. 83; Feltoronyi (1966), p. 66; Bowring (1840), pp. 28, 33–4, 53.

152 R. Dumke (1979), p. 11; Bowring (1940), pp. 19, 35–6, 53–5.

153 Dumke, ibid.

154 M. Kutz (1969), p. 191; O. Büsch (1971b), pp. 102–3; F.-W. Henning (1975), p. 161; M. Kitchen (1978), p. 58; L. Baar (1966), p. 127; K. Borchardt (1976), pp. 232–3; Robert A. Dickler (1975), pp. 286–7.

155 W. G. Hoffmann (1971, pp. 156–77; B. von Borries (1970), pp. 217, 221–3.

156 Based on M. Kutz (1974), Tables 34, 39, 58, 61. The calculations for 1833 are on a somewhat different basis, but are broadly comparable. Also see Léon (1978), iii, p. 471.

157 Based on Kutz (1974), Tables 74 and 76.

158 Ibid., pp. 204–5.

159 Ibid., Table 27.

160 Ibid., Tables 22 and 24.

161 Ibid., pp. 60–3, 69; B. von Borries (1970), Table 13 and p. 218. Yarn prices of a standard quality fell in Germany from 1.1 Pfennig per kg. in 1800 to 0.27 in 1836–8 and 0.21 in 1873–7; output per person engaged in spinning rose from 55 kg. in 1800 to 446 kg. in 1837 and 2.086 kg. in 1876. Kirchhain (1973), pp. 95, 113. It was the price fall in British exports which led the official British trade statistics to overstate greatly the British export values in those years. Kutz (1974), pp. 16 ff.; Léon (1978), iii, pp. 427–8; I. A. Glazier *et al.* (1975), pp. 12–14.

162 B. von Borries (1970), p. 217; Dumke (1979), p. 181.

163 Von Borries (1970), Table 14. There is a slight ambiguity here. Although the author seems mostly to include yarn, pig and bar iron, other metals, and skins and leather in this category, as one would expect (e.g. p. 96), yet in the price table, yarns are also included among 'textiles', Table 12, pp. 72–3; Kirchhain (1973), Table 2 and p. 234.

164 Von Borries (1970), pp. 121, 137–8.

165 Ibid., Table 45; also Benaerts (1933), pp. 224–5, 439, 489; Wrigley (1962), p. 29; K. W. Hardach (1965), p. 22; Kirchhain (1973), pp. 29–30; Bondi (1958), pp. 55, 57, 78, 87, 100, 129–30; Scheel (1892), pp. 549 ff.; Lambi (1963), p. 16.

166 Von Borries (1970), Table 46.

167 Richard Tilly (1978) quoting C. F. W. Dieterici (1849); H. Kisch (1959), p. 553; Marcel Rist (1970a), pp. 298 ff.; M. Kitchen (1978), p. 57; Lévy-Leboyer (1964), p. 169; Kindleberger (1975), p. 29; Vial (1967), p. 522; Dunham (1931, 1970), p. 191; van Houtte (1949), p. 220; Fischer (1962), p. 112. These examples could be multiplied.

168 Exactly this process has been described for Rhineland textiles, Gerhard Adelmann (1969), pp. 89–90. See also Horst Blumberg (1965), p. 30, quoting Gülich (1844); Bowring (1840), pp. 53–5.

169 Dumke (1979), p. 10; Kaufhold (1976), p. 356; Dupriez (1966a), p. 33, and Feltoronyi (1966), p. 253–7; F. Crouzet (1972), pp. 122–5.

170 J. R. Hicks (1953), esp. p. 127.

171 Dumke (1979), p. 16.

172 There is a large literature. For a sample, see Paul Bairoch (1976b), pp. 312–13; M. L. Greenhut (1966), pp. 462 ff.; G. Myrdal (1956), p. 228; Hla Myint (1958), 317–37; R. E. Caves (1967), p. 259; idem (1965) and (1971);

Douglass North (1955); idem (1961), chapters 10 and 11; Jan Tinbergen (1965), 116-25; Kindleberger (1964), p. 248; W. M. Corden (1971); K. G. Hilderbrand in *Econ. Hist. Ass.* (1978), pp. 29, 36. For similar views on Italy and Hungary, see ibid. G. Mori (p. 167), and Good and Ranki (p. 169).

173 Loc. Cit., pp. 127-8.

174 W. Schlote (n. d.), pp. 85-8.

175 Above all, Richard Tilly (1968), 179-96; K. Borchardt (1976), p. 241; for Russia, see Blackwell (1968), p. 44.

176 Cf. Forberger (1958), pp. 287-8, 300-1; H. Kisch (1962-3), esp. pp. 324-7; H. Winkel (1968), p. 22; Milward and Saul (1973), chapter 4; L. Baar (1966), p. 63; Joachim Kermann (1972), pp. 195-6; F. Mendels (1972), p. 245; Heckscher (1922), pp. 279, 306 *passim*. From the British point of view it was also a traumatic experience—the need to employ capital made redundant at the end of the war. S. D. Chapman (1979), pp. 55-6.

177 F. Crouzet (1972), p. 101; idem (1964); idem (1958).

178 This is the argument of Paul Bairoch (1976b).

179 The German equivalent of a not dissimilar idea, 'die gleichzeitige Ungleichzeitigkeit', sounds better. E. Bloch (1962), p. 104 and *passim*.

180 Paul Bairoch (1976a), p. 279.

181 Ibid., p. 307; idem (1976b), p. 155.

182 Paul Bairoch (1965), pp. 1100-7; also idem (1976b), p. 138. For other comparisons of the same kind, see e.g. Jan Craeybeckx (1970a), pp. 197-9; H. Matis (1972), pp. 25, 180-1, 332; W. G. Hoffmann (1963), p. 118; Jacques Godechot (1972), p. 37; Lyashchenko (1949), p. 673.

183 For the annual rates 1830-1913, see Paul Bairoch (1976a), p. 309, also (1976b), p. 139. For the gap in years, idem in *Economic History Association* (1978), Theme A. 4, p. 176.

184 Paul Bairoch (1976b), p. 188. In food consumption per head, however, she was caught up by the mid-nineteenth century. Also Léon (1978), iii, p. 70; Purš (1973), pp. 116-17, 162-4, 171; N. B. Ryder (1967), p. 27.

185 R. Zangheri (1974), p. 24.

186 Alexander Gerschenkron (1966b), p. 44.

187 Gerschenkron (1966b) and idem (1968b).

188 e.g. Steven L. Barsby (1969), 449-72.

189 Kindleberger (1964), pp. 183-6.

190 Werner Conze (1969), p. 81; P. Léon (1970), p. 340.

191 Some of the data on which this view is based are in Heinrich Rubner (1968), p. 472 and *passim*. Also D. M. Smith (1968), pp. 392-4; Vilar (1962), pp. 292-6; Schulze-Gävernitz (1899), p. 55; S.-E. Aström (1970).

192 This last suggestion is derived from an as yet unpublished paper by A. G. Ford. Also see Olga Crisp (1967a), p. 233, and Rondo Cameron (1967d), p. 306; R. A. Webster (1975), pp. 7-8.

193 C. P. Kindleberger (1951), 30-46; also Stephen H. Hymer and Stephen A. Resnick (1971).

194 See chapter 7 below. Also Paul Bairoch (1976b), p. 5.

195 This contradiction between Russian claims as a Great Power and her economic backwardness and dependent status increasingly dominated her political history in the nineteenth century. Laue (1960) and (1963); B. G. Litvak (1973) p. 109. Franco-British failures in the Crimea were the result of military incompetence, not lack of economic capability.

196 Tom Kemp (1969), p. 169; Clough (1964), pp. 76-81.

197 Gerschenkron (1968b), p. 161.
198 Quoted in idem (1977), p. 27; Hunecke (1978), pp. 24-5.

CHAPTER 5

1 A. Gerschenkron (1970), p. 108. Also see Irena Pietrzak-Pawlowska (1968), 183-90. For a different dividing-line between 'core' and 'border' see Liepmann (1938), p. 47.
2 Tom Kemp (1969), p. 10.
3 I. Wallerstein (1974), p. 350; Jerzy Topolski (1968), 3-12. A convenient chronological list of emancipation decrees will be found in Blum (1978), p. 356.
4 Jerome Blum (1957); M. M. Postan and John Hatcher (1978), 27-8; M. Malowist (1966); idem (1959); W. Rusinski (1968), 115-34; Stark (1934), pp. 27-8. For a slightly different interpretation, see L. Zytkowicz (1972), pp. 138-44; A. Maczak (1972), 674.
5 P. Léon (1970), pp. 67-8, also 336-41; Hermann Kellenbenz (1965), pp. 142-3; Slicher van Bath (1967), 60-1, 65; Jan de Vries (1974), pp. 169-82 and literature quoted there, W. S. Unger (1959).
6 H. Krüger (1958), pp. 26-7, 49; J. Leskiewicz (1972), 117; H. Schissler (1978), pp. 106-9; A. Maczak (1972); L. Zytkowicz (1972), pp. 147-51.
7 There is a large literature. Among the best accounts are F. Lütge (1963), pp. 119 ff.; R. B. D. Morier (1881); G. F. Knapp (1887); G. Franz (1976), p. 305; Albert Judeich (1863); K. D. Barkin (1970), pp. 23-8; A. Gerschenkron (1943), pp. 21-4; Robert A. Dickler (1975); Gerhard Heitz (1975), 45-54; Ernst Klein (1973), pp. 72-89; H. Schissler (1978).
8 Chapter 7 below.
9 J. Kahk and H. Ligi (1975); Andrejs Plakans (1975), 639-42.
10 Alicja Falniowska-Gradowska (1975), 173-5; Werner Conze (1969), pp. 77-8; Milward and Saul (1973), pp. 65-6.
11 Jerzy Topolski (1974) and (1971), 51-63.
12 Leonid Zytkowicz (1972); Janina Leskiewicz (1965); Witold Kula (1976); Wladyslaw Rusinski (1973).
13 Regina Chomac-Klimek (1975), 177-81; Julian Bartys (1968); Blum (1978), pp. 232-3; Barel (1968), pp. 141-3; Werner Conze (1969), pp. 79-80.
14 Lyashchenko (1949), pp. 309-10, 365-8.
15 Jerome Blum (1961), p. 332.
16 In practice this worked out at around 28 acres per household of 3 males (9.4 acres a head) on private land and c.45 acres (13.0-14.3) for state serfs. Vladimir P. Timoshenko (1932), pp. 50-1.
17 Blum (1961), pp. 460-1, 596-7.
18 Among a voluminous literature, see esp. Lyashchenko (1949), pp. 379 ff.; A. Gerschenkron (1966a), Julius Faucher (1881), 313-50; A. S. Milward and S. B. Saul (1977), pp. 367 ff., Haxthausen (1866), pp. 184-345.
19 By 1859 the private owners had mortgaged 66 per cent of their serfs. Blum (1961), p. 380.
20 Lyashchenko (1949), pp. 453, 518; Timoshenko (1932), p. 372.
21 A. Gerschenkron (1966b), pp. 119-21; idem (1968b), pp. 141-52, 163-5, 182-208; idem (1966a), pp. 735-5; Olga Crisp (1972), pp. 445-6; B. G. Litwak (1973), pp. 97-9; Willetts (1971), p. 114.
22 Milward and Saul (1977), pp. 62-5; Lütge (1963), p. 262; Sergij Vilfan

(1973); Jerome Blum (1948), pp. 49 ff.; Friedrich Lütge (1967), 153-70; Klima (1961), pp. 16-19; Mesaros (1961), pp. 81-4; Link (1949), pp. 48, 56, 59, 105; Stark (1934), pp. 52 ff.

23 J. Varga (1965); Ivan Erceg (1967), pp. 146-52.

24 F. Lütge (1967), p. 170; Karl Dinklage (1973), pp. 403-61; Link (1949), p. 183.

25 Alfred Hoffmann (1974), pp. 578-96; H. Matis (1972), pp. 33-42; Jaroslav Purš (1965), pp. 247-57; M. Scott Eddie (1967), p. 295; J. Blum (1948), pp. 232 ff.; I. T. Berend and G. Ranki (1973), pp. 484 ff.; idem (1974a), pp. 43 ff.; idem (1974b), pp. 42 ff.; Komlos (1979); D. Warriner (1965), pp. 11, 33; Kovacs (1961).

26 Florian Constantiniu (1973), pp. 66-82 and 83-96; Warriner (1965), p. 12; Milward and Saul (1977), pp. 68, 449-52; W. Zorn (1960), 506; Berend and Ranki (1974a), pp. 35-6, Daniel Chirot (1976), esp. pp. 92-100, 124-33; Gilbert Garrier (1978), iv, 431-2.

27 Berend and Ranki (1974a), pp. 36-9; M. Palairet (1977), 583; Warriner (1965), pp. 2-5, 14-15; Auty (1965), pp. 303, 375-6; Katus (1961).

28 e.g. Peet (1972); Blum (1978), esp. 53-6, 371-3.

29 Friedrich Vöchting (1951), pp. 68-72; K. R. Greenfield (1965), 1934; Hilowitz (1976), p. 23.

30 Milward and Saul (1977), pp. 222-30; Richard Herr (1958), pp. 99-114; Edward E. Malefakis (1970), pp. 4-5, 35 ff.; Morgado (1979), pp. 322-3; Sugenheim (1861), pp. 68-76; J. Harrison (1978), pp. 5-7.

31 R. Zangheri (1974); also see M. Boserup (1963), p. 213; Jean-Pierre Filippini (1978), iii, 546-52; Emile de Laveleye (1881), p. 470.

32 Lennart Jörberg (1969), pp. 259-60.

33 Alois Mika (1978), 225-57; A. Klima (1974), esp. pp. 52-5; idem (1959-60), 34-48, idem (1977); idem (1957); idem (1975); idem (1962); Klima and J. Macurek (1960), pp. 104-5; Peter Kriedte (1977a), p. 87; H. Freudenberger (1960), 383-406; Bernard Michel (1965); H. Matis (1972), pp. 68-9; J. Purš (1965), i, 190-6; Spulber (1966), p. 13.

34 Frantisek Dudek (1978), pp. 25-54; Bernard Michel (1965), p. 994.

35 Pavel Hapák (1978).

36 H. Matis (1972), pp. 28-9.

37 Herbert Hassinger (1964b), p. 146; S. B. Saul (1972), p. 50; J. Blum (1948), p. 42; Berend and Ranki (1974a), p. 35; Viktor Hofmann (1919); N. T. Gross (1973), iii, 248, 253-4.

38 H. Freudenberger (1974), p. 311; Miloslav Despot (1968), 141-56.

39 Colin Heywood (1977), tables 1 and 2; Eduard März (1968), pp. 15-18; R. Portal (1966), p. 806; and, in general, Thomas F. Huertas (1977) and the literature cited there.

40 H. Krüger (1958), pp. 59-61, 143, 277-80; K. Hinze (1963), pp. 80-1, 155-6; Alfred Hoffmann (1952), i, 493.

41 K.-G. Hildebrand (1958), 3-52; but see B. Boethius (1958), pp. 157-8; Eli F. Heckscher (1968), p. 178.

42 F.-X. Coquin (1978), iii, 41-4. The British figures may need some revisions. Also A. Baykov (1954), p. 139; Joseph T. Fuhrmann (1972), pp. 107-10, 248.

43 R. Portal (1950); William L. Blackwell (1968), pp. 20-3, 57 ff.; Milward and Saul (1977), pp. 357-8; Crisp (1976), pp. 60 ff.

44 Wolfgang Zorn (1961), p. 9.

45 W. O. Henderson (1967a), pp. 207-10; R. Forberger (1958), p. 9; J. Blum

(1961), pp. 308-17; Schulze-Gävernitz (1899), pp. 29-38; Tugan-Baranowski (1900), Part I, chapters 3 and 4.

46 W. L. Blackwell (1968), p. 38.

47 Lyashchenko (1940), p. 328; Henderson (1967a), p. 217; Godechot, in discussion, after 'L'industrialisation en Europe' (1972), p. 376; W. L. Blackwell (1968), p. 62.

48 S. Strumilin (1969), pp. 157-8; Lyashchenko (1949), pp. 332 ff.; Olga Crisp (1972), p. 444; Henderson (1967a), pp. 210-14; V. K. Yatsounski (1965); R. Portal (1966), pp. 813-14; W. L. Blackwell (1968), pp. 44 ff.; Schulze-Gävernitz (1899), pp. 52 ff.

49 Olga Crisp (1972), p. 444; Henderson (1967a), p. 208; Lyashchenko (1949), pp. 330, 338; Portal (1966), pp. 808-9.

50 Lyashchenko (1949), p. 337; Blackwell (1968), p. 42; J. Blum (1961), pp. 323-4.

51 Blackwell (1968), pp. 66-70.

52 Richard Herr (1958), pp. 123-4; J. C. La Force (1965).

53 Jordi Nadal (1972); J. Harrison (1978), p. 15.

54 By F. M. Nifo, quoted in Pierre Vilar (1962), ii, 10.

55 Le Roy Ladurie (1974), p. 144; Pierre Vilar (1972); idem (1962), i, 297-305; ii, 77, 109, 189 ff., 242-4; Richard Herr (1958), pp. 135 ff.; J. C. La Force (1965), pp. 15-17, 142-3; Jordi Nadal (1973), iv, 606-10; J. Harrison (1977); idem (1978), pp. 16, 58-9.

56 Gino Luzzatto (1969), pp. 221-2; K. R. Greenfield (1965), pp. 81-6, 114; F. Vöchting (1951), pp. 79-80.

57 The general case is made in Paul H. Cootner (1963), pp. 273-83.

58 Lyashchenko (1949), p. 514 (the totals do not add up in the original), p. 512. Also Joseph Metzer (1974), and idem (1976).

59 F. Delaisi (1929), pp. 54-7.

60 Lyashchenko (1949), pp. 514-15, 533.

61 Quoted in Olga Crisp (1972), p. 462.

62 Quoted in Blackwell (1968), p. 317. Also R. Portal (1966), p. 813; Müller-Link (1977), p. 27; Falkus (1979), p. 10; Léon (1978), iv, p. 165.

63 Karl Bachinger (1973), 278-322; Berend and Ranki (1973), pp. 478-80 and (1974a), p. 73; Alfred Hoffmann (1974), p. 592; V. Sandor (1956), 154.

64 Ernest Lémonon (1913), p. 24; Gino Luzzatto (1969), pp. 214, 222; Fenoaltea (1971), pp. 337-8; Milward and Saul (1977), p. 245.

65 Milward and Saul (1977), pp. 244-5; David R. Ringrose (1970), pp. 13-16; P. Léon (1970), p. 158; Richard Herr (1958), p. 131.

66 Quoted in Nadal (1973), p. 552.

67 K.-G. Hildebrand (1960), pp. 275-7; J. Lee (1969).

68 Milward and Saul (1977), pp. 440-3, 497, 532-3; Anne-Marie James (1965), p. 146; F. Delaisi (1929), pp. 57-8; Berend and Ranki (1974a), pp. 75, 80.

69 Sima Lieberman (1970), pp. 101-2; J. Nadal (1973), p. 541; John R. Lampe (1975), 3-4.

70 Olga Crisp, (1967a), pp. 233-5.

71 There is now a large literature, but see esp. Pierre Léon (1977-8), v, 477-82, vi, 98; David Herlihy, in *Economic History Association* (1978), 'A' Themes, p. 59.

72 Adna F. Weber (1968, 1899); Max Weber (1976), ii, Cap. 9, sec. 7. Also e.g. André Armengaud (1973), iii, pp. 32-4. International comparisons reach the height of absurdity with the attempt to set up mathematical 'rules' of the ratios which city populations should bear to each other and to a country's total.

73 Quoted in H. Krüger (1958), p. 260, also see pp. 280-1; F. Braudel (1973), p. 416; L. Baar (1966), p. 25; O. Büsch (1971b), p. 142.

74 K. Hinze (1963), p. 171.

75 Braudel (1973), pp. 421 ff., W. L. Blackwell (1968), p. 98; Schulze-Gävernitz (1899), p. 58.

76 Julius Faucher (1881), p. 321; J. Blum (1961), pp. 280-1, 609-11; D. Brower (1977), 74-5, 79. Also see Zorn (1970), p. 503; Chirot (1976), pp. 145-6; R. Portal (1961), 38-40; A. Gerschenkron (1977), p. 251; Thiede (1976); Rozman (1976).

77 Gino Luzzatto (1969), p. 206.

78 F. Vöchting (1951), pp. 83-4; Braudel (1973), p. 417; T. Kemp (1969), p. 165.

79 D. R. Ringrose (1970), p. 5.

80 Tom Kemp (1978), p. 134.

81 F. Delaisi (1929), pp. 55-6.

82 Ringrose (1970); idem (1973). Close proximity to a successful economy may often be a danger: Francesco Vito (1969), p. 157, and Jean Valarché (1969), p. 212; T. Kemp (1969), pp. 163-4; Michael Rau (1977), p. 183.

83 G. Myrdal (1971), pp. 27-30; idem (1956), pp. 224-5; S. Groenman (1968), pp. 18-19.

84 G. Hohorst (1977), pp. 334-5; A. Gerschenkron (1968b), p. 223; Olga Crisp (1972), p. 462; E. A. G. Robinson (1969), p. xvi; Milward and Saul (1977), pp. 382-3; R. A. Webster (1975), p. 195.

85 A. Gerschenkron (1966b), p. 360, also pp. 44-50, 353-4; *Economic History Association* (1968), 'A' Themes, Paul Bairoch, pp. 176, 179; Tom Kemp (1969), pp. 176-7. It seems that the Gerschenkron assumption that the latecomers concentrate at once on producer goods is not borne out by the data, nor is this in any sense basic to the theory. S. L. Barsby (1969). In Hungary, indeed, backwardness is seen in the concentration on food processing. Berend and Ranki (1973), p. 512.

86 J. C. La Force (1965), pp. 167, 173-5; D. Ringrose (1970), pp. xxii. 13-14, 55; Milward and Saul (1977), pp. 532-6; R. A. Webster (1975), pp. 41-2, 106.

87 R. A. Webster (1975), pp. 7-8; Henderson (1967a), p. 205; D. Ringrose (1970), pp. 138-9; J. Nadal (1973), F. Vöchting (1951), pp. 74-5; M. Palairet (1977), pp. 584-5; J. Harrison (1978), pp. 36-42; Tortella-Casares (1977).

88 Michael R. Palairet (1978); Tom Kemp (1969), pp. 163-4; E. Lémonon (1913), p. 215; S. B. Clough and Carlo Livi (1956), 345-8; Arcadius Kahan (1967), 460-77; Alois Brusatti (1965), p. 85; J. K. Siegenthaler (1973), 393-4, 397-8; Caizzi (1962), Saville (1968), p. 19.

89 Angelo Tamborra (1974), 87-120.

90 Tom Kemp (1978), p. 163; Peet (1972); Liepmann (1938), pp. 193-4.

91 Milward and Saul (1977), pp. 456, 463-4.

CHAPTER 6

1 François Caron (1978), iv, 111; Volker Hunecke (1978), p. 17.

2 H. A. Winkler (1974).

3 S. Groenman (1969), p. 32.

4 Berend and Ranki (1974a), p. 99.

5 William Ashworth (1977), 156-8; Svend Aage Hansen (1970), p. 7; Daniel

Chirot (1976), pp. 90-1, 119, 162-3; D. Kosäry (1975), 366; Berend and Ranki (1974a), p. 153; Koblik (1975), pp. 11-12.

6 Herbert Matis (1971), p. 152.

7 Richard L. Rudolph (1976), p. 19; Herbert Matis and Karl Bachinger (1973), p. 148; Ashworth (1977), p. 148; Herbert Matis (1972), p. 436.

8 K. M. Fink (1968), p. 28. For a similar picture of the regional distribution of railway lines, see Matis (1972), p. 397.

9 The argument is developed most effectively in Ashworth (1977), p. 144. Also see Paul Bairoch (1976b), p. 253; idem (1976a), p. 307; Jaroslav Purš (1973), Table 1, pp. 162-4; Matis and Bachinger (1973), p. 117; Matis (1972), pp. 180-1, 291, 330 ff.; Herbert Hassinger (1964b), pp. 112-13; N. T. Gross (1973), p. 266.

10 Thomas F. Huertas, Report on Ph.D. thesis in *JEcH* 38 (March 1978) and (1977), pp. 36-46; also Matis (1972) (1976a), p. 36; Waltershausen (1931), p. 348.

11 Paul Bairoch (1976a), p. 283; David F. Good (1974), 81; N. Gross (1968), 67; idem (1971); Matis and Bachinger (1973), pp. 124, 148; Matis (1972), p. 430.

12 Herbert Matis (1971), pp. 159 ff.; A. Gerschenkron (1977), pp. 46 ff.; D. F. Good (1974); idem (1978), 290-4; John Komlos (1978), 287-9; T. F. Huertas (1977), pp. 5-9; Eduard März (1968), pp. 57 ff., 375; Ashworth (1977), p. 145; Matis and Bachinger (1973), p. 232; Matis (1972), pp. 83, 153, 329, 441-6; N. Gross (1973), p. 269.

13 Pavla Horska (1978), p. 278; Ashworth (1977), p. 147; Matis and Bachinger (1973), pp. 220-2; Matis (1972), p. 334; Pounds (1958), pp. 131-2.

14 E. März (1968), p. 373.

15 T. F. Huertas (1977).

16 März (1968), pp. 313-14.

17 R. L. Rudolph (1976), p. 199; Matis (1972), p. 392.

18 A. Brusatti (1965), p. 70. The totals do not add up in the original.

19 Bernard Michel (1965), pp. 999-1001; D. F. Good (1977); Matis (1972), p. 370; März (1968), pp. 235-6, 271, 280, 301-2, 371; Gross (1973), pp. 258-9.

20 I. Grailer (1949), pp. 548-50; Matis (1972), pp. 316 ff,; Karl Bachinger (1973), pp. 282-3.

21 Berend and Ranki (1974a), p. 98; K. M. Fink (1968), p. 77.

22 Berend and Ranki (1974a), p. 62.

23 Matis (1972), p. 404; V. Sandor (1956), pp. 209-10; Berend and Ranki (1974a), pp. 101-4.

24 Scott M. Eddie (1972); V. Sandor (1956); F. Tremel (1958), 242-50; Berend and Ranki (1973); Berend and Ranki (1974a).

25 V. Sandor (1956), p. 197; Matis (1972), p. 423; Wolfgang Zorn (1970), pp. 505-6; D. Kosary (1975), p. 374.

26 Berend and Ranki (1974a), pp. 127, 152-3, 301; Zorn (1970), p. 518; T. Csato (1977), 405-9; V. Sandor (1956), p. 218; Warriner (1965), pp. 99-102.

27 Scott M. Eddie (1972), p. 300; A. Brusatti (1965), p. 79; K. M. Fink (1968), p. 64.

28 There are signs that the Hungarians also consciously used their monopoly of the Austrian market to drive up prices by limiting output. Scott M. Eddie (1971), esp. pp. 577, 583-5.

29 Berend and Ranki (1973), pp. 490 ff.

30 S. M. Eddie (1969); idem (1967) and (1968), esp. 200-1.

31 F. Tremel (1958), p. 249; Berend and Ranki (1974a), p. 78.

32 Matis (1972), p. 401; Alexander Eckstein (1955), pp. 175, 189; Gross (1973), p. 273; Berend and Ranki (1974a), pp. 56-7.

33 S. B. Saul (1972), p. 50; Wolfgang Zorn (1970), p. 517; V. Sandor (1956), pp. 200-2.

34 Report to Zürich Congress of the International, quoted in V. Hunecke (1978), p. 15; W. W. Rostow (1978), p. 439.

35 Luigi Bulferetti (1972), pp. 237-9.

36 Luciano Cafagna (1973), iv, 282-3; V. Hunecke (1978), p. 18.

37 Giorgio Mori (1975); Hunecke (1978), pp. 48-50; Sombart (1892), pp. 131, 137.

38 I. A. Glazier, V. N. Bandera, R. B. Berner (1975).

39 L. Cafagna (1973), pp. 285-6; Stefano Fenoaltea (1971-2), 325; Milward and Saul (1977), 246; F. Vöchting (1951), p. 84.

40 Fenoaltea (1971-2), pp. 337-8; R. A. Webster (1975), p. 6; T. Kemp (1969), pp. 165-8; E. Lémonon (1913), pp. 23-5.

41 G. Mori (1975), p. 86.

42 Paul Bairoch (1976a), pp. 282-3, 286, 307.

43 By 1913, 21.6% of the population lived in the North-West, which had 58% of the larger-scale industry and 48.9% of the country's horsepower. L. Cafagana (1973), p. 323; Also Mori (1979), pp. 73-4.

44 R. Zangheri (1974), pp. 26, 29, 39; Gino Luzzatto (1969), pp. 208-9, 222; E. Lémonon (1913), p. xvi.

45 S. B. Saul (1972), p. 55.

46 Jon S. Cohen (1967), 363-4; L. Cafagna (1973), p. 297; Milward and Saul (1977), 262 ff.; V. Hunecke (1978), p. 107; S. B. Clough (1964), p. 93 ff.

47 Jon S. Cohen (1967), p. 366; R. A. Webster (1975); S. B. Clough (1964), pp. 125 ff.; Waltershausen (1931), p. 593; Tamborra (1974), pp. 97-8; Mori (1979), pp. 65 ff.; G. Fua (1965), pp. 12 ff.

48 Paul Bairoch (1976b), pp. 247-52; A. Gerschenkron (1970), pp. 124-5; idem (1966b), pp. 72 ff.; idem (1968b), p. 98 and *passim*; Milward and Saul (1977), p. 257 and *passim*; Barry Supple (1973), iii, 341-3.

49 Gianni Toniolo (1977); also see Frank J. Coppa (1970).

50 T. Kemp (1969), p. 175.

51 F. Vöchting (1951), pp. 92, 222; S. B. Clough and C. Livi (1956), p. 336; L. Saville (1968), Caizzi (1962); R. S. Eckaus (1961); Barzanti (1965), pp. 27 ff.; D. M. Smith (1968), pp. 390-473; S. B. Clough (1964), pp. 165-7; Podbielski (1974), p. 4.

52 R. A. Webster (1975), p. 48; F. Vöchting (1951), p. 238; Paul Bairoch (1976b), p. 250.

53 François Caron (1978), iv, p. 102; A. Gerschenkron (1966b), pp. 361-2; Kurt Albert Gerlach (1911), pp. 169 ff. Paul Bairoch makes a distinction between those small countries which opted for complementarity with a dominant economy, and those which set out to compete with them on the basis of favourable raw materials or specialized skills. For the latter, exports rose less fast, but their output rose faster. However, the distinction is not very clear and some, like Sweden, fitted both. (1976b), p. 260.

54 K. Berrill (1963), pp. 295-6; S. A. Hansen (1970), pp. 60-1; K.-G. Hildebrand (1972), p. 310; Axel Nielsen (1933), pp. 519, 577-81; Gerlach (1922), pp. 363-9; G. Myrdal (1956), p. 98; Lars Sandberg (1978), 655; Lennart Jörberg (1973), iv, 479.

55 Bairoch (1976a), pp. 307, 309. Figures in parentheses are partly estimated. Also (1976b), pp. 154-7; Jörberg (1973), pp. 377-9; Sandberg (1979), p. 225.

56 Gerlach (1911), p. 6.

57 Bairoch (1976b), p. 250; Gerlach (1911), pp. 17, 197; Erik Helmer Pederson

(1975), 109; S. Helmfrid (1974); E. F. Heckscher (1968), p. 256; S. Lieberman (1970), p. 44; Semmingsen (1972).

58 Lars G. Sandberg (1978), idem (1979); Koblik (1975), pp. 11-12; M. Drake (1979), pp. 288-90.

59 Gerlach (1911), pp. 29 ff., Bairoch (1976b), pp. 263-6; A. Nielsen (1933), pp. 528 ff.; Wolf von Arnim (1951); Hildebrand (1972), p. 306 and R. Cameron (1972), p. 311; A. H. Hollmann (1904); H. Bergtrup, H. Lund, P. Manniche (1929); L. Jörberg (1973), pp. 394-9.

60 Gerlach (1911), pp. 52 ff.; A. Nielsen (1933), pp. 542-8; Kjeld Bjerke (1955), pp. 124-9.

61 Kristof Glamann (1960), p. 125; S. A. Hansen (1970), pp. 14 ff.; L. Jörberg (1973), p. 408.

62 Heckscher (1968), pp. 167, 217-19; Hildebrand (1972), p. 307; Boethius (1958), p. 155.

63 Heckscher (1968), pp. 225-31, 240-3; K. -G. Hildebrand (1972), pp. 275-81; idem in *Economic History* (1978), 'A' Themes, p. 36; L. Jörberg (1973), p. 446.

64 L. Jörberg (1969), pp. 272, 277 ff.

65 Hildebrand (1972), pp. 308-9; Heckscher (1968), p. 224; L. Jörberg (1973), pp. 442, 475.

66 In the 1870s, only the British and American were larger, Edvard Bull (1960), pp. 262-3, 267, 270; E. Jutikkala (1960), pp. 152-4; S. Lieberman (1970), pp. 119-30; L. Jörberg (1973), p. 430; Sejersted (1968).

67 S. Lieberman (1970), pp. 78, 115, 152-6; L. Jörberg (1973), p. 426.

68 S. Lieberman (1970), pp. 133-8; L. Jörberg (1973), pp. 432-6; E. Bull (1960), pp. 268-9.

69 Henk Van Dijk, in *Economic History* (1978), Part I, 'A' Themes, pp. 104-5; J. Mokyr (1974), p. 383; idem (1975), pp. 288 ff.; Jan de Vries (1978), 89-90, 97.

70 Robert Demoulin (1938), p. 108; J. Mokyr (1974), pp. 370-2; Bläsing (1973), p. 107.

71 J. C. Boogman (1968), p. 140; Joel Mokyr (1975), p. 298; Bläsing (1973), pp. 82-6.

72 This is the argument of Richard T. Griffiths in an unpubl. cyclost. paper read to the Economic History Conference (1978); Joel Mokyr (1976a), pp. 94 ff.; Jan de Vries (1978), pp. 160-2; Dhont and Bruwier (1973), pp. 358-60.

73 Jan de Vries (1978), pp. 160-2, 211.

74 J. A. van Houtte (1972), 116; Jan de Vries (1978), esp. pp. 162-3, 173, 182. Brugmans dated the industrialization period 1870-1914. Brugmans (1961), p. 312 and *passim*.

75 Paul Bairoch (1976a), p. 307; Purš (1973), pp. 162-4.

76 Olga Crisp (1972), p. 436; V. K. Yatsounsky (1965), pp. 288, 306. Also see W. Ashworth (1977), p. 150, and Gregory Grossman (1973), iv, 490; Goldsmith (1961), p. 442.

77 G. Grossman (1973), p. 489.

78 Olga Crisp (1972), pp. 450-1, 455; A. Baykov (1954), p. 143; K. W. Hardach (1967), p. 59.

79 Milward and Saul (1977), pp. 400-1; B. R. Mitchell, 'Statistical Appendix' in Cipolla (1973), pp. 789-90; P. I. Lyashchenko (1949), pp. 491-3; M. E. Falkus (1972), p. 55.

80 W. O. Henderson (1967a), pp. 224-6; A. Kahan (1967), pp. 460, 467; A. Gerschenkron (1977), p. 54.

81 Lyashchenko (1949), pp. 527–30.

82 W. O. Henderson (1967a), pp. 210 ff.; Milward and Saul (1977), 404–5; Schulze-Gävernitz (1899), pp. 95–7, 112–22.

83 Daniel Brower (1977).

84 R. Portal (1966), pp. 829–36, 853–5; Berend and Ranki (1974a), p. 132; Andrzej Jezierski (1969); Irena Petrzak-Pawlowska (1970); Pounds (1958), pp. 123–6, Spulber (1966), p. 15; R. E. Johnson (1979); Kahan (1978), p. 269.

85 Yatsounsky (1965), pp. 301, 303; Milward and Saul (1977), pp. 406–9, 416; Lyashchenko (1949), pp. 540 ff., 671–2; Henderson (1967a), pp. 215–17; Crisp (1976), pp. 64–5.

86 Milward and Saul (1977), 409.

87 R. Portal (1966), pp. 837, 844.

88 Milward and Saul (1977), 387 ff.; Olga Crisp (1972), p. 456; Th. H. von Laue (1954), pp. 221 ff., M. E. Falkus (1972), pp. 61–74.

89 Milward and Saul (1977), 403; also G. Grossman (1973), p. 489; also Goldsmith (1961); Thalheim (1971), pp. 89–95.

90 A. Gerschenkron (1966b), pp. 126 ff.; idem (1970), pp. 122–3; idem (1963) and (1947a), W. O. Henderson (1967a), pp. 228–9. For an early expression of the view that Russia's backwardness determined the course of her economic history, see Th. H. v. Laue (1954), p. 218.

91 M. E. Falkus (1972), pp. 46, 79 ff.

92 P. I. Lyashchenko (1949), pp. 531, 708 ff.; Olga Crisp (1972), pp. 457–8; R. Portal (1966), pp. 849–51; 863; Falkus (1972), p. 83.

93 P. I. Lyashchenko (1949), pp. 673 ff; Olga Crisp (1972), pp. 465–6.

94 This is the conclusion of Roger Portal (1954), pp. 213–14.

95 J. Nadal (1972); Pierre Vilar (1972); Paul Bairoch (1976b), p. 254; Tortella-Casares (1977); Baklanoff (1978), p.6; J. Harrison (1978), pp. 54–6, 62.

96 E. E. Malefakis (1970), p. 12.

97 J. Nadal (1973), pp. 580–3, 593–5; Milward and Saul (1977), p. 238; Pierre Vilar (1972), p. 421; J. Harrison (1978), pp. 69 ff.; Vicens (1959), pp. 592–601.

98 Paul Bairoch (1976a), p. 286.

99 In 1816–51, 35 per cent of the credit absorbed by the Paris Bourse was for the Spanish public debt, and in 1869–73 Spain was the second largest recipient, after Russia, of credit raised on the London Stock Exchange. But the terms were onerous, and Spain sometimes defaulted. J. Nadal (1973), pp. 539–43, 555; H. Kellenbenz (1965), p. 168.

100 Henry Kamen (1978); David Ringrose (1970) and (1973); Wittfogel (1932), p. 724.

101 J. Nadal (1973), pp. 559, 598, 610; R. Cameron (1972) pp. 530–1; Gilbert Garrier (1978), iv, 409.

102 Paul Bairoch (1976b), p. 250; Milward and Saul (1977), 226; Gilbert Garrier (1978), p. 421; Morgado (1979), pp. 322–3.

103 Paul Bairoch (1976a), p. 307; Wolfgang Zorn (1970), p. 501; John R. Lampe (1975).

104 Berend and Ranki (1974a), pp. 88, 106; Milward and Saul (1977), 430, 436, 443–4; N. Todorov (1972), 121–8; Wolfgang Zorn (1970); Tamborra (1974).

105 W. Ashworth (1977), p. 151; Michael Palairet (1977); Nicola Vuco (1975), 121–2; John R. Lampe (1975), p. 68; Milward and Saul (1977), 434; Berend and Ranki (1974a), pp. 139 ff.; Spulber (1966), pp. 94–5; Warriner (1965), pp. 21–2.

106 The industrial backwardness of the Italian South as against the North was

noticed as early as the late seventeenth century. Domenico Sella (1968-9), 237. Also W. Ashworth (1977), p. 157; F. Tremel (1958), p. 244.

107 F. Voigt, K. Otto, G. Unterburg, H. Trerich (1968), pp. 396-7; Schremmer (1978), pp. 206-7.

108 Olga Crisp (1972), pp. 237-8; Institut de Science Économique de l'Université Catholique de Sacré-Cœur (1968), p. 277; A. Baykov (1954), pp. 140-1; Jerome Blum (1961), p. 343; J. C. La Force (1965), p. 177; F. Vöchting (1951), pp. 17 ff.

109 W. O. Henderson (1967a), pp. 203, 222; Milward and Saul (1977), 352-3, 380, 406-9; Olga Crisp (1972), pp. 437-8; A. Baykov (1954), pp. 140-2; Jerome Blum (1961), pp. 280-3; P. I. Lyashchenko (1949), p. 367; Haxthausen (1856), i, p. 390; Schultze Gävernitz (1899), p. 122.

110 Witold Kula (1976), p. 162.

111 J. C. La Force (1965), p. 168.

112 David R. Ringrose (1970), p. v; Richard Herr (1958), p. 131.

113 K. Greenfield (1965), p. 67; Jan de Vries (1976), pp. 168-70; Clough and Livi (1956), pp. 345-8; J. K. Siegenthaler (1973), p. 406; Francesco Vito (1968), pp. 211-12.

114 Jerome Blum (1948), p. 94; H. Matis and Karl Bachinger (1973), p. 203; Milward and Saul (1977), p. 433.

115 e.g. P. Prandke (1968), pp. 119-20; Sociological Institute of the University of Utrecht (1968), p. 328; Voigt, Otto. Unterberg, Trerich (1968), p. 391.

116 M. Penouil (1969), p. 101; R. E. Caves (1967), p. 255; G. Myrdal (1956), p. 167; Centre Européen (1968), Discussion, p. 78.

117 E. A. G. Robinson (1969b), pp. x-xi, and Francesco Vito (1968), p. 214; Milward and Saul (1977), pp. 528-31; François Caron (1978), iii, p. 409; H. Matis (1972), p. 423; W. Ashworth (1977), p. 156; W. A. Lewis (1978), pp. 164-6.

118 Jerome Blum (1961), pp. 280, 609.

119 Chapter 5, last section.

120 Milward and Saul (1977), 369, 515-16; F. Delaisi (1929), pp. 54-6; Pierre Vilar (1972), p. 431; F. B. Tipton (1976), pp. 612-13; P. I. Lyashchenko (1949), p. 498; R. A. Webster (1975), p. 89; William L. Blackwell (1968), p. 37; Waltershausen (1931), p. 348.

121 M. Despot (1969), p. 142.

122 Sigurd Klatt (1959), p. 373; Olga Crisp (1972), p. 461; A. Gerschenkron (1966b), pp. 362-3; K. R. Greenfield (1965), pp. xiv-xv, 134-5; Matis and Bachinger (1973), p. 114.

123 W. Dlugoborski (1973), p. 23.

124 Chapter 3 above.

125 *Economic History* (1978), Theme B. 7, pp. 32, 33, 36; A. Gerschenkron (1966b), p. 62; E. A. G. Robinson (1969b), pp. 21-5; S. Groenman (1969); P. Léon (1970), p. 358; F. Delaisi (1929), pp. 47 ff.; R. A. Webster (1975), p. 16; J. C. La Force (1965), p. 168; Clough and Livi (1956), pp. 345-8; V. Sandor (1956), p. 140; J. K. Siegenthaler (1973); V. Hunecke (1978), esp. pp. 121, 54-5; Polonski (1975), pp. 3-5.

126 W. L. Blackwell (1968), p. 36; W. O. Henderson (1967a), p. 205. Also Alois Brusatti (1971), p. 142.

127 A. Gerschenkron (1968b), p. 210; W. O. Henderson (1967a), p. 204; Milward and Saul (1977), 395; M. Lévy-Leboyer (1964), p. 104; Peter Borscheid (1978), pp. 42 ff.; E. Lémonon (1913), p. 215; F. Vöchting (1951), p. 92; H. Matis (1971), pp. 152-4; Berend and Ranki (1974a), pp. 24 ff.; Haxthausen (1856),

ii, pp. 177-8; Tugan-Baranowski (1900), pp. 520 ff.; Schulze-Gävernitz (1899), pp. 131, 141; Crisp (1976), pp. 167-9; Crisp (1978), esp. pp. 326, 370 ff., 381, 402-3.

128 A. Gerschenkron (1966b), pp. 69-70.

129 Pavel Hapák (1978), pp. 321-7; A. Gerschenkron (1977), p. 46; H. Matis (1972), p. 427; M. C. MacLennan (1968), pp. 43-4; Institut de . . . Sacré Cœur (1968), p. 278.

130 e.g. J. A. Dunlevy and H. A. Gemery (1978), 902; Svenningsen (1972).

131 *Economic History* (1978), Theme B. 7, p. 35; R. Cameron (1972), pp. 528-9; François Caron (1978), iv, p. 102.

132 Chapter 5, last section.

133 Francesco Vito (1968), p. 213.

134 e.g. A. Gerschenkron (1966b), pp. 47-62.

135 Olga Crisp (1972), pp. 437-8.

136 Aubin and Zorn (1976), p. 600; H. Matis (1972), p. 36; Matis and Bachinger (1973), p. 114; Milward and Saul (1977), 460-4; J. Nadal (1973), p. 543; J. C. La Force (1965), p. 177; Spulber (1966), pp. 67-8; Waltershausen (1931), p. 348.

CHAPTER 7

1 An excellent study linking the various movements touched upon here is E. J. Hobsbawm (1964). Also see Hans Kohn (1945) and Hugh Seton-Watson (1971), esp. chapter 11; W. Roepke (1942), p. 74.

2 R. H. Dumke (1976), esp. chapter 1; Gerhard Bondi (1958), p. 47. For the wavering southern German states, the lax Austrian customs administration was an insignificant reason for rejecting closer association with Austria in 1862. L. Maenner (1928), p. 13.

3 Pierre Chaunu (1964), 165-76, esp. p. 174.

4 August Lösch (1944), pp. 140-4.

5 René Gendarme (1954), pp. 42-3, 94-5.

6 S. B. Saul (1972a). Also W. Arthur Lewis (1978), p. 68.

7 Hans Rosenberg (1978), p. 166.

8 Paul Bairoch (1976b), esp. pp. 117 ff.

9 Ibid., pp. 43-6; K. R. Greenfield (1965), pp. 9-10; Walter Bodmer (1960), p. 346; H. Pirenne (1948), vii, 166; G. Mori (1975); Frank J. Coppa (1970), p. 743; Werner Sombart (1892), i, 83-91; Ernest Mahaim (1892); Henri Réus and G. S. Endt (1892); William Scharing (1892); Prof. Fahlbeck (1892), p. 307; V. Wittschewsky (1892), pp. 364-6; Emil Frey (1892), all ibid.

10 A. L. Dunham (1971), p. 19; A. Sartorius von Waltershausen (1931), p. 305; Barry M. Ratcliffe (1978); C. P. Kindleberger (1964), p. 283; Percy Ashley (1920), pp. 295-6.

11 C. P. Kindleberger (1975), 20-55; Dunham (1971); Marcel Rist (1970a); Barry M. Ratcliffe (1973), 582-613; Paul Bairoch (1976b), pp. 221-9; P. Ashley (1920), pp. 297-301.

12 S. v. Waltershausen (1931), pp. 305 ff. Also Kindleberger (1975); Karl F. Helleiner (1973); Ernest Mahaim (1892), pp. 214-24; Emil Frey (1892), pp. 463 ff.; Walther Lotz (1892), pp. 35 ff.; Joachim F. E. Bläsing (1973), pp. 171-8; Herbert Matis (1973), p. 40; Hans Rosenberg (1978), pp. 150-60; Karl Heinz Werner (1949), pp. 388, 406; Olga Crisp (1972), p. 448; M. E. Falkus (1972), p. 58; K. A. Gerlach (1911), pp. 86 ff.

13 Walter Lotz (1892), pp. 128 ff.

14 Ibid., pp. 138 ff.; Ivo Nicolai Lambi (1963), Hans Rosenberg (1978), pp. 109–10; W. O. Henderson (1967a), p. 49; L. Maenner (1928), pp. 22–40; Karl W. Hardach (1967); P. Ashley (1920), p. 41 and *passim*.

15 Duty in marks per ton:

	1879	*1885*	*1887*
Wheat	10	30	50
Rye	10	30	50
Barley	5	15	25
Oats	10	15	40

16 Olga Crisp (1953–4), p. 161; M. E. Falkus (1972), p. 58; R. Portal (1966), pp. 801, 824; P. I. Lyashchenko (1949), pp. 557–8; Schulze-Gävernitz (1899), pp. 244–83, 351.

17 W. Sombart (1892), pp. 94–100; Frank J. Coppa (1970), pp. 750–1; S. v. Waltershausen (1931), p. 504.

18 Paul Bairoch (1976b), p. 53.

19 A good summary will be found in Hermann Gross (1962), 100–4.

20 Paul Bairoch (1976b), p. 53, and F. Caron (1978), iv, 172, based on a League of Nations Study. 'Average tariffs' is a dubious concept and may involve double counting, but the general rank order is a fair enough representation. On this problem also see H. Liepmann (1938), pp. 20 ff., and Footnote 74, chapter 8, below.

21 This may be generalized as a conflict between producer and consumer interests: e.g. Anthony Downs (1957).

22 For a good example, see R. Poidevin (1971), 47–62. For the painful process of downward revision, see Karl F. Helleiner (1973).

23 S. B. Clough (1964), pp. 116–17; P. Ashley (1920), pp. 323–7.

24 A. Brusatti (1965), p. 80; Berend and Ranki (1974a), pp. 89–91; K. M. Fink (1968), pp. 75–6; Leo Pasvolsky (1928), pp. 57–60; P. Ashley (1920), pp. 334–6.

25 See esp. Horst Müller-Link (1977). Also Martin Kitchen (1978), p. 206; W. O. Henderson (1967a), p. 49; P. Ashley (1920), pp. 69–74.

26 Hungary also had some industry and mining, particularly in her border regions, but political power was in the undisputed hands of the large landowners.

27 A. Peez (1892), i, 167–93; H. Matis (1972), pp. 370 ff.; N. Gross (1962), pp. 103–5.

28 Frank J. Coppa (1970).

29 M. Kitchen (1978), esp. p. 244 and *passim*; A. Gerschenkron (1943); Kenneth D. Barkin (1970).

30 A good summary will be found in M. Kitchen (1978), pp. 215 ff. Also Kenneth D. Barkin (1970); A. Gerschenkron (1943), pp. 58 ff.; Hans-Jürgen Puhle (1966); W. Roepke (1931), p. 73; A. Kahan (1967), pp. 14 ff.; Michael Tracy (1964), pp. 92–5; P. Ashley (1920), pp. 92–108.

31 K. W. Deutsch and Alexander Eckstein (1961) and A. K. Cairncross and J. Faaland (1951), 26; and see discussion in C. P. Kindleberger (1964), p. 269 and Richard E. Caves (1971).

32 Pierre Léon (1978), v, 27.

33 Paul Bairoch (1976b), pp. 78–9; Richard E. Caves (1971), p. 425; Milward and Saul (1977), 469–72; W. A. Lewis (1978), p. 29; W. Schlote (n. d.), pp. 49–51. Also Walther G. Hoffmann (1971), p. 151; S. v. Waltershausen (1931), pp. 259–61, 419.

34 R. E. Caves (1967), p. 128; C. Iversen (1936); K. Borchardt (1976), p. 730.

35 According to W. A. Lewis, the fall in grain prices had the further significance of holding back Eastern European industrialization (1978), p. 165; also see Gerschenkron (1943), pp. ix-x.

36 A. H. Hollmann (1904), pp. 1-2.

37 Max Sering (1887), p. 530; 'Imports of Grain before and after the Repeal of the Corn Laws' (1866), 445-51.

38 W. A. Lewis argued that it was this failure to keep up American output (as well as the slowing-down of the Australian wool supply) which was behind the Kondratieff upturn in prices in the 1890s (1978), pp. 80-1, 93, also E. G. Nourse (1924).

39 R. F. Crawford (1895), 87-9, 92, 94-5. Also see Robert M. Stern (1960), 46-9; W. Malenbaum (1953), pp. 39-40; Helling (1977), p. 122.

40 C. K. Harley (1978), 866; Michael Tracy (1964), pp. 22, 36.

41 Max Sering (1887), p. 530.

42 It had been 906 m. b. in 1931-40.

43 Their yields had, if anything, dropped even further behind the advanced regions by 1913, but were growing absolutely. Pierre Léon (1978), iv, 409; Nicolas Spulber (1966), pp. 84-5; Schulze-Gävernitz (1899), p. 359.

44 W. W. Rostow (1978), pp. 147, 164-5; also S. v. Waltershausen (1931), pp. 524-5. By comparison, total agricultural output in Europe rose only from an index of 75.3 in 1871-80 to 119.7 in 1909-13. Paul Bairoch (1976b), p. 333.

45 R. F. Crawford (1895), p. 101; W. W. Rostow (1978), pp. 164-5; Th. B. Veblen (1892), 70-103.

46 Lyashchenko (1949), pp. 468-9.

47 Also see C. P. Kindleberger (1951).

48 J. Nadal (1973), pp. 557-9; S. v. Waltershausen (1931), p. 624; J. Vicens Vives (1959), pp. 626-8.

49 In 1913 only 5% of British grain imports came from Europe. For Germany, the main continental importer, 25% of the imports of wheat and 93% of her imported barley were European in origin. William Woodruff (1973), iv, 719-23.

50 Max Sering (1887), pp. 555-7; W. H. Dawson (1904), p. 10; M. Tracy (1964), p. 36; P. Ashley (1920), p. 97; W. Malenbaum (1975), p. 118; H. Liepmann (1938), pp. 62, 371-2.

51 I. N. Lambi (1963), p. 230; Heinz Haushofer (1972), p. 207; G. Bondi (1958), pp. 92, 135; Sering (1887), p. 543; Helling (1977), p. 135.

52 C. K. Harley (1978), p. 866.

53 V. P. Timoshenko (1932), p. 372. A metric quintal equalled 100 kg. or 0.1 ton = 220 lbs.

54 Doreen Warriner (1964), p. 51; Berend and Ranki (1974a), p. 151.

55 R. M. Stern (1960), pp. 58-9.

56 Berend and Ranki (1974a), p. 151.

57 R. M. Stern (1960), pp. 58-9.

58 A. Peez (1892), esp. pp. 175 ff., 187, 338-9.

59 Berend and Ranki (1973), pp. 490-9; S. M. Eddie (1967), p. 308. Also Pal Sandor (1961); G. Szabad (1961).

60 N. Spulber (1966), pp. 63, 84; D. Chirot (1976), pp. 123-4; Berend and Ranki (1974a), p. 151; Milward and Saul (1977), 453.

61 Berend and Ranki (1974a), p. 55; L. Katus (1961), p. 143.

62 It need hardly be stressed that the use of postal services was proportional to the level of industrialization and the standard of living. Milward and Saul (1977),

Tables 95, 96.

63 S. Pollard (1974), chapter 5. S. v. Waltershausen (1931), pp. 278 ff.; 474 ff.

64 Milward and Saul (1977), 494-501; M. Kitchen (1978), pp. 275-6.

65 William Ashworth (1962), pp. 204, 211.

66 e.g. W. Dlugoborski (1973), pp. 22-6, 38; A. Gerschenkron (1977), p. 46; Sune Åkerman (1975), 167-79; Berend and Ranki (1974a), p. 33; F. Delaisi (1929), p. 63, Adolph Jensen (1969), ii, pp. 288-9; F. Burgdörfer (1969), ii, pp. 333, 347-9; Michael Drake (1979a), p. 307. The concept of 'allocation theory' does not add much, apart from a more neutral tone, to this understanding. John A. Tomaske (1971), 852-3.

67 Paul Bairoch (1976b), p. 115.

68 Achille Viallate (1928), p. 164; R. E. Webster (1975), p. 49; S. B. Clough (1964), p. 139; S. v. Waltershausen (1931), p. 457; H. Matis (1972), p. 427; Felix Klezl (1969), ii, p. 402; Gustav Thirring (1969), ii, p. 413, 430-1; Anna Maria Ratti (1969), ii, pp. 448-9.

69 Normal Angell (1910).

70 *Zum Ewigen Frieden*, quoted in W. Roepke (1945), p. 93.

71 Lawrence Schofer (1975), pp. 7, 24-5; H. Haushofer (1972), pp. 209-10. The hostility was particularly deep in Upper Silesia, where tariffs had divided a single natural region into three parts at enormous economic cost. Pounds (1958), pp. 133 ff., 147.

72 M. Kitchen (1978), pp. 200-2; Hans Rosenberg (1978), pp. 112-14.

73 Wilhelm Roepke (1959), p. 85.

74 David Mitrany (1936), p. 40, also pp. 43-7, 194.

75 Rudolf Hilferding (1968), p. 458.

76 G. Myrdal (1964), p. 32.

CHAPTER 8

1 Gerschenkron (1943), pp. 7-8.

2 Domestic 'democracy' of pressure groups, as Sir Arthurs Salter has shown so eloquently, further complicated matters by driving official representatives to be more narrow-mindedly nationalist than they otherwise might have been. John Bell Condliffe (1951), p. 484.

3 O. Delle-Donne (1928), p. 81; Wilhelm Roepke (1954), pp. 37-8; also idem (1944). However, Roepke's contrast between the 'bright sunny day' of the immediate pre-war years and the 'polar night' thereafter (*Internationale Ordnung*, p. 11) is too strongly drawn, as is Paul Brandt's wistful glance at the pre-war world economy as a 'land of wishful dreams' (1922). The war was part of the process, not its sole cause.

4 Harry G. Johnson (1967), p. 1. Also, e.g. H. V. Hodson (1938), p. 52.

5 Derek H. Aldcroft (1978), pp. 14-16.

6 Ibid., p. 19; Gerd Hardach (1973), p. 292.

7 W. A. Lewis (1952), 127-8; E. L. Bogart (1920); I. Svennilson (1954), pp. 18-19.

8 Hardach (1973), p. 295.

9 League of Nations (1945), pp. 134-7. Germany reached her pre-war level of industrial production only in 1927, the United Kingdom in 1929, according to those calculations. According to Paul Bairoch, total gross national product at

market prices in Europe including Russia reached its pre-war level only in 1925, excluding Russia in 1924. On a per capita basis, only seven of the thirteen belligerent countries for which data exist had reached their pre-war GNP level by 1924. (1976a), pp. 292, 297. Also see Svennilson (1954), p. 37.

10 Henri Morsel (1978), v, 49-53.

11 W. A. Lewis (1965), pp. 23-33; Alec Nove (1969), p. 91; Berend and Ranki (1974a), p. 104.

12 K. Laursen and J. Pedersen (1964).

13 H. V. Hodson (1938), pp. 14-15, 26-29.

14 Aldcroft (1978), p. 34.

15 Ibid., pp. 63-4; Achille Viallate (1928), p. 24; W. S. and E. S. Woytinsky (1955), pp. 745-8; R. A. C. Parker (1969), pp. 243-5; Arndt (1963), pp. 9-12, 27; also p. 286 below. Both the payment and the non-payment helped to fan 'self-righteous nationalism': 'to avoid paying interest and amortizations to foreigners became almost a noble sport'. Roepke (1942), p. 77.

16 G. Hardach (1973), pp. 263-4.

17 For the classic statements, see J. M. Keynes (1919) and E. Mantoux (1946).

18 William Ashworth (1962), pp. 225-31; Henri Morsel (1978), v, 155.

19 She paid in the period some 10½ milliard marks (4½ in kind and 6 across the exchanges), and received 17-18½ milliard marks (9 long-term, 5-5½ short-term loans, and 3-4 miscellaneous capital).

20 Aldcroft (1978), pp. 75-8.

21 W. A. Lewis (1965), p. 57; Woytinsky (1955), pp. 202-4; Carlo Zacchia (1973), v, 578.

22 H. V. Hodson (1938), pp. 4-7.

23 D. Mitrany (1936), pp. 172-82; Ashworth (1962), pp. 220-2; J. B. Condliffe (1951), p. 481; Leo Pasvolsky (1928), pp. 71, 548-9; M. S. Gordon (1941), p. 19.

24 Berend and Ranki (1974a), pp. 174-8.

25 H. G. Johnson (1967), p. 2. Also Frederick Hertz (1947), pp. 86-7.

26 N. Gross (1968), pp. 104-8; L. Pasvolsky (1928), pp. 270-4.

27 W. A. Lewis (1965), pp. 20-1; D. Mitrany (1936), pp. 165-6; F. Hertz (1947), pp. 115-16; N. Spulber (1966), pp. 69-72, 112-14; L. Pasvolsky (1928), pp. 259-60.

28 D. Mitrany (1936), p. 192. Also see F. Hertz (1947), pp. 218-23; L. Pasvolsky (1928), pp. 65-75, 85; Royal Institute of International Affairs (1939), pp. 14-15, 22.

29 F. Hertz (1947), p. 10, also pp. 65-6; A. Viallate (1928), p. 192.

30 It need hardly be stressed that this was not a matter of small versus large nations. Some small countries like Holland, Switzerland, and Sweden fought no economic wars, and while small countries usually harmed only themselves, the economic nationalism of countries like the USA and Germany also harmed others. W. Roepke (1954), p. 184.

31 N. Spulber (1966), pp. 5-6, 35-6.

32 Svennilson (1954), p. 26 and *passim*.

33 I. T. Berend and G. Ranki (1978), 396-400; N. Spulber (1966), pp. 5-6, 35-6.

34 Paul Bairoch (1976a), p. 297.

35 E. Jutikkala (1960), pp. 153-61.

36 N. Spulber (1966), p. 58.

37 G. M. Sorokin (1967), i, 151, iii, 225, 229; A. Gerschenkron (1966b), pp.

199-233. Economic History Association (1978), Part I, *Pre-Industrial Period in Europe*, p. 168 (Teichova); Berend and Ranki (1974a), p. 301.

38 Only 3 per cent of agricultural dwellings had electricity. G. M. Sorokin (1967), iii, 136-7.

39 It was Delaisi's basic plea that the West should help agrarian Europe, 'Europe B', and thereby help itself by injections of capital (1929). Also Aldcroft (1978), p. 49; N. Spulber (1966), pp. 39-40; Berend and Ranki (1974a), pp. 180-4, 229-39; idem (1978), pp. 401-2, 245; G. M. Sorokin (1967), i, 155; I. Pietrzak-Pawlowska (1968), pp. 193-6.

40 N. Spulber (1966), p. 57.

41 Pietrzak-Pawlowska (1968), p. 196; Andrzej Jesierski and Zbigniew Landau (1970), 344; D. Warriner (1939), pp. xviii-xix, 20, 47; Alexander Eckstein (1955), pp. 165, 182; N. Spulber (1966), p. 87; K. Mandelbaum (1961), p. 23; RIIA (1939), pp. 115-16; Berend and Ranki (1974a), pp. 306-7; idem (1978), p. 404.

42 Czechoslovakia was the exception: small holdings there led at once to rising output. D. H. Aldcroft (1978), pp. 28, 48, 58-9; H. Gollwitzer (1978), 539; L. Katus (1961), pp. 157-8; H. Schissler (1978), pp. 186-93; Berend and Ranki (1974a), Table 8-2; F. Hertz (1947), pp. 100 ff.; G. M. Sorokin (1967), iii, 89; L. Pasvolsky (1928), pp. 249, 363-4, 421, 507; Jedruszczak (1972), pp. 201-3; Polonsky (1975), pp. 7-11; Royal Institute of International Affairs (1938), pp. 29-30, 105-9; Seton-Watson (1945) pp. 77-9.

43 N. Spulber (1966), p. 56.

44 See esp. D. Warriner (1939), pp. xxvi-xxviii, 22-49, 61-78, 138; Berend and Ranki (1974a), pp. 295-6; idem (1978), pp. 390-1; D. B. Grigg (1976), p. 141; P. N. Rosenstein-Rodan (1943), 202-11; K. Mandelbaum (1961); P. E. P. (1945), p. 39; Wilbert E. Moore (1945); Seton-Watson (1945), pp. 97-9. For a contrary view, see Berdj Kenadjian (1961-2), 216-23; Harry Oshima (1958), 259-264.

45 Berend and Ranki (1974a), pp. 193-5; L. Pasvolsky (1928), 18-19; United Nations (1961), vi, pp. 16-17; Royal Institute of International Affairs (1938), p. 110.

46 Pietrzak-Pawlowska (1968), pp. 193-5; D. Mitrany (1936), pp. 199-200.

47 K. Mandelbaum (1961), p. 3; D. B. Grigg (1976), pp. 147, 161; D. Warriner (1939), p. 12; W. Roepke (1959), pp. 79-82; H. Liepmann (1938), p. 364.

48 Pierre Guillaume (1978), v, 16; A. Viallate (1928), p. 31.

49 A. Viallate (1928), p. 161; Wladimir Woytinsky (1930), pp. 61-2; Svennilson (1954), pp. 65-6.

50 Paul Bairoch (1976a), p. 297.

51 Pierre Léon (1978), v, 430-5; Richard Herr (1971), pp. 120-1, 144; J. Fontana and Jordi Nadal (1973), vi, 461-83; Raymond Carr (1966), pp. 401-5; J. Harrison (1978), p. 89.

52 Theodore H. von Laue (1964); A. Gerschenkron (1970), p. 116; idem (1966a) and other works. For an opposite view, 'the Soviet Revolution appeared as the first powerful reaction to the impact of the Industrial Revolution from the world outside the dominant North Atlantic countries', see J. B. Condliffe (1951), p. 570.

53 There was unemployment in the 1920s, reaching a maximum of 1.6 million in 1929, or 12 per cent of the labour force. A. Nove (1969), p. 115.

54 R. Portal (1966), p. 866.

55 Alexander Baykov (1946), pp. 8, 22, 29, 41; A. Nove (1969), pp. 68, 113; A. Gerschenkron (1947), 218; Lazar Volin (1970), p. 163.

56 John P. Hardt (1968), pp. 7-8; Jerzy Karcz (1968), p. 113; Gregory Grossmann (1973), pp. 122-3.

57 Stanley H. Cohn (1968), p. 27.

58 A. Nove (1969), pp. 40 ff., 78-9; Maurice Dobb (1966), pp. 122-3.

59 G. M. Sorokin (1967), i, 121-2; R. Portal (1966), p. 868; R. Lorenz (1965).

60 A. Baykov (1946), p. 17.

61 A. Nove (1969), chapter 4.

62 G. M. Sorokin (1967), i, 140; Kaser (1978), pp. 486-9.

63 M. Dobb (1966), pp. 164 ff.

64 A. Nove (1969), pp. 119 ff.; Alexander Erlich (1960); J. P. Hardt (1968), pp. 8-11; Stanley H. Cohn (1970), pp. 18-24; Nicholas Spulber (1964).

65 W. A. Lewis (1965), p. 126; J. P. Hardt (1968), pp. 3-4, 13.

66 S. H. Cohn (1970), pp. 12-13; M. Dobb (1966), pp. 217-21; A. Baykov (1946), pp. 131 ff.

67 L. Volin (1970), pp. 189-98; A. Nove (1969), pp. 110-11, 162; A. Erlich (1960), chapter 9.

68 A. Nove (1969), pp. 158-9; M. Lewin (1968).

69 A. Baykov (1946), pp. 193-6; A. Nove (1969), pp. 160-1, 170-4; L. Volin (1970), pp. 197-8. 211; W. A. Lewis (1965), p. 131.

70 Index of Russian agriculture on the inter-war territory (1913 = 100)

	1928	Av. 1936-9
Gross Output	105	105
Gross output per capita	100	88
Farm marketing p. Urban Head	96	78
Food marketing p. Urban Head	93	74

J. F. Karcz (1968), 'Soviet Agriculture', p. 113; Also L. Volin (1970), pp. 177, 224 ff.; M. Dobb (1966), p. 246.

71 A. Nove (1969), pp. 166, 180-6; L. Volin (1970), pp. 213-56.

72 S. H. Cohn (1970), p. 28; M. Dobb (1966), pp. 261, 326; Abram Bergson (1978), p. 122; Gregory Grossman (1973), pp. 505-6; Alfred Zauberman (1973), vi, 589; S. H. Cohn (1968); W. A. Lewis (1965), p. 125.

73 M. Dobb (1966), pp. 311, 326; M. P. Kim (1960), pp. 291-2.

74 No satisfactory way has yet been found of expressing a tariff system fairly in comparison with another by a single figure. The League of Nations method, of comparing total duties levied with total imports, ignores the effect which very high tariffs have of preventing imports altogether. Cf. F. Hertz (1947), pp. 70-1; Berend and Ranki (1974a), pp. 205-6; Woytinsky (1955), pp. 273-6; O. Delle-Donne (1928), pp. 189 ff.; and, in general, H. Liepmann (1938), pp. 17 ff., and A. Loveday (1928), 487-529.

75 League of Nations (1942), pp. 18, 32; idem (1943), p. 7.

76 League of Nations (1942), p. 131. Also W. Roepke (1954), pp. 27-8.

77 League of Nations (1942), pp. 22-42, 101-2; Aldcroft (1978), pp. 49-50; W. A. Lewis (1965), p. 164; C. Zacchia (1973), v, pp. 516-17.

78 A. Viallate (1928), pp. 154-5; W. Ashworth (1962), p. 233; H. V. Hodson (1938), pp. 34, 37; W. A. Lewis (1978), pp. 226-7; Pierre Léon (1978), v, 169, 187; C. P. Kindleberger (1973), pp. 86-94; J. B. Condliffe (1951), p. 481; Michael Tracy (1964), pp. 117-19; Ernst Klein (1973), pp. 157, 165-8; W. Malenbaum (1953), p. 5; W. Arndt (1963), pp. 9-10.

79 A. Gerschenkron (1943), pp. 116 ff., 293; N. Spulber (1966), p. 32; F. Hertz (1947), pp. 123-7; Berend and Ranki (1974a), p. 207; Ernst Klein (1973),

pp. 261-2; M. Tracy (1964), p. 121; Malenbaum (1953), pp. 106, 120, 127-53, 238-9; Svennilson (1954), esp. pp. 88-91, 243, Roepke (1942), pp. 118-49.

80 The terms of trade between world primary products and manufactures, at 100 in 1913, fell to 88.9 in 1929 and a low of 65.1 in 1932, to recover somewhat thereafter. W. A. Lewis (1952), pp. 117-18. Also idem (1965), p. 56; H. Morsel (1978), pp. 171, 180; C. Kindleberger (1973), pp. 143, 188; Berend and Ranki (1974a), p. 244. Commodity valorization schemes on the basis of world cartels were not generally effective before the mid-1930s: W. A. Lewis (1965), pp. 172-4; H. V. Hodson (1938), pp. 41-50, 235-57; Svennilson (1954), pp. 86-7, 92; J. W. F. Rowe (1936); Royal Institute of International Affairs (1938), pp. 143 ff.

81 See, e.g., C. P. Kindleberger (1973), pp. 104 ff.

82 H. V. Hodson (1938), p. 154; W. Malenbaum (1953), p. 111; H. Liepmann (1938), p. 331.

83 K. W. Hardach (1967), pp. 280-1.

84 H. V. Hodson (1938), pp. 100-4; Berend and Ranki (1974a), p. 262; League of Nations (1942), p. 52; W. A. Lewis (1965), p. 151; Woytinsky (1955), p. 277; J. B. Condliffe (1951), p. 492; M. Tracy (1964), pp. 122-5. The most-favoured-nation clause, it is worthy of note, now became a hindrance rather than a help in lowering barriers, as no one wished to offer concessions for fear of having to extend them to earlier treaty partners—unless, indeed, commodities could be suitably defined. Thus the Germans specified milk produced at certain altitudes as a commodity so as to exclude the Alpine Swiss suppliers from the trade. L. Pasvolsky (1928), p. 118; League of Nations (1942), pp. 118-19; Malenbaum (1953), pp. 13-18, 116 ff.; M. S. Gordon (1941), pp. 31-2.

85 H. Liepmann (1938), p. 415.

86 League of Nations (1942), p. 67 and idem (1943), p. 19.

87 Berend and Ranki (1974a), pp. 259-60; D. H. Aldcroft (1978), p. 111; H. V. Hodson (1938), p. 106; W. A. Lewis (1965), p. 65; Philip Friedmann (1976), 114-16; RIIA (1939), pp. 119-20, 131, 145-8, 160, 171-2. M. S. Gordon (1941), chapter 4. By 1937, the 'blocked section' of world trade, operating under exchange control, amounted to 29.5 per cent of the total. Roepke (1942), pp. 36-7.

88 Henri Morsel (1978), v, 322 ff.; W. A. Lewis (1965), pp. 92-3; C. P. Kindleberger (1973), p. 240; H. V. Hodson (1938), pp. 324-8; M. S. Gordon (1941), pp. 81-4, 89-96, 178-85; H. Henderson (1955), p. 265; Arndt (1963), pp. 180-97.

89 Kindleberger (1973), p. 305, quoting Hubert Henderson.

90 Kindleberger (1973), pp. 240-1; P. Friedmann (1976); W. A. Lewis (1965), pp. 93-4, 170; Aldcroft (1978), pp. 112-13; H. V. Hodson (1938), p. 108; Berend and Ranki (1974a), pp. 267-91; A. Basch (1944); W. Ashworth (1962), pp. 248-9; D. Warriner (1939), pp. 55-6; L. Pasvolsky (1928), pp. 85, 137; H. Gross (1962), pp. 111-13; RIIA (1939), pp. 135-7, 149-50, 186-200; Political and Economic Planning (1937), pp. 59-63, 228-9; M. S. Gordon (1941), pp. 160-5; Arndt (1963), pp. 192-5; H. Henderson (1955), pp. 266-70; L. Neal (1979); Berend and Ranki (1974a), pp. 120-2.

91 Kindleberger (1973), pp. 281-2; H. Morsel (1978), pp. 321-3; League of Nations (1942), pp. 70-5; Aldcroft (1978), p. 112; W. Ashworth (1962), p. 243; W. A. Lewis (1965), p. 169; PEP (1937), pp. 55-69. Actual bilateral clearing, however, affected a maximum of 12 per cent of world trade. J. B. Condliffe (1951), pp. 729-30; M. S. Gordon (1941), pp. 130-3.

92 W. A. Lewis (1965), pp. 66, 83-4; H. V. Hodson (1938), pp. 161-71; League of Nations (1942), pp. 58-9; H. Tennenbaum (1944), pp. 84, 129, 181-2;

H. Gross (1962), pp. 110-11; Svennilson (1954), pp. 176, 198; H. Liepmann (1938), pp. 376-8; M. S. Gordon (1941), pp. 444-78.

93 W. A. Lewis (1965), pp. 58, 149, also p. 122; H. Morsel (1978), p. 171; A. K. Cairncross and J. Faaland (1952), 29, 32; Kindleberger (1973), p. 172; P. L. Yates (1959), pp. 30-1, 39, 43, 227; J. B. Condliffe (1951), pp. 488-9, 495; Woytinsky (1955), pp. 39-43; M. Tracy (1964), pp. 136-7; A. Coppé (1972), pp. 18-19; A. Maizels (1963), chapter 4, pp. 150-61, and his data show the ratio of trade to production to have been falling as early as the 1920s (pp. 80-1), *pace* his own statement that this occurred only in the 1930s.

94 League of Nations (1942), p. 67; also Kindleberger (1973), pp. 191, 278-9.

95 Berend and Ranki (1974a), p. 247. Also N. Spulber (1966), p. 75; F. Hertz (1947), p. 80; Hans Raupach (1972), pp. 236-45.

96 Kindleberger (1973), pp. 298, also 204, 211-12, 257; H. V. Hodson (1938), pp. 148-9, 230; League of Nations (1942), pp. 57, 61, 74, 83-7; J. B. Condliffe (1951), pp. 497-500; RIIA (1939), pp. 24-5; Woytinsky (1955), pp. 260-1; H. Liepmann (1938), pp. 349 ff.

97 H. Morsel (1978), pp. 313-14; W. A. Lewis (1965), pp. 59-60, 156-7.

98 Hans Jaeger (1972), p. 135.

99 Kindleberger (1973), p. 26.

100 League of Nations (1942), p. 72.

101 e.g. Forrest Capie (1978), 309-409; Ph. Friedmann (1978), 148-80.

102 W. Roepke (1954), p. 175.

103 Lionel Robbins (1934), pp. 196-8; H. Liepmann (1938), pp. 379-81.

CHAPTER 9

1 Angus Maddison (1973), v, 469-70; D. H. Aldcroft (1978), pp. 133-4.

2 Maddison (1973), pp. 468-72; Aldcroft (1978), pp. 134-8; Berend and Ranki (1974a), pp. 334-40; M. M. Postan (1967), pp. 12-13; Wladislaw Sliwka (1948), p. 58; A. Jezierski and Z. Landau (1970), p. 331; B. Dmytryshyn (1977), pp. 561-2.

3 W. Sliwka (1948), p. 54. Also D. H. Aldcroft (1978), p. 128.

4 Postan (1967), pp. 22-3.

5 Maddison (1973), p. 474.

6 W. Sliwka (1948), p. 91; Maddison (1973), pp. 474-5.

7 For a good summary, see D. H. Aldcroft (1978), pp. 144-5. For a break-down of the total gross sum of $53 billion made available by the US Government to Europe from mid-1945, see Maddison (1973), p. 475.

8 Based on United Nations (1950) and (1951) summarized in Aldcroft (1978), p. 150.

9 E. F. Denison (1967).

10 Maddison (1973), p. 444; Paul Bairoch (1976a), p. 309; United Nations *Yearbook* II (1977); also see Aldcroft (1978), pp. 163-70; Angus Maddison (1964), p. 30.

11 Maddison (1973), pp. 478, 488, 494.

12 Miriam Camps (1967).

13 Fritz Hellwig (1975).

14 Uwe Kitzinger (1963), pp. 52-4, offers a good summary.

15 For a theoretical consideration, see Jacob Viner (1953); J. E. Meade (1955); also J. J. Allen (1960), esp. chapters 2, 5, 8, 14, and pp. 229-30; W. Roepke (1945), pp. 309-11. For some estimates, Bela Balassa, chapters 4 and 5.

16 e.g. Kenneth J. Twitchett (1976); Miriam Camps (1964).
17 International Chamber of Commerce (1955).
18 Postan (1967), pp. 109 ff.
19 A. Maddison (1964), p. 166; Carlo Zacchia (1973), v, pp. 600-1, Table 41; United Nations. *Yearbook* (1977). Also Aldcroft (1978), pp. 167, 182.
20 E. -S. Kirschen (1969), pp. 41 ff.; Hans O. Lundström (1967), pp. 130-52.
21 Kirschen (1969), pp. 16-17; Arnold M. Rose (1969), pp. 45-52; C. P. Kindleberger (1967), pp. 177-82.
22 A. M. Rose (1969), pp. 13-44; Kindleberger (1967), pp. 186-94; Paine (1977).
23 Turkey, lying mostly in Asia, is treated here as in UN publications as an Asiatic country.
24 Postan (1967), pp. 173-85; OECD (1974), Tables 1 and 2.
25 OECD (1974), Table 9 and Para. 1.7.
26 Paul Bairoch (1976a), p. 307; Maddison (1973), p. 488; H. Hasenpflug (1977), pp. 110-12.
27 Santiago Garcia-Echevarria (1964), esp. pp. 21-32, 71-5.
28 International Bank for Reconstruction and Development (1963), esp. pp. 267, 290, 329, 365; R. Herr (1971), pp. 242-50.
29 J. Fontana and J. Nadal (1973), pp. 516-23; Donges (1976), p. 158 and *passim*; J. Harrison (1978), p. 150; A. Wright (1977), pp. 2 ff.; Baklanoff (1978), pp. 19-29, 43, 59.
30 L. T. Pinto (1960), pp. 183-4; OECD (1970a), esp. pp. 5-21, 38, 53; Nuno Alves Morgado (1979a), pp. 326-7; Baklanoff (1978), pp. 120, 176.
31 Karl-Herrmann Buck (1977); Xenophon Zolotas (1977).
32 Sergio Barzanti (1965), p. 89.
33 Among them, see S. Barzanti (1965); OECD (1973); idem (1970b); Centre Européen (1968); E. A. G. Robinson (1969).
34 S. Barzanti (1965), pp. 95 ff., *Economic History* (1978), pp. 169-70 (Graziani); Richard S. Eckhaus (1961), 285-317; Lloyd Saville (1968); Vera Lutz (1962), esp. chapters 5-7.
35 G. M. Sorokin (1967), i, 123-8, 181-212. Berend and Ranki (1974a), pp. 434-50; D. Warriner (1964), pp. xxiii-xxiv; UN Economic Commission for Europe (1960), p. vi/5; Berend and Ranki (1974b), p. 136.
36 G. M. Sorokin (1967), ii, 304-9, iii, 44-5, 69, 173-7, 259-87, 289-322, 381-409; Michael Kaser (1967), pp. 63-79, 162.
37 Werner Gumpel (1977), ii, pp. 155-85; Harriet Matejka (1972), ii, pp. 187-224; John Pinder (1971), 119-36; D. H. Aldcroft (1978), pp. 224-5, 230-1; Alfred Zauberman (1964), pp. 316 ff., 324-8; G. M. Sorokin (1967), ii, 324, 357-9.
38 M. Kaser (1967), pp. 140-4; A. Jezierski (1969), p. 14; G. M. Sorokin (1967), ii, 301, 306, 350-2, 429; Altiero Spinelli (1971); Michael Kaser (1971); A. Zauberman (1964), pp. 276-8.
39 G. M. Sorokin (1967), iii, 62.
40 Paul Bairoch (1976b), pp. 307, 309; United Nations, *Yearbook*; United Nations (1972), pp. 6-8; Also see Aldcroft (1978), p. 210; Maddison (1973), pp. 444, 478.
41 e.g. Aldcroft (1978), pp. 215-22. Conversely, each tried to become autarkic also in food, so that e.g. Czechoslovakia expanded her high-cost agriculture. Kaser (1967), pp. 216-17.
42 Kaser (1967), p. 137.
43 United Nations (1972), pp. 48-9; G. M. Sorokin (1967), i, 170, ii, 164, iii,

262. Eastern methods of calculation, sometimes known as 'gross gross' in the West, tend to include much double counting and thus exaggerate the growth-rates. We are concerned here, however, only with their relation to each other. Zauberman (1964), pp. 112-20.

44 G. M. Sorokin (1967), ii, 39-40, 276; Zauberman (1964), pp. 284-7.

45 D. Warriner (1964), pp. xiv-xv.

46 G. M. Sorokin (1967), i, 156, 455-6, 466, ii, 134; Zauberman (1964), pp. 43, 55; Aldcroft (1978), pp. 210-11.

47 N. J. G. Pounds (1958), p. 195, quoting Jan Wszelaki.

48 Maddison (1973), pp. 488, 496; UNECE, *Survey of 1960* p. iv/8, 15-28, and *Survey of 1971*, pp. 56 ff., 132-3.

49 Aldcroft (1978), p. 213; United Nations. *Yearbook.* Also Zauberman (1964), pp. 59-60, 77-80; D. Warriner (1964), pp. xviii-xix; Nicolas Spulber (1966), pp. 84-5; J. Blum (1978), p. 145; Hanna Jedruszczak (1972), 209.

50 K. Mihailovic (1969), p. 266.

51 G. M. Sorokin (1967), ii, 73 ff., Jezierski and Landau (1970), p. 346; Pavel Turcan (1969), p. 243; B. Winarski (1969), p. 286. For the G. D. R. see Pohl (1979), p. 287.

52 L. Köszegi (1969), p. 307; K. Mihailovic (1969), pp. 269-70; G. M. Sorokin (1967), iii, 77.

Bibliography

Abbreviations

AER	American Economic Review
AgHR	Agricultural History Review
AmHistR	American Historical Review
Annales ESC	Annales, Économies, Sociétés, Civilisations
BusHistR	Business History Review
CEHE	Cambridge Economic History of Europe
EcHR	Economic History Review
EJ	Economic Journal
EngHR	English Historical Review
ExplEcH	Explorations in Economic History
Ges and Ges	Geschichte und Gesellschaft
HistZ	Historische Zeitschrift
IntRevSocH	International Review of Social History
JahrbfWg	Jahrbuch für Wirtschaftsgeschichte
JahrbNS	Jahrbücher für Nationalökonomie und Statistik
JEcH	Journal of Economic History
JEuropEcH	Journal of European Economic History
JPE	Journal of Political Economy
JRStatS	Journal of the Royal Statistical Society
OEP	Oxford Economic Papers
ParlP	Parliamentary Papers
QJE	Quarterly Journal of Economics
RevEcStat	Review of Economic Statistics
RevEcStud	Review of Economic Studies
RevHES	Revue d'Histoire Économique et Sociale
RevHist	Revue Historique
ScandEcHR	Scandinavian Economic History Review
StudHistOec	Studia Historiae Oeconomicae
TransRHS	Transactions of the Royal Historical Society
VSWG	Vierteljahrschrift für Social- und Wirtschaftsgeschichte
YorksBull	Yorkshire Bulletin of Economic and Social Research
ZfN	Zeitschrift für Nationalökonomie
ZgSW	Zeitschrift für die Gesamte Staatswissenschaft

(NB: Place of publication is London, unless stated otherwise)

ABEL, Wilhelm, *Geschichte der deutschen Landwirtschaft vom frühen Mittelalter bis zum 19. Jahrhundert* (Stuttgart, 1962, 1967).
— *Massenarmut und Hungerkrisen im vorindustriellen Deutschland* (Göttingen, 1972).

ACHILLES, Walter, 'Die Bedeutung des Flachsanbaues im südlichen Niedersachsen' in KELLENBENZ (1975).

ADELMAN, Irma, and MORRIS, Cynthia Taft, 'The Role of Institutional Influences in Patterns of Agricultural Development', *JEcH* 39 (1979), 159-76.

ADELMANN, Gerhard, 'Structural Change in the Rhenish Linen and Cotton Trades at the Outset of Industrialization', in CROUZET, CHALONER, and STERN (1969).

AIKIN, J., *A Description of the Country from Thirty to Forty Miles around Manchester* (1795).

ALDCROFT, Derek H., *The European Economy 1914-1970* (1978).

ALLEN, G. C., 'An Eighteenth-Century Combination in the Copper-mining Industry', *EJ* 33 (1923), 74-85.

— *The Industrial Development of Birmingham and the Black Country* (1929).

ALLEN, James Jay, *The European Common Market and the GATT* (Washington, 1960).

ALMQUIST, Eric L., 'Pre-Famine Ireland and the Theory of European Proto-Industrialization', *JEcH* 39 (1979), 699-718.

ALONSO, W., 'Location Theory', in NEEDLEMAN (1968).

AMES, E., and ROSENBERG, N., 'Changing Technological Leadership and Industrial Growth', in ROSENBERG, N. (1971).

ANDERSON, Otto, 'Denmark', in LEE, W. R. (1979a).

ANDERSON, B. L., 'The Attorney and the Early Capital Market in Lancashire', in HARRIS, J. R. (1969).

ANDERSON, B. L., and COTTRELL, P. L. 'Another Victorian Capital Market: A Study of Banking and Bank Investors on Merseyside', *EcHR* 28 (1975), 598-615.

ANDERSON, Michael, *Family Structure in Nineteenth Century Lancashire* (Cambridge, 1971).

ANGELL, Norman, *The Great Illusion* (1910).

ARGAVALA, A. N., and SINGH, J. P., *Economics of Underdevelopment* (1963).

ARMENGAUD, A., 'Les débuts de la population dans les campagnes toulousaines', *Annales ESC* 6 (1951), 172-8.

— (ed.), *Études sur la vie rurale dans la France de l'Est* (Dijon, 1966).

— 'Population in Europe 1700-1914', in CIPOLLA (1973), iii.

ARNDT, H. W., *The Economic Lessons of the Nineteen-Thirties* (1944).

ARNIM, Wolf von, *Die Landwirtschaft Dänemarks als Beispiel intensiver Betriebsgestaltung bei starker weltwirtschaftlicher Verflechtung* (Kiel, 1951).

ASHLEY, Percy, *Modern Tariff History* (1920 ed.).

ASHTON, T. S., 'The Bill of Exchange and Private Banks in Lancashire', in T. S. ASHTON and R. S. SAYERS (eds.), *Papers in English Monetary History* (Oxford, 1953).

— 'Some Statistics of the Industrial Revolution in Britain', in E. M. Carus-Wilson (ed.), *Essays in Economic History*, iii (1962).

— *The Industrial Revolution 1760-1830* (1970).

ASHWORTH, William, *A Short History of the International Economy since 1850* (1962 ed.).

— 'Typologies and Evidence: Has Nineteenth-Century Europe a Guide to Economic Growth?' *EcHR* 30 (1977), 140-58.

ASTRÖM, Sven-Erik, 'English Timber Imports from Northern Europe in the Eighteenth Century', *ScandEcHR* 18 (1970), 12-32.

ATKINSON, Frank, *Some Aspects of the Woollen and Worsted Trade in Halifax*

(Halifax, 1956).

ATLANTIC INSTITUTE, *Europas Zukunft zwischen Ost und West* (Baden-Baden, 1971).

AUBIN, Hermann, and ZORN, Wolfgang, *Handbuch der deutschen Wirschafts- und Sozialgeschichte* (vol. 2, Stuttgart, 1976).

BAAR, Lothar, *Die Berliner Industrie in der industriellen Revolution* (Berlin, 1966).

BAASCH, Ernst, *Holländische Wirtschaftsgeschichte* (Jena, 1927).

BACHINGER, Karl, 'Das Verkehrswesen', in BRUSATTI (1973).

BAGWELL, P. S., *The Transport Revolution from 1770* (1974).

BAINES, Edward, *History of the Cotton Manufacture in Great Britain* (1835, repr. 1966).

BAIROCH, Paul 'Niveaux de développement économique de 1810 à 1910', *Annales ESC* 20 (1965), 1091-117.

— 'Europe's Gross National Product 1800-1975' *JEuropEcH* 5 (1976a), 273-340.

— *Commerce extérieur et développement économique de l'Europe au XIXe siècle* Paris, Hague, 1976b).

BANKLANOFF, Eric N., *The Economic Transformation of Spain and Portugal* (NY, 1978).

BALASSA, Bela, *Theory of Economic Integration* (1962).

— *Trade Liberalization Among Industrial Countries* (NY, 1967).

— 'Effective Protection in Developing Countries', in BHAGWATI *et al.* (1971).

BALDWIN, Robert E., *et al.*, *Trade, Growth and Balance of Payments: Essays in Honour of Gottfried Haberler* (Chicago, Amsterdam, 1965).

BALLOT, Charles, *L'introduction du machinisme dans l'industrie française* (Lille, Paris, 1923).

BARBOUR, Violet, *Capitalism in Amsterdam in the Seventeenth Century* (Baltimore, 1950).

BAREL, Yves, *Le développement économique de la Russie tsariste* (Paris, Hague, 1968).

BARKER, T. C., 'The Beginnings of the Canal Age', in Leslie S. Pressnell (ed.), *Studies in the Industrial Revolution* (1960).

— *The Glassmakers-Pilkington 1826-1976* (1977).

— 'Lord Salisbury, Chairman of the Great Eastern Railway 1868-72', in MARRINER (1978).

BARKER, T. C., and HARRIS, J. R., *A Merseyside Town in the Industrial Revolution : St. Helens* (1954).

BARKER, T. C., and SAVAGE, C. I., *An Economic History of Transport in Britain* (1974 ed.).

BARKHAUSEN, Max, 'Government Control and Free Enterprise in West Germany and the Low Countries in the Eighteenth Century', in EARLE (1974).

BARKIN, Kenneth D., *The Controversy over German Industrialization 1890-1902* (Chicago, 1970).

BARSBY, Steven L., 'Economic Backwardness and the Characteristics of Development', *JEcH* 29 (1969), 449-72.

BARTYS, Julian, 'Die Anfänge der Mechanisierung in der polnischen Landwirtschaft', *StudHistOec* 3 (1968), 135-57.

BARZANTI, Sergio, *The Underdeveloped Areas within the Common Market* (Princeton, NJ, 1965).

BASCH, A., *The Danube Basin and the German Economic Sphere* (1944).

BASTIE, V., 'Paris et l'Ile de France au temps de la révolution des chemins de fer

(1856-1880)' in MOLLAT, Michel (ed.), *Histoire de l'Île de France et de Paris* (Toulouse, 1971).

BAUER, P. T., and YAMEY, B. S., *The Economics of Underdeveloped Countries* (1957).

BAXTER, John L., *The Origins of the Social War in South Yorkshire . . .c.1750-1855* (unpubl. Ph. D. thesis, Sheffield, 1977).

BAYKOV, Alexander, *The Development of the Soviet Economic System.* Cambridge, 1944, repr. 1970).

— 'The Economic Development of Russia', *EcHR* 7 (1954), 137-49.

BECKETT, J. V., 'Onset of Industrialization in West Cumberland *c.* 1630-1750, in PALMER (1977?).

BEER, Adolf, *Die österreichische Handelspolitik im 19. Jahrhundert* (Vienna, 1891, repr. 1972).

BENAERTS, Pierre, *Les origines de la grande industrie Allemande* (Paris, 1933).

BENEDIKT, Heinrich, *Die wirtschaftliche Entwicklung in der Franz-Joseph-Zeit* (Vienna, Munich, 1958).

BENSUSAN-BUTT, D. M., *On Economic Growth, an Essay in Pure Theory* (Oxford, 1960).

BEREND, Ivan T., and RANKI, György 'Ungarns wirtschaftliche Entwicklung 1849-1918', in BRUSATTI (1973).

— — *Economic Development in East-Central Europe in the 19th and 20th Centuries (NY, 1974a).*

— — *Hungary. A Century of Economic Development* (Newton Abbot, 1974b).

— — 'L'évolution économique de l'Europe orientale entre les deux guerres mondiales', *AnnalesESC* 33 (1978), 389-407.

BERGERON, Louis, 'Les effets de la Révolution française et les French Wars' in LÉON (1978), iii.

— 'Investment and Industry in Lorraine', in POLLARD (1980).

BERGIER, Jean-Francois, *Problèmes de l'histoire économique de la Suisse* (Berne, 1968).

— *Naissance et croissance de la Suisse industrielle* (Berne, 1974).

BERGMAN, M., 'The Potato Blight in the Netherlands and its Social Consequences' *IntRevSocH* 12 (1967), 390-431.

BERGMANN, Jürgen, 'Das "alte Handwerk" im Übergang', in BÜSCH (1971a).

BERGSON, Abram, *Planning and Productivity under Soviet Socialism* (NY, 1968).

— *Productivity and the Social System—The USSR and the West* (Cambridge, Mass., 1978).

BERINDEI, Dan, *et al.* (eds.) *Die Bauern Mittel- und Osteuropas im Wandel des 18. und 19. Jahrhunderts* (Cologne, Vienna, 1973).

— 'Die Lage der Bauernschaft . . . in der Periode des organischen Reglements (1831-1858)', in BERINDEI (1973).

BERKNER, Lutz K., 'Inheritance, Land Tenure and Peasant Family Structure: a German Regional Comparison', in GOODY, Jack, THIRSK, Joan and THOMPSON, E. P. (eds.), *Family and Inheritance. Rural Society in Western Europe 1200-1800* (Cambridge, 1976).

BERKNER, Lutz, and MENDELS, Franklin, F., 'Inheritance Systems, Family Structure, and Demographic Patterns in Western Europe. 1700-1900', in TILLY, Charles (ed.), *Historical Studies of Changing Fertility* (Princeton, NJ, 1978).

BERRILL, Kenneth, 'Foreign Capital and Take-Off', in ROSTOW (1963).

BEST, Heinrich, 'Die regionale Differenzierung interessenpolitischer Orientierung im frühindustriellen Deutschland', in FREMDLING and TILLY (1979).

BEZUCHA, Robert J., *The Lyon Uprising of 1834* (Cambridge, Mass., (1974).

BHAGWATI, Jagdish, 'Immizerating Growth: A Geometric Note', *RevEcStud* 25 (1958), 201-5.

BHAGWATI, Jagdish N., *et al.* (eds.), *Trade, balance of payments and growth. Papers in international economics in Honour of Charles P. Kindleberger* (Amsterdam, Oxford, 1971).

BIRCH, Alan, *The Economic History of the British Iron and Steel Industry 1784-1879* (1967).

BIRCH, A., and FLINN, M. W., 'The English Steel Industry before 1856, with special reference to the development of the Yorkshire steel industry', *YorksBull* 6 (1954).

BIUCCHI, B. M., 'Switzerland, 1700-1914', in CIPOLLA (1973), iv.

Bjerke, Kjeld, 'The National Product of Denmark, 1870-1952', in INTERNA-TIONAL ASSOCIATION (1955).

BLACK, Cyril E. (ed.), *The Transformation of Russian Society. Aspects of Social Change since 1861* (Cambridge, Mass., 1960).

BLACK, R. D. Collison, 'The Irish Experience in Relation to the Theory and Policy of Economic Development', in YOUNGSON (1972).

BLACKWELL, William L., *The Beginnings of Russian Industrialization 1800-1860* (Princeton, NJ, 1968).

BLÄSING, Joachim F. E., *Das goldene Delta und sein eisernes Hinterland* (Leiden, 1973).

BLAISDELL, Donald C., *European Financial Control and the Ottoman Empire* (NY, 1966).

BLANCHARD, M., 'The Railway Policy of the Second Empire', in CROUZET, CHALONER, and STERN (1969).

BLASCHKE, Karlheinz, 'Industrialisierung und Bevölkerung in Sachsen im Zeitraum von 1830 bis 1890', in HISTORISCHE RAUMFORSCHUNG (1965).

— *Bevölkerungsgeschichte von Sachsen bis zur industriellen Revolution* (Weimar, 1967).

BLAUG, M., 'The Productivity of Capital in the Lancashire Cotton Industry during the Nineteenth Century', *EcHR* 13 (1961), 358-81.

— 'A Case of Emperor's Clothes: Perroux' Theories of Economic Domination', *Kyklos* 17 (1964).

BLOCH, Ernst, *Erbschaft dieser Zeit* (Frankfurt-Main, 1962).

BLUM, Jerome, *Noble Landowners and Agriculture in Austria 1815-1848* (Baltimore, 1948).

— 'The Rise of Serfdom in Eastern Europe', *American Historical Review*, 62 (1957), 807-36.

— *Lord and Peasant in Russia* (Princeton, NJ, 1961).

— *The End of the Old Order in Rural Europe* (Princeton, NJ, 1978).

BLUMBERG, Horst, *Die deutsche Textilindustrie in der industriellen Revolution* (Berlin, 1965).

BOCH, Rudolf, *Zur Entwicklung der Forschungsansätze der Proto-Industrialisierung* (Unpubl. Staatsexamen Bielefeld, 1977).

BODMER, Walter, *Die Entwicklung der schweizerischen Textilwirtschaft* (Zürich, 1960).

BOETHIUS, B., 'Swedish Iron and Steel, 1600-1955', *ScandEcHR* 6 (1958), 144-5.

BÖVENTER, Edwin von, 'Towards a United Theory of Spatial Economic Structure', in DEAN, Robert D., *et al.*, *Spatial Economic Theory* (NY, 1970).

BOG, Ingemar, *et al.* (eds.), *Wirtschaftliche und soziale Strukturen im säkulären Wandel. Festschrift für Wilhelm Abel* (Hanover, 1974).

BOGART, E. L., *Direct and Indirect Costs of the Great World War* (1920).

BOMBACH, Gottfried, 'Quantitative und monetäre Aspekte des Wirteschafts-wachstums', in W. G. HOFFMANN, (ed.), *Finanz-und währungspolitische Bedingungen stetigen Wirtschaftswachstums* (Berlin, 1959).

BONDI, Gerhard, *Deutschlands Außenhandel 1815-1870* (Berlin, 1958).

BOOGMAN, J. C., 'The Netherlands in the European Scene', in J. S. BROMLEY and E. H. KOSSMANN (eds.), *Britain and the Netherlands in Europe* (1968).

BOOKER, John, *Essex and the Industrial Revolution* (Chelmsford, 1974).

BORCHARDT, K., 'Regionale Wachstumsdifferenzierung in Deutschland im 19. Jahrhundert', in LÜTGE (1968).

— 'Zur Frage des Kapitalmangels in der ersten Hälfte des 19. Jahrhunderts in Deutschland', in BRAUN, *et al.*, (1972).

— 'Wirtschaftliches Wachstum und Wechsellagen 1800-1914', in AUBIN and ZORN (1976).

BORRIES, Bodo von, *Deutschlands Außenhandel 1836-1856* (Stuttgart, 1970).

BORSCHEID, Peter, *Textilarbeiterschaft in der Industrialisierung* (Stuttgart,1978).

— 'Arbeitskräftepotential, Wanderung und Wohlstandsgefälle, in FREMDLING and TILLY 1979).

BORTS, G. H., 'The Equalisation of Returns and Regional Economic Growth', *AER* 50 (1960), 319-47.

BORTS, G. H., and STEIN, T. L., 'Regional Growth and Maturity in the United States', in NEEDLEMAN (1968).

BOSERUP, M., 'Agrarian Structure—Take-Off', in ROSTOW, (1963).

BOUVIER, Jean, 'The Banking Mechanism in France in the late 19th Century', in CAMERON (1970a).

BOWDEN, Witt, *Industrial Society in England towards the End of the Eighteenth Century* (NY, 1925, London 1965).

BOWRING, John, *Report on the Prussian Commercial Union (ParlP* 1840).

BRANDT, Paul, *Die Zerstörung der Weltwirtschaft* (Berlin, 1922).

BRAUDEL, Fernand, *Capitalism and Material Life 1400-1800* (NY, 1973).

BRAUDEL, Fernand, *et al.* (eds.), *Conjoncture économique, structures sociales* (Paris, Hague, 1974).

BRAUDEL, Fernand, and LABROUSSE, Ernest (eds.), *Histoire économique et sociale de la France* (3 vols, Paris, vol. 2, 1970, vol. 3, 1976).

BRAUN, Hans-Joachim, *Technologische Beziehungen zwischen Deutschland und England von der Mitte des 17. bis zum Ausgang des 18. Jahrhunderts* (Düsseldorf, 1974).

BRAUN, Rudolf, *Industrialisierung und Volksleben* (Zürich, Stuttgart, 1960).

— 'The Rise of a Rural Class of Industrial Entrepreneurs', *Journal of World History* 10 (1967), 551-66.

BRAUN, Rudolf, *et al.*, *Industrielle Revolution: Wirtschaftliche Aspekte* (Cologne, Berlin, 1972).

BRAUNS, Heinrich, *Der Übergang von der Handweberei zum Fabrikbetrieb in der niederrheinischen Samt- und Seidenindustrie* (Leipzig, 1906).

BREPOHL, W., *Der Aufbau des Ruhrvolkes* (Recklinghausen, 1948).

BROADBRIDGE, S. A., 'The Sources of Railway Share Capital', in M. C. REED, (ed.), *Railways in the Victorian Economy* (Newton Abbot, 1969).

— *Studies in Railway Expansion and the Capital Market: England 1825-1873* (1970).

BROWER, Daniel, 'L'urbanisation russe à la fin du XIXe siècle', *Annales ESC* 32 (1977), 70–86.

BROWN, Robert, *General View of the Agriculture of the West Riding of Yorkshire* (1793 and 1799).

BRUGMANS, J. J., *Paardenkracht en Mensenmacht* (Hague, 1961, 1969).

BRUNNER, Otto, 'Das "ganze Haus" und die alteuropäische Ökonomik' in *Neue Wege der Sozialgeschichte* (Göttingen, 1956).

BRUSATTI, Alois, *Österreichische Wirtschaftspolitik vom Josephinismus zum Ständestaat* (Vienna, 1965).

— 'Österreich am Vorabend des industriellen Zeitalters', in INSTITUT FÜR ÖSTERREICHKUNDE (1971).

— (ed.), *Die Habsburgermonarchie 1848-1918* (vol. 1, Vienna, 1973).

BUCKATZSCH, E. J., 'Places of Origin of a Group of Immigrants into Sheffield', *EcHR* 2 (1950), 303–6.

BUCK, Karl-Hermann, 'Griechenlands Beitritt zur EG—Cui Bono', in HASEN-PFLUG and KOHLER (1977).

BUSCH, Otto, *Militärsystem und Sozialleben im alten Preußen 1713-1807* (Berlin, 1962).

— (ed.), *Untersuchungen zur Geschichte der frühen Industrialisierung* (Berlin, 1971a).

— *Industrialisierung und Gewerbe im Raum Berlin/Brandenburg* (Berlin, 1971b).

BULFERETTI, Luigi, 'Le déclin de l'influence des sources énergétiques... dans l'Italie du XIXe siècle', in LEON, CROUZET, GASCON, (1972).

BULL, Edvard, 'Industrialisation as a Factor in Economic Growth', PREMIÈRE CONFERENCE (1960).

BUNZL, Karl, *Klassenkampf in the Diaspora* (Vienna, 1975).

BURGESS, Keith, *Origins of British Industrial Relations* (1975).

BURGDÖRFER, F., 'Migration across the frontiers of Germany', in WILLCOX (1931, 1696).

BUTT, John, 'The Scottish Cotton Industry during the Industrial Revolution, 1780-1840', in CULLEN (1977).

BUTTLER, Friedrich, *Growth Pole Theory and Economic Development* (Farnborough, 1975).

BYLUND, Erik, 'Industrial Location Policy and the Problem of the Sparsely Populated Areas in Sweden' in E. A. G. Robinson (1969).

BYTHELL, Duncan, *The Handloom Weavers* (Cambridge, 1969).

CAFAGNA, Luciano, 'The Industrial Revolution in Italy, 1830-1914' in CIPOLLA (1973), iv.

CAICCI, B., 'The Main Themes in the History of the Southern Question', *Banca Nationale del Lavoro Quarterly Review* 15 (1962), 383–410.

CAIRD, James, *English Agriculture in 1850-1* (1852, 1968).

CAIRNCROSS, A. K., and FAALAND, J., 'Long-Term Trends in Europe's Trade', *EJ* 62 (1952), 25–34.

CAMERON, Rondo, 'Some French Contributions to the Industrial Development of Germany', *JEcH* 16 (1956a), 281-321.

— 'Founding of the Bank of Darmstadt' *ExplEcH* 8 (1956b), 113–30.

— *France and the Economic Development of Europe* (Princeton, NJ, 1961).

— (ed.), *Banking in the Early Stages of Industrialization* (1967a).

— 'France 1800-1870', (1967b) in CAMERON (1967a).

— 'Belgium 1800-1875', (1967c), in *ibid.*

— 'Conclusions' (1967d), in *ibid.*

— (ed.), *Essays in French Economic History* (Homewood, Ill., 1970a).
— 'L'économie francaise: passé, présent, avenir', *Annales ESC* 25 (1970b), 1418-33.
— 'Pourquoi l'industrialisation européenne fut-elle si inégale?', in LEON, CROUZET, GASCON (1972).
CAMPBELL, R. H., *Carron Company* (Edinburgh, 1961).
— *Scotland Since 1707* (Oxford, 1971).
CAMPS, Miriam, *Britain and the European Community 1955-1963* (1964).
— *European Unification in the Sixties* (1967).
— 'Ist Europa nicht mehr aktuell?' ATLANTIC INSTITUTE (1971).
CAPIE, Forrest, 'The British Tariff and Industrial Protection in the 1930's', *EcHR* 31 (1978).
CARON, F., 'L'évolution économique depuis un siècle', in Jean RICHARD (ed.), *Histoire de la Bourgogne* (Toulouse, 1979).
— 'French Railroad Investment, 1850-1914', in CAMERON (1970a).
— in LÉON (1978), iii, pp. 385-504, iv, pp. 69-206.
CARR, Raymond, *Spain 1808-1939* (Oxford, 1966).
CARTER, Alice, 'The Dutch and the English Public Debt in 1777' 59-61, and 'Dutch Foreign Investment 1738-1800', 322-40, *Economica* 20 (1953).
CASPARD, Pierre, 'L'accumulation du capital dans l'indiennage au XVIIIème siècle', *Revue du Nord*, 61 (1979), 115-24.
CAULIER-MATHY, N., *La modernisation des charbonnages liégeois pendant la première moitié du 19e siècle* (Paris, 1971).
CAVES, Richard E., 'Vent for Surplus Models of Trade and Growth', in BALDWIN (1965).
— *Trade and Economic Structure, Models and Methods* (Cambridge, Mass., 1967).
— 'Export-led Growth and the New Economic History' in BHAGWATI (1971).
CAYEZ, Pierre, 'Industrielle und regionale Entwicklung im 19. Jahrhundert. Das Beispiel von Lyon', in POLLARD (1980).
CENTRE EUROPEEN DE COORDINATION ET DE DOCUMENTATION EN SCIENCES SOCIALES, *Regional Disequilibrium in Europe* (Brussels, 1968).
CHAMBERLAIN, Neil W., 'Training and Human Capital', in SPENCER and WORONIAK (1967).
CHAMBERS, J. D., 'The Worshipful Company of Framework Knitters (1657-1779)', *Economica* 9 (1929), 296-329.
— *Nottinghamshire in the Eighteenth Century* (1932).
— 'Enclosure and Labour Supply in the Industrial Revolution', *EcHR* 5 (1953), 319-43.
— *The Vale of Trent 1670-1800* (n. d.).
— *Population, Economy and Society in Pre-Industrial England* (1972).
CHAMBON, R. *L'Histoire de la verrerie en Belgique* (Brussels, 1955).
CHAPMAN, S. D., *The Early Factory Masters* (Newton Abbot, 1967).
— *The Cotton Industry in the Industrial Revolution* (1972a).
— 'The Genesis of the British Hosiery Industry 1600-1750', *Textile History* 3 (1972), 7-50.
— 'Industrial Capital Before the Industrial Revolution', in HARTE and PONTING (1973).
— *The Devon Cloth Industry in the Eighteenth Century* (Torquay, 1978).
— 'Financial Restraints on the Growth of Firms in the Cotton Industry, 1790-1850', *EcHR* 32 (1979), 50-69.

CHASSAGNE, Serge, 'La diffusion rurale de l'industrie cotonnière en France (1750-1850)', *Revue du Nord* 61 (1979), 97-114.

CHAUNU, H. and P., *Seville et l'Atlantique* (vol. 1, Paris, 1955).

CHAUNU, Pierre, 'Histoire quantitative et histoire sociale', *Cahiers Vilfredo Pareto*, 3 (1964), 165-76.

—— 'Réflexions sur l'échec industriel de la Normandie', in LEON, CROUZET, GASCON (1972).

CHAYANOV, A. V., *Theory of Peasant Economy* (1966).

CHECKLAND, S. G., 'The British City Region', in POLLARD (1980).

CHILDREN'S EMPLOYMENT COMMISSION (MINES), *First Report*, *ParlP* (1842), XV. 380.

CHIROT, Daniel, *Social Change in a Peripheral Society. The Creation of a Balkan Country* (NY, 1976).

CHIVA, I., 'Causes sociologiques du sous-développement régional: L'example Corse', *Cahiers Internationaux de Sociologie* 24 (1958), 141-7.

CHOMAC-KLIMEK, Regina, 'Investment Expenditure in Farms in the Congress Kingdom of Poland at the turn of the 19th and 20th Century', *StudHistOec* 10 (1975), 177-81.

CHURCH, Roy A., *Economic and Social Change in a Midland Town: Victorian Nottingham 1815-1900* (1966).

CIPOLLA, Carlo M., *The Economic History of World Population* (Harmondsworth, 1962, 1972).

—— (ed.), *Fontana Economic History of Europe* (6 vols., 1973).

CLAPHAM, J. H., 'The Transference of the Worsted Industry from Norfolk to the West Riding', *EJ*, 20 (1910), 195-210.

—— *The Economic Development of France and Germany 1815-1914* (Cambridge, 1928 ed.).

—— *An Economic History of Modern Britain* (Cambridge, vol. 1, 1967 ed., vol. 2, 1936 ed.).

CLARKSON, L. A., *The Pre-Industrial Economy of England 1500-1700* (1971).

CLENDENNING, P. H., 'William Gomm. A Case Study of the Foreign Entrepreneur in 18th Century Russia', *JEuropEcH* 6 (1977), 535-48.

CLIFFE LESLIE, T. E., 'The Land System in France' in PROBYN (1881).

CLOUGH, Shepard B., 'Retardative Factors in French Economic History', *JEcH* 6 Suppl. (1946), 91-102.

CLOUGH, Shepard B., *The Economic History of Modern Italy* (NY, 1964).

CLOUGH, Shepard B., and LIVI, Carlo. 'Economic Growth in Italy. An Analysis of the Uneven Development of North and South', *JEcH* 16 (1956), 334-49.

CLOW, A. and N., *The Chemical Revolution* (1952).

COHEN, Jon S., 'Financing Industrialization in Italy, 1894-1914: The Partial Transformation of a Late-Comer', *JEcH* 27 (1967), 363-82.

COHN, Stanley H., *Economic Development in the Soviet Union* (Lexington, Mass., 1970).

—— 'The Soviet Economy: Performance and Growth' in TREML (1968).

COLE, Charles W., *Colbert and a Century of French Mercantilism* (2 vols., NY, 1939).

—— *French Mercantilism 1683-1700* (NY, 1971 repr.).

COLEMAN, D. C., 'Growth and Decay during the Industrial Revolution: The Case of East Anglia', *ScandEcHR* 10 (1962), 115-27.

—— 'An Innovation and its Diffusion: the "New Draperies"', *EcHR* 22 (1969), 417-29.

—— 'Textile Growth', in HARTE and PONTING (1973).
—— *The Economy of England 1450-1750* (1977).
COLLINS, E. J. T., 'Labour Supply and Demand in European Agriculture 1800-1880', in JONES and WOOLF (1974).
CONDLIFFE, John Bell, *The Commerce of Nations* (1951).
CONSTANTINIU, F., 'Fürstliche Reform und Bojarenreaktion: die Lage der rumänischen Bauernschaft im Zeitalter des aufgeklärten Absolutismus', in BERINDEI (1973).
CONZE, Werner, 'The Effects of Nineteenth-Century Liberal Agrarian Reforms on Social Structure in Central Europe', in CROUZET, CHALONER, and STERN (1969).
—— *Sozialgeschichte der Familie in der Neuzeit Europas* (Stuttgart, 1976).
COOPER, J. P., 'In Search of Agrarian Capitalism', *Past and Present* 80 (1978).
COOTNER, Paul H., 'Social Overhead Capital and Economic Growth', in ROSTOW (1963).
COPPA, Frank J., 'The Italian Tariff and the Conflict Between Agriculture and Industry', *JEcH* 30 (1970), 742-69.
COPPÉ, A., 'International Consequences of the Great Crisis', in VAN DER WEE (1972).
COQUIN, François Xavier, in LÉON (1978), iii, pp. 39-50, 208-25.
CORDEN, W. M., 'The Effects of Trade on the Rate of Growth', in BHAGWATI *et al.* (1971).
CORNWALL, John, *Modern Capitalism, its Growth and Transformation* (1977).
COURT, W. H. B., *The Rise of the Midland Industries 1600-1838* (1938, 1953).
CRAEYBECKX, Jan, 'The beginnings of the Industrial Revolution in Belgium', in CAMERON (1970a).
CRAFTS, N. F. R., 'Industrial Revolution in England and France: Some Thoughts on the Question: "Why was England First"?', *EcHR* 30 (1977).
—— 'Entrepreneurship and a Probabilistic View of the British Industrial Revolution', *EcHR* 31 (1878).
CRAWFORD, R. F., 'An Inquiry into Wheat Prices and Wheat Supply', *JRStatS* 53 (1895), 75-111.
CRAWFORD, W. H., 'The Influence of the Landlord in Eighteenth-Century Ulster', in CULLEN and SMOUT (1977).
—— 'The Rise of the Linen Industry', in CULLEN (1969).
CRISP, Olga, 'Russian Financial Policy and the Gold Standard at the end of the Nineteenth Century', *EcHR* 6 (1953-4), 156-72.
—— 'Russia, 1860-1914', in CAMERON (1967a).
—— 'The Pattern of Russian Industrialisation up to 1914', in LÉON, CROUZET, GASCON (1972).
—— *Studies in the Russian Economy Before 1914* (1976).
—— 'Labour and Industrialization in Russia', *CEHE* 7/2 (1978), pp. 308-415.
CROUZET, François, *L'Economie britannique et le blocus continental* (Paris, 2 vols., 1958).
—— 'Les origines du sous-développement économique du Sud-Ouest', *Annales du Midi* (1959) 71-9.
—— 'War, Blockade and Economic Change in Europe, 1792-1815', *JEcH* 24 (1964), 567-90.
—— 'An Annual Index of French Industrial Production in the 19th Century', in CAMERON (1970a).
—— 'Essai de construction d'un indice annuel de la production industrielle française

au 19e siècle', *Annales ESC* 25 (1970b) 56-99.
— 'Western Europe and Great Britain: Catching up in the first half of the 19th Century', in YOUNGSON (1972).
— 'Encore la croissance économique française au 19e siècle', *Revue du Nord* 54 (1972b), 271-88.
— *Capital Formation in the Industrial Revolution* (1972c).
— 'French Economic History in the 19th Century Reconsidered', *History* 59 (1974).
— 'When the Railways were built: A French Engineering Firm during the "Great Depression" and After', in MARRINER (1978).
— *L'Économie de la Grande-Bretagne Victorienne* (Paris, 1978b).
CROUZET, F., CHALONER, W. H., and STERN, W. M. (eds.), *Essays in European Economic History 1789-1914* (1969).
CRUMP, W. B., *The Leeds Woollen Industry 1780-1820* (Leeds, 1931).
CSATO, T., 'The Development of Internal Trade in East Central, and South-East Europe', *Acta Historica* 23 (1977), 397-439.
CULLEN, L. M., 'Problems in the Interpretation and Revision of Eighteenth-Century Irish Economic History', *TransRHS* 5th S., 17 (1967), 1-22.
— *Anglo-Irish Trade 1660-1800* (Manchester, 1968a).
— 'Irish History Without the Potato', *Past and Present*, 40 (1968b), 72-83.
— *The Formation of the Irish Economy* (Cork, 1969).
— *An Economic History of Ireland Since 1660* (1972).
CULLEN, L. M., and SMOUT, T. C., *Comparative Aspects of Scottish and Irish Economic and Social History 1600-1900*, (Edinburgh, 1977).
— 'Economic Growth in Scotland and Ireland', in CULLEN and SMOUT (1977b).
CURTISS, John Shelton (ed.), *Essays in Russian and Soviet History* (Leiden, 1963).
CZECHOSLOVAK AND WORLD HISTORY INSTITUTE, *Economic History*, 2 (Prague, 1978).
DANIELS, George W., *The Early English Cotton Industry* (Manchester, 1920).
DAVIN, Louis, E., 'The Structural Crisis of a Regional Economy. A Case Study: The Walloon Area', in ROBINSON, E. A. G., (1969).
DAVIS, R., 'English Foreign Trade, 1700-1774', *EcHR* 15 (1962-3), 285-303.
— *The Rise of the Atlantic Economies* (1973).
DAWSON, W. H., *Protection in Germany* (1904).
DEANE, Phyllis, 'The Output of the British Woollen Industry in the 18th Century', *JEcH*, 17 (1957), 207-23.
— *The First Industrial Revolution* (Cambridge, 1965).
DEANE, Phyllis, and COLE, W. A., *British Economic Growth 1688-1959* (Cambridge, 1969).
DECHESNE, Laurent, *Industrie drapière de la Vesdre avant 1800* (Paris, Liege, 1926).
DEFOE, Daniel, *Advantages to Scotland by an Incorporate Union with England* (Edinburgh, 1706a).
— *Fifth Essay on Removing National Prejudices* (Edinburgh, 1706b).
— *A Tour Through the Whole Island of Great Britain* (2 vols, 1962 ed.).
DELAISI, François, *Les deux Europes* (Paris, 1929).
DELLE-DONNE, O., *European Tariff Policies since the World War* (NY, 1928).
DEMOULIN, Robert, *Guillaume Ier et la transformation des Provinces Belges (1815-1830)* (Paris, 1938).

DENISON, E. F., *Why Growth Rates Differ* (Washington, 1967).

DEPREZ, P., 'The Demographic Development of Flanders in the Eighteenth Century', in GLASS and EVERSLEY (1965).

DESPOT, Miloslav, 'Über die Entstehung und Entwicklung der Manufakturen in Kroatien bis zum Jahre 1948' *StudHistOec* 4 (1969), 141-56.

DESPRESCHINS, A., *Liévin Bauwens et sa famille* (Bruges, 1954).

DEUTSCH, Karl W., and ECKSTEIN, Alexander, 'National Industrialisation and the Declining Share of the International Economic Sector'. *World Politics* 13 (1961), 267-99.

DEVINE, T. M., 'The Colonial Traders and Industrial Investment in Scotland c. 1700-1815', *EcHR* 29 (1976), 1-13.

— 'Colonial Commerce and the Scottish Economy c.1739-1815', in CULLEN and SMOUT (1977).

— 'Temporary Migration and the Scottish Highlanders in the Nineteenth Century', *EcHR* 32 (1979), 344-59.

DEYON, Pierre, 'La diffusion rurale des industries textiles en Flandre française', *Revue du Nord* 61 (1979), 83-95.

DHONT, J., 'The Cotton Industry at Ghent during the French Regime', in CROUZET, CHALONER, and STERN (1969).

DHONT, Jan, and BRUWIER, Marinette, 'The Low Countries 1700-1914', in CIPOLLA (1973), iv.

DICKLER, Robert A., 'Organization and Change in Productivity in Eastern Prussia', in PARKER and JONES (1975).

DICKSON, David, 'Aspects of the Rise and Decline of the Irish Cotton Industry', in CULLEN and SMOUT (1977).

DIETZ, Walter, *Die Wuppertaler Garnnahrung* (Neustadt/Aisch, 1957).

— 'Die Wuppertaler Garnnahrung', in JORDAN and WOLF (1977).

DILLEN, J. G. van, 'Economic Fluctuations and Trade in the Netherlands, 1650-1750', in EARLE (1974).

DINKLAGE, Karl, 'Die landwirtschaftliche Entwicklung', in BRUSATTI (1973).

DLUGOBORSKI, Waclaw, *The Influx of Labour to Industry in the Countries of Central and Eastern Europe (1850-1918)* (Jablonna, 1973a).

— 'Peasant Economy in the Coal and Smelting Regions of Middle-East Europe Before and During the Early Period of Industrialisation', *StudHistOec* 10 (1975), 125-32.

— 'Wirtschafliche Region und politische Grenzen: Die Industrialisierung des oberschlesischen Kohlenbeckens' in POLLARD (1980).

DMYTRYSHYN, Basil, *A History of Russia* (Englewood Cliffs, NJ, 1977).

DOBB, Maurice, *Soviet Economic Development since 1917* (1966 ed.).

DODD, A. H., *The Industrial Revolution in North Wales* (Cardiff, 1933).

DOLLINGER, Philippe (ed.), *Histoire de l'Alsace* (Toulouse, 1970).

DONGES, J. B., *La Industrialización en España* (Barcelona, 1971).

DOVRING, Folke, 'The Transformation of European Agriculture', *CEHE*, vi, (1966), pp. 604-72.

DOWNS, Anthony, *An Economic Theory of Democracy* (NY, 1957).

DRAKE, Michael, 'Norway', in LEE (1979a).

DREYFUS, François-G., in LÉON (1978), iii.

DUDEK, Frantisek, 'The Transition from the Mechano-Chemical Manufactory Type Plant to the Factory', in CZECHOSLAVAK AND WORLD HISTORY INSTITUTE (1978).

DUMKE, R. H., *The Political Economy of German Economic Unification* (Unpubl.

Ph. D. Dissertation, Wisconsin, 1976).

—— 'Anglo-Deutscher Handel und Frühindustrialisierung in Deutschland 1822–1865', *Ges and Ges* 5 (1979), 175–200.

DUNHAM, Arthur Louis, *The Anglo-French Treaty of Commerce of 1860* (NY, 1971 ed.).

—— *The Industrial Revolution in France 1815–1848* (NY, 1955).

DUNLEVY, J. A., and GEMERY, H. A., 'Economic Opportunity and the Response of "Old" and "New" Migrants to the United States', *JEcH* 38 (1978).

DUNN, Matthias, *View of the Coal Trade of the North of England* (Newcastle/Tyne, 1844).

DUPÂQUIER, Jacques, 'Les aventures démographiques comparées de la France et l'Irlande (XVIIIe–XXe siècle)', *Annales ESC* 33 (1978), 143–55.

DUPRIEZ, Leon H., BARDOS, Feltorony, N., SZAPARI, G., and PEEMANS, J. -P., *Diffusion du progrès et convergence des prix* (2 vols., Louvain, Paris, 1966, 1970).

—— 'Principes et problèmes d'interprétation', in DUPRIEZ *et al.* (1966b).

DURAND, John D. (ed.), *World Population: Special Number of Annals of the American Academy of Political and Social Sciences* (1967).

—— 'A Long-Range View of World Population Growth', in DURAND (1967b).

DURIE, Alastair J., 'The Scottish Linen Industry in the Eighteenth Century: Some Aspects of Expansion', in CULLEN and SMOUT (1977).

EARLE, E. M. (ed.), *Modern France. Problems of the Third and Fourth Republic* (Princeton, NJ, 1951).

EARLE, Peter (ed.), *Essays in European Economic History 1500–1800* (Oxford, 1974).

EASTERLIN, R. A., 'Regional Growth in income: long-term tendencies', in KUZNETS, S., MILLER, R. A., and EASTERLIN, R. A., *Population Redistribution and Economic Growth, United States 1870–1950* (Philadelphia, 1960a).

—— 'Interregional Differences in Per Capita Incomes, Population and Total Income. 1840–1950', *Conference on Research in Income and Wealth* vol. 24, (Princeton, NJ, 1960b), pp. 73–140.

—— 'Effects of Population Growth on the Economic Development of Developing Countries', in DURAND (1967).

ECKAUS, Richard S., 'The North-South Differential in Italian Economic Development', *JEcH*, 21 (1961), 285–317.

ECKSTEIN, Alexander, 'National Income and Capital Formation in Hungary 1900–1950', in INTERNATIONAL ASSOCIATION FOR RESEARCH IN INCOME AND WEALTH (1955).

ECONOMIC HISTORY, *Second International Congress*, Aix-en-Provence in 1962 (Paris, Hague, 1965).

—— *Seventh International Congress* (Edinburgh, 1978).

EDDIE, Scott, M. 'The Changing Pattern of Landownership in Hungary 1867–1914', *EcHR* 20 (1967), 293–310.

—— 'Agricultural Production and Output per Worker in Hungary, 1870–1913', *JEcH* 28 (1968).

—— 'Die Landwirtschaft als Quelle des Arbeitskraft-Angebots', *VSGW* 56 (1969).

—— 'Farmers' Reactions to Price in Large-Estate Agriculture: Hungary 1870–1913', *EcHR* 24 (1971), 571–88.

—— 'The Terms of Trade as a Tax on Agriculture: Hungary's Trade with Austria, 1883–1913', *JEcH* 32 (1972), 298–315.

EDWARDS, J. K., 'The Decline of the Norwich Textile Industry', *YorksBull* 16 (1964), 31–41.

EISTERT, Ekkehard, *Die Beeinflussung des Wirtschaftswachstums in Deutschland von 1883 bis 1913 durch das Bankensystem* (Berlin, 1970).

EISTERT, Ekkehard, and RINGEL, Johannes, 'Die Finanzierung des wirtschaftlichen Wachstums durch die Banken', in HOFFMANN (1971).

ELLISON, Thomas, *The Cotton Trade of Great Britain* (1886, 1968).

ENCISO, A. González, and MERINO, J. Patricio, 'The Public Sector and Economic Growth in Eighteenth Century Spain', *JEuropEcH* 8 (1979), 553–92.

ENGRAND, Charles, 'Concurrences et complémentarités des villes et des campagnes: les manufactures picards de 1780 à 1815' *Revue du Nord* 61 (1979), 61–81.

ERCEG, Ivan, 'Die theresianischen Reformen in Kroatien', in HAUSHOFER and BOELCKE (1967).

ERLICH, Alexander, 'The Soviet Industrialization Debate, 1924–1928' (Cambridge, Mass, 1960).

EVERLING, Ulrich, 'Integrative politische Probleme der Erweiterung der EG', in HASENPFLUG and KOHLER (1977).

FABER, J. A., 'Anpassung friesischer Bauern und Veränderungen im Preis- und Kostengefüge während des 18. Jahrhunderts', in BOG (1974).

FABER, Karl-Georg, 'Was ist eine Geschichtslandschaft', in PETRY (1968).

FAHLBECK, Professor, 'Die Handelspolitik Schwedens und Norwegens', in VEREIN FÜR SOCIALPOLITIK (1892), i.

FALKUS, M. E., *The Industrialization of Russia 1700–1914* (1972).

—— 'Aspects of Foreign Investment in Tsarist Russia'', *JEuropEcH* 8 (1979), 5–36.

FALNIOWSKA-GRADOWSKA, Alicja, 'Some Remarks on Rental System in Southern Poland', *StudHistOec* 10 (1975), 173–5.

FARNIE, D. A., *The English Cotton Industry and the World Market 1815–1896* (Oxford, 1979).

FAUCHER, Julius, 'The Russian Agrarian Legislation of 1861', in PROBYN (1881).

FECHNER, Hermann, *Wirtschaftsgeschichte der deutschen Provinz Schlesien in der Zeit ihrer provinziellen Selbständigkeit 1741–1806* (Breslau, 1907).

FEIS, H., *Europe, the World's Banker 1870–1914* (New Haven, 1930).

FELTONRONYI, Nicholas B., 'Allemagne-Angleterre 1792–1913', in DUPRIEZ *et al.* (1966).

FENOALTEA, Stefano, 'Railroads and Italian Industrial Growth', *ExplEcH* 9 (1971–2), 325–51.

—— 'The Discipline and They: Notes on Counterfactual Methodology and the "New Economic History"', *JEuropEcH* 2 (1973).

FILIPINI, Jean-Pierre, 'L'Espagne et l'Italie', in LÉON (1978), iii, pp. 540–56.

FINK, Krisztina Maria, *Die österreichisch-ungarische Monarchie als Wirtschaftsgemeinschaft* (Munich, 1968).

FISCHER, Wolfram, *Der Staat und die Anfänge der Industrialisierung in Baden 1800–1850* (vol. l, Berlin, 1962).

—— 'Government Activity and Industrialization in Germany', in ROSTOW (1963).

—— (ed.), *Wirtschafts- und Sozialgeschichtliche Probleme der frühen Industrialisierung* (Cologne, Berlin, 1968).

—— 'Das Verhältnis von Staat und Wirtschaft in Deutschland am Beginn der Industrialisierung', in BRAUN *et al.* (1972).

—— *Wirtschaft und Gesellschaft im Zeitalter der Industrialisierung* (Göttingen, 1972b).

—— 'Rural Industrialization and Population Change', *Comparative Studies in Society and History* 15 (1973), 158-70.
—— 'Rekrutierung und Ausbildung', in Reinhard KOSELLECK (ed.). *Studien zum Beginn der modernen Welt* (Stuttgart, 1977).
FLINN, M. W., 'The Stabilization of Mortality in Pre-Industrial Western Europe', *JEuropEcH* 3 (1974), 285-318.
—— Malthus, Emigration and Potatoes in the Scottish North-West, 1770-1870' in CULLEN and SMOUT, (1977).
FOHLEN, Claude, *L'industrie textile au temps du second empire* (Paris, 1956).
—— 'Charbon et révolution industrielle en France', in Louis TRENARD (ed.), *Charbon et sciences humaines* (Paris, 1966).
—— 'The Industrial Revolution in France', in CAMERON (1970).
—— 'France, 1700-1914', in CIPOLLA, (1973), iv.
FORBERGER, Rudolf, *Die Manufaktur in Sachsen vom Ende des 16. bis zum Anfang des 19. Jahrhunderts* (Berlin, 1958).
FOSTER, John, *Class Struggle in the Industrial Revolution* (1974).
FOURASTIÉ, Jean, *Le Grand Espoir du XXe siècle* (Paris, 1963).
FRANK, André Gunder, *On Capitalist Underdevelopment* (Bombay, 1975).
FRANZ, Günther, 'Landwirtschaft 1800-1850', in AUBIN and ZORN (1976).
FREMDLING, Rainer, *Eisenbahnen und deutsches Wirtschaftswachstum 1840-1879* (Dortmund, 1975).
—— 'Modernisierung und Wachstum der Schwerindustrie in Deutschland 1830-1860', *Ges and Ges* 5 (1979), 201-27.
FREMDLING, Rainer, and TILLY, Richard D., *Industrialisierung und Raum. Studien zur regionalen Differenzierung im Deutschland des 19. Jahrhunderts* (Stuttgart, 1979).
FREMDLING, Rainer, and HOHORST, Gerd, 'Marktintegration der deutschen Wirtschaft im 19. Jahrhundert', in FREMDLING and TILLY (1979).
FREMDLING, Rainer, PIERENKEMPER, Toni, and TILLY, R. H., 'Regionale Differenzierung in Deutschland als Schwerpunkt der wissenschaftlichen Forschung', in FREMDLING and TILLY (1979).
FREUDENBERGER, Herman, 'The Woolen-Goods Industry of the Habsburg Monarchy in the Eighteenth Century', *JEcH* 20 (1960), 383-406.
—— *The Waldstein Woolen Mill—Noble Entrepreneurship in Eighteenth-Century Bohemia* (Boston, 1963).
—— 'The Mercantilist Proto-Factories', *Business History Review* 40 (1966), 167-89.
—— 'State Intervention as an Obstacle to Economic Growth in the Habsburg Monarchy', *JEcH* 27 (1967), 493-509.
—— 'Die Struktur der frühindustriellen Fabrik im Umriss (mit besonderer Berücksichtigung Böhmens)' in FISCHER (1968).
—— 'Das Arbeitsjahr', in BOG (1974).
FREUDENBERGER, Herman, and MENSCH, Gerhard, *Von der Provinzstadt zur Industrieregion* (Göttingen, 1975).
FREY, Emil, 'Die schweizerische Handelspolitik der letzten Jahrzehnte', in VEREIN FÜR SOCIALPOLITIK (1892), i.
FRIDLIZIUS, G., 'Sweden', in LEE, W. R. (1979a).
FRIED, Pankraz, 'Reagrarisierung Südbayerns seit dem 19. Jahrhundert', in KELLENBENZ (1975).
FRIEDMAN, Philip, 'The Welfare Costs of Bilateralism: German–Hungarian Trade, 1933-1938', *ExplEcH* 13 (1976), 113-26.
—— 'An Econometric Model of National Income, Commercial Policy and the Level

of International Trade: The Open Economies of Europe 1924–1938', *JEcH* 38 (1978), 148–80.

FRIEDMANN, J., 'A formal theory of polarized development', in *Growth Centres in Regional Economic Development.* (NY, 1972).

FUA, Giorgio, *Notes on Italian Economic Growth 1861–1964* (Milan, 1965).

FUHRMANN, Joseph T., *The Origins of Capitalism in Russia* (Chicago, 1972).

GALE, W. K. V., 'Development of Industrial Technology—The Black Country 1700–1900', in *Birmingham and its Industrial Region. A Scientific Survey* (1950).

GARDEN, Maurice, *Lyons et les Lyonnais au XVIIIe siècle* (Paris, 1970).

—— in LÉON, (1978), iii, pp. 13–20, 39–50.

GARCIA-ECHEVARRIA, Santiago, *Wirtschaftsentwicklung Spaniens unter dem Einfluß der europäischen Integration* (Cologne and Opladen, 1964).

GARHOFER, Emil, 'Hundert Jahre österreichische Gewerbepolitik' in Mayer (1949).

GARRIER, Gilbert, in LÉON, (1978), iv, pp. 13–68, 397–454.

GASTEYGER, Kurt 'Introduction', in ATLANTIC INSTITUTE (1971).

GATTRELL, V. A. C., 'Labour, Power and the Size of Firms in Lancashire Cotton in the Second Quarter of the Nineteenth Century', *EcHR* 30 (1977).

GEIGER, Reed G., *The Anzin Coal Company 1800–1833* (Newark, Del., 1974).

GENDARME, René, *La Région du Nord. Essai d'analyse économique* (Paris, 1954).

GEORGE, Dorothy, *London Life in the Eighteenth Century* (1925).

GERARD, Martin, 'Évolution de l'agriculture en Auxois de 1840 à 1939', in ARMENGAUD (1966).

GERLACH, Kurt Albert, *Dänemarks Stellung in der Weltwirtschaft* (Jena, 1911).

GERSCHENKRON, Alexander, *Bread and Democracy in Germany* (NY, 1943).

—— 'The Rate of Industrial Growth in Russia since 1885', *JEcH* Suppl. 7 (1947a), 144–74.

—— 'The Soviet indices of industrial production', *RevEcStat* 29 (1947b).

—— 'The Early Phase of Industrialization in Russia: Afterthoughts and Counter-thoughts', in ROSTOW (1963).

—— 'Agrarian Policies and Industrialization in Russia 1861–1917', *CEHE* 6/2, pp. 706–800 (1966a).

—— *Economic Backwardness in Historical Perspective* (Cambridge, Mass., 1966b).

—— 'Die Vorbedingungen der europäischen Industrialisierung im 19. Jahrhundert', in FISCHER (1968).

—— *Continuity in History and Other Essays* (Cambridge, Mass., 1968b).

—— *Europe in the Russian Mirror* (Cambridge, 1970).

—— *An Economic Spurt That Failed* (Princeton, NJ, 1977).

GILBOY, Elizabeth, W., *Wages in Eighteenth-Century England* (Cambridge, Mass., 1934).

GILL, Conrad, and BRIGGS, Asa, *History of Birmingham* (1952).

GILLE, Bertrand, *La sidérurgie française au XIXe siècle* (Geneva, 1968).

—— *La Banque en France au XIXe siècle* (Geneva, 1970).

—— 'Banking and Industrialisation in Europe, 1730–1914', in CIPOLLA (1973), iii.

GILLET, Marcel, 'The Coal Age and the rise of Coalfields in the North and the Pas-de-Calais', in CROUZET, CHALONER, and STERN (1969).

—— *Les Charbonnages du Nord de la France au XIXe siècle* (Paris, Hague, 1973).

—— 'Structures et conjoncture: Houille et métallurgie en France au début du XXe siècle', in BRAUDEL *et al.* (1974).

GIRARD, L., *La Politique des travaux publics du Second Empire* (Paris, 1952).
— 'Transport', *CEHE* (1966) 6/1, pp. 212-73.
GLAMANN, Kristof, 'Industrialization as a Factor in Economic Growth in Denmark since 1700', in PREMIÈRE CONFÉRENCE INTERNATIONALE (1960).
GLASS, D. V., and EVERSLEY, D. E. C. (ed.), *Population in History* (1965).
GLASS, D. V., and GREBENIK, E., 'World Population, 1800-1950' *CEHE* 6/1 (1966), pp. 60-138.
GLAZIER, I. A., BANDERA, V. N., BERNER, R. B., 'Terms of Trade between Italy and the United Kingdom 1815-1913', *JEuropEcH* 4 (1975), 5-48.
GODECHOT, Jacques, 'L'industrialisation en Europe à l'époque révolutionnaire', in LÉON, CROUZET, GASCON (1972).
GOEBEL. Klaus, 'So wurden sie Wuppertaler', in JORDAN and WOLF (1977).
GOLDSMITH, Raymond W., 'The Economic Growth of Tsarist Russia 1860-1913', *Economic Development and Cultural Change* 9 (1961), 441-75.
GOLDSTROM, J. M., 'The Industrialisation of the North-East', in CULLEN (1969).
GOLLWITZER, H., 'Demokratische Agrarbewegungen als europäisches Phänomen im 20. Jahrhundert', *Historische Zeitschrift* 227 (1978), 529-51.
GOOD, David F., 'Stagnation and "Take-Off" in Austria, 1873-1913', *EcHR* 27 (1974), 72-87.
— 'Financial Integration in late Nineteenth-Century Austria', *JEcH* 37 (1977), 890-910.
— 'The Great Depression and Austrian Growth after 1873', *EcHR* 31 (1978), 290-94.
GORDON, Margaret S., *Barriers to World Trade. A Study of Recent Commercial Policy* (NY, 1941).
GOUBERT, Pierre, 'Sociétés rurales françaises du XVIIIe siècle', in BRAUDEL *et al.* (1974).
GRAILER, Iring, 'Das österreichische Verkehrswesen im Wandel eines Jahrhunderts', in MAYER (1949).
GRANTHAM, George W., 'Scale and Organisation in French Farming', in PARKER and JONES (1975).
GRAS, Christian, and LIVET, Georges (eds.), *Régions et régionalisme en France du XVIIIe siècle à nos jours* (Paris, 1977).
GRAVIER, J.-F., *Paris et le désert français* (Paris, 1947).
— *L'Aménagement du territoire et l'avenir des régions françaises* (Paris, 1964).
GREEN, E. R. R., *The Lagan Valley 1800-1850: a local History of the Industrial Revolution* (1949).
GREENFIELD, Kent Roberts, *Economics and Liberalism in the Risorgimento* (Baltimore, 1965 ed.).
GREENHUT, M. L., 'Needed—a Return to the Classics in Regional Economic Development Theory', *Kyklos* 19 (1966), 461-80.
GREGORY, Paul A., 'The Russian Balance of Payments, the Gold Standard, and Monetary Policy', *JEcH* 39 (1979), 379-99.
GRIFFITHS, Richard T., 'Models of Development: The Netherlands 1830-1870 —A Preliminary Investigation' (unpubl. cyclost., 1978).
GRIGG, D. B., 'Population Pressure and Agricultural Change', *Progress in Geography* 8 (1976), 135-76.
GROENMAN, S., 'General Impressions', in CENTRE EUROPÉEN (1968).
— 'Social Aspects of Backwardness in Developed Countries', in ROBINSON (1969).

GROSS, Hermann, 'Mitteleuropäische Handelspolitik 1890-1938 und der Donauraum', *Der Donauraum* 7, Parts 2-3 (1962), 100-14.

GROSS, Nachum, 'Austrian Industrial Statistics 1880/5 and 1911/13' *ZgSW* 124 (1968), 35-69.

—— 'Economic Growth and the Consumption of Coal in Austria and Hungary 1831-1913', *JEcH* 31 (1971), 898-916.

—— 'The Industrial Revolution in the Habsburg Monarchy, 1750-1914', in CIPOLLA (1973), iv.

GROSSMAN, Gregory, 'The Industrialization of Russia and the Soviet Union', CIPOLLA (1973), iv.

GUENEAU, Louis *Lyon et le commerce de la soie* (NY, 1973 ed.).

GUICHONNET, Paul, 'Vers de nouvelles formes d'industrialisation: le type alpin, l'expérience italienne', in LEON, CROUZET, GASCON (1972).

GUIGNET, Philippe, 'Adaptations, mutations et survivances proto-industrielles dans le textile du Cambresis et du Valenciennois du XVIIIe au début du XXe siècle', *Revue du Nord* 61 (1979), 27-59.

GUILLAUME, Pierre, in LEON, (1978), v, pp. 59-72, 395-429.

HABAKKUK, H. J., 'Family Structure and Economic Change in Nineteenth-Century Europe', *JEcH* 15 (1955), 1-12.

—— *Population Growth and Economic Development Since 1750* (Leicester, 1971).

HABERLER, Gottfried, 'Some Problems in the Pure Theory of International Trade', *EJ* 60 (1950), 232-40.

—— *Der Internationale Handel* (Berlin, Heidelberg, NY 1970 ed.).

HADFIELD, Charles, *British Canals* (1959).

—— *The Canals of South Wales and the Border* (1960).

HÄPKE, Rudolf, *Die Entstehung der holländischen Wirtschaft* (Berlin, 1928).

HAGEMANN, Wilhelm, *Das Verhältnis der deutschen Großbanken zur Industrie* (Berlin, 1931).

HAGEN, Everett, E., 'An Economic Justification for Protectionism' *QJE* 72 (1958), 496-514.

HAMEROW, Theodore S., *Restoration, Revolution, Reaction. Economics and Politics in Germany 1815-1871* (Princeton, NJ, 1958, 1966).

HAMILTON, H., 'Scotland's Balance of Payments Problem in 1762' *EcHR* 5 (1953), 344-57.

—— 'The Failure of the Ayr Bank, 1772', *EcHR* 8 (1956), 405-17.

—— *An Economic History of Scotland in the Eighteenth Century* (Oxford, 1963).

—— *The English Brass and Copper Industries to 1800* (1967).

HAMM, Michael F. (ed.), *The City in Russian History* (Lexington, Kentucky, 1976).

HANSEN, Niles M., 'Unbalanced Growth and Regional Development', *Western Economic Journal* 4 (1965-6), 3-14.

HANSEN, Svend Aage, *Early Industrialisation in Denmark* (Copenhagen, 1970).

HAPAK, Pavel, 'The Migration of Manpower and Emigration From Slovakia' in CZECHOSLOVAK AND WORLD HISTORY (1978).

HARDACH, Gerd H., *Der soziale Status des Arbeiters in der Frühindustrialisierung* (Berlin, 1969).

—— *Der erste Weltkrieg 1914-1918* (Munich 1973).

—— *Die wirtschaftlichen and sozialen Folgen des ersten Weltkriegs* (Cyclost., 1979).

HARDACH, Karl, *Die Bedeutung der wirtschaftlichen Faktoren bei der Wiedereinführung der Eisen- und Getreidezölle in Deutschland 1879* (Berlin, 1967).

HARDT, John P., 'Soviet Economic Development and Policy Alternatives', in TREML and FARRELL (1968).

HARLEY, C. Knick, 'Western Settlement and the Price of Wheat' *JEcH* 38 (1978), 865–78.

HARRIS, J. R., *The Copper King: a Biography of Thomas Williams of Llanidan* (Liverpool, 1964).

— (ed.), *Liverpool and Merseyside. Essays in the economic and social history of the port and its hinterland* (1969).

— 'Attempts to transfer English steel techniques to France in the eighteenth century', in MARRINER (1978).

HARRISON, Joseph, 'The Origins of Modern Industrialism in the Basque Country', *Sheffield Studies in Economic and Social History*, 2 (1977).

— *An Economic History of Modern Spain* (NY, 1978).

HARTE, N. B., and PONTING, K. G. (eds.), *Textile History and Economic History* (Manchester, 1973).

HARTE, N. B., 'The Rise of Protection in the English Linen Trade, 1690–1790', in HARTE and PONTING' (1973b).

HARTWELL, R. M. (ed.), *The Causes of the Industrial Revolution in England* (1967).

— *The Industrial Revolution and Economic Growth* (1971).

HASENPFLUG, Hajo, and KOHLER, Beate (eds.), *Die Süd-Erweiterung der Europäischen Gemeinschaft. Wende oder Ende der Integration* (Hamburg, 1977).

HASENPFLUG, Hajo, 'Industrie- und agrarpolitische Probleme der bietritts-kandidaten', in HASENPFLUG and KOHLER (1977).

HASSINGER, Herbert, 'Der Außenhandel der Habsburgermonarchie in der zweiten Hälfte des 18. Jahrhunderts', in LÜTGE (1964a).

— 'Der Stand der Manufakturen in den deutschen Erbländern der Habsburger-monarchie am Ende des 18. Jahrhunderts', in LÜTGE (1964b).

HAU, Michel, 'Un cas de déséquilibre régional: La Champagne', in GRAS and LIVET (1977).

— 'Energiekosten und Industrialisierung der französischen Regionen von der Mitte des XIX Jh. bis zum ersten Weltkrieg', in POLLARD (1980).

HAUSER, Albert, *Schweizerische Wirtschafts- und Sozialgeschichte* (Erlenbach-Zürich, Stuttgart, 1961).

HAUSHOFER, Heinz, *Die deutsche Landwirtschaft im technischen Zeitalter* (Stuttgart, 1963, 1972).

HAUSHOFER, Heinz, and BOELCKE, Willi A., *Wege und Forschungen der Agrargeschichte. Festschrift zum 65. Geburtstag von Günther Franz* (Frankfurt, 1967).

HAVINDEN, Michael, 'The Southwest: A Case for De-Industrialisation' in PALMER (?1977).

HAWKE, G. R., *Railways and Economic Growth in England and Wales 1840–1870* (Oxford, 1970).

HAXTHAUSEN, Baron von, *The Russian Empire. Its People, Institutions, and Resources* (1856, 1968, 2 vols.).

— *Die ländliche Verfassung Rußlands. Ihre Entwicklung und ihre Feststellung in der Gesetzgebung von 1861* (Leipzig, 1866).

HEATH, John, 'Industrial Development of the Erewash Valley and its adjacent Areas', in PALMER, (?1977).

HEATON, Herbert, *The Yorkshire Woollen and Worsted Industries* (Oxford, 1965 ed.).

HECHTER, Michael, 'Regional Inequality and National Integration: The Case of the British Isles', *Journal of Social History*, 5 (1971-2), 96-117.
HECKSCHER, Eli F., *The Continental System. An Economic Interpretation* (Oxford, 1922).
— *Mercantilism* (2 vols., 1955).
— 'The Effects of Foreign Trade on the Distribution of Incomes', repr. in *Readings in the Theory of International Trade* (1961 ed.).
— *An Economic History of Sweden* (Cambridge, Mass., 1968 ed.).
HEGGEN, Alfred, *Erfindungsschutz und Industrialisierung in Preußen 1793-1877* (Göttingen, 1975).
HEITZ, Gerhard, 'Bauer und Gemeinde vor und zu Beginn der industriellen Revolution', *StudHistOec* 10 (1975), 45-54.
HELLEINER, Karl F., *Free Trade and Frustration: Anglo-Austrian Negotiations 1860-70* (Toronto, 1973).
HELLING, Gertrud, *Nahrungsmittel-Produktion und Weltaussenhandel seit Anfang des 19. Jahrhunderts* (Berlin, 1977).
HELLWIG, Fritz, 'Wirtschaftsentwicklung und Grenzen im Raum Saarland-Lothringen-Luxemburg', *Blätter für deutsche Landesgeschichte* 111 (1975), 159-71.
HELMFRID, S., 'Bevölkerungswachstum und Agrarstruktur', in BOG (1974).
HENDERSON, Hubert Douglas, *The Inter-War Years and Other Papers* (Oxford. 1955).
HENDERSON, W. O., *Britain and Industrial Europe 1750-1870* (Liverpool, (1954).
— 'The Genesis of the Industrial Revolution in France and Germany in the 18th Century', *Kyklos* 9 (1956), 190-207.
— *Studies in the Economic Policy of Frederick the Great* (1963).
— *The Industrial Revolution on the Continent. Germany, France, Russia, 1800-1914* (1967a, ed.).
— *The State and the Industrial Revolution in Prussia 1740-1870* (Liverpool, 1967b).
HENNING, Friedrich-Wilhelm, 'Industrialisierung und dörfliche Einkommensmöglichkeiten', in KELLENBENZ (1975).
HERMAN, Léon M., 'The Promise of Economic Self-Sufficiency under Soviet Socialism', in TREML (1968).
HERMANSEN, Tormod, 'Development Poles and Development Centres in National and Regional Development', in KUKLINSKI (1972).
HERR, Richard, *The Eighteenth-Century Revolution in Spain* (Princeton, NJ, 1958).
— *Spain* (Englewood Cliffs, NJ, 1971).
HERSCH, Liebmann, 'International Migration of the Jews', in WILLCOX (1969), ii.
HERTZ, Frederick, *The Economic Problem of the Danubian States* (1947).
HEY, David, 'A Dual Economy in South Yorkshire', *AgHR* 17 (1970).
— 'The Chronology of the Onset of Industralisation in the Sheffield Region', in PALMER (?1977).
HEYWOOD, Colin, *The Cotton Industry in France, 1750-1850* (Loughborough, 1977).
HICKS, J. R., 'An Inaugural Lecture', *OEP* 5 (1953), 117-35.
HIGGINS, Benjamin, 'Regional Interactions, the Frontiers and Economic Growth', in KUKLINSKI (1972).

HILDEBRANDT, Karl-Gustaf, 'Foreign Markets for Swedish Iron in the 18th Century', *ScandEcHR* 6 (1958) 3-52.
—— 'Sweden', in PREMIÈRE CONFERENCE INTERNATIONALE (1960).
—— 'Les traits charactéristiques de l'industrialisation des pays scandinaves et la Finlande au XIXe siècle', in LÉON, CROUZET, GASCON (1972).
HILFERDING, Rudolf, *Das Finanzkapital* (Frankfurt/Main, 1968 ed.).
HILOWITZ, Jane, *Economic Development and Social Change in Sicily* (Cambridge, Mass., 1976).
HINDESS, Barry, and HIRST, Paul Q., *Pre-Capitalist Modes of Production* (1975).
HINZE, Kurt, *Die Arbeiterfrage zu Beginn des modernen Kapitalismus in Branden-burg-Preußen 1685-1806* (Berlin, 1963 ed.).
HIPPEL, Wolfgang von, 'Bevölkerungsentwicklung und Wirtschaftsstruktur im Königreich Württemberg 1815/65', in U. ENGELHARDT, Volker SELLIN, Horst STUKE (eds.), *Soziale Bewegung und politische Verfassung* (Stuttgart, 1976).
HISTORISCHE RAUMFORSCHUNG, *Raumordnung im 19. Jahrhundert* (2 vols., Hanover, 1965 and 1967).
HOBSBAWM, E. J., *An Age of Revolution in Europe 1789-1848* (1962).
—— *Industry and Empire. An Economic History of Britain since 1750* (1968).
HODGEN, Margaret T., *Change and History* (NY, 1952).
HODGES, T. M., 'Early Banking in Cardiff', *EcHR* 18 (1948), 84-90.
HODSON, H. V., *Slump and Recovery 1929-1937. A Survey of World Economic Affairs* (1938).
HÖHMANN, Hans-Hermann, KASER, Michael C., THALHEIM, Karl C. (eds.), *Die Wirtschaftsordnungen Osteuropas im Wandel* (2 vols, Freiburg/Breisgau, 1972).
HOFFMANN, Alfred, *Wirtschaftsgeschichte des Landes Oberösterreich* (Linz, 1952).
—— 'Die Agrarisierung der Industriebauern in Österreich', *Zeitschrift für Agrargeschichte und Agrarsoziologie* 20 (1971), 66.
—— 'Das Kaisertum Österreich als Agrarstaat im Zeitalter des Neoabsolutismus (1849-1867)', in BOG (1974).
—— 'Zur Problematik der agrarischen Nebengewerbe und der Reagrarisierung', in KELLENBENZ (1975).
HOFFMANN, Walther G., *The Growth of Industrial Economics* (Manchester, 1958).
—— 'The Take-Off in Germany', in ROSTOW (1963).
—— (ed.), *Untersuchungen zum Wachstum der deutschen Wirtschaft* (Tübingen, 1971).
—— 'Wachstumsschwankungen in der deutschen Wirtschaft', in HOFFMANN (1971b).
HOFFMANN, Walther G., and MÜLLER, J. H., *Das deutsche Volkseinkommen 1851-1957* (Tübingen, 1959).
HOFFMANN, Walther G., GRUMBACH, Fritz, HESSE, Helmut, *Das Wachstum der deutschen Wirtschaft seit der Mitte des 19. Jahrhunderts* (Berlin, Heidelberg, NY, 1965).
HOFMANN, H. A., 'Deutschlands erste Eisenbahn als Beispiel unternehmerischer Planung', in HISTORISCHE RAUMFORSCHUNG (1967).
HOFMANN, Victor, *Beiträge zur neueren österreichischen Wirtschaftsgeschichte* (Vienna, 1919).
HOHENBERG, Paul, 'Change in Rural France in the Period of Industrialization 1830-1914', *JEcH* 32 (1972), 219-40.

HOHORST, Gerd, *Wirtschaftswachstum und Bevölkerungsentwicklung in Preußen 1816 bis 1914* (Münster and Bielefeld, 1977).
—— 'Marktintegration der deutschen Wirtschaft im 19. Jahrhundert', in FREMD-LING and TILLY (1979).
—— 'Regionale Entwicklungsunterschiede im Industrialisierungsprozess Preußens', in POLLARD (1980).
HOLDERNESS, B. A., *Pre-Industrial England: Economy and Society 1500–1750* (1976).
HOLLAND, Stuart, *The Regional Problem* (NY, 1976).
HOLLMANN, A. H., *Die Entwicklung der dänischen Landwirtschaf* (Berlin, 1904).
HOLT, John, *General View of the Agriculture of the County of Lancaster* (1795).
HOLTFRERICH, Carl-Ludwig. *Quantitative Wirtschaftsgeschichte des Ruhr-kohlenbergbaus im 19. Jahrhundert* (Dortmund, 1973).
HONEY, W. B., *English Pottery and Porcelain* (1949).
HOOVER, Edgar M., 'Some Old and New Issues in Regional Development', in ROBINSON (1969).
HORSKA, Pavla, 'On the Problem of Urbanisation in the Czech Lands at the Turn of the 19th and 20th Centuries', in CZECHOSLOVAK AND WORLD HISTORY INSTITUTE (1978).
HOSKINS, W. G., *Industry, Trade and People of Exeter 1688–1800* (Exeter, 1968 ed.).
HOTH, Wolfgang, *Die Industrialisierung einer rheinischen Gewerbestadt—dargestellt am Beispiel Wuppertal* (Cologne, 1975).
HOUILLIER, 'L'évolution dans la paix', in DOLLINGER (1970).
HOUTTE, François-Xavier van, *L'Evolution de l'industrie textile en Belgique et dans le monde de 1800 à 1939* (Louvain, 1949).
HOUTTE, J. A. van, 'Stadt und Land in der Geschichte des flandrischen Gewerbes im Spätmittelalter und in der Neuzeit', in LÜTGE (1965).
—— 'Economic Development of Belgium and the Netherlands from the Beginning of the Modern Era', *JEuropEcH* 1 (1972), 100–20.
—— *An Economic History of the Low Countries, 800–1800* (1977).
HUBER, Paul B., 'Regionale Expansion und Entleerung im Deutschland des 19. Jh.: eine Folge der Eisenbahnentwicklung?', in FREMDLING and TILLY (1979).
HUCK, Gerhard, and REULECKE, Jürgen (eds.), '. . . und reges Leben ist überall sichtbar!' (Neustadt/Aisch, 1978).
HUERTAS, Thomas F., *Economic Growth and Economic Policy in a Multi-national Setting. (The Habsburg Monarchy, 1841–1865* (NY, 1977).
HUFBAUER, G. C.., *Synthetic Materials and the Theory of International Trade* (1966).
HUGHES, Edward, *North Country Life in the Eighteenth Century* (1952).
HUGHES, Thomas Parke, 'Comment on Paper by Brittain and Robinson', *JEcH* 34 (1974), 126–30.
—— 'Regional Technological Style' (unpubl.).
HUNECKE, Volker, *Arbeiterschaft und industrielle Revolution in Mailand 1859–1892* (Göttingen, 1978).
HUNT, E. H., *Regional Wage Variation in Britain, 1850–1914* (Oxford, 1973).
HUTTMAN, John P., 'Modernization of Irish Peasant Agriculture under the Impact of Land Reform 1850–1915', *StudHistOec* 10 (1975), 81–108.
HYDE, C. K., *Technological Change and the British Iron Industry 1700–1870* Princeton, NJ, 1977).

HYMER, Stephen, and RESNICK, Stephen, 'A Model of an Agrarian Economy with Nonagricultural Activities', *AER* 59 (1969), 493-506.
— — 'International Trade and Uneven Development', in BHAGWATI *et al.* (1971).
INGRAM, J. C., 'State and Regional Payments Mechanisms', in NEEDLEMAN (1968).
INKSTER, Ian, *Meiji Economic Development in Perspective: Revisionist Comments upon the Industrial Revolution in Japan* (cyclost., 1978).
INSTITUT D'ÉCONOMIE RÉGIONALE DE SUD-OUEST, 'France', in CENTRE EUROPÉEN (1968).
INSTITUT DE SCIENCE ÉCONOMIQUE DE L'UNIVERSITÉ CATHOLIQUE DE SACRE-CŒUR, MILAN, 'Italie', in CENTRE EUROPÉEN (1968).
INSTITUT FÜR ÖSTERREICHKUNDE, *Die Wirtschaftsgeschichte Österreichs* (Vienna, 1971).
INTERNATIONAL ASSOCIATION FOR RESEARCH IN INCOME AND WEALTH, *Income and Wealth*, Series 5 (1955).
INTERNATIONAL BANK FOR RECONSTRUCTION AND DEVELOPMENT, *The Economic Development of Spain* (Baltimore, 1963).
INTERNATIONAL CHAMBER OF COMMERCE, *GATT, an Analysis and Appraisal of the General Agreement on Tariffs and Trade* (1955).
INTERNATIONAL CONGRESS ON ECONOMIC HISTORY, *6th Congress, Copenhagen* (1974).
IPPOLITO, Richard, 'The Effects of the "Agricultural depression" on Industrial Demand in England in 1730-1750', *Economica* 42 (1975), 298-312.
ISARD, Walter, *Location and Space Economy* (NY, 1956).
— *Methods of Regional Analysis: an Introduction to Regional Science* (Cambridge, Mass., 1960).
IVERSEN, C., *Some Aspects of International Capital Movements* (Copenhagen, 1936).
JACKSON, Gordon, *Hull in the Eighteenth Century: A Study in Economic History* (1972).
JACQUEMINS, G., 'Histoire de la Crise économique des Flandres 1845-1880', Academie Royale de Belgique, *Mémoires* 26 (1929), 11-472.
JAEGER, Hans, 'Business in the Great Depression', in WEE (1972).
JAMES, Anne-Marie, 'Sidérurgie et chemins de fer en France', in RUSSO (1965).
JAMES, John, *History of the Worsted Manufacture in England* (1857, 1968).
JEDRUSZCZAK, Hanna, 'Land Reform and Economic Development in the People's Democracies of Europe', *StudHistOec* 7 (1972), 199-211.
JENKINS, D. T., *West Riding Wool Textile Industry 1770-1835* (Westbury, 1975).
— 'Early Factory Development in the West Riding of Yorkshire, 1770-1800', in HARTE and PONTING (1973).
JENKINS, J. G. (ed.), *The Wool Textile Industry in Great Britain* (1972).
JENKS, Leland Hamilton, *The Migration of British Capital to 1875* (1971 ed.).
JENSEN, Adolph, 'Migration Statistics of Denmark, Norway and Sweden', in WILLCOX (1969).
JEREMY, David J., 'Damming the Flood: British Government Efforts to Check the Outflow of Technicians and Machinery, 1780-1843', *BusHistR* 5 (1977), 1-34.
JERSCH-WENZEL, Stefi, 'Der Einfluß zugewanderter Minoritäten als Wirtschaftsgruppe auf die Berliner Wirtschaft in vor- und frühindustrieller Zeit', in BÜSCH (1971a).

JEWETT, Llewellyn F. W., *The Wedgwoods* (1865).

JEZIERSKI, Andrzej, 'The Role of Eastern Markets in the Development of Polish Industry in the Light of the Balance of Trade Estimate of Nineteenth-Century Poland', *StudHistOec* 4 (1969), 13–28.

JEZIERSKI, Andrzej, and LANDAU, Zbigniew, 'The Directions of the Economic Development of People's Poland in the Years 1944–1969', *StudHistOec* 5 (1970), 329–49.

JOHN, A. H., *The Industrial Development of South Wales 1750–1850*, (Cardiff, 1950).

—— 'Aspects of English Economic Growth in the First Half of the Eighteenth Century', *Economica* 28 (1961), 176–90.

—— 'The Industrial Development of South Wales, 1750–1914', in LÉON, CROUZET, GASCON (1972).

JOHNSON, B. L. C., and WISE, M. J., 'The Black Country' and 'The Changing Regional Pattern during the Eighteenth Century', in *Birmingham and its Industrial Region. A Scientific Survey* (1950).

JOHNSON, Harry G., 'Opitimal Trade Intervention in the Presence of Domestic Distortions', in BALDWIN, *et al.* (1965).

—— (ed.), *Economic Nationalism in Old and New States* (Chicago, 1967).

—— 'The Theory of Trade and Growth: a Diagrammatic Analysis', in BHAGWATI *et al.* (1971).

JOHNSON, Henry, 'South Staffordshire Coalfield', in TIMMINS (1967).

JOHNSON, Robert Eugene, *Peasant and Proletarian. The Working Class of Moscow in the Late Nineteenth Century* (Leicester, 1979).

JONES, E. L., 'Agriculture and Economic Growth in England 1660–1750: Agricultural Change', *JEcH* 25 (1965), 1–18.

—— 'Agricultural Origins of Industry', *Past and Present* 40 (1968a), 58–71.

—— 'Le origini agricole dell' industria', *Studi storici* 9 (1968b), 564–93.

—— *Agriculture and the Industrial Revolution* (Oxford, 1974a).

—— 'The Constraints on Economic Growth in Southern England 1650–1850', *THIRD INTERNATIONAL CONFERENCE OF ECONOMIC HISTORY (1965)* (1974b).

—— 'Environment, Agriculture and Industrialization in Europe', *Agricultural History* 51 (1977), 491–502.

JONES, E. L., and WOOLF, S. J., *Agrarian Change and Economic Development. The Historical Problem* (1974).

—— —— 'Introduction: the Historical Role of Agrarian Change in Economic Development', in JONES and WOOLF (1974b).

JONES, John, 'Iron Trades in South Staffordshire', in TIMMINS (1967).

JONES, S. R. H., 'The Development of Needle Manufacturing in the West Midlands before 1750', *EcHR* 31 (1978), 354–68.

JONGE, J. A. de, 'Industrial Growth in the Netherlands 1850–1914' *Acta Historiae Neerlandicae* 5 (1971), 159–212.

JÖRBERG, Lennart, 'Structural Change and Economic Growth: Sweden in the Nineteenth Century', in CROUZET, CHALONER, STERN (1969).

—— 'The Industrial Revolution in the Nordic Countries', in CIPOLLA (1973), iv.

JORDAN, Horst, and WOLF, Heinz, *Werden und Wachsen der Wuppertaler Wirtschaft* (Wuppertal, 1977).

JOSTOCK, Paul, 'The Long-Term Growth of National Income in Germany', in INTERNATIONAL ASSOCIATION (1955).

Journal of the Royal Statistical Society (no author): 'The Imports of Grain before and after the Repeal of the Corn Laws', *JRStatS* 29 (1966), 445–51.

JUDEICH, Albert, *Die Grundentlastung in Deutschland* (Leipzig, 1863).

JÜNGST, Ernst, 'Bergbau und Hüttenindustrie', in MOST *et al.* (1931).

JUILLARD, Étienne, *L'Europe rhénane* (Paris, 1968).

JUTIKKALA, E., 'Industrialization as a Factor in Economic Growth in Finland', in PREMIÈRE CONFERENCE (1960).

KAHAN, Arcadius, 'Government Policies and the Industrialization of Russia', *JEcH* 27 (1967), 460–77.

— 'Capital Formation during the Period of Early Industrialization in Russia 1890–1913', *CEHE* 7/2 (1978), pp. 265–307.

KAHK, J., and LIGI, H., 'The Peasant Household in Estonia at the Eve of Industrialization', *StudHistOec* 10 (1975), 133–44.

KAMEN, Henry, 'The Decline of Spain: A Historical Myth?' *Past and Present* 81 (1978), 24–50.

KARCZ, Jerzy F., 'Soviet Agriculture, A Balance Sheet', in TREML (1968).

KASER, Michael, *COMECON, Integration Problems of the Planned Economies* (1965).

— 'Change in East-West Trade', in ATLANTIC INSTITUTE (1971).

— 'Russian Entrepreneurship', *CEHE* 7/2 (1978), pp. 416–93.

KATUS, L., 'Die Haptzüge der kapitalistischen Entwicklung der Landwirtschaft in den südslawischen Gebieten der Österreich-Ungarischen Monarchie', in SANDOR and HANAK (1961).

KAUFHOLD, Karl Heinrich, 'Handwerk und Industrie 1800–1850', in AUBIN and ZORN (1976).

KELLENBENZ, Hermann, 'Ländliches Gewerbe und bäuerliches Unternehmertum in Westeuropa vom Spätmittelalter bis ins 18. Jahrhundert', ECONOMIC HISTORY (1962).

— 'Der deutsche Außenhandel gegen Ausgang des 18. Jahrhunderts', in LÜTGE (1963).

— 'Landverkehr, Fluß- und Seeschiffahrt im europäischen Handel', in Michel MOLLAT (ed.), *Les Grandes Voies maritimes dans le monde. XVe-XIXe siècles* (Paris, 1965).

— 'Rural Industries in the West from the End of the Middle Ages to the Eighteenth Century', in EARLE (1974).

— (ed.), *Agrarisches Nebengewerbe und Formen der Reagrarisierung im Spätmittelalter und 19./20. Jahrhundert* (Stuttgart, 1975).

— 'Verkehrs- und Nachrichtenwesen, 1800–1850', in AUBIN and ZORN (1976).

KELLETT, J. R. 'The Breakdown of Gild and Corporation Control over the Handicraft and Retail Trade in London', *EcHR* 10 (1957-8), 381–94.

KEMP, Murray, 'Technological Change, the Terms of Trade and Welfare', *EJ* 65 (1955), 467–8.

KEMP, Tom, *Industrialization in Nineteenth-Century Europe* (1969).

— *Historical Patterns of Industrialization* (1978).

KENADJIAN, Nerdj, 'Disguised Unemployment in Underdeveloped Countries', *ZfN* 21 (1961-2), 216–23.

KENWOOD, A. G., 'Fixed Capital Formation on Merseyside, 1800–1913' *EcHR* 31 (1978), 214–37.

KERMANN, Joachim, *Die Manufakturen im Rheinland 1750–1833* (Bonn, 1972a).

— 'Die Manufakturen im Rheinland 1750–1833' *Rheinisches Archiv* 82 (1972b), 117–91.

KEYNES, J. M., *The Economic Consequences of the Peace* (1919).

KIESEWETTER, Hubert, 'Bevölkerung, Erwerbstätige und Landwirtschaft im Königreich Sachsen 1815-1871', in POLLARD (1980).

KIM, M. P., 'USSR Industrial Development', in PREMIÈRE CONFÉRENCE (1960).

KILLICK, J. R., and THOMAS, W. A., 'The Provincial Stock Exchanges, 1830-1870', *EcHR* (1970), 96-111.

KINDLEBERGER, C. P., 'Group Behaviour in International Trade', *JPE* 59 (1951), 30-46.

—— *Economic Growth in France and Britain 1851-1950* (Cambridge, Mass., 1964).

—— *Europe's Postwar Growth. The Role of Labour Supply* (Cambridge, Mass., 1967).

—— *The World in Depression 1929-1939* (1973).

—— 'Germany's Overtaking of England, 1806-1914' *Weltwirtschaftliches Archiv* 3 (1975a), 253-81, 477-504.

—— 'The Rise of Free Trade in Western Europe 1820-1875', *JEcH* 35 (1975b), 20-55.

—— 'Theory and Policy in International Economics since 1918', ECONOMIC HISTORY, 7th INTERNATIONAL CONGRESS, Theme B. 10 (1978).

KIRCHHAIN, Günter, *Das Wachstum der deutschen Baumwollindustrie* (Münster, Diss., 1973).

KIRSCHEN, Étienne-Sadi, with BLOCH, Henry Simon and BASSETT, William Bruce, *Financial Integration in Western Europe* (NY, 1969).

KISCH, Herbert, 'The Textile Industries in Silesia and the Rhineland: a Comparative Study in Industrialization', *JEcH* 19 (1959), 541-64.

—— 'The Impact of the French Revolution on the Lower Rhine Textile Districts —Some comments on Economic Development and Social Change', *EcHR* 25 (1962-3), 304-27.

—— 'From Monopoly to Laissez-Faire: the Early Growth of the Wupper Valley Textile Trades', *JEuropEcH* 1 (1972), 298-407.

KITCHEN, Martin, *The Political Economy of Germany 1815-1914* (1978).

KITZINGER, Uwe, *The Politics and Economics of European Integration* (NY, 1963).

KLAASSEN, L. H., KLEIN, P. W., PAELINK, J. H. P., 'Very Long-Term Evolution of a System of Regions', INTERNATIONAL CONGRESS ON ECONOMIC-HISTORY (1974) Themes: Relations between Regions of Uneven Economic Development.

KLATT, Sigurd, *Zur Theorie der Industrialisierung* (Cologne, Opladen, 1959).

KLEIN, Ernst, 'Die Anfänge der Industrialisierung Württembergs in der ersten Hälfte des 19. Jahrhunderts', in HISTORISCHE RAUMFORSCHUNG (1967).

—— 'Der Staat als Unternehmer im saarländischen Steinkohlenbergbau 1750-1850', *VSWG* 57 (1970), 323-49.

—— *Geschichte der deutschen Landwirtschaft im Industriezeitalter* (Wiesbaden, 1973).

—— 'Der Steinkohlenbergbau an der Saar während der siebziger Jahre des 19. Jahrhunderts', in BOG *et al.* (1974).

KLEZL, Felix, 'Austria', in WILLCOX (1969) ii.

KLIMA, Arnost, 'Industrial Development in Bohemia 1648-1781' *Past and Present* 11 (1957), 87-99.

—— 'English Merchant Capital in Bohemia in the Eighteenth Century', *EcHR* 12 (1959-60), 34-48.

— 'Ein Beitrag zur Agrarfrage in der Revolution von 1848 in Böhmen', in SANDOR and HANÁK (1961).
— 'The Domestic Industry and the Putting-Out System (Verlagssystem) in the Period of Transition from Feudalism to Capitalism', in ECONOMIC HISTORY (1962).
— 'The Role of Rural Domestic Industry in Bohemia in the 18th Century', *EcHR* 27 (1974), 48–56.
— 'The Beginnings of the Machine-Building Industry in the Czech lands in the First Half of the 19th Century', *JEuropEcH* 4 (1975), 49–78.
— 'Industrial Growth and Entrepreneurship in the Early stages of Industrialization in the Czech lands', *JEuropEcH* 6 (1977), 549–74.
KLIMA, Arnost, and MAČUREK J., 'La question de la transition du feodalisme au capitalisme en Europe centrale', XI Congrès International des Sciences Historiques, *Rapports*, iv, *Histoire Moderne* (Göteborg, Stockholm, Uppsala, 1960).
KMENTA, Jan, 'Economic Theory and Transfer of Technology', in SPENCER and WORONIAK (1967).
KNAPP, G. F., *Die Bauernbefreiung und der Ursprung der Landarbeiter* (Leipzig, 1887).
KOBLIK, Steven (ed.), *Sweden's Development from Poverty to Affluence 1750–1970* (Minnesota, 1975).
KÖLLMANN, Wolfgang, 'Demographische Konsequenzen der Industrialisierung in Preußen', in LEON, CROUZET, GASCON (1972).
— *Bevölkerung in der industriellen Revolution* (Göttingen, 1974).
— 'Zur Bedeutung der Regionalgeschichte im Rahmen struktur- und sozialgeschichtlicher Konzeptionen' *Archiv für Sozialgeschichte* 15 (1975), 43–60.
— 'Bevölkerungsgeschichte 1800–1970', in AUBIN and ZORN (1976).
— Das Wuppertal in der deutschen Geschichte', in JORDAN and WOLF (1977).
KÖSZEGI, L., 'Development Problems of Backward areas in Hungary' in ROBINSON (1969)..
KOHN, Hans, *The Idea of Nationalism* (NY, 1945).
KOMLOS, John Austro-Hungarian Agricultural Development 1827–1877, *JEuropEcH* 8 (1979), 37–60.
KOSÁRY, D., 'Les antecédents de la Révolution industrielle en Hongrie: hypothèses et réalités', *Acta Historica* 21 (1975), 365–75.
KOSELLECK, Reinhard, *Preußen zwischen Reform und Revolution* (Stuttgart, 1967).
KOVACS, J., 'Zur Frage der siebenbürgischen Bauernbefreiung und der Entwicklung der kapitalistischen Landwirtschaft nach 1848' in SANDOR and HANÁK (1961).
KRAUSE, Max, *A. Borsig, Berlin 1837–1902* (Berlin, 1902).
KRAVIS, I. B., 'Wages and Foreign Trade', *RevEcStat* 38 (1956), 14–30.
— 'Availability and Other Influences on the Commodity Composition of Trade', *JPE* 64 (1956b), 143–55.
— 'Trade as a Handmaiden of Growth: Similarities between the Nineteenth and Twentieth Centuries', *EJ* 80 (1970), 850–72.
KRIEDTE, Peter, MEDICK, Hans, SCHLUMBOHM, Jürgen, *Industrialisierung vor der Industrialisierung* (Göttingen, 1977).
KRIEDTE, Peter, 'Genese, agrarischer Kontext und Weltmarktbedingungen', in KRIEDTE *et al.* (1977a).

—— 'Die Proto-Industrialisierung zwischen Industrialisierung und De-Industriali-
  sierung', in KRIEDTE (1977b).
KROKER, Werner, *Wege zur Verbreitung technologischer Kenntnisse zwischen
  England und Deutschland in der zweiten Hälfte des 18. Jahrhunderts* (Berlin,
  1971).
KRÜGER, Horst, *Zur Geschichte der Manufakturen und der Manufakturarbeiter
  in Preußen* (Berlin, 1958).
KUKLINSKI Antoni (ed.), *Growth Poles and Growth Centres in Regional Planning*
  (Paris, Hague, 1972).
KUKLINSKI A., and PETRELLA, R., *Growth Poles and Regional Policies* (Hague,
  1972).
KULA, Witold, *An Economic Theory of the Feudal System* (1976).
KUSKE, Bruno, 'Wirtschaftsraum und Mensch', in MOST, KUSKE, WEBER (1931).
—— *Wirtschaftsgeschichte Westfalens in Leistung und Verflechtung mit den Nach-
  barländern bis zum 18. Jahrhundert* (Münster, 1949).
KUTZ, Martin, 'Die deutsch-britischen Handelsbeziehungen von 1790 bis zur
  Gründung des Zollvereins', *VSWG* 56 (1969), 178-214.
—— *Deutschlands Außenhandel von der französischen Revolution bis zur Gründung
  des Zollvereins* (Wiesbaden, 1974).
KUZNETS, Simon, 'The State as a Unit in Study of Economic Growth', *JEcH* 11
  (1951), 25-41.
—— 'Economic Growth of Small Nations', in ROBINSON (1960).
—— 'Notes on the Take-Off', in ROSTOW (1963).
—— *Economic Growth and Structure* (NY, 1965).
—— *Modern Economic Growth* (New Haven, 1966).
LA FORCE, James Clayburn, *The Development of the Spanish Textile Industry
  1750-1800* (Berkeley, Los Angeles, 1965).
LAMBI, Ivo Nikolai, *Free Trade and Protection in Germany 1868-1879* (Wies-
  baden, 1963).
LAMPE, John R., 'Variations of Unsuccessful Industrialisation: The Balkan
  States Before 1914', *JEcH* 35 (1975), 56-85.
LANDER, J. E., *International Economic History. Industrialisation and the World
  Economy 1830-1950* (1967).
LANDES, D. S., 'French Entrepreneurship', *JEcH* 9 (1949), 45-61.
—— 'French Business and the Business Man', in EARLE (1951).
—— *The Unbound Prometheus. Technological Change and Industrial Development
  in Western Europe from 1750 to the Present* (Cambridge, 1969a).
—— 'The Old Bank and the New: the Financial Revolution of the Nineteenth Cen-
  tury', in CROUZET, CHALONER, STERN (1969b).
LANE, Frederick C., 'The Role of Governments in Economic Growth in Early
  Modern Times', *JEcH* 35 (1975), 8-17.
LANGTON, John, *The Geography of the South Lancashire Mining Industry
  1590-1799* (Unpubl. Ph. D., Univ. of Wales, 1969).
LARGE, P. F. W., 'Agricultural Change and Urban Growth in the West Midlands.
  1660-1760' (Unpubl., 1978).
LASLETT, Peter, *The World We Have Lost* (1965).
—— 'Familie und Industrialisierung: eine "starke Theorie"', in CONZE (1976).
LASUEN, J. R., 'On Growth Poles', *Urban Studies* 6 (1969).
LAUE, Theodore H. von, 'Einige politische Folgen der russischen Wirtschafts-
  planung um 1900', *Forschungen zur Osteuropäischen Geschichte* 1 (1954),
  217-38.

—— 'The State and the Economy', in BLACK, Cyril E. (ed.), *The Transformation of Russian Society* (Cambridge, Mass., 1960).

—— 'The Crises in the Russian Polity', in CURTISS (1963).

—— *Sergei Witte and the Industrialization of Russia* (NY, 1963b).

—— *Why Lenin? Why Stalin? A reappraisal of the Russian Revolution, 1900-1930* Philadelphia, 1964).

LAURENT, Robert, 'Octroi Archives as Source of Urban Social and Economic History', in CAMERON (1970a).

LAURSEN, K., and PEDERSEN, J., *The German Inflation 1918-1923* (Amsterdam 1964).

LAVELEYE, Emile D., 'The Land System of Belgium and Holland', in PROBYN (1881).

LAVERGNE, L. de, *Économie rurale de la France* (Paris, 1877).

LEAGUE OF NATIONS, *Commercial Policy in the Inter-War Period: International Proposals and National Policies* (Geneva, 1942).

—— *Quantitative Trade Controls* (Geneva, 1943).

—— *Industrialization and Foreign Trade* (Geneva, 1945).

LEBRUN, Pierre, *L'Industrie de la laine à Verviers, pendant le XVIIIe et le début du XIXe siècle* (Liège, 1948).

—— 'L'industrialisation en Belgique au XIXe siècle', in LÉON, CROUZET, GASCON (1972).

LEE, C. H., *Regional Economic Growth in the United Kingdom since the 1880's* (Maidenhead, 1971).

—— 'Regional Structural Change in the Long Run: Great Britain 1841-1971', in POLLARD, (1980).

LEE, Everett S., 'A Theory of Migration', *Demography* 3 (1966), 47-57.

LEE, J., 'The Railways in Irish History', in CULLEN (1969).

LEE, W. Robert, *Population Growth, Economic Development and Social Change in Bavaria, 1750-1850* (NY, 1977).

—— (ed.), *European Demography and Economic Growth* (1979a).

—— 'Germany', in LEE (1979b).

—— 'Regionale Differenzierung im Bevölkerungswachstum Deutschlands im frühen neunzehnten Jahrhundert', in FREMDLING and TILLY (1979c).

LEIBENSTEIN, Harvey, 'Population Growth and the Take-Off Hypothesis', in ROSTOW (1963).

LELEUX, Fernand, *Liévin Bauwens, industriel gantois* (Paris, 1969).

LÉMONON, Ernest, *L'Italie économique et sociale (1861-1912)* (Paris, 1913).

LENMAN, Bruce, *An Economic History of Modern Scotland 1660-1976* (1977).

LÉON, Pierre, 'L'industrialisation en France en tant que facteurs de croissance économique, du début du XVIIIe siècle à nos jours', in PREMIÈRE CONFÉRENCE (1960).

—— *Les Techniques métallurgiques dauphinoises au dix-huitième siècle* (Paris, 1961).

—— *Économies et sociétés préindustrielles* (vol. 2, Paris, 1970).

—— 'Structure du commerce extérieur et évolution industrielle de la France à la fin du XVIIIe siècle', in BRAUDEL *et al.* (1974).

—— (ed.), *Histoire économique et sociale du monde* (6 vols., Paris, 1977-8).

LÉON, Pierre, CROUZET, François, GASCON, Richard, *L'Industrialisation en Europe au XIXe siècle* (Paris, 1972).

LE ROY LADURIE, Emmanuel, *The Peasants of Languedoc* (Urbana, Ill., 1974).

LESKIEWICZ, Janina, 'Les entraves sociales au développement de la "nouvelle agriculture" en Pologne', in ECONOMIC HISTORY (1965).

—— 'Land Reform in Poland (1764–1870)', *JEuropEcH* (1972), 435–48.

LESTOCQUOY, Jean (ed.), *Histoire du Pas-de-Calais* (Arras, 1946).

—— *Histoire de la Flandre et de l'Artois* (Paris, 1948).

LEUILLOT, Paul, 'The Industrial Revolution in France', *JEcH* 17 (1957), 245–54.

—— *L'Alsace au début du XIXe siècle* (vol. 2, Paris, 1959).

LEVEN, C. L., 'Regional and Interregional Accounts in Perspective' in NEEDLE-MAN (1968).

LEVINE, David, 'Proletarianization, Economic Opportunity and Population Growth', in CONZE (1976).

LÉVY, Maurice, *Histoire économique et sociale de la France dépuis 1848* (Paris, 3 vols., 1952).

LÉVY, Robert, *Histoire économique de l'industrie cotonnière en Alsace* (Paris, 1912).

LÉVY-LEBOYER, Maurice, *Les banques européennes et l'industrialisation dans la première moitié du XIX siècle* (Paris, 1964).

—— 'La croissance économique en France au XIXe siècle. Résultats préliminaires', *Annales ESC* 23 (1968a), 788–807.

—— 'Le processus de l'industrialisation: le cas de l'Angleterre et de la France', *RevHist* 239 (1968b), 281–98.

—— 'La décélération de l'économie française dans la seconde moitié du 19e siècle', *RevHES* 49 (1971).

—— 'Capital Investment and Economic Growth in France, 1820–1930', *CEHE* 7/1 (1978), pp. 231–95.

LEWIN, M., *Russian Peasants and Soviet Power* (1968).

LEWIS, G. R., *The Stannaries. A Story of the English Tin Miner* (1908).

LEWIS, M. J. T., *Early Wooden Railways* (1970).

LEWIS, W. Arthur, 'World Production, Prices and Trade, 1870–1960', *Manchester School* 20 (1952), 105–38.

—— *Economic Survey 1919–1939* (1965).

—— *Growth and Fluctuations 1870–1913* (1978).

LIEBERMAN, Sima, *The Industrialization of Norway, 1800–1920* (Oslo, Bergen, Tromsö, 1970).

LIEPMANN, H., *Tariff Levels and the Economic Unity of Europe* (1938).

LILLEY, Samuel, 'Technological Progress and the Industrial Revolution 1700–1914', in CIPOLLA (1973), iii.

LINDER, S. B., 'Trade and Technical Efficiency', in BHAGWATI *et al.* (1971).

LINDSTROM, Diane, 'The Industrial Revolution in America', in POLLARD (1980).

LINK, Edith Murr, *The Emancipation of the Austrian Peasant 1740–1798* (NY, 1949).

LIPSON, E., *The History of the Woollen and Worsted Industries* (1921, 1965).

LITWAK, B. G., 'Die Voraussetzungen für den Niedergang der Leibeigenschaft und die Gründe für die Reform des Jahres 1861 in Rußland', in BERINDEI *et al.* (1973).

LIVET, Georges, 'LE XVIIIe siècle et l'esprit des lumières', in DOLLINGER (1970).

—— 'Bourgeoisie et capitalisme à Strasbourg au XVIIIe siècle', in BRAUDEL *et al.* (1974).

LLOYD, G. I. H., *The Cutlery Trades* (1968).

LLOYD-PRITCHARD, M. F., 'The Decline of Norwich', *EcHR* 3 (1951), 371-7.

LÖSCH, August, *Die räumliche Ordnung der Wirtschaft* (Jena, 1944 ed.).

LONG, W. Harwood, *A Survey of the Agriculture of Yorkshire* (1969).

LONGFIELD, M., *Three Lectures on Commerce* (Dublin 1835, repr. 1931).

LORENZ, Richard, *Anfänge der bolschewistischen Industriepolitik* (Cologne, 1965).

LOTZ, Walther, 'Die Ideen der deutschen Handelspolitik von 1860-1891', in VEREIN (1892) ii.

LOUGH, J., 'France under Louis XIV', *New Cambridge Modern History*, v (Cambridge , 1969).

LOVEDAY, A., 'Tariff Level Indices', *JRStatS* 112 (1928), 487-529.

LOWERSON, John, 'Sussex and Industrialisation: Economic Depression and Restrictive Elements 1700-1840', in PALMER (?1977).

LÜTGE, Friedrich, *Die Mitteldeutsche Grundherrschaft* (Jena, 1934).

— *Geschichte der deutschen Agrarverfassung* (Stuttgart, 1963).

— *Die wirtschaftliche Situation in Deutschland und Österreich um die Wende vom 18. zum 19. Jahrhundert* (Stuttgart, 1964).

— 'Die Robot-Abolition unter Kaiser Joseph II', in HAUSHOFER and BOELCKE (1967).

— (ed.), *Wirtschaftliche und soziale Probleme der gewerblichen Entwicklung im 15.- 16. und 19. Jahrhundert* (Stuttgart, 1968).

LUNDGREEN, Peter, 'Schulbildung und Frühindustrialisierung in Berlin/Preußen', in BÜSCH (1971a).

LUNDSTRÖM, Hans O., *Capital Movements and Economic Integration* (Leyden, 1967).

LUTZ, Vera. *Italy: A Study in Economic Development* (1962).

LUZZATTO, Gino, 'The Italian Economy in the First Decade after Unification', in CROUZET, CHALONER, STERN (1969).

LYASHCHENKO, Peter I., *History of the National Economy of Russia to the 1917 Revolution* (NY, 1949).

MACDOUGALL, G. D. A., 'British and American Exports: A Study Suggested by the Theory of Comparative Costs', *EJ* 61 (1951), 697-724, and 62 (1952), 487-521.

MACLENNAN, M. C., 'Regional Development Policies for Backward Regions', in CENTRE EUROPÉEN (1968).

— 'Regional Policy in the United Kingdom', in ROBINSON (1969).

MADDISON, Angus, *Economic Growth in the West* (1964).

— 'Economic Policy and Performance in Europe 1913-1970', in CIPOLLA (1973) v.

MACZAK, Antoni, 'Agricultural and Livestock Production in Poland: Internal and Foreign Markets', *JEuropEcH* 1 (1972), 671-80.

MAENNER, Ludwig, *Deutschlands Wirtschaft und Liberalismus in der Krise von 1879* (Berlin, 1928).

MÄRZ, Eduard, *Österreichische Industrie- und Bankpolitik in der Zeit Franz Josephs I* (Vienna, Frankfurt, Zürich, 1968).

MAGER, F., *Geschichte des Bauerntums und der Bodenkultur im Lande Mecklenburg* (Berlin, 1955).

MAHAIM, Ernest, 'La politique commerciale de la Belgique', in VEREIN (1892) i.

MAIZELS, Alfred, *Industrial Growth and World Trade* (Cambridge, 1963).

MALEFAKIS, Edward E., *Agrarian Reform and Peasant Revolution in Spain* (New Haven, 1970).

MALENBAUM, Wilfred, *The World Wheat Economy 1885-1939* (Cambridge, Mass., 1953).

MALOWIST, M., 'The Economic and Social Development of the Baltic Countries from the Fifteenth to the Seventeenth Centuries', *EcHR* 12 (1959), 177-89.

—— 'The Problem of the Inequality of Economic Development in Europe in the Later Middle Ages', *EcHR* 19 (1966).

MANDELBAUM, K., *The Industrialisation of Backward Areas* (Oxford, 1945, 1961).

MANN, Julia de L., *Documents Illustrating the Wiltshire Textile Trades in the Eighteenth Century* (Devizes, 1964).

—— *The Cloth Industry of the West of England from 1640-1880* (Oxford, 1971).

MANNICHE, P., *The Folk High Schools of Denmark and the Development of a Farming Community* (Copenhagen, 1929).

MANOILESCO, M., *The Theory of Protection* (1931).

MANTOUX, E., *The Carthaginian Peace or the Economic Consequences of Mr. Keynes* (1946).

MANTOUX, Paul, *The Industrial Revolution of the Eighteenth Century* (1961).

MARCHAND, Hans, *Säkularstatistik der deutschen Eisenindustrie* (Essen, 1939).

—— MARCY, G., 'How far can foreign trade . . . confer upon small nations the advantages of large nations', in ROBINSON (1960).

MARCZEWSKI, Jean, 'Some Aspects of the Economic Growth of France 1660-1958', *Economic Development and Cultural Change* 9 (1961), 369-86.

—— 'The Take-Off hypothesis and French experience' in ROSTOW (1963).

—— 'Le produit physique de l'économie française de 1789 à 1913', *Cahiers de l'I.S.E.A.*, A. F. 4, No. 163 (1965), pp. vii–cliv.

MARKOVITCH, Tihomir J., 'L'industrie française de 1789 à 1964', in MARCZEWSKI (1965).

—— 'The Dominant Sectors of French Industry', in CAMERON (1970a).

—— 'La croissance industrielle sous l'ancien régime', *Annales ESC* 31 (1976), 644-55.

MARRINER, Sheila (ed.), *Business and Business Men. Studies in Business, Economic and Accounting History* (Liverpool, 1978).

MARSHALL, Alfred, *Money, Credit and Commerce* (1923).

MARSHALL, J. D., *Furness and the Industrial Revolution* (Barrow/Furn., 1958).

MARTIN, Gerard, 'Évolution de l'agriculture en Auxois de 1840 à 1939', in ARMENGAUD (1966).

MARTIN, Germain, *La Grande Industrie sous le règne de Louis XIV* (NY, 1971).

MASCHKE, Erich, 'Industrialisierungsgeschichte und Landesgeschichte', *Blätter für deutsche Landesgeschichte* 103 (1967), 71-84.

—— 'Outline of the History of German Cartels from 1873 to 1914', in CROUZET, CHALONER, STERN (1969).

MATHIAS, Peter, *The Brewing Industry of England 1700-1830* (Cambridge, 1959).

—— 'Agriculture and the Brewing and Distilling Industries in the Eighteenth Century', in JONES, E. L. (ed.), *Agriculture and Economic Growth in England 1650-1815* (1967).

—— *The First Industrial Nation: An Economic History of Great Britain 1700-1914* (1969).

—— 'British Industrialisation: Unique or Not?', in LÉON, CROUZET, GASCON (1972).

— 'Skills and Diffusion of Innovations from Britain in the Eighteenth Century', *TransRHS* 5th S., 25 (1975), 93-113.

MATIS, Herbert, 'Die Wirtschaft der Franzisko-Josephinischen Epoche', in INSTITUT FÜR ÖSTERREICHKUNDE (1971).

— *Österreichs Wirtschaft 1848-1913* (Berlin, 1972).

— 'Leitlinien der österreichischen Wirtschaftspolitik 1848-1918', in BRUSATTI (1973).

MATIS, Herbert, BACHINGER, Karl, 'Österreichs industrielle Entwicklung', in BRUSATTI (1973).

MATZERATH, Horst, 'Industrialisierung, Mobilität und sozialer Wandel am Beispiel der Städte Rheydt und Rheindahlen', in KAELBLE, Hartmut, *et al.*, *Probleme der Modernisierung in Deutschland* (Opladen, 1978).

MAUERSBERG, Hans, 'Betriebsform-Modelle der alten Industrien im Strukturwandel', in LÜTGE (1964).

— *Deutsche Industrien im Zeitgeschehen eines Jahrhunderts* (Stuttgart, 1966).

MAURO, Frédéric, 'Pour une théorie du capitalisme commerical', *VSWG* 42 (1955), 117-21.

MAYER, Hans (ed.), *Hundert Jahre österreichische Wirtschaftsentwicklung 1848-1948* (Vienna, 1949).

MAYHEW, Henry, *London Labour and the London Poor* (4 vols., NY, 1967 ed.).

MCCLOY, Shelby T., *Government Assistance in Eighteenth-Century France* (Philadelphia, 1977 ed.).

MCCORD, Norman, 'Northern England, some Points of Regional Interest', in POLLARD (1980).

MCCORD, Norman, and ROWE, D. J., 'Industrialisation and Urban Growth in North-Eastern England', *IntRevSocH* 22 (1977), 30-64.

MCDONALD, D. F., *Scotland's Shifting Population 1770-1850* (Glasgow, 1937).

MCKINNON, R. I., 'On Misunderstanding the Capital Constraint in LDC's: the Consequences of Trade Policy', in BHAGWATI *et al.* (1971).

MEADE, J. E., *The Theory of Customs Union* (Amsterdam, 1955).

MEDICK, Hans, 'Zur Strukturellen Funktion in Haushalt und Familie . . . die proto-industrielle Familienwirtschaft', in CONZE (1976).

— 'The Proto-Industrial Family Economy', *Social History* 3 (1976b), 291-315.

— 'Die proto-industrielle Familienwirtschaft', in KRIEDTE *et al.* (1977a).

— 'Struktur und Funktion der Bevölkerungsentwicklung im proto-industriellen System', in KRIEDTE *et al.* (1977b).

MEGERLE, Klaus, 'Regionale Differenzierung des Industrialisierungsprozesses: Überlegungen am Beispiel Württembergs', in FREMDLING and TILLY (1979).

MENDELS, Franklin F., 'Industrialization and Population Pressure in 18th Century Flanders' (Report on Ph. D. thesis), *JEcH* 31 (1971), 269-71.

— 'Proto-Industrialization: the First Phase of the Industrialization Process', *JEcH* 32 (1972), 241-61.

— 'Agriculture and Peasant Industry in 18th-Century Flanders', in PARKER and JONES (1975).

— 'La composition du ménage paysan en France au XIXe siècle: une analyse économique de production domestique', *Annales ESC* 33 (1978), 780-802.

— 'Seasons and Regions in Agriculture and Industry During the Process of Industrialization', in POLLARD (1980).

MÉSAROŠ, J., 'Die Expropriation des Bauerntums . . . in der Slowakei in der zweiten Hälfte des 19. Jahrhunderts', in SÁNDOR and HANÁK (1961).

METZER, Jacob, 'Railroad Development and Market Integration: The Case of Tsarist Russia', *JEcH* 34 (1974), 529-50.
— 'Railroads in Tsarist Russia. Direct Gains and Implications', *ExplEcH* 13 (1976), 85-112.
MEYER, J. R., 'Regional Economics, a Survey', in NEEDLEMAN (1968).
MICHEL, Bernard, 'La révolution industrielle dans les pays tchèques au XIXe siècle', *Annales ESC* 20 (1965), 984-1005.
— in LÉON, iii, 513-23.
MIECK, Ilja, *Preußische Gewerbepolitik in Berlin 1806-1844* (Berlin, 1965).
MIHAILOVIČ, K., 'On the Yugoslav Experience in Backward Areas', in ROBINSON (1969).
MIKA, Alois, 'On the Economic Status of Czech Towns in the Period of Late Feudalism', in CZECHOSLOVAK AND WORLD HISTORY INSTITUTE (1978).
MILL, James, *Elements of Political Economy* (1844, NY 1965 repr.).
MILL, John Stuart, *Principles of Political Economy* (1948, NY 1965 repr.).
MILWARD, A. S., and SAUL, S. B., *The Economic Development of Continental Europe 1780-1870* (1973).
— — *The Development of the Economies of Continental Europe 1850-1914* (1977).
MINCHINTON, W. E., 'Bristol—Metropolis of the West in the Eighteenth Century', *TransRHS* 5th S. 4 (1954).
— — *The British Tinplate Industry* (Oxford, 1957).
— — *Industrial South Wales 1750-1914* (1969).
MIRABEAU, Comte de, *De la monarchie prussienne sous Frédéric le Grand* (4 vols, London, 1788).
MITCHELL, B. R., 'The Coming of the Railway and United Kingdom Economic Growth', *JEcH* 24 (1964), 315-36.
— *European Historical Statistics 1750-1870* (1976 ed.).
MITCHELL, B. R., and DEANE, Phyllis, *Abstract of British Historical Statistics* (Cambridge, 1962).
MITRANY, David, *The Effect of the War on South-Eastern Europe* (New Haven, 1936).
MITTERAUER, Michael, 'Auswirkungen von Urbanisierung und Frühindustrialisierung auf die Familienverfassung an Beispielen des österreichischen Raums', in CONZE (1976).
MOFFIT, Louis W., *England on the Eve of the Industrial Revolution* (1925).
MOKYR, Joel, 'Industrial Revolution in the Low Countries', *JEcH* 34 (1974), 365-91.
— 'Capital, Labour and the Delay in the Industrial Revolution in the Netherlands', *Economisch en Sociaal-Historisch Jaarboek* 38 (1975), 280-99.
— *Industrialization in the Low Countries 1795-1850* (New Haven, 1976a).
— 'Growing-up and the Industrial Revolution in Europe', *ExplEcH* 13 (1976b), 371-96.
— 'Demand vs. Supply in the Industrial Revolution', *JEcH* 37 (1977), 981-1008.
MONAGHAN, J. J., 'The Rise and Fall of the Belfast Cotton Industry', *Irish Historical Studies* 3 (1942-3), 1-17.
MOORE, Wilbert E., *Economic Demography of Eastern and Southern Europe* (Geneva, 1945).
MORGADO, Nuno Alves, 'Portugal', in LEE (1979a).
MORI, Giorgio, 'The Genesis of Italian Industrialization', *JEcH* (1975), 79-94.

—— 'The Process of Industrialization in General and the Process of Industrialization in Italy', *JEuropEcH* 8 (1979), 61–82.

MORIER, R. B. D., 'The Agrarian Legislation of Prussia during the Present Century', in PROBYN (1881).

MORINEAU, M., 'Was there an agricultural revolution in 18th-century France?' in CAMERON (1970a).

MORONEY, J. R., and WALKER J. M., 'A Regional Test of the Heckscher-Ohlin Hypothesis', in NEEDLEMAN (1968).

MORSEL, Henri, in LÉON (1978), v, pp. 27–58, 145–88, 297–341.

MOST, Otto, 'Binnenschiffahrt und Kanalbau im 19. Jahrhundert', in HISTORISCHE RAUMFORSCHUNG (1967).

MOST, Otto, KUSKE, Bruno, WEBER, Heinrich, *Wirtschaftskunde für Rheinland und Westfalen* (Berlin, 1931).

MOTTEK, Hans, *Wirtschaftsgeschichte Deutschlands* (vols. 1 and 2, Berlin 1964).

MÜLLER-LINK, Horst, *Industrialisierung und Agrarpolitik. Preußen-Deutschland und des Zarenreich von 1860 bis 1890* (Göttingen, 1977).

MUNDELL, Robert A., and SWOBODA, Alexander K. (eds.), *Monetary Problems of the International Economy* (Chicago, 1969).

MUNTING, R., 'Ransome's in Russia: An English Agricultural Engineering Company's Trade with Russia to 1917', *EcHR* 13 (1978), 257–69.

MURPHY, J. J., 'Retrospect and Prospect', in SPENCER and WORONIAK (1967).

MURRAY, Adam, *General View of the Agriculture of the County of Warwick* (1813).

MUSSON, A. E., 'Critical Influence of the Industrial Revolution in Great Britain', in RATCLIFFE, B. M., *Great Britain and Her World* (Manchester, 1975).

—— 'Industrial Motive Power in the United Kingdom 1800–1870', *EcHR*, 29 (1976), 415–39.

—— *The Growth of British Industry* (1978).

MUSSON, A. E., and ROBINSON, Eric, *Science and Technology in the Industrial Revolution* (Manchester, 1969).

MYINT, Hla, 'The Classical Theory of International Trade and the Underdeveloped Countries', *EJ* 68 (1958), 317–37.

MYRDAL, Gunnar, *An International Economy. Problems and Prospects* (NY, 1956, 1964).

—— *Economic Theory and Underdeveloped Regions* (NY, 1971).

NADAL, Jordi, 'Industrialisation et désindustrialisation du sud-ouest espagnol', in LÉON, CROUZET, GASCON (1972).

—— 'Spain, 1830–1914', in CIPOLLA (1973), iv.

NEAL, Larry, 'The Economics and Finance of Bilateral Clearing Agreements in Germany, 1934–8', *EcHR* 32 (1979), 391–404.

NEEDLEMAN, L. (ed.), *Regional Analysis. Selected Readings* (Harmondsworth, 1968).

NEWELL, William H., 'The Agricultural Revolution in Nineteenth-Century France', *JEcH* 33 (1973), 697–731.

—— *Population Change and Agricultural Development in Nineteenth Century France* (Ann Arbor, 1972).

NIELSEN, Axel, *Dänische Wirtschaftsgeschichte* (Jena, 1933).

NORTH, Douglass C., 'Location Theory and Regional Economic Growth', *JPE* 63 (1955), 243–58.

—— *The Economic Growth of the United States 1790–1860* (NY, 1961, 1966).

NOURSE, E. G., *American Agriculture and European Markets* (NY, 1924).

NOVE, Alec, *An Economic History of the U.S.S.R.* Harmondsworth, 1969).
— 'Russia as an Emergent Country', in YOUNGSON (1972).
OBERLÄNDER, Erwin, *Russia Enters the Twentieth Century 1894-1917* (NY, 1971).
OBLENSKY-OSSINSKY, V. V., 'Emigration from and Immigration into Russia', in WILLCOX (1969).
O'BRIEN, P. K., 'Agriculture and the Industrial Revolution', *EcHR* 30 (1977).
O'BRIEN, Patrick, and KEYDER, Caglar, *Economic Growth in Britain and France 1780-1914* (1978).
OCKENFELS, Hans Dieter, *Regionalplanung und Wirtschaftswachstum. Dargestellt am Beispiel Frankreichs* (Diss., Bonn, 1969).
OHLIN, Bertil, *Interregional and International Trade* (Cambridge, Mass., 1933, 1968).
ORGANISATION DE COOPÉRATION ET DE DÉVELOPPEMENT ÉCONOMIQUE, *Portugal* (Paris, 1970a).
ORGANISATION FOR ECONOMIC CO-OPERATION AND DEVELOPMENT, *The Regional Factor in Economic Development* (Paris, 1970b).
— *Issues of Regional Policies* (Paris, 1973).
— *Agricultural Policy of the E.E.C.* (Paris, 1974).
OSHIMA, Harry, 'Underemployment in Backward Economies—an Empirical Comment', *JPE* 66 (1958), 259-64.
PAINE, Suzanne, 'The Changing Role of Migrant Labour in the Advanced Capitalist Economies of Western Europe', in GRIFFITHS, Richard T. (ed.), *Government, Business and Labour in European Capitalism* (1977).
PALAIRET, Michael, 'Merchant Enterprise and the Development of the Plumbased Trades in Serbia 1847-1911', *EcHR* 30 (1977), 582-601.
— 'The Peasantry of Serbia and the Burden of a Fiscal Revolution 1862-1911' (Unpubl. cylost;, 1978), publ. later as 'Fiscal Pressure and Peasant Impoverishment in Serbia before World War I', *JEcH* 39 (1979), 719-740.
PALMADE, Guy P., *French Capitalism in the Nineteenth Century* (Newton Abbot, 1972).
PALMER, Marilyn (ed.), *The Onset of Industrialisation* (Nottingham, n.d., ?1977).
PANTA, Lorenzo del, 'Italy', in LEE (1979a).
PARISET, E., *Histoire de la fabrique lyonnaise* (Lyons, 1902).
PARKER, R. A. C., *Europe 1919-45* (1969).
PARKER, William N., 'Economic Development in Historical Perspective', in ROSENBERG (1971).
— 'Technology, Resources and Economic Change in the West', in YOUNGSON (1972).
PARKER, William N., and JONES, Eric L., (eds.), *European Peasants and their Markets* (Princeton, NY, 1975).
PARKINSON, C. N., *The Rise of the Port of Liverpool* (Liverpool, 1952).
PARLIAMENTARY PAPERS (*ParlP*), *Report of the Committee on the Woollen Manufacture of England* (1806) (268) iii.
PASVOLSKY, Leo, *Economic Nationalism of the Danubian States* (NY, 1928).
PEDERSEN, Erik H., 'Modernization of the Danish Peasant and Cottager Agriculture during . . . 1860-1880', *StudHistOec* 10 (1975), 109-13.
PEEMANS, Jean Philippe, 'Congo-Belgique', in DUPRIEZ *et al.* (1970).
PEET, Richard, 'Influence of the British Market on Agriculture and Related Economic Development in Europe Before 1860', *Institute of British Geographers* 56 (1972), 1-20.

PEEZ, A., 'Die österreichische Handelspolitik der letzten 25 Jahre', in VEREIN (1892) i.

PENOUIL, M., 'An Appraisal of Regional Development Policy in the Aquitaine Region', in ROBINSON (1969).

PERLOFF, Harvey S., DUNN, Edgar S. Jr., LAMPARD, Eric E., MUTH, Richard F., *Regions, Resources and Economic Growth* (Baltimore, 1960).

PERROUX, François, 'Economic Spaces: Theory and Applications', *QJE* 64 (1950), 89–104.

—— 'Prise de vues sur la croissance de l'économie française 1780–1950', in INTER-NATIONAL ASSOCIATON (1955).

—— *L'économie du XXe siècle* (Paris, 1961, 1969).

—— 'Matériaux pour une analyse de la croissance économique', *Cahiers de l'I.N.S.E.A.*, Série D, No. 8 (1965).

PEUCKERT, Will-Erich, *Volkskunde des Proletariats. I. Aufgang der proletarischen Kultur* (Frankfurt/Main, 1931).

PIERENKEMPER, Toni, 'Die Schwerindustrie in Oberschlesien und im west-fälischen Ruhrgebiet 1852–1913', *Zeitschrift für Unternehmergeschichte* 24 (1979).

—— 'Entrepreneurs in Heavy Industry: Upper Silesia and the Westphalian Ruhr Region, 1852–1913', *Business History Review* (1979b).

—— 'Regionale Differenzierung im östlichen Ruhrgebiet von 1850–1887; dargestellt am Beispiel der Einführung der Dampfkraft', FREMDLING and TILLY (1979).

PIETRZAK-PAWLOWSKA, Irena, 'Industrialisation des territoires européens arrierés au XIXe siècle', *StudHistOec* 3 (1968), 181–200.

—— 'Die polnischen Gebiete in der Periode der europäischen industriellen Revolu-tion', *StudHistOec* 5 (1970), 173–90.

PINDER, John, 'EEC, EFTA and COMECON', in ATLANTIC INSTITUTE (1971).

—— 'Europe in the World Economy 1920–1970', in CIPOLLA (1973), vi.

PINSON, Monique, 'La sidérurgie française', in RUSSO (1965).

PINTO, L. T., 'The Problem of Portuguese Economic Development', in ROBINSON (1960).

PIRENNE, Henri, *Histoire de Belgique* (vol. 7, Brussels, 1948).

PIUZ, Anne-Marie, 'Note sur l'industrie des indiennes à Genève au XVIIIe siècle', in LÉON, CROUZET, GASCON (1972).

PLAKANS, Andrejs, 'Seignorial Authority and Peasant Family Life: The Baltic Area in the Eighteenth Century', *Journal of Interdisciplinary History* 5 (1975), 629–854.

PLATT, D. C. M., 'British Portfolio Investment Overseas before 1870's: Some Doubts', *EcHR* 33 (1980), 1–16.

PODBIELSKI, Gisela, *Italy: Development and Crisis in the Post-War Economy* (Oxford, 1974).

POHL, Reinhard (ed.), *Handbook of the Economy of the German Democratic Republic* (Farnborough, 1979).

POIDEVIN, R., 'Protectionnisme et relations internationales: l'exemple du Tarif douanier français de 1910', *RevHist* 497 (1971), 47–62.

POLITICAL AND ECONOMIC PLANNING, *Economic Development in South-East Europe* (Oxford, 1945).

—— *Report on International Trade* (1937).

POLLARD, Sidney, 'The Ethics of the Sheffield Outrages', *Transactions of the Hunter Archaeological Society*, 7 (1954), 118–39.

—— *A History of Labour in Sheffield 1850-1939* (Liverpool, 1959).
—— (ed.), *The Sheffield Outrages* (Bath, 1971).
—— 'Industrialisation and the European Economy', *EcHR* 26 (1973), 636-48.
—— *European Economic Integration 1850-1970* (1974).
—— 'Industrialization and Integration of the European Economy', in BÜSCH, Otto, *et al.* (ed.), *Industrialisierung und die europäische Wirtschaft im 19. Jahrhundert* (Berlin, 1975).
—— (ed.), *Region und Industrialisierung* (Göttingen, 1980).
POLONSKY, Antony, *The Little Dictators. The History of Eastern Europe since 1918* (1975).
PONTING, K. G., *Baines' Account of the Woollen Manufacture of England* (NY, 1970).
—— *The Woollen Industry of South-West England* (Bath, 1971).
—— 'The Structure of the Wiltshire-Somerset Border Woollen Industry, 1816-40', in HARTE and PONTING (1973).
PORTAL, Roger, *L'Oural au XVIIIe siècle* (Paris, 1950).
—— 'Das Problem einer industriellen Revolution in Rußland im 19. Jahrhundert', *Forschungen zur Osteuropäischen Geschichte* 1 (1954), 205-16.
—— 'Aux origines d'une bourgeoisie industrielle en Russie', *Revue d'histoire moderne et contemporaine* 8 (1961), 35-60.
—— 'The Industrialization of Russia', *CEHE* 6/2 (1966), pp. 801-72.
POSNER, Michael, 'International Trade and Technical Change', *OEP* 13 (1961), 323-41.
POST, John D., 'A Study in Meteorological and Trade Cycle History: The Economic Crisis Following the Napoleonic Wars', *JEcH* 34 (1974), 315-49.
POSTAN, M. M., *An Economic History of Western Europe 1945-1964* (1967).
POSTAN, M. M., and HATCHER, John, 'Population and Class Relations in Feudal Society', *Past and Present* 78 (1978).
POUNDS, Norman J. G., *The Upper Silesian Industrial Region* (Bloomington, 1958).
—— *The Ruhr. A Study in Historical and Economic Geography* (NY, 1968).
POUNDS, Norman J. G., and PARKER, William N., *Coal and Steel in Western Europe* (Bloomington, 1957).
POUTARD, J., Les Disparités régionales dans la croissance de l'agriculture française (Paris, 1965).
PRABANDER, G. L. de, 'Discussion', in INTERNATIONAL CONGRESS (1974), Themes: Relations between Regions of Uneven Economic Development.
PRANDKE, P., 'Austria', in CENTRE EUROPÉEN (1968).
PRED, Allan, *The External Relations of Cities During 'Industrial Revolution'* (Chicago, 1962).
—— *Behaviour and Location: Foundations for a Geographic and Dynamic Location Theory* (Lund, 1967).
PREMIÈRE CONFÉRENCE INTERNATIONALE D'HISTOIRE ÉCONOMIQUE, Stockholm, 1960 (Paris, Hague, 1960).
PRESSNELL, L. S., 'Public Moneys and the Development of English Banking', *EcHR* 5 (1953), 378-97.
—— *Country Banking in the Industrial Revolution* (Oxford, 1956).
PREST, John *The Industrial Revolution in Coventry* (1960).
PRICE, Roger, *The Economic Modernisation of France* (1975).
PRIESTLEY, Joseph, *Historical Account of the Navigable Rivers, Canals and Railways throughout Great Britain* (1831, repr. 1967).

PROBYN, J. W. (ed.), *Systems of Land Tenure in Various Countries* (1881).
PUHLE, Hans-Jürgen, *Agrarische Interessenpolitik und preußischer Konservatismus* (Hanover, 1966).
PURŠ, Jaroslav, 'Die Aufhebung der Hörigkeit und die Grundentlastung in den böhmischen Ländern', *Economic History, 2nd International Congress*, 1962 (Paris, Hague, 1965).
—— 'Struktur und Dynamik der industriellen Entwicklung in Böhmen im letzten Viertel des 18. Jahrhunderts', *JahrbfWg* (1965b), 160-96.
—— 'La diffusion asynchronique de la traction à vapeur dans l'industrie en Europe au 19e siècle', *Historica* 18 (1973), 139-79.
QUESTED, R., *The Russo-Chinese Bank: A Multinational Base of Tsarism in China* (Birmingham, 1977).
RADCLIFFE, W., *The Origins of Power Loom Weaving* (Stockport, 1828).
RAISTRICK, A., *Dynasty of Ironfounders: the Darbys of Coalbrookdale* (1953).
RAPPARD, William E., *La révolution industrielle et les origines de la protection légale du travail en Suisse* (Berne, 1914).
RATCLIFFE, Barry M., 'Napoleon III and the Anglo-French Commercial Treaty of 1860: a Reconsideration', *JEuropEcH* 2 (1973), 582-613.
—— 'The Tariff Reform Campaign in France 1831-36', *JEuropEcH* 7 (1978), 61-138.
RATTI, Anna Maria, 'Italian Migration Movements, 1876-1926', in WILLCOX (1931, 1969).
RAUPACH, Hans, 'The Impact of the Great Depression on Eastern Europe', in WEE (1972).
RAYBOULD, T. J., *The Economic Emergence of the Black Country* (Newton Abbot, 1973).
REACH, Angus Bethune, *Manchester and the Textile Districts in 1849* (Helmshore, 1972).
REDDY, W. M., 'The Textile Trade and the Language of the Crowd at Rouen 1752-1871', *Past and Present* 74 (1977), 62-89.
REDFORD, Arthur, *Labour Migration in England 1800-1850* (Manchester, 1926, London 1964).
—— *Manchester Merchants and Foreign Trade 1794-1858* (Manchester, 1934).
REDLICH, F., and FREUDENBERGER, H., 'The Industrial Development of Europe: Reality, Symbols, Images', *Kyklos* 17 (1964), 372-401.
REED, M. C., *Investment in Railways in Britain 1820-1844* (1975).
REINHARD, Marcel, ARMENGAUD, André, DUPAQUIER, Jacques, *Histoire générale de la population mondiale* (Paris, 1968).
RÉMOND, André, *John Holker, manufacturier et grand fonctionnaire en France au XVIIIe siècle, 1719-1786* (Paris, 1946).
REULECKE, Jürgen, 'Nachzügler und Pionier zugleich: das bergische Land und der Beginn der Industrialisierung in Deutschland', in POLLARD, (1980).
—— 'Die industrielle Entwicklung des Wuppertals', in JORDAN and WOLF (1977).
RÉUS, Henri de, and ENDT, G. S., 'Die Handelspolitik der Niederlande', in VEREIN FÜR SOCIALPOLITIK (1892), i.
REYNOLDS, Lloyd G., 'Economic Development with Surplus Labour: Some Complications', *OEP* 21 (1969), 89-103.
RICARDO, David, *On the Principles of Political Economy and Taxation* (1817, Sraffa ed., vol. 1, 1970).
RICHARDSON, Harry W., *Elements of Regional Economics* (Harmondsworth, 1969).

—— *Regional Growth Theory* (1973).

RIDEN, P. 'The Output of the British Iron Industry before 1870', *EcHR* 30 (1977), 442–59.

RIESSER, Jacob, *The Great German Banks and their Concentration* (Washington, 1911).

RIMMER, Gordon, 'The Industrial Profile of Leeds 1740–1840', *Thoresby Society Publications* L. 113 (1967).

RINGEL, Hermann, *Bergische Wirtschaft zwischen 1790 und 1860* (Remscheid, 1966).

RINGROSE, David R., *Transportation and Economic Stagnation in Spain 1750–1850* (Durham, NC, 1970).

—— 'The Impact of a New Capital City: Madrid, Toledo and the New Castile 1560–1660', *JEcH* 33 (1973), 761–91.

RIST, Marcel, 'A French Experiment with Free Trade: the Treaty of 1860', in CAMERON (1970a).

RITTER, Ulrich Peter, *Die Rolle des Staates in den Frühstadien der Industrialisierung* (Berlin, 1961).

ROBBINS, Lionel, *The Great Depression* (1934).

ROBBINS, Michael, *The Railway Age* (1962).

ROBERTS, Charles A., 'Interregional Per Capita Income Differentials and Convergence: 1880–1950', *JEcH* 39 (1979), 101–12.

ROBERTS, R. O., 'Bank of England Branch Discounting 1826–59', *Economica* 25 (1958), 230–45.

ROBINSON, E. A. G., (ed.), *Economic Consequences of the Size of Nations* (1960).

—— (ed.), *Backward Areas in Advanced Countries* (1969).

—— 'Location Theory, Regional Economics and Backward Areas', in ROBINSON (1969b).

ROEHL, Richard, 'French Industrialisation, a Reconsideration' *ExplEcH* 13 (1976), 233–81.

ROEPKE Wilhelm, *Welwirtschaft und Außenhandelspolitik* (Berlin, Vienna, 1931).

—— *International Economic Disintegration* (1942).

—— *Civitas Humana* (Zürich, 1944).

—— *Internationale Ordnung* (Eerlenbach, Zürich, 1945).

—— *L'Économie mondiale aux XIXe et XXe siècles* (Geneva, 1959).

ROESSINGH, H. K., 'Village and Hamlet in a Sandy Region of the Netherlands in the Middle of the 18th Century', *Acta Historiae Neerlandicae* 4 (1970), 105–29.

ROGERS, Alan, 'Industrialisation and the Local Community', in POLLARD (1980).

ROOSA, R. A., 'Russian Industrialists Look to the Future: Thoughts on Economic Development', in CURTISS (1963).

ROSE, Arnold M., *Migrants in Europe. Problems of Acceptance and Adjustments* (Minneapolis, 1969).

ROSENBERG, Hans *Machteliten und Wirtschaftskonjunkturen* (Göttingen, 1978).

ROSENBERG, Nathan (ed.), *The Economics of Technological Change* (Harmondsworth, 1971).

—— *Perspectives in Technology* (Cambridge, 1976).

ROSENSTEIN-RODAN, P. N., 'Problems of Industrialisation of Eastern and South-Eastern Europe', *EJ* 53 (1943), 202–11.

ROSTOW, W. W., *The Stages of Economic Growth* (Cambridge, 1960a).
— *The Process of Economic Growth* (Oxford, 1960b).
— (ed.), *The Economics of Take-Off into Sustained Growth* (1963).
— 'Introduction and Epilogue', in ROSTOW (1963b).
— 'Leading Sectors and the Take-Off', in ROSTOW (1963c).
— *The World Economy, History and Prospect* (Austin, Texas, 1978).
ROWE, David J., 'The Economy of the North-East', *Northern History* 6 (1971),
    117-47.
— 'The Chronology of the Onset of Industrialisation in North-East England', in
    PALMER (?1977).
ROWE, John, *Cornwall in the Age of the Industrial Revolution* (Liverpool, 1953).
ROWE, J. W. F., *Markets and Men. A Study of Artificial Control Schemes in
    Some Primary Industries* (Cambridge, 1936).
ROWLANDS, Marie, 'Industrialization and Social Change in the West Midlands
    1560-1760', in PALMER (?1977).
ROYAL INSTITUTE OF INTERNATIONAL AFFAIRS, *The Baltic States*
    (1938).
— *South-Eastern Europe* (1939).
ROZMAN, Gilbert, 'Comparative Approaches to Urbanization: Russia 1750-1800',
    in HAMM (1976).
RUBNER, Heinrich, 'Forstwirtschaft und Industrialisierung (besonders Frank-
    reich)', in FISCHER (1968).
RUDOLPH, Richard L., *Banking and Industrialization in Austria-Hungary* (Cam-
    bridge, 1976).
RUSINSKI, Wladislaw, 'The Role of the Polish Territories in the European Trade in
    the Seventeenth and Eighteenth Centuries', *StudHistOec* 3 (1968), 115-34.
— Strukturwandlungen der bäuerlichen Bevölkerung Polens im 16.- 18. Jahr-
    hundert', *StudHistOec* 7 (1972), 99-119.
— 'Veränderungen in der Struktur und ökonomischen Lage der polnischen
    Bauernschaft an der Wende vom 18. zum 19. Jahrhundert', in BERINDEI
    (1973).
RUSSO F., 'Sidérurgie et croissance économique en France et en Grande Bretagne
    (1735-1913)' *Cahiers de l'I.N.S.E.A.* T. 5, No. 158 (1965).
RUTTAN, Vernon W., 'Structural Retardation and the Modernization of French
    Agriculture: A Skeptical View', *JEcH* 38 (1978), 714-28.
RYDER, Norman B., 'The Character of Modern Fertility', in DURAND (1967).
SAALFELD, D., 'Einkommensverhältnisse und Lebenserhaltungskosten städt-
    ischer Populationen in der Übergangsperiode zum Industriezeitalter', in BOG
    (1974).
SABARRA, Eda, *A Social History of Germany 1648-1914* (1977).
SAINT-LÉON, Étienne Martin, *Histoire des corporations de Métiers, dépuis leur
    origines jusqu'à leur suppression en 1791* (Paris, 1922).
SALTER, W. E. G., *Productivity and Technical Change* (Cambridge, 1960).
SAMUEL, Raphael, 'The Workshop of the World: Steam Power and Hand Tech-
    nology in mid-Victorian Britain', *History Workshop* 3 (1977), 6-72.
SANCHEZ-ALBORNOZ, Nicholas, 'Congruence among Spanish Economic Regions
    in the 19th Century', *JEuropEcH* 3 (1974), 725-45.
SANDBERG, Lars G., 'Movements in the Quality of British Cotton Textile Ex-
    ports 1815-1913', *EcHR* 28 (1968), 1-27.
— 'Banking and Economic Growth in Sweden Before World War I', *JEcH* 38
    (1978), 650-80.

— 'The Case of the Impoverished Sophisticate: Human Capital and Swedish Economic Growth before World War I', *JEcH* 39 (1979), 225-41.

SANDER, Hartmut, 'Bevölkerungsexplosion im 19. Jahrhundert', in JORDAN and WOLF (1977).

SÁNDOR, Pal, 'Die Agrarkrise am Ende des 19. Jahrhunderts und der Großgrundbesitz in Ungarn', in SÁNDOR and HANÁK (1961).

SÁNDOR, V., 'Die großindustrielle Entwicklung in Ungarn 1867-1919', *Acta Historica* 3 (1956), 139-247.

SÁNDOR, V., and HANÁK, P. (eds.), *Studien zur Geschichte der österreich-ungarischen Monarchie* (Budapest, 1961).

SAUL, S. B., *The Myth of the Great Depression 1873-1896* (1972a).

— The Nature and Diffusion of Technology', in YOUNGSON (1972b).

SAVILLE, Lloyd, *Regional Economic Development in Italy* (Cambridge, 1968).

SAWYER, J. C., 'Stresses in the Structure of Modern France', in EARLE (1951).

SCHARING, William, 'Die Handelspolitik Dänemarks 1864-1891', in VEREIN (1892), i.

SCHEEL, H. von, 'Der auswärtige Handel des Deutschen Zollgebiets im letzten Jahrzehnt', in VEREIN (1892), i.

SCHISSLER, Hanna, *Preußische Agrargesellschaft im Wandel* (Göttingen, 1978).

SCHLOTE, Werner, *British Overseas Trade from 1700 to the 1930's* (Oxford, n. d.: German ed. 1938).

SCHLUMBOHM, Jürgen, 'Produktionsverhältnisse, Produktivkräfte, Krisen in der Proto-Industrialisierung', in KRIEDTE (1977a).

— 'Exkurs zur Bedeutung der politisch-industriellen Rahmenbedingungen in der Proto-Industrialisierung', in KRIEDTE (1977b).

SCHMIDT, K.-H., 'Die Rolle des Kleingewerbes in regionalen Wachstumsprozessen in der zweiten Hälfte des 19. Jahrhunderts', in BOG (1974).

SCHÖLLER, Paul, 'Les transformations économiques de la Belgique de 1832 à 1844', *Bulletin de l'Institut de Recherches Économiques et Sociales* 14 (1948), 526-96.

SCHOFER, Lawrence, *The Formation of a Modern Labour Force: Upper Silesia 1865-1914* (Berkeley and L. A., 1975).

SCHREMMER, Eckart, *Die Bauernbefreiung in Hohenlohe* (Stuttgart, 1963).

— *Die Wirtschaft Bayerns. Vom hohen Mittelalter bis zum Beginn der Industrialisierung* (Munich, 1970).

— 'Standortausweitung der Warenproduktion im langfristigen Wirtschaftswachstum', *VSWG* 59 (1972), 1-40.

— 'Zusammenhänge zwischen Katastersteuersystem, Wirtschaftswachstum und Wirtschaftsstruktur im 19. Jahrhundert', in BOG (1974).

— 'Überlegungen zur Bestimmung des gewerblichen und des agrarischen Elements in einer Region', in KELLENBENZ (1975).

— 'The Textile Industry in South Germany 1750-1850', *Textile History* 7 (1976).

— 'Industrielle Rückständigkeit und strukturstabilisierender Fortschritt', in H. KELLENBENZ, *Wirtschaftliches Wachstum* (Stuttgart, 1978).

— 'Der südhessische Odenwald', *Zeitschrift für Agrargeschichte und Agrarsoziologie* 27 (1979), 1-18.

SCHULTE, Fritz, *Die Entwicklung der gewerblichen Wirtschaft in Rheinland-Westfalen im 18. Jahrhundert* (Cologne, 1959).

SCHULZE-GÄVERNITZ, Gerhard von, *Volkswirtschaftliche Studien aus Rußland* (Leipzig, 1899).

SCITOVSKY, Tibor, 'International Trade and Economic Integration as a Means of Overcoming the Disadvantages of Small Nations', in ROBINSON (1960).

SCOVILLE, W. C., *The Persecution of Huguenots and French Economic Development 1680-1720* (Berkeley, 1960).

SÉE, Henri, 'Remarques sur le caractère de l'industrie rurale en France et les causes de son extension au XVIII siècle', *RevHist* 142 (1923), 47-53.

—— *Histoire économique de la France* (2 vols., Paris, 1939, 1942).

SEJERSTED, Francis, 'Aspects of Norwegian Timber Trade in the 1840's and 50's', *ScandEcHR* 16 (1968), 137-54.

SELLA, Domenico, 'Industrial Production in Seventeenth-Century Italy: A Reappraisal', *ExplEcH* 6 (1968-9), 235-53.

SEMMINGSEN, Ingrid, 'Emigration from Scandinavia', *ScandEcHR* 20 (1972), 45-60.

SERING, Max, *Die landwirtschaftliche Konkurrenz Nordamerikas in Gegenwart und Zukunft* (Leipzig, 1887).

—— *Deutsche Agrarpolitik auf geschichtlicher und landeskundlicher Grundlage* (Leipzig, 1934).

SETON-WATSON, Hugh, *Eastern Europe between the Wars 1918-1941* (Cambridge, 1945).

—— *Nations and States. An Enquiry into the Origins of Nations and the Politics of Nationalism* (1977).

SEWARD, David, 'The Wool Textile Industry 1750-1960', in JENKINS (1972).

SHAPIRO, Seymour, *Capital and the Cotton Industry in the Industrial Revolution* (Ithaca, NY, 1967).

SHAW, Simeon, *History of the Staffordshire Potteries* (Hanley, 1829).

SHERMAN, Dennis, 'Governmental Policy Towards Joint-Stock Business Organization in Mid-Nineteenth-Century France', *JEuropEcH* 3 (1974), 149-68.

—— 'Governmental Responses to Economic Modernization in Mid-Nineteenth-Century France', *JEuropEcH* 6 (1977), 717-36.

SIEBERT, Horst, *Regionales Wirtschaftswachstum und interregionale Mobilität* (Tübingen, 1970).

SIEGENTHALER, Jürg, 'A Scale Analysis of Nineteenth-Century Industrialization, *ExplEcH* 10 (1972), 75-101.

—— 'Sicilian Economic Changes Since 1860', *JEuropEcH* 2 (1973), 363-415.

SINGLETON, Fred, *Industrial Revolution in Yorkshire* (Clapham, 1970).

SLAVEN, Anthony, *The Development of the West of Scotland: 1750-1960* (1975).

SLICHER VAN BATH, B. H., *The Agrarian History of Western Europe A. D. 500-1850* (1963).

—— 'The Yield of Different Crops (mainly cereals) in Relation to the Seed c.1810-1820', *Acta Historiae Neerlandicae* 2 (1967), 26-106.

SLIWKA, Wladislaw, *Les Mouvements internationaux et la réconstruction économique de l'Europe* (Paris, 1948).

SMITH, Adam, *Wealth of Nations* (1970 ed., vol. 1).

SMITH, Denis Mack, *A History of Sicily: Modern Sicily After 1713* (1968).

SMITH, Michael S., 'Thoughts on the Evolution of the French Capitalist Community in the XIXth Century', *JEuropEcH* 7 (1978), 139-44.

SMITH, T. E., 'The Control of Mortality', in DURAND (1967).

SMOUT, T. C., *A History of the Scottish People 1560-1830* (1969).

SNELLER, Z.-W., 'La naissance de l'industrie rurale dans les pays-bas au XVIIe et XVIIIe siècles', *Annales d'histoire économique et sociale* 1 (1929), 193-202.

SOCIOLOGICAL INSTITUTE, STATE UNIVERSITY OF UTRECHT, 'The Netherlands', in CENTRE EUROPÉEN (1968).

SOLO, R., 'The Capacity to Assimilate an Advanced Technology', in ROSENBERG (1971).

SOMBART, Werner, 'Die Handelspolitik Italiens seit der Einigung des Königreichs', in VEREIN (1892).

SONTAG, John P., 'Tsarist Debts and Tsarist Foreign Policy', *Slavic Review* 27 (1968), 529–41.

SOROKIN, G. M. (ed.), *Sozialistisches Weltsystem* (4 volumes, 3 vols. publ., Berlin, 1967).

SPENCER, Daniel L., and WORONIAK, Alexander (eds.), *The Transfer of Technology to Developing Countries* (NY, 1967).

SPENCER, Herbert, *Principles of Sociology* (vol. 2, 1902 ed.).

SPINELLI, Altiero, 'On New East-West Relations', in ATLANTIC INSTITUTE (1971).

SPREE, Reinhard, *Wachstumstrends und Konjunkturzyklen in der deutschen Wirtschaft von 1820 bis 1913* (Göttingen, 1978).

SPULBER, Nicholas, *Soviet Strategy for Economic Growth* (Bloomington, 1964).

—— *The State and Economic Development in Eastern Europe* (NY, 1966).

STARK, Werner, *Ursprung und Aufstieg des landwirtschaftlichen Großbetriebs in den böhmischen Ländern* (Brno, Prague, Leipzig, Vienna, 1934).

STEINBERG, Heinz Günter, 'Die Entwicklung des Ruhrgebiets von 1840 bis 1914', in HISTORISCHE RAUMFORSCHUNG (1967).

—— *Die Entwicklung des Ruhrgebietes. Eine wirtschafts- und sozialgeographische Studie* (Düsseldorf, 1967b).

STEINKOHLENBERGBAU IN SCHLESIEN (Hanover, 1947).

STERN, Robert M., 'A Century of Food Exports', *Kyklos* 13 (1960), 44–61.

STOIANOVICH, Traian, 'The Conquering Balkan Orthodox Merchant', *JEcH* 20 (1960), 234–313.

STRUMILIN, S., 'Industrial Crises in Russia', in CROUZET, CHALONER, STERN (1969).

SUGENHEIM, Samuel, *Geschichte der Aufhebung der Leibeigenschaft und Hörigkeit in Europa bis um die Mitte des 19. Jahrhunderts* (St. Petersburg 1861, repr. Aalen 1966).

SUPPLE, Barry, 'Talking about Economic Development', in YOUNGSON (1972).

—— 'The State and the Industrial Revolution, 1700-1914', in CIPOLLA (1973), iii.

SVENNILSON, Ingvar, *Growth and Stagnation in the European Economy* (Geneva, 1954).

—— 'The Concept of the Nation and its Relevance to Economic Analysis', in ROBINSON, (1960).

—— 'The Transfer of Industrial Know-How to Non-Industrialized Countries', in K. BERRILL (ed.), *Economic Development* (1964).

SWEEZY, P. M., *Monopoly and Competition in the English Coal Trade 1550-1850* (Cambridge, Mass., 1938).

SZABAD, György, 'Das Anwachsen der Ausgleichtendenz der Produktenpreise im Habsburgerreich um die Mitte des 19. Jahrhunderts', in SÁNDOR and HANÁK (1961).

SZAPARY, Georges, 'Europe-États-Unis 1899-1962', in DUPRIEZ *et al.* (1966).

TAMBORRA, Angelo, 'The Rise of Italian Industry and the Balkans (1900-1914)', *JEuropEcH* 3 (1974), 87–120.

TANN, Jennifer, 'The Employment of Power in the West of England Textile Industry, 1790-1840', in HARTE and PONTING (1973).

TANN, Jennifer, and BRECKIN, M. J., 'The International Diffusion of the Watt Engine, 1775-1825', *EcHR* 31 (1978), 541-64.

TARLÉ, Eugene, *L'Industrie dans les campagnes en France à la fin de l'ancien régime* (Paris, 1910).

TAUSSIG, F. W., *International Trade* (NY, 1927).

TAYLOR, A. J., 'The Sub-Contract System in the British Coal Industry', in L. S. PRESSNELL (ed.), *Studies in the Industrial Revolution* (1960).

TAYLOR, George V., 'Types of Capitalism in Eighteenth-Century France', *EngHR* 79 (1964), 478-97.

TENNENBAUM, Henrik, *Central and Eastern Europe in World Economy* (1944).

TERLINDEN, Ch., 'La politique économique de Guillaume Ier, roi de Pays-Bas, en Belgique', *RevHist* 139 (1922), 1-39.

THALHEIM, K. C., 'Russia's Economic Development', in OBERLÄNDER (1971).

THIEDE, Roger L., 'Industry and Urbanization in New Russia', in HAMM (1976).

THIENEL, Ingrid, *Städtewachstum im Industrialisierungsprozess des 19. Jahrhunderts: das Berliner Beispiel* (Berlin, NY, 1973).

THIMME, Paul, *Straßenbau and Straßenpolitik zur Zeit der Gründung des Zollvereins 1825-35* (Stuttgart, 1931)

THIRRING, Gustav, 'Hungarian Migration of Modern Times', in WILLCOX (1969), ii.

THIRSK, Joan, 'Industries in the Countryside', in F. J. FISHER (ed.), *Essays in the Economic and Social History of Tudor and Stuart England* (Cambridge, 1961).

—— 'The Fantastical Folly of Fashion: The English Stocking Knitting Industry, 1500-1700', in HARTE and PONTING (1973).

THOMAS, John, *The Rise of the Staffordshire Potteries* (Somerset, 1971).

THOMPSON, E. P., *The Making of the English Working Class* (1963).

THOMPSON, E. P., and YEO, Eileen, *The Unknown Mayhew* (1971).

THORNER, Daniel, 'Peasant Economy as a Category in Economic History', ECONOMIC HISTORY (1962).

THÜNEN, Johann Heinrich von, *Der isolierte Staat, in Beziehung auf Landwirtschaft und Nationalökonomie* (1842, Stuttgart, 1966 ed.).

THUILLIER, Guy, 'La métallurgie rhénane de 1800 à 1830', *Annales ESC* 16 (1961), 877-907.

TIEBOUT, C. M., 'Regional and Interregional Output Models: An Appraisal', in NEEDLEMAN (1968).

TILLY, Richard, *Financial Institutions and Industrialization in the Rhineland 1850-1870* (Madison, 1966).

—— 'The Political Economy of Public Finance and the Industrialization of Prussia 1815-1866', *JEcH* 26 (1966), 484-97.

—— 'Germany 1815-1870', in CAMERON (1967a).

—— 'Finanzielle Aspekte der preußischen Industrialisierung 1815-1870', in FISCHER (1968).

—— 'Los von England', *ZgSW* 124 (1968b), 179-96.

—— 'Verkehrs- und Nachrichtenwesen 1850-1914', in AUBIN and ZORN (1976).

—— 'Capital Formation in Germany in the Nineteenth Century', *CEHE* 7/1 (1978), pp. 382-441.

TIMMINS, Samuel, *Birmingham and the Midland Hardware District* (1866, repr. 1967).

— 'The Industrial History of Birmingham', in TIMMINS (1967b).

TIMOSHENKO, Vladimir P., *Agricultural Russia and the Wheat Problem* (Stanford, Cal., 1932).

TINBERGEN, Jan, 'International, National, Regional and Local Industries', in BALDWIN (1965).

TIPTON, Frank B., *Regional Variations in the Economic Development of Germany during the Nineteenth Century* (Middletown, Conn., 1976).

TODOROV, N., 'The Genesis of Capitalism in the Balkan Provinces of the Ottoman Empire in the Nineteenth Century' *ExplEcH* 7 (1969-70), 313-24.

TOMASKE, John A., 'The Determinants of Inter-Country Differences in European Emigration 1881-1900', *JEcH* 31 (1971), 840-53.

TONIOLO, Gianni, 'Effective Protection and Industrial Growth: the Case of Italian Engineering, 1898-1913', *JEuropEcH* 6 (1977), 659-74.

TOPOLSKI, Jerzy, 'Cases of Dualism in the Economic Development of Modern Europe', *StudHistOec* 3 (1968), 3-12.

— 'La réfeodalisation dans l'économie des grands domaines en Europe centrale et oreintale (XVIe-XVIIIe ss.)', *StudHistOec* 6 (1971), 51-63.

— 'Economic Decline in Poland from the Sixteenth to the Eighteenth Centuries', in EARLE (1974).

TORTELLA-CASARES, Gabriel, *Banking, Railroads and Industry in Spain, 1829-1874* (NY, 1977).

TOUTAIN, J.-C., 'La produit de l'agriculture francaise de 1700 à 1958', *Cahiers de l'I.N.S.E.A.*, No. 115 and Suppl. (Paris, 1961).

TOYNBEE, A., *Lectures on the Industrial Revolution in England* (1884).

TRACY, Michael, *Agriculture in Western Europe* (NY, 1964).

TREMEL, Ferdinand, 'Die industrielle Entwicklung in Ungarn in 1867-1900', *VSWG* 45 (1958), 242-50.

TREML, Vladimir G., with Farrell, R. (eds.), *The Development of the Soviet Economy. Plan and Performance* (NY, 1968).

TRIFFIN, R., 'The Size of the Nation and its Vulnerability to Economic Nationalism', in ROBINSON (1960).

TRINDER, Barrie, *The Industrial Revolution in Shropshire* (London and Chichester, 1973).

TROELTSCH, W., *Die Calwer Zeughauscompagnie* (Jena, 1897).

TUCKER, Josiah, *Four Tracts on Political and Commercial Subjects* (Gloucester, 1776 ed.).

TUGAN-BARANOWSKY, M., *Geschichte der russischen Fabrik* (Berlin, 1900).

TUPLING, G. H., *The Economic History of Rossendale* (Manchester, 1927).

TURCAN, Pavel, 'The Development of a Backward Area in Czechoslovakia', in ROBINSON, (1969).

TWITCHETT, Kenneth J. (ed.), *Europe and the World. The External Relations of the Common Market* (1976).

UNGER, R. W., *Dutch Shipbuilding before 1800* (Amsterdam, 1978).

— 'Trade Through the Sound in the Seventeenth and Eighteenth Centuries', *EcHR* 12 (1959), 206-21.

UNITED NATIONS, *Yearbook of International Accounts* (Annual).

UNITED NATIONS, ECONOMIC COMMISSION FOR EUROPE, *Economic Survey of Europe* in 1950, 1951 etc. (Geneva, annual). (N.B.: Year of appearance in the year after the reference data.)

— E.C.E. *The European Economy from the 1950's to the 1970's* (NY, 1972).

UNWIN, George, *Samuel Oldknow and the Arkwrights* (Manchester, 1924).

VALARCHÉ, Jean, 'The Backward Region of Friburg in Switzerland', in ROBIN-
SON, (1969).
VALENSI, Lucette, in LÉON, (1978), iii, pp. 557-86.
VAMPLEW, Wray, 'The Railways and the Iron Industry: A Study of their Re-
lationship in Scotland', in M. C. REED (ed.), *Railways and the Victorian
Economy* (Newton Abbot, 1969).
VARGA, J., *Typen und Probleme des bäuerlichen Grundbesitzes in Ungarn
1767-1849* (Budapest, 1965).
VEBLEN, Th. B., 'The Price of Wheat since 1867', *JPE* (1890), 70-103.
VEREIN FÜR SOCIALPOLITIK (eds.), *Die Handelspolitik der wichtigeren
Kulturstaaten* (Leipzig, 1892, 2 vols.).
VERNON, Raymond, 'International Investment and International Trade in the
Product Cycle', *QJE* 80 (1966), 190-207.
VEYRASSAT-HERREN, Béatrice, 'Les centres de gravité de l'industrialisation
en Suisse au XIXe siècle: le rôle du coton', in LÉON, CROUZET, GASCON
(1972).
VIAL, Jean, *L'Industrialisation de la sidérurgie française 1814-1864* (Paris, Hague,
2 vols., 1967).
VIALLATE, Achille, *Le Monde économique 1918-1927* (Paris, 1928).
VICENS VIVES, J., *Manual de Historia Económica de España* (Barcelona, 1959).
— *Cataluna en el siglo XIX* (Madrid, 1961).
VIDALENC, J., 'Naissance de la Normandie contemporaine (1789-1814)', in
Michel de BOUARD (ed.), *Histoire de la Normandie* (Toulouse, 1970).
VILAR, Pierre, 'Agricultural Progress and the Economic Background in Eighteenth-
Century Catalonia', *EcHR* 11 (1958-9), 113-20.
— *La Catalogne dans l'Espagne moderne* (Paris, 3 vols., 1962).
— 'La Catalogne industrielle: réflexions sur un démarrage et sur un destin', in
LÉON, CROUZET, GASCON (1972).
VILFAN, Sergej, 'Die Agrarsozialpolitik von Maria Theresia bis Kudlich', in
BERINDEI (1973).
VINER, Jacob. *The Customs Union Issue* (NY, 1953a).
— *International Trade and Economic Development* (Oxford, 1953b).
VITO, F., 'Typologie des régions en retard', in CENTRE EUROPÉEN (1968).
VÖCHTING, Friedrich, *Die italienische Südfrage. Entstehung und Problematik
eines wirtschaftlichen Notstandgebietes* (Berlin, 1951).
VOIGT, Fritz, FRERICH, Johannes, RADEL, Rainer, UNTERBERG, Gerd, *Wirt-
schaftliche Entleerungsgebiete in Industrieländern* (Cologne, Opladen, 1969).
VOIGT, F., OTTO K., UNTERBERG, G., FRERICH, H., 'Federal Republic of
Germany', in CENTRE EUROPÉEN (1968).
VOLIN, Lazar, *A Century of Russian Agriculture. From Alexander II to Khrush-
chev* (Cambridge, Mass., 1970).
VOLTZ, Dr (ed.), *Handbuch des Oberschlesischen Industriebezirks* (Katowitz,
1913).
VRIES, Jan de, *The Dutch Rural Economy in the Golden Age, 1500-1700* (New
Haven, 1974).
— 'Peasant Demand Patterns and Economic Development: Friesland 1550-1750',
in PARKER and JONES, (1975).
— *Economy of Europe in an Age of Crisis. 1600-1750* (Cambridge, 1976).
— 'An Enquiry into the Behaviour of Wages in the Dutch Republic and the
Southern Netherlands, 1580-1800, *Acta Historiae Neerlandicae* 10 (1978),
79-97.

VUČO, Nikola, 'Les effets de la révolution industrielle sur le développement de l'agriculture en Serbie au XIX siècle', *StudHistOec* 10 (1975), 121–23.

WADSWORTH, Alfred P., and MANN, Julia de Lacy, *The Cotton Trade and Industrial Lancashire 1600–1780* (Manchester 1931, repr. 1965).

WALLE Étienne van der, 'France', in LEE (1979a).

WALLERSTEIN, Immanuel, *The Modern World System* (NY, 1974).

WALTERSHAUSEN, A. Sartorius von. *Die Entstehung der Weltwirtschaft* (Jena, 1931).

WARRINER, Doreen, *Economics of Peasant Farming* (1939), repr. 1964).

— (ed.), *Contrasts in Emerging Societies* (1965).

WEATHERILL, L., *The Pottery Trade and North Staffordshire 1660–1700* (1971).

WEBER, Adna F., *The Growth of Cities in the Nineteenth Century* (1899, repr. Ithaca, NY, 1968).

WEBER, Max, *Wirtschaft und Gesellschaft* (Tübingen, 1976).

WEBSTER, R. A., *Industrial Imperialism in Italy 1908–1915* (Berkeley, L. A., 1975).

WEE, Herman van der (ed.), *The Great Depression* (Hague, 1972).

— 'Agrarian Developments in the Low Countries as Reflected in Tithe and Rent Statistics 1250–1800', in Antoni MACZAK (ed.), *Resources in Economic History* Part 1, 7th International Economic History Congress, (Edinburgh, 1978).

WELLS, Louis T., 'International Trade: the Product Cycle Approach', in *The Product Life Cycle and International Trade* (Boston, Mass., 1972).

WELLS, Roger A. E., *Dearth and Distress in Yorkshire 1793–1802* (York, Borthwick Papers No. 52, 1977).

WENDEL, Hugo, *The Evolution of Industrial Freedom in Prussia 1845–1849* (NY, (1920).

WERNER, Karl Heinz, 'Österreichs Industrie- und Außenhandelspolitik 1848–1948', in MAYER (1949).

WHYMAN, John, 'Industrialisation by fits and starts: the Kentish Experience', in PALMER (?1977).

WIEL, Paul, *Das Ruhrgebiet in Vergangenheit und Gegenwart* (Essen, 1963).

— *Wirtschaftsgeschichte des Ruhrgebietes* (Essen, 1970).

WILD, M. T., 'The Yorkshire Wool Textile Industry', in JENKINS (1972).

WILLCOX, Walter F., *International Migrations* (NY, 2 vols., 1931, repr. 1969).

— 'Increase of the Population of the Earth and of the Continents since 1650', in WILLCOX (1969b), ii.

WILLETTS, H. T., 'The Agrarian Problem', in OBERLÄNDER (1971).

WILLIAMSON, J. G., 'Regional Inequality and the Process of National Developments: a Description of the Pattern', in NEEDLEMAN (1968).

WILSON, Charles, *England's Apprenticeship 1603–1763* (1965).

— 'The Decline of the Netherlands', in *Economic History and the Historians* (1969).

WILSON, R. G., *Gentleman Merchants. The Merchant Community in Leeds 1700–1830* (Manchester, 1971).

— 'The Supremacy of the Yorkshire Cloth Industry in the Eighteenth Century', in HARTE and PONTING (1973).

WINARSKI, B., 'The Programming and Development Policy of Backward Areas in National Economic Planning in Poland' in ROBINSON (1969).

WINKEL, Harald, *Die Ablösungskapitalien aus der Bauernbefreiung in West- und Süddeutschland* (Stuttgart, 1968).

WINKLER, H. A. (ed.), *Organisierter Kapitalismus* (Göttingen, 1974).

WITTFOGEL, K. A., 'Die natürlichen Ursachen der Wirtschaftsgeschichte', *Archiv für Sozialwissenschaft und Sozialpolitik* 67 (1932), 466–731.

WITTRAM, Reinhard, *Das Nationale als europäisches Problem* (Göttingen, 1954).

WITTSCHEWKSY, V., 'Die Zoll- und Handelspolitik Rußlands während der letzten Jahrzehnte', in VEREIN (1892), i.

WOLF, M., 'Éléments pour la construction d'un indice de la production industrielle dans le Nord 1815–1914', *Revue du Nord* 54 (1972), 289–316.

WOODRUFF, William, 'The Emergence of an International Economy 1700–1914', in CIPOLLA (1973), iv.

WOYTINSKY, W., *Die Vereinigten Staaten von Europa* (Berlin, 1926).

— *Tatsachen und Zahlen Europas* (Vienna, 1930).

WOYTINSKY, W. S. and E. S., *World Commerce and Governments. Trends and Outlook* (NY, 1955).

WRIGHT, Alison, *The Spanish Economy 1959–1976* (1977).

WRIGHT, H. R. C., *Free Trade and Protection in the Netherlands 1860–1913* (Cambridge, 1953).

WRIGLEY, E. A., *Industrial Growth and Population Change* (Cambridge, 1962).

— 'The Process of Modernization and the Industrial Revolution in England', *Journal of Interdisciplinary History* 3 (1972), 225–59.

— 'The Supply of Raw Materials in the Industrial Revolution', *EcHR* 15 (1962).

— 'A Simple Model of London's Importance in Changing English Society and Economy 1650–1750', *Past and Present* 37 (1967), 44–70.

— *Population and History* (1969).

WYSOCKI, Josef, 'Landwirtschaftlicher Nebenerwerb und soziale Sicherheit', in KELLENBENZ (1975).

YATES, P. Lamartine, *Forty Years of Foreign Trade* (1959).

YATSOUNSKY, V. K., 'Formation en Russie de la grande industrie textile sur la base de la production rurale', in ECONOMIC HISTORY, 2nd Congress (1965).

YOUNG, Arthur, *Six Months Tour Through the North of England* (4 vols., 1771).

YOUNGSON, A. J. (ed.), *Economic Development in the Long Run* (1972).

ZANGHERI, R., 'The historical relationship between agricultural and economic development in Italy', in JONES and WOLF (1974).

ZAUBERMAN, Alfred, *Industrial Progress in Poland, Czechoslovakia, and East Germany 1937–1962* (1964).

— 'Russia and Eastern Europe 1920–1970', in CIPOLLA (1973), vi.

ZIEKURSCH, Johannes, *Hundert Jahre schlesische Agrargeschichte* (Breslau, 1915).

ZIPF, G. K., 'The $\frac{P1P2}{D}$ hypothesis: on the Intercity Movement of Persons', *American Sociological Review* 11 (1946), 677–86.

ZOGRAFSKI, Dančo, 'Die wirtschaftlich-finanzielle Penetration der Großmächte auf den Balkan gegen Ende des XIX. Jahrhunderts', *StudHistOec* 7 (1972), 121–28.

ZOLOTAS, Xenophon, 'Griechenland: zum EWG Beitritt bereit', in HASENPFLUG und KOHLER (1977).

ZORN, Wolfgang, 'Schwerpunkte der deutschen Ausfuhrindustrie im 18. Jahrhundert', *JahrbNS* 173 (1961), 422–47.

— 'Binnenwirtschaftliche Verflechtungen um 1800', in LÜTGE (1964).

— 'Eine Wirtschaftskarte Deutschlands um 1820 als Spiegel der gewerblichen Entwicklung', *JahrbNS* 179 (1966), 344–55.

— 'Umrisse der frühen Industrialisierung: Südosteuropa im 19. Jahrhundert', *VSWG* 57 (1970), 500–33.
— 'L'industrialisation de l'Allemagne de Sud au XIXe siècle, in LÉON, CROUZET, GASCON (1972).
ZWAHR, Helmut, *Zur Konstituierung des Proletariats als Klasse* (Berlin, 1978).
ZYTKOWICZ, Leonid, 'The Peasant's Farm and the Landlord's Farm in Poland from the 16th to the Middle of the 18th Century', *JEuropEcH* 1 (1972), 135–54.

Index